AMERICA'S HISTORY

NINTH EDITION

CONCISE EDITION

VOLUME 2: SINCE 1865

Rebecca Edwards
Vassar College

Eric Hinderaker
University of Utah

Robert O. Self
Brown University

James A. Henretta
University of Maryland

bedford/st.martin's
Macmillan Learning
Boston | New York

For Bedford/St. Martin's

Vice President, Editorial, Macmillan Learning Humanities: *Edwin Hill*
Program Director for History: *Michael Rosenberg*
Senior Program Manager for History: *William J. Lombardo*
History Marketing Manager: *Melissa Rodriguez*
Director of Content Development: *Jane Knetzger*
Senior Developmental Editor: *Leah Strauss*
Senior Content Project Manager: *Gregory Erb*
Senior Workflow Project Manager: *Lisa McDowell*
Production Supervisor: *Robert Cherry*
Media Project Manager: *Tess Fletcher*
Composition: *Jouve*
Cartographer: *Mapping Specialists, Ltd.*
Photo Editor: *Sheena Goldstein*
Photo Researcher: *Naomi Kornhauser*
Permissions Editor: *Kalina Ingham*
Permissions Researcher: *Eve Lehmann*
Senior Art Director: *Anna Palchik*
Text Design: *Maureen McCutcheon*
Cover Design: *William Boardman*
Cover Art: *Queensboro Bridge, New York*, c. 1935 (oil on canvas), Campbell, Blendon Reed
    (1872–1969)/Museum of the City of New York, USA/Bridgeman Images
Printing and Binding: *LSC Communications*

Manufactured in the United States of America.
2   1   0   9   8   7
f   e   d   c   b   a

For information, write: Bedford/St. Martin's, 75 Arlington Street, Boston, MA 02116

ISBN: 978-1-319-05953-8 (Combined Edition)
ISBN: 978-1-319-06058-9 (Volume 1)
ISBN: 978-1-319-06059-6 (Volume 2)

Acknowledgments

Preface
Why This Book This Way

History classrooms present a unique dilemma. How do we offer our students a basic understanding of key events and facts while inviting them to see the past not as a rote list of names and dates but as the fascinating, conflicted prelude to their lives today? How do we teach our students to think like historians? As scholars and teachers who go into the classroom every day, the authors of *America's History, Concise Edition* know these challenges well. We have composed the ninth edition to help instructors meet them. *America's History* has long been known for its breadth, balance, and ability to explain to students not just what happened, but *why*. The latest edition of the Concise Edition preserves and builds on those strengths. The Concise Edition provides our signature approach to history in a smaller, more affordable trim size. Featuring the full narrative of the parent text and select features, images, maps, and pedagogical tools, the Concise Edition continues to incorporate the latest and best scholarship in the field in an accessible, student-friendly manner.

The foundation of our approach lies in a commitment to an integrated history. *America's History, Concise Edition* combines traditional "top down" narratives of political and economic history with "bottom up" narratives of the lived experiences of ordinary people. Our goal is to help students achieve a richer understanding of politics, diplomacy, war, economics, intellectual and cultural life, and gender, class, and race relations by exploring how developments in all these areas were interconnected. Our analysis is fueled by a passion for exploring big, consequential questions. How did a colonial slave society settled by people from four continents become a pluralist democracy? How have struggles for liberty, equality, and justice informed the American experience? To whom has the "American Dream" appealed—and who has achieved it, or experienced disillusionment or exclusion? How has the experience of war shaped American politics, society, and culture? Questions like these help students understand what's at stake as we study the past. In *America's History, Concise Edition* we provide an integrated historical approach and bring a dedication to *why history matters* to bear on the full sweep of America's past.

One of the most exciting developments in this edition is the attention we have devoted to fresh interpretations of the colonial, early national, and antebellum periods. Since his arrival as a new author on the eighth edition, Eric Hinderaker, an expert in Native American and early American history, has invigorated the chapters on Native, colonial European, and African societies and the revolutionary Atlantic world of the eighteenth century, bringing them in line with the most current historical scholarship. Rebecca Edwards, an expert in women's and gender history and nineteenth-century electoral politics, has done the same for the chapters covering the antebellum decades and the "long Progressive Era" of the late nineteenth and early twentieth centuries. These authors have integrated coverage of slavery and the South's economy and society into all the pre–Civil War chapters. They have also consolidated antebellum coverage, enabling teachers to move more efficiently through this material, and have updated coverage of the Civil War. Robert Self, whose work explores the relationship between urban and suburban politics, social movements, and the state, has updated the twentieth- and twenty-first-century chapters, with special attention to Chapter 30, which chronicles the extraordinary events of the most recent decades. Together, we strive to ensure that energy and creativity, as well as our wide experience in the study of history, infuse every page that follows.

In this edition, we bid a fond and deeply appreciative adieu to James Henretta, one of the original authors of *America's History* and its ballast and intellectual leader for eight editions. Professor Emeritus at the University of Maryland, and soon to be an emeritus author, James will use his retirement to pursue a variety of personal and scholarly endeavors. His influence on this book, and his name on the title page, will continue for some time, but he will no longer participate in our cycles of revision. We wish him the best and thank him for sustaining *America's History* for so many years and for his commitment to the highest standards of scholarship and prose.

In our contemporary digital world, facts and data are everywhere. What students crave is analysis. As it has since its inception, *America's History* provides students with a comprehensive explanation and interpretation of events, a guide to why history unfolded as it did and a road map for understanding the world in which we live. The core of a textbook is its narrative, and we have endeavored to make ours clear, accessible, and lively. In it, we focus not only on the marvelous diversity of peoples who came to call themselves Americans but also on the institutions that have forged a common national identity. More than ever, we daily confront the collision of our past with the demands of the future and the shrinking distance between Americans and others around the globe. To help students meet these challenges, we call attention to connections with the histories of Canada, Latin America, Europe, Africa, and Asia, drawing links between events in the United States and those elsewhere.

Of course, the contents of this book are only helpful if students read and assimilate the material before coming to class. So that students will come to class prepared, they can receive access to **LearningCurve** — an adaptive, online learning tool that helps them master content — when they purchase the **LaunchPad e-Book** (which is free when bundled with the print book). To learn more about the benefits of LearningCurve and LaunchPad, see the "Versions and Supplements" section on page x.

A Nine-Part Framework Highlights Key Developments

One of the greatest strengths of *America's History, Concise Edition* is its part structure, which helps students identify the key forces and major developments that shaped each era. A four-page part opener introduces each of the nine parts, using analysis, striking images, and a detailed **thematic timeline** to orient students to major developments and themes of the period. **Thematic Understanding** questions ask students to consider periodization and make connections among chapters. By organizing U.S. history into nine distinct periods, rather than just thirty successive chapters, we encourage students to trace changes and continuities over time and to grasp connections between political, economic, social, and cultural events.

In this edition, as in earlier ones, we have refined the part structure to reflect the most up-to-date scholarship. Part 4 now focuses more tightly on the history of the emerging republic, ending with the U.S.-Mexico War rather than in 1860. Part 5 offers expanded coverage of immigration, while Part 6 gives more emphasis to economic and intellectual debates during the era of industrialization. Part 9 extends to the end of Obama's presidency and the emergence of Donald Trump, linking political upheavals in this era to earlier events and themes.

Part 1, "Transformations of North America, 1491–1700," highlights the diversity and complexity of Native Americans prior to European contact, examines the transformative impact of European intrusions and the Columbian Exchange, and emphasizes the experimental quality of colonial ventures. Part 2, "British North America and the Atlantic World, 1607–1763," explains the diversification of British North America and the rise of the British Atlantic world and emphasizes the importance of contact between colonists and Native Americans and imperial rivalries among European powers. Part 3, "Revolution and Republican Culture, 1754–1800," traces the rise of colonial protest against British imperial reform, outlines the ways that the American Revolution challenged the social order, and explores the processes of conquest, competition, and consolidation that followed it.

Part 4, "Overlapping Revolutions, 1800–1848," traces the transformation of the economy, society, and culture of the new nation; the creation of a democratic polity; and growing sectional divisions. Part 5, "Consolidating a Continental Union, 1844–1877," covers the conflicts generated by America's empire building in the West, including sectional political struggles that led to the Civil War and national consolidation of power during and after Reconstruction. Part 6, "Industrializing America: Upheavals and Experiments, 1877–1917," examines the transformations brought about by the rise of corporations and a powerhouse industrial economy; immigration and a diverse, urbanizing society; and movements for progressive reform.

Part 7, "Domestic and Global Challenges, 1890–1945," explores America's rise to world power, the cultural transformations and political conflicts of the 1920s, the Great Depression, and the creation of the New Deal welfare state. Part 8, "The Modern State and the Age of Liberalism, 1945–1980," addresses the postwar period, including America's new global leadership role during the Cold War; the expansion of federal responsibility during a new "age of liberalism"; and the growth of mass consumption and the middle class. Finally, Part 9, "Globalization and the End of the American Century, 1980 to the Present," discusses the conservative political ascendancy of the 1980s; the end of the Cold War and rising conflict in the Middle East; and globalization and increasing social inequality.

Helping Students Work with Primary and Secondary Sources

America's History has long emphasized primary sources. In addition to weaving lively quotations throughout the narrative, we offer students substantial excerpts from historical documents — letters, diaries, autobiographies, public testimony, and more — and numerous figures that give students practice working with data. These documents allow students to experience the past through the words and perspectives of those who lived it, to understand how historians make sense of the past using data, and to gain skill in interpreting historical evidence.

To sharpen the ability of students to think historically, and to expose them to diverse historical views, we have added a new feature in this edition, called **Interpretations**. The new **Interpretations** feature brings historical argumentation directly into each chapter. Students read short, accessible passages from two scholarly works of history that offer different interpretations of the same event or period. By examining the passages side by side, and responding to the questions we pose, students learn how historians interpret evidence, weigh facts, and arrive at their conclusions. This feature highlights how *history* is a way of thinking and analyzing, rather than an inert set of facts.

Each of the thirty chapters of *America's History, Concise Edition* contains an **Interpretations** feature in addition to two primary source–based features, continued from the eighth edition.

The **America in Global Context** feature, developed for the previous edition, uses primary sources and data to situate U.S. history in a global context while giving students practice in comparison and data analysis. These features appear in every chapter on topics as diverse as the fight for women's rights in France and the United States, an examination of labor laws after emancipation in Haiti and the United States, the loss of human life in World War I, the global protests of 1968, and an analysis of the worldwide economic malaise of the 1970s.

We are excited to retain and reinvigorate a dynamic feature to aid you in teaching historical thinking skills that we developed for the eighth edition. A **Thinking Like a Historian** feature in every chapter includes five to eight brief primary sources organized around a central theme, such as "Beyond the Proclamation Line," "Making Modern Presidents," and "The Suburban Landscape of Cold War America." Students are asked to analyze the documents and complete a Putting It All Together assignment that asks them to synthesize and use the evidence to create an argument.

Those using LaunchPad will have access to an additional primary source feature. **Analyzing Voices**, a two-page feature in each chapter, helps students learn to think critically by comparing primary source texts written or spoken from two or more perspectives. New topics include "Susanna Martin, Accused Witch," "Native Americans and European Empires," "To Secede or Not to Secede?" "The Omaha Platform," "Race and Geography in the Civil Rights Era," and "The Toll of War," about the Vietnam War.

Because we understand how important primary sources are to the study of history, we are also pleased to offer for **free**, when packaged, the companion reader, *Sources for America's History*, featuring a wealth of additional documents.

As in past editions, an outstanding **visual program** engages students' attention and gives them practice in working with visual sources. The ninth edition features over one hundred and fifty paintings, cartoons, illustrations, photographs, and charts, most of them in full color and more than a quarter new to this edition. Informative captions set the illustrations in context and provide students with background for making their own analysis of the images in the book. Keenly aware that students lack geographic literacy, we have included dozens of **maps** that show major developments in the narrative, each with a caption to help students interpret what they see.

Taken together, these documents, figures, maps, and illustrations provide instructors with a trove of teaching materials, so that *America's History, Concise Edition* offers not only a compelling narrative, but also — right in the text — the rich documentary materials that instructors need to bring the past alive and introduce students to historical analysis.

Helping Students Understand the Narrative

The study aids in the ninth edition have been strengthened to support students in their understanding of the material and in their development of historical thinking skills. **Identify the Big Idea** questions at the start of every chapter guide student reading and focus their attention on identifying not just what happened, but why. Chapter chronologies have been moved from the last page of the chapter to the third, to enable students to more readily grasp the major events and developments as they begin to read. A variety of learning tools from the beginning to the end of each chapter support this big idea focus. As they read, students will gain proficiency in historical thinking skills via **marginal review questions** that ask students to "Identify Causes," "Trace Change over Time," and "Understand Points of View," among other skills. New **Section Review Questions** help students articulate the main points of each section of a chapter. Where students are likely to stumble over a key concept, we boldface it in the text where it is first mentioned and provide a **new on-page glossary** that defines the term.

The revised and expanded Chapter Review section provides a set of **Review Questions** that restate the individual section review questions, a **Thematic Understanding** question, and **Making Connections** questions that ask students to consider broader historical issues, developments, and continuities and changes over time. **Terms to Know** provides a list of **Key Concepts and Events** and **Key People** students should know. Lastly, a **Key Turning Points** question reminds students of important events and asks them to consider periodization.

Helping Instructors Teach with Digital Resources

As noted, *America's History, Concise Edition* is offered in Macmillan's premier learning platform, **LaunchPad**, an intuitive, interactive e-Book and course space. Free when packaged with the print text or available at a low price when used alone, LaunchPad grants students and teachers access to a wealth of online tools and resources built specifically for our text to enhance reading comprehension and promote in-depth study.

Developed with extensive feedback from history instructors and students, *LaunchPad for America's History* includes the complete narrative of the print book, the companion reader, *Sources for America's History,* and **LearningCurve**, an adaptive learning tool that is designed to get students to read before they come to class. With **new source-based questions in the test bank and in the LearningCurve** and the ability to **sort test**

bank questions by chapter learning objectives, instructors now have more ways to test students on their understanding of sources and narrative in the book.

This edition also includes **Guided Reading Exercises** that prompt students to be active readers of the chapter narrative and auto-graded **primary source quizzes** to test comprehension of written and visual sources. These features, plus **additional primary source documents, video sources and tools for making video assignments, map activities, flash cards,** and **customizable test banks,** make LaunchPad a great asset for any instructor who wants to enliven American history for students.

New Updates to the Narrative

In the new edition, we continue to offer instructors a bold account of U.S. history that reflects the latest, most exciting scholarship in the field. Throughout the book, we have given increased attention to political culture and political economy, including the history of capitalism, using this analysis to help students understand how society, culture, politics, and the economy informed one another.

The opening chapters incisively analyze the processes by which European colonization transformed the Western Hemisphere. They emphasize the way Native Americans shaped, and were shaped by, the contact experience—a focus that carries through the ninth edition in a continental perspective and sustained coverage of Native Americans, the environment, and the West in every era. These chapters highlight the varied and tenuous nature of experiments in colonization; in doing so, they stress the opportunity, as well as the instability and violence, inherent in the colonial enterprise. And they trace the rise of British North America, the Atlantic world, and the many revolutions—in print, consumption, and politics—that transformed the eighteenth century.

In the early nineteenth-century chapters, coverage of the South and slavery has been integrated throughout, to give more emphasis to the economic and political clout of the "Cotton Kingdom" and its "peculiar institution." Antebellum urban culture and Irish and German immigration also get more attention. The 1850s and the secession crisis receive more extended treatment, showing students that there was no direct or inevitable path from the Kansas-Nebraska Act to war. The Civil War chapter has been extensively revised to reflect recent scholarship, balancing military and technological history with crucial diplomatic and political events, while conveying the experiences of civilians, self-liberated former slaves, refugees, and soldiers.

In the post–Civil War chapters, enhanced coverage of gender, ethnicity, and race includes greater emphasis on gay and lesbian history and Asian and Latino immigration, alongside the entire chapter devoted to the civil rights movement, a major addition to the last edition. Finally, we have kept up with recent developments with an expanded section on the Obama presidency and the election of 2016. Students keen to understand contemporary political developments will find in the post–World War II chapters a strong political and economic narrative that helps them contextualize the very recent past.

Acknowledgments

We are grateful to the following scholars and teachers who reported on their experiences with the eighth edition or reviewed features of the new edition. Their comments often challenged us to rethink or justify our interpretations and always provided a check on accuracy down to the smallest detail.

Roger Carpenter, *University of Louisiana at Monroe*
Petra DeWitt, *Missouri University of Science and Technology*
Blake Ellis, *Lone Star College–CyFair*
Roger Greenland, *Mineral Area College*
Daniel Haworth, *University of Houston–Clear Lake*
Alan Lehmann, *Blinn College*
Philbert Martin, *San Jacinto College*
Suzanne McCormack, *Community College of Rhode Island*
William Morgan, *Lone Star College–Montgomery*
Daniel Murphree, *University of Central Florida*
Manfred Silva, *El Paso Community College*
Andrew Slap, *East Tennessee State University*
Whitney Snow, *Midwestern State University*
Michael Wise, *University of North Texas*

As the authors of *America's History*, we know better than anyone else how much this book is the work of other hands and minds. We are especially grateful to Kevin B. Sheets of the State University of New York at Cortland for his peerless help in assembling the material for the new Interpretations feature. We are indebted to the team at Bedford/ St. Martin's: Michael Rosenberg, William J. Lombardo, Jane Knetzger, Laura Arcari, Nathan Odell, Blythe Robbins, Leah Strauss, and Kathryn Abbott, who asked the right questions and suggested a multitude of improvements. Greg Erb did a masterful job consulting with the authors and seeing the book through the production process. Melissa Rodriguez and Janie Pierce-Bratcher in the marketing department understood how to communicate our vision to teachers; they and the members of college and high school sales forces did wonderful work in helping this edition reach the classroom. We also thank the rest of our editorial and production team for their dedicated efforts: Media Editor Tess Fletcher; Editorial Assistant Lexi DeConti; copyeditor Susan Zorn; proofreaders Deborah Heimann and Diana George; indexer Rebecca McCorkle; art researchers Naomi Kornhauser and Sheena Goldstein; and text permissions researchers Eve Lehmann and Kalina Ingham. Finally, we want to express our appreciation for the assistance of Michelle Whalen and the U.S. historians at Vassar College — Robert Brigham, Miriam Cohen, James Merrell, and Quincy Mills — for their invaluable help and advice. Many thanks to all of you for your contributions to this new edition of *America's History*.

Rebecca Edwards
Eric Hinderaker
Robert O. Self

Versions and Supplements

Adopters of *America's History* and their students have access to abundant print and digital resources and tools, the acclaimed Bedford Series in History and Culture volumes, and much more. The LaunchPad course space for *America's History* provides access to the narrative as well as a wealth of primary sources and other features, along with assignment and assessment opportunities at the ready. See below for more information, visit the book's catalog site at **macmillanlearning.com**, or contact your local Bedford/St. Martin's sales representative.

Get the Right Version for Your Class

To accommodate different course lengths and course budgets, *America's History* is available in several different versions and formats to best suit your course needs. The comprehensive *America's History* includes a full-color art program and a robust set of features. The Concise Edition also provides the full narrative, with a streamlined art and feature program, at a lower price. The Value Edition offers a trade-sized two-color option with the full narrative and selected art and maps at a steeper discount. The Value Edition is also offered at the lowest price point in loose-leaf, and all versions are available as e-Books. For the best value of all, package a new print book with LaunchPad at no additional charge to get the best each format offers — a print version for easy portability with a LaunchPad interactive e-Book and course space with LearningCurve and loads of additional assignment and assessment options.

- **Combined Volume** (Chapters 1–30): available in paperback, Concise, Value, and e-Book formats and in LaunchPad
- **Volume 1: To 1877** (Chapters 1–15): available in paperback, Concise, Value, loose-leaf, and e-Book formats and in LaunchPad
- **Volume 2: Since 1865** (Chapters 14–30): available in paperback, Concise, Value, loose-leaf, and e-Book formats and in LaunchPad

As noted below, any of these volumes can be packaged with additional titles for a discount. To get ISBNs for discount packages, visit **macmillanlearning.com** for the comprehensive version or Value Edition or contact your Bedford/St. Martin's representative.

![LaunchPad macmillan learning] Assign LaunchPad — an Assessment-Ready Interactive e-Book and Course Space

Available for discount purchase on its own or for packaging with new books at no additional charge, LaunchPad is a breakthrough solution for history courses. Intuitive and easy to use for students and instructors alike, LaunchPad is ready to use as is and can be edited, customized with your own material, and assigned quickly. *LaunchPad for America's History* includes Bedford/St. Martin's high-quality content all in one place, including the full interactive e-Book and the companion reader *Sources for America's History*, plus LearningCurve formative quizzing, guided reading activities designed to help students read actively for key concepts, autograded quizzes for each primary source, and chapter summative quizzes. Through a wealth of formative and summative assessments, including the adaptive learning program of LearningCurve (see the full description below), students gain confidence and get into their reading before class. These features, plus additional primary source documents, video sources and tools for making video assignments, map activities, flash cards, and customizable test banks, make LaunchPad an invaluable asset for any instructor.

LaunchPad easily integrates with course management systems, and with fast ways to build assignments, rearrange chapters, and add new pages, sections, or links, it lets teachers build the courses they want to teach and hold students accountable. For more information, visit **launchpadworks.com**, or to arrange a demo, contact us at **history @macmillan.com**.

Assign LearningCurve So Your Students Come to Class Prepared

Students using LaunchPad receive access to LearningCurve for *America's History*. Assigning LearningCurve in place of reading quizzes is easy for instructors, and the reporting features help instructors track overall class trends and spot topics that are giving students trouble so they can adjust their lectures and class activities. This online learning tool is popular with students because it was designed to help them rehearse content at their own pace in a non-threatening, gamelike environment. The feedback for wrong answers provides instructional coaching and sends students back to the book for review. Students answer as many questions as necessary to reach a target score, with repeated chances to revisit material they haven't mastered. When LearningCurve is assigned, students come to class better prepared.

iClicker, Active Learning Simplified

iClicker offers simple, flexible tools to help you give students a voice and facilitate active learning in the classroom. Students can participate with the devices they already bring to class using our iClicker Reef mobile apps (which work with smart phones, tablets, or laptops) or iClicker remotes. We've now integrated iClicker with Macmillan's LaunchPad to make it easier than ever to synchronize grades and promote engagement — both in and out of class. iClicker Reef access cards can also be packaged with LaunchPad or your textbook at a significant savings for your students. To learn more, talk to your Macmillan Learning representative or visit us at **www.iclicker.com**.

Take Advantage of Instructor Resources

Bedford/St. Martin's has developed a rich array of teaching resources for this book and for this course. They range from lecture and presentation materials and assessment tools to course management options. Most can be found in LaunchPad or can be downloaded or ordered at **macmillanlearning.com**.

Bedford Coursepack for Blackboard, Canvas, Brightspace by D2L, or Moodle. We can help you integrate our rich content into your course management system. Registered instructors can download coursepacks that include our popular free resources and book-specific content for *America's History*. Visit **macmillanlearning.com** to find your version or download your coursepack.

Instructor's Resource Manual. The instructor's manual offers both experienced and first-time instructors tools for presenting textbook material in engaging ways. It includes content learning objectives, annotated chapter outlines, and strategies for teaching with the textbook, plus suggestions on how to get the most out of LearningCurve and a survival guide for first-time teaching assistants.

Guide to Changing Editions. Designed to facilitate an instructor's transition from the previous edition of *America's History* to this new edition, this guide presents an overview of major changes as well as changes in each chapter.

Online Test Bank. The test bank includes a mix of fresh, carefully crafted multiple-choice, matching, short-answer, and essay questions for each chapter. Many of the multiple-choice questions feature a map, an image, or a primary source excerpt as the prompt. All questions appear in Microsoft Word format and in easy-to-use test bank software that allows instructors to add, edit, re-sequence, filter by question type or learning objective, and print questions and answers. Instructors can also export questions into a variety of course management systems. This test bank is tagged to book-specific learning outcomes and to the Texas Higher Education Coordinating Board's Student Learning Outcomes for History 1301 (U.S. History to 1877) and History 1302 (U.S. History Since 1865).

The Bedford Lecture Kit:* Lecture Outlines, Maps, and Images.** Look good and save time with ***The Bedford Lecture Kit. These presentation materials include fully customizable multimedia presentations built around chapter outlines that are embedded with maps, figures, and images from the textbook and are supplemented by detailed instructor notes on key points and concepts.

America in Motion: Video Clips for U.S. History. Set history in motion with *America in Motion*, an instructor DVD containing dozens of short digital movie files of events in twentieth-century American history. From the wreckage of the battleship *Maine* to FDR's fireside chats, to Ronald Reagan speaking before the Brandenburg Gate, *America in Motion* engages students with dynamic scenes from key events and challenges them to think critically. All files are classroom-ready, edited for brevity, and easily integrated with presentation slides or other software for electronic lectures or assignments. An accompanying guide provides each clip's historical context, ideas for use, and suggested questions.

Print, Digital, and Custom Options for More Choice and Value

For information on free packages and discounts up to 50%, visit **macmillanlearning .com**, or contact your local Bedford/St. Martin's sales representative.

NEW *Sources for America's History,* **Ninth Edition.** This primary source collection provides a revised and expanded selection of sources to accompany *America's History,* Ninth Edition. *Sources for America's History* provides a broad selection of over 225 primary source documents as well as editorial apparatus to help students understand the sources. *To support the structure of the parent text, unique document sets at the end of each part present sources that illustrate the major themes of each section.* This companion reader is an exceptional value for students and offers plenty of assignment options for instructors. Available free when packaged with the print text and included in the LaunchPad e-Book. Also available on its own as a downloadable PDF e-Book.

NEW Bedford Tutorials for History. Designed to customize textbooks with resources relevant to individual courses, this collection of brief units, each 16 pages long and loaded with examples, guides students through basic skills such as using historical evidence effectively, working with primary sources, taking effective notes, avoiding plagiarism and citing sources, and more. Up to two tutorials can be added to a Bedford/St. Martin's history survey title at no additional charge, freeing you to spend your class time focusing on content and interpretation. For more information, visit **macmillan learning.com/historytutorials**.

NEW Bedford Document Collections for U.S. History. This source collection provides a flexible and affordable online repository of discovery-oriented primary source projects ready to assign. Each curated project — written by a historian about a favorite topic — poses a historical question and guides students step by step through analysis of primary sources. Examples include What Caused the Civil War? The California Gold Rush: A Trans-Pacific Phenomenon; and War Stories: Black Soldiers and the Long Civil Rights Movement. For more information, visit **macmillanlearning.com**. Available free when packaged.

NEW Bedford Document Collections Custom Print Modules. Choose one or two document projects from the collection (see above) and add them in print to a Bedford/ St. Martin's title, or select several to be bound together in a custom reader created specifically for your course. Either way, the modules are affordably priced. For more information, contact your Bedford/St. Martin's representative.

The Bedford Series in History and Culture. More than one hundred titles in this highly praised series combine first-rate scholarship, historical narrative, and important primary documents for undergraduate courses. Each book is brief, inexpensive, and focused on a specific topic or period. Revisions of several best-selling titles, such as *The Cherokee Removal: A Brief History with Documents* by Theda Perdue; *Narrative of the Life of Frederick Douglass,* edited by David Blight; and *The Triangle Fire: A Brief History with Documents* by Jo Ann Argersinger, are now available. For a complete list of titles, visit **macmillanlearning.com**. Package discounts are available.

Rand McNally Atlas of American History. This collection of more than eighty full-color maps illustrates key events and eras from early exploration, settlement, expansion, and immigration to U.S. involvement in wars abroad and on U.S. soil. Introductory pages for each section include a brief overview, timelines, graphs, and photos to quickly establish a historical context. Free when packaged.

The Bedford Glossary for U.S. History. This handy supplement for the survey course gives students historically contextualized definitions for hundreds of terms — from *abolitionism* to *zoot suit* — that they will encounter in lectures, reading, and exams. Free when packaged.

Trade Books. Titles published by sister companies Hill and Wang; Farrar, Straus and Giroux; Henry Holt and Company; St. Martin's Press; Picador; and Palgrave Macmillan are available at a 50% discount when packaged with Bedford/St. Martin's textbooks. For more information, visit **macmillanlearning.com/tradeup**.

A Pocket Guide to Writing in History. Updated to reflect changes made in the 2017 *Chicago Manual of Style* revision, this portable and affordable reference tool by Mary Lynn Rampolla provides reading, writing, and research advice useful to students in all history courses. Concise yet comprehensive advice on approaching typical history assignments, developing critical reading skills, writing effective history papers, conducting research, using and documenting sources, and avoiding plagiarism — enhanced with practical tips and examples throughout — has made this slim reference a best-seller. Package discounts are available.

A Student's Guide to History. This complete guide to success in any history course provides the practical help students need to be successful. In addition to introducing students to the nature of the discipline, author Jules Benjamin teaches a wide range of skills, from preparing for exams to approaching common writing assignments, and explains the research and documentation process with plentiful examples. Package discounts are available.

Going to the Source: The Bedford Reader in American History. Developed by Victoria Bissell Brown and Timothy J. Shannon, this reader combines a rich diversity of primary and secondary sources with in-depth instructions for how to use each type of source. Mirroring the chronology of the U.S. history survey, each of the main chapters familiarizes students with a single type of source — from personal letters to political cartoons — while focusing on an important historical episode such as the Cherokee Removal or the 1894 Pullman Strike. The reader's wide variety of chapter topics and sources provokes students' interest as it teaches them the skills they need to successfully interrogate historical sources. Package discounts are available.

America Firsthand. With its distinctive focus on first-person accounts from ordinary people, this primary documents reader by Anthony Marcus, John M. Giggie, and David Burner offers a remarkable range of perspectives on America's history from those who lived it. Popular Points of View sections expose students to different perspectives on a specific event or topic. Package discounts are available.

Contents

PART 5 Consolidating a Continental Union, 1844–1877   *(continued)*

Maps, Figures, and Tables

Special Features

THINKING LIKE A HISTORIAN

14

Reconstruction
1865–1877

CHAPTER

On the last day of April 1866, black soldiers in Memphis, Tennessee, turned in their weapons as they mustered out of the Union army. The next day, whites who resented the soldiers' presence provoked a clash. At a street celebration where African Americans shouted "Hurrah for Abe Lincoln," a white policeman responded, "Your old father, Abe Lincoln, is dead and damned."

IDENTIFY THE BIG IDEA

What goals did Republican policymakers, ex-Confederates, and freedpeople pursue during Reconstruction? To what degree did each succeed?

The scuffle that followed precipitated three days of white violence and rape that left forty-eight African Americans dead and dozens more wounded. Mobs burned black homes and churches and destroyed all twelve of the city's black schools.

Unionists were appalled. They had won the Civil War, but where was the peace? Ex-Confederates murdered freedmen and flagrantly resisted federal control. After the Memphis attacks, Republicans in Congress proposed a new measure that would protect African Americans by defining and enforcing U.S. citizenship rights. Eventually this bill became the most significant law to emerge from Reconstruction, the Fourteenth Amendment to the Constitution.

Andrew Johnson, however—the Unionist Democrat who became president after Abraham Lincoln's assassination—refused to sign the bill. In May 1865, while Congress was adjourned, Johnson had implemented his own Reconstruction plan. It extended amnesty to all southerners who took a loyalty oath, except for a few high-ranking Confederates. It also allowed states to reenter the Union as soon as they revoked secession, abolished slavery, and relieved their new state governments of financial burdens by repudiating Confederate debts. A year later, at the time of the Memphis carnage, all ex-Confederate states had met Johnson's terms. The president rejected any further intervention.

Johnson's vetoes, combined with ongoing violence in the South, angered Unionist voters. In the political struggle that ensued, congressional Republicans seized the initiative from the president and enacted a sweeping program that became known as Radical Reconstruction. One of its key achievements, the Fifteenth Amendment, would have been unthinkable a few years earlier: voting rights for African American men.

Black southerners, though, had additional, urgent priorities. "We have toiled nearly all our lives as slaves [and] have made these lands what they are," a group of South Carolina petitioners declared. They pleaded for "some provision by which we as Freedmen can obtain a Homestead." Though northern Republicans and freedpeople agreed that black southerners must have physical safety and the right to vote, former slaves also wanted economic independence. Northerners sought, instead, to revive cash-crop plantations with wage labor. Reconstruction's eventual failure stemmed from the conflicting goals of lawmakers, freedpeople, and relentlessly hostile ex-Confederates.

Celebrating the Fifteenth Amendment, 1870 This lithograph depicts a celebration in Baltimore on May 15, 1870. With perhaps 200,000 people attending, the grand parade and orations marked passage of the Fifteenth Amendment, which enfranchised men irrespective of "race, color, or previous condition of servitude." The heroes depicted at the top are Martin Delany, the first black man to become an officer in the U.S. Army; abolitionist Frederick Douglass, born in slavery on Maryland's Eastern Shore; and Mississippi senator Hiram Rhodes Revels. The images at the bottom carried the following captions: "Liberty Protects the Marriage Altar," "The Ballot Box is open to us," and "Our Representative Sits in the National Legislature." Such lithographs, widely printed and sold, capture the pride, hope, and optimism of Reconstruction — but the optimism was not to last. Library of Congress.

CHAPTER CHRONOLOGY

As you read, ask yourself why this chapter begins and ends with these dates and try to identify the links among related events.

1864 ▶ Wade-Davis Bill passed by Congress but killed by Lincoln's pocket veto	**1870** ▶ Ku Klux Klan at peak of power ▶ Congress passes Enforcement Laws to suppress Klan ▶ Fifteenth Amendment ratified ▶ Victoria Woodhull declares her support for "free love"
1865 ▶ Freedmen's Bureau established ▶ Lincoln assassinated; Andrew Johnson succeeds him as president ▶ Johnson implements restoration plan ▶ Ex-Confederate states pass Black Codes to limit freedpeople's rights	**1872** ▶ Grant reelected; Crédit Mobilier scandal emerges
	1873 ▶ Panic of 1873 ushers in severe economic depression ▶ Supreme Court severely curtails Reconstruction in *Slaughter-House Cases*
1866 ▶ Civil Rights Act passes over Johnson's veto ▶ Major Republican gains in congressional elections	**1874** ▶ Sweeping Democratic gains in congressional elections
1867 ▶ Reconstruction Act	**1875** ▶ Whiskey Ring and other scandals undermine Grant administration ▶ *Minor v. Happersett:* Supreme Court rules that Fourteenth Amendment does not extend voting rights to women ▶ Beecher-Tilton scandal dominates headlines
1868 ▶ Impeachment of Andrew Johnson ▶ Fourteenth Amendment ratified ▶ Ulysses S. Grant elected president	
	1877 ▶ Rutherford B. Hayes becomes president ▶ Federal Reconstruction ends

The Struggle for National Reconstruction

Ten Percent Plan
A plan proposed by President Abraham Lincoln during the Civil War, but never implemented, that would have granted amnesty to most ex-Confederates and allowed each rebellious state to return to the Union as soon as 10 percent of its voters had taken a loyalty oath and the state had approved the Thirteenth Amendment.

Wade-Davis Bill
A bill proposed by Congress in July 1864 that required an oath of allegiance by a majority of each state's adult white men, new governments formed only by those who had never taken up arms against the Union, and permanent disenfranchisement of Confederate leaders. The plan was passed but pocket vetoed by President Abraham Lincoln.

Congress clashed with President Johnson, in part, because the framers of the Constitution did not anticipate a civil war or provide for its aftermath. Had Confederate states legally left the Union when they seceded? If so, then their reentry required action by Congress. If not — if even during secession they had retained U.S. statehood — then restoring them might be an administrative matter, best left to the president. Lack of clarity on this fundamental question made for explosive politics.

Presidential Approaches: From Lincoln to Johnson

As wartime president, Lincoln had offered a plan similar to Johnson's. It granted amnesty to most ex-Confederates and allowed each rebellious state to return to the Union as soon as 10 percent of its voters had taken a loyalty oath and the state had approved the Thirteenth Amendment, abolishing slavery. But even amid defeat, Confederate states rejected this **Ten Percent Plan** — an ominous sign for the future. In July 1864, Congress proposed a tougher substitute, the **Wade-Davis Bill**, that required an oath of allegiance by a majority of each state's adult white men, new governments formed only by those who had never taken up arms against the Union, and permanent disenfranchisement of Confederate leaders. Lincoln defeated the Wade-Davis Bill with a pocket veto, leaving it unsigned when Congress adjourned. At the same time, he opened talks with key congressmen, aiming for a compromise.

On April 14, 1865, Lincoln was shot by John Wilkes Booth while watching a play at Ford's Theatre. We will never know what would have happened had Lincoln lived.

His death precipitated grief and political turmoil. As a special train bore the president's flag-draped coffin home to Illinois, thousands of Americans lined the railroad tracks in mourning. Furious and grief-stricken, many Unionists blamed all Confederates for the acts of southern sympathizer John Wilkes Booth and his accomplices in the murder. At the same time, Lincoln's death left the presidency in the hands of Andrew Johnson, a man utterly lacking in Lincoln's moral sense and political judgment.

Johnson was a self-styled "common man" from the hills of eastern Tennessee. Trained as a tailor, he built his political career on the support of farmers and laborers. Loyal to the Union, Johnson had refused to leave the U.S. Senate when Tennessee seceded. After federal forces captured Nashville in 1862, Lincoln appointed Johnson as Tennessee's military governor. In the election of 1864, placing Lincoln and this War Democrat on the ticket together had seemed a smart move, designed to promote unity. But after Lincoln's death, Johnson's disagreement with Republicans, combined with his belligerent and contradictory actions, wreaked political havoc.

The new president and Congress confronted a set of problems that would have challenged even Lincoln. During the war, Unionists had insisted that rebel leaders were a small minority and most white southerners wanted to rejoin the Union. With even greater optimism, Republicans hoped the defeated South would accept post-war reforms. Ex-Confederates, however, contested that plan through both violence and political action. New southern state legislatures, created under Johnson's limited Reconstruction plan, moved to restore slavery in all but name. In 1865, they enacted **Black Codes**, designed to force former slaves back to plantation labor. Like similar laws passed in other places after slavery ended, the codes reflected plantation owners' economic interests (America in Global Context). They imposed severe penalties on blacks who did not hold full-year labor contracts and also set up procedures for taking black children from their parents and apprenticing them to former slave masters.

Faced with these developments, Johnson gave all the wrong signals. He had long talked tough against southern planters. But in practice, Johnson allied himself with ex-Confederate leaders, forgiving them when they appealed for pardons. White southern leaders were delighted. "By this wise and noble statesmanship," wrote a Confederate legislator, "you have become the benefactor of the Southern people." Northerners and freedmen were disgusted. The president had left Reconstruction "to the tender mercies of the rebels," wrote one Republican. An angry Union veteran in Missouri called Johnson "a traitor to the loyal people of the Union." Emboldened by Johnson's indulgence, ex-Confederates began to filter back into the halls of power. When Georgians elected Alexander Stephens, former vice president of the Confederacy, to represent them in Congress, many outraged Republicans saw this as the last straw.

Black Codes
Laws passed by southern states after the Civil War that denied ex-slaves the civil rights enjoyed by whites, punished vague crimes such as "vagrancy" or failing to have a labor contract, and tried to force African Americans back to plantation labor systems that closely mirrored those in slavery times.

Congress Versus the President

Under the Constitution, Congress is "the judge of the Elections, Returns and Qualifications of its own Members" (Article 1, Section 5). Using this power, Republican majorities in both houses had refused to admit southern delegations when Congress convened in December 1865, effectively blocking Johnson's program. Hoping to mollify Congress, some southern states dropped the most objectionable provisions

Labor Laws After Emancipation: Haiti and the United States

Many government officials agreed with former masters on the need to control rural workers. Often planters themselves or allied with the planter class, they believed that economic strength and public revenue depended on plantation export crops and that workers would not produce those without legal coercion.

This was true in the British Caribbean and also Haiti, which eventually, after a successful slave revolt ending in 1803, became an independent republic led by former slaves and, in particular, by propertied free men of color. In the passage below, a British observer describes a rural labor code adopted by Haiti's government in 1826. Despite the law, Haiti's large plantations did not revive; the island's economy, even more than that of the U.S. South, came to be dominated by small-scale, impoverished farmers.

The Code of Laws before us is one that could only have been framed by a legislature composed of proprietors of land, having at their command a considerable military power, of which they themselves were the leaders; for a population whom it was necessary to compel to labour. . . .

The choice of a master, altho' expressly reserved to the labourer, is greatly modified by the clauses which restrain the labourer from quitting the section of country to which he belongs; and from the absence of any clause compelling proprietors to engage him; so that the cultivator must consent to bind himself to whomsoever may be willing to engage him, or remain in prison, to be employed among convicts. . . .

The Code begins (Article 1) by declaring Agriculture to be the foundation of national prosperity; and then decrees (Article 3), That all persons, excepting soldiers, and civil servants of the State, professional persons, artizans, and domestic servants, shall cultivate the soil. The next clause (Article 4), forbids the inhabitants of the country quitting it to dwell in towns or villages; and every kind of wholesale or retail trade is forbidden (Article 7) to be exercised by persons dwelling in the country.

Further articles stipulate that any person dwelling in the country, not being the owner or occupier of land, and not having bound himself in the manner directed, . . . shall be considered a vagabond, be arrested, and taken before a Justice, who, after reading the Law to him, shall commit him to jail, until he consent to bind himself according to law.

. . . Those who are hired from a job-master [labor agent], . . . are entitled to receive half the produce, after deducting the expences of cultivation; [those who are bound to the proprietor directly], one-fourth of the gross produce of their labour. . . . Out of their miserable pittance, these Haitian labourers are to provide themselves and their children with almost every thing, and to lay by a provision for old age. . . .

These, with the regulations already detailed, clearly shew what is intended to be the condition of the labouring population of Haiti. I must not call it slavery; the word is objectionable; but few of the ingredients of slavery seem to be wanting.

QUESTIONS FOR ANALYSIS

1. Compare this Haitian law with the Black Codes briefly adopted by ex-Confederate states, and with the sharecropping system that evolved in the United States during Reconstruction (p. 476). What did these labor systems — or proposed systems — have in common? How did they differ?

2. Why would the Haitian government, led by men of color, enact such laws? What considerations other than race might have shaped their views, and why?

from their Black Codes. But at the same time, antiblack violence erupted in various parts of the South.

Congressional Republicans concluded that the federal government had to intervene. Back in March 1865, Congress had established the **Freedmen's Bureau** to aid displaced blacks and other war refugees. In early 1866, Congress voted to extend the bureau, gave it direct funding for the first time, and authorized its agents to investigate southern abuses. Even more extraordinary was the **Civil Rights Act of 1866**, which declared formerly enslaved people to be citizens and granted them equal protection and rights of contract, with full access to the courts.

These bills provoked bitter conflict with Johnson, who vetoed them both. Johnson's racism, hitherto publicly muted, now blazed forth: "This is a country for white men, and by God, as long as I am president, it shall be a government for white men." Galvanized, Republicans in Congress gathered two-thirds majorities and overrode both vetoes, passing the Civil Rights Act in April 1866 and the Freedmen's Bureau law four months later. Their resolve was reinforced by continued upheaval in the South. In addition to the violence in Memphis, twenty-four black political leaders and their allies in Arkansas were murdered and their homes burned.

Anxious to protect freedpeople and reassert Republican power in the South, Congress took further measures to sustain civil rights. In what became the **Fourteenth Amendment** (1868), it declared that "all persons born or naturalized in the United States" were citizens. No state could abridge "the privileges or immunities of citizens of the United States"; deprive "any person of life, liberty, or property, without due process of law"; or deny anyone "equal protection." In a stunning increase of federal power, the Fourteenth Amendment declared that when people's essential rights were at stake, national citizenship henceforth took priority over citizenship in a state.

Johnson opposed ratification, but public opinion had swung against him. In the 1866 congressional elections, voters gave Republicans a 3-to-1 majority in Congress. Power shifted to the so-called Radical Republicans, who sought sweeping transformations in the defeated South. The Radicals' leader in the Senate was Charles Sumner of Massachusetts, the fiery abolitionist who in 1856 had been nearly beaten to death by South Carolina congressman Preston Brooks. Radicals in the House followed Thaddeus Stevens of Pennsylvania, a passionate advocate of freedmen's political and economic rights. With such men at the fore, and with congressional Republicans now numerous and united enough to override Johnson's vetoes on many questions, Congress proceeded to remake Reconstruction.

Radical Reconstruction

The **Reconstruction Act of 1867**, enacted in March, divided the conquered South into five military districts, each under the command of a U.S. general (Map 14.1). To reenter the Union, former Confederate states had to grant the vote to freedmen and deny it to leading ex-Confederates. Each military commander was required to register all eligible adult males, black as well as white; supervise state constitutional conventions; and ensure that new constitutions guaranteed black suffrage. Congress would readmit a state to the Union once these conditions were met and the new state legislature ratified the Fourteenth Amendment. Johnson vetoed the Reconstruction Act, but Congress overrode his veto (Table 14.1).

Freedmen's Bureau
Government organization created in March 1865 to aid displaced blacks and other war refugees. Active until the early 1870s, it was the first federal agency in history that provided direct payments to assist those in poverty and to foster social welfare.

Civil Rights Act of 1866
Legislation passed by Congress that nullified the Black Codes and affirmed that African Americans should have equal benefit of the law.

Fourteenth Amendment
Constitutional amendment ratified in 1868 that made all native-born or naturalized persons U.S. citizens and prohibited states from abridging the rights of national citizens, thus giving primacy to national rather than state citizenship.

Reconstruction Act of 1867
An act that divided the conquered South into five military districts, each under the command of a U.S. general. To reenter the Union, former Confederate states had to grant the vote to freedmen and deny it to leading ex-Confederates.

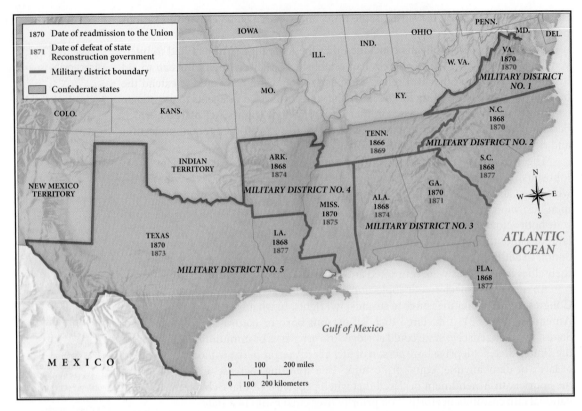

MAP 14.1 Reconstruction
The federal government organized the Confederate states into five military districts during congressional Reconstruction. For the states shown in this map, the first date indicates when that state was readmitted to the Union; the second date shows when Republicans lost control of the state government. All the ex-Confederate states rejoined the Union between 1868 and 1870, but the periods of Radical government varied widely. Republicans lasted only a few months in Virginia; they held on until the end of Reconstruction in Louisiana, Florida, and South Carolina.

The Impeachment of Andrew Johnson In August 1867, Johnson fought back by "suspending" Secretary of War Edwin M. Stanton, a Radical, and replacing him with Union general Ulysses S. Grant, believing Grant would be a good soldier and follow orders. Johnson, however, had misjudged Grant, who publicly objected to the president's machinations. When the Senate overruled Stanton's suspension, Grant—now an open enemy of Johnson—resigned so Stanton could resume his place as secretary of war. On February 21, 1868, Johnson formally dismissed Stanton. The feisty secretary of war responded by barricading himself in his office, precipitating a crisis.

Three days later, for the first time in U.S. history, legislators in the House of Representatives introduced articles of impeachment against the president, employing their constitutional power to charge high federal officials with "Treason, Bribery, or other high Crimes and Misdemeanors." The House serves, in effect, as the prosecutor in such cases, and the Senate serves as the court. The Republican majority brought

Table 14.1

Primary Reconstruction Laws and Constitutional Amendments

Law (Date of Congressional Passage)	Key Provisions
Thirteenth Amendment (December 1865[*])	Prohibited slavery
Civil Rights Act of 1866 (April 1866)	Defined citizenship rights of freedmen
	Authorized federal authorities to bring suit against those who violated those rights
Fourteenth Amendment (June 1866[†])	Established national citizenship for persons born or naturalized in the United States
	Prohibited the states from depriving citizens of their civil rights or equal protection under the law
	Reduced state representation in House of Representatives by the percentage of adult male citizens denied the vote
Reconstruction Act of 1867 (March 1867)	Divided the South into five military districts, each under the command of a Union general
	Established requirements for readmission of ex-Confederate states to the Union
Tenure of Office Act (March 1867)	Required Senate consent for removal of any federal official whose appointment had required Senate confirmation
Fifteenth Amendment (February 1869[‡])	Forbade states to deny citizens the right to vote on the grounds of race, color, or "previous condition of servitude"
Ku Klux Klan Act (April 1871)	Authorized the president to use federal prosecutions and military force to suppress conspiracies to deprive citizens of the right to vote and enjoy the equal protection of the law

[*] Ratified by three-fourths of all states in December 1865.
[†] Ratified by three-fourths of all states in July 1868.
[‡] Ratified by three-fourths of all states in March 1870.

eleven counts of misconduct against Johnson, most relating to infringement of the powers of Congress. After an eleven-week trial in the Senate, thirty-five senators voted for conviction — one vote short of the two-thirds majority required. Twelve Democrats and seven Republicans voted for acquittal. The dissenting Republicans felt that removing a president for defying Congress was too damaging to the constitutional system of checks and balances. But despite the president's acquittal, Congress had shown its power. For the brief months remaining in his term, Johnson was largely irrelevant.

Election of 1868 and the Fifteenth Amendment The impeachment controversy made Grant, already the Union's greatest war hero, a Republican idol as well. He easily won the party's presidential nomination in 1868. Although he supported congressional

Reconstruction, Grant also urged sectional reconciliation. His Democratic opponent, former New York governor Horatio Seymour, almost declined the nomination because he understood that Democrats could not yet overcome the stain of disloyalty. Grant won by an overwhelming margin, receiving 214 out of 294 electoral votes. Republicans retained two-thirds majorities in both houses of Congress.

In February 1869, following this smashing victory, Republicans produced the era's last constitutional amendment, the Fifteenth. It protected male citizens' right to vote irrespective of race, color, or "previous condition of servitude." Despite Radical Republicans' protests, the amendment left room for a poll tax (paid for the privilege of voting) and literacy requirements. Both were concessions to northern and western states that sought such provisions to keep immigrants and the "unworthy" poor from the polls. Congress required the four states remaining under federal control to ratify the measure as a condition for readmission to the Union. A year later, the **Fifteenth Amendment** became law.

Passage of the Fifteenth Amendment, despite its limitations, was an astonishing feat. Elsewhere in the Western Hemisphere, lawmakers had left emancipated slaves in a condition of semi-citizenship, with no voting rights. But, like almost all Americans, congressional Republicans had extraordinary faith in the power of the vote. Many African Americans agreed. "The colored people of these Southern states have cast their lot with the Government," declared a delegate to Arkansas's constitutional convention, "and with the great Republican Party. . . . The ballot is our only means of protection." In the election of 1870, hundreds of thousands of African Americans voted across the South, in an atmosphere of collective pride and celebration.

Women's Rights Denied

Passage of the Fifteenth Amendment was a bittersweet victory for national women's rights leaders, who had campaigned for the ballot since the Seneca Falls Convention of 1848. They hoped to secure voting rights for women and African American men at the same time. As Elizabeth Cady Stanton put it, women could "avail ourselves of the strong arm and the blue uniform of the black soldier to walk in by his side." The protected categories for voting in the Fifteenth Amendment could have read "race, color, *sex*, or previous condition of servitude." But that word proved impossible to obtain.

Enfranchising black men had clear benefits for the authors of Reconstruction. It punished ex-Confederates and ensured Republican support in the South. But women's party loyalties were more divided, and a substantial majority of northern voters — all men, of course — opposed women's enfranchisement. Even Radicals feared that this "side issue" would overburden their program. Influential abolitionists such as Wendell Philips refused to campaign for women's suffrage, fearing it would detract from the focus on black men. Philips criticized women's leaders for being "selfish." "Do you believe," Stanton hotly replied, "the African race is entirely composed of males?"

By May 1869, the former allies were at an impasse. At a convention of the Equal Rights Association, black abolitionist and women's rights advocate Frederick Douglass pleaded for white women to consider the situation in the South and allow black male suffrage to take priority. "When women, because they are women, are hunted down, . . . dragged from their homes and hung upon lamp posts," Douglass said, "then

Fifteenth Amendment
Constitutional amendment ratified in 1869 that forbade states to deny citizens the right to vote on grounds of race, color, or "previous condition of servitude."

American Woman Suffrage Association
A women's suffrage organization led by Lucy Stone, Henry Blackwell, and others who remained loyal to the Republican Party, despite its failure to include women's voting rights in the Reconstruction amendments. Stressing the urgency of voting rights for African American men, AWSA leaders held out hope that once Reconstruction had been settled, it would be women's turn.

National Woman Suffrage Association
A suffrage group headed by Elizabeth Cady Stanton and Susan B. Anthony that stressed the need for women to lead organizations on their own behalf. The NWSA focused exclusively on women's rights — sometimes denigrating men of color in the process — and took up the battle for a federal women's suffrage amendment.

they will have an urgency to obtain the ballot equal to our own." Some women's suffrage leaders joined Douglass in backing the Fifteenth Amendment without the word *sex*. But many, especially white women, rejected Douglass's plea. One African American woman remarked that they "all go for sex, letting race occupy a minor position." Embittered, Elizabeth Cady Stanton lashed out against "Patrick and Sambo and Hans and Ung Tung," maligning uneducated freedmen and immigrants who could vote while educated white women could not. Douglass's resolution in support of the Fifteenth Amendment failed, and the convention broke up.

A rift thus opened in the women's movement. The majority, led by Lucy Stone, reconciled themselves to disappointment. Organized into the **American Woman Suffrage Association**, they remained loyal to the Republican Party in hopes that once Reconstruction had been settled, it would be women's turn. A group led by Elizabeth Cady Stanton and Susan B. Anthony struck out in a new direction. They saw that, once the Reconstruction amendments had passed, women's suffrage was unlikely in the near future. Stanton declared that woman "must not put her trust in man." The new organization she headed, the **National Woman Suffrage Association** (NWSA), focused exclusively on women's rights and took up the battle for a federal suffrage amendment.

OUT IN THE COLD.

"Out in the Cold" Though many women, including African American activists in the South, went to the polls in the early 1870s to test whether the new Fourteenth Amendment had given them the vote, federal courts subsequently rejected women's voting rights. Only Wyoming and Utah territories fully enfranchised women. At the same time, revised naturalization laws allowed immigrant men of African descent — though not of Asian descent — to become citizens. With its crude Irish, African, and Chinese racial caricatures, this 1884 cartoon from the humor magazine *The Judge* echoes the arguments of some white suffragists: though men of races stereotyped as inferior had been enfranchised, white women were not. The woman knocking on the door is also a caricature, with her harsh appearance and masculine hat. Library of Congress.

In 1873, NWSA members decided to test the new constitutional amendments. Suffragists all over the United States, including some black women in the South, tried to register and vote. Most were turned away. In an ensuing lawsuit, suffrage advocate Virginia Minor of Missouri argued that the registrar who denied her a ballot had violated her rights under the Fourteenth Amendment. In ***Minor v. Happersett*** (1875), the Supreme Court dashed such hopes. It ruled that suffrage rights were not inherent in citizenship; women were citizens, but state legislatures could deny women the vote if they wished.

Women's rights advocates began to focus narrowly on suffrage as their movement suffered backlash from controversies over sexual freedom. After Victoria Woodhull,

Minor v. Happersett
A Supreme Court decision in 1875 that ruled that suffrage rights were not inherent in citizenship and had not been granted by the Fourteenth Amendment, as some women's rights advocates argued. Women were citizens, the Court ruled, but state legislatures could deny women the vote if they wished.

a flamboyant young woman from Ohio, became the nation's first female stockbroker on Wall Street, she won notoriety by denouncing marriage as a form of tyranny. She urged that women be "trained like men," for independent thought and economic self-sufficiency. Particularly sensational was Woodhull's insistence, in a speech in New York in 1871, that "I am a free lover. I have an inalienable, constitutional, and natural right to love whom I may, to love as long or as short a period as I can; to change that love every day if I please."

Beecher-Tilton scandal
A trial, triggered by revelations made by free love advocate and journalist Victoria Woodhull, that exposed unconventional sexual relationships among a leading New York abolitionist pastor and his congregants, discrediting radical Reconstruction by associating some of its advocates with alleged sexual immorality.

Woodhull helped trigger the **Beecher-Tilton scandal**, a sensational trial that dominated headlines in the mid-1870s. She accused Brooklyn Congregationalist minister Henry Ward Beecher, a staunch Republican and abolitionist from a famous reform family, of secretly being a free lover himself. For making allegations of adultery, Woodhull was tried on obscenity charges, briefly jailed, and released. Beecher was then sued by the husband of a congregant with whom he had allegedly had an affair. The results of the trial were inconclusive, but the relentless publicity, including the publication of intimate letters, damaged the reputation of everyone involved. Many Americans concluded that Radical Republicans wanted to go too far, and that, in private, former abolitionists like Beecher and his congregants were behaving immorally. Social conservatives, including ex-Confederates in the South, gleefully watched leading abolitionists get their come-uppance. Women's rights advocates, who had welcomed Victoria Woodhull as an ally, soon distanced themselves from her free love proclamations. Leaders such as Susan B. Anthony decided that the only way to win the vote was to practice and advocate strict sexual respectability.

Despite these defeats and embarrassments, Radical Reconstruction had created the conditions for a nationwide women's rights movement. Some argued for suffrage as part of a broader expansion of democracy. Others, on the contrary, saw white women's votes as a possible counterweight to the votes of African American or Chinese men (while opponents pointed out that black and immigrant women would likely be enfranchised, too). When Wyoming Territory gave women full voting rights in 1869, its governor received telegrams of congratulation from around the world. Afterward, contrary to dire predictions, female voters in Wyoming did not appear to neglect their homes, abandon their children, or otherwise "unsex" themselves. Women's suffrage could no longer be dismissed as the absurd notion of a tiny minority. It had become a serious issue for national debate.

> **IN YOUR OWN WORDS** What factors explain how Reconstruction policies unfolded between 1865 and 1870, and what was the impact on different groups of Americans?

The Meaning of Freedom

While political leaders wrangled in Washington, emancipated slaves acted on their own ideas about freedom. Emancipation meant many things: the end of punishment by the lash; the ability to move around; reunion of families; and opportunities to build schools and churches and to publish and read newspapers. Foremost among freedpeople's demands were voting rights and economic autonomy. Former Confederates opposed these goals. Most southern whites believed the proper place for blacks was as "servants and inferiors," as a Virginia planter testified to Congress. Mississippi's governor, elected under President Johnson's plan, vowed that "ours is and it shall ever be, a government of white men." Meanwhile, as Reconstruction unfolded, it became clear that on economic questions, southern blacks and northern Republican policymakers did not see eye to eye.

The Quest for Land

During the Civil War, wherever Union forces had conquered portions of the South, rural black workers had formed associations that agreed on common goals and even practiced military drills. After the war, when resettlement became the responsibility of the Freedmen's Bureau, thousands of rural blacks hoped for land distributions. But Johnson's amnesty plan, which allowed pardoned Confederates to recover property seized during the war, blasted such hopes. In October 1865, for example, Johnson ordered General Oliver O. Howard, head of the Freedmen's Bureau, to restore plantations on South Carolina's Sea Islands to white property holders. Dispossessed blacks protested: "Why do you take away our lands? You take them from us who have always been true, always true to the Government! You give them to our all-time enemies! That is not right!" Former slaves resisted efforts to evict them. Led by black Union veterans, they fought pitched battles with former slaveholders and bands of ex-Confederate soldiers. But white landowners, sometimes aided by federal troops, generally prevailed.

Freed Slaves and Northerners: Conflicting Goals On questions of land and labor, freedmen in the South and Republicans in Washington seriously differed. The economic revolution of the antebellum period had transformed New England and the Mid-Atlantic states. Believing similar development could revolutionize the South, most congressional leaders sought to restore cotton as the country's leading export, and they envisioned former slaves as wageworkers on cash-crop plantations, not independent farmers. Only a handful of Republican leaders, like Thaddeus Stevens, argued that freed slaves had earned a right to land grants, through what Lincoln had referred to as "four hundred years of unrequited toil." Stevens proposed that southern plantations be treated as "forfeited estates of the enemy" and broken up into small farms for former slaves. "Nothing will make men so industrious and moral," Stevens declared, "as to let them feel that they are above want and are the owners of the soil which they till."

Today, most historians of Reconstruction agree with Stevens: policymakers did not do enough to ensure freedpeople's economic security. Without land, former slaves were left poor and vulnerable. At the time, though, Stevens had few allies. A deep veneration for private property lay at the heart of his vision, but others interpreted the same principle differently: they defined ownership by legal title, not by labor invested. Though often accused of harshness toward the defeated Confederacy, most Republicans — even Radicals — could not imagine "giving" land to former slaves. The same congressmen, of course, had no difficulty giving away homesteads on the frontier that had been taken from Indians. But they were deeply reluctant to confiscate white-owned plantations.

Some southern Republican state governments did try, without much success, to use tax policy to break up large landholdings and get them into the hands of poorer

whites and blacks. In 1869, South Carolina established a land commission to buy property and resell it on easy terms to the landless; about 14,000 black families acquired
farms through the program. But such initiatives were the exception, not the rule. Over
time, some rural blacks did succeed in becoming small-scale landowners, especially
in Upper South states such as Virginia, North Carolina, and Tennessee. But it was an
uphill fight, and policymakers provided little aid.

Wage Labor and Sharecropping   Without land, most freedpeople had few options
but to work for former slave owners. Landowners wanted to retain the old gang-labor
system, with wages replacing the food, clothing, and shelter that slaves had once
received. Southern planters — who had recently scorned the North for the cruelties of
wage labor — now embraced waged work with apparent satisfaction. Maliciously
comparing black workers to free-roaming pigs, landowners told them to "root, hog, or
die." Former slaves found themselves with rock-bottom wages; it was a shock to find
that emancipation and "free labor" did not prevent a hardworking family from nearly
starving.

African American workers used a variety of tactics to fight back. As early as
1865, alarmed whites across the South reported that former slaves were holding mass
meetings to agree on "plans and terms for labor." Such meetings continued through the
Reconstruction years. Facing limited prospects at home, some workers left the fields
and traveled long distances to seek better-paying jobs on the railroads or in turpentine
and lumber camps. Others — from rice cultivators to laundry workers — organized
strikes.

At the same time, struggles raged between employers and freedpeople over
women's work. In slavery, African American women's bodies had been the sexual
property of white men. Protecting black women from such abuse, as much as possible,
was a crucial priority for freedpeople. When planters demanded that black women go
back into the fields, African Americans resisted resolutely. "I seen on some plantations,"
one freedman recounted, "where the white men would . . . tell colored men that their
wives and children could not live on their places unless they work in the fields. The
colored men [answered that] whenever they wanted their wives to work they would
tell them themselves."

There was a profound irony in this man's definition of freedom: it designated a
wife's labor as her husband's property. Some black women asserted their independence and headed their own households, though this was often a matter of necessity
rather than choice. For many freedpeople, the opportunity for a stable family life was
one of the greatest achievements of emancipation. Many enthusiastically accepted the
northern ideal of domesticity. Missionaries, teachers, and editors of black newspapers
urged men to work diligently and support their families, and they told women
(though many worked for wages) to devote themselves to motherhood and the home
(Interpretations).

Even in rural areas, former slaves refused to work under conditions that recalled
slavery. There would be no gang work, they vowed: no overseers, no whippings, no
regulation of their private lives. Across the South, planters who needed labor were
forced to yield to what one planter termed the "prejudices of the freedmen, who desire
to be masters of their own time." In a few areas, wage work became the norm — for

What did the Thirteenth Amendment really accomplish? The answer may seem self-evident: it abolished slavery. But how free were newly emancipated slaves during the years immediately following the war, in comparison to earlier and later decades? For historians who measure change over time, it is a question worth asking.

Formerly enslaved people sought out and reunited with family members they could find who had been sold to other regions during slavery. They also founded businesses, churches, and schools and worked to secure economic stability and political rights. The ideological, political, and economic system that had sustained slavery prior to the Civil War, however, did not entirely disappear. Gender made a difference: as they had under slavery, the experiences of women differed from those of men. Historians Tera W. Hunter and Jacqueline Jones focus on the postwar experiences of freedwomen to understand what changes emancipation brought to their lives and to assess how much freedom they were able to secure.

How Free Were Freedwomen in Reconstruction?

TERA W. HUNTER

SOURCE: Tera W. Hunter, *To Joy My Freedom: Southern Black Women's Lives and Labors After the Civil War* (Cambridge: Harvard University Press, 1997), 28.

African-American women decided to quit work over such grievances as low wages, long hours, and unpleasant tasks. . . . [I]t was an effective strategy to deprive employers of complete power over their labor. . . . Occasional refusals to sell their labor or self-imposed limits enabled working-class women to conduct their own family and community affairs in ways that mitigated the demands of white supremacy and the market economy.

JACQUELINE JONES

SOURCE: Jacqueline Jones, *Labor of Love, Labor of Sorrow: Black Women, Work and the Family from Slavery to the Present* (New York: Vintage Books, 1986), 7.

[B]lack working women . . . lacked the control over their own productive energies and material resources. . . . Though perhaps "freed" or "liberated" from narrow sex-role conventions, they remained tied to overwhelming wage-earning and child-rearing responsibilities. . . . [W]hen measured against traditional standards of power — usually defined in terms of wealth; personal autonomy; and control over workers, votes, or inheritances — black wives and mothers had little leverage with which to manipulate the behavior of their kinfolk.

QUESTIONS FOR ANALYSIS

1. How does each historian assess the impact of the Reconstruction era on freedwomen?
2. Name two factors that each historian considers when evaluating freedom for freedwomen during Reconstruction.
3. What evidence from the chapter supports or refutes the interpretation that emancipation empowered freedwomen in the years following the Civil War?

example, on the giant sugar plantations of Louisiana financed by northern capital. But cotton planters lacked money to pay wages, and sometimes, in lieu of a wage, they offered a share of the crop. Freedmen, in turn, paid their rent in shares of the harvest.

Thus the Reconstruction years gave rise to a distinctive system of cotton agriculture known as **sharecropping**, in which freedmen worked as renters, exchanging their labor for the use of land, house, implements, and sometimes seed and fertilizer. Sharecroppers typically turned over half of their crops to the landlord (Map 14.2). In a credit-starved agricultural region that grew crops for a world economy, sharecropping was an effective strategy, enabling laborers and landowners to share risks and returns. But it was a very unequal relationship. Starting out penniless, sharecroppers had no way to make it through the first growing season without borrowing for food and supplies.

Country storekeepers stepped in. Bankrolled by northern suppliers, they furnished sharecroppers with provisions and took as collateral a lien on the crop, effectively assuming ownership of croppers' shares and leaving them only what remained after debts had been paid. Crop-lien laws enforced lenders' ownership rights to the crop

sharecropping
The labor system by which landowners and impoverished southern farmworkers, particularly African Americans, divided the proceeds from crops harvested on the landowner's property. With local merchants providing supplies — in exchange for a lien on the crop — sharecropping pushed farmers into cash-crop production and often trapped them in long-term debt.

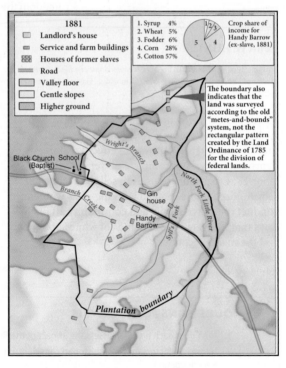

MAP 14.2 The Barrow Plantation, 1860 and 1881
This map is a modern redrawing of one that first appeared in the popular magazine *Scribner's Monthly* in April 1881, accompanying an article about the Barrow plantation. Comparing the 1860 map of this central Georgia plantation with the 1881 map reveals the impact of sharecropping on patterns of black residence. In 1860, the slave quarters were clustered near the planter's house. In contrast, by 1881 the sharecroppers were scattered across the plantation's 2,000 acres, having built cabins on the ridges between the low-lying streams. The surname *Barrow* was common among the sharecropping families, which means almost certainly that they had been slaves who, years after emancipation, still had not moved on. For sharecroppers, freedom meant not only their individual lots and cabins but also the school and church shown on the map.

share. Once indebted at a store, sharecroppers became easy targets for exorbitant prices, unfair interest rates, and crooked bookkeeping. As cotton prices declined in the 1870s, more and more sharecroppers fell into permanent debt. If the merchant was also the landowner or conspired with the landowner, debt became a pretext for forced labor, or peonage.

Sharecropping arose in part because it was a good fit for cotton agriculture. Cotton, unlike sugarcane, could be raised efficiently by small farmers (provided they had the lash of indebtedness always on their backs). We can see this in the experience of other regions that became major producers in response to the global cotton shortage set off by the Civil War. In India, Egypt, Brazil, and West Africa, variants of the sharecropping system emerged. Everywhere international merchants and bankers, who put up capital, insisted on passage of crop-lien laws. Indian and Egyptian villagers ended up, like their American counterparts, permanently under the thumb of furnishing merchants.

By 1890, three out of every four black farmers in the South were tenants or sharecroppers; among white farmers, the ratio was one in three. For freedmen, sharecropping was not the worst choice, in a world

Picking Cotton in Mississippi After emancipation most African Americans in the South, lacking land or capital, continued to work in agriculture. Through sharecropping and other arrangements, they sought as much autonomy and control over their work as they could obtain. Many families made it a priority for women to work in the home and children to attend school. At harvest time, however, everyone was needed in the fields. The Granger Collection, New York.

where former masters threatened to impose labor conditions that were close to slavery. But the costs were devastating. With farms leased on a year-to-year basis, neither tenant nor owner had much incentive to improve the property. The crop-lien system rested on expensive interest payments — money that might otherwise have gone into agricultural improvements or to meet human needs. And sharecropping committed the South inflexibly to cotton, a crop that generated the cash required by landlords and furnishing merchants. The result was a stagnant farm economy that blighted the South's future. As Republican governments tried to remake the region, they confronted not only wartime destruction but also the failure of their hopes that free labor would create a modern, prosperous South, built in the image of the industrializing North. Instead, the South's rural economy remained mired in widespread poverty and based on an uneasy compromise between landowners and laborers.

Republican Governments in the South

Between 1868 and 1871, all the former Confederate states met congressional stipulations and rejoined the Union. Protected by federal troops, Republican administrations in these states retained power for periods ranging from a few months in

Virginia to nine years in South Carolina, Louisiana, and Florida. These governments remain some of the most misunderstood institutions in all U.S. history. Ex-Confederates never accepted their legitimacy. Many other whites agreed, focusing particularly on the role of African Americans who began to serve in public office. "It is strange, abnormal, and unfit," declared one British visitor to Louisiana, "that a *negro* Legislature should deal . . . with the gravest commercial and financial interests." During much of the twentieth century, historians echoed such critics, condemning Reconstruction leaders as ignorant and corrupt. These historians shared the racial prejudices of the British observer: black men were simply unfit to govern.

In fact, Reconstruction governments were ambitious. They were hated, in part, because they undertook impressive reforms in public education, family law, social services, commerce, and transportation. Like their northern allies, southern Republicans admired the economic and social transformations that had occurred in the North before the Civil War and worked energetically to import them.

The southern Republican Party included former Whigs, a few former Democrats, black and white newcomers from the North, and southern African Americans. From the start, its leaders faced the dilemma of racial prejudice. In the upcountry, white Unionists were eager to join the party but sometimes reluctant to work with black allies. In most areas, the Republicans also desperately needed African Americans, who constituted a majority of registered voters in Alabama, Florida, South Carolina, and Mississippi.

For a brief moment in the late 1860s, black and white Republicans joined forces through the Union League, a secret fraternal order. Formed in border states and northern cities during the Civil War, the league became a powerful political association that spread through the former Confederacy. Functioning as a grassroots wing of Radical Republicanism, it pressured Congress to uphold justice for freedmen. After blacks won voting rights, the league organized meetings at churches and schoolhouses to instruct freedmen on political issues and voting procedures. League clubs held parades and military drills, giving a public face to the new political order.

The Freedmen's Bureau also supported grassroots Reconstruction efforts. Though some bureau officials sympathized with planters, most were dedicated, idealistic men who tried valiantly to reconcile opposing interests. Bureau men kept a sharp eye out for unfair labor contracts and often forced landowners to bargain with workers and tenants. They advised freedmen on economic matters; provided direct payments to desperate families, especially women and children; and helped establish schools. In cooperation with northern aid societies, the bureau played a key role in founding African American colleges and universities such as Fisk, Tougaloo, and the Hampton Institute. These institutions, in turn, focused on training teachers. By 1869, there were more than three thousand teachers instructing freedpeople in the South. More than half were themselves African Americans.

Ex-Confederates viewed the Union League, Freedmen's Bureau, and Republican Party as illegitimate forces in southern affairs, and they resented the political education of freedpeople. They referred to southern whites who supported Reconstruction as scalawags — an ancient Scots-Irish term for worthless animals — and denounced northern whites as carpetbaggers, self-seeking interlopers who carried all their property in cheap suitcases called carpetbags. Such labels glossed over the actual diversity of white Republicans. Many arrivals from the North, while motivated by personal profit, also brought capital and skills. Interspersed with ambitious schemers were reformers hoping to advance freedmen's rights. So-called scalawags were even more varied. Some southern Republicans were former slave owners; others were ex-Whigs or even ex-Democrats who hoped to attract northern capital. But most hailed from the backcountry and wanted to rid the South of its slaveholding aristocracy, believing slavery had victimized whites as well as blacks.

Southern Democrats' contempt for black politicians, whom they regarded as ignorant field hands, was just as misguided as their stereotypes about white Republicans. Many African American leaders in the South came from the ranks of antebellum free blacks. Others were skilled men like Robert Smalls of South Carolina, who as a slave had worked for wages that he turned over to his master. Smalls, a steamer pilot in Charleston harbor, had become a war hero when he escaped with his family and other slaves and brought his ship to the Union navy. Buying property in Beaufort after the war, Smalls became a state legislator and later a congressman. Blanche K. Bruce, another former slave, had been tutored on a Virginia plantation by his white father; during the war, he escaped and established a school for freedmen in Missouri. In 1869, he moved to Mississippi and became, five years later, Mississippi's second black U.S. senator. Political leaders such as Smalls and Bruce were joined by northern blacks — including ministers, teachers, and Union veterans — who moved south to support Reconstruction.

During radical Reconstruction, such men fanned out into plantation districts and recruited former slaves to participate in politics. Literacy helped freedman Thomas Allen, a Baptist minister and shoemaker, win election to the Georgia legislature. "The colored people came to me," Allen recalled, "and I gave them the best instructions I could. I took the *New York Tribune* and other papers, and in that way I found out a great deal, and I told them whatever I thought was right." Though never proportionate to their numbers in the population, blacks became officeholders across the South. In South Carolina, African Americans constituted a majority in the lower house of the legislature in 1868. Over the course of Reconstruction, twenty African Americans served in state administrations as governor, lieutenant governor, secretary of state, or lesser offices. More than six hundred became state legislators, and sixteen were congressmen.

Both white and black Republicans had big plans. Their southern Reconstruction governments eliminated property qualifications for the vote and abolished Black Codes. Their new state constitutions expanded the rights of married women, enabling them to own their own property and wages — "a wonderful reform," one white woman in Georgia wrote, for "the cause of Women's Rights." Like their counterparts in the North, southern Republicans also believed in using government to foster economic growth. Seeking to diversify the economy beyond cotton agriculture, they poured money into railroads and other projects.

In myriad ways, Republicans brought southern state and city governments up to date. They outlawed corporal punishments such as whipping and branding. They established hospitals and asylums for orphans and the disabled. South Carolina offered free public health services, while Alabama provided free legal representation for defendants who could not pay. Some municipal governments paved streets and installed streetlights. Petersburg, Virginia, established a board of health that offered free medical care during the smallpox epidemic of 1873. Nashville, Tennessee, created soup kitchens for the poor.

Most impressive of all were achievements in public education, where the South had lagged woefully. Republicans viewed education as the foundation of a true democratic order. By 1875, over half of black children were attending school in Mississippi, Florida, and South Carolina. African Americans of all ages rushed to the newly established schools, even when they had to pay tuition. They understood why slaveholders had criminalized slave literacy: the practice of freedom rested on the ability to read newspapers, labor contracts, history books, and the Bible. A school official in Virginia reported that freedpeople were "*crazy* to learn." One Louisiana man explained why he was sending his children to school, even though he needed their help in the field. It was "better than leaving them a fortune; because if you left them even five hundred dollars, some man having more education than they had would come along and cheat them out of it all." Thousands of white children, particularly girls and the sons of poor farmers and laborers, also benefitted from new public education systems. Young white women's graduation from high school, an unheard-of occurrence before the Civil War, became a celebrated event in southern cities and towns.

Southern Reconstruction governments also had their flaws — flaws that would become more apparent as the 1870s unfolded. In the race for economic development, for example, state officials allowed private companies to hire out prisoners to labor in mines and other industries, in a notorious system known as **convict leasing**. Corruption was rife and conditions horrific. In 1866, Alabama's governor leased 200 state convicts to a railroad construction company for the grand total of $5. While they labored to build state-subsidized lines such as the Alabama and Chattanooga, prisoners were housed at night in open, rolling cages. Physical abuse was common and medical care nonexistent. At the start of 1869, Alabama counted 263 prisoners available for leasing; by the end of the year, a staggering 92 of them had died. While convict leasing expanded in later decades, it began during Reconstruction, supported by both Republicans and Democrats.

convict leasing
Notorious system, begun during Reconstruction, whereby southern state officials allowed private companies to hire out prisoners to labor under brutal conditions in mines and other industries.

Building Black Communities

Enslaved African Americans had built networks of religious worship and mutual aid, but these operated largely in secret. After emancipation, southern blacks could engage in open community building. In doing so, they cooperated with northern missionaries and teachers, both black and white, who came to help in the great work of freedom. "Ignorant though they may be, on account of long years of oppression, they exhibit a desire to hear and to learn, that I never imagined," reported African American minister Reverend James Lynch, who traveled from Maryland to the Deep South. "Every word you say while preaching, they drink down and respond to, with an earnestness that sets your heart all on fire."

Independent churches quickly became central community institutions, as blacks across the South left white-dominated congregations, where they had sat in segregated balconies, and built churches of their own. These churches joined their counterparts in the North to become national denominations, including, most prominently, the National Baptist Convention and the African Methodist Episcopal Church. Black churches served not only as sites of worship but also as schools, social centers, and meeting halls. Ministers were often political spokesmen as well. As Charles H. Pearce, a black Methodist pastor in Florida, declared, "A man in this State cannot do his whole duty as a minister except he looks out for the political interests of his people." Religious leaders articulated the special destiny of freedpeople as the new "Children of Israel."

The flowering of black churches, schools, newspapers, and civic groups was one of the most enduring initiatives of the Reconstruction era. Dedicated teachers and charity leaders embarked on a project of "race uplift" that never ceased thereafter, while black entrepreneurs were proud to build businesses that served their communities. The issue of desegregation — sharing public facilities with whites — was a trickier one. Though some black leaders pressed for desegregation, they were keenly aware of the backlash this was likely to provoke. Others made it clear that they preferred their children to attend all-black schools, especially if they encountered hostile or condescending white teachers and classmates. Many had pragmatic concerns. Asked whether she wanted her boys to attend an integrated school, one woman in New Orleans said no: "I don't want my children to be pounded by . . . white boys. I don't send them to school to fight, I send them to learn."

At the national level, congressmen wrestled with similar issues as they debated an ambitious civil rights

Fisk Jubilee Singers, 1873 Fisk University in Nashville, Tennessee, was established in 1865 to provide higher education for African Americans from all across the South. When funds ran short in 1871, enterprising students formed the Jubilee Singers choral group (bottom) and toured to raise money for the school. They performed African American spirituals and folk songs, such as "Swing Low, Sweet Chariot," arranged in ways that appealed to white audiences, making this music nationally popular for the first time. In 1872, the group performed for President Grant at the White House. Money raised by this acclaimed group saved Fisk from bankruptcy and built the university's imposing Jubilee Hall (top). Private Collection/© Look and Learn/Illustrated Papers Collection/Bridgeman Images.

bill championed by Radical Republican senator Charles Sumner. Sumner first introduced his bill in 1870, seeking to enforce, among other things, equal access to schools, public transportation, hotels, and churches. Due to a series of defeats and delays, the bill remained on Capitol Hill for five years. Opponents charged that shared public spaces would lead to race mixing and intermarriage. Some sympathetic Republicans

To see a call for passage of the Civil Rights Act from an African American Congress, along with other primary sources from this period, see *Sources for America's History*.

Civil Rights Act of 1875
A law that required "full and equal" access to jury service and to transportation and public accommodations, irrespective of race.

feared a backlash, while others questioned whether, because of the First Amendment, the federal government had the right to regulate churches. On his deathbed in 1874, Sumner exhorted a visitor to remember the civil rights bill: "Don't let it fail." In the end, the Senate removed Sumner's provision for integrated churches, and the House removed the clause requiring integrated schools. But to honor the great Massachusetts abolitionist, Congress passed the **Civil Rights Act of 1875**. The law required "full and equal" access to jury service and to transportation and public accommodations, irrespective of race. It was the last such act for almost a hundred years — until the Civil Rights Act of 1964.

> **IN YOUR OWN WORDS** What goals were southern freedmen and freedwomen able to achieve in the post–Civil War years, and why? What goals were they not able to achieve, and why not?

The Undoing of Reconstruction

Sumner's death marked the waning of Radical Reconstruction. That movement had accomplished more than anyone dreamed a few years earlier. But a chasm had opened between the goals of freedmen, who wanted autonomy, and policymakers, whose first priorities were to reincorporate ex-Confederates into the nation and build a powerful national economy. Meanwhile, the North was flooded with one-sided, racist reports such as James M. Pike's influential book *The Prostrate State* (1873), which claimed South Carolina was in the grip of "black barbarism." Events of the 1870s deepened the northern public's disillusionment. Scandals rocked the Grant administration, and an economic depression curbed both private investment and public spending. At the same time, northern resolve was worn down by continued ex-Confederate resistance and violence. Only full-scale military intervention could reverse the situation in the South, and by the mid-1870s the North had no political willpower to renew the occupation.

The Republicans Unravel

Republicans had banked on economic growth to underpin their ambitious program, but their hopes were dashed in 1873 by the sudden onset of a severe worldwide depression. In the United States, the initial panic was triggered by the bankruptcy of the Northern Pacific Railroad, backed by leading financier Jay Cooke. Cooke's supervision of Union finances during the Civil War had made him a national hero; his downfall was a shock, and since Cooke was so well connected in Washington, it raised suspicions that Republican financial manipulation had caused the depression. Officials in the Grant administration deepened public resentment toward their party when they rejected pleas to increase the money supply and provide relief from debt and unemployment.

The impact of the depression varied in different parts of the United States. Farmers suffered a terrible plight as crop prices plunged, while industrial workers faced layoffs and sharp wage reductions. Within a year, 50 percent of American iron manufacturing had stopped. By 1877, half the nation's railroad companies had filed for bankruptcy. Rail construction halted. With hundreds of thousands thrown out of work, people took to the road. Wandering "tramps," who camped by railroad tracks and knocked on doors to beg for work and food, terrified prosperous Americans.

In addition to discrediting Republicans, the depression directly undercut their policies, most dramatically in the South. The ex-Confederacy was still recovering from the ravages of war, and its new economic and social order remained fragile. The bold policies of southern Republicans — for education, public health, and grants to railroad builders — cost a great deal of money. Federal support, through programs like the Freedmen's Bureau, had begun to fade even before 1873. Republicans had banked on major infusions of northern and foreign investment capital; for the most part, these failed to materialize. Investors who had sunk money into Confederate bonds, only to have those repudiated, were especially wary. The South's economy grew more slowly than Republicans had hoped, and after 1873, growth screeched to a halt. State debts mounted rapidly, and as crushing interest on bonds fell due, public credit collapsed.

Not only had Republican officials failed to anticipate a severe depression; during the era of generous spending, considerable funds had also been wasted or had ended up in the pockets of corrupt officials. Two swindlers in North Carolina, one of them a former Union general, were found to have distributed more than $200,000 in bribes and loans to legislators to gain millions in state funds for rail construction. Instead of building railroads, they used the money to travel to Europe and speculate in stocks and bonds. Not only Republicans were on the take. "You are mistaken," wrote one southern Democrat to a northern friend, "if you suppose that all the evils . . . result from the carpetbaggers and negroes. The Democrats are leagued with them when anything is proposed that promises to pay." In South Carolina, when African American congressman Robert Smalls was convicted of taking a bribe, the Democratic governor pardoned him in exchange for an agreement that federal officials would drop an investigation of Democratic election fraud.

One of the depression's most tragic results was the failure of the Freedman's Savings and Trust Company. This private bank, founded in 1865, had worked closely with the Freedmen's Bureau and Union army across the South. Former slaves associated it with the party of Lincoln, and thousands responded to northerners' call for thrift and savings by bringing their small deposits to the nearest branch. African American farmers, entrepreneurs, churches, and charitable groups opened accounts at the bank. But in the early 1870s, the bank's directors sank their money into risky loans and speculative investments. In June 1874, the bank failed.

Some Republicans believed that, because the bank had been so closely associated with the U.S. Army and federal agencies, Congress had a duty to step in. Even one southern Democrat argued that the government was "morally bound to see to it that not a dollar is lost." But in the end, Congress refused to compensate the 61,000 depositors. About half recovered small amounts — averaging $18.51 — but the others received nothing. The party of Reconstruction was losing its moral gloss.

The Disillusioned Liberals As a result of the depression and rising criticism of postwar activist government, a revolt emerged in the Republican Party. It was led by influential intellectuals, journalists, and businessmen who believed in **classical liberalism**: free

classical liberalism
The political ideology of individual liberty, private property, a competitive market economy, free trade, and limited government. The ideal is a *laissez faire* or "let alone" policy, in which government does the least possible, particularly in reference to economic policies such as tariffs and incentives for industrial development. Attacking corruption and defending private property, late-nineteenth-century liberals generally called for elite governance and questioned the advisability of full democratic participation.

trade, small government, low property taxes, and limitation of voting rights to men of education and property. Liberals responded to the massive increase in federal power, during the Civil War and Reconstruction, by urging a policy of *laissez faire*, in which government "let alone" business and the economy. In the postwar decades, laissez faire advocates never succeeded in ending federal policies such as the protective tariff and national banking system (Chapter 16), but their arguments helped roll back Reconstruction. Unable to block Grant's renomination for the presidency in 1872, the dissidents broke away and formed a new party under the name Liberal Republican. Their candidate was Horace Greeley, longtime publisher of the *New York Tribune* and veteran reformer and abolitionist. The Democrats, still in disarray, also nominated Greeley, notwithstanding his editorial diatribes against them. A poor campaigner, Greeley was assailed so severely that, as he said, "I hardly knew whether I was running for the Presidency or the penitentiary."

Grant won reelection overwhelmingly, capturing 56 percent of the popular vote and every electoral vote. Yet Liberal Republicans had shifted the terms of debate. The agenda they advanced — smaller government, restricted voting rights, and reconciliation with ex-Confederates — resonated with Democrats, who had long advocated limited government and were working to reclaim their status as a legitimate national party. Liberalism thus crossed party lines, uniting disillusioned conservative Republicans with Democrats who denounced government activism. E. L. Godkin of *The Nation* and other classical liberal editors played key roles in turning northern public opinion against Reconstruction. With unabashed elitism, Godkin and others claimed that freedmen were unfit to vote. They denounced universal suffrage, which "can only mean in plain English the government of ignorance and vice."

Crédit Mobilier

A sham corporation set up by shareholders in the Union Pacific Railroad to secure government grants at an enormous profit. Organizers of the scheme protected it from investigation by providing gifts of its stock to powerful members of Congress.

The second Grant administration gave liberals plenty of ammunition. The most notorious scandal involved **Crédit Mobilier**, a sham corporation set up by shareholders in the Union Pacific Railroad to secure government grants at an enormous profit. Organizers of the scheme protected it from investigation by providing gifts of Crédit Mobilier stock to powerful members of Congress. Controversy over this railroad scandal arose even before Grant's reelection; by 1875 another scandal emerged involving the so-called "Whiskey Ring," a network of liquor distillers and treasury agents who defrauded the government of millions of dollars of excise taxes on whiskey. The ringleader was Grant's private secretary, Orville Babcock. Others went to prison, but Grant stood by Babcock, possibly perjuring himself to save his secretary from jail. The stench of scandal permeated the White House.

Counterrevolution in the South

While northerners became preoccupied with scandals and the shock of economic depression, ex-Confederates seized power in the South. Most believed (as northern liberals had also begun to argue) that southern Reconstruction governments were illegitimate "regimes." Led by the planters, ex-Confederates staged a massive insurgency to take back the South.

When they could win at the ballot box, southern Democrats took that route. They got ex-Confederate voting rights restored and campaigned against "negro rule." But when force was necessary, southern Democrats used it. Present-day Americans, witnessing political violence in other countries, seldom remember that our own history includes the overthrow of elected governments by paramilitary groups. But this is exactly how Reconstruction ended in many parts of the South. Ex-Confederates terrorized Republicans, especially in districts with large proportions of black voters. Black political leaders were shot, hanged, beaten to death, and in one case even beheaded. Many Republicans, both black and white, went into hiding or fled for their lives. Southern Democrats called this violent process "Redemption"—a heroic name that still lingers today, even though this seizure of power was murderous and undemocratic.

No one looms larger in this bloody story than Nathan Bedford Forrest, a decorated Confederate general. Born in poverty in 1821, Forrest had risen to become a big-time slave trader and Mississippi planter. A fiery secessionist, Forrest had formed a Tennessee Confederate cavalry regiment, fought bravely at the battle of Shiloh, and won fame as a daring raider. On April 12, 1864, his troops perpetrated one of the war's worst atrocities, the massacre at Fort Pillow, Tennessee, of black Union soldiers who were trying to surrender.

After the Civil War, Forrest's determination to uphold white supremacy altered the course of Reconstruction. William G. Brownlow, elected as Tennessee's Republican governor in 1865, was a tough man, a former prisoner of the Confederates who was not shy about calling his enemies to account. Ex-Confederates struck back with a campaign of terror, targeting especially Brownlow's black supporters. Amid the mayhem, ex-Confederates formed the first **Ku Klux Klan** group in late 1865 or early 1866. As it proliferated across the state, the Klan turned to Forrest, who had been trying, unsuccessfully, to rebuild his prewar fortune. Late in 1866, at a secret meeting in Nashville, Forrest donned the robes of Grand Wizard. His activities are mostly cloaked in mystery, but there is no mistake about his goals: the Klan would strike blows against the despised Republican government of Tennessee.

In many towns, the Klan became virtually identical to the Democratic Party. Klan members—including Forrest—dominated Tennessee's delegation to the Democratic national convention of 1868. At home, the Klan unleashed a murderous campaign of terror, and though Governor Brownlow responded resolutely, in the end Republicans cracked. The Klan and similar groups—organized under such names as the White League and Knights of the White Camelia—arose in other states. Vigilantes burned freedmen's schools, beat teachers, attacked Republican gatherings, and murdered political opponents. By 1870, Democrats had seized power in Georgia and North Carolina and were making headway across the South. Once they took power,

Ku Klux Klan
Secret society that first undertook violence against African Americans in the South after the Civil War but was reborn in 1915 to fight the perceived threats posed by African Americans, immigrants, radicals, feminists, Catholics, and Jews.

Ku Klux Klan Mask White supremacists of the 1870s organized under many names and wore many costumes, not simply (or often) the white cone-shaped hats that were made famous later, in the 1920s, when the Klan underwent a nationwide resurgence. Few masks from the 1870s have survived. The horns and fangs on this one, from North Carolina, suggest how Klan members sought to strike terror in their victims, while also hiding their own identities. North Carolina Museum of History.

they slashed property taxes and passed other laws favorable to landowners. They terminated Reconstruction programs and cut funding for schools, especially those teaching black students.

In responding to the Klan between 1869 and 1871, the federal government showed it could still exert power effectively in the South. Determined to end Klan violence, Congress held extensive hearings and in 1870 passed laws designed to protect freedmen's rights under the Fourteenth and Fifteenth Amendments. These so-called **Enforcement Laws** authorized federal prosecutions, military intervention, and martial law to suppress terrorist activity. Grant's administration made full use of these new powers. In South Carolina, where the Klan was deeply entrenched, U.S. troops occupied nine counties, made hundreds of arrests, and drove as many as 2,000 Klansmen from the state.

This assault on the Klan, while raising the spirits of southern Republicans, revealed how dependent they were on Washington. "No such law could be enforced by state authority," one Mississippi Republican observed, "the local power being too weak." But northern Republicans were growing disillusioned with Reconstruction, while in the South, prosecuting Klansmen was an uphill battle against all-white juries and unsympathetic federal judges. After 1872, prosecutions dropped off. Meanwhile, the Texas government fell to the Democrats in 1873 and Alabama and Arkansas fell in 1874.

Enforcement Laws
Acts passed in Congress in 1870 and signed by President U. S. Grant that were designed to protect freedmen's rights under the Fourteenth and Fifteenth Amendments. Authorizing federal prosecutions, military intervention, and martial law to suppress terrorist activity, the Enforcement Laws largely succeeded in shutting down Klan activities.

Reconstruction Rolled Back

As divided Republicans debated how to respond, voters in the congressional election of 1874 handed them one of the most stunning defeats of the nineteenth century. Responding especially to the severe depression that gripped the nation, they removed almost half of the party's 199 representatives in the House. Democrats, who had held 88 seats, now commanded an overwhelming majority of 182. "The election is not merely a victory but a revolution," exulted a Democratic newspaper in New York.

After 1874, with Democrats in control of the House, Republicans who tried to shore up their southern wing had limited options. Bowing to election results, the Grant administration began to reject southern Republicans' appeals for aid. Events in Mississippi showed the outcome. As state elections neared there in 1875, paramilitary groups such as the Red Shirts operated openly. Mississippi's Republican governor, Adelbert Ames, a Union veteran from Maine, appealed for U.S. troops, but Grant refused. "The whole public are tired out with these annual autumnal outbreaks in the South," complained a Grant official, who told southern Republicans that they were responsible for their own fate. Facing a rising tide of brutal murders, Governor Ames — realizing that only further bloodshed could result — urged his allies to give up the fight. Brandishing guns and stuffing ballot boxes, Democratic "Redeemers" swept the 1875 elections and took control of Mississippi. By 1876, Reconstruction was largely over. Republican governments, backed by token U.S. military units, remained in only three southern states: Louisiana, South Carolina, and Florida. Elsewhere, former Confederates and their allies took power.

The Supreme Court Rejects Equal Rights Though ex-Confederates seized power in southern states, new landmark constitutional amendments and federal laws remained in force. If the Supreme Court had left these intact, subsequent generations of civil rights advocates could have used the federal courts to combat racial discrimination and violence. Instead, the Court closed off this avenue for the pursuit of justice, just as it dashed the hopes of women's rights advocates.

As early as 1873, in a group of decisions known collectively as the **Slaughter-House Cases**, the Court began to undercut the power of the Fourteenth Amendment. In *Slaughter-House* and a related ruling, *U.S. v. Cruikshank* (1876), the justices argued that the Fourteenth Amendment offered only a few, rather trivial federal protections to citizens (such as access to navigable waterways). In *Cruikshank* — a case that emerged from a gruesome killing of African American farmers by ex-Confederates in Colfax, Louisiana, followed by a Democratic political coup — the Court ruled that voting rights remained a state matter unless the state itself violated those rights. If former slaves' rights were violated by individuals or private groups (including the Klan), that lay beyond federal jurisdiction. The Fourteenth Amendment did not protect citizens from armed vigilantes, even when those vigilantes seized political power. The Court thus gutted the Fourteenth Amendment. In the **Civil Rights Cases** (1883), the justices also struck down the Civil Rights Act of 1875, paving the way for later decisions that sanctioned segregation. The impact of these decisions endured well into the twentieth century.

The Political Crisis of 1877

After the grim election results of 1874, Republicans faced a major battle in the presidential election of 1876. Abandoning Grant, they nominated Rutherford B. Hayes, a former Union general who was untainted by corruption and — even more important — hailed from the key swing state of Ohio. Hayes's Democratic opponent was New York governor Samuel J. Tilden, a Wall Street lawyer with a reform reputation. Tilden favored home rule for the South, but so, more discreetly, did Hayes. With enforcement on the wane, Reconstruction did not figure prominently in the campaign, and little was said about the states still led by Reconstruction governments: Florida, South Carolina, and Louisiana.

Once returns started coming in on election night, however, those states loomed large. Tilden led in the popular vote and seemed headed for victory until sleepless politicians at Republican headquarters realized that the electoral vote stood at 184 to 165, with the 20 votes from Florida, South Carolina, and Louisiana still uncertain. If Hayes took those votes, he would win by a margin of 1. Citing ample evidence of Democratic fraud and intimidation, Republican officials certified all three states for Hayes. "Redeemer" Democrats who had taken over the states' governments submitted their own electoral votes for Tilden. When Congress met in early 1877, it confronted two sets of electoral votes from those states.

The Constitution does not provide for such a contingency. All it says is that the president of the Senate (in 1877, a Republican) opens the electoral certificates before the House (Democratic) and the Senate (Republican) and "the Votes shall then be counted" (Article 2, Section 1). Suspense gripped the country. There was talk of inside deals or a new election — even a violent coup. Finally, Congress appointed an electoral commission to settle the question. The commission included seven Republicans, seven Democrats, and, as the deciding member, David Davis, a Supreme Court justice not known to have fixed party loyalties. Davis, however, disqualified himself by accepting an Illinois Senate seat. He was replaced by Republican justice Joseph P. Bradley, and by a vote of 8 to 7, on party lines, the commission awarded the election to Hayes.

Slaughter-House Cases
A group of decisions begun in 1873 in which the Court began to undercut the power of the Fourteenth Amendment to protect African American rights.

Civil Rights Cases
A series of 1883 Supreme Court decisions that struck down the Civil Rights Act of 1875, rolling back key Reconstruction laws and paving the way for later decisions that sanctioned segregation.

The South's "Lost Cause"

After Reconstruction ended, many white southerners celebrated the Confederacy as a heroic "Lost Cause." Through organizations such as the Sons of Confederate Veterans and United Daughters of the Confederacy, they profoundly influenced the nation's memories of slavery, the Civil War, and Reconstruction.

1. **Commemorative postcard of living Confederate flag, Robert E. Lee Monument, Richmond, Virginia, 1907.** *An estimated 150,000 people gathered in 1890 to dedicate this statue — ten times more than had attended earlier memorial events.*

Source: The Library of Virginia.

HUMAN CONFEDERATE FLAG   "And 'Twill Live In Song and Story Though Its Folds Are In the Dust"

2. **From the United Daughters of the Confederacy Constitution, 1894.** *The United Daughters of the Confederacy (UDC), founded in 1894, grew in three years to 136 chapters and by the late 1910s counted a membership of 100,000.*

The objects of this association are historical, educational, memorial, benevolent, and social: To fulfill the duties of sacred charity to the survivors of the war and those dependent on them; to collect and preserve material for a truthful history of the war; to protect historic places of the Confederacy; to record the part taken by the Southern women . . . in patient endurance of hardship and patriotic devotion during the struggle; to perpetuate the memory of our Confederate heroes and the glorious cause for which they fought; to cherish the ties of friendship among members of this Association; to endeavor to have used in all Southern schools only such histories as are just and true.

3. **McNeel Marble Co. advertisement in *Confederate Veteran* magazine, 1905.**

To the Daughters of the Confederacy: In regard to that Confederate monument which your Chapter has been talking about and planning for since you first got organized. Why not buy it NOW and have it erected before all the old veterans have answered the final roll call? Why wait and worry about raising funds? Our terms to U.D.C. Chapters are so liberal and our plans for raising funds are so effective as to obviate the necessity of either waiting or worrying. During the last three or four years we have sold Confederate monuments to thirty-seven of your sister Chapters. . . . Our designs, our prices, our work, our business methods have pleased them, and we can please you. What your sister Chapters have done, you can do. . . . WRITE TO-DAY.

4. **Confederate veteran's letter, *Confederate Veteran* magazine, 1910.** *An anonymous Georgian who had served in Lee's army sent the following letter to the veterans' magazine after attending a reunion in Memphis.*

Reunion gatherings are supposed to be for the benefit of the old veterans; but will you show us where the privates, the men who stood the hardships and did the fighting, have any consideration when they get to the city that is expected to entertain them? . . . [In Memphis, I] stopped at the school building, where there were at least twenty-five or thirty old veterans lying on the ground, and had been there all night. All this while the officers were being banqueted, wined, dined, and quartered in the very best hotels; but the private must shift for himself, stand around on the street, or sit on the curbstone. He must march if he is able, but the officers ride in fine carriages. Pay more attention to the men of the ranks—men who did service! I always go prepared to pay my way; but I do not like to be ignored.

5. **Matthew Page Andrews, *The Women of the South in War Times*, 1923.** *Matthew Page Andrews's* The Women of the South in War Times, *approved by the UDC, was a popular textbook for decades in schools throughout the South.*

The Southern people of the "old regime" have been pictured as engaged primarily in a protracted struggle for the maintenance of negro slavery. . . . Fighting on behalf of slavery was as far from the minds of these Americans as going to war in order to free the slaves was from the purpose of Abraham Lincoln, whose sole object, frequently expressed by him, was to "preserve the Union." . . .

That, in the midst of war, there were almost no instances of arson, murder, or outrage committed by the negroes of the South is an everlasting tribute to the splendid character of the dominant race and their moral uplift of a weaker one. . . . When these negroes were landed on American shores, almost all were savages taken from the lowest forms of jungle life. It was largely the women of the South who trained these heathen people, molded their characters, and, in the second and third generations, lifted them up a thousand years in the scale of civilization.

6. **Susie King Taylor, *Reminiscences of My Life in Camp with the 33d United States Colored Troops, Late 1st S.C. Volunteers*, 1902.** *Susie King Taylor, born in slavery in Georgia in 1848, fled with her uncle during the Civil War and served as a nurse in the Union army.*

I read an article, which said the ex-Confederate Daughters had sent a petition to the managers of the local theatres in Tennessee to prohibit the performance of "Uncle Tom's Cabin," claiming it was exaggerated (that is, the treatment of the slaves), and would have a very bad effect on the children who might see the drama. I paused and thought back a few years of the heart-rending scenes I have witnessed. . . . I remember, as if it were yesterday, seeing droves of negroes going to be sold, and I often went to look at them, and I could hear the auctioneer very plainly from my house, auctioning these poor people off.

Do these Confederate Daughters ever send petitions to prohibit the atrocious lynchings and wholesale murdering and torture of the negro? Do you ever hear of them fearing this would have a bad effect on the children? Which of these two, the drama or the present state of affairs, makes a degrading impression upon the minds of our young generation? In my opinion it is not "Uncle Tom's Cabin." . . . It does not seem as if our land is yet civilized.

SOURCES: (2) *Minutes of the Seventh Annual Meeting of the United Daughters of the Confederacy* (Nashville, TN: Press of Foster & Webb, Printers, 1901), 235; (3) *Confederate Veteran*, 1905; (4) *Confederate Veteran*, Vol. XVIII (Nashville, TN: S. A. Cunningham, 1910); (5) Matthew Page Andrews, ed., *The Women of the South in War Times* (Baltimore: The Norman, Remington Co., 1923), 3–4, 9–10; (6) Susie King Taylor, *Reminiscences of My Life in Camp* (Boston: Published by the author, 1902), 65–66.

ANALYZING THE EVIDENCE

1. What do sources 2 and 3 tell us about the work of local UDC chapters? What does the advertisement suggest about the economy of the postwar South?

2. What can you infer from these sources about the situation in the South after the Civil War? Why might women have played a particularly important role in memorial associations?

3. Compare and contrast sources 4 and 6. Who did "Lost Cause" associations serve, and how is this connected to issues of class and race?

4. How does source 5 depict slaves? Slaveholders? Is this an accurate account of the history of the South, and how does this compare to source 4? What do these different interpretations suggest about the legacy of "Redemption"?

PUTTING IT ALL TOGETHER

"Lost Cause" advocates often stated that their work was not political. To what extent was this true, based on the evidence here? What do these documents suggest about the influence of the Lost Cause, and also the limitations and challenges it faced? What do they tell us about the legacies of Reconstruction more broadly?

In the House of Representatives, outraged Democrats vowed to stall the final count of electoral votes so as to prevent Hayes's inauguration on March 4. But in the end, they went along, partly because Tilden himself urged that they do so. Hayes had publicly indicated his desire to offer substantial patronage to the South, including federal funds for education and internal improvements. He promised "a complete change of men and policy," naively hoping he could count on support from old-line southern Whigs and protect black voting rights. Hayes was inaugurated on schedule. He expressed hope in his inaugural address that the federal government could serve "the interests of both races carefully and equally." But, setting aside the U.S. troops who were serving on border duty in Texas, only 3,000 Union soldiers remained in the South. As soon as the new president ordered them back to their barracks, the last Republican administrations in the South collapsed. Reconstruction had ended.

Lasting Legacies

In the short run, the political events of 1877 had little impact on most southerners. Much of the work of "Redemption" had already been done. What mattered was the long, slow decline of Radical Republican power and the corresponding rise of Democrats in the South and nationally. It was obvious that so-called Redeemers in the South had assumed power through violence. But many Americans, including prominent classical liberals who shaped public opinion, believed the Democrats had overthrown corrupt, illegitimate governments. Thus the end justified the means. After 1874, those who deplored the results had little political traction. The only remaining question was how far Reconstruction would be rolled back.

The South never went back to the antebellum status quo. Sharecropping, for all its flaws and injustices, was not slavery. Freedmen and freedwomen managed to resist gang labor and work on their own terms. They also established their right to marry, read and write, worship as they pleased, and travel in search of a better life — rights that were not easily revoked. Across the South, black farmers overcame great odds to buy and work their own land. African American businessmen built thriving enterprises. Black churches and community groups sustained networks of mutual aid. Parents sacrificed to send their children to school, and a few proudly watched their sons and daughters graduate from college.

Reconstruction had also shaken, if not fully overturned, the legal and political framework that had made the United States a white man's country. This was a stunning achievement, and though hostile courts and political opponents undercut it, no one ever repealed the Thirteenth, Fourteenth, or Fifteenth Amendments. They remained in the Constitution, and the civil rights movement of the twentieth century would return and build on this framework (Chapter 26).

Still, in the final reckoning, Reconstruction failed. The majority of freedpeople remained in poverty, and by the late 1870s their political rights were also eroding. Vocal advocates of smaller government argued that Reconstruction had been a mistake; pressured by economic hardship, northern voters abandoned their southern Unionist allies. One of the enduring legacies of this process was the way later Americans remembered Reconstruction itself. After "Redemption," generations of schoolchildren were taught that ignorant, lazy blacks and corrupt whites had imposed illegitimate Reconstruction "regimes" on the South. White southerners won national support for their celebration of a heroic Confederacy (Thinking Like a Historian).

One of the first historians to challenge these views was the great African American intellectual W. E. B. Du Bois. In *Black Reconstruction in America* (1935), Du Bois meticulously documented the history of African American struggle, white vigilante violence, and national policy failure. If Reconstruction, he wrote, "had been conceived as a major national program . . . whose accomplishment at any price was well worth the effort, we should be living today in a different world." His words still ring true, but in 1935 historians ignored him. Not a single scholarly journal reviewed Du Bois's important book. Ex-Confederates had lost the war, but they won control over the nation's memory of Reconstruction.

Meanwhile, though their programs failed in the South, Republicans carried their nation-building project into the West, where their policies helped consolidate a continental empire. There, the federal power that had secured emancipation created the conditions for the United States to become an industrial power and a major leader on the world stage.

> **IN YOUR OWN WORDS** Why and how did federal Reconstruction policies falter in the South?

Summary

Postwar Republicans faced two tasks: restoring rebellious states to the Union and defining the role of emancipated slaves. After Lincoln's assassination, his successor, Andrew Johnson, hostile to Congress, unilaterally offered the South easy terms for reentering the Union. Exploiting this opportunity, southerners adopted oppressive Black Codes and put ex-Confederates back in power. Congress impeached Johnson and, though failing to convict him, seized the initiative and placed the South under military rule. In this second, or radical, phase of Reconstruction, Republican state governments tried to transform the South's economic and social institutions. Congress passed innovative civil rights acts and funded new agencies like the Freedmen's Bureau. The Fourteenth Amendment defined U.S. citizenship and asserted that states could no longer supersede it, and the Fifteenth Amendment gave voting rights to formerly enslaved men. Debate over this amendment precipitated a split among women's rights advocates, since women did not win inclusion.

Freedmen found that their goals conflicted with those of Republican leaders, who counted on cotton to fuel economic growth. Like southern landowners, national lawmakers envisioned former slaves as wageworkers, while freedmen wanted their own land. Sharecropping, which satisfied no one completely, emerged as a compromise suited to the needs of the cotton market and an impoverished, credit-starved region.

Nothing could reconcile ex-Confederates to Republican government, and they staged a violent counterrevolution in the name of white supremacy and "Redemption." Meanwhile, struck by a massive economic depression, northern voters handed Republicans a crushing defeat in the election of 1874. By 1876, Reconstruction was dead. Rutherford B. Hayes's narrow victory in the presidential election of that year resulted in withdrawal of the last Union troops from the South. A series of Supreme Court decisions also undermined the Fourteenth Amendment and civil rights laws, setting up legal parameters through which, over the long term, disenfranchisement and segregation would flourish.

CHAPTER 14 REVIEW

TERMS TO KNOW   *Identify and explain the significance of each term below.*

Key Concepts and Events

Ten Percent Plan (p. 464)

Wade-Davis Bill (p. 464)

Black Codes (p. 465)

Freedmen's Bureau (p. 467)

Civil Rights Act of 1866 (p. 467)

Fourteenth Amendment (p. 467)

Reconstruction Act of 1867 (p. 467)

Fifteenth Amendment (p. 470)

American Woman Suffrage Association (p. 471)

National Woman Suffrage Association (p. 471)

Minor v. Happersett (p. 471)

Beecher-Tilton scandal (p. 472)

sharecropping (p. 476)

convict leasing (p. 480)

Civil Rights Act of 1875 (p. 482)

classical liberalism (p. 483)

Crédit Mobilier (p. 484)

Ku Klux Klan (p. 485)

Enforcement Laws (p. 486)

Slaughter-House Cases (p. 487)

Civil Rights Cases (p. 487)

Key People

Andrew Johnson (p. 465)

Charles Sumner (p. 467)

Thaddeus Stevens (p. 467)

Ulysses S. Grant (p. 468)

Elizabeth Cady Stanton (p. 470)

Victoria Woodhull (p. 471)

Robert Smalls (p. 479)

Blanche K. Bruce (p. 479)

Nathan Bedford Forrest (p. 485)

REVIEW QUESTIONS   *Answer these questions to demonstrate your understanding of the chapter's main ideas.*

1. What factors explain how Reconstruction policies unfolded between 1865 and 1870, and what was the impact on different groups of Americans?

2. What goals were southern freedmen and freedwomen able to achieve in the post–Civil War years, and why? What goals were they not able to achieve, and why not?

3. Why and how did federal Reconstruction policies falter in the South?

4. Look again at the events listed under "American and National Identity" on the thematic timeline on page 388. Some historians have argued that, during this era, the United States moved, politically and socially, from being a loose union of states to being a more unified and inclusive *nation*. To what extent do you agree? Use the events of Reconstruction as evidence in making your case.

MAKING CONNECTIONS   *Recognize the larger developments and continuities within and across chapters.*

1. Ex-Confederates were not the first Americans to engage in violent protest against what they saw as tyrannical government power. Imagine, for example, a conversation between a participant in Shays's Rebellion (Chapter 6) and a southern Democrat who participated in the overthrow of a Republican government in his state. How would each describe his grievances? Whom would he name as enemies? Compare and contrast the tactics of these and other violent protests against government power in the United States. To what extent did these groups succeed?

2. Return to the image at the start of this chapter (p. 463), which shows a celebration in Baltimore after ratification of the Fifteenth Amendment. Note the various activities depicted, as representations of the impact of emancipation and voting rights for black men. How might an African American family at the time have understood the image? What about a southern white family opposed to the Fifteenth Amendment?

KEY TURNING POINTS   *Refer to the chapter chronology on page 464 for help in answering the question below.*

Identify two crucial turning points in the course of Reconstruction. What caused those shifts in direction, and what were the results?

15

CHAPTER

Conquering a Continent
1860–1890

On May 10, 1869, Americans poured into the streets for a giant party. In big cities, the racket was incredible. Cannons boomed and train whistles shrilled. New York fired a hundred-gun salute at City Hall. Congregations sang anthems, while the less religious gathered in saloons to celebrate with whiskey. Philadelphia's joyful throngs reminded an observer of the day, four years earlier, when news had arrived of Lee's surrender.

IDENTIFY THE BIG IDEA

How did U.S. policymakers seek to stimulate the economy and integrate the trans-Mississippi west into the nation, and how did this affect people living there?

The festivities were prompted by a long-awaited telegraph message: executives of the Union Pacific and Central Pacific railroads had driven a golden spike at Promontory Point, Utah, linking up their lines. Unbroken track now stretched from the Atlantic to the Pacific. A journey across North America could be made in less than a week.

transcontinental railroad

The railway line completed on May 10, 1869, that connected the Central Pacific and Union Pacific lines, enabling goods to move by railway from the eastern United States all the way to California.

The first **transcontinental railroad** meant jobs and money. San Francisco residents got right to business: after firing a salute, they loaded Japanese tea on a train bound for St. Louis, marking California's first overland delivery to the East. In coming decades, trade and tourism fueled tremendous growth west of the Mississippi. San Francisco, which in 1860 had handled $7.4 million in imports, increased that figure to $49 million over thirty years. The new railroad would, as one speaker predicted in 1869, "populate our vast territory" and make America "the highway of nations."

The railroad was also a political triumph. Victorious in the Civil War, Republicans saw themselves as heirs to the American System envisioned by antebellum Whigs. They believed government intervention in the economy was the key to nation building. But unlike Whigs, whose plans had met stiff Democratic opposition, Republicans enjoyed a decade of unparalleled federal power. They used it vigorously: U.S. government spending per person, after skyrocketing in the Civil War, remained well above earlier levels. Republicans believed that national economic integration was the best guarantor of lasting peace. As a New York minister declared, the federally supported transcontinental railroad would "preserve the Union."

The minister was wrong on one point. He claimed the railroad was a peaceful achievement, in contrast to military battles that had brought "devastation, misery, and woe." In fact, creating a continental empire caused plenty of woe. Regions west of the Mississippi could only be incorporated if the United States subdued Native peoples and established favorable conditions for international investors — often at great domestic cost. And while conquering the West helped make the United States into an industrial power, it also deepened America's rivalry with European empires and created new patterns of exploitation.

The Great West In the wake of the Civil War, Americans looked westward. Republicans implemented an array of policies to foster economic development in the "Great West." Ranchers, farmers, and lumbermen cast hungry eyes on the remaining lands held by Native Americans. Steamboats and railroads, both visible in the background of this image, became celebrated as symbols of the expanding reach of U.S. economic might. This 1881 promotional poster illustrates the bountiful natural resources to be found out west, as well as the land available for ranching, farming, and commerce. The men in the lower left corner are surveying land for sale. Library of Congress.

As you read, ask yourself why this chapter begins and ends with these dates and identify the links among related events.

1859 ▶ Comstock silver lode discovered in Nevada	**1873** ▶ United States begins to move to gold standard
1862 ▶ Homestead Act	**1876** ▶ Battle of Little Big Horn
▶ Dakota Sioux uprising in Minnesota	**1877** ▶ Nez Perce forcibly removed from ancestral
▶ Morrill Act funds public state universities	homelands in Northwest
1864 ▶ Sand Creek massacre of Cheyennes in	▶ *Munn v. Illinois* Supreme Court decision
Colorado	**1879** ▶ Exoduster migration to Kansas
▶ Yosemite Valley reserved as public park	▶ John Wesley Powell presents *Report on the Lands of*
1865 ▶ Long Drive of Texas longhorns begins	*the Arid Region of the United States*
1866 ▶ Fetterman massacre	**1880s** ▶ Rise of the Ghost Dance movement
1868 ▶ Burlingame Treaty with China	**1885** ▶ Sitting Bull tours with Buffalo Bill's Wild West
1869 ▶ Transcontinental railroad completed	**1886** ▶ Dry cycle begins on the plains
▶ Wyoming women's suffrage	▶ Chiricahua Apache leader Geronimo surrenders
1870 ▶ Utah women's suffrage	**1887** ▶ Dawes Severalty Act
1872 ▶ General Mining Act	**1890** ▶ Massacre of Sioux Ghost Dancers at Wounded
▶ Yellowstone National Park created	Knee, South Dakota

The Republican Vision

Reshaping the former Confederacy was only part of Republicans' plan for a reconstructed nation. They remembered the era after Andrew Jackson's destruction of the Second National Bank as one of economic chaos, when the United States had become vulnerable to international creditors and market fluctuations. Land speculation on the frontier had provoked extreme cycles of boom and bust. Failure to fund a transcontinental railroad had left different regions of the country disconnected. This, Republicans believed, had helped trigger the Civil War, and they were determined to set a new direction.

Even while the war raged, Congress made vigorous use of federal power, launching the transcontinental rail project and a new national banking system. Congress also raised the **protective tariff** on a range of manufactured goods, from textiles to steel, and on some agricultural products, like wool and sugar. At federal customhouses in each port, foreign manufacturers who brought merchandise into the United States had to pay import fees. These tariff revenues gave U.S. manufacturers, who did not pay the fees, a competitive advantage in America's vast domestic market.

protective tariff
A tax or duty on foreign producers of goods coming into or imported into the United States; tariffs gave U.S. manufacturers a competitive advantage in America's gigantic domestic market.

The economic depression that began in 1873 set limits on Republicans' economic ambitions, just as it hindered their Reconstruction plans in the South. But their policies continued to shape the economy. Though some historians argue that the late nineteenth century was an era of *laissez faire* or unrestrained capitalism, in which government sat passively by, the industrial United States was actually the product of a massive public-private partnership in which government played critical roles.

The New Union and the World

The United States emerged from the Civil War with new leverage in its negotiation with European countries, especially Great Britain, whose navy dominated the seas.

Britain, which had allowed Confederate raiding ships such as CSS *Alabama* to be built in its shipyards, submitted afterward to arbitration and paid the United States $15.5 million in damages. Flush with victory, many Americans expected more British and Spanish territories to drop into the Union's lap. Senator Charles Sumner proposed, in fact, that Britain settle the *Alabama* claims by handing over Canada.

Such dreams were a logical extension of pre–Civil War conquests, especially in the U.S.-Mexico War. With the coasts now linked by rail, merchants and manufacturers looked across the Pacific, hungry for trade with Asia.

Union victory also increased U.S. economic influence in Latin America. While the United States was preoccupied with its internal war, France had deposed Mexico's government and installed an emperor. On May 5, 1867, Mexico overthrew the French invaders and executed Emperor Maximilian. But while Mexico regained independence, it lay open to the economic designs of its increasingly powerful northern neighbor.

A new model emerged for asserting U.S. power in Latin America and Asia: not by direct conquest, but through trade. The architect of this vision was William Seward, secretary of state from 1861 to 1869 under presidents Abraham Lincoln and Andrew Johnson. A New Yorker of grand ambition and ego, Seward believed, like many contemporaries, that Asia would become "the chief theatre of [world] events" and that commerce there was key to America's prosperity. He urged the Senate to purchase sites in both the Pacific and the Caribbean for naval bases and refueling stations. When Japan changed policy and tried to close its ports to foreigners, Seward dispatched U.S. naval vessels to join those of Britain, France, and the Netherlands in reopening trade by force. At the same time, Seward urged annexation of Hawaii. He also predicted that the United States would one day claim the Philippines and build a Panama canal.

Seward's short-term achievements were modest. Exhausted by civil war, Americans had little enthusiasm for further military exploits. Seward achieved only two significant victories. In 1868, he secured congressional approval for the **Burlingame Treaty** with China, which guaranteed the rights of U.S. missionaries in China and set official terms for the emigration of Chinese laborers, some of whom were already clearing farmland and building railroads in the West. That same year, Seward negotiated the purchase of Alaska from Russia. After the Senate approved the deal, Seward waxed poetic:

Burlingame Treaty An 1868 treaty that guaranteed the rights of U.S. missionaries in China and set official terms for the emigration of Chinese laborers to work in the United States.

> Our nation with united interests blest
> Not now content to poise, shall sway the rest;
> Abroad our empire shall no limits know,
> But like the sea in endless circles flow.

Many Americans scoffed at the purchase of Alaska, a frigid arctic tract that skeptics nicknamed "Seward's Icebox." But the secretary of state mapped out a path his Republican successors would follow thirty years later in an aggressive bid for global power.

Integrating the National Economy

Closer to home, Republicans focused on transportation infrastructure. Railroad development in the United States began well before the Civil War, with the first locomotives arriving from Britain in the early 1830s. Unlike canals or roads, railroads offered the promise of year-round, all-weather service. Locomotives could run in the dark and never needed to rest, except to take on coal and water. Steam engines crossed high mountains and rocky gorges where pack animals could find no fodder and canals could never reach. West of the Mississippi, railroads opened vast regions for farming, trade, and tourism. A transcontinental railroad executive was only half-joking when he said, "The West is purely a railroad enterprise."

Governments could choose to build and operate railroads themselves or promote construction by private companies. Unlike most European countries, the United States chose the private approach. The federal government, however, provided essential loans, subsidies, and grants of public land. States and localities also lured railroads with offers of financial aid, mainly by buying railroad bonds. Without this aid, rail networks would have grown much more slowly and would probably have concentrated in urban regions. With it, railroads enjoyed an enormous—and reckless—boom. By 1900, virtually no corner of the country lacked rail service (Map 15.1). At the same time, U.S. railroads built across the border into Mexico (America in Global Context).

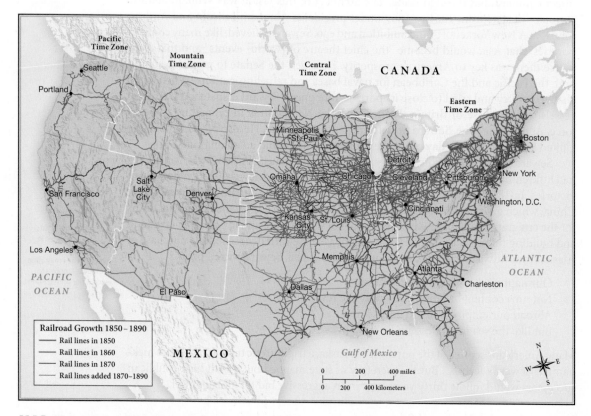

MAP 15.1 Expansion of the Railroad System, 1850–1890

In 1850, the United States had 9,000 miles of rail track; by 1890, it had 167,000 miles, including transcontinental lines terminating in San Francisco, Los Angeles, and Seattle. The tremendous burst of construction during the last twenty years of that period essentially completed the nation's rail network, although there would be additional expansion for the next two decades. The main areas of growth were in the South and in lands west of the Mississippi. Time zones—an innovation introduced not by government entities, but by railroad corporations in 1883—are marked by the white lines.

The Santa Fe Railroad in Mexico and the United States

Map 15.2, based on an 1885 traveler's guide published by the Atchison, Topeka, and Santa Fe Railroad, includes the company's U.S. lines and also those of its Mexican Central Railroad, an ATSF subsidiary that crossed the border and terminated at Guaymas and Mexico City, Mexico. The dots represent the many stops that the trains made along the routes between major cities. Most Mexican railroads in this era were built and operated by U.S. companies. As you analyze this map, consider the significance of imported Mexican raw materials and agricultural products to the U.S. economy.

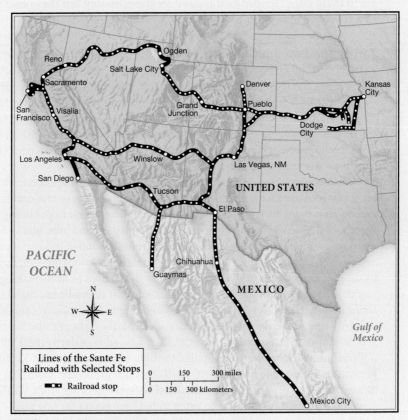

MAP 15.2 The Santa Fe Railroad System, 1885

QUESTIONS FOR ANALYSIS

1. In what directions could passengers and freight travel on ATSF lines in each country? What does this suggest about the objectives of railroad companies like this one?

2. Based on this evidence, how might Mexicans have experienced the arrival of railroads differently from residents of the western United States?

Railroad companies transformed American capitalism. They adopted a legal form of organization, the corporation, that enabled them to raise private capital in prodigious amounts. In earlier decades, state legislatures had chartered corporations for specific public purposes, binding these creations to government goals and oversight. But over the course of the nineteenth century, legislatures gradually began to allow any business to become a corporation by simply applying for a state charter. Among the first corporations to become large interstate enterprises, private railroads were much freer than earlier companies to do as they pleased. After the Civil War, they received lavish public aid with few strings attached. Their position was like that of American banks in late 2008 after the big federal bailout: even critics acknowledged that public aid to these giant companies was good for the economy, but they observed that it also lent government support to fabulous accumulations of private wealth.

Tariffs and Economic Growth   Along with the transformative power of railroads, Republicans' protective tariffs helped build other U.S. industries, including textiles and steel in the Northeast and Midwest and, through tariffs on imported sugar and wool, sugar beet farming and sheep ranching in the West. Tariffs also funded government itself. In an era when the United States did not levy income taxes, tariffs provided the bulk of treasury revenue. The Civil War had left the Union with a staggering debt of $2.8 billion. Tariff income erased that debt and by the 1880s generated huge budget *surpluses* — a circumstance hard to imagine today.

As Reconstruction faltered, tariffs came under political fire. Democrats argued that tariffs taxed American consumers by denying them access to low-cost imported goods and forcing them to pay subsidies to U.S. manufacturers. Republicans claimed, conversely, that tariffs benefitted workers because they created jobs, blocked low-wage foreign competition, and safeguarded America from the kind of industrial poverty that had arisen in Europe. According to this argument, tariffs helped American men earn enough to support their families; wives could devote themselves to homemaking, and children could go to school, not the factory. For protectionist Republicans, high tariffs were akin to the abolition of slavery: they protected and uplifted the most vulnerable workers.

In these fierce debates, both sides were partly right. Protective tariffs did play a powerful role in economic growth. They helped transform the United States into a global industrial power. Eventually, though, even protectionist Republicans had to admit that Democrats had a point: tariffs had not prevented industrial poverty in the United States. Corporations accumulated massive benefits from tariffs but failed to pass them along to workers, who often toiled long hours for low wages. Furthermore, tariffs helped foster trusts, corporations that dominated whole sectors of the economy and wielded near-monopoly power. The rise of large private corporations and trusts generated enduring political problems.

Munn v. Illinois
An 1877 Supreme Court case that affirmed that states could regulate key businesses, such as railroads and grain elevators, if those businesses were "clothed in the public interest."

The Role of Courts   While fostering growth, most historians agree, Republicans did not give government enough regulatory power over the new corporations. State legislatures did pass hundreds of regulatory laws after the Civil War, but interstate companies challenged them in federal courts. In *Munn v. Illinois* (1877), the Supreme Court affirmed that states could regulate key businesses, such as railroads and grain elevators, that were "clothed in the public interest." However, the justices feared that too many state and local regulations would impede business and fragment the national marketplace. Starting in the 1870s, they interpreted the "due process" clause of the new Fourteenth Amendment — which dictated that no state could "deprive any person of life, liberty, or property, without due process of law" — as shielding corporations from excessive regulation. Ironically, the Court refused to use the same amendment to protect the rights of African Americans.

In the Southwest as well, federal courts promoted economic development at the expense of racial justice. Though the United States had taken control of New Mexico and Arizona after the U.S.-Mexico War, much land remained afterward in the hands of Mexican farmers and ranchers. Many lived as *peónes*, under long-standing agreements with landowners who held large tracts originally granted by the Spanish crown. The post–Civil War years brought railroads and an influx of land-hungry Anglos. New Mexico's governor reported indignantly that Mexican shepherds were often "asked" to leave their ranges "by a cowboy or cattle herder with a brace of pistols at his belt and a Winchester in his hands."

Existing land claims were so complex that Congress eventually set up a special court to rule on land titles. Between 1891 and 1904, the court invalidated most traditional claims, including those of many New Mexico *ejidos*, or villages owned collectively by their communities. Mexican Americans lost about 64 percent of the contested lands. In addition, much land was sold or appropriated through legal machinations like those of a notorious cabal of politicians and lawyers known as the Santa Fe Ring. The result was displacement of thousands of Mexican American villagers and farmers. Some found work as railroad builders or mine workers; others, moving into the sparse high country of the Sierras and Rockies where cattle could not survive, developed sheep raising into a major enterprise.

Silver and Gold In an era of nation building, U.S. and European policymakers sought new ways to rationalize markets. Industrializing nations, for example, tried to develop an international system of standard measurements and even a unified currency. Though these proposals failed as each nation succumbed to self-interest, governments did increasingly agree that, for "scientific" reasons, money should be based on gold, which was thought to have an intrinsic worth above other metals. Great Britain had long held to the **gold standard**, meaning that paper notes from the Bank of England could be backed by gold held in the bank's vaults. During the 1870s and 1880s, the United States, Germany, France, and other countries also converted to gold.

Beforehand, these nations had been on a bimetallic standard: they issued both gold and silver coins, with respective weights fixed at a relative value. The United States switched to the gold standard in part because treasury officials and financiers were watching developments out west. Geologists accurately predicted the discovery of immense silver deposits, such as Nevada's Comstock Lode, without comparable new gold strikes. A massive influx of silver would clearly upset the long-standing ratio. Thus, with a law that became infamous to later critics as the **"Crime of 1873,"** Congress chose gold. It directed the U.S. Treasury to cease minting silver dollars and, over a six-year period, retire Civil War–era greenbacks (paper dollars) and replace them with notes from an expanded system of national banks. After this process was complete in 1879, the treasury exchanged these notes for gold on request. (Advocates

gold standard
The practice of backing a country's currency with its reserves of gold. In 1873 the United States, following Great Britain and other European nations, began converting to the gold standard.

"Crime of 1873"
A term used by those critical of an 1873 law directing the U.S. Treasury to cease minting silver dollars, retire Civil War–era greenbacks, and replace them with notes backed by the gold standard from an expanded system of national banks.

of bimetallism did achieve one small victory: the Bland-Allison Act of 1878 required the U.S. Mint to coin a modest amount of silver.)

By adopting the gold standard, Republican policymakers sharply limited the nation's money supply, to the level of available gold. The amount of money circulating in the United States had been $30.35 per person in 1865; by 1880, it fell to only $19.36 per person. Today, few economists would sanction such a plan, especially for an economy growing at breakneck speed. They would recommend, instead, increasing money supplies to keep pace with development. But at the time, policymakers remembered rampant antebellum speculation and the hardships of inflation during the Civil War. The United States, as a developing country, also needed to attract investment capital from Britain, Belgium, and other European nations that were on the gold standard. Making it easy to exchange U.S. bonds and currency for gold encouraged European investors to send their money to the United States.

Republican policies fostered exuberant growth and a breathtakingly rapid integration of the economy. Railroads and telegraphs tied the nation together. U.S. manufacturers amassed staggering amounts of capital and built corporations of national and even global scope. With its immense, integrated marketplace of workers, consumers, raw materials, and finished products, the United States was poised to become a mighty industrial power.

> **IN YOUR OWN WORDS** What federal policies contributed to the rise of America's industrial economy, and what were their results?

Incorporating the West

Homestead Act
The 1862 act that gave 160 acres of free western land to any applicant who occupied and improved the property. This policy led to the rapid development of the American West after the Civil War; facing arid conditions in the West, however, many homesteaders found themselves unable to live on their land.

Republicans wanted farms as well as factories. As early as 1860, popular lyrics hailed the advent of "Uncle Sam's Farm":

> A welcome, warm and hearty, do we give the sons of toil,
> To come west and settle and labor on Free Soil;
> We've room enough and land enough, they needn't feel alarmed —
> Oh! Come to the land of Freedom and vote yourself a farm.

The **Homestead Act** (1862) gave 160 acres of federal land to any applicant who occupied and improved the property. Republicans hoped the bill would help build up the interior West, which was inhabited by Indian peoples but remained "empty" on U.S. government survey maps.

land-grant colleges
Authorized by the Morrill Act of 1862, land-grant colleges were public universities founded to broaden educational opportunities and foster technical and scientific expertise. These universities were funded by the Morrill Act, which authorized the sale of federal lands to raise money for higher education.

Implementing this plan required innovative policies. The same year it passed the Homestead Act, Congress also created the federal Department of Agriculture and, through the Morrill Act, set aside 140 million federal acres that states could sell to raise money for public universities. The goal of these **land-grant colleges** was to broaden educational opportunities and foster technical and scientific expertise. After the Civil War, Congress also funded a series of geological surveys, dispatching U.S. Army officers, scientists, and photographers to chart unknown western terrain and catalog resources.

To a large extent, these policies succeeded in incorporating lands west of the Mississippi. The United States began to exploit its western empire for minerals, lumber, and other raw materials. But for ordinary Americans who went west, dreams often outran reality. Well-financed corporations, not individual prospectors, reaped most of the profits from western mines, while the Great Plains environment proved resistant to ranching and farming.

Mining Empires

In the late 1850s, as easy pickings in the California gold rush diminished, prospectors scattered in hopes of finding riches elsewhere. They found gold at many sites, including Nevada, the Colorado Rockies, and South Dakota's Black Hills (Map 15.3). As news of each strike spread, remote areas turned overnight into mob scenes of prospectors, traders, prostitutes, and saloon keepers. At community meetings, white prospectors made their own laws, often using them as an instrument for excluding Mexicans, Chinese, and blacks.

The silver from Nevada's **Comstock Lode**, discovered in 1859, built the boomtown of Virginia City, which soon acquired fancy hotels, a Shakespearean theater, and even its own stock exchange. In 1870, a hundred saloons operated in Virginia City, brothels lined D Street, and men outnumbered women 2 to 1. In the 1880s, however, as the Comstock ore gave out, Virginia City suffered the fate of many mining camps: it became a ghost town. What remained was a ravaged landscape with mountains of debris, poisoned water sources, and surrounding lands stripped of timber.

In hopes of encouraging development of western resources, Congress passed the General Mining Act of 1872, which allowed those who discovered minerals on federally owned land to work the claim and keep all the proceeds. (The law — including the $5-per-acre fee for filing a claim — remains in force today.) Americans idealized the notion of the lone, hardy mining prospector with his pan and his mule, but digging into deep veins of underground ore required big money. Consortiums of powerful investors, bringing engineers and advanced equipment, generally extracted the most wealth. This was the case for the New York trading firm Phelps Dodge, which invested in massive copper mines and smelting operations on both sides of the U.S.-Mexico border. The mines created jobs in new towns like Bisbee and Morenci, Arizona — but with dangerous conditions and low pay, especially for those who received the segregated "Mexican wage." Anglos, testified one Mexican mine worker, "occupied decorous residences . . . and had large amounts of money," while "the Mexican population and its economic condition offered a pathetic contrast." He protested this affront to "the most elemental principles of justice."

The rise of western mining created an insatiable market for timber and produce from the Pacific Northwest. Seattle and Portland grew rapidly as supply centers,

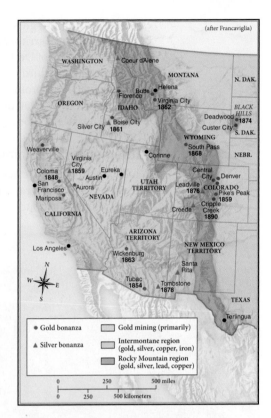

MAP 15.3 Mining Frontiers, 1848–1890
The Far West was America's gold country because of its geological history. Veins of gold and silver form when molten material from the earth's core is forced up into fissures caused by the tectonic movements that create mountain ranges, such as the ones that dominate the far western landscape. It was these veins, the product of mountain-forming activity many thousands of years earlier, that prospectors began to discover after 1848 and furiously exploit. Although widely dispersed across the Far West, the lodes that they found followed the mountain ranges bisecting the region and bypassing the great plateaus not shaped by the ancient tectonic activity.

Comstock Lode
A vein of silver ore discovered in Nevada in 1859, leading to one of the West's most important mining booms. The lode was so rich that a Confederate expedition tried unsuccessfully to capture it during the Civil War; its output significantly altered the ratio of silver in circulation, leading to changes in monetary policy.

especially during the great gold rushes of California (after 1848) and the Klondike in Canada's Yukon Territory (after 1897). Residents of Tacoma, Washington, claimed theirs was the "City of Destiny" when it became the Pacific terminus for the Northern Pacific, the nation's third transcontinental railroad, in 1887. But rival businessmen in Seattle succeeded in promoting their city as the gateway to Alaska and the Klondike. Seattle, a town with 1,000 residents in 1870, grew over the next forty years to a population of a quarter million.

Cattlemen on the Plains

While boomtowns arose across the West, hunters began transforming the plains. As late as the Civil War years, great herds of bison still roamed this region. But over-hunting and the introduction of European animal afflictions, like the bacterial disease

Cowboys, Real and Mythic   As early as the 1860s, popular dime novels such as this one (right) celebrated the alleged ruggedness, individual freedoms, and gun-slinging capabilities of western cowboys. (Note that this 1888 story, like most dime novels, was published in New York.) Generations of young Americans grew up on stories of frontier valor and "Cowboys versus Indians." In fact, cowboys like the ones depicted in the photograph were really wageworkers on horseback. An ethnically diverse group, including many blacks and Hispanics, they earned perhaps $25 a month, plus meals and a bed in the bunkhouse, in return for long hours of grueling, lonesome work.   Left: Getty Images. Right: Denver Public Library, Western History Collection/Bridgeman Images.

brucellosis, were already decimating the herds. In the 1870s, hide hunters finished them off so thoroughly that at one point fewer than two hundred bison remained in U.S. territory. Hunters hidden downwind, under the right conditions, could kill four dozen at a time without moving from the spot. They took hides but left the meat to rot, an act of vast wastefulness that shocked Native peoples.

Removal of the bison opened opportunities for cattle ranchers. South Texas provided an early model for their ambitious plans. By the end of the Civil War, about five million head of longhorn cattle grazed on Anglo ranches there. In 1865, the Missouri Pacific Railroad reached Sedalia, Missouri, far enough west to be accessible as Texas reentered the Union. A longhorn worth $3 in Texas might command $40 at Sedalia. With this incentive, ranchers inaugurated the Long Drive, hiring cowboys to herd cattle hundreds of miles north to the new rail lines, which soon extended into Kansas. At Abilene and Dodge City, Kansas, ranchers sold their longhorns and trail-weary cowboys crowded into saloons. These cow towns captured the nation's imagination as symbols of the Wild West, but the reality was much less exciting. Cowboys, many of them African Americans and Latinos, were really farmhands on horseback who worked long, harsh hours for low pay.

North of Texas, public grazing lands drew investors and adventurers eager for a taste of the West. By the early 1880s, as many as 7.5 million cattle were overgrazing the plains' native grasses. A cycle of good weather postponed disaster, which arrived in 1886: record blizzards and bitter cold. An awful scene of rotting carcasses greeted cowboys as they rode onto the range that spring. Further hit by a severe drought the following summer, the cattle boom collapsed.

Thanks to new strategies, however, cattle ranching survived and became part of the integrated national economy. As railroads reached Texas and ranchers there abandoned the Long Drive, the invention of barbed wire — which enabled ranchers and farmers to fence large areas cheaply and easily on the plains, where wood was scarce and expensive — made it easier for northern cattlemen to fence small areas and feed animals on hay. Stockyards appeared beside the rapidly extending railroad tracks, and trains took these gathered cattle to giant slaughterhouses in cities like Chicago, which turned them into cheap beef for customers back east.

Homesteaders

Republicans envisioned the Great Plains dotted with small farms, but farmers had to be persuaded that crops would grow there. Powerful interests worked hard to overcome the popular idea that the grassland was the Great American Desert. Railroads, eager to sell land the government had granted them, advertised aggressively. Land speculators, transatlantic steamship lines, and western states and territories joined the campaign.

Newcomers found the soil beneath the native prairie grasses deep and fertile. Steel plows enabled them to break through the tough roots, while barbed wire provided cheap, effective fencing against roaming cattle. European immigrants brought strains of hard-kernel wheat that tolerated the extreme temperatures of the plains. As if to confirm promoters' optimism, a wet cycle occurred between 1878 and 1886, increasing rainfall in the arid regions east of the Rockies. Americans decided that **"rain follows the plow"**: settlement and farming of the plains was increasing rainfall. Some

"rain follows the plow"
An unfounded theory that settlement and farming of the Great Plains caused an increase in rainfall.

attributed the rain to soil cultivation and tree planting, while others credited God. One Harvard professor proposed that steel railroad tracks attracted moisture. Such optimists would soon learn their mistake.

The motivation for most settlers, American or immigrant, was to better themselves economically. Union veterans, who received favorable terms in staking homestead claims, played a major role in settling Kansas and other plains states. When severe depression hit northern Europe in the 1870s, Norwegians and Swedes joined German emigrants in large numbers. At the peak of "American fever" in 1882, more than 105,000 Scandinavians left for the United States. Swedish and Norwegian became the primary languages in parts of Minnesota and the Dakotas.

For some African Americans, the plains represented a promised land of freedom. In 1879, a group of black communities left Mississippi and Louisiana in a quest to escape poverty and white violence. Some 6,000 blacks departed together, most carrying little but the clothes on their backs and faith in God. They called themselves **Exodusters**, participants in a great exodus to Kansas. The 1880 census reported 40,000 blacks there, by far the largest African American concentration in the West aside from Texas, where the expanding cotton frontier attracted hundreds of thousands of black migrants.

Exodusters
African Americans who walked or rode out of the Deep South following the Civil War, many settling on farms in Kansas in hopes of finding peace and prosperity.

For newcomers, taming the plains differed from pioneering in antebellum Iowa or Oregon. Dealers sold big new machines to help with plowing and harvesting. Western wheat traveled by rail to giant grain elevators and traded immediately on world markets. Hoping frontier land values would appreciate rapidly, many farmers planned to profit from selling acres as much as (or more than) from their crops. In boom times, many rushed into debt to acquire more land and better equipment. All these enthusiasms — for cash crops, land speculation, borrowed money, and new technology — bore witness to the conviction that farming was, as one agricultural journal remarked, a business "like all other business."

Women in the West   Early miners, lumbermen, and cowboys were overwhelmingly male, but homesteading was a family affair. The success of a farm depended on the work of wives and children who tended the garden and animals, preserved food, and helped out at harvest time. Some women struck out on their own: a study of North Dakota found between 5 and 20 percent of homestead claims filed by single women, often working land adjacent to that of sisters, brothers, and parents. Family members thus supported one another in the difficult work of farming, while easing the loneliness many newcomers felt. Looking back with pride on her homesteading days, one Dakota woman said simply, "It was a place to stay and it was mine."

While promoting farms in the West, Republicans clashed with the distinctive religious group that had already settled Utah: Mormons, or members of the Church of Jesus Christ of Latter-day Saints (LDS). After suffering persecution in Missouri and Illinois, Mormons had moved west to Utah in the 1840s, attracting many working-class converts from England as well. Most Americans at the time were deeply hostile to Mormonism, especially the LDS practice of plural marriage — sanctioned by church founder Joseph Smith — through which some Mormon men married more than one wife.

Mormons had their own complex view of women's role, illustrated by the career of Mormon leader Emmeline Wells. Born Emmeline Woodward in New Hampshire,

Wells converted to Mormonism at age thirteen along with her mother and joined the exodus to Utah in 1848. After her first husband abandoned her when he left the church, Wells became the seventh wife of church elder Daniel Wells. In 1870, due in part to organized pressure from Wells and other Mormon women, the Utah legislature granted full voting rights to women, becoming the second U.S. territory to do so (after Wyoming, in 1869). The measure increased LDS control, since most Utah women were Mormons, while non-Mormons in mining camps were predominantly male. It also recognized the central role of women in Mormon life.

Amid the constitutional debates of Reconstruction, polygamy and women's voting rights became intertwined issues. Encouraged by other plural wives, Wells began in 1877 to write for a Salt Lake City newspaper, the *Woman's Exponent*. She served as editor for forty years and led local women's rights groups. At first, Utah's legislature blocked Wells's candidacy in a local election, based on her sex. But when Utah won statehood in 1896, Wells had the pleasure of watching several women win seats in the new legislature, including Dr. Martha Hughes Cannon, a physician and Mormon plural wife who became the first American woman to serve in a state senate. Like their counterparts in other western states, Utah's women experienced a combination of severe frontier hardships and striking new opportunities.

Environmental Challenges Homesteaders faced a host of challenges, particularly the natural environment of the Great Plains. Clouds of grasshoppers could descend and destroy a crop in a day; a prairie fire or hailstorm could do the job in an hour. In spring, homesteaders faced sudden, terrifying tornados, while their winter experiences in the 1870s added the word *blizzard* to America's vocabulary. On the plains, also, water and lumber were hard to find. Newly arrived families often cut dugouts into hillsides and then, after a season or two, erected houses made of turf cut from the ground.

Over the long term, homesteaders discovered that the western grasslands did not receive enough rain to grow wheat and other grains. As the cycle of rainfall shifted from wet to dry, farmers as well as ranchers suffered. "A wind hot as an oven's fury . . . raged like a pestilence," reported one Nebraskan, leaving "farmers helpless, with no weapon against this terrible and inscrutable wrath of nature." By the late 1880s, some recently settled lands emptied as homesteaders fled in defeat — 50,000 from the Dakotas alone. It became obvious that farming in the arid West required methods other than those used east of the Mississippi.

Clearly, 160-acre homesteads were the wrong size for the West: farmers needed either small irrigated plots or immense tracts for dry farming, which involved deep planting to bring subsoil moisture to the roots and quick harrowing after rainfalls to slow evaporation. Dry farming developed most fully on huge corporate farms in the Red River Valley of North Dakota. But even family farms, the norm elsewhere, could not survive on less than 300 acres of grain. Crop prices were too low, and the climate too unpredictable, to allow farmers to get by on less.

In this struggle, settlers regarded themselves as nature's conquerors, striving, as one pioneer remarked, "to get the land subdued and the wilde nature out of it." Much about its "wilde nature" was hidden to the newcomers. They did not know that destroying biodiversity, which was what farming the plains really meant, opened pathways for exotic, destructive pests and weeds, and that removing native grasses left the soil vulnerable to erosion. By the turn of the twentieth century, about half the nation's cattle and sheep, one-third of its cereal crops, and nearly three-fifths of its wheat came from the Great Plains. But in the drier parts of the region, it was not a sustainable achievement. This renowned breadbasket was later revealed to be, in the words of one historian, "the largest, longest-run agricultural and environmental miscalculation in American history."

John Wesley Powell, a one-armed Union veteran, predicted the catastrophe from an early date. Powell, employed by the new U.S. Geological Survey, led a famous expedition in the West in which his team navigated the rapids of the Colorado River through the Grand Canyon in wooden boats. In his *Report on the Lands of the Arid Region of the United States* (1879), Powell told Congress bluntly that 160-acre homesteads would not work in dry regions. Impressed with the success of Mormon irrigation projects in Utah, Powell urged the United States to follow their model. He proposed that the government develop the West's water resources, building dams and canals and organizing landowners into local districts to operate them. Doubting that rugged individualism would succeed in the West, Powell proposed massive cooperation under government control.

After heated debate, Congress rejected Powell's plan. Critics accused him of playing into the hands of large ranching corporations; boosters were not yet willing to give up the dream of small homesteads. But Powell turned out to be right. Though environmental historians do not always agree with Powell's proposed solutions, they point to his *Report on Arid Lands* as a cogent critique of what went wrong on the Great Plains. Later, federal funding paid for dams and canals that supported intensive agriculture in many parts of the West.

The First National Park

Powell was not the only one rethinking land use. The West's incorporation into the national marketplace occurred with such speed that some Americans began to fear rampant overdevelopment. Perhaps the federal government should not sell off all its public land, but instead hold and manage some of it. Amid the heady initiatives of Reconstruction, Congress began to preserve sites of unusual natural splendor. As early as 1864, Congress gave 10 square miles of the Yosemite Valley to California for "public use, resort, and recreation." (In 1890, Yosemite reverted to federal control.) In 1872, Congress set aside 2 million acres of Wyoming's Yellowstone Valley as the world's first national park: preserved as a public holding, it would serve as "a public park or pleasuring ground for the benefit and enjoyment of the people."

Yellowstone National Park
Established in 1872 by Congress, Yellowstone was the United States's first national park.

Railroad tourism, which developed side by side with other western industries, was an important motive for the creation of **Yellowstone National Park**. The Northern Pacific Railroad lobbied Congress vigorously to get the park established. Soon, luxury Pullman cars ushered visitors to Yellowstone's hotel, operated by the railroad itself. But creation of the park was fraught with complications. Since no one knew exactly what a "national park" was or how to operate it, the U.S. Army was dispatched to take charge; only in the early 1900s, when Congress established many more parks in the West, did consistent management policies emerge. In the meantime, soldiers spent much of their time arresting Native peoples who sought to hunt on Yellowstone lands.

Thomas Moran, *Grand Canyon of the Yellowstone*, 1872 In 1871, English-born artist Thomas Moran joined Ferdinand Hayden's expedition to the Yellowstone Valley on behalf of the U.S. Geological Survey, an important new federal agency dedicated to mapping and exploring the West, as well as undertaking scientific investigations of flora, fauna, and potential mineral and timber resources. Moran's painting, along with photographs by William Henry Jackson and other eyewitness testimony to Yellowstone's uniqueness and beauty, helped introduce the American public to their first new national park. The painting remains property of the federal government, who commissioned Hayden's expedition, and hangs in the Smithsonian American Art Museum. Smithsonian American Art Museum, Washington, D.C./Art Resource, NY.

The creation of Yellowstone was an important step toward an ethic of respect for land and wildlife. So was the 1871 creation of a **U.S. Fisheries Commission**, which made recommendations to stem the decline in wild fish; by the 1930s, it merged with other federal wildlife bureaus to become the U.S. Fish and Wildlife Service. At the same time, eviction of Indians showed that defining small preserves of "uninhabited wilderness" was part of conquest itself. In 1877, for example, the federal government forcibly removed the Nez Perce tribe from their ancestral land in what is now Idaho, Washington, and Oregon. Under the leadership of young Chief Joseph, the Nez Perce tried to flee to Canada. After a journey of 1,100 miles, they were forced to surrender just short of the border. During their trek, five bands crossed Yellowstone; as a Nez Perce named Yellow Wolf recalled, they "knew that country well." For thirteen days, Nez Perce men raided the valley for supplies, waylaying several groups of tourists. The conflict made national headlines. Easterners, proud of their new "pleasuring ground," were startled to find that it remained a site of Native resistance. Americans were not settling an empty West. They were *un*settling it by taking it from Native peoples who already lived there.

U.S. Fisheries Commission
A federal bureau established in 1871 that made recommendations to stem the decline in wild fish. Its creation was an important step toward wildlife conservation and management.

IN YOUR OWN WORDS What factors led to transformation of the trans-Mississippi west after the Civil War?

A Harvest of Blood: Native Peoples Dispossessed

Before the Civil War, when most Americans believed the prairie could not be farmed, Congress reserved the Great Plains for Indian peoples. But in the era of steel plows and railroads, policymakers suddenly had the power and desire to incorporate the whole region. The U.S. Army fought against the loosely federated Sioux — the major power on the northern grasslands — as well as other peoples who had agreed to live on reservations but found conditions so desperate that they fled (Map 15.4). These "reservation wars," caused largely by local violence and confused federal policies, were messy and bitter. Pointing to failed military campaigns, army atrocities, and egregious

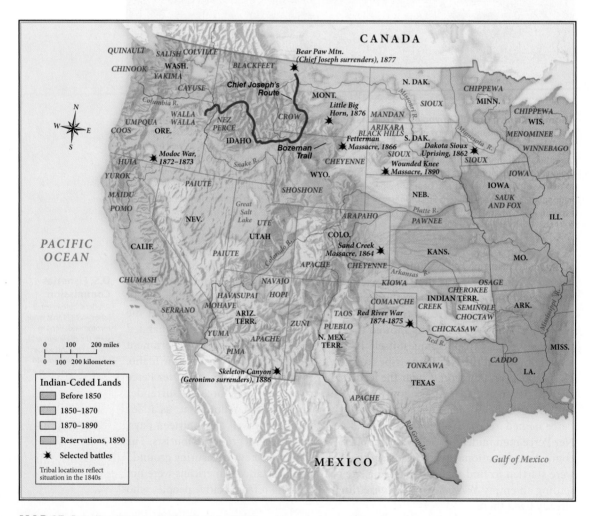

MAP 15.4 Indian Country in the West, to 1890
As settlement pushed onto the Great Plains after the Civil War, Native peoples put up bitter resistance but ultimately to no avail. Over a period of decades, they ceded most of their lands to the federal government, and by 1890 they were confined to scattered reservations.

corruption in the Indian Bureau, reformers called for new policies that would destroy Native peoples' traditional lifeways and "civilize" them — or, as one reformer put it, "kill the Indian and save the man."

The Civil War and Indians on the Plains

In August 1862, the attention of most Unionists and Confederates was riveted on General George McClellan's failing campaign in Virginia. But in Minnesota, the Dakota Sioux were increasingly frustrated. In 1858, the year Minnesota secured statehood, they had agreed to settle on a strip of land reserved by the government, in exchange for receiving regular payments and supplies. But Indian agents, contractors, and even Minnesota's territorial governor pocketed most of the funds. When the Dakotas protested that their children were starving, state officials dismissed their appeals. Corruption was so egregious that one leading Minnesotan, Episcopal bishop Henry Whipple, wrote an urgent appeal to President James Buchanan. "A nation which sows robbery," he warned, "will reap a harvest of blood."

Whipple's prediction proved correct. During the summer of 1862, a decade of anger boiled over. In a surprise attack, Dakota fighters fanned out through the Minnesota countryside, killing immigrants and burning farms. They planned to sweep eastward to St. Paul but were stopped at Fort Ridgely. In the end, more than four hundred whites lay dead, including women and children from farms and small towns. Thousands fled; panicked officials telegraphed for aid, spreading hysteria from Wisconsin to Colorado.

Minnesotans' ferocious response to the uprising set the stage for further conflict. A hastily appointed military court, bent on revenge, sentenced 307 Dakotas to death, making it clear that rebellious Indians would be treated as criminals rather than warriors. President Abraham Lincoln reviewed the trial records and commuted most of the sentences but authorized the deaths of 38 Dakota men. They were hanged just after Christmas 1862 in the largest mass execution in U.S. history. Two months later, Congress canceled all treaties with the Dakotas, revoked their annuities, and expelled them from Minnesota. The scattered bands fled west to join nonreservation allies.

As the uprising showed, the Civil War created two dangerous conditions in the West, compounding the problems already caused by corruption. With the Union army fighting the Confederacy, western whites felt vulnerable to Indian attacks. They also discovered they could fight Indians with minimal federal oversight. In the wake of the Dakota uprising, worried Coloradans favored a military campaign against the Cheyennes — allies of the Sioux — even though the Cheyennes had shown little evidence of hostility. Colorado militia leader John M. Chivington, an aspiring politician, determined to quell public anxiety and make his career.

In May 1864, Cheyenne chief Black Kettle, fearing his band would be attacked, consulted with U.S. agents, who instructed him to settle along Sand Creek in eastern Colorado until a treaty could be signed. On November 29, 1864, Chivington's Colorado militia attacked the camp while most of the men were out hunting, slaughtering more than a hundred women and children. "I killed all I could," one officer testified later. "I think and earnestly believe the Indian to be an obstacle to civilization and should be exterminated." Captain Silas Soule, who served under Chivington but refused to give his men the order to fire, dissented. "It was hard to see little children on their knees," he wrote later, "having their brains beat out by men professing to be civilized."

Chivington's men rode back for a celebration in Denver, where they hung Cheyenne scalps (and women's genitals) from the rafters of the Apollo Theater.

The northern plains exploded in conflict. Infuriated by the **Sand Creek massacre**, Cheyennes carried war pipes to the Arapahos and Sioux, who attacked and burned white settlements along the South Platte River. Ordered to subdue these peoples, the U.S. Army failed miserably: officers could not even locate the enemy, who traveled rapidly in small bands and knew the country well. A further shock occurred in December 1866 when 1,500 Sioux warriors executed a perfect ambush, luring Captain William Fetterman and 80 soldiers from a Wyoming fort and wiping them out. With the **Fetterman massacre**, the Sioux succeeded in closing the Bozeman Trail, a private road under army protection that had served as the main route into Montana.

General William Tecumseh Sherman, now commanding the army in the West, swore to defeat defiant Indians. But the Union hero met his match on the plains. Another year of fighting proved expensive and inconclusive. In 1868, the Sioux, led by the Oglala band under Chief Red Cloud, told a peace commission they would not sign any treaty unless the United States pledged to abandon all its forts along the Bozeman Trail. The commission agreed. Red Cloud had won.

In the wake of these events, eastern public opinion turned against the Indian wars, which seemed at best ineffective, at worst brutal. Congress held hearings on the slaughter at Sand Creek. Though Chivington, now a civilian, was never prosecuted, the massacre became an infamous example of western vigilantism. By the time Ulysses Grant entered the White House in 1869, the authors of Reconstruction in the South also began to seek solutions to what they called the "Indian problem."

Grant's Peace Policy

Grant inherited an Indian policy in disarray. Federal incompetence was highlighted by yet another mass killing of friendly Indians in January 1870, this time on the Marias River in Montana, by an army detachment that shot and burned to death 173 Piegans (Blackfeet). Having run out of other options, Grant introduced a peace policy, based on recommendations from Christian advisors. He offered selected appointments to the reformers — including many former abolitionists — who had created such groups as the Indian Rights Association and the Women's National Indian Association (Interpretations).

Rejecting the virulent anti-Indian stance of many westerners, reformers argued that Native peoples had the innate capacity to become equal with whites. They believed, however, that Indians could achieve this only if they embraced Christianity and white ways. Reformers thus aimed to destroy indigenous languages, cultures, and religions. Despite humane intentions, their condescension was obvious. They ignored dissenters like Dr. Thomas Bland of the National Indian Defense Association, who suggested that instead of an "Indian problem" there might be a "white problem" — refusal to permit Indians to follow their own lifeways. To most nineteenth-century Americans, such a notion was shocking and uncivilized. Increasingly dismissive of blacks' capacity for citizenship and hostile toward "heathen" Chinese immigrants, white Americans were even less willing to understand and respect Indian cultures. They believed that in the modern world, Native peoples were fated for extinction (Thinking Like a Historian).

Sand Creek massacre
The November 29, 1864, massacre of more than one hundred peaceful Cheyennes, largely women and children, by John M. Chivington's Colorado militia.

Fetterman massacre
A massacre in December 1866 in which 1,500 Sioux warriors lured Captain William Fetterman and 80 soldiers from a Wyoming fort and attacked them. With the Fetterman massacre the Sioux succeeded in closing the Bozeman Trail, the main route into Montana.

What Factors Motivated America's Indian Policies?

In the latter nineteenth century, the U.S. government adopted a number of policies designed to eliminate the "Indian problem" by eliminating the Indian: first through military engagement, then through a program of assimilation. The Dawes Severalty Act of 1887, for example, distributed tribal lands among individual Native Americans to break apart reservations and tribal identities. Indian children were often placed in boarding schools under white supervision, where they learned English and were introduced to Christianity.

Scholars have not always agreed on how to explain the motivations of late-nineteenth-century reformers. Two historians, Francis Paul Prucha and Margaret D. Jacobs, interpret this period and America's Indian policies in different ways.

FRANCIS PAUL PRUCHA

SOURCE: Francis Paul Prucha, *The Indian in American Society: From the Revolutionary War to the Present* (Berkeley: University of California Press, 1985), 19.

The treaty system ended in 1871, when Congress decided that no more treaties would be made with Indian tribes . . . but the paternalism of the federal government toward the Indians continued . . . [under the] Board of Indian Commissioners . . . [which included] a remarkable collection of high-minded Christian philanthropists, suffused with a spirit of benevolence, who epitomized the evangelical religious atmosphere of the nineteenth century. For better or for worse, the American Indians fell into the hands of this group and their successors.

MARGARET D. JACOBS

SOURCE: Margaret D. Jacobs, *White Mother to a Dark Race: Settler Colonialism, Maternalism, and the Removal of Indigenous Children in the American West and Australia, 1880–1940* (Lincoln: University of Nebraska Press, 2009), 25, 88.

[O]fficials often proclaimed that they were ushering in a new age of dealing fairly and kindly with . . . indigenous inhabitants. Yet these new policies actually entailed one of the most draconian measures possible: the removal of indigenous children from their kin . . . to be raised in distant institutions. . . . [I]nstead of watching from the sidelines as male government officials designed and carried out policies of indigenous child removal, many white women reformers campaigned for a greater role in setting public policy for indigenous peoples and became deeply implicated in this phase of settler colonialism.

QUESTIONS FOR ANALYSIS

1. Identify two ways these two historians differ in their description of America's Indian policies.
2. According to these two historians, what role did gender play in shaping policies toward Native Americans?
3. To what extent does this chapter support one or the other of these historians' interpretations of America's Indian policies?

Representing Indians

The documents below, designed for white audiences, all depict American Indians in the West.

1. **Buffalo Bill Cody's Wild West advertisement, 1899.** *Cody never called the Wild West a "show," placing tremendous emphasis on its allegedly authentic reenactments of events.*

SOURCE: Library of Congress.

2. **Lewis Henry Morgan, *Ancient Society*, 1877.** *Morgan, a leading American anthropologist, studied the Iroquois and other Native peoples. In 1877 he published an influential theory of human development, ranking various peoples in their "progress" from the "lowest stage of savagery" through the pinnacle of "civilization" — northern Europeans.*

Some tribes and families have been left in geographical isolation to work out the problems of progress. . . . [Others] have been adulterated through external influence. Thus, while Africa was and is an ethnical chaos of savagery and barbarism, Australia and Polynesia were in savagery, pure and simple. . . . The Indian family of America, unlike any other existing family, exemplified the condition of mankind in three successive ethnical periods. . . . The far northern Indians and some of the coast tribes of North and South America were in the Upper Status of savagery; the partially Village Indians east of the Mississippi were in the Lower Status of barbarism, and the Village Indians of North and South America were in the Middle Status. . . .

Commencing, then, with the Australians and Polynesians, following with the American Indian tribes, and concluding with the Roman and Grecian, who afford the highest exemplifications respectively of the six great stages of human progress, the sum of their united experiences may be supposed fairly to represent that of the human family. . . . We are dealing substantially, with the ancient history and condition of our own remote ancestors.

Status of Civilization (from Morgan, *Ancient Society*, 1877)	
I. Lower Status of Savagery	From the Infancy of the Human Race to the commencement of the next Period.
II. Middle Status of Savagery	From the acquisition of a fish subsistence and a knowledge of the use of fire . . .
III. Upper Status of Savagery	From the Invention of the Bow and Arrow . . .
IV. Lower Status of Barbarism	From the Invention of the Art of Pottery . . .
V. Middle Status of Barbarism	From the Domestication of animals on the Eastern hemisphere, and in the Western from the cultivation of maize and plants by Irrigation . . .
VI. Upper Status of Barbarism	From the Invention of the process of Smelting Iron Ore, with the use of iron tools . . .
VII. Civilization	From the Invention of writing, to the present time.

3. Touring Indian Country, 1888 and 1894. *Hoping to lure eastern tourists, the Northern Pacific Railroad published an annual journal,* Wonderland, *describing the natural splendors and economic progress of the West, as seen from its rail lines.*

We are now in the far-famed Yellowstone Valley. . . . There are but few Indians now to be seen along the line of the railroad, and those are engaged in agricultural and industrial pursuits. The extinction of the buffalo has rendered the Indian much more amenable to the civilizing influences brought to bear upon him than he formerly was, and very fair crops of grain are being raised at some of the agencies. At the Devil's Lake agency, for example, 60,000 bushels of wheat have been raised by the [Sioux and Chippewa] Indians in a single season. . . .

[The Crows'] great reservation is probably the garden spot of Montana, and the throwing open of a large portion of it to [white] settlement, which cannot long be delayed, will assuredly give an immense impetus to the agricultural interests of the Territory. . . .

The Flatheads have probably 10,000 or more horses and 5,000 or 6,000 cattle. . . . As ranchers and farmers the Flatheads are a success. It would be a matter of surprise to some people who think that the only good Indian is a dead Indian, to see the way some of the women handle sewing machines.

SOURCES: (2) Lewis H. Morgan, *Ancient Society* (New York: Henry Holt and Company, 1878), 12–13, 16–18; (3) John Hyde, *Wonderland* (St. Paul, 1888), 21, and (1894), 27.

4. Gertrude Käsebier, photograph of Joe Black Fox, 1898. *One of the first women to become a professional photographer, Käsebier here depicts Joe Black Fox relaxing with a cigarette. Black Fox, an Oglala Sioux, toured with Buffalo Bill's Wild West in 1900.*

SOURCE: Photographic History Collection, National Museum of American History, Smithsonian Institution.

ANALYZING THE EVIDENCE

1. Compare the depiction of the Plains Indians and Buffalo Bill Cody in source 1. How does source 4 differ from source 1? From Edward Curtis's depiction of Little Plume and Yellow Kidney (p. 518), in which all traces of modern life were erased? How might these depictions of "actual life" have shaped their audience's understanding of the West?

2. What bases did Morgan use for his rankings in source 2? How did he define the relationship between American Indians and whites (whom he refers to, in this passage, as "we")? Why did he suggest that Indians offered a unique opportunity for study?

3. Imagine that you were a wealthy, well-educated tourist preparing to travel west in 1900. Which of these documents would you most likely have encountered in advance? How might they have shaped your expectations and experiences?

4. These documents had different creators: an artist, a scholar, and two sets of entrepreneurs. What audiences did they have in mind? How do you think this affected their messages?

PUTTING IT ALL TOGETHER

Using these sources and your knowledge of the period, analyze the myths and realities of Native American life in the late nineteenth century.

Indian Boarding Schools   Reformers focused their greatest energy on educating the next generation. Realizing that acculturation — adoption of white ways — was difficult when children lived at home, agents and missionaries created off-reservation schools. Native families were exhorted, bullied, and bribed into sending their children to these schools, where, in addition to school lessons, boys learned farming skills and girls practiced housekeeping. "English only" was the rule; students were punished if they spoke their own languages. Mourning Dove, a Salish girl from what is now Washington State, remembered that her school "ran strictly. We never talked during meals without permission, given only on Sunday or special holidays. Otherwise there was silence — a terrible silent silence. I was used to the freedom of the forest, and it was hard to learn this strict discipline. I was punished many times before I learned." The Lakota boy Plenty Kill, who at boarding school received the new name Luther, remembered his loneliness and fear upon arrival: "The big boys would sing brave songs, and that would start the girls to crying. . . . The girls' quarters were about a hundred and fifty yards from ours, so we could hear them." After having his hair cut short, Plenty Kill felt a profound change in his identity. "None of us slept well that night," he recalled. "I felt that I was no more Indian, but would be an imitation of a white man."

Even in the first flush of reform zeal, Grant's policies faced major hurdles. Most Indians had been pushed off traditional lands and assigned to barren ground that would have defeated the most enterprising farmer. Poverty and dislocation left Indians especially vulnerable to the ravages of infectious diseases like measles and scarlet fever. At the same time, Quaker, Presbyterian, and Methodist reformers fought turf battles among themselves and with Catholic missionaries. Many traders and agents also continued to steal money and supplies from people they were supposed to protect. In the late 1870s, Rutherford B. Hayes's administration undertook more housecleaning at the Bureau of Indian Affairs, but corruption lingered.

From the Indians' point of view, reformers often became just another interest group in a crowded field of whites sending hopelessly mixed messages. The attitudes of individual army representatives, agents, and missionaries ranged from courageous and sympathetic to utterly ruthless. Many times, after chiefs thought they had reached a face-to-face agreement, they found it drastically altered by Congress or Washington bureaucrats. Nez Perce leader Joseph observed that "white people have too many chiefs. They do not understand each other. . . . I cannot understand why so many chiefs are allowed to talk so many different ways, and promise so many different things." A Kiowa chief agreed: "We make but few contracts, and them we remember well. The whites make so many they are liable to forget them. The white chief seems not to be able to govern his braves."

Native peoples were nonetheless forced to accommodate, as independent tribal governance and treaty making came to an end. Back in the 1830s, the U.S. Supreme Court had declared Indians no longer sovereign but rather "domestic dependent nations." On a practical basis, however, both the U.S. Senate and agents in the field continued to negotiate treaties as late as 1869. Two years later, the House of Representatives, jealous of Senate privileges, passed a bill to abolish all treaty making with Indians. The Senate agreed, provided that existing treaties remained in force. It was one more step in a long, torturous erosion of Native rights. Eventually, the U.S. Supreme Court ruled in *Lone Wolf v. Hitchcock* (1903) that Congress could make whatever Indian policies it chose, ignoring

To see a longer excerpt of Mourning Dove's autobiography, along with other primary sources from this period, see **Sources for America's History**.

Lone Wolf v. Hitchcock
A 1903 Supreme Court ruling that Congress could make whatever Indian policies it chose, ignoring all existing treaties.

all existing treaties. That same year, in *Ex Parte Crow Dog*, the Court ruled that no Indian was a citizen unless Congress designated him so. Indians were henceforth wards of the government. These rulings remained in force until the New Deal of the 1930s.

Breaking Up Tribal Lands Reformers' most sweeping effort to assimilate Indians was the **Dawes Severalty Act** (1887), the dream of Senator Henry L. Dawes of Massachusetts, a leader in the Indian Rights Association. Dawes saw the reservation system as an ugly relic of the past. Through severalty — division of tribal lands — he hoped to force Indians onto individual landholdings, partitioning reservations into homesteads, just like those of white farmers. Supporters of the plan believed that landownership would encourage Indians to assimilate. It would lead, as Dawes wrote, to "a personal sense of independence." Individual property, echoed another reformer, would make the Indian man "intelligently selfish, . . . with a *pocket that aches to be filled with dollars!*"

The Dawes Act was a disaster. It played into the hands of whites who coveted Indian land and who persuaded the government to sell them land that was not needed for individual allotments. In this and other ways, the Bureau of Indian Affairs (BIA) implemented the law carelessly, to the outrage of Dawes. In Indian Territory, a commission seized more than 15 million "surplus" acres from Native tribes by 1894, opening the way for whites to convert the last federal territory set aside for Native peoples into the state of Oklahoma. In addition to catastrophic losses of collectively held property, Native peoples lost 66 percent of their individually allotted lands between the 1880s and the 1930s, through fraud, BIA mismanagement, and pressure to sell to whites.

Dawes Severalty Act

The 1887 law that gave Native Americans severalty (individual ownership of land) by dividing reservations into homesteads. The law was a disaster for Native peoples, resulting over several decades in the loss of 66 percent of lands held by Indians at the time of the law's passage.

The End of Armed Resistance

As the nation consolidated control of the West in the 1870s, Americans hoped that Grant's peace policy was solving the "Indian problem." In the Southwest, such formidable peoples as the Kiowas and Comanches had been forced onto reservations. The Diné or Navajo nation, exiled under horrific conditions during the Civil War but permitted to reoccupy their traditional land, gave up further military resistance. An outbreak among California's Modoc people in 1873 — again, humiliating to the army — was at last subdued. Only Sitting Bull, a leader of the powerful Lakota Sioux on the northern plains, openly refused to go to a reservation. When pressured by U.S. troops, he repeatedly crossed into Canada, where he told reporters that "the life of white men is slavery. . . . I have seen nothing that a white man has, houses or railways or clothing or food, that is as good as the right to move in open country and live in our own fashion."

In 1874, the Lakotas faced direct provocation. Lieutenant Colonel George Armstrong Custer, a brash self-promoter who had graduated last in his class at West Point, led an expedition into South Dakota's Black Hills and loudly proclaimed the discovery of gold. Amid the severe depression of the 1870s, prospectors rushed in. The United States, wavering on its 1868 treaty, pressured Sioux leaders to sell the Black Hills. The chiefs said no. Ignoring this answer, the government demanded in 1876 that all Sioux gather at the federal agencies. The policy backfired: not only did Sitting Bull refuse to report, but other Sioux, Cheyennes, and Arapahos slipped away from reservations to join him. Knowing they might face military attack, they agreed to live together for the summer in one great village numbering over seven thousand people. By June, they were camped on the Little Big Horn River in what is now southeastern Montana. Some of the young men wanted to organize raiding parties, but elders counseled against it. "We [are] within our treaty rights as hunters," they argued. "We must keep ourselves so."

The U.S. Army dispatched a thousand cavalry and infantrymen to drive the Indians back to the reservation. Despite warnings from experienced scouts — including Crow Indian allies — most officers thought the job would be easy. Their greatest fear was that the Indians would manage to slip away. But amid the nation's centennial celebration on the Fourth of July 1876, Americans received dreadful news. On June 26 and 27, Lieutenant Colonel Custer, leading the 7th Cavalry as part of a three-pronged effort to surround the Indians, had led 210 men in an ill-considered assault on Sitting Bull's camp. The Sioux and their allies had killed the attackers to the last man. "The Indians," one Oglala woman remembered, "acted just like they were driving buffalo to a good place where they could be easily slaughtered."

As retold by the press in sensational (and often fictionalized) accounts, the story of Custer's "last stand" quickly served to justify American conquest of Indian "savages." Long after Americans forgot the massacres of Cheyenne women and children at Sand Creek and of Piegan people on the Marias River, prints of the **Battle of Little Big Horn**

Battle of Little Big Horn
The 1876 battle begun when American cavalry under George Armstrong Custer attacked an encampment of Sioux, Arapaho, and Cheyenne Indians who were resisting removal to a reservation. Custer's force was annihilated, but with whites calling for U.S. soldiers to retaliate, the Native American military victory was short-lived.

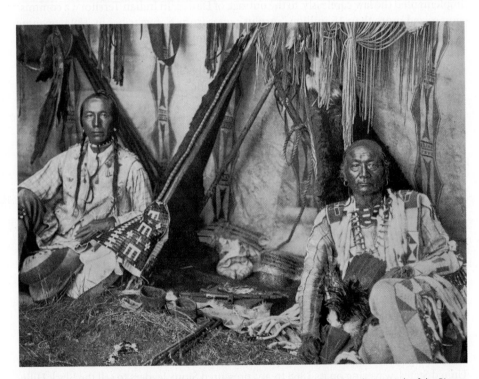

Little Plume and Yellow Kidney Photographer Edward S. Curtis took this photograph of the Piegan (Blackfeet) leader Little Plume and his son Yellow Kidney. Curtis's extensive collection of photographs of Native Americans remains a valuable resource for historians. However, Curtis altered his images to make his Native subjects seem more "authentic": though Indians made widespread use of nonnative furniture, clothes, and other consumer goods (such as Singer sewing machines), Curtis removed those from the frame. He also retouched photographs to remove items such as belts and watches. Note the circular "shadow" here, against the lodge wall, near Little Plume's right arm: the original photograph included a clock. Library of Congress.

hung in barrooms across the country. William F. "Buffalo Bill" Cody, in his traveling Wild West performances, enacted a revenge killing of a Cheyenne man named Yellow Hand in a tableau Cody called "first scalp for Custer." Notwithstanding that the tableau featured a white man scalping a Cheyenne, Cody depicted it as a triumph for civilization.

Little Big Horn proved to be the last military victory of Plains Indians against the U.S. Army. Pursued relentlessly after Custer's death and finding fewer and fewer bison to sustain them, Sioux parents watched their children starve through a bitter winter. Slowly, families trickled into the agencies and accommodated themselves to reservation life (Map 15.5). The next year, the Nez Perces, fleeing for the Canadian border, also surrendered. The final holdouts fought in the Southwest with Chiricahua Apache leader Geronimo. Like many others, Geronimo had accepted reservation life but found conditions unendurable. Describing the desolate land the tribe had been allotted, one Apache said it had "nothing but cactus, rattlesnakes, heat, rocks, and insects. . . . Many, many of our people died of starvation." When Geronimo took up arms in protest, the army recruited other Apaches to track him and his band into the hills; in September 1886, he surrendered for the last time. The Chiricahua Apaches never returned to their homeland. The United States had completed its military conquest of the West.

Strategies of Survival

Though the warpath closed, many Native peoples continued secretly to practice traditional customs. Away from the disapproving eyes of agents and teachers, they passed on their languages, histories, and traditional arts and medicine to younger generations. Frustrated missionaries often concluded that little could be accomplished because bonds of kinship and custom were so strong. Parents also hated to relinquish their children to off-reservation boarding schools. Thus more and more Indian schools ended up on or near reservations; white teachers had to accept their pupils' continued participation in the rhythms of Indian community life.

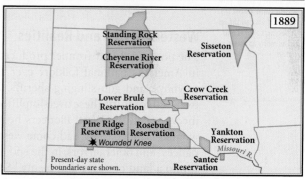

MAP 15.5 The Sioux Reservations in South Dakota, 1868–1889

In 1868, when they bent to the demand that they move onto the reservation, the Sioux thought they had gained secure rights to a substantial part of their ancestral hunting grounds. But harsh conditions on reservations led to continuing military conflicts. Land-hungry whites exerted continuous local pressure, and officials in Washington repeatedly changed the terms of Sioux landholdings—always eroding Native claims.

Selectively, most indigenous peoples adopted some white ways. Many parents urged their sons and daughters to study hard, learn English, and develop skills to help them succeed in the new world they confronted. Even Sitting Bull announced in 1885 that he wanted his children "to be educated like the white children are." Some Indian students grew up to be lawyers, doctors, and advocates for their people, including writers and artists who interpreted Native experiences for national audiences. One of the most famous was a Santee Sioux boy named Ohiyesa, who became Dr. Charles Eastman. Posted to the Pine Ridge Reservation in South Dakota, Eastman practiced medicine side by side with traditional healers, whom he respected, and wrote popular books under his Sioux name. He remembered that when he left for boarding school, his father had said, "We have now entered upon this life, and there is no going back. . . . Remember, my boy, it is the same as if I sent you on your first war-path. I shall expect you to conquer."

Nothing exemplified this syncretism, or cultural blending, better than the **Ghost Dance movement** of the late 1880s and early 1890s, which fostered American Indian peoples' hope that they could, through sacred dances, resurrect the bison and call a great storm to drive whites back across the Atlantic. The Ghost Dance drew on Christian elements as well as Native ones. As the movement spread from reservation to reservation — Paiutes, Arapahos, Sioux — indigenous peoples developed new forms of pan-Indian identity and cooperation.

White responses to the Ghost Dance showed continued misunderstanding and lethal exertion of authority. In 1890, when a group of Lakota Sioux Ghost Dancers left their South Dakota reservation, they were pursued by the U.S. Army, who feared that further spread of the religion would provoke war. On December 29, at **Wounded Knee**, the 7th Cavalry caught up with fleeing Lakotas and killed at least 150 — perhaps as many as 300. Like other massacres, this one could have been avoided. The deaths at Wounded Knee stand as a final indictment of decades of relentless U.S. expansion, white ignorance and greed, chaotic and conflicting policies, and bloody mistakes.

Western Myths and Realities

The post–Civil War frontier produced mythic figures who have played starring roles in America's national folklore ever since: "savage" Indians, brave pioneers, rugged cowboys, and gun-slinging sheriffs. Far from being invented by Hollywood in the twentieth century, these oversimplified characters emerged in the era when the nation incorporated the West. Pioneers helped develop the mythic ideal. As one Montana woman claimed, they had come west "at peril of their lives" and faced down "scalp dances" and other terrors; in the end, they "conquered the wilderness and transformed it into a land of peace and plenty." Some former cowboys, capitalizing on the popularity of dime novel Westerns, spiced up their memoirs for sale. Eastern readers were eager for stories like *The Life and Adventures of Nat Love* (1907), written by a Texas cowhand who had been born in slavery in Tennessee and who, as a rodeo star in the 1870s, had won the nickname "Deadwood Dick."

No myth-maker proved more influential than Buffalo Bill Cody. Unlike those who saw the West as free or empty, Bill understood that the United States had taken it by conquest. Ironically, his famous Wild West, which he insisted was not a "show" but an authentic representation of frontier experience, provided one of the few employment options for Plains Indians. To escape harsh reservation conditions, Sioux and

Ghost Dance movement
Religion of the late 1880s and early 1890s that combined elements of Christianity and traditional Native American religion. It fostered Plains Indians' hope that they could, through sacred dances, resurrect the great bison herds and call up a storm to drive whites back across the Atlantic.

Wounded Knee
The 1890 massacre of Sioux Indians by American cavalry at Wounded Knee Creek, South Dakota. Sent to suppress the Ghost Dance, soldiers caught up with fleeing Lakotas and killed as many as three hundred.

Cheyenne men signed on with Bill and demonstrated their riding skills for cheering audiences across the United States and Europe, chasing buffalo and attacking U.S. soldiers and pioneer wagons in the arena. Buffalo Bill proved to be a good employer to Native men, including Lakota Sioux leader Sitting Bull, who toured with Bill's Wild West in 1885. Black Elk, another Lakota Sioux man who joined Cody's operation, recalled that Bill was generous and "had a strong heart." But Black Elk had a mixed reaction to the Wild West. "I liked the part of the show we made," he told an interviewer, "but not the part the Wasichus [white people] made." As he observed, the Wild West of the 1880s was at its heart a celebration of U.S. military conquest.

At this same moment of transition, a young historian named Frederick Jackson Turner reviewed recent census data and proclaimed the end of the frontier. Up to 1890, he wrote, a clear, westward-moving line had existed between "civilization and savagery." The frontier experience, Turner argued, shaped Americans' national character. It left them a heritage of "coarseness and strength, combined with acuteness and inquisitiveness," as well as "restless, nervous energy."

Today, historians reject Turner's depiction of Indian "savagery" — and his contradictory idea that white pioneers in the West claimed empty "free land." Many scholars have noted that frontier conquest was both violent and incomplete. The Dust Bowl of the 1930s, as well as more recent cycles of drought, have repeated late-nineteenth-century patterns of hardship and depopulation on the plains. During the 1950s and 1960s, also, uranium mining rushes in the West mimicked earlier patterns of boom and bust, leaving ghost towns in their wake. Turner himself acknowledged that the frontier had both good and evil elements. He noted that in the West, "frontier liberty was sometimes confused with absence of all effective government." But in 1893, when Turner first published "The Significance of the Frontier in American History," eager listeners heard only the positives. They saw pioneering in the West as evidence of American exceptionalism: of the nation's unique history and destiny. They claimed that "peaceful" American expansion was the opposite of European empires — ignoring the many military and economic similarities. Although politically the American West became a set of states rather than a colony, historians today emphasize the legacy of conquest that is central to its (and America's) history.

Less than two months after the massacre at Wounded Knee, General William T. Sherman died in New York. As the nation marked his passing with pomp and oratory, commentators noted that his career reflected a great era of conquest and consolidation of national power. Known primarily for his role in defeating the Confederacy, Sherman's first military exploits had been against Seminoles in Florida. Later, during the U.S.-Mexico War, he had gone west with the U.S. Army to help claim California. After the Civil War, the general went west again, supervising the forced removal of Sioux and Cheyennes to reservations.

When Sherman graduated from West Point in 1840, the United States had counted twenty-six states, none of them west of Missouri. At his death in 1891, the nation boasted forty-four states, stretching to the Pacific coast. The United States now rivaled Britain and Germany as an industrial giant, and its dynamic economy was drawing immigrants from around the world. Over the span of Sherman's career, the United States had become a major player on the world stage. It had done so through the kind of fierce military conquest that Sherman made famous, as well as through bold expansions of federal authority to foster economic expansion. From the wars and policies of Sherman's lifetime, the children and grandchildren of Civil War heroes inherited a vast empire. In the coming decades, it would be up to them to decide how they would use the nation's new power.

> **IN YOUR OWN WORDS** In the late nineteenth century, what strategies did Native peoples in the West pursue in response to dispossession of their lands and efforts to assimilate them?

Summary

Between 1861 and 1877, the United States completed its conquest of the continent. After the Civil War, expansion of railroads fostered integration of the national economy. Republican policymakers promoted this integration through protective tariffs, while federal court rulings facilitated economic growth and strengthened corporations. To attract foreign investment, Congress placed the nation on the gold standard. Federal officials also pursued a vigorous foreign policy, acquiring Alaska and asserting U.S. power indirectly through control of international trade in Latin America and Asia.

An important result of economic integration was incorporation of the Great Plains. Cattlemen built an industry linked to the integrated economy, in the process nearly driving the native bison to extinction. Homesteaders confronted harsh environmental conditions as they converted the grasslands for agriculture. Republicans championed homesteader families as representatives of domesticity, an ideal opposed to Mormon plural marriage in Utah. Homesteading accelerated the rapid, often violent, transformation of western environments. Perceiving this transformation, federal officials began setting aside natural preserves such as Yellowstone, often clashing with Native Americans who wished to hunt there.

Conflicts led to the dispossession of Native American lands. During the Civil War, whites clashed with the Sioux and their allies. Grant's peace policy sought to end this conflict by forcing Native Americans to acculturate to European-style practices. Indian armed resistance continued through the 1880s, ending with Geronimo's surrender in 1886. Thereafter, Native Americans survived by secretly continuing their traditions and selectively adopting white ways. Due in part to the determined military conquest of this period, the United States claimed a major role on the world stage. Frontier myths shaped Americans' view of themselves as rugged individualists with a unique national destiny.

CHAPTER 15 REVIEW

TERMS TO KNOW *Identify and explain the significance of each term below.*

Key Concepts and Events

transcontinental railroad (p. 494)	Burlingame Treaty (p. 497)	gold standard (p. 501)	land-grant colleges (p. 502)
protective tariff (p. 496)	*Munn v. Illinois* (p. 500)	"Crime of 1873" (p. 501)	Comstock Lode (p. 503)
		Homestead Act (p. 502)	

"rain follows the plow" (p. 505)

Exodusters (p. 506)

Yellowstone National Park (p. 508)

U.S. Fisheries Commission (p. 509)

Sand Creek massacre (p. 512)

Fetterman massacre (p. 512)

Lone Wolf v. Hitchcock (p. 516)

Dawes Severalty Act (p. 517)

Battle of Little Big Horn (p. 518)

Ghost Dance movement (p. 520)

Wounded Knee (p. 520)

Key People

William Seward (p. 497)

Emmeline Wells (p. 506)

John Wesley Powell (p. 508)

Chief Joseph (p. 509)

Sitting Bull (p. 517)

George Armstrong Custer (p. 517)

William F. "Buffalo Bill" Cody (p. 519)

Geronimo (p. 519)

Ohiyesa (Dr. Charles Eastman) (p. 520)

Frederick Jackson Turner (p. 521)

REVIEW QUESTIONS   *Answer these questions to demonstrate your understanding of the chapter's main ideas.*

1. What federal policies contributed to the rise of America's industrial economy, and what were their results?

2. What factors led to transformation of the trans-Mississippi west after the Civil War?

3. In the late nineteenth century, what strategies did Native peoples in the West pursue in response to dispossession of their lands and efforts to assimilate them?

4. Review the events listed under "American and National Identity" and "Migration and Settlement" on the thematic timeline on pages 388–389. Between the 1840s and the 1870s, what distinctive patterns of racial and ethnic conflict occurred in the West? What were the results for different ethnic and racial groups?

MAKING CONNECTIONS   *Recognize the larger developments and continuities within and across chapters.*

1. During the Reconstruction years, Republican policymakers made sweeping policy decisions — especially having to do with land rights, voting rights, and education — that shaped the future of African Americans in the South and American Indians in the West. In an essay, compare U.S. policies toward the two groups. What assumptions and goals underlay each effort to incorporate racial minorities into the United States? To what extent did each effort succeed or fail, and why? How did the actions of powerful whites in each region shape the results?

2. Consider the image at the start of this chapter, "The Great West" (p. 495), which depicts how many Americans of the era thought the West *ought* to look when settlement was complete. Look at the other images in Chapter 15 that show what the natural and built environments of the West *really* looked like. What do you conclude from this comparison about the impact or the limits of U.S. policies in the West?

KEY TURNING POINTS   *Refer to the chapter chronology on page 496 for help in answering the question below.*

The military, political, and economic events of the Civil War years (1861–1865) are often treated as largely occurring in the Northeast and South — at places such as Shiloh, Gettysburg, and Washington, D.C. What impact did these developments have on the West, and what were their legacies?

Industrializing America: Upheavals and Experiments

1877–1917

Touring the United States around 1900, a Hungarian Catholic abbot named Count Péter Vay visited the steel mills of Pittsburgh. "Fourteen-thousand tall chimneys . . . discharge their burning sparks and smoke incessantly," he reported. He was moved by the plight of fellow Hungarians, laboring "wherever the heat is most insupportable, the flames most scorching." One worker had just been killed in a foundry accident. Vay, attending the funeral, worried that immigration was "of no use except to help fill the moneybags of the insatiable millionaires."

Vay witnessed America's emergence as an industrial power, the subject of Part 6 of *America's History*. We begin Part 6 in 1877 because the transformations wrought by capitalism drove the nation's most urgent controversies after the end of the Civil War and Reconstruction. Key working-class reform and protest movements developed new strategies and arguments in the four decades that followed the end of Reconstruction. The Democratic Party, traditionally hostile to strong central government but pressured in new directions by grassroots groups like the People's Party of the 1890s, began to advocate for new measures to address poverty and rein in growing corporate power. By 1910, thousands of middle-class and elite Americans had adopted their own reform visions. As ex-president Theodore Roosevelt declared, American citizens needed to "control the mighty commercial forces which they have called into being."

Part 6 ends in 1917 because we, like many other historians, see U.S. participation in World War I as a key turning point that helped bring about some measures that progressives had sought for decades, such as national women's suffrage, prohibition, and government ownership of railroads. As we shall see in Part 7, the aftermath of World War I also revealed the limits of those reforms. ▶

Corporations and Conflicts

Library of Congress.

Giant corporations developed global networks of production, marketing, and finance by innovating technically and developing ruthless tactics such as predatory pricing. Corporations' complex structures opened new careers for managers and "pink-collar workers," but wageworkers, including African Americans and millions of newly arrived immigrants, endured low pay, health hazards, and frequent unemployment. In addition to creating labor unions to protest such conditions, workers forged political alliances with farmers, who also found themselves economically vulnerable. Along with an eight-hour day and union recognition, workers agitated for, and won, Chinese exclusion.

A Diverse, Urban Society

National Archives.

The values of thrift, piety, and domesticity faced challenges in the era of industrialization. Women took prominent roles in public life, while Charles Darwin's theory of evolution prompted some thinkers to justify economic inequality as a law of nature. Writers and artists experimented with realism and abstraction. People of religious faith had diverse reactions to these upheavals.

The nation's fast-growing cities offered enticing consumer pleasures, while also housing millions of impoverished immigrants. Cities proved challenging to govern, and reformers denounced the immigrant-supported political machines that controlled them. By 1900, however, some machine leaders helped lead urban progressive experiments.

Reform Initiatives

Library of Congress.

Progressive reformers — a diverse group who were not at all united — sought to enhance democracy, limit corporate power, ameliorate poverty, and protect the environment. Though Republican President Theodore Roosevelt championed landmark legislation (1901–1909), much reform energy passed to other parties. During the presidency of Woodrow Wilson (1913–1921), Democrats enacted an impressive slate of laws, including new recognition of labor rights. Meanwhile, the Populist, Socialist, and Progressive parties proposed more radical responses to poverty and concentrated wealth. While none of these parties won national power, their ideas helped influence the shape of the emerging modern state.

Industrializing America: Upheavals and Experiments 1877–1917

AMERICAN AND NATIONAL IDENTITY	POLITICS AND POWER	WORK, EXCHANGE, AND TECHNOLOGY
1870 • Association for the Advancement of Women founded (1873) • National Farmers' Alliances form (1875–early 1880s) • San Francisco mob attacks Chinatown (1877)	• Greenback-Labor Party elects fifteen congressmen (1878)	• Economic depression (1873–1879) • Alexander Graham Bell invents telephone (1876) • Great Railroad Strike (1877)
1880 • Knights of Labor peaks (1884) • Haymarket Square violence in Chicago (1886) • American Federation of Labor founded (1886)	• Pendleton Act (1883) • Peak of Woman's Christian Temperance Union (1880s) • Interstate Commerce Act (1887) • Hull House founded (1889)	• John D. Rockefeller creates Standard Oil trust (1882) • First skyscraper completed in Chicago (1885) • American Federation of Labor founded (1886)
1890 • Lockout at Homestead, Pennsylvania (1892) • Sierra Club founded (1892) • National Association of Colored Women founded (1896)	• Disfranchisement in South (1890–1905) • People's Party founded (1890) • *Plessy v. Ferguson* (1896) • William McKinley elected president (1896)	• Severe depression hits (1893) • Corporate mergers in key industries • First subway line opens in Boston (1897) • Birth of modern advertising
1900 • Women's Trade Union League founded (1903) • Industrial Workers of the World founded (1905) • National Association for the Advancement of Colored People founded (1909)	• McKinley assassinated; Theodore Roosevelt assumes presidency (1901) • Food and Drug Administration established (1906) • Hepburn Act (1906)	• J. P. Morgan creates U.S. Steel (1901) • Women's Trade Union League founded (1903) • International Workers of the World founded (1905) • *Muller v. Oregon* (1908)
1910	• Woodrow Wilson wins presidency (1912) • Sixteenth and Seventeenth Amendments (1913) • Federal Reserve created (1913)	• Triangle Fire at Triangle Shirtwaist Company, New York (1911) • Supreme Court orders Standard Oil divided (1911)

Thematic Understanding:

This timeline arranges some of the important events of this period into themes. What was the relationship of the two severe economic depressions listed under "Work, Exchange, and Technology" to political reform? Did reform tend to come during or after periods of economic crisis? Why do you think this was the case? In what ways did Americans respond politically to the depression of the 1870s? What continuities and changes do you see in their responses to the next severe depression, in the 1890s? Minnesota Historical Society.

CULTURE AND SOCIETY	MIGRATION AND SETTLEMENT	GEOGRAPHY AND THE ENVIRONMENT	AMERICA IN THE WORLD
• Comstock Act (1873) • Baseball's National League founded (1876)		• First national park created at Yellowstone (1872) • Yellow fever epidemic devastates Memphis, Tennessee (1878)	• Social Darwinism gains acceptance • Hostility toward Chinese immigrants grows
• William Dean Howells calls for realism in literature • Booker T. Washington founds Tuskegee Institute (1881) • Birth of American football	• Congress passes Chinese Exclusion Act (1882) • Mass immigration of Russian Jews (1880s) • American Protective Association (1887)	• Hatch Act (1887) • Industrialization and urban growth cause rising pollution	• Rapid industrialization draws immigrants from around the world • Chinese Exclusion Act (1882–1943)
• Jacob Riis publishes *How the Other Half Lives* (1890) • World's Columbian Exposition in Chicago (1893)	• New York's Ellis Island opens (1892)	• John Muir founds Sierra Club (1892) • "Bicycle craze" and rise of hiking and camping get more Americans outdoors	• Gorras Blancas confront wealthy Anglo interests in New Mexico • Ellis Island opens (1892) • *Plessy v. Ferguson* (1896)
• First World Series (1903) • Robert Hunter publishes *Poverty* (1904) • Upton Sinclair's *The Jungle* published (1906) • Walter Dill Scott publishes *The Psychology of Advertising* (1908)	• Migration of African Americans to northern cities increases • New York passes Tenement House Law (1901) • Mutual aid societies form to help immigrants	• Antiquities Act (1906) • National Audubon Society forms (1901) • Newlands Reclamation Act (1902) • U.S. Forest Service created (1905)	• Rising immigration from Eastern and Southern Europe • Height of eugenics (1900s–1920s) • Increasing numbers of blacks move to cities; responses include "race riots" by whites
• Armory Show of modern art held in New York City (1913)		• National Park Service created (1916)	• Peak of foreign missions activity by American Protestant churches (1915)

Row labels (left axis): 1870, 1880, 1890, 1900, 1910

16

CHAPTER

Industrial America: Corporations and Conflicts
1877–1911

F or millions of his contemporaries, Andrew Carnegie exemplified American success. Arriving from Scotland as a poor twelve-year-old in 1848, Carnegie found work as an errand boy for the Pennsylvania Railroad and rapidly scaled the managerial ladder. In 1865, he struck out on his own as an iron manufacturer, selling to friends in the railroad business. Encouraged by Republican tariffs to enter the steel industry, he soon built a massive steel mill outside Pittsburgh where a state-of-the-art Bessemer converter made steel refining dramatically more efficient. With Carnegie leading the way, steel became a major U.S. industry, reaching annual production of 10 million metric tons by 1900 — almost as much as the *combined* output of the world's other top producers, Germany (6.6 million tons) and Britain (4.8 million).

At first, skilled workers at Carnegie's mill in Homestead, Pennsylvania, earned good wages. They had a strong union, and Carnegie affirmed workers' right to organize. But Carnegie — confident that new machinery enabled him to replace many skilled laborers — eventually decided that collective bargaining was too expensive. In the summer of 1892, he withdrew to his estate in Scotland, leaving his partner Henry Clay Frick in command. A former coal magnate and veteran foe of labor, Frick was well qualified to do the dirty work. He announced that after July 1, members of the Amalgamated Association of Iron and Steel Workers would be locked out of the Homestead mill. If they wanted to return to work, they would have to abandon the union and sign new individual contracts. Frick fortified the mill and prepared to hire replacement workers. The battle was on.

At dawn on July 6, barges chugging up the Monongahela River brought dozens of private armed guards from the Pinkerton Detective Agency, hired by Carnegie to defend the plant. Locked-out workers opened fire, starting a gunfight that left seven workers and three Pinkertons dead. Frick appealed to Pennsylvania's governor, who sent the state militia to arrest labor leaders on charges of riot and murder. Most of the locked-out workers lost their jobs. The union was dead.

As the **Homestead lockout** showed, industrialization was a controversial and often bloody process. During the half century after the Civil War, more and more Americans worked not as independent farmers or artisans but as employees of large corporations. Conditions of work changed for people of all economic classes. Drawn by the dynamic economy, immigrants arrived from around the globe. These transformations provoked working people, including farmers as well as industrial workers, to organize and defend their interests.

IDENTIFY THE BIG IDEA

What new opportunities and risks did industrialization bring, and how did it reshape American society?

Homestead lockout

The 1892 lockout of workers at the Homestead, Pennsylvania, steel mill after Andrew Carnegie refused to renew the union contract. Union supporters attacked the guards hired to close them out and protect strike-breakers who had been employed by the mill, but the National Guard soon suppressed this resistance and Homestead, like other steel plants, became a non-union mill.

Marianna Mine Disaster The bituminous mines of Marianna, Pennsylvania, and many other rich sites provided the coal that fueled American industrial growth. On November 28, 1908, an explosion in the mine killed 158 workers. Many were American-born; some were Irish, Welsh, Italian, and Polish immigrants. Here, a horse-drawn wagon carries bodies recovered from the mine. Such catastrophes laid bare the human cost of industrialization. Marianna was one among many: in the same decade, disasters at Scofield, Utah; Jacobs Creek, Pennsylvania; Monongah, West Virginia; and Cherry, Illinois, each killed over 200 men. Library of Congress.

CHAPTER CHRONOLOGY

As you read, ask yourself why this chapter begins and ends with these dates and identify the links among related events.

1863 ▸ Cleveland, Ohio, becomes nation's petroleum refining center	**1882** ▸ John D. Rockefeller creates Standard Oil trust ▸ Congress passes Chinese Exclusion Act
1865 ▸ Chicago's Union Stock Yards opens	**1884** ▸ Knights of Labor at peak of membership
1867 ▸ National Grange of the Patrons of Husbandry founded	**1885** ▸ Rock Springs massacre of Chinese miners
1869 ▸ Knights of Labor founded	**1886** ▸ Haymarket Square violence ▸ American Federation of Labor (AFL) founded
1873 ▸ Panic followed by severe economic depression	**1887** ▸ Hatch Act ▸ Interstate Commerce Act
1875 ▸ John Wanamaker opens nation's first department store in Philadelphia	**1889** ▸ New Jersey passes law enabling trusts to operate in the state
1876 ▸ Alexander Graham Bell invents the telephone	**1892** ▸ Homestead lockout
1877 ▸ San Francisco mob attacks Chinatown ▸ Great Railroad Strike ▸ First Farmers' Alliances form in South and West	**1893** ▸ Severe depression hits, causes mass unemployment and wave of corporate mergers
1878 ▸ Greenback-Labor Party elects fifteen congressmen	**1901** ▸ J. P. Morgan creates U.S. Steel, America's first billion-dollar corporation
1879 ▸ Henry George publishes *Progress and Poverty*	**1908** ▸ Walter Dill Scott publishes *The Psychology of Advertising* ▸ Marianna, Pennsylvania, mine disaster
1880s ▸ Violence in Russia and Eastern Europe prompts mass immigration of Jews to United States	

 To see a longer excerpt of "The Gospel of Wealth," along with other primary sources from this period, see **Sources for America's History**.

Gospel of Wealth
Andrew Carnegie's argument that corporate leaders' success showed their "fitness" to lead society and that poverty demonstrated, on the contrary, lack of "fitness" to compete in the new economy. Carnegie advocated, however, that wealthy men should use their fortunes for the public good.

The Rise of Big Business

In the late 1800s, industrialization in Europe and the United States revolutionized the world economy. It brought large-scale commercial agriculture to many parts of the globe and prompted millions of migrants — both skilled workers and displaced peasants — to cross continents and oceans in search of jobs. Industrialization also created a production glut. The immense scale of agriculture and manufacturing caused a long era of deflation, when prices dropped worldwide (Figure 16.1).

Falling prices normally signal low demand for goods and services, and thus stagnation. In England, a mature industrial power, the late nineteenth century did bring economic decline. But in the United States, production expanded. Between 1877 and 1900, Americans' average real per capita income increased from $388 to $573. In this sense, Andrew Carnegie was right when he argued that, even though industrialization increased the gap between rich and poor, everyone's standard of living rose. In his famous 1889 essay "Wealth" — later called the **Gospel of Wealth** — he observed that "the poor enjoy what the rich could not before afford. What were the luxuries have become the necessaries of life."

Technological and business efficiencies allowed American firms to grow, invest in new equipment, and earn profits even as prices for their products fell. Growth depended, in turn, on America's large and growing population, expansion into the West, and an integrated national marketplace. In many fields, large corporations became the dominant form of business.

Innovators in Enterprise

As rail lines stretched westward between the 1850s and 1880s, operators faced a crisis. As one Erie Railroad executive noted, a superintendent on a 50-mile line could personally attend to every detail. But supervising a 500-mile line was impossible; trains ran late, communications failed, and trains crashed. Managers gradually invented systems to solve these problems. They distinguished top executives from those responsible for day-to-day operations. They departmentalized operations by function — purchasing, machinery, freight traffic, passenger traffic — and established clear lines of communication. They perfected cost accounting, which allowed an industrialist like Carnegie to track expenses and revenues carefully and thus follow his Scottish mother's advice: "Take care of the pennies, and the pounds will take care of themselves." This **management revolution** created the internal structure adopted by many large, complex corporations.

During these same years, the United States became an industrial power by tapping North America's vast natural resources, particularly in the West. Industries that had once depended on water power began to use prodigious amounts of coal. Steam engines replaced human and animal labor, and kerosene replaced whale oil and wood. By 1900, America's factories and urban homes were converting to electric power. With new management structures and dependency on fossil fuels (oil, coal, natural gas), corporations transformed both the economy and the country's natural and built environments.

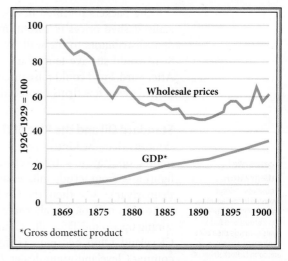

FIGURE 16.1 Business Activity and Wholesale Prices, 1869–1900

This graph shows the key feature of the performance of the late-nineteenth-century economy: while output was booming, wholesale prices were, on the whole, falling. Thus, while workers often struggled with falling wages — especially during decades of severe economic crisis — consumer products also became cheaper to buy.

management revolution
An internal management structure adopted by many large, complex corporations that distinguished top executives from those responsible for day-to-day operations and departmentalized operations by function.

Production and Sales After Chicago's Union Stock Yards opened in 1865, middlemen shipped cows by rail from the Great Plains to Chicago and from there to eastern cities, where slaughter took place in local butchertowns. Such a system — a national livestock market with local processing — could have lasted, as it did in Europe. But Gustavus Swift, a shrewd Chicago cattle dealer, saw that local slaughterhouses lacked the scale to utilize waste by-products and cut labor costs. To improve productivity, Swift invented the assembly line, where each wageworker repeated the same slaughtering task over and over.

Swift also pioneered **vertical integration**, a model in which a company controlled all aspects of production from raw materials to finished goods. Once his engineers designed a cooling system, Swift invested in a fleet of refrigerator cars to keep beef fresh as he shipped it eastward, priced below what local butchers could afford. In cities that received his chilled meat, Swift built branch houses and fleets of delivery wagons. He also constructed factories to make fertilizer and chemicals from the by-products of slaughter, and he developed marketing strategies for those products as well. Other Chicago packers followed Swift's lead. By 1900, five firms, all vertically integrated, produced nearly 90 percent of the meat shipped in interstate commerce.

vertical integration
A business model in which a corporation controlled all aspects of production from raw materials to packaged products. "Robber barons," or industrial innovators such as Gustavus Swift and Andrew Carnegie, pioneered this business form at the end of the Civil War.

Big packers invented new sales tactics. For example, Swift & Company periodically slashed prices in certain markets to below production costs, driving independent distributors to the wall. With profits from its sales elsewhere, a large firm like Swift could survive temporary losses in one locality until competitors went under. Afterward, Swift could raise prices again. This technique, known as predatory pricing, helped give a few firms unprecedented market control.

Standard Oil and the Rise of the Trusts

No one used ruthless business tactics more skillfully than the king of petroleum, John D. Rockefeller. After inventors in the 1850s figured out how to extract kerosene — a clean-burning fuel for domestic heating and lighting — from crude oil, enormous oil deposits were discovered at Titusville, Pennsylvania. Just then, the Civil War severely disrupted whaling, forcing whale-oil customers to look for alternative lighting sources. Overnight, a forest of oil wells sprang up around Titusville. Connected to these Pennsylvania oil fields by rail in 1863, Cleveland, Ohio, became a refining center. John D. Rockefeller was then an up-and-coming Cleveland grain dealer. (He, like Carnegie and most other budding tycoons, hired a substitute to fight for him in the Civil War.) Rockefeller had strong nerves, a sharp eye for able partners, and a genius for finance. He went into the kerosene business and borrowed heavily to expand. Within a few years, his firm — Standard Oil of Ohio — was Cleveland's leading refiner.

Like Carnegie and Swift, Rockefeller succeeded through vertical integration: to control production and sales all the way from the oil well to the kerosene lamp, he took a big stake in the oil fields, added pipelines, and developed a vast distribution network. Rockefeller allied with railroad executives, who, like him, hated the oil market's boom-and-bust cycles. What they wanted was predictable, high-volume traffic, and they offered Rockefeller secret rebates that gave him a leg up on competitors.

horizontal integration
A business concept invented in the late nineteenth century to pressure competitors and force rivals to merge their companies into a conglomerate. John D. Rockefeller of Standard Oil pioneered this business model.

trust
A small group of associates that hold stock from a group of combined firms, managing them as a single entity. Trusts quickly evolved into other centralized business forms, but progressive critics continued to refer to giant firms like U.S. Steel and Standard Oil as "trusts."

Rockefeller also pioneered a strategy called **horizontal integration**. After driving competitors to the brink of failure through predatory pricing, he invited them to merge their local companies into his conglomerate. Most agreed, often because they had no choice. Through such mergers, Standard Oil wrested control of 95 percent of the nation's oil refining capacity by the 1880s. In 1882, Rockefeller's lawyers created a new legal form, the **trust**. It organized a small group of associates — the board of trustees — to hold stock from a group of combined firms, managing them as a single entity. Rockefeller soon invested in Mexican oil fields and competed in world markets against Russian and Middle Eastern producers.

Other companies followed Rockefeller's lead, creating trusts to produce such products as linseed oil, sugar, and salt. Many expanded

A "Gusher" in Pennsylvania Late nineteenth-century Americans tapped large petroleum fields in western Pennsylvania and later in Texas, developing an array of uses for kerosene and other fossil fuels. This 1880 sketch of an oil well shows what happened when drillers struck an underground petroleum pocket that was under pressure.
Everett Collection.

sales and production overseas. As early as 1868, Singer Manufacturing Company established a factory in Scotland to produce sewing machines. By World War I, such brands as Ford and General Electric had become familiar around the world.

Distressed by the development of near monopolies, reformers began to denounce "the trusts," a term that in popular usage referred to any large corporation that seemed to wield excessive power. Some states outlawed trusts as a legal form. But in an effort to attract corporate headquarters to its state, New Jersey broke ranks in 1889, passing a law that permitted the creation of holding companies and other combinations. Delaware soon followed, providing another legal haven for consolidated corporations. A wave of mergers further concentrated corporate power during the depression of the 1890s, as weaker firms succumbed to powerful rivals. By 1900, America's largest one hundred companies controlled a third of the nation's productive capacity. Purchasing several steel companies in 1901, including Carnegie Steel, J. P. Morgan created U.S. Steel, the nation's first billion-dollar corporation. Such familiar firms as DuPont and Eastman Kodak assumed dominant places in their respective industries (Interpretations).

Assessing the Industrialists The work of men like Swift, Rockefeller, and Carnegie was controversial in their lifetimes and has been ever since. Carnegie, in his "Wealth" essay, argued that corporate titans attained their wealth through talent, proving they deserved their success. He also declared, however, that wealth was a "public trust" and that every elite man, after providing for his family, had a patriotic obligation to give away his millions to benefit education and other worthy causes. Carnegie advocated a near 100 percent inheritance tax on privately held wealth: inheriting large sums, he believed, discouraged young people's initiative, just as "handouts" of food or shelter to the poor discouraged them from working. Carnegie rejected both, viewing Social Darwinism, or "survival of the fittest," as the key principle of the new order (see Chapter 17).

Historians' opinions of the first industrial titans have tended to be harsh in eras of economic crisis, when the shortcomings of corporate America appear in stark relief. During the Great Depression of the 1930s, a historian coined the term *robber barons*, which is still used today. In periods of prosperity, both scholars and the public have tended to view early industrialists more favorably, calling them *industrial statesmen*.

Some scholars have argued that industrialists benefitted the economy by replacing the chaos of market competition with a "visible hand" of planning and expert management. But one recent study of railroads asserts that the main skills of early tycoons (as well as those of today) were cultivating political "friends," defaulting on loans, and lying to the public. Whether we consider the industrialists heroes, villains, or something in between, it is clear that the corporate economy was not the creation of just a few individuals, however famous or influential. It was a systemic transformation of the economy.

A National Consumer Culture As they integrated vertically and horizontally, corporations innovated in other ways. Companies such as Bell Telephone and Westinghouse set up research laboratories. Steelmakers invested in chemistry and materials science to make their products cheaper, better, and stronger. Mass markets brought an appealing array of goods to consumers who could afford them. Railroads

How Modern Were Late-Nineteenth-Century Corporations?

The modern corporation emerged in the late nineteenth century as both a cause and consequence of industrialization and the expansion of the capitalist system. Unlike smaller manufacturing and mercantile businesses of the early nineteenth century, which were often owned and operated by a single person or family, these sprawling and complex organizations developed elaborate administrative structures and employed a bureaucracy of managers to run daily operations. But were these professionals any good?

Historians Alfred D. Chandler Jr. and Richard White examine the railroad as the key industry pioneering the development of the modern corporation. In both accounts, the managerial class was central to this process because, unlike owners, who were often uninvolved stockholders, the managers oversaw the day-to-day running of these multifaceted organizations. Chandler and White, however, interpret the success of these managers and their corporations in different ways.

ALFRED D. CHANDLER JR.

SOURCE: Alfred D. Chandler Jr., *The Visible Hand: The Managerial Revolution in American Business* (Cambridge: The Belknap Press of Harvard University Press, 1977), 12, 87.

The visible hand of management replaced the invisible hand of market forces. . . . [S]afe, regular, reliable movement of goods and passengers, as well as the continuing maintenance and repair of locomotives, rolling stock, and track, roadbed, stations, roundhouses, and other equipment, required . . . special skills and training which could only be commanded by a full-time salaried manager. . . . This career orientation and the specialized nature of tasks gave the railroad managers an increasingly professional outlook on their work.

RICHARD WHITE

SOURCE: Richard White, *Railroaded: The Transcontinentals and the Making of Modern America* (New York: W. W. Norton & Company, 2011), xxix–xxxii.

[Railroads] were not the harbingers of order, rationality, and effective large-scale organization. . . . Managers blamed their failures on accidents and contingent events, but they also used them to cover their mistakes and claim quite fortuitous results as the fruits of their planning. . . . [The railroad corporations] not only failed to institute the order they desired; they also just plain failed and repeatedly needed rescuing by the state and the courts. . . . The transcontinental railroads are sometimes fetishized as the ultimate manifestation of modern rationality, but, when seen from within, these astonishingly mismanaged railroads are the anteroom to mystery.

QUESTIONS FOR ANALYSIS

1. Name two ways that each of these two historians evaluates the success of late-nineteenth-century corporations.
2. What are the key differences between Chandler's assessment of corporate planning and White's?
3. Besides railroads, what other examples from this chapter demonstrate the growth of the modern corporation described by either Chandler or White?

whisked Florida oranges and other fresh produce to the shelves of grocery stores. Retailers such as F. W. Woolworth and the Great Atlantic and Pacific Tea Company (A&P) opened chains of stores that soon stretched nationwide.

The department store was pioneered in 1875 by John Wanamaker in Philadelphia. These megastores displaced small retail shops, tempting customers with large show windows and Christmas displays. Like industrialists, department store magnates developed economies of scale that enabled them to slash prices. An 1898 newspaper advertisement for Macy's Department Store urged shoppers to "read our books, cook in our saucepans, dine off our china, wear our silks, get under our blankets, smoke our cigars, drink our wines — Shop at Macy's — and Life will Cost You Less and Yield You More Than You Dreamed Possible."

While department stores became urban fixtures, Montgomery Ward and Sears built mail-order empires. Rural families from Vermont to California pored over the companies' annual catalogs, making wish lists of tools, clothes, furniture, and toys. Mail-order companies used money-back guarantees to coax wary customers to buy products they could not see or touch. "Don't be afraid to make a mistake," the Sears catalog counseled. "Tell us what you want, in your own way." By 1900, America counted more than twelve hundred mail-order companies.

The active shaping of consumer demand became, in itself, a new enterprise. Outdoors, advertisements appeared everywhere: in New York's Madison Square, the Heinz Company installed a 45-foot pickle made of green electric lights. Tourists had difficulty admiring Niagara Falls because billboards obscured the view. By 1900, companies were spending more than $90 million a year ($2.3 billion today) on print advertising, as the press itself became a mass-market industry. Rather than charging subscribers the cost of production, magazines began to cover their costs by selling ads. Cheap subscriptions built a mass readership, which in turn attracted more advertisers. In 1903, the *Ladies' Home Journal* became the first magazine with a million subscribers.

The Corporate Workplace

Before the Civil War, most American boys had hoped to become farmers, small-business owners, or independent artisans. Afterward, more and more Americans — both male and female — began working for someone else. Because they wore white shirts with starched collars, those who held professional positions in corporations became known as white-collar workers, a term differentiating them from blue-collar employees, who labored with their hands. For a range of employees — managers and laborers, clerks and salespeople — the rise of corporate work had wide-ranging consequences.

Managers and Salesmen As the managerial revolution unfolded, the headquarters of major corporations began to house departments handling specific activities such as purchasing and accounting. These departments were supervised by middle managers, something not seen before in American industry. Middle managers took on entirely new tasks, directing the flow of goods, labor, and information throughout the enterprise. They were key innovators, counterparts to the engineers in research laboratories who, in the same decades, worked to reduce costs and improve efficiency.

Corporations also needed a new kind of sales force. In post–Civil War America, the drummer, or traveling salesman, became a familiar sight on city streets and in remote country stores. Riding rail networks from town to town, drummers introduced merchants to new products, offered incentives, and suggested sales displays. They built nationwide distribution networks for such popular consumer products as cigarettes and Coca-Cola. By the late 1880s, the leading manufacturer of cash registers produced a sales script for its employees' conversations with local merchants. "Take for granted that he will buy," the script directed. "Say to him, 'Now, Mr. Blank, what color shall I make it?' . . . Handing him your pen say, 'Just sign here where I have made the cross.'"

With such companies in the vanguard, sales became systematized. Managers set individual sales quotas and awarded prizes to top salesmen, while those who sold too little were singled out for remedial training or dismissal. Executives embraced the ideas of business psychologist Walter Dill Scott, who published *The Psychology of Advertising* in 1908. Scott's principles — which included selling to customers based on their presumed "instinct of escape" and "instinct of combat" — were soon taught at Harvard Business School. Others also promised that a "scientific attitude" would "attract attention" and "create desire."

Telephone Operators, 1888 Like other women office workers, these switchboard operators enjoyed relatively high pay and comfortable working conditions — especially in the early years of the telephone industry, before operators' work routines speeded up. These young women worked for the Central Union Telephone Company in Canton, Ohio. Courtesy of the Ohio History Connection , AL00129.

Women in the Corporate Office Beneath the ranks of managers emerged a new class of female office workers. Before the Civil War, most clerks at small firms had been young men who expected to rise through the ranks. In a large corporation, secretarial work became a dead-end job, and employers began assigning it to women. By the turn of the twentieth century, 77 percent of all stenographers and typists were female; by 1920, women held half of all low-level office jobs.

For white working-class women, clerking and office work represented new opportunities. In an era before most families had access to day care, mothers most often earned money at home, where they could tend children while also taking in laundry, caring for boarders, or doing piecework (sewing or other assembly projects, paid on a per-item basis). Unmarried daughters could enter domestic service or factory work, but clerking and secretarial work were cleaner and better paid.

New technologies provided additional opportunities for women. The rise of the telephone, introduced by inventor Alexander Graham Bell in 1876, was a notable example. Originally intended for business use on local exchanges, telephones were eagerly adopted by residential customers. Thousands of young women found work as telephone opera-tors. By 1900, more than 4 million women worked for wages. About a third worked in domestic service; another third in industry; the rest in office work, teaching, nursing, or sales. As new occupations arose, the percentage of wage-earning women in domes-tic service dropped dramatically, a trend that continued in the twentieth century.

On the Shop Floor

Despite the managerial revolution at the top, skilled craft workers — almost all of them men — retained considerable autonomy in many industries. A coal miner, for exam-ple, was not an hourly wageworker but essentially an independent contractor, paid by the amount of coal he produced. He provided his own tools, worked at his own pace, and knocked off early when he chose. The same was true for puddlers and roll-ers in ironworks; molders in stove making; and machinists, glass blowers, and skilled workers in many other industries. Such workers abided by the stint, a self-imposed limit on how much they would produce each day. This informal system of restricting output infuriated efficiency-minded engineers, but to the workers it signified personal dignity, manly pride, and brotherhood with fellow employees. One shop in Lowell, Massachusetts, posted regulations requiring all employees to be at their posts by the time of the opening bell and to remain, with the shop door locked, until the closing bell. A machinist promptly packed his tools, declaring that he had not "been brought up under such a system of slavery."

Skilled workers — craftsmen, inside contractors, and foremen — enjoyed a high degree of autonomy. But those who paid helpers from their own pocket could also exploit them. Subcontracting arose, in part, to enable manufacturers to distance themselves from the consequences of shady labor practices. In Pittsburgh steel mills, foremen were known as "pushers," notorious for driving their gangs mercilessly. On the other hand, industrial labor operated on a human scale, through personal rela-tionships that could be close and enduring. Striking craft workers would commonly receive the support of helpers and laborers, and labor gangs would sometimes walk out on behalf of a popular foreman.

As industrialization advanced, however, workers increasingly lost the indepen-dence characteristic of craft work. The most important cause of this was the **deskilling** of labor under a new system of mechanized manufacturing that men like meatpacker Gustavus Swift had pioneered and that automobile maker Henry Ford would soon call mass production. Everything from typewriters to automobiles came to be assem-bled from standardized parts, using machines that increasingly operated with little human oversight. A machinist protested in 1883 that the sewing machine industry was so "subdivided" that "one man may make just a particular part of a machine and may not know anything whatever about another part of the same machine." Such a worker, noted an observer, "cannot be master of a craft, but only master of a fragment." Employers, who originally favored automatic machinery because it increased output, quickly found that it also helped them control workers and cut labor costs. They could pay unskilled workers less and replace them easily.

By the early twentieth century, managers sought to further reduce costs through a program of industrial efficiency called **scientific management**. Its inventor, a metal-cutting expert named Frederick W. Taylor, recommended that employers eliminate

deskilling
The elimination of skilled labor under a new system of mechanized manufac-turing, in which workers completed discrete, small-scale tasks rather than crafting an entire product. With deskilling, employers found they could pay workers less and replace them more easily.

scientific management
A system of organizing work developed by Frederick W. Taylor in the late nineteenth century. It was designed to coax maximum output from the individual worker, increase efficiency, and reduce production costs.

all brain work from manual labor, hiring experts to develop rules for the shop floor. Workers must be required to "do what they are told promptly and without asking questions or making suggestions." In its most extreme form, scientific management called for engineers to time each task with a stopwatch; companies would pay workers more if they met the stopwatch standard. Taylor assumed that workers would respond automatically to the lure of higher earnings. But scientific management was not, in practice, a great success. Implementing it proved to be expensive, and workers stubbornly resisted. Corporate managers, however, adopted bits and pieces of Taylor's system, and they enthusiastically agreed that decisions should lie with "management alone." Over time, in comparison with businesses in other countries, American corporations created a particularly wide gap between the roles of managers and those of the blue-collar workforce.

Blue-collar workers had little freedom to negotiate, and their working conditions deteriorated markedly as deskilling and mass production took hold. At the same time, industrialization brought cheaper products that enabled many Americans to enjoy new consumer products — if they could avoid starvation. From executives down to unskilled workers, the hierarchy of corporate employment contributed to sharper distinctions among three economic classes: the wealthy elite; an emerging, self-defined "middle class"; and a struggling class of workers, who bore the brunt of the economy's new risks and included many Americans living in dire poverty. As it wrought these changes, industrialization prompted intense debate over inequality (Thinking Like a Historian).

Health Hazards and Pollution   Industrialized labor also damaged workers' health. In 1884, a study of the Illinois Central Railroad showed that, over the previous decade, one in twenty of its workers had been killed or permanently disabled by an accident on the job. For brakemen — one of the most dangerous jobs — the rate was one in seven. Due to lack of regulatory laws and inspections, mining was 50 percent more dangerous in the United States than in Germany; between 1876 and 1925, an average of over two thousand U.S. coal miners died each year from cave-ins and explosions. Silver, gold, and copper mines were also not immune from such tragedies, but mining companies resisted demands for safety regulation.

Extractive industries and factories also damaged nearby environments and the people who lived there. In big cities, poor residents suffered from polluted air and the dumping of noxious by-products into the water supply. Mines like those in Leadville, Colorado, contaminated the land and water with mercury and lead. Alabama convicts, forced to work in coal mines, faced brutal working conditions and fatal illnesses caused by the mines' contamination of local water. At the time, people were well aware of many of these dangers, but workers had an even more urgent priority: work. Pittsburgh's belching smokestacks meant coughing and lung damage, but they also meant running mills and paying jobs.

Unskilled Labor and Discrimination   As managers deskilled production, the ranks of factory workers came to include more and more women and children, who were almost always unskilled and low paid. Men often resented women's presence in factories, and male labor unions often worked to exclude women — especially wives, who they argued should remain in the home. Women vigorously defended their right to work. On hearing accusations that married women worked only to buy frivolous luxuries, one female worker in a Massachusetts shoe factory wrote a heated response to the local newspaper: "When the husband and father cannot provide for his wife and children, it is perfectly natural that the wife and mother should desire to work. . . . Don't blame married women if the land of the free has become a land of slavery and oppression."

In 1900, one of every five children under the age of sixteen worked outside the home. Child labor was most widespread in the ex-Confederacy. Here, a low-wage industrial sector emerged after Reconstruction, leading commentators to hail the region as a more economically diversified **New South** (Map 16.1). Textile mills sprouted in the Carolinas and Georgia, recruiting workers from surrounding farms; whole families often worked in the mills. Many children also worked in Pennsylvania

New South
A nickname for the former Confederate states, used by boosters to describe the region's economic diversification and growth of industrial jobs in the post–Civil War era. Because of the region's poverty, many of those industries were extractive (such as coal and timber), and some (like textiles) were low-wage and involved considerable child labor.

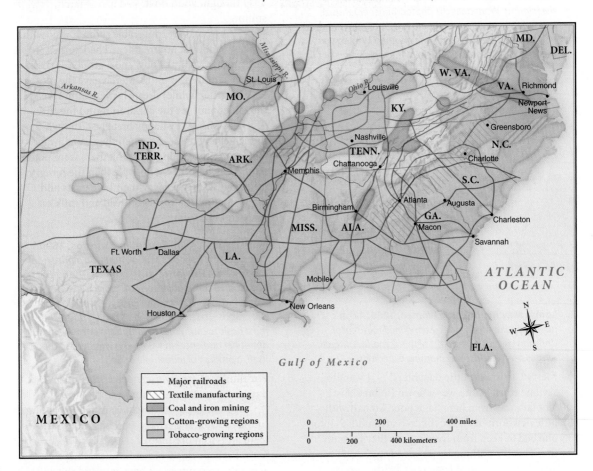

MAP 16.1 The New South, 1900
The economy of the Old South focused on raising staple crops, especially cotton and tobacco. In the New South, staple agriculture continued to dominate, but industrial regions also evolved, producing textiles, coal, and iron. By 1900, the South's industrial pattern was well defined, though the region still served — like the West — as a major producer of raw materials for the industrial region that stretched from New England to Chicago.

Poverty and Food

Amid rising industrial poverty, food emerged as a reference point. How much was too little, or too much? If some Americans were going hungry, how should others respond? The documents below show some contributions to these debates.

1. **Lewis W. Hine, "Mealtime, New York Tenement," 1910.** *Hine was an influential photographer and reformer. He took a famous series of photographs at Ellis Island, remarking that he hoped Americans would view new immigrants in the same way they thought of the Pilgrims. What does the photographer emphasize in the living conditions of this Italian immigrant family and their relationships with one another? Why do you think Hine photographed them at the table?*

Source: Pictorial Press Ltd./Alamy Stock Photo.

2. **Louisa May Alcott, *Little Women*, 1869.** *Alcott's novel, popular for decades, exemplified the ideal of Christian charity. At the start of this scene, Mrs. March returns from a Christmas morning expedition.*

Merry Christmas, little daughters! . . . I want to say one word before we sit down [to breakfast]. Not far away from here lies a poor woman with a little newborn baby. Six children are huddled into one bed to keep from freezing, for they have no fire. There is nothing to eat. . . . My girls, will you give them your breakfasts as a Christmas present?

. . . For a minute no one spoke, only a minute, for Jo exclaimed impetuously, I'm so glad you came before we began!

May I go and help . . . ? asked Beth eagerly.

I shall take the cream and the muffins, added Amy. . . . Meg was already covering the buckwheats and piling the bread into one big plate.

I thought you'd do it, said Mrs. March, smiling.

. . . A poor, bare, miserable room it was, with broken windows, no fire, ragged bedclothes, a sick mother, wailing baby, and a group of pale, hungry children. . . . Mrs. March gave the mother tea and gruel [while] the girls meantime spread the table [and] set the children round the fire. . . .

That was a very happy breakfast, though they didn't get any of it. And when they went away, leaving comfort behind, I think there were not in all the city four merrier people than the hungry little girls who gave away their breakfasts and contented themselves with bread and milk on Christmas morning.

3. **Mary Hinman Abel, *Promoting Nutrition*, 1890.** *This excerpt is from a cookbook that won a prize from the American Public Health Association. The author had studied community cooking projects in Europe and worked to meet the needs of Boston's poor. How does she propose to feed people on 13 cents a day — her most basic menu? What assumptions does she make about her audience? In what ways was her cookbook, itself, a product of industrialization?*

For family of six, average price 78 cents per day, or 13 cents per person.

. . . I am going to consider myself as talking to the mother of a family who has six mouths to feed, and no more money than this to do it with. Perhaps this woman has never kept accurate accounts. . . . I have in mind the wife [who has] time to attend to the housework and children. If a woman helps earn, as in a factory, doing most of her housework after she comes home at night, she must certainly have more money than in the first case in order to accomplish the same result.

. . . The Proteid column is the one that you must look to most carefully because it is furnished at the most expense, and it is very important that it should not fall below the figures I have given [or] your family would be undernourished.

[Sample spring menu]
Breakfast. Milk Toast. Coffee.
Dinner. Stuffed Beef's Heart. Potatoes stewed with Milk. Dried Apple Pie. Bread and Cheese. Corn Coffee.
Supper. Noodle Soup (from Saturday). Boiled Herring. Bread. Tea.

Proteids. (oz.)	21.20
Fats. (oz.)	14.39
Carbohydrates. (oz.)	77.08
Cost in Cents.	76

4. **Werner Sombart, *Why Is There No Socialism in the United States?*, 1906.** *Sombart, a German sociologist, compared living conditions in Germany and the United States in order to answer the question above. What conclusion did he reach?*

The American worker eats almost three times as much meat, three times as much flour and four times as much sugar as his German counterpart. . . . The American worker is much closer to the better sections of the German middle class than to the German wage-labouring class. He does not merely eat, but dines. . . .

It is no wonder if, in such a situation, any dissatisfaction with the "existing social order" finds difficulty in establishing itself in the mind of the worker. . . . All Socialist utopias came to nothing on roast beef and apple pie.

5. **Helen Campbell, *Prisoners of Poverty*, 1887.** *A journalist, Campbell investigated the conditions of low-paid seamstresses in New York City who did piecework in their apartments. Like Abel (source 3), she tried to teach what she called "survival economics." Here, a woman responds to Campbell's suggestion that she cook beans for better nutrition.*

"Beans!" said one indignant soul. "What time have I to think of beans, or what money to buy coal to cook 'em? What you'd want if you sat over a machine fourteen hours a day would be tea like lye to put a back-bone in you. That's why we have tea always in the pot, and it don't make much odds what's with it. A slice of bread is about all. . . . We'd our tea an' bread an' a good bit of fried beef or pork, maybe, when my husband was alive an' at work. . . . It's the tea that keeps you up."

6. **Julian Street, Show and Extravagance, 1910.** *Street, a journalist, was invited to an elite home in Buffalo, New York, for a dinner that included cocktails, fine wines, caviar, a roast, Turkish coffee, and cigars.*

Before we left New York there was newspaper talk about some rich women who had organized a movement of protest against the ever-increasing American tendency toward show and extravagance. . . . Our hostess [in Buffalo] was the first to mention it, but several other ladies added details. . . .

"We don't intend to go to any foolish extremes," said one. . . . "We are only going to scale things down and eliminate waste. There is a lot of useless show in this country which only makes it hard for people who can't afford things. And even for those who can, it is wrong. . . . Take this little dinner we had tonight. . . . In future we are all going to give plain little dinners like this."

"*Plain?*" I gasped. . . . "But I didn't think it had begun yet! I thought this dinner was a kind of farewell feast — that it was —"

Our hostess looked grieved. The other ladies of the league gazed at me reproachfully. . . . "Didn't you notice?" asked my hostess. . . .

"Notice *what*?"

"That we didn't have champagne!"

SOURCES: (2) Louisa May Alcott, *Little Women*, Part 2, Chapter 2 at xroads.virginia.edu/~HYPER/ALCOTT/ch2.html; (3) Mary Hinman Abel, *Practical, Sanitary, and Economic Cooking Adapted to Persons of Moderate and Small Means* (American Public Health Association, 1890), 143–154; (4) Werner Sombart, *Why Is There No Socialism in the United States?*, trans. Patricia M. Hocking and C. T. Husbands (White Plains, NY: International Arts and Sciences Press, 1976), 97, 105–106; (5) Helen Campbell, *Prisoners of Poverty* (Cambridge, MA: University Press, 1887), 123–124; (6) Julian Street, *Abroad at Home* (New York: The Century Co., 1915), 37–39.

1. These documents were created by journalists and reformers. What audiences did they seek to reach? Why do you think they all focused on food?

2. Imagine a conversation among these authors. How might we account for the differences in Sombart's and Campbell's findings? How might Hine, Abel, and Campbell respond to Alcott's vision of charitable Christian acts?

PUTTING IT ALL TOGETHER

Using the documents above and your knowledge from this chapter, write a short essay explaining some challenges and opportunities faced by different Americans in the industrializing era — including those of the wealthy elite, emerging middle class, skilled blue-collar men, and very poorest unskilled laborers. How did labor leaders and reformers seek to persuade prosperous Americans to concern themselves with workers' problems? To what dominant values did they appeal?

Child Labor For many working-class families, children's wages — even though they were low — made up an essential part of the household income. These boys worked the night shift in a glass factory in Indiana. Lewis Hine, an investigative photographer for the National Child Labor Committee, took their picture at midnight, as part of a campaign to educate more prosperous Americans about the widespread employment of child labor and the harsh conditions in which many children worked. Library of Congress.

coal fields, where death and injury rates were high. State law permitted children as young as twelve to labor with a family member, but turn-of-the-century investigators estimated that about 10,000 additional boys, at even younger ages, were illegally employed in the mines.

Also at the bottom of the pay scale were most African Americans. Corporations and industrial manufacturers widely discriminated against them on the basis of race, and such prejudice was hardly limited to the South. After the Civil War, African American women who moved to northern cities were largely barred from office work and other new employment options; instead, they remained heavily concentrated in domestic service, with more than half employed as cooks or servants. African American men confronted similar exclusion. America's booming vertically integrated corporations turned black men away from all but the most menial jobs. In 1890, almost a third of black men worked in personal service. Employers in the North and West recruited, instead, a different kind of low-wage labor: newly arrived immigrants.

> **IN YOUR OWN WORDS** What new business practices arose in the late-nineteenth-century United States, and what impact did they have on employees, consumers, and the environment?

Immigrants, East and West

Across the globe, industrialization set people in motion with the lure of jobs. Between the Civil War and World War I, over 25 million immigrants entered the United States. The American working class became truly global, including not only people of African and Western European descent but also Southern and Eastern Europeans, Mexicans, and Asians. In 1900, census-takers found that more than 75 percent of San Francisco and New York City residents had at least one parent who was foreign-born.

In the new industrial order, immigrants made an ideal labor supply. They took the worst jobs at low pay, and during economic downturns tens of thousands returned to their home countries, reducing the shock of unemployment in the United States. But many native-born Americans viewed immigrants with hostility, through the lens of racial, ethnic, and religious prejudices. They also feared that immigrants would take more coveted jobs and erode white men's wages. For immigrants themselves, America could be disorienting, liberating, and disappointing.

Newcomers from Europe

Mass migration from Western Europe had started in the 1840s, when more than one million Irish fled a terrible famine. In the following decades, as Europe's population grew rapidly and agriculture became commercialized, peasant economies suffered, first in Germany and Scandinavia, then across Austria-Hungary, Russia, Italy, and the Balkans. This upheaval displaced millions of rural people. Some went to Europe's mines and factories; others headed for South America and the United States (Map 16.2; America in Global Context).

"America was known to foreigners," remembered one Jewish woman from Lithuania, "as the land where you'd get rich." But the reality was much harsher. Even in the age of steam, a transatlantic voyage was grueling. For ten to twenty days, passengers in steerage class crowded below decks, eating terrible food and struggling with seasickness. An investigator who traveled with immigrants from Naples asked, "How can a steerage passenger remember that he is a human being when he must

Emigrants and Destinations, 1881–1915

The United States received more new residents than any other nation during the era of industrialization, but it was not the only place where emigrants (those departing) became immigrants (those arriving). The graph below shows six major destinations for emigrants from four European countries.

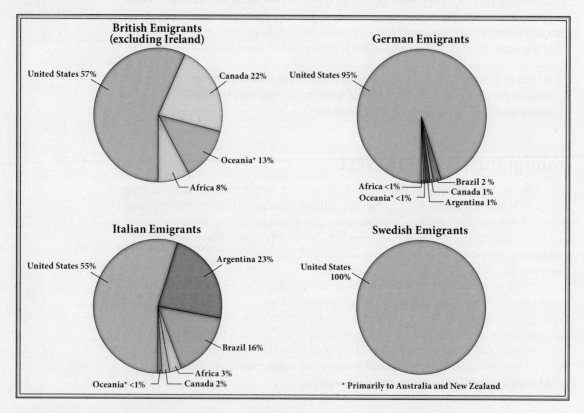

FIGURE 16.2 **Major Destinations for Emigrants, 1881–1915**

QUESTIONS FOR ANALYSIS

1. What might account for the different emigration patterns shown here?
2. What choices and limitations might each group of emigrants have faced in choosing the country to which they emigrated?
3. Do these figures suggest anything about the conditions various groups may have encountered in different countries, upon arrival?

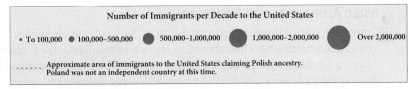

MAP 16.2 Sources of European Immigration to the United States, 1871–1910
Around 1900, Americans began to speak of the "new" immigration. They meant the large numbers of immigrants arriving from Eastern and Southern Europe — Poles, Slovaks and other Slavic peoples, Yiddish-speaking Jews, Greeks, and Italians — who overwhelmed the still substantial number of immigrants from the British Isles and Northern Europe.

first pick the worms from his food?" After 1892, European immigrants were routed through the enormous receiving station at New York's Ellis Island.

Some immigrants brought skills. Many Welshmen, for example, arrived in the United States as experienced tin-plate makers; Germans came as machinists and carpenters, Scandinavians as sailors. But industrialization required, most of all, increasing quantities of unskilled labor. As poor farmers from Italy, Greece, and Eastern Europe arrived in the United States, heavy, low-paid labor became their domain.

In an era of cheap railroad and steamship travel, many immigrants expected to work and save for a few years and then head home. More than 800,000 French Canadians moved to New England in search of textile jobs, many families with hopes of scraping together enough savings to return to Quebec and buy a farm. Thousands of men came alone, especially from Ireland, Italy, and Greece. Many single Irishwomen also immigrated. But some would-be sojourners ended up staying a lifetime, while immigrants who had expected to settle permanently found themselves forced to leave by an accident or sudden economic depression. One historian has estimated that a third of immigrants to the United States in this era returned to their home countries.

Along with Italians and Greeks, Eastern European Jews were among the most numerous arrivals. The first American Jews, who numbered around 50,000 in 1880, had been mostly of German Jewish descent. In the next four decades, more than 3 million poverty-stricken Jews arrived from Russia, Ukraine, Poland, and other parts of Eastern Europe, transforming the Jewish presence in the United States. Like other immigrants, they sought economic opportunity, but they also came to escape religious repression.

Wherever they came from, immigrants took a considerable gamble in traveling to the United States. Some prospered quickly, especially if they came with education, money, or well-placed business contacts. Others, by toiling many years in harsh conditions, succeeded in securing a better life for their children or grandchildren. Still others met with catastrophe or early death. One Polish man who came with his parents in 1908 summed up his life over the next thirty years as "a mere struggle for bread." He added: "Sometimes I think life isn't worth a damn for a man like me. . . . Look at my wife and kids — undernourished, seldom have a square meal." But an Orthodox Russian Jewish woman told an interviewer that she "thanked God for America," where she had married, raised three children, and made a good life. She "liked everything about this country, especially its leniency toward the Jews."

Asian Americans and Exclusion

Compared with Europeans, newcomers from Asia faced even harsher treatment. The first Chinese immigrants had arrived in the late 1840s during the California gold rush. After the Civil War, the Burlingame Treaty between the United States and China opened the way for increasing numbers to emigrate. Fleeing poverty and upheaval in southern China, they, like European immigrants, filled low-wage jobs in the American economy. The Chinese confronted threats and violence. "We kept indoors after dark for fear of being shot in the back," remembered one Chinese immigrant to California. During the depression of the 1870s, a rising tide of racism was especially extreme in the Pacific coast states, where the majority of Chinese immigrants lived. "The Chinese must go!" railed Dennis Kearney, leader of the California Workingmen's Party, who referred to Asians as "almond-eyed lepers." Incited by Kearney in July 1877, a mob burned San Francisco's Chinatown and beat up residents. In the 1885 Rock Springs massacre in Wyoming, white men burned the local Chinatown and murdered at least twenty-eight Chinese miners.

Despite such atrocities, some Chinese managed to build profitable businesses and farms. Many did so by filling the only niches native-born Americans left open to them: running restaurants and laundries. Facing intense political pressure, Congress in 1882 passed the **Chinese Exclusion Act**, specifically barring Chinese laborers from entering the United States. Each decade thereafter, Congress renewed the law and tightened its provisions; it was not repealed until 1943. Exclusion barred almost all Chinese women, forcing husbands and wives to spend many years apart when men took jobs in the United States.

Asian immigrants made vigorous use of the courts to try to protect their rights. In a series of cases brought by Chinese and later Japanese immigrants, the U.S. Supreme Court ruled that all persons born in the United States had citizenship rights that could not be revoked, even if their parents had been born abroad. Nonetheless,

Chinese Exclusion Act
The 1882 law that barred Chinese laborers from entering the United States. It continued in effect until the 1940s.

well into the twentieth century, Chinese immigrants (as opposed to native-born Chinese Americans) could not apply for citizenship. Meanwhile, Japanese and a few Korean immigrants also began to arrive; by 1909, there were 40,000 Japanese immigrants working in agriculture, 10,000 on railroads, and 4,000 in canneries. In 1906, the U.S. attorney general ruled that Japanese and Koreans, like Chinese immigrants, were barred from citizenship.

The Chinese Exclusion Act created the legal foundations on which far-reaching exclusionary policies would be built in the 1920s and after (Chapter 21). To enforce the law, Congress and the courts gave sweeping new powers to immigration officials, transforming the Chinese into America's first illegal immigrants. Drawn, like others, by the promise of jobs in America's expanding economy, Chinese men stowed away on ships or walked across the borders. Disguising themselves as Mexicans — who at that time could freely enter the United States — some perished in the desert as they tried to reach California.

Some would-be immigrants, known as paper sons, relied on Chinese residents in the United States, who generated documents falsely claiming the newcomers as American-born children. Paper sons memorized pages of information about their supposed relatives and hometowns. The San Francisco earthquake of 1906 helped their cause by destroying all the port's records. "That was a big chance for a lot of Chinese," remembered one immigrant. "They forged themselves certificates saying they could go back to China and bring back four or five sons, just like that!" Such persistence ensured that, despite the harsh policies of Chinese exclusion, the flow of Asian immigrants never fully ceased.

> **IN YOUR OWN WORDS**   What factors encouraged immigrants to seek entry into the United States, and how did their experiences differ?

Labor Gets Organized

In the American political system, labor has typically been weak. Industrial workers cluster in cities, near factories and jobs; compared with small towns and rural areas, urban areas have been underrepresented in bodies such as the U.S. Senate and the presidential electoral college, in which representation is calculated by state, rather than (or in addition to) individuals. This problem became acute in the era of industrialization, and it has lingered. Even today, the twenty-two U.S. senators elected from Alaska, Idaho, Iowa, Maine, Mississippi, Montana, New Mexico, North Dakota, Vermont, West Virginia, and Wyoming represent a smaller number of people, *combined*, than the two U.S. senators who represent heavily urban California.

Faced with this obstacle, labor advocates could adopt one of two strategies. First, they could try to make political alliances with sympathetic rural voters who shared their problems. Second, they could reject politics and create narrowly focused trade unions to negotiate directly with employers. In general, labor advocates emphasized the first strategy between the 1870s and the early 1890s, and the latter in the early twentieth century. Across this era, while industrialization made America increasingly rich and powerful, it also brought large-scale conflict between labor and capital.

The Emergence of a Labor Movement

Great Railroad Strike of 1877
A nationwide strike of thousands of railroad workers and labor allies, who protested the growing power of railroad corporations and the steep wage cuts imposed by railroad managers amid a severe economic depression that had begun in 1873.

The problem of industrial labor entered Americans' consciousness dramatically with the **Great Railroad Strike of 1877**. Protesting steep wage cuts amid the depression that had begun in 1873, thousands of railroad workers walked off the job. Broader issues were at stake. "The officers of the road," reported strike leader Barney Donahue in upstate New York, "were bound to break the spirit of the men, and any or all organizations they belonged to." He believed railroad companies wanted to block workers from "all fellow-ship for mutual aid." The strike brought rail travel and commerce to a halt. Thousands of people poured into the streets of Buffalo, Pittsburgh, and Chicago to protest the economic injustice wrought by railroads — as well as fires caused by stray sparks from locomotives and injuries and deaths on train tracks in urban neighborhoods. When Pennsylvania's governor sent state militia to break the strike, Pittsburgh crowds reacted by burning rail-road property and overturning locomotives. Similar clashes between police and protest-ers occurred in other cities across the country, from Galveston, Texas, to San Francisco.

The 1877 strike left more than fifty people dead and caused $40 million worth of damage, primarily to railroad property. "It seemed as if the whole social and political structure was on the very brink of ruin," wrote one journalist. For their role in the strike, many railroad workers were fired and blacklisted: railroad companies circulated their names on a "do not hire" list to prevent them from getting any work in the industry. In the aftermath of the strike, the U.S. government created the National Guard, intended not to protect Americans against foreign invasion but to enforce order at home.

Watching the upheavals of industrialization, some radical thinkers pointed out its impact on workers. Among the most influential was Henry George, whose book *Progress and Poverty* (1879) was a best-seller for decades after publication. George warned that Americans had been too optimistic about the impact of railroads and man-ufacturing, which they hoped would — after an initial period of turmoil — bring pros-perity to all. George believed the emerging industrial order meant permanent poverty. Industrialization, he wrote, was driving a wedge through society, lifting the fortunes of professionals and the middle class but pushing the working class down by forcing them into deskilled, dangerous, and low-paid labor. George's proposed solution, a fed-eral "single tax" on landholdings, did not win widespread support, but his insightful diagnosis of the problem helped encourage radical movements for economic reform.

Many rural people believed they faced the same problems as industrial workers. In the new economy, they found themselves at the mercy of large corporations, from equipment dealers who sold them harvesters and plows to railroads and grain elevators that shipped and stored their products. Though farmers appeared to have more indepen-dence than corporate employees, many felt trapped in a web of middlemen who chipped away at their profits while international forces robbed them of decision-making power.

Farmers denounced not only corporations but also the previous two decades of government efforts to foster economic development — policies that now seemed wrongheaded. Farmers' advocates argued that high tariffs forced rural families to pay too much for basic necessities while failing to protect America's great export crops, cotton and wheat. At the same time, they charged, Republican financial policies ben-efitted banks, not borrowers. Farmers blamed railroad companies for taking govern-ment grants and subsidies to build but then charging unequal rates that privileged big manufacturers. From the farmers' point of view, public money had been used to build giant railroad companies that turned around and exploited ordinary people.

The most prominent rural protest group of the early postwar decades was the National Grange of the Patrons of Husbandry, founded in 1867. Like industrial workers, Grange farmers sought to counter the rising power of corporate middle-men through cooperation and mutual aid. Local Grange halls brought farm families together for recreation and conversation. The Grange set up its own banks, insurance companies, and grain elevators, and, in Iowa, even a farm implement factory. Many Grange members also advocated political action, building independent local parties that ran on anticorporate platforms.

During the 1870s depression, Grangers, labor advocates, and local workingmen's parties forged a national political movement, the **Greenback-Labor Party**. In the South, Greenbackers protested the collapse of Reconstruction and urged that every man's vote be protected. Across the country, Greenbackers advocated laws to regulate corporations and enforce an eight-hour workday to reduce long, grueling work hours. They called for the federal government to print more greenback dollars and increase the amount of money in circulation; this, they argued, would stimulate the economy, create jobs, and help borrowers by allowing them to pay off debts in dollars that, over time, slowly decreased in value. Greenbackers, like many industrial labor leaders, subscribed to the ideal of **producerism**: they dismissed middlemen, bankers, lawyers, and investors as idlers who lived off the sweat of people who worked with their hands. As a Pittsburgh worker put it in an 1878 poem, it was not the money-handlers or executives at the top but the "noble sons of Labor . . . who with bone, and brain, and fiber make the nation's wealth."

The Greenback movement radicalized thousands of farmers, miners, and industrial workers. In Alabama's coal-mining regions, black and white miners cooperated in the party. Texas boasted seventy African American Greenback clubs. In 1878, Greenback-Labor candidates won more than a million votes, and the party elected fifteen congressmen nationwide. In the Midwest, Greenback pressure helped trigger a wave of economic regulatory actions known as **Granger laws**. By the early 1880s, twenty-nine states had created railroad commissions to supervise railroad rates and policies; others appointed commissions to regulate insurance and utility companies. Such early regulatory efforts were not always effective, but they were crucial starting points for reform. While short-lived, the Greenback movement created the foundation for more sustained efforts to regulate big business.

The Knights of Labor

The most important union of the late nineteenth century, the **Knights of Labor**, was founded in 1869 as a secret society of garment workers in Philadelphia. In 1878, as the Greenback movement reached its height, some Knights served as delegates to Greenback-Labor conventions. Like Grangers, Knights believed that ordinary people needed control over the enterprises in which they worked. They proposed to set up shops owned by employees, transforming America into what they called a cooperative commonwealth. In keeping with this broad-based vision, the order practiced open membership, irrespective of race, gender, or field of employment — though, like other labor groups, the Knights excluded Chinese immigrants.

The Knights had a strong political bent. They believed that only electoral action could bring about many of their goals, such as government regulation of corporations and laws that required employers to negotiate during strikes. Their 1878 platform denounced the "aggressiveness of great capitalists and corporations." "If we

Greenback-Labor Party
A national political movement calling on the government to increase the money supply in order to assist borrowers and foster economic growth; "Greenbackers" also called for greater regulation of corporations and laws enforcing an eight-hour workday.

producerism
The argument that real economic wealth is created by workers who make their living by physical labor, such as farmers and craftsmen, and that merchants, lawyers, bankers, and other middlemen unfairly gain their wealth from such "producers."

Granger laws
Economic regulatory laws passed in some midwestern states in the late 1870s, triggered by pressure from farmers and the Greenback-Labor Party.

Knights of Labor
The first mass labor organization created among America's working class. Founded in 1869 and peaking in strength in the mid-1880s, the Knights of Labor attempted to bridge boundaries of ethnicity, gender, ideology, race, and occupation to build a "universal brotherhood" of all workers.

desire to enjoy the full blessings of life," the Knights warned, "a check [must] be placed upon unjust accumulation, and the power for evil of aggregated wealth." Among their demands were workplace safety laws, prohibition of child labor, a federal tax on the nation's highest incomes, public ownership of telegraphs and railroads, and government recognition of workers' right to organize. The Knights also advocated personal responsibility and self-discipline. Their leader, Terence Powderly, warned that the abuse of liquor robbed as many workers of their wages as did ruthless employers.

Growing rapidly in the 1880s, the Knights' union was sprawling and decentralized. It included not only skilled craftsmen such as carpenters, ironworkers, and beer brewers but also textile workers in Rhode Island, domestic workers in Georgia, and tenant farmers in Arkansas. Knights organized workingmen's parties to advocate a host of reforms, ranging from an eight-hour workday to cheaper streetcar fares and better garbage collection in urban areas. One of their key innovations was hiring a full-time women's organizer, Leonora Barry. An Irish American widow who was forced into factory work after her husband's death, Barry became a labor advocate out of horror at the conditions she experienced on the job. To the discomfort of some male Knights, she investigated and exposed widespread evidence of sexual harassment on the job.

The Knights' growth in the 1880s showed the grassroots basis of labor activism. Powderly tried to avoid strikes, which he saw as costly and risky. But the organization's greatest growth resulted from spontaneous, grassroots striking. In 1885, thousands of workers on the Southwest Railroad walked off the job to protest wage cuts; afterward, they telegraphed the Knights and asked to be admitted as members. The strike enhanced the Knights' reputation among workers and built membership to 750,000. By the following year, local assemblies had sprung up in every state and almost every county in the United States.

anarchism
The advocacy of a stateless society achieved by revolutionary means. Feared for their views, anarchists became scapegoats for the 1886 Haymarket Square bombing.

Haymarket Square
The May 4, 1886, conflict in Chicago in which both workers and policemen were killed or wounded during a labor demonstration called by local anarchists. The incident created a backlash against all labor organizations, including the Knights of Labor.

Just as the Knights reached this pinnacle of influence, an episode of violence brought them down. In 1886, a protest at the McCormick reaper works in Chicago led to a clash with police that left four strikers dead. (Three unions, including a Knights of Labor assembly, had struck, but the Knights had reached an agreement and returned to work. Only the machinists' union remained on strike when the incident occurred.) Chicago was a hotbed of **anarchism**, the revolutionary advocacy of a stateless society. Local anarchists, many of them German immigrants, called a protest meeting the next day, May 4, 1886, at **Haymarket Square**. When police tried to disperse the crowd, someone threw a bomb that killed several policemen. Officers responded with gunfire. In the trial that followed, eight anarchists were found guilty of murder and criminal conspiracy. All were convicted, not on any definitive evidence that one of them threw the bomb (the bomber's identity remains unknown) but on the basis of their antigovernment speeches. Four of the eight were executed by hanging, one committed suicide in prison, and the others received long sentences.

The Haymarket violence profoundly damaged the American labor movement. Seizing on resulting antiunion hysteria, employers took the offensive. They broke strikes with mass arrests, tied up the Knights in expensive court proceedings, and forced workers to sign contracts pledging not to join labor organizations. The Knights of Labor never recovered. In the view of the press and many prosperous Americans, they were tainted by their alleged links with anarchism. Struggles between industrialists and workers had created bitter divides.

Farmers and Workers: The Cooperative Alliance

In the aftermath of Haymarket, the Knights' cooperative vision did not entirely fade. A new rural movement, the **Farmers' Alliance**, arose to take up many of the issues that Grangers and Greenbackers had earlier sought to address. Founded in Texas during the depression of the 1870s, the Farmers' Alliance spread across the plains states and the South, becoming by the late 1880s the largest farmer-based movement in American history. A separate Colored Farmers' Alliance arose to represent rural African Americans. The harsh conditions farmers were enduring—including drought in the West and plunging global prices for corn, cotton, and wheat—intensified the movement's appeal. Traveling Alliance lecturers exhorted farmers to "stand as a great conservative body against . . . the growing corruption of wealth and power."

Like earlier movements, Alliance leaders pinned their initial hopes on cooperative stores and exchanges that would circumvent middlemen. Cooperatives gathered farmers' orders and bought in bulk at wholesale prices, passing the savings along. Alliance cooperatives achieved notable victories in the late 1880s. The Dakota Alliance, for example, offered members cheap hail insurance and low prices on machinery and farm supplies. The Texas Alliance established a huge cooperative enterprise to market cotton and provide farmers with cheap loans. When cotton prices fell further in 1891, however, the Texas exchange failed. Other cooperatives also suffered from chronic underfunding and lack of credit, and they faced hostility from merchants and lenders they tried to circumvent.

The Texas Farmers' Alliance thus proposed a federal price-support system for farm products, modeled on the national banks. Under this plan, the federal government would hold crops in public warehouses and issue loans on their value until they could be profitably sold. When Democrats—still wary of big-government schemes—declared the idea too radical, Alliances in Texas, Kansas, South Dakota, and elsewhere decided to create a new political party, the Populists (see Chapter 19). In this venture, the Alliance cooperated with the weakened Knights of Labor, seeking to use rural voters' substantial clout on behalf of urban workers who shared their vision.

By this time, farmer-labor coalitions had made a considerable impact on state politics. But state laws and commissions were proving ineffective against corporations of national and even global scope. It was difficult for Wisconsin, for instance, to enforce new laws against a railroad company whose lines might stretch from Chicago to Seattle and whose corporate headquarters might be in Minnesota. Militant farmers and labor advocates demanded federal action.

In 1887, responding to this pressure, Congress and President Grover Cleveland passed two landmark laws. The Hatch Act provided federal funding for agricultural research and education, meeting farmers' demands for government aid to agriculture. The **Interstate Commerce Act** counteracted a Supreme Court decision of the previous year, *Wabash v. Illinois* (1886), that had struck down states' authority to regulate railroads. The act created the Interstate Commerce Commission (ICC), charged with investigating interstate shipping, forcing railroads to make their rates public, and suing in court when necessary to make companies reduce "unjust or unreasonable" rates.

Though creation of the ICC was a direct response to farmer-labor demands, its final form represented a compromise. Radical leaders wanted Congress to establish a direct set of rules under which railroads must operate. If a railroad did not comply,

Farmers' Alliance
A rural movement founded in Texas during the depression of the 1870s that spread across the plains states and the South. The Farmers' Alliance advocated cooperative stores and exchanges that would circumvent middlemen, and it called for greater government aid to farmers and stricter regulation of railroads.

Interstate Commerce Act
An 1887 act that created the Interstate Commerce Commission (ICC), a federal regulatory agency designed to oversee the railroad industry and prevent collusion and unfair rates.

Industrial Violence: A Dynamited Mine, 1894 Strikes in the western mining regions pitted ruthless owners, bent on control of their property and workforce, against fiercely independent miners who knew how to use dynamite. Some of the bloodiest conflicts occurred in Colorado mining towns, where the Western Federation of Miners (WFM) had strong support and a series of Republican governors sent state militia to back the mine owners. Violence broke out repeatedly between the early 1890s and the 1910s. At Victor, Colorado, in May 1894, as dozens of armed sheriffs' deputies closed in on angry WFM members occupying the Strong Mine in protest, the miners blew up the mine's shaft house and boiler. Showered with debris, the deputies boarded the next train out of town. Because Colorado then had a Populist governor, Davis Waite, who sympathized with the miners and ordered the deputies to disband, this strike was one of the few in which owners and miners reached a peaceful settlement — a temporary victory for the union. Denver Public Library, Western History Collection/Bridgeman Images.

any citizen could take the company to court; if the new rules triggered bankruptcy, the railroad could convert to public ownership. But getting such a plan through Congress proved impossible. Lawmakers more sympathetic to business called instead for an expert commission to oversee the railroad industry. In a pattern that repeated frequently over the next few decades, the commission model proved more acceptable to the majority of congressmen.

The ICC faced formidable challenges. Though the new law forbade railroads from reaching secret rate-setting agreements, evidence was difficult to gather and secret "pooling" continued. A hostile Supreme Court also undermined the commission's powers. In a series of sixteen decisions over the two decades after the ICC was created, the Court sided with railroads fifteen times. The justices delivered a particularly hard blow in 1897 when they ruled that the ICC had no power to interfere with shipping rates. Nonetheless, the ICC's existence was a major achievement. In the early twentieth century, Congress would strengthen the commission's powers, and the ICC would become one of the most powerful federal agencies charged with overseeing private business.

Another Path: The American Federation of Labor

While the Knights of Labor exerted political pressure, other workers pursued a different strategy. In the 1870s, printers, ironworkers, bricklayers, and other skilled workers organized nationwide trade unions. These "brotherhoods" focused on the everyday needs of workers in skilled occupations. Trade unions sought a closed shop — with all jobs reserved for union members — that kept out lower-wage workers. Union rules specified terms of work, sometimes in minute detail. Many unions emphasized mutual aid. Because working on the railroads was a high-risk occupation, for example, brotherhoods of engineers, brakemen, and firemen pooled contributions into funds that provided accident and death benefits. Above all, trade unionism asserted craft workers' rights as active decision-makers in the workplace, not just cogs in a management-run machine.

In the early 1880s, many trade unionists joined the Knights of Labor coalition. But the aftermath of the Haymarket violence persuaded them to leave and create the separate **American Federation of Labor** (AFL). The man who led them was Samuel Gompers, a Dutch-Jewish cigar maker whose family had immigrated to New York in 1863. Gompers headed the AFL for nearly forty years. He believed the Knights relied too much on electoral politics, where victories were likely to be limited, and he did not share their sweeping critique of capitalism. The AFL, made up of relatively skilled and well-paid workers, was less interested in challenging the corporate order than in winning a larger share of its rewards.

Having gone to work at age ten, Gompers always contended that what he missed at school he more than made up for in the shop, where cigar makers paid one of their members to read to them while they worked. As a young worker-intellectual, Gompers gravitated to New York's radical circles, where he participated in lively debates about which strategies workingmen should pursue. Partly out of these debates, and partly from his own experience in the Cigar Makers Union, Gompers hammered out a doctrine that he called pure-and-simple unionism. *Pure* referred to membership: strictly limited to workers, organized by craft and occupation, with no reliance on outside advisors or allies. *Simple* referred to goals: only those that immediately benefitted workers — better wages, hours, and working conditions. Pure-and-simple unionists distrusted politics. Their aim was collective bargaining with employers.

On one level, pure-and-simple unionism worked. The AFL was small at first, but by 1904 its membership rose to more than two million. In the early twentieth century, it became the nation's leading voice for workers, lasting far longer than movements like the Knights of Labor. The AFL's strategy — personified by Gompers — was well suited to an era when Congress and the courts were hostile to labor. By the 1910s, the political climate would become more responsive; at that later moment, Gompers would soften his antipolitical stance and join the battle for new labor laws (Chapter 19).

What Gompers gave up most crucially, in the meantime, was the inclusiveness of the Knights. By comparison, the AFL was far less welcoming to women and blacks; it included mostly skilled craftsmen. There was little room in the AFL for department-store clerks and other service workers, much less the farm tenants and domestic servants whom the Knights had organized. Despite the AFL's success among skilled craftsmen, the narrowness of its base was a problem that would come back to haunt the labor movement later on. Gompers, however, saw that corporate titans and their political allies held tremendous power, and he advocated what he saw as the most

American Federation of Labor
Organization created by Samuel Gompers in 1886 that coordinated the activities of craft unions and called for direct negotiation with employers in order to achieve benefits for skilled workers. Like other trade unions, the AFL called for the closed shop — all employees had to be union members — to keep out low-wage competition and strengthen unions' bargaining power with employers.

practical defensive plan. In the meantime, the upheaval wrought by industrialization spread far beyond the workplace, transforming every aspect of American life.

> **IN YOUR OWN WORDS** How did the key institutions and goals of the labor movement change between 1877 and 1900, and what gains and losses resulted from these shifts?

Summary

The end of the Civil War ushered in the era of American big business. Exploiting the continent's vast resources, vertically integrated corporations emerged as the dominant business form, and giant companies built near monopolies in some sectors of the economy. Corporations devised new modes of production, distribution, and marketing, extending their reach through the department store, the mail-order catalog, and the new advertising industry. These developments laid the groundwork for mass consumer culture. They also offered emerging jobs in management, sales, and office work.

Rapid industrialization drew immigrants from around the world. Until the 1920s, most European and Latin American immigrants were welcome to enter the United States, though they often endured harsh conditions after they arrived. Asian immigrants, by contrast, faced severe discrimination. The Chinese Exclusion Act blocked all Chinese laborers from coming to the United States; it was later extended to other Asians, and it built the legal framework for broader forms of exclusion.

Nationwide movements for workers' rights arose in response to industrialization. During the 1870s and 1880s, coalitions of workers and farmers, notably the Knights of Labor and the Farmers' Alliance, sought political solutions to what they saw as large corporations' exploitation of working people. Pressure from such movements led to the first major attempts to regulate corporations, such as the federal Interstate Commerce Act. Radical protest movements were weakened, however, after public condemnation of anarchist violence in 1886 at Chicago's Haymarket Square. Meanwhile, trade unions such as the American Federation of Labor organized skilled workers and negotiated directly with employers, becoming the most popular form of labor organization in the early twentieth century.

CHAPTER 16 REVIEW

TERMS TO KNOW   *Identify and explain the significance of each term below.*

Key Concepts and Events

Homestead lockout (p. 528)	vertical integration (p. 531)	deskilling (p. 537)	Chinese Exclusion Act (p. 546)
Gospel of Wealth (p. 530)	horizontal integration (p. 532)	scientific management (p. 537)	Great Railroad Strike of 1877 (p. 548)
management revolution (p. 531)	trust (p. 532)	New South (p. 539)	

Greenback-Labor Party
  (p. 549)
producerism (p. 549)

Granger laws (p. 549)
Knights of Labor (p. 549)
anarchism (p. 550)

Haymarket Square
  (p. 550)
Farmers' Alliance (p. 551)

Interstate Commerce Act
  (p. 551)
American Federation of
  Labor (p. 553)

Key People

Andrew Carnegie (p. 530)
Gustavus Swift (p. 531)

John D. Rockefeller (p. 532)
Henry George (p. 548)

Terence Powderly (p. 550)
Leonora Barry (p. 550)

Samuel Gompers (p. 553)

REVIEW QUESTIONS   *Answer these questions to demonstrate your understanding of the chapter's main ideas.*

1. What new business practices arose in the late-nineteenth-century United States, and what impact did they have on employees, consumers, and the environment?

2. What factors encouraged immigrants to seek entry into the United States, and how did their experiences differ?

3. How did the key institutions and goals of the labor movement change between 1877 and 1900, and what gains and losses resulted from these shifts?

4. Review the events listed under "Politics and Power," "Migration and Settlement," and "Work, Exchange, and Technology" on the thematic timeline on pages 526–527. How did industrialization as an *economic* process transform American society and politics?

MAKING CONNECTIONS   *Recognize the larger developments and continuities within and across chapters.*

1. Compare the two phases of industrialization experienced in the nineteenth-century United States: one before the Civil War (Chapter 8) and one afterward (discussed in this chapter). What factors drove each period of economic expansion? What kinds of new industries arose, and in which regions and locations? In what ways were workers' experiences similar in the two periods, and how did they differ? What political challenges arose with each wave of industrialization?

2. Return to the chapter-opening photograph (p. 529), taken in the aftermath of a terrible mining accident in Pennsylvania. Imagine, first, that the young man in the middle of the picture, facing the camera, is the nephew of an Irish immigrant miner who was killed in the explosion. In the voice of this young man, write a letter to the editor of the local paper explaining what lessons Americans should take from the disaster. Now imagine instead that the young man has enrolled in business school to become a manager; he is the son of a Scottish-born executive in the mining company, and Andrew Carnegie is his hero. In the voice of this young man, write a letter to the editor explaining what lessons Americans should take from the disaster.

KEY TURNING POINTS   *Refer to the chapter chronology on page 530 for help in answering the questions below.*

In the era of industrialization, what events prompted the rise of labor unions and other reform groups that called for stronger government responses to corporate power?

Before 1900, what key events or turning points marked reformers' successes and failures?

17

CHAPTER

Making Modern American Culture
1880–1917

Between 1888 and 1900, American archaeologists conducted their first explorations in what is now Iraq, at the site of the ancient city of Nippur. Leaders of the expedition included Protestant ministers and the editor of the national *Sunday-School Times*. Their goal was to practice biblical archaeology: to confirm the truth of Old Testament accounts of Babylon. As one participant wrote, they sought to blend a "spirit of Christian enlightenment" with modern "scientific inquiry." The expeditions unearthed thousands of cuneiform tablets, which Jewish and Christian linguists and anthropologists used to reveal much about ancient Assyrian society. Some investigators found that these discoveries strengthened their faith in biblical truth. Others were not so sure.

As shown by the Babylonian expeditions, a passion for scientific inquiry swept the late-nineteenth-century United States, often inspired by religious teachings but ultimately calling into question many tenets of faith. Between the 1870s and the 1910s, a stunning series of scientific discoveries — from dinosaur fossils to telescopic observations of nebulae — challenged long-held beliefs. Biological theories of evolution prompted fierce debate, but so did the effects of technological innovations such as medical vaccines and electric chairs. While science gained popularity, religion hardly faded. In fact, religious diversity grew, as immigrants brought new faiths to the United States and Protestants responded with innovations of their own.

At the same time, industrialization reshaped class identities and generated an alluring consumer culture. Lavish urban department stores catered to middle-class customers, while working-class men and women enjoyed vaudeville shows. Americans of all backgrounds and classes mingled at baseball games and summer amusement parks. An older ethos of duty, self-restraint, and moral uplift gave way to expectations of leisure and fun. As African Americans and women claimed a right to education and public space — the opportunity to shop, dine, and travel freely — they built powerful reform movements. At the same time, the pressures of the industrial workplace led to aggressive calls for masculine fitness, exemplified by the rise of sports. Here, too, scientific research sparked debates over the body, gender, and race. Americans found themselves living in a modern world — one in which many of their grandparents' beliefs and practices might no longer apply.

IDENTIFY THE BIG IDEA

How did the changes wrought by industrialization shape Americans' identities, beliefs, and culture?

ELECTRIC TOWER
PAN-AMERICAN EXPOSITION 1901.

Tourist Postcard of the Electric Tower, 1901 The Pan-American Exposition in Buffalo, New York, featured displays and exhibits from across the Western Hemisphere. Like other world's fairs it celebrated technology, and the 389-foot tower, crowned with "The Goddess of Light," became what one observer called a "fitting . . . focal point" for "the Age of Electricity." Inside the tower were restaurants and a promenade near the top from which viewers could view the Exposition grounds. The Exposition's director of sculpture, influenced by Social Darwinism, used the fair's layout to illustrate "the intellectual progress of man," with the Tower of Light representing "the culmination of man's intellectual and physical mastery of Nature." Courtesy, University Archives, State University of New York at Buffalo.

CHAPTER CHRONOLOGY

As you read, ask yourself why this chapter begins and ends with these dates and identify the links among related events.

1870s ▶ Social Darwinism gains growing acceptance	**1893** ▶ Chicago World's Columbian Exposition
1873 ▶ Comstock Act	**1894** ▶ United Daughters of the Confederacy founded
1874 ▶ Woman's Christian Temperance Union founded	**1895** ▶ Booker T. Washington delivers Atlanta Compromise address
1876 ▶ Baseball's National League founded ▶ Appalachian Mountain Club founded	**1896** ▶ National Association of Colored Women founded ▶ Charles Sheldon publishes *In His Steps* ▶ *Plessy v. Ferguson* legalizes "separate but equal" doctrine
1879 ▶ Salvation Army established in the United States	
1881 ▶ Tuskegee Institute founded	
1885 ▶ Mississippi State College for Women founded	**1900** ▶ Lacey Act protects wildlife
1887 ▶ American Protective Association founded to oppose immigration	**1903** ▶ First World Series ▶ First National Wildlife Refuge established
1890 ▶ National American Woman Suffrage Association founded ▶ Daughters of the American Revolution founded	**1906** ▶ Antiquities Act
	1913 ▶ Armory Show of modern art held in New York City
1892 ▶ Elizabeth Cady Stanton delivers "solitude of self" speech to Congress ▶ John Muir founds Sierra Club	**1915** ▶ Peak of foreign missions activity by American Protestant churches
	1916 ▶ National Park Service created

Science and Faith

In the early nineteenth century, most Americans believed the world was about six thousand years old. No one knew what lay beyond the solar system. By the 1910s, paleontologists were classifying Jurassic dinosaurs, astronomers had identified distant galaxies, and physicists were beginning to measure the speed of light. Many scientists and ordinary Americans accepted Charles Darwin's theory of evolution, though exactly how "natural selection" worked — and its implications for religious belief — remained contested.

Scientific discoveries received widespread publicity through a series of great world's fairs, most famously Chicago's 1893 World's Columbian Exposition, held (a year late) to mark the four-hundredth anniversary of Columbus's first voyage to America. At the fairgrounds, visitors strolled through enormous buildings that displayed the latest inventions in industry, machinery, and transportation. They marveled over steam engines, weather-forecasting equipment, and moving sidewalks. At dusk they gathered to watch the fair buildings illuminated with strings of electric lights. One observer called the exposition "a vast and wonderful university of the arts and sciences."

It is hardly surprising, amid these achievements, that "fact worship" became a central feature of American intellectual life. Researchers in many fields argued that one could rely only on hard facts to understand the "laws of life." In their enthusiasm, some economists and sociologists rejected all social reform as sentimental. Fiction writers and artists kept a more humane emphasis, but they made use of similar methods — close observation and attention to real-life experience — to create works of realism. Meanwhile, other Americans struggled to reconcile scientific discoveries with religious faith.

Darwinism and Its Critics

Evolution — the idea that species are not fixed, but ever changing — was not a simple idea on which all scientists agreed. In his immensely influential 1859 book, *On the Origin of Species*, British naturalist Charles Darwin argued that all creatures struggle to survive. When individual members of a species are born with random genetic mutations that better suit them for their environment — for example, camouflage coloring for a moth — these characteristics, since they are genetically transmissible, become dominant in future generations. Many scientists rejected this theory of natural selection. They followed a line of thinking laid out by French biologist Jean Baptiste Lamarck, who argued, unlike Darwin, that individual animals or plants could acquire transmittable traits within a single lifetime. A rhinoceros that fought fiercely, in Lamarck's view, could build up a stronger horn; its offspring would then be born with that trait.

Evolution and Capitalism Darwin himself disapproved of the word *evolution* (which does not appear in his book) because it implied upward progress. In his view, natural selection was blind: environments and species changed randomly. Others were less scrupulous about drawing sweeping conclusions from Darwin's work. In the 1870s, British philosopher Herbert Spencer spun out an elaborate theory of how human society advanced through ruthless competitive struggle, resulting in "survival of the fittest." He applied this particularly to capitalism and industry.

The doctrine of **Social Darwinism**, as Spencer's idea became (confusingly) known, found its American champion in William Graham Sumner, a sociology professor at Yale. Competition, said Sumner, was a law of nature, like gravity. Who were the fittest? "Millionaires," Sumner declared. Their success showed they were "naturally selected." Sumner's views bolstered the pride and self-justification of industrial titans such as Andrew Carnegie, who loved Herbert Spencer's works and invited him to tour Pittsburgh. (Spencer was not impressed.) "The concentration of capital is necessary for meeting the demands of our day," was the message Carnegie took from Spencer. Similarly, John D. Rockefeller of Standard Oil declared that "the growth of a large business is merely a survival of the fittest. This is not an evil tendency of business. It is merely the working out of a law of nature and a law of God."

Social Darwinism
An idea, actually formulated not by Charles Darwin but by British philosopher and sociologist Herbert Spencer, that human society advanced through ruthless competition and the "survival of the fittest."

Even in the heyday of Social Darwinism, Spencer and Sumner's views were controversial. Many thinkers objected to the application of biological findings to the realm of economics and society. They pointed out that Darwin had observed finches and tortoises, not human institutions. Sociologist Lester Frank Ward argued that humanity "progresses through the *protection* of the weak," not through ruthless competition. "Man," he wrote, "through his intelligence, has labored successfully to resist the law of nature." Ward suggested, tongue in cheek, that if Americans subscribed to a doctrine of "survival of the fittest," they should abolish police and fire departments, irrigation works, and flood control. Social Darwinism, such critics argued, was simply an excuse for the worst excesses of industrialization. By the early twentieth century, intellectuals revolted against Sumner and his allies.

Eugenics   Meanwhile, though, some of the most dubious applications of evolutionary ideas were codified into new reproductive laws based on **eugenics**, a so-called science of human breeding. Eugenicists argued that mentally deficient people should be prevented from reproducing. They proposed to sterilize those deemed "unfit," especially residents of state asylums for the insane or mentally disabled. In early-twentieth-century America, almost half of the states enacted eugenics laws. By the time eugenics subsided in the 1930s, tens of thousands of people had been sterilized, with California and Virginia taking the lead. Women in Puerto Rico and other U.S. imperial possessions (see Chapter 20) also suffered from eugenic policies.

Advocates of eugenics had a broad impact. Because they associated mental unfitness with "lower races"—including people of African, Asian, and Native American descent—their arguments lent support to Jim Crow segregation laws and racial discrimination. In a wave of legislation beginning in the 1870s and peaking in the 1910s, most states in the South and West passed laws prohibiting interracial marriage, claiming that only separation of the races could foster human advancement. By warning that immigrants from Eastern and Southern Europe would dilute white Americans' racial purity, eugenicists helped win passage of immigration restriction in the 1920s.

Religion: Diversity and Innovation

By the turn of the twentieth century, emerging scientific and cultural paradigms posed a significant challenge to religious faith. Some Americans argued that science and modernity would sweep away religion altogether. Contrary to such predictions, American religious practice remained vibrant. Protestants developed creative new responses to the challenges of industrialization, while millions of newcomers built institutions for worship and religious education.

Immigrant Faiths   Arriving in the United States in large numbers, Catholics and Jews wrestled with similar questions. To what degree should they adapt to Protestant-dominated American society? Should the education of clergy be changed? Should children attend religious or public schools? What happened if they married outside the faith? Among Catholic leaders, Bishop John Ireland of Minnesota argued that "the principles of the Church are in harmony with the interests of the Republic." But traditionalists, led by Archbishop Michael A. Corrigan of New York, disagreed. They sought to insulate Catholics from the pluralistic American environment. Indeed, by 1920, almost two million children attended Catholic elementary schools nationwide, and Catholic dioceses operated fifteen hundred high schools. Catholics as well as Jews feared some of the same threats that distressed Protestants: industrial poverty and overwork kept working-class people away from worship services, while new consumer pleasures enticed many of them to go elsewhere.

Faithful immigrant Catholics were anxious to preserve familiar traditions from Europe, and they generally supported the Church's traditional wing. But they also wanted religious life to express their ethnic identities. Italians, Poles, and other new arrivals wanted separate parishes where they could celebrate their customs, speak their languages, and establish their own parochial schools. When they became numerous enough, they also demanded their own bishops. Since the demand for ethnic parishes implied local control of church property, the Catholic hierarchy, dominated

eugenics
An emerging "science" of human breeding in the late nineteenth century that argued that mentally deficient people should be prevented from reproducing.

by Irish Americans, felt that the integrity of the Church was at stake. With some strain, however, the Catholic Church managed to satisfy the diverse needs of the immigrant faithful. It met the demand for representation, for example, by appointing immigrant priests as auxiliary bishops within existing dioceses.

In the same decades, many prosperous native-born Jews embraced Reform Judaism, abandoning such religious practices as keeping a kosher kitchen and conducting services in Hebrew. This was not the way of Yiddish-speaking Jews from Eastern Europe, who arrived in large numbers after the 1880s. Generally much poorer and eager to preserve their own traditions, they founded Orthodox synagogues, often in vacant stores, and practiced Judaism as they had at home.

But in Eastern Europe, Judaism had been an entire way of life, one not easily replicated in a large American city. "The very clothes I wore and the very food I ate had a fatal effect on my religious habits," confessed the hero of Abraham Cahan's novel *The Rise of David Levinsky* (1917). "If you . . . attempt to bend your religion to the spirit of your surroundings, it breaks. It falls to pieces." Levinsky shaved off his beard and plunged into the Manhattan clothing business. Orthodox Judaism survived the transition to America, but like other immigrant religions, it had to renounce its claims to some of the faithful.

Protestant Innovations One of the era's dramatic religious developments—facilitated by global steamship and telegraph lines—was the rise of Protestant foreign missions. From a modest start before the Civil War, this movement peaked around 1915, a year when American religious organizations sponsored more than nine thousand overseas missionaries, supported at home by armies of volunteers, including more than three million women. A majority of Protestant missionaries served in Asia, with smaller numbers posted to Africa and the Middle East. Most saw American-style domesticity as a central part of evangelism, and missionary societies sent married couples into the field. Many unmarried women also served overseas as missionary teachers, doctors, and nurses, though almost never as ministers. "American woman," declared one Christian reformer, has "the exalted privilege of extending over the world those blessed influences, that are to renovate degraded man."

Protestant missionaries won converts, in part, by providing such modern services as medical care and women's education. Some missionaries developed deep bonds of respect with the people they served. Others showed considerable condescension toward the "poor heathen," who in turn bristled at their assumptions (America in Global Context). One Presbyterian, who found Syrians uninterested in his gospel message, angrily denounced all Muslims as "corrupt and immoral." By imposing their views of "heathen races" and attacking those who refused to convert, Christian missionaries sometimes ended up justifying Western imperialism.

Cultural imperialism abroad reflected attitudes at home. Starting in Iowa in 1887, militant Protestants created a powerful political organization, the **American Protective Association** (APA), which for a brief period in the 1890s counted more than two million members. This virulently nativist group expressed outrage at the existence of separate Catholic schools while demanding, at the same time, that all public school teachers be Protestants. The APA called for a ban on Catholic officeholders, arguing that they were beholden to an "ecclesiastic power" that was "not created

American Protective Association
A powerful political organization of militant Protestants, which for a brief period in the 1890s counted more than two million members. In its virulent anti-Catholicism and calls for restrictions on immigrants, the APA prefigured the revived Ku Klux Klan of the 1920s.

Christianity in the United States and Japan

During the 1893 Chicago World's Columbian Exhibition, a Parliament of Religions brought together representatives of prominent faiths for discussion. English-speaking Protestants dominated the program, but several Asian representatives included Kinzo Hirai, a lay Buddhist from Japan. In his speech, Hirai reviewed Japan's experiences with the United States since Commodore Matthew C. Perry "opened" the country in 1853.

I do not understand why the Christian lands have ignored the rights and advantages of forty million souls of Japan for forty years. . . . One of the excuses offered by foreign nations is that our country is not yet civilized. Is it the principle of civilized law that the rights and profits of the so-called uncivilized, or the weaker, should be sacrificed? As I understand it, the spirit and necessity of law is to protect the rights and profits of the weaker against the aggression of the stronger. . . .

From the religious source, the claim is made that the Japanese are idolaters and heathen. . . . [A]dmitting for the sake of argument that we are idolaters and heathen, is it Christian morality to trample upon the rights and advantages of a non-Christian nation, coloring all their natural happiness with the dark stain of injustice? . . .

You send your missionaries to Japan and they advise us to be moral and believe Christianity. We like to be moral, we know that Christianity is good; and we are very thankful for this kindness. But at the same time our people are rather perplexed. . . . For when we think that the treaty stipulated in the time of feudalism, when we were yet in our youth, is still clung to by the powerful nations of Christendom; when we find that every year a good many western vessels of seal fishery are smuggled into our seas; when legal cases are always decided by the foreign authorities in Japan unfavorably to us; when some

years ago a Japanese was not allowed to enter a university on the Pacific coast of America because of his being of a different race; when a few months ago the school board in San Francisco enacted a regulation that no Japanese should be allowed to enter the public school there; when last year the Japanese were driven out in wholesale from one of the territories of the United States; when our business men in San Francisco were compelled by some union not to employ Japanese assistants and laborers, but the Americans; when there are some in the same city who speak on the platform against those of us who are already here; when there are many who go in procession hoisting lanterns marked "Japs must go"; when the Japanese in the Hawaiian Islands were deprived of their suffrage; when we see some western people in Japan who erect before the entrance to their houses a special post upon which is the notice, "No Japanese is allowed to enter here" — just like a board upon which is written, "No dogs allowed"; when we are in such a situation, notwithstanding the kindness of the western nations from one point of view, who send their missionaries to us, that we unintelligent heathens are embarrassed and hesitate to swallow the sweet and warm liquid of the heaven of Christianity, will not be unreasonable.

Source: *The World's Parliament of Religions*, ed. John Henry Barrows (Chicago: Parliament Publishing Co., 1893), 444–450.

QUESTIONS FOR ANALYSIS

1. What is Hirai's attitude toward American Christians?
2. Of what events is Hirai aware that are taking place in the United States? How does this shape his view of Christian missions in Japan?
3. How might American delegates to the Parliament, especially Protestant missionaries, have responded to Hirai?

and controlled by American citizens." In its virulent anti-Catholicism and calls for restrictions on immigrants, the APA prefigured the revived Ku Klux Klan of the 1920s (Chapter 21).

The APA arose, in part, because Protestants found their dominance challenged. Millions of Americans, especially in the industrial working class, were now Catholics or Jews. Overall, in 1916, Protestants still constituted about 60 percent of Americans affiliated with a religious body. But they faced formidable rivals: the number of practicing Catholics in 1916 — 15.7 million — was greater than the number of Baptists, Methodists, and Presbyterians combined.

Some Protestants responded to the urban, immigrant challenge by evangelizing among the unchurched. They provided reading rooms, day nurseries, vocational classes, and other services. The goal of renewing religious faith through dedication to justice and social welfare became known as the **Social Gospel**. Its goals were epitomized by Charles Sheldon's novel *In His Steps* (1896), which told the story of a congregation that resolved to live by Christ's precepts for one year. "If church members were all doing as Jesus would do," Sheldon asked, "could it remain true that armies of men would walk the streets for jobs, and hundreds of them curse the church, and thousands of them find in the saloon their best friend?"

The Salvation Army, which arrived from Great Britain in 1879, also spread a gospel message among the urban poor, offering assistance that ranged from soup kitchens to shelters for former prostitutes. When all else failed, down-and-outers knew they could count on the Salvation Army, whose bell ringers became a familiar sight on city streets. The group borrowed up-to-date marketing techniques and used the latest business slang in urging its Christian soldiers to "hustle."

The Salvation Army succeeded, in part, because it managed to bridge an emerging divide between Social Gospel reformers and Protestants who were taking a different theological path. Disturbed by what they saw as rising secularism, conservative ministers and their allies held a series of Bible Conferences at Niagara Falls between 1876 and 1897. The resulting "Niagara Creed" reaffirmed the literal truth of the Bible and the certain damnation of those not born again in Christ. By the 1910s, a network of churches and Bible institutes had emerged from these conferences. They called their movement **fundamentalism**, based on their belief in the fundamental truth of the Bible.

Fundamentalists and their allies made particularly effective use of revival meetings. Unlike Social Gospel advocates, revivalists said little about poverty or earthly justice, focusing not on the matters of the world, but on heavenly redemption. The pioneer modern evangelist was Dwight L. Moody, a former Chicago shoe salesman and YMCA official who won fame in the 1870s. Eternal life could be had for the asking, Moody promised. His listeners needed only "to come forward and take, TAKE!" Moody's successor, Billy Sunday, helped bring evangelism into the modern era. More often than his predecessors, Sunday took political stances based on his Protestant beliefs. Condemning the "booze traffic" was his greatest cause. Sunday also denounced unrestricted immigration and labor radicalism. "If I had my way with these ornery wild-eyed Socialists," he once threatened, "I would stand them up before a firing squad." Sunday supported some progressive reform causes; he opposed child labor, for example, and advocated voting rights for women. In other ways, his views anticipated the nativism and antiradicalism that would dominate American politics after World War I.

Social Gospel
A movement to renew religious faith through dedication to public welfare and social justice, reforming both society and the self through Christian service.

fundamentalism
A term adopted by Protestants, between the 1890s and the 1910s, who rejected modernism and historical interpretations of scripture and asserted the literal truth of the Bible. Fundamentalists have historically seen secularism and religious relativism as markers of sin that will be punished by God.

Realism in the Arts

realism
A movement that called for writers and artists to picture daily life as precisely and truly as possible.

Inspired by the quest for facts, American authors rejected nineteenth-century romanticism and what they saw as its unfortunate product, sentimentality. Instead, they took up literary **realism**. In the 1880s, editor and novelist William Dean Howells called for writers "to picture the daily life in the most exact terms possible." By the 1890s, a younger generation of writers pursued this goal. Theodore Dreiser dismissed unrealistic novels that always had "a happy ending." In *Main-Travelled Roads* (1891), based on the struggles of his midwestern farm family, Hamlin Garland turned the same unsparing eye on the hardships of rural life. Stephen Crane's *Maggie: A Girl of the Streets* (1893), privately printed because no publisher would touch it, described the seduction, abandonment, and death of a slum girl.

Some authors believed realism did not go far enough to overturn sentimentalism. Jack London spent his teenage years as a factory worker, sailor, and tramp. In stories such as "The Law of Life" (1901), he dramatized what he saw as the harsh reality of an uncaring universe. American society, he said, was "a jungle wherein wild beasts eat and are eaten." Similarly, Stephen Crane tried to capture "a world full of fists." London and Crane suggested that human beings were not so much rational shapers of their own destinies as blind victims of forces beyond their control — including their own subconscious impulses.

America's most famous writer, Samuel Langhorne Clemens, who took the pen name of Mark Twain, came to an equally bleak view. Though he achieved enormous success with such lighthearted books as *The Adventures of Tom Sawyer* (1876), Clemens courted controversy with *The Adventures of Huckleberry Finn* (1884), notable for its indictment of slavery and racism. In his novel *A Connecticut Yankee in King Arthur's Court* (1889), which ends with a bloody, technology-driven slaughter of Arthur's knights, Mark Twain became one of the bitterest critics of America's idea of progress. Afterward, Clemens was devastated by the loss of his wife and two daughters, as well as by failed investments and bankruptcy. An outspoken critic of imperialism and foreign missions, Twain eventually denounced Christianity itself as a hypocritical delusion. Like his friend the industrialist Andrew Carnegie, Clemens "got rid of theology."

modernism
A movement that questioned the ideals of progress and order, rejected realism, and emphasized new cultural forms. Modernism became the first great literary and artistic movement of the twentieth century and remains influential today.

By the time Clemens died in 1910, American artists had laid the groundwork for **modernism**, which rejected traditional canons of artistic taste. Questioning the whole idea of progress and order, modernists focused on the subconscious and "primitive" mind. Above all, they sought to overturn convention and tradition. Poet Ezra Pound exhorted, "Make it new!" Modernism became the first great literary and artistic movement of the twentieth century.

In the visual arts, new technologies influenced aesthetics. By 1900, some photographers argued that their "true" representations made painting obsolete. But painters invented their own forms of realism. Nebraska-born artist Robert Henri became fascinated with life in the great cities. "The backs of tenement houses are living documents," he declared, and he set out to put them on canvas. Henri and his followers, notably John Sloan and George Bellows, called themselves the New York Realists. Critics derided them as the Ash Can school because they chose subjects that were not conventionally beautiful.

In 1913, realists participated in one of the most controversial events in American art history, the Armory Show. Housed in an enormous National Guard building in New York, the exhibit introduced America to modern art. Some painters whose work

Arthur B. Davies, *Dancers,* **1914–1915** Artist Arthur Davies (1862–1928) was one of the primary organizers of New York's 1913 Armory Show, which introduced Americans to modernist art. An associate of John Sloan and other New York realists, Davies experimented with an array of painting styles, as well as printmaking and tapestry making. This painting dates from a three-year period, just after the Armory Show, in which Davies experimented with Cubist techniques. Detroit Institute of Arts, USA/Gift of Ralph Harman Booth/ Bridgeman Images.

appeared at the show were experimenting with cubism, characterized by abstract, geometric forms. Along with works by Henri, Sloan, and Bellows, organizers featured paintings by European rebels such as Pablo Picasso. America's academic art world was shocked. One critic called cubism "the total destruction of the art of painting." But as the exhibition went on to Boston and Chicago, more than 250,000 people crowded to see it.

A striking feature of both realism and modernism, as they developed, was that many leading writers and artists were men. In making their work strong and modern, they also strove to assert their masculinity. Paralleling Theodore Roosevelt's call for "manly sports," they denounced nineteenth-century culture as hopelessly feminized. Stephen Crane called for "virility" in literature. Jack London described himself as a "man's man, . . . lustfully roving and conquering." Artist Robert Henri banned small brushes as "too feminine." In their own ways, these writers and artists contributed to a broad movement to masculinize American culture.

IN YOUR OWN WORDS How did Charles Darwin's theory of evolution and other scientific ideas impact American culture and intellectual life in the late nineteenth century? What uses did nonscientists make of such ideas?

Commerce and Culture

Debates over faith, science, and society affected Americans in widely different ways, partly because divisions between rural and urban life, and between affluent and poor Americans, were growing. As the United States industrialized, the terms *middle class* and *working class* came widely into use. Americans adopted these broad identities not only in the workplace but also in their leisure time. As professionals and corporate managers prospered, they and their families enjoyed rising income and an array of tempting ways to spend their dollars. Celebrating these new technological wonders, Americans hailed inventors as heroes. The most famous, Thomas Edison, operated an independent laboratory rather than working for a corporation. Edison, like many of the era's businessmen, was a shrewd entrepreneur who focused on commercial success. He and his colleagues helped introduce such lucrative products as the incandescent lightbulb and the phonograph.

Even working-class Americans enjoyed cheaper products delivered by global trade and mass production, from bananas and cigarettes to colorful dime novels and magazines. Edison's moving pictures, for example, first found popularity among the urban working class. Consumer culture appeared, at least, to be democratic: anyone could eat at a restaurant or buy a rail ticket for the "ladies' car" — as long as she or he could pay. In practice, though, well-to-do Americans enjoyed new amenities at much higher rates. Consumer culture thus became a site of struggle over class inequality, race privilege, and proper male and female behavior.

Consumer Spaces

America's public spaces — from election polls to saloons and circus shows — had long been boisterous and male-centered. A woman who ventured there without a male chaperone risked damaging her reputation (or worse). But the rise of new businesses encouraged change. To attract an eager public, purveyors of consumer culture invited women and families, especially those of the middle class, to linger in department stores and enjoy new amusements.

No one promoted commercial domesticity more successfully than showman P. T. Barnum, who used the country's expanding rail network to develop his famous traveling circus. Barnum condemned earlier circus managers who had opened their tents to "the rowdy element." Proclaiming children as his key audience, he created family entertainment for diverse audiences (though in the South, black audiences sat in segregated seats or attended separate shows). He promised middle-class parents that his circus would teach children courage and promote the benefits of exercise. To encourage women's attendance, Barnum emphasized the respectability and refinement of his female performers.

Department stores also lured middle-class women by offering tearooms, children's play areas, umbrellas, and clerks to wrap and carry every purchase. Store credit plans enabled well-to-do women to shop without handling money in public. Such tactics succeeded so well that New York's department store district became known as Ladies' Mile. Boston department store magnate William Filene called the department store an "Adamless Eden."

These Edens were reserved for the elite and middle classes. Though bargain basements and neighborhood stores served working-class families, big department stores used vagrancy laws and police to discourage the "wrong kind" from entering. Working-class women gained access primarily as clerks, cashiers, and cash girls, who at age twelve or younger served as internal store messengers, carrying orders and change for $1.50 a week. The department store was no Eden for these women, who worked long hours on their feet, often dealing with difficult customers. Nevertheless, many clerks claimed their own privileges as shoppers, making enthusiastic use of employee discounts and battling employers for the right to wear their fashionable purchases while they worked in the store.

In similar ways, class status was marked by the ways technology entered American homes. The rise of electricity, in particular, marked the gap between affluent urban consumers and rural and working-class families. In elite houses, domestic servants began to use — or find themselves replaced by — an array of new devices, from washing machines to vacuum cleaners. When Alexander Graham Bell invented the telephone in 1876, entrepreneurs introduced the device for business use, but it soon found eager residential customers, especially among the affluent. Telephones changed etiquette and social relations for middle-class suburban women — while providing their working-class counterparts with new employment as operators or "hello girls."

Railroads also reflected the emerging privileges of professional families. Finding prosperous Americans eager for excursions, railroad companies, like department stores, made things comfortable for middle-class women and children. Boston's South Station boasted of its modern amenities, including "everything that the traveler needs down to cradles in which the baby may be soothed." Rail cars manufactured by the famous Pullman Company of Chicago set a national standard for taste and elegance. Part of their appeal was the chance for people of modest means to emulate the rich. An experienced train conductor observed that the wives of grocers, not millionaires, were the ones most likely to "sweep . . . into a parlor car as if the very carpet ought to feel highly honored by their tread."

First-class "ladies' cars" soon became sites of struggle for racial equality. For three decades after the end of the Civil War, state laws and railroad regulations varied, and African Americans often succeeded in securing seats. One reformer noted, however, "There are few ordeals more nerve-wracking than the one which confronts a colored woman when she tries to secure a Pullman reservation in the South and even in some parts of the North." When they claimed first-class seats, black women often faced confrontations with conductors, resulting in numerous lawsuits in the 1870s and 1880s. Riding the Chesapeake & Ohio line in 1884, young African American journalist Ida B. Wells was told to leave. "I refused," she wrote later, "saying that the [nearest alternative] car was a smoker, and as I was in the ladies' car, I proposed to stay." Wells resisted, but the conductor and a baggage handler threw her bodily off the train. Returning home to Memphis, Wells sued and won in local courts, but Tennessee's supreme court reversed the ruling.

In 1896, the U.S. Supreme Court settled such issues decisively, but not justly. The case, **_Plessy v. Ferguson_**, was brought by civil rights advocates on behalf of Homer Plessy, a New Orleans resident who was one-eighth black. Ordered to leave a first-class car and move to the "colored" car of a Louisiana train, Plessy refused and was arrested. The Court ruled that such segregation did not violate the Fourteenth Amendment as

Plessy v. Ferguson
An 1896 Supreme Court case that ruled that racially segregated railroad cars and other public facilities, if they claimed to be "separate but equal," were permissible according to the Fourteenth Amendment.

long as blacks had access to accommodations that were "separate but equal" to those of whites. "Separate but equal" was a myth: segregated facilities in the South were flagrantly inferior. **Jim Crow** segregation laws, named for a stereotyped black character who appeared in minstrel shows, clearly discriminated, but the Court allowed them to stand.

Jim Crow
Laws that required separation of the races, especially blacks and whites, in public facilities. This system of racial segregation in the South lasted a century, from after the Civil War until the 1960s.

Jim Crow laws applied to public schools and parks and also to emerging commercial spaces — hotels, restaurants, streetcars, trains, and eventually sports stadiums and movie theaters. Placing a national stamp of approval on segregation, the *Plessy* decision remained in place until 1954, when the Court's *Brown v. Topeka Board of Education* ruling finally struck it down (Chapter 26). Until then, blacks' exclusion from first-class "public accommodations" was one of the most painful marks of racism. The *Plessy* decision, like the rock-bottom wages earned by twelve-year-old girls at Macy's, showed that consumer culture could be modern and innovative without being politically progressive. Business and consumer culture were shaped by, and themselves shaped, racial and class injustices.

Masculinity and the Rise of Sports

Industrialization changed expectations in the workplace. Traditionally, the mark of a successful American man was economic independence: he was his own boss. Now, tens of thousands worked for other men in big companies and in offices, rather than using their muscles. Would the professional American male, through his concentration on "brain work," become "weak, effeminate, [and] decaying," as one editor warned? How could well-to-do men assert their independence if work no longer required them to prove themselves physically? How could they develop toughness and strength? One answer was athletics.

Young Men's Christian Association
Introduced in Boston in 1851, the YMCA promoted muscular Christianity, combining evangelism with athletic facilities where men could make themselves "clean and strong."

"Muscular Christianity" The **Young Men's Christian Association** (YMCA) was one of the earliest and most successful promoters of athletic fitness. Introduced in Boston in 1851, the group promoted muscular Christianity, combining evangelism with gyms and athletic facilities where men could make themselves "clean and strong." Focusing first on white-collar workers, the YMCA developed a substantial industrial program after 1900. Railroad managers and other corporate titans hoped YMCAs would foster a loyal and contented workforce, discouraging labor unrest. Business leaders also relied on sports to build physical and mental discipline and help men adjust their bodies to the demands of the industrial clock. Sports honed men's competitive spirit, they believed; employer-sponsored teams instilled teamwork and company pride.

Working-class men had their own ideas about sports and leisure, and YMCAs quickly became a site of negotiation. Could workers come to the "Y" to play billiards or cards? Could they smoke? At first, YMCA leaders said no, but to attract working-class men they had to make concessions. As a result, the "Y" became a place where middle-class and working-class customs blended — or existed in uneasy tension. At the same time, YMCA leaders innovated. Searching for winter activities in the 1890s, YMCA instructors invented the new indoor games of basketball and volleyball.

For elite Americans, meanwhile, country clubs flourished; both men and women could enjoy tennis, golf, and swimming facilities as well as social gatherings. By the turn of the century — perhaps because country club women were encroaching on their athletic turf — elite men took up even more aggressive physical sports, including boxing, weightlifting, and martial arts. As early as 1890, future president Theodore Roosevelt argued that such "virile" activities were essential to "maintain and defend this very civilization." "Most masterful nations," he claimed, "have shown a strong taste for manly sports." Roosevelt, son of a wealthy New York family, became one of the first American devotees of jujitsu. During his presidency (1901–1909), he designated a judo room in the White House and hired an expert Japanese instructor. Roosevelt also wrestled and boxed, urging other American men — especially among the elite — to increase their leadership fitness by pursuing the "strenuous life."

America's Game Before the 1860s, the only distinctively American game was Native American lacrosse, and the most popular team sport among European Americans was cricket. After the Civil War, however, team sports became a fundamental part of American manhood, none more successfully than baseball. A derivative of cricket, the game's formal rules had begun to develop in New York in the 1840s and 1850s; its popularity spread in military camps during the Civil War. Afterward, the idea that baseball "received its baptism in the bloody days of our Nation's direst danger," as one promoter put it, became part of the game's mythology.

Until the 1870s, most amateur players were clerks and white-collar workers who had the leisure time to play and the income to buy their own uniforms. Business frowned on baseball and other sports as a waste of time, especially for working-class men. But late-nineteenth-century employers came to see baseball, like other athletic pursuits, as a benefit for workers. It provided fresh air and exercise, kept men out of saloons, and promoted discipline and teamwork. Players on company-sponsored teams, wearing uniforms emblazoned with their employers' names, began to compete on paid work time. Baseball thus set a pattern for how other American sports developed. Begun among independent craftsmen, it was taken up by elite men anxious to prove their strength and fitness. Well-to-do Americans then decided the sport could benefit the working class.

Big-time professional baseball arose with the launching of the National League in 1876. The league quickly built more than a dozen teams in large cities, from the Brooklyn Trolley Dodgers to the Cleveland Spiders. Team owners were, in their own right, profit-minded entrepreneurs who shaped the sport to please consumers (Interpretations). Wooden grandstands soon gave way to concrete and steel stadiums. By 1900, boys collected lithographed cards of their favorite players, and the baseball cap came into fashion. In 1903, the Boston Americans defeated the Pittsburgh Pirates in the first World Series. American men could now adopt a new consumer identity — not as athletes, but as fans.

Rise of the Negro Leagues Baseball stadiums, like first-class rail cars, were sites of racial negotiation and conflict. In the 1880s and 1890s, major league managers hired a few African American players. As late as 1901, the Baltimore Orioles succeeded in signing Charlie Grant, a light-skinned black player from Cincinnati, by renaming him Charlie Tokohoma and claiming he was Cherokee. But as this subterfuge suggested, black players were increasingly barred. A Toledo team received a threatening note

To see a longer excerpt of Theodore Roosevelt's views on sports, along with other primary sources from this period, see *Sources for America's History*.

INTERPRETATIONS

Was Professional Baseball a Pastime or a Business Monopoly — or Both?

By the late nineteenth century, baseball was already hailed as America's national pastime. Supported by a willing press promoting baseball's all-American virtues, the game sparked community pride. Fans cheered the home team, followed star players, and enjoyed the fresh air and warm sunlight of an afternoon amusement. Baseball, many said, taught young boys life lessons about teamwork, the virtue of sacrificing for another, and fair play. Historians have begun to challenge this nostalgic and romantic history. Here, scholars Steven A. Riess and Stuart Banner examine the professional game as a reflection of the political, economic, and cultural developments of the age.

STEVEN A. RIESS

SOURCE: Steven A. Riess, *Touching Base: Professional Baseball and American Culture in the Progressive Era* (Urbana: University of Illinois Press, 1999), 98.

Major league club owners were primarily men of new affluence, often Irish Catholics or German Jews. . . . These owners had important political connections that helped their sporting businesses succeed. . . . This created a fascinating paradox since WASPs [white, Anglo-Saxon Protestants] and other accultur-ated Americans regarded baseball as the institution that best epitomized the finest American beliefs, traditions, and values. Yet the baseball magnates were urban politicians, often machine politicians, who symbolized all that progressive small-town Americans believed was wrong with and destructive to American society.

STUART BANNER

SOURCE: Stuart Banner, *The Baseball Trust: A History of Baseball's Antitrust Exemption* (New York: Oxford University Press, 2013), 4–6.

The reserve clause would be a standard term in player contracts for nearly a century. . . . The teams first considered establishing limits on salaries, but they decided that it would be easier if they simply ceased competing with each other to hire the best players. Each club was accordingly allowed to reserve . . . players for the ensuing season. . . . Once a club reserved a player, the other clubs would treat him as if he were already under contract. . . . The result was an unusual system of labor relations, in which players were effectively bound for life to the teams that first signed them. . . . Even in the late nineteenth century, when workers throughout the economy had few rights enforceable against their employers, baseball stood out as a business in which the rules governing labor were conspicuously one-sided.

QUESTIONS FOR ANALYSIS

1. Identify one similarity and one difference in the way Riess and Banner describe the turn-of-the-century history of baseball.
2. How does their focus on the economics and politics of baseball change the story typically told about our "national pastime"?
3. From your reading of the excerpts and the textbook chapter, identify two specific ways baseball reflects broader developments in American history during this period.

before one game in Richmond, Virginia: if their "negro catcher" played, he would be lynched. Toledo put a substitute on the field, and at the end of the season the club terminated the black player's contract.

Shut out of white leagues, players and fans turned to all-black professional teams, where black men could showcase athletic ability and race pride. Louisiana's top team, the New Orleans Pinchbacks, pointedly named themselves after the state's black Reconstruction governor. By the early 1900s, such teams organized into separate **Negro Leagues**. Though players suffered from erratic pay and rundown ball fields, the leagues thrived until the desegregation of baseball after World War II. In an era of stark discrimination, they celebrated black manhood and talent. "I liked the way their uniform fit, the way they wore their cap," wrote an admiring fan of the Newark Eagles. "They showed a style in almost everything they did."

Negro Leagues
Professional baseball teams formed for and by black players, after the main national leagues began to exclude all African American players in the 1890s. Enduring until the desegregation of baseball after World War II, the leagues enabled black men to showcase athletic ability and race pride, but their working conditions and wages were much less desirable than those of players in the white leagues.

American Football The most controversial sport of the industrializing era was football, which began at elite colleges during the 1880s. The great powerhouse was the

Football Practice, Chilocco Indian School, 1911 Football became widely popular, spreading from Ivy League schools and state universities to schools like this one, built on Cherokee land in Oklahoma. The uniforms of this team, typical of the day, show very limited padding and protection—a factor that contributed to high rates of injury and even death on the field. As they practiced in 1911, these Chilocco students had an inspiring model to look up to: in that year Jim Thorpe, a fellow Oklahoman and a member of the Sac and Fox tribe, was winning national fame by leading the all-Indian team at Pennsylvania's Carlisle School to victory against Harvard. Thorpe, one of the finest athletes of his generation, went on to win gold medals in the pentathlon and decathlon at the 1912 Olympics in Stockholm, Sweden. National Archives.

Yale team, whose legendary coach Walter Camp went on to become a watch manufacturer. Between 1883 and 1891, under Camp's direction, Yale scored 4,660 points; its opponents scored 92. Drawing on the workplace model of scientific management, Camp emphasized drill and precision. He and other coaches argued that football offered perfect training for the competitive world of business. The game was violent: six players' deaths in the 1908 college season provoked a public outcry. Eventually, new rules protected quarterbacks and required coaches to remove injured players from the game. But such measures were adopted grudgingly, with supporters arguing that they ruined football's benefits in manly training.

Like baseball and the YMCA, football attracted sponsorship from business leaders hoping to divert workers from labor activism. The first professional teams emerged in western Pennsylvania's steel towns, soon after the defeat of the steelworkers' union. Carnegie Steel executives organized teams in Homestead and Braddock; the first league appeared during the anthracite coal strike of 1902. Other teams arose in the midwestern industrial heartland. The Indian-Acme Packing Company sponsored the Green Bay Packers; the future Chicago Bears, first known as the Decatur Staleys, were funded by a manufacturer of laundry starch. Like its baseball equivalent, professional football encouraged men to buy in as spectators and fans.

The Great Outdoors

As the rise of sports suggests, by the 1890s elite and middle-class Americans began to see Victorian culture as stuffy and claustrophobic. They revolted by heading outdoors. A craze for bicycling swept the country; in 1890, at the height of the mania, U.S. manufacturers sold an astonishing ten million bikes. Women were not far behind men in taking up athletics. By the 1890s, even elite women, long confined to corsets and heavy clothes that restricted their movement, donned lighter dresses and pursued archery and golf. Artist Charles Gibson became famous for his portraits of the Gibson Girl, an elite beauty depicted on the tennis court or swimming at the beach. The Gibson Girl personified the ideal of "New Women," more educated, athletic, and independent than their mothers.

Those with money and leisure time used railroad networks to get to the national parks of the West, which, as one senator put it, became a "breathing-place for the national lungs." People of more modest means began to take up camping. As early as 1904, California's Coronado Beach offered tent rentals for $3 a week. A decade later, campgrounds and cottages in many parts of the country catered to a working-class clientele. In an industrial society, the outdoors became associated with leisure and renewal rather than danger and hard work. One journalist, reflecting on urban life from the vantage point of a western vacation, wrote, "How stupid it all seems: the mad eagerness of money-making men, the sham pleasures of conventional society." In the wilderness, he wrote, "your blood clarifies; your brain becomes active. You get a new view of life."

As Americans searched for such renewal in remnants of unexploited land, the nation's first environmental movement arose. John Muir, who fell in love with the Yosemite Valley in 1869, became the most famous voice for wilderness. Raised in a stern Scots Presbyterian family on a Wisconsin farm, Muir knew much of the Bible by heart. He was a keen observer who developed a deeply spiritual relationship with the natural world. His contemporary Mary Austin, whose book *Land of Little Rain* (1905) celebrated the austere beauty of the California desert, called him "a devout man." In cooperation with his editor at *Century* magazine, Muir founded the **Sierra Club** in 1892. Like the earlier Appalachian Mountain Club, founded in Boston in 1876, the Sierra Club dedicated itself to preserving and enjoying America's great mountains.

Encouraged by such groups, national and state governments set aside more public lands for preservation and recreation. The United States substantially expanded its park system and, during Theodore Roosevelt's presidency, extended the reach of national forests. Starting in 1872 with the preservation of Yellowstone in Wyoming, Congress had begun to set aside land for national parks. In 1916, President Woodrow Wilson provided comprehensive oversight of these national parks, signing an act creating the **National Park Service** (Map 17.1). A year later, the system numbered thirteen parks — including Maine's Acadia, the first east of the Mississippi River.

Environmentalists also worked to protect wildlife. By the 1890s, several state Audubon Societies, named in honor of antebellum naturalist John James Audubon, banded together to advocate broader protections for wild birds, especially herons and egrets, which were being slaughtered by the thousands for their plumes. They succeeded in winning the Lacey Act (1900), which established federal penalties for selling specified birds, animals, and plants. Soon afterward, state organizations joined together to form the National Audubon Society. Women played prominent roles in the movement, promoting boycotts of hats with plumage. In 1903, President Theodore Roosevelt created the first National Wildlife Refuge at Pelican Island, Florida.

Sierra Club

An organization founded in 1892 that was dedicated to the enjoyment and preservation of America's great mountains (including the Sierra Nevadas) and wilderness environments. Encouraged by such groups, national and state governments began to set aside more public lands for preservation and recreation.

National Park Service

A federal agency founded in 1916 that provided comprehensive oversight of the growing system of national parks.

MAP 17.1 **National Parks and Forests, 1872–1980**
Yellowstone, the first national park in the United States, dates from 1872. In 1893, the federal government began to intervene to protect national forests. Without Theodore Roosevelt, however, the national forest program might have languished; during his presidency, he added 125 million acres to the forest system, plus six national parks in addition to several that had already been created during the 1890s. America's national forest and park systems remain one of the most visible and beloved legacies of federal policy innovation in the decades between the Civil War and World War I.

Antiquities Act
A 1906 act that allowed the U.S. president to use executive powers to set aside, as federal monuments, sites of great environmental or cultural significance. Theodore Roosevelt, the first president to invoke the act's powers, used them to preserve the Grand Canyon.

Roosevelt also expanded preservation under the **Antiquities Act** (1906), which enabled the U.S. president, without congressional approval, to set aside "objects of historic and scientific interest" as national monuments. Two years later, Roosevelt used these powers to preserve 800,000 acres at Arizona's magnificent Grand Canyon. The act proved a mixed blessing for conservation. Monuments received weaker protection than national parks did; many fell under the authority of the U.S. Forest Service, which permitted logging and grazing. Business interests thus lobbied to have coveted lands designated as monuments rather than national parks so they could more easily exploit resources. Nonetheless, the creation of national monuments offered some protection, and many monuments (such as Alaska's Katmai) later obtained park status. The expanding network of parks and monuments became popular places to hike, camp, and contemplate natural beauty.

The great outdoors provided new opportunities for women with the means to travel. One writer, advising women to enjoy mountain hikes, hinted at liberating possibilities: "For those loving freedom and health," he recommended "short skirts, pantlets, stout shoes, tasty hat." And like other leisure venues, "wilderness" did not remain in the hands of elite men and women. As early as the late 1880s, the lakes and hiking trails of the Catskill Mountains became so thronged with working-class tourists from nearby New York City, including many Jewish immigrants, that elite visitors began to segregate themselves into gated summer communities. They thus preserved the "seclusion and privacy" that they snobbishly claimed as the privilege of those who could demonstrate "mental and personal worth."

At the state level, meanwhile, new game laws triggered conflicts between elite conservationists and the poor. Shifting from year-round subsistence hunting to a limited, recreational hunting season brought hardship to poor rural families who depended on game for food. Regulation brought undeniable benefits: it suppressed such popular practices as songbird hunting and the use of dynamite to kill fish. Looking back on the era before game laws, one Alabama hunter remembered that "the slaughter was terrific." But while game laws prevented further extinctions like that of the passenger pigeon, which vanished around 1900, they made it harder for rural people to support themselves through subsistence hunting and fishing.

> **IN YOUR OWN WORDS** How did industrialization change Americans' ideas about appropriate leisure activities for men and women of various social classes?

Women, Men, and the Solitude of Self

Speaking to Congress in 1892, women's rights advocate Elizabeth Cady Stanton described what she called the "solitude of self." Stanton rejected the claim that women did not need equal rights because they enjoyed men's protection. "The talk of sheltering woman from the fierce storms of life is the sheerest mockery," she declared. "They beat on her from every point of the compass, just as they do on man, and with more fatal results, for he has been trained to protect himself."

Stanton's argument captured one of the dilemmas of industrialization: the marketplace of labor brought both freedom and risk, and working-class women were particularly vulnerable. At the same time, middle-class women — expected to engage in selfless community service — often saw the impact of industrialization more clearly than fathers, brothers, and husbands did. In seeking to address alcoholism, poverty, and other social and economic ills, they gained a new sense of their own collective power. Women's protest and reform work thus helped lay the foundations for progressivism (Chapter 19) and modern women's rights.

Changing Families

The average American family, especially in the middle class, decreased in size during the industrial era. In 1800, white women who survived to menopause had borne an average of 7.0 children; by 1900, the average was 3.6. On farms and in many working-class families, youngsters counted as assets on the family balance sheet: they worked in fields or factories. But parents who had fewer sons and daughters could concentrate their resources, educating and preparing each child for success in the new economy. Among the professional classes, education became a necessity, while limiting family size became, more broadly, a key to upward mobility.

Several factors limited childbearing. Americans married at older ages, and many mothers tried to space pregnancies more widely — as their mothers and grandmothers had — by nursing children for several years, which suppressed fertility. By the late nineteenth century, as vulcanized rubber became available, couples also had access to a range of other contraceptive methods, such as condoms and diaphragms. With pressure for family limitation rising, these methods were widely used and apparently effective. But couples rarely wrote about them. Historians' evidence comes from the occasional frank diary and from the thriving success of the mail-order contraceptive industry, which advertised

Portrait of a Middle-Class American Family This photograph of the Hedlund family was taken on July 4, 1911, on the front porch of their home in St. Paul, Minnesota. Christian, Grace, and Anna Hedlund appear on the top row, Louis and George on the bottom. Families like this one — with three children — were becoming typical among the middle class, in contrast to larger families in earlier generations. This photo was taken by twenty-one-year-old Joseph Pavlicek, a recent immigrant from Eastern Europe who was boarding with the Hedlunds. Pavlicek bought fireworks for the children to celebrate the holiday. He remembered being so proud and grateful to be in America that his heart "was nearly bursting." Minnesota Historical Society.

prominently and shipped products — wrapped in discreet brown paper packages — to customers nationwide.

Reluctance to talk about contraceptives was understandable, since information about them was stigmatized and, after 1873, illegal to distribute. During Reconstruction, Anthony Comstock, crusading secretary of the New York Society for the Suppression of Vice, secured a federal law banning "obscene materials" from the U.S. mail. The **Comstock Act** (1873) prohibited circulation of almost any information about sex and birth control — even in private letters. Comstock won support for the law, in part, by appealing to parents' fears that young people were receiving sexual information through the mail, promoting the rise of "secret vice." Though critics charged Comstock with high-handed interference in private matters, others supported his work, fearful of the rising tide of pornography, sexual information, and contraceptives made available by industrialization. A committee of the New York legislature declared Comstock's crusade "wholly essential to the safety and decency of the community." It appears, however, that Comstock had little success in stopping the lucrative and popular trade in contraceptives.

Comstock Act
An 1873 law that prohibited circulation of "obscene literature," defined as including most information on sex, reproduction, and birth control.

Education

In the industrial economy, the watchword for young people who hoped to secure good jobs was *education*. A high school diploma — now a gateway to a college degree — was valuable for boys who hoped to enter professional or managerial work. Daughters attended in even larger numbers than their brothers. Parents of the Civil War generation, who had witnessed the plight of war widows and orphans, encouraged girls to prepare themselves for teaching or office jobs, work before marriage, and gain skills they could fall back on, "just in case." By 1900, 71 percent of Americans between the ages of five and eighteen attended school. That figure rose further in the early twentieth century, as public officials adopted laws requiring school attendance.

Most high schools were coeducational, and almost every high school featured athletics. Recruited first as cheerleaders for boys' teams, girls soon established field hockey and other sports of their own. Boys and girls engaged in friendly — and sometimes not-so-friendly — rivalry in high school. In 1884, a high school newspaper in Concord, New Hampshire, published this poem from a disgruntled boy who caricatured his female classmates:

> We know many tongues of living and dead,
> In science and fiction we're very well read,
> But we cannot cook meat and cannot make bread
> And we've wished many times that we were all dead.

A female student shot back a poem of her own, denouncing male students' smoking habit:

> But if boys will smoke cigarettes
> Although the smoke may choke them,
> One consolation still remains —
> *They kill the boys that smoke them.*

The rate of Americans attending college had long hovered around 2 percent; driven by public universities' expansion, the rate rose in the 1880s, reaching 8 percent by 1920.

Much larger numbers attended a growing network of business and technical schools. "GET A PLACE IN THE WORLD," advertised one Minneapolis business college in 1907, "where your talents can be used to the best advantage." Typically, such schools offered both day and night classes in subjects such as bookkeeping, typewriting, and shorthand.

The needs of the new economy also shaped the curriculum at more traditional collegiate institutions. State universities emphasized technical training and fed the growing professional workforce with graduates trained in fields such as engineering. Many private colleges distanced themselves from such practical pursuits; their administrators argued that students who aimed to be leaders needed broad-based knowledge. But they modernized course offerings, emphasizing French and German, for example, rather than Latin and Greek. Harvard, led by dynamic president Charles W. Eliot from 1869 to 1909, pioneered the liberal arts. Students at the all-male college chose from a range of electives, as Eliot called for classes that developed each young man's "individual reality and creative power."

In the South, one of the most famous educational projects was Booker T. Washington's Tuskegee Institute, founded in 1881. Washington both taught and exemplified the goal of self-help; his autobiography, *Up from Slavery* (1901), became a best-seller. Because of the deep poverty in which most southern African Americans lived, Washington concluded that "book education" for most "would be almost a waste of time." He focused instead on industrial education. Students, he argued, would "be sure of knowing how to make a living after they had left us." Tuskegee sent female graduates into teaching and nursing; men more often entered the industrial trades or farmed by the latest scientific methods.

Washington gained national fame in 1895 with his **Atlanta Compromise** address, delivered at the Cotton States Exposition in Atlanta, Georgia. For the exposition's white organizers, the racial "compromise" was inviting Washington to speak at all. It was a move intended to show racial progress in the South. Washington, in turn, delivered an address that many interpreted as approving racial segregation. Stating that African Americans had, in slavery days, "proved our loyalty to you," he assured whites that "in our humble way, we shall stand by you . . . ready to lay down our lives, if need be, in defense of yours." The races could remain socially detached: "In all things that are purely social we can be as separate as the fingers, yet one as the hand in all things essential to mutual progress." Washington urged, however, that whites join him in working for "the highest intelligence and development of all."

Whites greeted this address with enthusiasm, and Washington became the most prominent black leader of his generation. His soothing rhetoric and style of leadership, based on avoiding confrontation and cultivating white patronage and private influence, was well suited to the difficult years after Reconstruction. Washington believed that money was color-blind, that whites would respect economic success. He represented the ideals of millions of African Americans who hoped education and hard work would erase white prejudice. That hope proved tragically overoptimistic. As the tide of disfranchisement and segregation rolled in, Washington would come under fire from a younger generation of race leaders who argued that he accommodated too much to white racism.

In addition to African American education, women's higher education expanded notably. In the Northeast and South, women most often attended single-sex institutions,

Atlanta Compromise
An 1895 address by Booker T. Washington that urged whites and African Americans to work together for the progress of all. Delivered at the Cotton States Exposition in Atlanta, the speech was widely interpreted as approving racial segregation.

including teacher-training colleges. For affluent families, private colleges offered an education equivalent to men's — for an equally high price. Vassar College started the trend when it opened in 1861; Smith, Wellesley, and others followed. Anxious doctors warned that these institutions were dangerous: intensive brain work would unsex young women and drain energy from their ovaries, leading them to bear weak children. But as thousands of women earned degrees and suffered no apparent harm, fears faded. Single-sex higher education for women spread from private to public institutions, especially in the South, where the Mississippi State College for Women (1885) led the way.

Coeducation was more prevalent in the Midwest and West, where many state universities opened their doors to female students after the Civil War. Women were also admitted to most African American colleges founded during Reconstruction. By 1910, 58 percent of America's colleges and universities were coeducational. While students at single-sex institutions forged strong bonds with one another, women also gained benefits from learning with men. When male students were friendly, they built comfortable working relationships; when men were hostile, women learned coping skills that served them well in later employment or reform work. One doctor who studied at the University of Iowa remembered later that he and his friends mercilessly harassed the first women who entered the medical school. But when the women showed they were good students, the men's attitudes changed to "wholesome respect."

Whether or not they got a college education, more and more women recognized, in the words of Elizabeth Cady Stanton, their "solitude of self." In the changing economy, they could not always count on fathers and husbands. Women who needed to support themselves could choose from dozens of guidebooks such as *What Girls Can Do* (1880) and *How to Make Money Although a Woman* (1895). The Association for the Advancement of Women, founded in 1873 by women's college graduates, defended women's higher education and argued that women's paid employment was a positive good.

Today, many economists argue that education and high-quality jobs for women are keys to reducing poverty in the developing world. In the United States, that process also led to broader gains in women's political rights. As women began to earn advanced degrees, work for wages and salaries, and live independently, it became harder to argue that women were "dependents" who did not need to vote.

Toward Women's Emancipation

maternalism
The belief that women should contribute to civic and political life through their special talents as mothers, Christians, and moral guides. Maternalists put this ideology into action by creating dozens of social reform organizations.

As the United States confronted industrialization, middle-class women steadily expanded their place beyond the household, building reform movements and taking political action. Starting in the 1880s, women's clubs sprang up and began to study such problems as pollution, unsafe working conditions, and urban poverty. So many formed by 1890 that their leaders created a nationwide umbrella organization, the General Federation of Women's Clubs. Women justified such work through the ideal of **maternalism**, appealing to their special role as mothers. Maternalism was an intermediate step between domesticity and modern arguments for women's equality. "Women's place is Home," declared the journalist Rheta Childe Dorr. But she added, "Home is the community. The city full of people is the Family. . . . Badly do the Home and Family need their mother."

Women's Temperance Activism One maternalist goal was to curb alcohol abuse by prohibiting liquor sales. The **Woman's Christian Temperance Union** (WCTU), founded after a series of women's grassroots campaigns in 1874, spread rapidly after 1879, when charismatic Frances Willard became its leader. More than any other group of the late nineteenth century, the WCTU launched women into reform. Willard knew how to frame political demands in the language of feminine self-sacrifice. "Womanliness first," she advised her followers; "afterward, what you will." WCTU members vividly described the plight of abused wives and children when men suffered in the grip of alcoholism. Willard's motto was "Home Protection," and though it placed all the blame on alcohol rather than other factors, the WCTU became the first organization to identify and combat domestic violence.

The prohibitionist movement drew activists from many backgrounds. Middle-class city dwellers worried about the link between alcoholism and crime, especially in the growing immigrant wards. Rural citizens equated liquor with big-city sins such as prostitution and political corruption. Methodists, Baptists, Mormons, and members of other denominations condemned drinking for religious reasons. Immigrants passionately disagreed, however: Germans and Irish Catholics enjoyed their Sunday beer and saw no harm in it. Saloons were a centerpiece of working-class leisure and community life, offering free lunches, public toilets, and a place to share neighborhood news. Thus, while some labor unions advocated voluntary temperance, attitudes toward prohibition divided along ethnic, religious, and class lines.

WCTU activism led some leaders to raise radical questions about the shape of industrial society. As she investigated alcohol abuse, Willard increasingly confronted poverty, hunger, unemployment, and other industrial problems (Thinking Like a Historian). Across the United States, WCTU locals founded soup kitchens and free libraries. They introduced a German educational innovation, the kindergarten. They investigated prison conditions. Though she did not persuade most prohibitionists to follow her lead, Willard declared herself a Christian Socialist and urged more attention to workers' plight. She advocated laws establishing an eight-hour workday and abolishing child labor.

Willard also called for women's voting rights, lending powerful support to the independent suffrage movement that had emerged during Reconstruction. Controversially, the WCTU threw its energies behind the Prohibition Party, which exercised considerable clout during the 1880s. Women worked in the party as speakers, convention delegates, and even local candidates. Liquor was big business, and powerful interests mobilized to block antiliquor legislation. In many areas — particularly the cities — prohibition simply did not gain majority support. Willard retired to England, where she died in 1898, worn and discouraged by many defeats. But her legacy was powerful. Other groups took up the cause, eventually winning national prohibition after World War I.

Through its emphasis on human welfare, the WCTU encouraged women to join the national debate over poverty and inequality of wealth. Some became active in the People's Party of the 1890s, which welcomed women as organizers and stump speakers. Others led groups such as the National Congress of Mothers, founded in 1897, which promoted better child-rearing techniques in rural and working-class families. The WCTU had taught women how to lobby, raise money, and even run for office.

Woman's Christian Temperance Union

An organization advocating the prohibition of liquor that spread rapidly after 1879, when charismatic Frances Willard became its leader. Advocating suffrage and a host of reform activities, it launched tens of thousands of women into public life and was the first nationwide organization to identify and condemn domestic violence.

Frances Willard, one of late-nineteenth-century America's most dynamic and admired reformers, rose to leadership of the Woman's Christian Temperance Union (WCTU) in the 1870s, when she was in her thirties. She built the WCTU, which had emerged from a series of spontaneous protests in Ohio in the 1870s, into a powerful national organization, touring the West, the ex-Confederacy, and Europe and reaching out to African Americans, immigrants, and farmer-labor organizations. Urging women to view alcohol abuse in a broad context, she famously challenged them to "Do Everything": start libraries, soup kitchens, and kindergartens; advocate prison reform; oppose prostitution; work for women's suffrage; and elect male prohibitionists to office—or run as candidates themselves. Though the WCTU had limited electoral success, it trained tens of thousands of women in strategies for civic engagement.

WCTU Women "Do Everything"

1. Consequences of Intemperance, 1874. *In songs, lectures, personal testimony, and illustrations like this one, prohibitionists described—sometimes luridly—the effects of alcoholism.*

Source: Library of Congress.

2. Frances E. Willard, *Hints and Helps in Our Temperance Work*, 1875. Hints and Helps *was one of Willard's first guidebooks for WCTU members.*

An attempt has here been made to anticipate questions that arise in the minds of Christian women who are willing to labor in the temperance cause, but not informed concerning plans of organization or methods of work. . . .

Write to your state secretary for a list of the best speakers available to you.

Observe the 23rd of December, the anniversary of the [1873 Ohio] crusade, by special exercises, in which men, women, and children all participate.

Get correct statistics of intemperance in *your own town*, and have them kept before the people. These will tell more than imported figures. Interest the press in your work. Wherever practicable, edit a column in the local newspaper. . . .

Whatever you neglect, keep up your *prayer-meeting*, and so far as possible get men and women in the bondage of strong drink to come there and sign the pledge and seek "the Lord behind the pledge." But while you are thus caring for the sick and wounded, do not forget that, after all, your most effective work is *drilling the juvenile troops*, and carrying your peaceful war right into the ranks of the men who vote. . . .

So far as possible, enlist *the pastors and the churches*. Seek to influence each church to become practically *a Temperance Society*. . . .

Write in a blank-book this agreement: "We, the undersigned, believing it to be for the greatest numbers' greatest good, agree to pay our employees on Monday (or the first of the week) instead of on Saturday night, from this time henceforth." Get all the business men to sign it. . . .

Seek to multiply places and sources of rational recreation for the young. If possible, induce each church in the town to fit up one of its apartments as a reading-room and place for social gatherings. . . .

Homes for Inebriates — both men and women — should be established in our cities, and the Women's Unions can do much to aid in this enterprise, by soliciting aid from the state and municipal governments and from the public. . . .

Drinking fountains for "man and beast" ought to be erected by our Unions in every city, town, and village. . . .

During the session of the legislature the Woman's State Union should plan for a convention or a series of mass-meetings at the capital. . . .

3. **Frances Willard on "Home Protection," 1879.** *Early in her career Willard took on the controversial issue of women's suffrage. By the late 1880s, most state WCTUs in the Northeast, Midwest, and West took up suffrage advocacy.*

"Home Protection" is the general name given to a movement already endorsed by the W.C.T. Unions of eight states, the object of which is to secure for all women above the age of twenty-one years the ballot as one means for the protection of their homes from the devastation caused by the legalized traffic in strong drink. . . .

We want [the] ballot because the liquor traffic is entrenched in law, and law grows out of the will of majorities. . . . As steam can be applied to locomotion only through an engine, and as electricity can be utilized only through a battery, so, in a Republic, we can condense the opinion of this majority of women into law only through the magical little paper which falls

As snowflakes fall upon the sod;

But executes a freeman's will

As lightnings do the will of God.

4. **Frances E. W. Harper, "The Woman's Christian Temperance Union and the Colored Woman," 1888.** *Writer and activist Frances E. W. Harper became one of the most prominent African American leaders in the WCTU. As Harper notes, black women worked largely in separate unions, sometimes by choice, but more often because white women insisted on maintaining all-white unions.*

Victor Hugo has spoken of the nineteenth century as being woman's era, and among the most noticeable epochs of this era is the uprising of women against the twin evils of slavery and intemperance. . . . In the great anti-slavery conflict women had borne a part, but after the storm cloud of battle had rolled away, it was found that an enemy, old and strong and deceptive, was warring against the best interests of society; not simply an enemy to one race, but an enemy to all races. . . . To dislodge this enemy, to put prohibition not simply on the statute book, but in the heart and conscience of a nation, embracing within itself such heterogeneous classes, is no child's play. . . .

One of the pleasantest remembrances of my connection with the Woman's Christian Temperance Union was the kind and hospitable reception I met in the Missouri State Convention, [whose] President, Mrs. Hoffman, . . . declared that the color-line was eliminated. A Superintendent was chosen at that meeting for colored work in the State. . . . Our work is divided into about forty departments, [including] departments for parlor meetings, juvenile and evangelistic work. . . . The Union held meetings in Methodist and Baptist churches, and opened in the African Methodist Episcopal Church an industrial school for children. . . . Some of the Unions . . . took the initiative for founding an orphan asylum for colored children. . . .

In the farther South separate State Unions have been formed. Southern white women, it may be, fail to make in their minds the discrimination between social equality and Christian affiliation. . . . Whether or not the members of the farther South will subordinate the spirit of caste to the spirit of Christ, time will show. . . .

5. **Frances Willard on her bicycle in Evanston, Illinois, 1893.** *Willard was in her fifties and in failing health when the United States was swept up in a bicycle craze, but she nonetheless undertook to show worried parents that bike riding was safe and fun for women and girls. As she reported in* A Wheel Within a Wheel, *biking gave girls self-confidence and an independent spirit to meet the challenges of the "wider world." Here, her two stenographers help her with her bicycle, which she nicknamed Gladys.*

6. Rozette Hendrix, Minnesota's WCTU president, reports on the Union's work, 1912. *Although Frances Willard died in 1898 and newer groups such as the Anti-Saloon League captured public attention, the WCTU continued organizing until the passage of national prohibition in 1920 (Chapter 21). This report suggests the diversity of its interests and alliances.*

Years ago the women began a war against child labor and also to procure compulsory educational laws, and sentiment has been created and much done along these lines. By the revision of our own state laws children under sixteen years of age are prohibited from employment in factories . . . and children under sixteen years of age are required to be in school. . . .

There is an aroused interest along all lines of Purity, not only in work done by our own organization but by others. A National Society of Moral Hygiene to promote sex teaching has been started, and an American Vigilance Association has been formed . . . [whose] purpose is the suppression of commercialized vice. . . . We have secured in our state such laws as are necessary for the suppression of [sex] traffic except the Injunction and Abatement measure which we failed of getting last session because of lack of time, and which we hope to get at our coming legislature. . . .

During the past year another state has been added to those already giving full suffrage. . . .

[As one doctor puts it], "How absurd that women who suffer most because of intemperance should not be permitted to have anything to do with settling the question of the saloon." Women who are the home makers are the ones who are most concerned in these matters and when they have had a chance to vote, they have shown their interest. . . .

We are out to win. We are in the midst of a battle for statewide prohibition and we shall never know defeat, victory may be delayed but it will come. God lives and right will prevail. . . . Have you not caught the vision of the homes protected, children free from the evils of drink, the tears wiped from the faces of mothers, sisters, and wives. Let us . . . work and pray as we never have before, for the homes, for the boys and the girls of Minnesota.

SOURCES: (2) Frances Willard, *Hints and Helps in Our Temperance Work*, in Carolyn De Swarte Gifford and Amy R. Slagell, eds., *Let Something Good Be Said: Speeches and Writings of Frances E. Willard* (Urbana: University of Illinois Press, 2007), 12–14; (3) Frances E. Willard, *Home Protection Manual* (New York: Independent, 1879), 4–5; (4) *A.M.E. Church Review* 12 (1888): 313–316; (6) Rozette Hendrix, "President's Annual Address," *Minutes of the Thirty-Sixth Annual Meeting of the WCTU of the State of Minnesota* (Minneapolis: Thurston & Gould, 1912), in Kathryn Kish Sklar and Thomas Dublin, eds., *Women and Social Movements in the United States, 1600–2000*, accessed through Vassar College Library at library.vassar.edu, Jan. 3, 2017.

ANALYZING THE EVIDENCE

1. How did Willard and other prohibitionists craft their public appeals? Use evidence from the sources to explain what values and identities WCTU leaders hoped would motivate others to join.

2. In addition to outlawing the manufacture and sale of liquor, the WCTU worked for a range of other measures. What policy recommendations appear in these documents? How might antiliquor work have led women to advocate these other policies?

3. Which Americans were likely most receptive to the WCTU's message, and why? Who may have been indifferent or hostile, and why?

PUTTING IT ALL TOGETHER

Using evidence from these sources and your knowledge of the period, write an essay responding to Frances Harper's comment, drawn from Victor Hugo, that the late nineteenth century was "women's era." What roles did the WCTU play in women's activism and women's rights?

Willard wrote that "perhaps the most significant outcome" of the movement was women's "knowledge of their own power."

Women, Race, and Patriotism As in temperance work, women played central roles in patriotic movements and African American community activism. Members of the Daughters of the American Revolution (DAR), founded in 1890, celebrated the memory of Revolutionary War heroes. Equally influential was the United Daughters of the Confederacy (UDC), founded in 1894 to extol the South's "Lost Cause." The UDC's elite southern members shaped Americans' memory of the Civil War by constructing monuments, distributing Confederate flags, and promoting school textbooks that defended the Confederacy and condemned Reconstruction. The UDC's work helped build and maintain support for segregation and disfranchisement (see Chapter 14, Thinking Like a Historian).

African American women did not sit idle in the face of this challenge. In 1896, they created the **National Association of Colored Women**. Through its local clubs, black women arranged for the care of orphans, founded homes for the elderly, advocated temperance, and undertook public health campaigns. Such women shared with white women a determination to carry domesticity into the public sphere. Journalist Victoria Earle Matthews hailed the American home as "the foundation upon which nationality rests, the pride of the citizen, and the glory of the Republic." She and other African American women used the language of domesticity and respectability to justify their work.

One of the most radical voices was Ida B. Wells, who as a young Tennessee schoolteacher sued the Chesapeake & Ohio Railroad for denying her a seat in the ladies' car (see p. 567). In 1892, a white mob in Memphis invaded a grocery store owned by three of Wells's friends, angry that it competed with a nearby white-owned store. When the black store owners defended themselves, wounding several of their attackers, all three were lynched. Grieving their deaths, Wells left Memphis and urged other African Americans to join her in boycotting the city's white businesses. As a journalist, she launched a one-woman campaign against lynching. Wells's investigations demolished the myth that lynchers were reacting to the crime of rape; she showed that the real cause was more

National Association of Colored Women

An organization created in 1896 by African American women to provide community support. Through its local clubs, the NACW arranged for the care of orphans, founded homes for the elderly, advocated temperance, and undertook public health campaigns.

SOUTHERN HORRORS.
LYNCH LAW
IN ALL
ITS PHASES

Miss IDA B. WELLS,

Price, · · · Fifteen Cents.

THE NEW YORK AGE PRINT,
1892.

Ida B. Wells In 1887, Ida Wells (Wells-Barnett after she married in 1895) was thrown bodily from a train in Tennessee for refusing to vacate her seat in a section reserved for whites, launching her into a lifelong crusade for racial justice. Her mission was to expose the evil of lynching in the South. This image is the title page of a pamphlet she published in 1892. Schomburg Center, NYPL/Art Resource, NY.

often economic competition, a labor dispute, or a consensual relationship between a white woman and a black man. Settling in Chicago, Wells became a noted and accomplished reformer, but in an era of increasing racial injustice, few whites supported her cause.

The largest African American women's organization arose within the National Baptist Church (NBC), which by 1906 represented 2.4 million black churchgoers. Founded in 1900, the Women's Convention of the NBC funded night schools, health clinics, kindergartens, day care centers, and prison outreach programs. Adella Hunt Logan, born in Alabama, exemplified how such work could lead women to demand political rights. Educated at Atlanta University, Logan became a women's club leader, teacher, and suffrage advocate. "If white American women, with all their mutual and acquired advantage, need the ballot," she declared, "how much more do Black Americans, male and female, need the strong defense of a vote to help secure them their right to life, liberty, and the pursuit of happiness?"

Women's Rights   Though it had split into two rival organizations during Reconstruction (Chapter 14), the movement for women's suffrage reunited in 1890 in the **National American Woman Suffrage Association** (NAWSA). Soon afterward, suffragists built on earlier victories in the West, winning full ballots for women in Colorado (1893), Idaho (1896), and Utah (1896, reestablished as Utah gained statehood). Afterward, movement leaders were discouraged by a decade of state-level defeats and Congress's refusal to consider a constitutional amendment. But suffrage again picked up momentum after 1911 (Map 17.2). By 1913, most women living west of the Mississippi River had the ballot. In other localities, women could vote in municipal elections, school elections, or liquor referenda.

The rising prominence of the women's suffrage movement had an ironic result: it prompted some women — and men — to organize against it, in groups such as the National Association Opposed to Woman Suffrage (1911). Antisuffragists argued that it was expensive to add so many voters to the rolls; wives' ballots would just "double their husbands' votes" or worse, cancel them out, subjecting men to "petticoat rule." Some antisuffragists also argued that voting would undermine women's special roles as disinterested reformers: no longer above the fray, they would be plunged into the "cesspool of politics." In short, women were "better citizens without the ballot." Such arguments helped delay passage of national women's suffrage until after World War I.

By the 1910s, some women moved beyond suffrage to take a public stance for what they called **feminism** — women's full political, economic, and social equality. A famous site of sexual rebellion was New York's Greenwich Village, where radical intellectuals, including many gays and lesbians, created a vibrant community. Among other political activities, women there founded the Heterodoxy Club (1912), open to any woman who pledged not to be "orthodox in her opinions." The club brought together intellectuals, journalists, and labor organizers. Almost all supported suffrage, but they had a more ambitious view of what was needed for women's liberation. "I wanted to belong to the human race, not to a ladies' aid society," wrote one divorced journalist who joined Heterodoxy. Feminists argued that women

National American Woman Suffrage Association
Women's suffrage organization created in 1890 by the union of the National Woman Suffrage Association and the American Woman Suffrage Association. Up to national ratification of suffrage in 1920, the NAWSA played a central role in campaigning for women's right to vote.

feminism
The ideology that women should enter the public sphere not only to work on behalf of others, but also for their own equal rights and advancement. Feminists moved beyond advocacy of women's voting rights to seek greater autonomy in professional careers, property rights, and personal relationships.

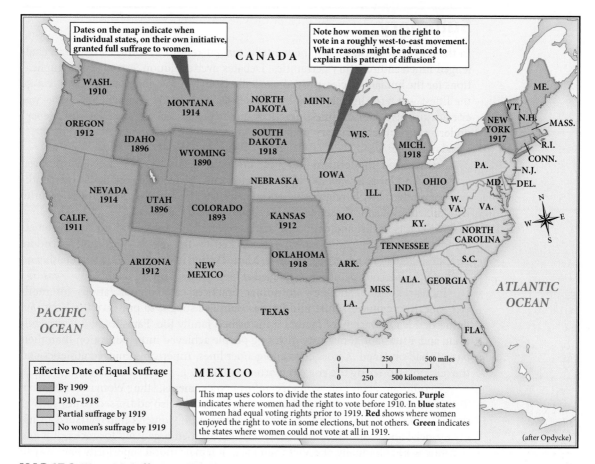

Dates on the map indicate when individual states, on their own initiative, granted full suffrage to women.

Note how women won the right to vote in a roughly west-to-east movement. What reasons might be advanced to explain this pattern of diffusion?

Effective Date of Equal Suffrage
- By 1909
- 1910–1918
- Partial suffrage by 1919
- No women's suffrage by 1919

This map uses colors to divide the states into four categories. **Purple** indicates where women had the right to vote before 1910. In **blue** states women had equal voting rights prior to 1919. **Red** shows where women enjoyed the right to vote in some elections, but not others. **Green** indicates the states where women could not vote at all in 1919.

(after Opdycke)

MAP 17.2 Women's Suffrage, 1890–1919

By 1909, after more than sixty years of agitation, only four lightly populated western states had granted women full voting rights. A number of other states offered partial suffrage, limited to voting for school boards and such issues as taxes and local referenda on whether or not to permit the sale of liquor licenses (the so-called local option). Between 1910 and 1918, as the effort shifted to the struggle for a constitutional amendment, eleven states joined the list granting full suffrage. The West remained the most progressive region in granting women's voting rights; the most stubborn resistance lay in the ex-Confederacy.

should not simply fulfill expectations of feminine self-sacrifice; they should work on their own behalf. As the United States entered the modern era, then, greater advocacy for women's rights proved to be — like new consumer spaces, literary realism, and appreciation for wilderness — another unexpected transformation wrought by industrialization.

IN YOUR OWN WORDS How did women's public activism impact American politics and society?

Summary

In the era of industrialization, new intellectual currents, including Darwinism, challenged nineteenth-century certainties. Debates over evolution, especially its implications for the human species, proved particularly intense and long-lasting. "Survival of the fittest"—a term invented not by Charles Darwin, but by Herbert Spencer — was cited to justify ruthless business practices and inequalities of wealth. Eugenic "science" underlay such discriminatory practices as forced sterilization and laws against interracial marriage.

Science and modernism did not, however, displace religion. Newly arrived Catholics and Jews, as well as old-line Protestants, adapted their faiths to the conditions of modern life. Foreign missions spread the Christian gospel around the world, with mixed results for those receiving the message.

In the arts, realist and naturalist writers rejected both romanticism and the tenets of domesticity. Many Americans were shocked by the results, including Theodore Dreiser's scandalous novel *Sister Carrie*, Mark Twain's rejection of Christian faith, and the boldly modernist paintings displayed at New York's Armory Show.

Industrialization and new consumer practices created foundations for modern American culture. While middle-class families sought to preserve the Victorian domestic ideal, a variety of factors transformed family life. Families had fewer children, and a substantial majority of young people achieved more education than their parents had obtained. Across class and gender lines, Americans enjoyed athletics and the outdoors, fostering the rise of environmentalism.

Among an array of women's reform movements, the Woman's Christian Temperance Union sought prohibition of liquor, but it also addressed issues such as domestic violence, poverty, and education. Members of women's clubs pursued a variety of social and economic reforms, while other women organized for race uplift and patriotic work. Gradually, the Victorian ideal of female moral superiority gave way to modern claims for women's equal rights.

CHAPTER 17 REVIEW

TERMS TO KNOW   *Identify and explain the significance of each term below.*

Key Concepts and Events

Social Darwinism (p. 559)	modernism (p. 564)	National Park Service (p. 573)	National Association of Colored Women (p. 583)
eugenics (p. 560)	*Plessy v. Ferguson* (p. 567)	Antiquities Act (p. 574)	
American Protective Association (p. 561)	Jim Crow (p. 568)	Comstock Act (p. 576)	National American Woman Suffrage Association (p. 584)
	Young Men's Christian Association (p. 568)	Atlanta Compromise (p. 577)	
Social Gospel (p. 563)		maternalism (p. 578)	
fundamentalism (p. 563)	Negro Leagues (p. 571)	Woman's Christian Temperance Union (p. 579)	feminism (p. 584)
realism (p. 564)	Sierra Club (p. 573)		

Key People

Billy Sunday (p. 563)

Mark Twain (Samuel Langhorne Clemens) (p. 564)

Thomas Edison (p. 566)

John Muir (p. 572)

Booker T. Washington (p. 577)

Frances Willard (p. 579)

Ida B. Wells (p. 583)

REVIEW QUESTIONS *Answer these questions to demonstrate your understanding of the chapter's main ideas.*

1. How did Charles Darwin's theory of evolution and other scientific ideas impact American culture and intellectual life in the late nineteenth century? What uses did nonscientists make of such ideas?

2. How did industrialization change Americans' ideas about appropriate leisure activities for men and women of various social classes?

3. How did women's public activism impact American politics and society?

4. On the Part 6 thematic timeline (p. 527), review developments in "Culture and Society" and "Geography and the Environment." How did industrialization change Americans' relationship to the outdoors — to natural environments? What connections do you see between those changes and other, broader shifts in American society and culture?

MAKING CONNECTIONS *Recognize the larger developments and continuities within and across chapters.*

1. This chapter explains cultural transformation as largely the result of industrialization. That's true, but it's not the whole story: the Civil War also helped bring about change. Review the material in Chapters 13 and 14, on the Civil War and its aftermath, and then write an essay in which you explain how changes in American society during the Civil War and Reconstruction laid the groundwork for cultural change in the areas of race relations, reform, science, and religious faith.

2. Consider the images in "Portrait of a Middle-Class American Family" (p. 575) and the cover of Ida B. Wells's investigative report on lynchings (p. 583). What do women's dress, hair, and deportment suggest about expectations for women at the time? In what ways do these images suggest how standards might have been changing for younger women and girls?

KEY TURNING POINTS *Refer to the chapter chronology on page 558 for help in answering the question below.*

Some historians have argued that the 1890s was a crucial turning point in American culture — a decade when "modernity arrived." Based on events in this chapter, do you agree?

18

"Civilization's Inferno": The Rise and Reform of Industrial Cities
1880–1917

CHAPTER

Clarence Darrow, a successful lawyer from Ashtabula, Ohio, felt isolated and overwhelmed when he moved to Chicago in the 1880s. "There is no place so lonely to a young man as a great city," Darrow later wrote. "When I walked along the street I scanned every face I met to see if I could not perchance discover someone from Ohio." Instead, he saw a "sea of human units, each intent upon hurrying by." At one point, Darrow felt near despair. "If it had been possible I would have gone back to Ohio," he wrote, "but I didn't want to borrow the money, and I dreaded to confess defeat." Yet Darrow stayed in Chicago and eventually prospered, becoming one of the nation's most famous defense attorneys.

In the era of industrialization, more and more Americans had experiences like Darrow's. In 1860, the United States was rural: less than 20 percent of Americans lived in an urban area, defined by census-takers as a place with more than 2,500 inhabitants. By 1910, more Americans lived in cities (42.1 million) than had lived in the entire nation on the eve of the Civil War (31.4 million). The country now had three of the world's ten largest cities (America in Global Context). Though the Northeast remained by far the most urbanized region, the industrial Midwest was catching up. Seattle, San Francisco, and soon Los Angeles became hubs on the Pacific coast. Even the South boasted of thriving Atlanta and Birmingham. As journalist Frederic C. Howe declared in 1905, "Man has entered on an urban age." (See America in Global Context.)

The scale of industrial cities encouraged experiments that ranged from the amusement park to the art museum, the skyscraper to the subway. Yet the city's complexity also posed problems, some of them far worse than Clarence Darrow's loneliness. Brothels flourished, as did slums, pollution, disease, and corrupt political machines. Fast-talking hucksters enjoyed prime opportunities to fleece new-comers; homeless men slept in the shadows of the mansions of the superrich. One African American observer called the city "Civilization's Inferno." The locus of urgent problems, industrial cities became important sites of political innovation and reform.

IDENTIFY THE BIG IDEA

How did the rise of big cities shape American society and politics?

George Bellows, *New York* George Bellows, a member of the so-called Ash Can school of painters, was fascinated by urban life. In this 1911 painting, he depicts Madison Square during a winter rush-hour, crowded with streetcars, horse-drawn wagons, and pedestrians. If you could enter the world of this painting, what might you hear, feel, and smell as well as see? What does Bellows suggest about the excitement and challenges of life in the big city? Collection of Mr. and Mrs. Paul Mellon, National Gallery of Art.

CHAPTER CHRONOLOGY

As you read, ask yourself why this chapter begins and ends with these dates and identify the links among related events.

1871 ▶ First elevated railroad begins operation in New York	**1897** ▶ First subway line opened in Boston
1878 ▶ Yellow fever epidemic in Memphis, Tennessee	**1899** ▶ Central Labor Union protests in Cleveland ▶ National Consumers' League founded
1883 ▶ Metropolitan Opera opens in New York	**1901** ▶ New York passes Tenement House Law
1885 ▶ First skyscraper completed in Chicago	**1903** ▶ Women's Trade Union League founded
1887 ▶ First electric trolley system built in Richmond, Virginia	**1906** ▶ Upton Sinclair publishes *The Jungle* ▶ Food and Drug Administration established ▶ Atlanta race riot
1889 ▶ Jane Addams and Ellen Gates Starr found Hull House in Chicago	**1910** ▶ Mann Act prohibits transportation of prostitutes across state lines
1890 ▶ Jacob Riis publishes *How the Other Half Lives*	**1911** ▶ Triangle Fire at Triangle Shirtwaist Company in New York
1892 ▶ New York's Ellis Island opens	
1893 ▶ Ragtime introduced to national audiences at Chicago World's Columbian Exposition	

The New Metropolis

Mark Twain, arriving in New York in 1867, remarked, "You cannot accomplish anything in the way of business, you cannot even pay a friendly call without devoting a whole day to it. . . . [The] distances are too great." But new technologies allowed engineers and planners to reorganize urban geographies. Specialized districts began to include not only areas for finance, manufacturing, wholesaling, and warehousing but also immigrant wards, shopping districts, and business-oriented downtowns. It was an exciting and bewildering world.

The Shape of the Industrial City

Before the Civil War, cities served the needs of commerce and finance, not industry. Early manufacturing sprang up mostly in the countryside, where mill owners could draw water power from streams, find plentiful fuel and raw materials, and recruit workers from farms and villages. The nation's largest cities were seaports; urban merchants bought and sold goods for distribution into the interior or to global markets.

As industrialization developed, though, cities became sites for manufacturing as well as finance and trade. Steam engines played a central role in this change. With them, mill operators no longer had to depend on less reliable water power. Steam power also vastly increased the scale of industry. A factory employing thousands of workers could instantly create a small city such as Aliquippa, Pennsylvania, which belonged body and soul to the Jones and Laughlin Steel Company. Older commercial cities also industrialized. Warehouse districts converted to small-scale manufacturing. Port cities that served as immigrant gateways offered abundant cheap labor, an essential element in the industrial economy.

Mass Transit New technologies helped residents and visitors negotiate the industrial city. Steam-driven cable cars appeared in the 1870s. By 1887, engineer Frank Sprague designed an electric trolley system for Richmond, Virginia. Electricity from a central

AMERICA IN GLOBAL CONTEXT

The World's Biggest Cities, 1800–2000

This table lists the ten largest cities in the world, by population in millions, at the start of the nineteenth, twentieth, and twenty-first centuries.

TABLE 18.1

1800	
City	**Population**
Beijing, China	1.10 million
London, United Kingdom	0.86
Guangzhou, China	0.80
Istanbul, Turkey	0.57
Paris, France	0.55
Hangzhou, China	0.50
Edo (later Tokyo), Japan	0.49
Naples (later part of Italy)	0.43
Suzhou, China	0.39
Osaka, Japan	0.38

1900	
City	**Population**
London, United Kingdom	6.48 million
New York, United States	4.24
Paris, France	3.33
Berlin, Germany	2.42
Chicago, United States	1.72
Vienna, Austria	1.66
Tokyo, Japan	1.50
St. Petersburg, Russia	1.44
Philadelphia, United States	1.42
Manchester, United Kingdom	1.26

2000	
City	**Population**
Tokyo, Japan	34.45 million
Mexico City, Mexico	18.02
New York City/Newark, United States	17.85
São Paulo, Brazil	17.10
Mumbai (Bombay), India	16.09
Delhi, India	15.73
Shanghai, China	13.22
Calcutta, India	13.06
Buenos Aires, Argentina	11.85
Los Angeles, United States	11.81

QUESTIONS FOR ANALYSIS

1. In each year, how many of the world's ten largest cities were located in the United States? In what regions of the world were the other cities located? What does this tell us about the United States's role in the world at each of these historical moments?

2. The figures from 1900 and 2000 show, to a large degree, the effects of industrialization. What does the table suggest about its impact?

generating plant was fed to trolleys through overhead power lines, which each trolley touched with a pole mounted on its roof. Trolleys soon became the primary mode of transportation in most American cities. Congestion and frequent accidents, however, led to demands that trolley lines be moved off streets. The "el" or elevated railroad, which began operation as early as 1871 in New York City, became a safer alternative. Other urban planners built down, not up. Boston opened a short underground line in 1897; by 1904, a subway running the length of Manhattan demonstrated the full potential of high-speed underground trains.

Even before the Civil War, the spread of railroads led to growth of outlying residential districts for the well-to-do. The high cost of transportation effectively segregated these wealthy districts. In the late nineteenth century, the trend accelerated. Businessmen and professionals built homes on large, beautifully landscaped lots in outlying towns such as Riverside, Illinois, and Tuxedo Park, New York. In such places, affluent wives and children enjoyed refuge from the pollution and perceived dangers of the city.

Los Angeles entrepreneur Henry Huntington, nephew of a wealthy Southern Pacific Railroad magnate, helped foster an emerging suburban ideal as he pitched the benefits of southern California sunshine. Huntington invested his family fortune in Los Angeles real estate and transportation. Along his trolley lines, he subdivided property into lots and built rows of bungalows, planting the tidy yards with lush trees and tropical fruits. Middle-class buyers flocked to purchase Huntington's houses. One exclaimed, "I have apparently found a Paradise on Earth." Anticipating twentieth-century Americans' love for affordable single-family homes near large cities, Huntington had begun to invent southern California sprawl.

Skyscrapers By the 1880s, the invention of steel girders, durable plate glass, and passenger elevators began to revolutionize urban building methods. Architects invented the skyscraper, a building supported by its steel skeleton. Its walls bore little weight, serving instead as curtains to enclose the structure. Although expensive to build, skyscrapers allowed downtown landowners to profit from small plots of land. By investing in a skyscraper, a landlord could collect rent for ten or even twenty floors of space. Large corporations commissioned these striking designs as symbols of business prowess.

The first skyscraper was William Le Baron Jenney's ten-story Home Insurance Building (1885) in Chicago. Though unremarkable in appearance — it looked just like other downtown buildings — Jenney's steel-girder construction inspired the creativity of American architects. A **Chicago school** sprang up, dedicated to the design of buildings whose form expressed, rather than masked, their structure and function. The presiding genius of this school was architect Louis Sullivan, whose "vertical aesthetic" of set-back windows and strong columns gave skyscrapers a "proud and soaring" presence and offered plentiful natural light for workers inside. Chicago pioneered skyscraper construction, but New York, with its unrelenting demand for prime downtown space, took the lead by the late 1890s. The fifty-five-story Woolworth Building, completed in 1913, marked the beginning of Manhattan's modern skyline.

Chicago school
A school of architecture dedicated to the design of buildings whose form expressed, rather than masked, their structure and function.

The Electric City One of the most dramatic urban amenities was electric light. Gaslight, produced from coal gas, had been used for residential light since the early nineteenth century, but gas lamps were too dim to brighten streets and public spaces. In the 1870s, as generating technology became commercially viable, electricity proved far better. Electric arc lamps, installed in Wanamaker's department store in Philadelphia in 1878, astonished viewers with their brilliant illumination. Electric streetlights soon replaced gaslights on city streets.

Before it had a significant effect on industry, electricity gave the city its modern tempo. It lifted elevators, illuminated department store windows, and above all, turned night into day. Electric streetlights made residents feel safer; as one magazine put it in 1912, "A light is as good as a policeman." Nightlife became less risky and more appealing. One journalist described Broadway in 1894: "All the shop fronts are lighted, and the entrances to the theaters blaze out on the sidewalk." At the end of a long working day, city dwellers flocked to this free entertainment. Nothing, declared an observer, matched the "festive panorama" of Broadway "when the lights are on."

Newcomers and Neighborhoods

Explosive population growth made cities a world of new arrivals, including many young women and men arriving from the countryside. Traditionally, rural daughters had provided essential labor for spinning and weaving cloth, but industrialization relocated those tasks from the household to the factory. Finding themselves without a useful household role, many farm daughters sought paid employment. In an age of declining rural prosperity, many sons also left the farm and — like immigrants arriving from other countries — set aside part of their pay to help the folks at home. Explaining why she moved to Chicago, an African American woman from Louisiana declared, "A child with any respect about herself or hisself wouldn't like to see their mother and father work so hard and earn nothing. I feel it my duty to help."

America's cities also became homes for millions of overseas immigrants. Most numerous in Boston were the Irish; in Minneapolis, Swedes; in other northern cities, Germans. Arriving in a great metropolis, immigrants confronted many difficulties. One Polish man, who had lost the address of his American cousins, felt utterly alone after disembarking at New York's main immigration facility, Ellis Island, which opened in 1892. Then he heard a kindly voice in Polish, offering to help. "From sheer joy," he recalled, "tears welled up in my eyes to hear my native tongue." Such experiences suggest why immigrants stuck together, relying on relatives and friends to get oriented and find jobs. A high degree of ethnic clustering resulted, even within a single factory. At the Jones and Laughlin steelworks in Pittsburgh, for example, the carpentry shop was German, the hammer shop Polish, and the blooming mill Serbian. "My people . . . stick together," observed a son of Ukrainian immigrants. But he added, "We who are born in this country . . . feel this country is our home."

Patterns of settlement varied by ethnic group. Many Italians, recruited by *padroni*, or labor bosses, found work in northeastern and Mid-Atlantic cities. Their urban concentration was especially marked after the 1880s, as more and more laborers arrived from southern Italy. The attraction of America was obvious to one young man, who had grown up in a poor southern Italian farm family. "I had never gotten any wages of any kind before," he reported after settling with his uncle in New Jersey. "The work here was just as hard as that on the farm; but I didn't mind it much because I would receive what seemed to me like a lot." Amadeo Peter Giannini, who started off as a produce merchant in San Francisco, soon turned to banking. After the San Francisco earthquake in 1906, his Banca d'Italia was the first financial institution to reopen in the Bay area. Expanding steadily across the West, it eventually became Bank of America.

Like Giannini's bank, institutions of many kinds sprang up to serve ethnic urban communities. Throughout America, Italian speakers avidly read the newspaper *Il Progresso Italo-Americano*; Jews read the Yiddish-language *Jewish Daily Forward*, also published in New York. Bohemians gathered in singing societies, while New York Jews patronized a lively Yiddish theater. By 1903, Italians in Chicago had sixty-six **mutual aid societies**, most composed of people from a particular province or town.

mutual aid society
An urban aid society that served members of an ethnic immigrant group, usually those from a particular province or town. The societies functioned as fraternal clubs that collected dues from members in order to pay support in case of death or disability.

MAP 18.1 The Lower East Side, New York City, 1900
As this map shows, the Jewish immigrants dominating Manhattan's Lower East Side preferred to live in neighborhoods populated by those from their home regions of Eastern Europe. Their sense of a common identity made for a remarkable flowering of educational, cultural, and social institutions on the Jewish East Side. Ethnic neighborhoods became a feature of almost every American city.

These societies collected dues from members and paid support in case of death or disability on the job. Mutual benefit societies also functioned as fraternal clubs. "We are strangers in a strange country," explained one member of a Chinese *tong*, or mutual aid society, in Chicago. "We must have an organization (*tong*) to control our country fellows and develop our friendship."

Sharply defined ethnic neighborhoods such as San Francisco's Chinatown, Italian North Beach, and Jewish Hayes Valley grew up in every major city, driven by both discrimination and immigrants' desire to stick together (Map 18.1). In addition to patterns of ethnic and racial segregation, residential districts in almost all industrial cities divided along lines of economic class. Around Los Angeles's central plaza, Mexican neighborhoods diversified, incorporating Italians and Jews. Later, as the plaza became a site for business and tourism, immigrants were pushed into working-class neighborhoods like Belvedere and Boyle Heights, which sprang up to the east. Though ethnically diverse, East Los Angeles was resolutely working class; middle-class white neighborhoods grew up predominantly in West Los Angeles.

African Americans also sought urban opportunities. In 1900, almost 90 percent of American blacks still lived in the South, but increasing numbers had moved to cities such as Baton Rouge, Jacksonville, Montgomery, and Charleston, all of whose populations were more than 50 percent African American. Blacks also settled in northern cities, albeit not in the numbers that would arrive during the Great Migration of World War I. Though blacks constituted only 2 percent of New York City's population in

1910, they already numbered more than 90,000. These newcomers confronted conditions even worse than those for foreign-born immigrants. Relentlessly turned away from manufacturing jobs, most black men and women took up work in the service sector, becoming porters, laundrywomen, and domestic servants.

Blacks faced another urban danger: the so-called **race riot**, an attack by white mobs triggered by street altercations or rumors of crime. One of the most virulent episodes occurred in Atlanta, Georgia, in 1906. The violence was fueled by a nasty political campaign that generated sensational false charges of "negro crime." Roaming bands of white men attacked black Atlantans, invading middle-class black neighborhoods and in one case lynching two barbers after seizing them in their shop. The rioters killed at least twenty-four blacks and wounded more than a hundred. The disease of hatred was not limited to the South. Race riots broke out in New York City's Tenderloin district (1900); Evansville, Indiana (1903); and Springfield, Illinois (1908). By then, one journalist observed, "In every important Northern city, a distinct race-problem already exists which must, in a few years, assume serious proportions."

Whether they arrived from the South or from Europe, Latin America, or Asia, working-class city residents needed cheap housing near their jobs. They faced grim choices. As urban land values climbed, speculators tore down houses that were vacated by middle-class families moving away from the industrial core. In their place, they erected five- or six-story **tenements**, buildings that housed twenty or more families in cramped, airless apartments. Tenements fostered rampant disease and horrific infant mortality. In New York's Eleventh Ward, an average of 986 persons occupied each acre. One investigator in Philadelphia described twenty-six people living in nine rooms of a tenement. "The bathroom at the rear of the house was used as a kitchen," she reported. "One privy compartment in the yard was the sole toilet accommodation for the five families living in the house." African Americans often suffered most. A study of Albany, Syracuse, and Troy, New York, noted, "The colored people are relegated to the least healthful buildings."

Denouncing these conditions, reformers called for model tenements financed by public-spirited citizens willing to accept a limited return on their investment. When private philanthropy failed to make a dent, cities turned to housing codes. The most advanced was New York's Tenement House Law of 1901, which required interior courts, indoor toilets, and fire safeguards for new structures. The law, however, had no effect on the 44,000 tenements that already existed in Manhattan and the Bronx. Reformers were thwarted by the economic facts of urban development. Industrial workers could not afford transportation and had to live near their jobs; commercial development pushed up land values. Only high-density, cheaply built housing earned landlords a significant profit.

City Cultures

Despite their dangers and problems, industrial cities could be exciting places to live. In the nineteenth century, white middle-class Protestants had set the cultural standard; immigrants and the poor were expected to follow cues from their betters, seeking "uplift" and respectability. But in the cities, new mass-based entertainments emerged among the working classes, especially youth. These entertainments spread from the working class to the middle class — much to the distress of many middle-class parents. At the same time, cities became stimulating centers for intellectual life.

race riot
A term for an attack on African Americans by white mobs, triggered by political conflicts, street altercations, or rumors of crime. In some cases, such "riots" were not spontaneous but planned in advance by a group of leaders seeking to enforce white supremacy.

tenement
A high-density, cheap, five- or six-story housing unit designed for working-class urban populations. In the late nineteenth and early twentieth centuries, tenements became a symbol of urban immigrant poverty.

Some of the Amusements on the Pike.
Long Beach, Cal.

Amusement Park, Long Beach, California The origins of the roller coaster go back to a Switchback Railway installed at New York's Coney Island in 1884, featuring gentle dips and curves. By 1900, when the Jack Rabbit Race was constructed at Long Beach, California, the goal was to create the biggest possible thrill. Angelenos journeyed by trolley to Long Beach to take a dip in the ocean as well as to ride the new roller coaster — and the whip ride in the foreground. Private Collection/Photo © GraphicaArtis/ Bridgeman Images.

vaudeville theater
A type of professional stage show popular in the 1880s and 1890s that included singing, dancing, and comedy routines; it created a form of family entertainment for the urban masses that deeply influenced later forms, such as radio shows and television sitcoms.

Urban Amusements One enticing attraction was **vaudeville theater**, which arose in the 1880s and 1890s. Vaudeville customers could walk in anytime and watch a continuous sequence of musical acts, skits, magic shows, and other entertainment. First popular among the working class, vaudeville quickly broadened its appeal to include middle-class audiences. By the early 1900s, vaudeville faced competition from early movie theaters, or nickelodeons, which offered short films for a nickel entry fee. With distaste, one reporter described a typical movie audience as "mothers of bawling infants" and "newsboys, bootblacks, and smudgy urchins." By the 1910s, even working girls who refrained from less respectable amusements might indulge in a movie once or twice a week.

More spectacular were the great amusement parks that appeared around 1900, most famously at New York's Coney Island. These parks had their origins in world's fairs, whose paid entertainment areas had offered giant Ferris wheels and camel rides through "a street in Cairo." Entrepreneurs found that such attractions were big business. Between 1895 and 1904, they installed them at several rival amusement parks near Coney Island's popular beaches. The parks offered New Yorkers a chance to come by ferry, escape the hot city, and enjoy roller coasters, lagoon plunges, and "hootchy-kootchy" dance shows. Among the amazed observers was Cuban revolutionary José Martí, working as a journalist in the United States. "What facilities for every pleasure!" Martí wrote. "What absolute absence of any outward sadness or poverty! . . . The theater, the photographers' booth, the bathhouses!" He concluded that Coney Island epitomized America's commercial society, driven not by "love or glory" but by "a desire for gain." Similar parks grew up around the United States. By the summer of 1903, Philadelphia's Willow Grove counted three million visitors annually; so did two amusement parks outside Los Angeles.

Ragtime and City Blues Music also became a booming urban entertainment. By the 1890s, Tin Pan Alley, the nickname for New York City's song-publishing district, produced such national hit tunes as "A Bicycle Built for Two" and "My Wild Irish Rose." The most famous sold more than a million copies of sheet music, as well as audio recordings for the newly invented phonograph. To find out what would sell, publishers had musicians play at New York's working-class beer gardens and dance halls. One publishing agent, who visited "sixty joints a week" to test new songs, declared that "the best songs came from the gutter."

African American musicians brought a syncopated beat that began, by the 1890s, to work its way into mainstream hits like "A Hot Time in the Old Town Tonight." Black performers became stars in their own right with the rise of ragtime. This music, apparently named for its ragged rhythm, combined a steady beat in the bass (played with the left hand on the piano) with syncopated, off-beat rhythms in the treble (played with the right). Ragtime became wildly popular among audiences of all classes and races who heard in its infectious rhythms something exciting — a decisive break with Victorian hymns and parlor songs.

For the master of the genre, composer Scott Joplin, ragtime was serious music. Joplin, the son of former slaves, grew up along the Texas-Arkansas border and took piano lessons as a boy from a German teacher. He and other traveling performers introduced ragtime to national audiences at the Chicago World's Fair in 1893. Seeking to elevate African American music and secure a broad national audience, Joplin warned pianists, "It is never right to play 'Ragtime' fast." But his instructions were widely ignored. Young Americans embraced ragtime.

They also embraced each other, as ragtime ushered in an urban dance craze. By 1910, New York alone had more than five hundred dance halls. In Kansas City, shocked guardians of morality counted 16,500 dancers on the floor on a Saturday night; Chicago had 86,000. Some young Polish and Slovak women chose restaurant jobs rather than domestic service so they would have free time to visit dance halls "several nights a week." New dances like the Bunny Hug and Grizzly Bear were overtly sexual: they called for close body contact and plenty of hip movement. In fact, many of these dances originated in brothels. Despite widespread denunciation, dance mania quickly spread from the urban working classes to rural and middle-class youth.

By the 1910s, black music was achieving a central place in American popular culture. African American trumpet player and bandleader W. C. Handy, born in Alabama, electrified national audiences by performing music drawn from the cotton fields of the Mississippi Delta. Made famous when it reached the big city, this music became known as the **blues**. Blues music spoke of hard work and heartbreak, as in Handy's popular hit "St. Louis Blues" (1914):

> Got de St. Louis Blues jes blue as I can be,
> Dat man got a heart lak a rock cast in the sea,
> Or else he wouldn't gone so far from me.

Blues spoke to the emotional lives of young urbanites who were far from home, experiencing dislocation, loneliness, and bitter disappointment along with the thrills of city

blues
A form of American music that originated in the Deep South, especially from the black workers in the cotton fields of the Mississippi Delta.

life. Like Coney Island and other leisure activities, ragtime and blues helped forge new collective experiences in a world of strangers.

Ragtime and blues spread quickly and had a profound influence on twentieth-century American culture. By the time Handy published "St. Louis Blues," composer Irving Berlin, a Russian Jewish immigrant, was introducing altered ragtime pieces into musical theater — which eventually transferred to radio and film. Lyrics often featured sexual innuendo, as in the title of Berlin's hit song "If You Don't Want My Peaches (You'd Better Stop Shaking My Tree)." The popularity of such music marked the arrival of modern youth culture. Its enduring features included "crossover" music that originated in the black working class and a commercial music industry that brazenly appropriated African American musical styles.

New Sexual Freedoms   In the city, many young people found parental oversight weaker than it had been before. Amusement parks and dance halls helped foster the new custom of dating, which like other cultural innovations emerged first among the working class. Gradually, it became acceptable for a young man to escort a young woman out on the town for commercial entertainments rather than spending time at home under a chaperone's watchful eye. Dating opened a new world of pleasure, sexual adventure, and danger. Young women headed to dance halls alone to meet men; the term *gold digger* came into use to describe a woman who wanted a man's money more than the man himself.

But young women, not men, proved most vulnerable in the system of dating. Having less money to spend because they earned half or less of men's wages, working-class girls relied on the **"treat."** Some tried to maintain strict standards of respectability, keenly aware that their prospects for marriage depended on a virtuous reputation. Others became so-called charity girls, eager for a good time. Such young women, one investigator reported, "offer themselves to strangers, not for money, but for presents, attention and pleasure." For some women, sexual favors were a matter of practical necessity. "If I did not have a man," declared one waitress, "I could not get along on my wages." In the anonymous city, there was not always a clear line between working-class treats and casual prostitution.

Dating and casual sex were hallmarks of an urban world in which large numbers of residents were young and single. The 1900 census found that more than 20 percent of women in Detroit, Philadelphia, and Boston lived as boarders and lodgers, not in family units; the percentage topped 30 percent in St. Paul and Minneapolis. Single men also found social opportunities in the city. One historian has called the late nineteenth century the Age of the Bachelor, a time when being an unattached male lost its social stigma. With boardinghouses, restaurants, and abundant personal services, the city afforded bachelors all the comforts of home and, on top of that, an array of men's clubs, saloons, and sporting events.

Many industrial cities developed robust gay subcultures. New York's gay underground, for example, included an array of drinking and meeting places, as well as clubs and drag balls. Middle-class men, both straight and gay, frequented such venues for entertainment or to find companionship. One medical student remembered being taken to a ball at which he was startled to find five hundred gay and lesbian couples waltzing to "a good band." By the 1910s, the word *queer* had come into use as slang for *homosexual*. Though harassment was frequent and moral reformers like Anthony

"treat"
A form of heterosexual dating in which, given the male partner's higher wage level, he is expected to pay for food and entertainment, and the young woman is expected to provide sexual favors in return.

Comstock issued regular denunciations of sexual "degeneracy," arrests were few. Gay sex shows and saloons were lucrative for those who ran them (and for police, who took bribes to look the other way, just as they did for brothels). The exuberant gay urban subculture offered a dramatic challenge to Victorian ideals.

High Culture For elites, the rise of great cities offered an opportunity to build museums, libraries, and other cultural institutions that could flourish only in major metropolitan centers. Millionaires patronized the arts partly to advance themselves socially but also out of a sense of civic duty and national pride. As early as the 1870s, symphony orchestras emerged in Boston and New York. Composers and conductors soon joined Europe in new experiments. The Metropolitan Opera, founded in 1883 by wealthy businessmen, drew enthusiastic crowds to hear the innovative work of Richard Wagner. In 1907, the Met shocked audiences by presenting Richard Strauss's sexually scandalous opera *Salome*.

Art museums and natural history museums also became prominent new institutions in this era. The nation's first major art museum, the Corcoran Gallery of Art, opened in Washington, D.C., in 1869, while New York's Metropolitan Museum of Art settled into its permanent home in 1880. In the same decades, public libraries grew from modest collections into major urban institutions. The greatest library benefactor was steel magnate Andrew Carnegie, who announced in 1881 that he would build a library in any town or city that was prepared to maintain it. By 1907, Carnegie had spent more than $32.7 million to establish over a thousand libraries throughout the United States.

Urban Journalism Patrons of Carnegie's libraries could read, in addition to books, an increasing array of mass-market newspapers. Joseph Pulitzer, owner of the *St. Louis Post-Dispatch* and *New York World*, led the way in building his sales base with sensational investigations, human-interest stories, and targeted sections covering sports and high society. By the 1890s, Pulitzer faced a challenge from William Randolph Hearst (Thinking Like a Historian). The arrival of Sunday color comics featuring the "Yellow Kid" gave such publications the name **yellow journalism**, a derogatory term for mass-market newspapers. Hearst's and Pulitzer's sensational coverage was often irresponsible. In the late 1890s, for example, their papers helped whip up frenzied pressure for the United States to declare war against Spain (Chapter 20). But Hearst and Pulitzer also exposed scandals and injustices. They believed their papers should challenge the powerful by speaking to and for ordinary Americans.

Along with Hearst's and Pulitzer's stunt reporters, other urban journalists also worked to promote reform. New magazines such as *McClure's* introduced national audiences to reporters such as Ida Tarbell, who exposed the machinations of John D. Rockefeller, and David Graham Phillips, whose "Treason of the Senate," published in *Cosmopolitan* in 1906, documented the deference of U.S. senators — especially Republicans — to wealthy corporate interests. Theodore Roosevelt dismissed such writers as **muckrakers** who focused too much on the negative side of American life. The term stuck, but muckrakers' influence was profound. They inspired thousands of readers to get involved in reform movements and tackle the problems caused by industrialization.

yellow journalism
A derogatory term for newspapers that specialize in sensationalistic reporting. Yellow journalism is associated with the inflammatory reporting by the Hearst and Pulitzer newspapers leading up to the Spanish-American War in 1898.

muckrakers
A critical term, first applied by Theodore Roosevelt, for investigative journalists who published exposés of political scandals and industrial abuses.

IN YOUR OWN WORDS How did American cities change in the late nineteenth century?

Making Mass Media: Newspaper Empires

Among the businesses that served urban consumers were mass-market newspapers. Joseph Pulitzer's *New York World* led the way in the 1880s; a decade later Pulitzer had a powerful rival in the *New York Journal*, owned by William Randolph Hearst.

1. **R. F. Outcault's "The Yellow Kid" comic, *The World*, August 9, 1896.** *Pulitzer and Hearst introduced Sunday color comics, including "The Yellow Kid" (shown here on a bicycle). Working-class readers instantly recognized the "kid," slang that then referred to working-class immigrant children. The Kid, like other boys of his age, wore skirts; tenement toddlers' heads were shaved to discourage lice.*

HOGAN'S ALLEY FOLK HAVE A TROLLEY PARTY IN BROOKLYN.

SOURCE: Picture Research Consultants & Archives.

2. **Editorial, *Wheeling Register*, April 6, 1885.** *A West Virginia newspaper commented on a campaign by the New York World to complete the Statue of Liberty. Parts of the statue, donated by France, were languishing in New York City parks.*

The *New York World* is a liberty-loving journal. It has taken the responsibility of being foster mother to that much abused piece of bronze called the "BARTHOLDI statue." It begins to look as if the

World may nurse it to a successful termination by raising funds enough through public contributions to complete the pedestal upon which it is to stand. Success to the enterprise.

3. **"HOMELESS, HOPELESS! Nellie Bly in a Night Haunt of the City's Wretchedest of Women," *New York World*, February 9, 1896.** *Pulitzer and Hearst hired many "stunt reporters." The most famous was Elizabeth Jane Cochrane, who took her pen name, Nellie Bly, from a popular song. In 1892, sponsored by the World, Bly beat the record in Jules Verne's famous novel* Around the World in Eighty Days, *circumnavigating the world in seventy-two days. She filed many investigative pieces such as this one.*

An old woman stood with her back against the side of a building. Over her head was a ragged shawl that had once been red. Around her knees hung a limp and shapeless calico skirt. The rain and sleet were falling steadily and lay thick and slushy upon the streets.

I shivered as I stopped to watch. . . . If the old woman felt the cold she gave no sign. She stood motionless, peeping around the corner. Her eyes were fixed upon the door of the Oak Street Station-House.

Just then three small boys, unmindful of the weather, came trudging down the street . . . industriously gathering every white spot that showed upon the pavement to add to the black snowballs they held in their wet red hands.

Turning the corner suddenly they came upon the old woman. For a second they paused and looked at her and she glared at them. It reminded me of the way dogs behave when they turn a corner and espy a cat. . . . The old woman started on a frantic hobble across the street, the boys after her. Their black snowballs landed squarely and soakingly against her bent back. . . . The old woman shouted things as she ran, things that do not sound well and are never by any chance reproduced in print, but they seemed to increase the delight of the fiendish boys. . . . As fast as she could hobble she made for the station-house and the boys pursued her, pelting her.

4. **Lewis Wickes Hine, newsboys selling at a Hartford, Connecticut saloon, 9:30 P.M., March 1909.** *In addition to subscriptions and sales at newsstands, newspapers sold bundles of one hundred papers to boys and girls, who resold as many as they could. Photographer Lewis Hine's caption, included below, suggests one strategy for selling papers. Hine, working for the National Child Labor Committee, took many such images.*

A common case of "team work." The smaller boy . . . goes into one of the saloons and sells his "last" papers. Then comes out and his brother gives him more. Joseph said, "Drunks are me best customers. . . . Dey buy me out so I kin go home." He sells every afternoon and night. Extra late Saturday. At it again at 6 A.M.

Source: Library of Congress.

5. **Newsboys strike coverage, *New York Herald-Tribune*, July 25, 1899.** *As sales plummeted after the War of 1898, Pulitzer and other newspaper titans raised the cost of a newspaper bundle, for children who resold them, from 50 to 60 cents. Newsboys struck. They failed to get the 50-cent price reinstated, but the* World *and other companies agreed to buy back unsold papers, which they had not done before. Kid Blink, the strike leader, was blind in one eye.*

The newsboys' strike gathered new strength last night in a monster mass meeting held at New Irving Hall. . . . "Kid" Blink, who has been made Grand Master Workman of the union, led the procession. . . . The unbiased spectator last evening

could not fail to be impressed with the resolute, manly fight the little fellows are making. . . .

SPEECH OF "KID" BLINK

. . . Dis is de time when we'se got to stick togedder like glue! But der's one ting I want ter say before I goes any furder. I don't believe in gettin' no feller's papers frum him and tearin' 'em up. I know I done it. (Cries of "You bet you did!") But I'm sorry fer it. No! der ain't nuttin in dat. We know wot we wants and we'll git it. . . . Dem 10 cents is as good ter us as to de million-aires — maybe better. . . . We'll strike and restrike till we get it. . . . We'll stick togedder like plaster, won't we, boys?

The boys answered that they would.

6. **Circulation statistics for the *New York World* from *N. W. Ayer and Son's American Newspaper Annual and Directory*, 1910.**

Edition	Political affiliation	No. of Pages	Circulation
Morning	Democratic	16	361,412
Evening	Independent	12–16	410,259
Sunday	Democratic	56–72	459,663

Sources: (2) *Wheeling Register*, April 6, 1885; (3) *New York World*, February 9, 1896; (5) *New York Herald-Tribune*, July 25, 1899; (6) *N. W. Ayer and Son's American Newspaper Annual and Directory* (Philadelphia: N. W. Ayer and Son, 1910), 623.

ANALYZING THE EVIDENCE

1. Based on these sources, why do you think "yellow journalism" was popular and profitable? What audiences did it serve, and how?

2. Consider the tone and point of view of sources 1, 3, and 5. What do they suggest about American attitudes toward the urban poor?

3. What do these sources say about how Pulitzer and Hearst viewed their role as publishers? How might we compare their newspaper empires to other corporations of the industrial era (Chapter 16)?

PUTTING IT ALL TOGETHER

Write a brief essay in which you explain the ways in which the rise of mass-market newspapers might have contributed to and helped to publicize calls for progressive reform.

Governing the Great City

One of the most famous muckrakers was Lincoln Steffens, whose book *The Shame of the Cities* (1904), first published serially in *McClure's* magazine, denounced the corruption afflicting America's urban governments. Steffens used dramatic language to expose "swindling" politicians. He claimed, for example, that the mayor of Minneapolis had turned his city over to "outlaws." In St. Louis, "bribery was a joke," while Pittsburgh's Democratic Party operated a private company that handled most of the city's street-paving projects — at a hefty profit. Historians now believe that Steffens and other middle-class crusaders took a rather extreme view of urban politics; the reality was more complex. But charges of corruption could hardly be denied. As industrial cities grew with breathtaking speed, they posed a serious problem of governance.

Urban Machines

In the United States, cities relied largely on private developers to build streetcar lines and provide urgently needed water, gas, and electricity. This preference for business solutions gave birth to what one urban historian calls the "private city" — an urban environment shaped by individuals and profit-seeking businesses. Private enterprise, Americans believed, spurred great innovations — trolley cars, electric lighting, skyscrapers — and drove urban real estate development. Investment opportunities looked so tempting, in fact, that new cities sprang up almost overnight from the ruins of a catastrophic Chicago fire in 1871 and a major San Francisco earthquake in 1906. Real estate interests were often instrumental in encouraging streetcar lines to build outward from the central districts.

political machines
Complex, hierarchical party organizations such as New York's Tammany Hall, whose candidates remained in office on the strength of their political organization and their personal relationship with voters, especially working-class immigrants who had little alternative access to political power.

When contractors sought city business, or saloonkeepers needed licenses, they turned to **political machines**: local party bureaucracies that kept an unshakable grip on both elected and appointed public offices. A machine like New York's infamous Tammany Society — known by the name of its meeting place, Tammany Hall — consisted of layers of political functionaries. At the bottom were precinct captains who knew every city neighborhood and block; above them were ward bosses and, at the top, powerful citywide leaders, who had usually started at the bottom and worked their way up. Machines dispensed jobs and patronage, arranged for urban services, and devoted their energies to staying in office, which they did, year after year, on the strength of their political clout and popularity among urban voters.

For constituents, political machines acted as a rough-and-ready social service agency, providing jobs for the jobless or a helping hand for a bereaved family. Tammany ward boss George Washington Plunkitt, for example, reported that he arranged housing for families after their apartments burned, "fix[ing] them up until they get things runnin' again." Plunkitt was an Irishman, and so were most Tammany Hall leaders. But by the 1890s, Plunkitt's Fifteenth District was filling up with Italians and Russian Jews. On a given day (as recorded in his diary), he might attend an Italian funeral in the afternoon and a Jewish wedding in the evening. Wherever he went, he brought gifts, listened to his constituents' troubles, and offered a helping hand.

The favors dispensed by men like Plunkitt came via a system of boss control that was, as Lincoln Steffens charged, corrupt. Though rural, state, and national politics were hardly immune to such problems, cities offered flagrant opportunities for bribes and kickbacks. The level of corruption, as Plunkitt observed, was greater in cities, "accordin' to the opportunities." When politicians made contracts for city services, some of the money ended up in their pockets. In the 1860s, William Marcy Tweed, known as Boss Tweed, had made Tammany Hall a byword for corruption, until he was brought down in 1871 by flagrant overpricing of contracts for a lavish city courthouse. Thereafter, machine corruption became more surreptitious. Plunkitt declared that he had no need for outright bribes. He favored what he called "honest graft" — the profits that came to savvy insiders who knew where and when to buy land. Plunkitt made most of his money building wharves on Manhattan's waterfront.

Middle-class reformers condemned immigrants for supporting machines. But urban immigrants believed that few middle-class Americans cared about the plight of poor city folk like themselves. Machines were hardly perfect, but immigrants could rely on them for jobs, emergency aid, and the only public services they could hope to obtain. Astute commentators saw that bosses dominated city government because they provided what was needed, with no condescending moral judgments. As reformer Jane Addams put it, the ward boss was a "stalking survival of village kindness." Voters knew he was corrupt, but on election day they might say, "Ah, well, he has a big Irish heart. He is good to the widow and the fatherless," or, "he knows the poor." Addams concluded that middle-class reformers would only make headway if they set aside their prejudices, learned to "stand by and for and with the people," and did a better job of it than the machine bosses did.

Machine-style governments achieved some notable successes. They arranged (at a profit) for companies to operate streetcars, bring clean water and gaslight, and remove garbage. Nowhere in the world were there more massive public projects — aqueducts, sewage systems, bridges, and spacious parks — than in the great cities of the United States. The nature of this achievement can be grasped by comparing Chicago, Illinois, with Berlin, the capital of Germany, in 1900. At that time, Chicago's water-works pumped 500 million gallons of water a day, providing 139 gallons per resident; Berliners made do with 18 gallons each. Flush toilets, a rarity in Berlin, could be found in 60 percent of Chicago homes. Chicago lit its streets with electricity, while Berlin still relied mostly on gaslight. Chicago had twice as many parks as the German capital, and it had just completed an ambitious sanitation project that reversed the course of the Chicago River, carrying sewage into Lake Michigan, away from city residents.

These achievements were remarkable, because American municipal governments labored under severe political constraints. Judges did grant cities some authority: in 1897, for example, New York's state supreme court ruled that New York City was entirely within its rights to operate a municipally owned subway. Use of private land was also subject to whatever regulations a city might impose. But, starting with an 1868 ruling in Iowa, the American legal system largely classified the city as a "corporate entity" subject to state control. In contrast to state governments, cities had only a limited police power, which they could use, for example, to stop crime but not to pass more ambitious measures for public welfare. States, not cities, held most taxation power and received most public revenues. Machines and their private allies flourished, in part, because cities were starved for legitimate cash.

Thus money talked; powerful economic interests warped city government. Working-class residents — even those loyal to their local machines — knew that the newest electric lights and best trolley lines served affluent neighborhoods, where

To see a longer excerpt of the Jane Addams essay, along with other primary sources from this period, see *Sources for America's History*.

A Hint to Boards of Health In 1884, *Frank Leslie's Illustrated Newspaper* urged municipal and state boards of health to work harder to protect urban children. When this cartoon appeared, New Yorkers were reading shocking reports of milk dealers who diluted milk with borax and other chemicals. Note the range of health threats that the cartoonist identifies. Rutherford B. Hayes Presidential Center.

citizens had the most clout. Hilda Satt, a Polish immigrant who moved into a poor Chicago neighborhood in 1893, recalled garbage-strewn streets and filthy backyard privies. "The streets were paved with wooden blocks," she later wrote, "and after a heavy rainfall the blocks would become loose and float about in the street." She remembered that on one such occasion, local pranksters posted a sign saying, "The Mayor and the Aldermen are Invited to Swim Here." As cities expanded, the limitations of political machines became increasingly clear.

The Limits of Machine Government

The scale of urban problems became dramatically evident in the depression of the 1890s, when unemployment reached a staggering 25 percent in some cities. Homelessness and hunger were rampant; newspapers nationwide reported on cases of starvation, desperation, and suicide. To make matters worse, most cities had abolished the early-nineteenth-century system of outdoor relief, which provided public support for the indigent. Fearing the system promoted laziness among the poor, middle-class reformers had insisted on private, not public, charity. Even cities that continued to provide outdoor relief in the 1890s were overwhelmed by the magnitude of the crisis. Flooded with "tramps," police stations were forced to end the long-standing practice of allowing homeless individuals to sleep inside.

Faced with this crisis, many urban voters proved none too loyal to the machines when better alternatives arose. Cleveland, Ohio, for example, experienced eighty-three labor strikes between 1893 and 1898. Workers' frustration centered on corrupt businesses with close ties to municipal officials. The city's Central Labor Union, dissatisfied with Democrats' failure to address its concerns, worked with middle-class allies to build a thriving local branch of the People's Party (Chapter 19). Their demands for stronger government measures, especially to curb corporate power, culminated in city-wide protests in 1899 during a strike against the hated streetcar company. That year, more than eight thousand workers participated in the city's annual Labor Day parade. As they passed the mayor's reviewing stand, the bands fell silent and the unions furled their flags in a solemn protest against the mayor's failure to support their cause.

To recapture support from working-class Clevelanders, Democrats made a dramatic change in 1901, nominating Tom Johnson for mayor. Johnson, a reform-minded businessman, advocated municipal ownership of utilities and a tax system in which "monopoly and privilege" bore the main burdens. (Johnson once thanked Cleveland's city appraisers for raising taxes on his own mansion.) Johnson's comfortable victory transformed the Democrats into Cleveland's leading reform party. While the new mayor did not fulfill the whole agenda of the Central Labor Union and its allies, he became an advocate of publicly owned utilities and one of the nation's most famous and innovative reformers.

Like Johnson, other mayors began to oust machines and launch ambitious programs of reform. Some modeled their municipal governments on those of Glasgow, Scotland; Düsseldorf, Germany; and other European cities on the cutting edge of innovation. In Boston, Mayor Josiah Quincy built public baths, gyms, swimming pools, and playgrounds and provided free public concerts. Like other mayors, he battled streetcar companies to bring down fares. The scope of such projects varied. In 1912, San Francisco managed to open one small municipally owned streetcar line to compete with private companies. Milwaukee, Wisconsin, on the other hand, elected socialists who experimented with a sweeping array of measures, including publicly subsidized medical care and housing.

Republican Hazen Pingree, mayor of Detroit from 1890 to 1897, was a particularly noted reformer who worked for better streets and public transportation. During the depression, Pingree opened a network of vacant city-owned lots as community vegetable gardens. Though some people ridiculed "Pingree's Potato Patches," the gardens helped feed thousands of Detroit's working people during the harsh depression years. By 1901, a coalition of reformers who campaigned against New York's Tammany Hall began to borrow ideas from Pingree and other mayors. In the wealthier wards of New York, they promised to reduce crime and save taxpayer dollars. In working-class neighborhoods, they vowed to provide affordable housing and municipal ownership of gas and electricity. They defeated Tammany's candidates, and though they did not fulfill all of their promises, they did provide more funding for overcrowded public schools.

Reformers also experimented with new ways of organizing municipal government itself. After a devastating hurricane in 1900 killed an estimated six thousand people in Galveston, Texas, and destroyed much of the city, rebuilders adopted a commission system that became a nationwide model for efficient government. Leaders of the **National Municipal League** advised cities to elect small councils and hire professional city managers who would direct operations like a corporate executive. The league had difficulty persuading politicians to adopt its business-oriented model; it won its greatest victories in young, small cities like Phoenix, Arizona, where the professional classes held political power. Other cities chose, instead, to enhance democratic participation. As part of the Oregon System, which called for direct voting on key political questions, Portland voters participated in 129 municipal referendum votes between 1905 and 1913.

> **IN YOUR OWN WORDS** What problems did big cities pose for those who ran them, and how did political leaders try to meet those challenges?

Crucibles of Progressive Reform

The challenges posed by urban life presented rich opportunities for experimentation and reform. As happened in Cleveland with Tom Johnson's election as mayor, working-class radicals and middle-class reformers often mounted simultaneous challenges to political machines, and these combined pressures led to dramatic change. Many reformers pointed to the plight of the urban poor, especially children. Thus it is not surprising that **progressivism**, an overlapping set of movements to combat the ills of industrialization (Chapter 19), had important roots in the city. In the slums and

National Municipal League
A political reform organization that advised cities to elect small councils and hire professional city managers who would direct operations like a corporate executive.

progressivism
A loose term for the cause of political reformers — especially those from the elite and middle classes — who worked to improve the political system, fight poverty, conserve environmental resources, and increase government involvement in the economy. Giving their name to the "Progressive Era," such reformers were often prompted to act by fear that mass, radical protests by workers and farmers would spread, as well as by their desire to enhance social welfare and social justice.

tenements of the metropolis, reformers invented new forms of civic participation that shaped the course of national politics.

Fighting Dirt and Vice

As early as the 1870s and 1880s, news reporters drew attention to corrupt city governments, the abuse of power by large corporations, and threats to public health. Researcher Helen Campbell reported on tenement conditions in such exposés as *Prisoners of Poverty* (1887). Making innovative use of the invention of flash photography, Danish-born journalist Jacob Riis included photographs of tenement interiors in his famous 1890 book, *How the Other Half Lives*. Riis had a profound influence on Theodore Roosevelt when the future president served as New York City's police commissioner. Roosevelt asked Riis to lead him on tours around the tenements, to help him better understand the problems of poverty, disease, and crime.

Cleaning Up Urban Environments   One of the most urgent problems of the big city was disease. In the late nineteenth century, scientists in Europe came to understand the role of germs and bacteria. Though researchers could not yet cure epidemic diseases, they could recommend effective measures for prevention. Following up on New York City's victory against cholera in 1866 — when government officials instituted an effective quarantine and prevented large numbers of deaths — city and state officials began to champion more public health projects. With a major clean-water initiative for its industrial cities in the late nineteenth century, Massachusetts demonstrated that it could largely eliminate typhoid fever. After a horrific yellow fever epidemic in 1878 that killed perhaps 12 percent of its population, Memphis, Tennessee, invested in state-of-the-art sewage and drainage. Though the new system did not eliminate yellow fever, it unexpectedly cut death rates from typhoid and cholera, as well as infant deaths from water-borne disease. Other cities followed suit. By 1913, a nationwide survey of 198 cities found that they were spending an average of $1.28 per resident for sanitation and other health measures.

The public health movement became one of the era's most visible and influential reforms. In cities, the impact of pollution was obvious. Children played on piles of garbage, breathed toxic air, and consumed poisoned food, milk, and water. Infant mortality rates were shocking: in the early 1900s, a baby born to a Slavic woman in an American city had a 1 in 3 chance of dying in infancy. Outraged, reformers mobilized to demand safe water and better garbage collection. Hygiene reformers taught hand-washing and other techniques to fight the spread of tuberculosis.

Americans worked in other ways to make industrial cities healthier and more beautiful to live in. Many municipalities adopted smoke-abatement laws, though they had limited success with enforcement until the post–World War I adoption of natural gas, which burned cleaner than coal. Recreation also received attention. Even before the Civil War, urban planners had established sanctuaries like New York's Central Park, where city people could stroll, rest, and contemplate natural landscapes. By the turn of the twentieth century, the **"City Beautiful" movement** arose to advocate more and better urban park spaces. Though most parks still featured flower gardens and tree-lined paths, they also made room for skating rinks, tennis courts, baseball fields, and swimming pools. Many included play areas with swing sets and seesaws, promoted by the National Playground Association as a way to keep urban children safe and healthy (Interpretations).

"City Beautiful" movement
A turn-of-the-twentieth-century movement that advocated landscape beautification, playgrounds, and more and better urban parks.

Contemporary stereotypes often associate environmentalism with wild landscapes, but environmentalism had an early history in America's cities. The urban landscapes of the late nineteenth and early twentieth centuries were the focus of reformers' efforts to manage the ill effects of industrialization and overcrowding. Though progressive environmentalists responded in different ways, they shared the view that America's cities were in danger.

The evidence was all around them. The nation's industrial factories belched plumes of coal ash. The pigs and horses wandering unpaved city streets dropped manure. The waste from overcrowded tenements spilled onto city sidewalks. With an inadequate and frequently corrupt public works infrastructure, cities were easily viewed as environmental disasters. Armed with an ideal of the city, reformers embraced an environmental mission to transform America's urban spaces. But what goals of environmentalism did reformers prioritize? In the excerpts below, two historians, William H. Wilson and David Stradling, emphasize different approaches to Progressive Era urban environmentalism.

How Did Urban Progressive Reformers Approach Environmentalism?

WILLIAM H. WILSON

Source: William H. Wilson, *The City Beautiful Movement* (Baltimore: The Johns Hopkins University Press, 1989), 79–80, 86–87.

[T]hose who endorsed the City Beautiful [movement] were environmentalists. When they trumpeted the meliorative power of beauty, they were stating their belief in its capacity to shape human thought and behavior. . . . [T]he whole urban environment and the entire human experience within it were critical to the City Beautiful movement. If the city became the locus of harmony, mutual responsibility, and interdependence between classes, mediated by experts, then it would be a peaceful, productive place. . . . [A]dvocates found secular salvation for humans in their belief in a flexible, organic city. . . . City Beautiful praised flowers, shrubs, and trees for their enhancing, softening qualities in city settings . . . [and] urged grass plots, ground covers, flowers, and plant groupings . . . [and] treated naturalistic parks and parkways as precious assets.

DAVID STRADLING

Source: David Stradling, *The Nature of New York: An Environmental History of the Empire State* (Ithaca: Cornell University Press, 2010), 118–119.

Municipal health officials and city inspectors did make some advances against disease, especially through the improvement of the urban environment. They banned pigs from city streets, regulated notoriously unhealthy dairies inside city limits, and stepped up oversight of street cleaning and garbage removal. . . . [T]he Ladies Health Protective Association . . . shared a concern for the vile odors emanating from a manure handler along the East River . . . [and] the entire slaughterhouse district near . . . the tenements fouled by sickening smells and backed-up sewage. . . . [T]he association contacted business owners directly with their complaints, and . . . organized demonstrations at the offending locations, inviting the press to witness their lay inspections. . . . The women also gained considerable publicity when they brought their complaints to the Board of Health.

QUESTIONS FOR ANALYSIS

1. What different perspectives of Progressive Era environmentalism do these two historians emphasize?
2. What do these excerpts reveal about the different strategies and tactics urban environmental reformers pursued?
3. What characteristics of progressivism, as discussed in this textbook, are visible in the urban environmental movements described in these excerpts?

"FRIENDS" MEETING EMIGRANT GIRL AT THE DOCK

"The girl was met at New York by two 'friends' who took her in charge. These 'friends' were two of the most brutal of all the white slave traders who are in the traffic."
—U. S. Dist. Attorney Edwin W. Sims

Foreign girls are more helplessly at the mercy of white slave hunters than girls at home. Every year thousands of girls arriving in America from Italy, Sweden, Germany, etc., are never heard of again.

The Crusade Against "White Slavery" With the growth of large cities, prostitution was a major cause of concern in the Progressive Era. Though the number of sex workers per capita in the United States was probably declining by 1900, the presence of red light districts was obvious; thousands of young women (as well as a smaller number of young men) were exploited in the sex trade. This image appeared in *The Great War on White Slavery*, published by the American Purity Foundation in 1911. It illustrates how immigrant women could be ensnared in the sex trade by alleged "friends" who offered them work. Reformers' denunciations of "white slavery" show an overt racial bias: while antiprostitution campaigners reported on the exploitation of Asian and African American women, the victimization of white women received the greatest emphasis and most effectively grabbed the attention of prosperous, middle-class Americans. *The Great War on White Slavery*, by Clifford G. Roe, 1911. Courtesy Vassar College Special Collections.

Closing Red Light Districts Distressed by the commercialization of sex, reformers also launched a campaign against urban prostitution. They warned, in dramatic language, of the threat of white slavery, alleging (in spite of considerable evidence to the contrary) that large numbers of young white women were being kidnapped and forced into prostitution. In *The City's Perils* (1910), author Leona Prall Groetzinger wrote that young women arrived from the countryside "burning with high hope and filled with great resolve, but the remorseless city takes them, grinds them, crushes them, and at last deposits them in unknown graves."

Practical investigators found a more complex reality: women entered prostitution as a result of many factors, including low-wage jobs, economic desperation, abandonment, and often sexual and domestic abuse. Women who bore a child out of wedlock were often shunned by their families and forced into prostitution. Some working women and even housewives undertook casual prostitution to make ends meet. For decades, female reformers had tried to "rescue" such women and retrain them for more respectable employments, such as sewing. Results were, at best, mixed. Efforts to curb demand — that is, to focus on arresting and punishing men who employed prostitutes — proved unpopular with voters.

Nonetheless, with public concern mounting over "white slavery" and the payoffs machine bosses exacted from brothel keepers, many cities appointed vice commissions in the early twentieth century. A wave of brothel closings crested between 1909 and 1912, as police shut down red light districts in cities nationwide. Meanwhile, Congress passed the Mann Act (1910) to prohibit the transportation of prostitutes across state lines.

The crusade against prostitution accomplished its main goal, closing brothels, but in the long term it worsened the conditions under which many prostitutes worked. Though conditions in some brothels were horrific, sex workers who catered to wealthy clients made high wages and were relatively protected by madams, many of whom set strict rules for clients and provided medical care for their workers. In the wake of brothel closings, such women lost control of the prostitution business. Instead, almost all sex workers became "streetwalkers" or "call girls," more vulnerable to violence and often earning lower wages than they had before the antiprostitution crusade began.

The Movement for Social Settlements

Some urban reformers focused their energies on building a creative new institution, the **social settlement**. These community welfare centers investigated the plight of the urban poor, raised funds to address urgent needs, and helped neighborhood residents advocate on their own behalf. At the movement's peak in the early twentieth century, dozens of social settlements operated across the United States. The most famous, and one of the first, was **Hull House** on Chicago's West Side, founded in 1889 by Jane Addams and her companion Ellen Gates Starr. Their dilapidated mansion, flanked by saloons in a neighborhood of Italian and Eastern European immigrants, served as a spark plug for community improvement and political reform.

The idea for Hull House came partly from Toynbee Hall, a London settlement that Addams and Starr had visited while touring Europe. Social settlements also drew inspiration from U.S. urban missions of the 1870s and 1880s. Some of these, like the Hampton Institute, had aided former slaves during Reconstruction; others, like Grace Baptist in Philadelphia, arose in northern cities. To meet the needs of urban residents, missions offered employment counseling, medical clinics, day care centers, and sometimes athletic facilities in cooperation with the Young Men's Christian Association (YMCA).

Jane Addams, a daughter of the middle class, first expected Hull House to offer art classes and other cultural programs for the poor. But Addams's views quickly changed as she got to know her new neighbors and struggled to keep Hull House open during the depression of the 1890s. Addams's views were also influenced by conversations with fellow Hull House resident Florence Kelley, who had studied in Europe and returned a committed socialist. Dr. Alice Hamilton, who opened a pediatric clinic at Hull House, wrote that Addams came to see her settlement as "a bridge between the classes. . . . She always held that this bridge was as much of a help to the well-to-do as to the poor." Settlements offered idealistic young people "a place where they could live as neighbors and give as much as they could of what they had."

Addams and her colleagues believed that working-class Americans already *knew* what they needed. What they lacked were resources to fulfill those needs, as well as a political voice. These, settlement workers tried to provide. Hull House was typical in offering a bathhouse, playground, kindergarten, and day care center. Some settlements opened libraries and gymnasiums; others operated penny savings banks and cooperative kitchens where tired mothers could purchase a meal at the end of the day. (Addams humbly closed the Hull House kitchen when she found that her bland New England cooking had little appeal for Italians; her coworker, Dr. Alice Hamilton, soon investigated the health benefits of garlic.) At the Henry Street Settlement in New York, Lillian Wald organized visiting nurses to improve health in tenement wards. Addams, meanwhile, encouraged local women to inspect the neighborhood and bring back a list of dangers to health and safety. Together, they prepared a complaint to city council. The women, Addams wrote, had shown "civic enterprise and moral conviction" in carrying out the project themselves.

Social settlements took many forms. Some attached themselves to preexisting missions and African American colleges. Others were founded by energetic college graduates. Catholics ran St. Elizabeth Center in St. Louis; Jews, the Boston Hebrew Industrial School. Whatever their origins, social settlements were, in Addams's words, "an experimental effort to aid in the solution of the social and industrial problems which are engendered by the modern condition of life in a great city."

social settlement
A community welfare center that investigated the plight of the urban poor, raised funds to address urgent needs, and helped neighborhood residents advocate on their own behalf. Social settlements became a nationally recognized reform strategy during the Progressive Era.

Hull House
One of the first and most famous social settlements, founded in 1889 by Jane Addams and her companion Ellen Gates Starr in an impoverished, largely Italian immigrant neighborhood on Chicago's West Side.

Settlements served as a springboard for many other projects. Settlement workers often fought city hall to get better schools and lobbied state legislatures for new workplace safety laws. At Hull House, Hamilton investigated lead poisoning and other health threats at local factories. Her colleague Julia Lathrop investigated the plight of teenagers caught in the criminal justice system. She drafted a proposal for separate juvenile courts and persuaded Chicago to adopt it. Pressuring the city to experiment with better rehabilitation strategies for juveniles convicted of crime, Lathrop created a model for juvenile court systems across the United States.

Another example of settlements' long-term impact was the work of Margaret Sanger, a nurse who moved to New York City in 1911 and volunteered with a Lower East Side settlement. Horrified by women's suffering from constant pregnancies — and remembering her devout Catholic mother, who had died young after bearing eleven children — Sanger launched a crusade for what she called birth control. Her newspaper column, "What Every Girl Should Know," soon garnered an indictment for violating obscenity laws. The publicity that resulted helped Sanger launch a national birth control movement.

Settlements were thus a crucial proving ground for many progressive experiments, as well as for the emerging profession of social work, which transformed the provision of public welfare. Social workers rejected the older model of private Christian charity, dispensed by well-meaning middle-class volunteers to those in need. Instead, social workers defined themselves as professional caseworkers who served as advocates of social justice. Like many reformers of the era, they allied themselves with the new social sciences, such as sociology and economics, and undertook statistical surveys and other systematic methods for gathering facts. Social work proved to be an excellent opportunity for educated women who sought professional careers. By 1920, women made up 62 percent of U.S. social workers.

Cities and National Politics

Despite reform efforts, the problems wrought by industrialization continued to cause suffering in urban workplaces and environments. In 1906, journalist Upton Sinclair exposed some of the most extreme forms of labor exploitation in his novel *The Jungle*, which described appalling conditions in Chicago meatpacking plants. What caught the nation's attention was not Sinclair's account of workers' plight, but his descriptions of rotten meat and filthy packing conditions. With constituents up in arms, Congress passed the **Pure Food and Drug Act** (1906) and created the federal Food and Drug Administration to oversee compliance with the new law.

The impact of *The Jungle* showed how urban reformers could affect national politics. Even more significant was the work of Josephine Shaw Lowell, a Civil War widow from a prominent family. After years of struggling to aid poverty-stricken individuals in New York City, Lowell concluded that charity was not enough. In 1890, she helped found the New York Consumers' League to improve wages and working conditions for female store clerks. The league encouraged shoppers to patronize only stores where wages and working conditions were known to be fair. By 1899, the organization had become the **National Consumers' League** (NCL). At its head stood the outspoken and skillful Florence Kelley, a Hull House worker and former chief factory inspector of Illinois. Kelley believed that only government oversight could protect exploited workers. Under her crusading leadership, the NCL became one of the most powerful progressive organizations advocating worker protection laws.

Pure Food and Drug Act
A 1906 law regulating the conditions in the food and drug industries to ensure a safe supply of food and medicine.

National Consumers' League
Begun in New York, a national progressive organization that encouraged women, through their shopping decisions, to support fair wages and working conditions for industrial laborers.

Many labor organizations also began in a single city and then grew to national stature. One famous example was the **Women's Trade Union League**, founded in New York in 1903. Financed by wealthy women who supported its work, the league trained working-class leaders like Rose Schneiderman, who organized unions among garment workers. Although often frustrated by the patronizing attitude of elite sponsors, trade-union women joined together in the broader struggle for women's rights. When New York State held referenda on women's suffrage in 1915 and 1917, strong support came from Jewish and Italian precincts where unionized garment workers lived. Working-class voters hoped, in turn, that enfranchised women would use their ballots to help industrial workers.

Residents of industrial cities, then, sought allies in state and national politics. The need for broader action was made clear in New York City by a shocking event on March 25, 1911. On that Saturday afternoon, just before quitting time, a fire broke out at the Triangle Shirtwaist Company. The **Triangle Fire** quickly spread through the three floors the company occupied at the top of a ten-story building. Panicked workers discovered that, despite fire safety laws, employers had locked the emergency doors to prevent theft. Dozens of Triangle workers, mostly young immigrant women, were trapped in the flames. Many leaped to their deaths; the rest never reached the windows. The average age of the 146 people who died was just nineteen.

Shocked by this horrific event, New Yorkers responded with an outpouring of anger and grief that crossed ethnic, class, and religious boundaries. Many remembered that, only a year earlier, shirtwaist workers had walked off the job to protest abysmal safety and working conditions — and that the owners of Triangle, among other employers, had broken the strike. Facing demands for action, New York State appointed a factory commission that developed a remarkable program of labor reform: fifty-six laws dealing with such issues as fire hazards, unsafe machines, and wages and working hours for women and children. The chairman and vice chairman of the commission were Robert F. Wagner and Alfred E. Smith, both Tammany Hall politicians then serving in the state legislature. They established the commission, participated fully in its work, and marshaled party regulars to pass the proposals into law — all with the approval of Tammany. The labor code that resulted was the most advanced in the United States.

Tammany's response to the Triangle Fire showed that it was acknowledging its need for help. The social and economic problems of the industrial city had outgrown the power of party machines; only stronger state and national laws could bar industrial firetraps, alleviate sweatshop conditions, and improve slums. Politicians like Wagner and Smith saw that Tammany had to change or die. The fire had unforeseen further consequences. Frances Perkins, a Columbia University student who witnessed the horror of Triangle workers leaping from the windows to their deaths, decided she would devote her

Women's Trade Union League
A labor organization for women founded in New York in 1903 that brought elite, middle-class, and working-class women together as allies. The WTUL supported union organizing efforts among garment workers.

Triangle Fire
A devastating fire that quickly spread through the Triangle Shirtwaist Company in New York City on March 25, 1911, killing 146 people. In the wake of the tragedy, fifty-six state laws were passed dealing with such issues as fire hazards, unsafe machines, and wages and working hours for women and children. The fire also provided a national impetus for industrial reform.

Outrage after the Triangle Fire This graphic cartoon by John Sloan was titled "In Memoriam — The Real Triangle." It appeared in a prolabor newspaper, the *New York Call*. "How Long," asked the *Call*'s headline, "Will the Workers Permit Themselves to be Burned As Well As Enslaved in Their Shops?" Who benefitted from the rent, interest, and profit that Sloan names as causes of the fire? The Granger Collection, New York.

efforts to the cause of labor. Already active in women's reform organizations, Perkins went to Chicago, where she volunteered for several years at Hull House. In 1929, she became New York State's first commissioner of labor; four years later, during the New Deal (Chapter 22), Franklin D. Roosevelt appointed her as U.S. secretary of labor — the first woman to hold a cabinet post.

The political aftermath of the Triangle Fire demonstrated how challenges posed by industrial cities pushed politics in new directions, transforming urban government and initiating broader movements for reform. The nation's political and cultural standards had long been set by native-born, Protestant, middle-class Americans. By 1900, the people who thronged to the great cities helped build America into a global industrial power — and in the process, created an electorate that was far more ethnically, racially, and religiously diverse.

In the era of industrialization, some rural and native-born commentators warned that immigrants were "inferior breeds" who would "mongrelize" American culture. But urban political leaders defended cultural pluralism, expressing appreciation — even admiration — for immigrants, including Catholics and Jews, who sought a better life in the United States. At the same time, urban reformers worked to improve conditions of life for the diverse residents of American cities. Cities, then, and the innovative solutions proposed by urban leaders, held a central place in America's consciousness as the nation took on the task of progressive reform.

> **IN YOUR OWN WORDS** Why and how did large cities become what one commentator called "seedbeds for reform"?

Summary

After 1865, American cities grew at an unprecedented rate, and urban populations swelled with workers from rural areas and abroad. To move their burgeoning populations around, cities pioneered innovative forms of mass transit. Skyscrapers came to mark urban skylines, and new electric lighting systems encouraged nightlife. Neighborhoods divided along class and ethnic lines, with the working class inhabiting crowded, shoddily built tenements. Immigrants developed new ethnic cultures in their neighborhoods, while racism followed African American migrants from the country to the city. At the same time, new forms of popular urban culture bridged class and ethnic lines, challenging traditional sexual norms and gender roles. Popular journalism rose to prominence and helped build rising sympathy for reform.

Industrial cities confronted a variety of new political challenges. Despite notable achievements, established machine governments could not address urban problems through traditional means. Forward-looking politicians took the initiative and implemented a range of political, labor, and social reforms. Urban reformers also launched campaigns to address public health, morals, and welfare. They did so through a variety of innovative institutions, most notably social settlements, which brought affluent Americans into working-class neighborhoods to learn, cooperate, and advocate on behalf of their neighbors. Such projects began to increase Americans' acceptance of urban diversity and their confidence in government's ability to solve the problems of industrialization.

CHAPTER 18 REVIEW

TERMS TO KNOW   *Identify and explain the significance of each term below.*

Key Concepts and Events

Chicago school (p. 592)
mutual aid society (p. 593)
race riot (p. 595)
tenement (p. 595)
vaudeville theater (p. 596)
blues (p. 597)

"treat" (p. 598)
yellow journalism (p. 599)
muckrakers (p. 599)
political machines (p. 602)
National Municipal League (p. 605)

progressivism (p. 605)
"City Beautiful" movement (p. 606)
social settlement (p. 609)
Hull House (p. 609)
Pure Food and Drug Act (p. 610)

National Consumers' League (p. 610)
Women's Trade Union League (p. 611)
Triangle Fire (p. 611)

Key People

Scott Joplin (p. 597)
Tom Johnson (p. 604)

Jacob Riis (p. 606)
Jane Addams (p. 609)

Margaret Sanger (p. 610)
Upton Sinclair (p. 610)

Florence Kelley (p. 610)

REVIEW QUESTIONS   *Answer these questions to demonstrate your understanding of the chapter's main ideas.*

1. How did American cities change in the late nineteenth century?

2. What problems did big cities pose for those who ran them, and how did political leaders try to meet those challenges?

3. Why and how did large cities become what one commentator called "seedbeds for reform"?

4. Using the thematic timeline on pages 526–527, consider some of the ways in which mass migrations of people — both from other countries and from places within the United States — shaped industrial cities. How did this influence American society, culture, and national identity?

MAKING CONNECTIONS   *Recognize the larger developments and continuities within and across chapters.*

1. What broader economic changes that were occurring in the United States (Chapters 16 and 17) affected cities? How did urban dwellers' responses to these changes vary from those of farmers and other rural Americans?

2. Imagine that you have just arrived in a big American city in the early 1900s. Review the images of the amusement park (p. 596), "A Hint to Boards of

Health" (p. 604), the crusade against "white slavery," (p. 608), and Triangle Fire aftermath (p. 611). What do these images suggest about the problems and dangers you might encounter? What opportunities might appeal to you as a newcomer? On balance, do you think you want to stay, or turn around and head back home? Why? What factors shape your decision?

KEY TURNING POINTS   *Refer to the chapter chronology on page 590 for help in answering the questions below.*

Based on the chapter chronology and the chapter narrative, what tipping points can you identify when

Americans began to propose political solutions for urban industrial problems? What issues did they emphasize?

19

CHAPTER

Whose Government? Politics, Populists, and Progressives
1880–1917

"We are living in a grand and wonderful time," declared Kansas political organizer Mary E. Lease in 1891. "Men, women and children are in commotion, discussing the mighty problems of the day." This "movement among the masses," she said, was based on the words of Jesus: "Whatsoever ye would that men should do unto you, do ye even so unto them."

Between the 1880s and the 1910s, thousands of reformers like Lease confronted the problems of industrialization. Lease herself stumped not only for the People's Party, which sought more government regulation of the economy, but also for the Knights of Labor and Woman's Christian Temperance Union (WCTU), as well as for women's suffrage and public health.

Between the end of Reconstruction and the start of World War I, political reformers focused on four main goals: cleaning up politics, limiting the power of big business, reducing poverty, and promoting social justice. Historians call this period of agitation and innovation the Progressive Era. In the 1880s and 1890s, labor unions and farm groups took the lead in critiquing the industrial order and demanding change. But over time, more and more middle-class and elite Americans took up the call, earning the name *progressives*. On the whole, they proposed more limited measures than farmer-labor advocates did, but since they had more political clout, they often had greater success in winning new laws. Thus both radicals and progressives played important roles in advancing reform.

No single group defined the Progressive Era. On the contrary, reformers took opposite views on such questions as immigration, racial justice, women's rights, and imperialism. Leaders such as Theodore Roosevelt and Woodrow Wilson, initially hostile to the sweeping critiques of capitalism offered by radicals, gradually adopted bolder ideas. Dramatic political changes influenced the direction of reform. Close party competition in the 1880s gave way to Republican control between 1894 and 1910, followed by a period of Democratic leadership during Wilson's presidency (1913–1919). Progressives gave the era its name, not because they acted as a unified force, but because they engaged in diverse, energetic movements to improve America.

IDENTIFY THE BIG IDEA

How and why did Progressive Era reformers seek to address the problems of industrial America, and to what extent did they succeed?

Coxey's Army on the March, 1894 During the severe depression of the 1890s, Ohio businessman Jacob Coxey organized unemployed men for a peaceful march to the U.S. Capitol to plead for an emergency jobs program. They called themselves the Commonweal of Christ but won the nickname "Coxey's Army." Though it failed to win sympathy from Congress, the army's march on Washington — one of the nation's first — inspired similar groups to set out from many cities. Here, Coxey's group nears Washington, D.C. The man on horseback is Carl Browne, one of the group's leaders and a flamboyant publicist. As the marchers entered Washington, Coxey's seventeen-year-old daughter Mamie, dressed as the "Goddess of Peace," led the procession on a white Arabian horse. Library of Congress.

CHAPTER CHRONOLOGY

As you read, ask yourself why this chapter begins and ends with these dates and identify the links among related events.

1881 ▸ President James Garfield assassinated	**1902** ▸ Newlands Reclamation Act
1883 ▸ Pendleton Act establishes the Civil Service Commission	**1903** ▸ Elkins Act
	1904 ▸ Robert Hunter publishes *Poverty*
1890 ▸ Sherman Antitrust Act ▸ People's Party created in Kansas	**1905** ▸ Industrial Workers of the World founded ▸ Niagara Principles articulated
1893 ▸ Economic depression begins	**1906** ▸ Hepburn Act
1894 ▸ Coxey's Army marches on Washington, D.C.	**1908** ▸ *Muller v. Oregon* limits women's work hours
1895 ▸ John Pierpont Morgan arranges gold purchases to rescue U.S. Treasury	**1909** ▸ NAACP created
1896 ▸ William McKinley wins presidency	**1911** ▸ Supreme Court orders Standard Oil divided to overturn its monopoly power
1898 ▸ *Williams v. Mississippi* allows poll taxes and literacy tests for voters	**1912** ▸ Four-way election gives presidency to Woodrow Wilson
1900 ▸ William McKinley reelected	**1913** ▸ Sixteenth Amendment ▸ Seventeenth Amendment ▸ Federal Reserve Act
1901 ▸ Eugene Debs founds the Socialist Party of America ▸ McKinley assassinated; Theodore Roosevelt assumes presidency	**1914** ▸ Clayton Antitrust Act

Reform Visions, 1880–1892

In the 1880s, radical farmers' groups and the Knights of Labor provided a powerful challenge to industrialization (Chapter 16). At the same time, groups such as the WCTU (Chapter 17) and urban settlements (Chapter 18) laid the groundwork for progressivism, especially among women. Though they had different goals, these groups confronted similar dilemmas upon entering politics. Should they work through existing political parties? Create new ones? Or generate pressure from the outside? Reformers tried all these strategies.

Electoral Politics After Reconstruction

The end of Reconstruction ushered in a period of fierce partisan conflict. Republicans and Democrats traded control of the Senate three times between 1880 and 1894, and the House majority five times. Causes of this tight competition included northerners' disillusionment with Republican policies and the resurgence of southern Democrats, who regained a strong base in Congress. Dizzying population growth also changed the size and shape of the House of Representatives. In 1875, it counted 243 seats; two decades later, that had risen to 356. Between 1889 and 1896, entry of seven new western states — Montana, North and South Dakota, Washington, Idaho, Wyoming, and Utah — contributed to political instability.

Heated competition and the legacies of the Civil War drew Americans into politics. Union veterans donned their uniforms to march in Republican parades, while ex-Confederate Democrats did the same in the South. When politicians appealed to war loyalties, critics ridiculed them for "waving the bloody shirt": whipping up old animosities that ought to be set aside. For those who had fought or lost beloved family members in the conflict, however — as well as those struggling over African American rights in the South — war issues remained crucial. Many voters also had strong views on economic policies, especially Republicans' high protective tariffs. Proportionately more voters turned out in presidential elections from 1876 to 1892 than at any other time in American history.

The presidents of this era had limited room to maneuver in a period of narrow victories, when the opposing party often held one or both houses of Congress. Republicans Rutherford B. Hayes and Benjamin Harrison both won the electoral college but lost the popular vote. In 1884, Democrat Grover Cleveland won only 29,214 more votes than his opponent, James Blaine, while almost half a million voters rejected both major candidates (Map 19.1). With key states decided by razor-thin margins, both Republicans and Democrats engaged in vote buying and other forms of fraud. The fierce struggle for advantage also prompted innovations in political campaigning (Thinking Like a Historian).

Some historians have characterized this period as a *Gilded Age*, when politics was corrupt and stagnant and elections centered on "meaningless hoopla." The term *Gilded Age*, borrowed from the title of an 1873 novel cowritten by Mark Twain, suggested that America had achieved a glittery outer coating of prosperity and lofty rhetoric, but underneath suffered from moral decay. Economically, the term *Gilded Age* seems apt: as we have seen in previous chapters, a handful of men made spectacular fortunes, and their triumphs belied a rising crisis of poverty, pollution, and erosion of workers' rights. But political leaders were not

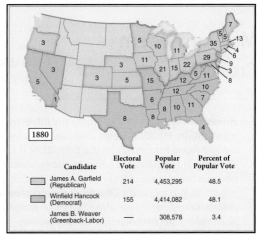

Candidate	Electoral Vote	Popular Vote	Percent of Popular Vote
James A. Garfield (Republican)	214	4,453,295	48.5
Winfield Hancock (Democrat)	155	4,414,082	48.1
James B. Weaver (Greenback-Labor)	—	308,578	3.4

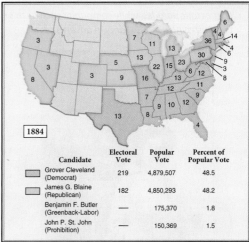

Candidate	Electoral Vote	Popular Vote	Percent of Popular Vote
Grover Cleveland (Democrat)	219	4,879,507	48.5
James G. Blaine (Republican)	182	4,850,293	48.2
Benjamin F. Butler (Greenback-Labor)	—	175,370	1.8
John P. St. John (Prohibition)	—	150,369	1.5

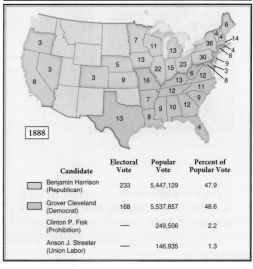

Candidate	Electoral Vote	Popular Vote	Percent of Popular Vote
Benjamin Harrison (Republican)	233	5,447,129	47.9
Grover Cleveland (Democrat)	168	5,537,857	48.6
Clinton P. Fisk (Prohibition)	—	249,506	2.2
Anson J. Streeter (Union Labor)	—	146,935	1.3

MAP 19.1 The Presidential Elections of 1880, 1884, and 1888

The anatomy of hard-fought, narrowly won presidential campaigns is evident in this trio of electoral maps. First, note the equal division of the popular vote between Republicans and Democrats. Second, note the persistent pattern of electoral votes, as states overwhelmingly went to the same party in all three elections. Here, we can identify who determined the outcomes — voters in swing states, such as New York and Indiana, whose vote shifted every four years and always in favor of the winning candidate.

Making Modern Presidents

Between 1880 and 1917, the stature and powers of the U.S. president grew in relation to those of Congress. Presidential campaign techniques also changed. The sources below shed light on candidates' increasing public visibility and new uses of campaign funds.

1. **Household sewing machine company advertisement, 1880s.** *President Grover Cleveland, a bachelor, married young Frances Folsom in a quiet White House ceremony in June 1886. The bride, a college graduate who was twenty-six years younger than her husband, proved wildly popular. The Clevelands never authorized political or commercial use of the First Lady's image. Nonetheless, over their objections, young women organized "Frankie Cleveland Clubs" to march in Democratic parades, while companies such as this one capitalized on her popularity in advertising.*

<small>SOURCE: Picture Research Consultants & Archives.</small>

2. **Account of Benjamin Harrison's front porch campaign in Indianapolis,** *New York Tribune,* **October 12, 1888.** *For much of the nineteenth century, presidential candidates left campaigning to*

their allies. A man who promoted himself risked appearing vain and greedy for office. By the 1880s, Republicans began to run "front porch campaigns": party leaders arranged for delegations to visit the candidate at home.

This morning General Harrison's home was surrounded by visitors, who had arrived in the city in the night and on the early morning trains. . . . There were many relic-hunters among the early visitors and they swarmed about the house, taking, without protest from any one, whatever they were pleased to seize. There is no longer a fence about the house to be converted into relics, and so the visitors are taking the trees now. The shrubbery has almost disappeared. . . . The informal reception began as soon as the General got up from [breakfast] and continued until afternoon. The first delegation was composed of representatives of the Cincinnati Republican Clubs. . . . A delegation from Belleville, Ill., which . . . had patiently waited for more than four hours, were next invited to enter the house, and they were accorded the usual handshaking reception. . . .

The parade early in the afternoon was the principal feature of the day's demonstration. Two hundred or more clubs participated and they came from all parts of the State, representing various classes and interests. . . . There were mounted men and men on foot, women in wagons and women in uniform marching, brass bands. . . .

On the balcony beside General Harrison stood his wife, with several of her lady friends.

3. **Henry George on money in politics,** *Wheeling Register,* **September 19, 1896.** *Reformer Henry George was among many who warned of the influence of corporate contributions, solicited brilliantly in 1896 by William McKinley's campaign manager, Mark*

Hanna. Short of funds, Democratic candidate William Jennings Bryan undertook exhausting nationwide speaking tours.

There is no question which of the great parties represents the house of Have and which the house of Want. . . . Democrat[s] are cramped for want of funds. . . . On the other hand there is practically "no end of money" at the disposal of the McKinley committees. . . .

As for the banks, the great railroad companies and insurance companies, who, even in ordinary times find it to their interest to help financially one, and frequently both, sides . . . , their purse strings are unloosed more freely than ever before, but only in one direction.

The danger to a republican form of government of a money interest in politics is so clear that it needs not to be dwelt upon. . . . The steady tendency of American legislation, national and state, has not merely been to create great special interests, but in the very effort to control them for the benefit of the public, to concern them directly in politics.

4. Theodore Roosevelt on the campaign trail, 1904.

Having watched Bryan's electrifying tours, Theodore Roosevelt became the first winning candidate to adopt the practice. In 1904, after a summer front porch campaign, he undertook a thirty-day speaking tour of the West. To cover as much ground as possible, Roosevelt often spoke from the last car of his train.

SOURCE: Library of Congress.

5. "Expenses of the Campaign," *Springfield Daily Republican*, September 22, 1900.

It is estimated that it costs $25,000,000 to elect a president of the United States. The annual allowance which the British Parliament makes to Queen Victoria is $1,925,000 . . . indicat[ing] that it is much cheaper to maintain a queen permanently than it is to elect a president. . . .

More than half of the money spent by both national and state committees goes for campaign orators. During the next three months it is estimated that the Republican national committee will have 3000 "spellbinders" traveling out of the Chicago headquarters and 2500 who will report to the New York office. . . .

The next largest item on the campaign bill is that for printing. . . . Each of the national committees will spend at least $500,000 in this way. Before the campaign is over it is estimated that both the Republican and Democratic committees will send out 100,000,000 separate documents. . . .

One more important branch of the work is the two house-to-house canvasses of the voters. . . . Hundreds of men are employed in each state, and the work of tabulating and classifying the results is by no means small. . . .

Some novel campaign methods will be adopted by both the great parties during the campaign just opening. The Republicans, it is stated, have decided to use phonographs. . . . Some eloquent party man . . . will deliver a speech before a phonographic record, from which any desired number of copies may be made . . . and sent far out into the rural districts, where it would be impossible for the more popular and important orators to go. . . .

Democrats, on the other hand, will pin their faith to stereopticons [an early slide projector].

SOURCES: (2) *New York Tribune*, October 12, 1888; (3) *Wheeling Register*, September 19, 1896; (5) *Springfield Daily Republican*, September 22, 1900.

blind to these problems, and the political scene was hardly idle or indifferent. Rather, Americans bitterly disagreed about what to do. Nonetheless, as early as the 1880s, Congress passed important new federal measures to clean up corruption and rein in corporate power. That decade deserves to be considered an early stage in the emerging Progressive Era (Interpretations).

New Initiatives One of the first reforms resulted from tragedy. On July 2, 1881, only four months after entering the White House, James Garfield was shot at a train station in Washington, D.C. ("Assassination," he had told a friend, "can no more be guarded against than death by lightning, and it is best not to worry about either.") After lingering for several agonizing months, Garfield died. Most historians now believe the assassin, Charles Guiteau, suffered from mental illness. But reformers then blamed the spoils system, arguing that Guiteau had murdered Garfield out of disappointment in the scramble for patronage, the granting of government jobs to party loyalists.

In the wake of Garfield's death, Congress passed the **Pendleton Act** (1883), establishing a nonpartisan Civil Service Commission to fill federal jobs by examination. Initially, civil service applied to only 10 percent of such jobs, but the act laid the groundwork for a sweeping transformation of public employment. By the 1910s, Congress extended the act to cover most federal positions; cities and states across the country enacted similar laws.

Civil service laws had their downside. In the race for government jobs, they tilted the balance toward middle-class applicants who could perform well on tests. "Firemen now must know equations," complained a critic, "and be up on Euclid too." But the laws put talented professionals in office and discouraged politicians from appointing unqualified party hacks. The civil service also brought stability and consistency to government, since officials did not lose their jobs every time their party lost power. In the long run, civil service laws markedly reduced corruption.

Leaders of the civil service movement included many classical liberals (Chapter 14): former Republicans who became disillusioned with Reconstruction and advocated smaller, more professionalized government. Many had opposed President Ulysses S. Grant's reelection in 1872. In 1884, they again left the Republican Party because they could not stomach its scandal-tainted candidate, James Blaine. Liberal Republicans — ridiculed by their enemies as Mugwumps (fence-sitters who had their "mugs" on one side and their "wumps" on the other) — helped elect Democrat Grover Cleveland. They believed he shared their vision of smaller government.

Pendleton Act
An 1883 law establishing a nonpartisan Civil Service Commission to fill federal jobs by examination. The Pendleton Act dealt a major blow to the "spoils system" and sought to ensure that government positions were filled by trained, professional employees.

INTERPRETATIONS

Were the "Gilded Age" and "Progressive Era" Separate Periods?

Starting in the 1920s, historians borrowed the title of *The Gilded Age*, an 1873 novel by Mark Twain and Charles Dudley Warner, to describe the late-nineteenth-century United States. "Gilded" implies a false impression of beauty: though American politics and society glittered on the outside, according to this view, they were dull or rotten underneath. Following this view, historians have described the years between 1870 and 1900 as marked by political stagnation and corruption, rampant greed and corporate ruthlessness, *laissez faire* government, and ineffective "dud presidents." Only after 1900 did a more optimistic, reform-minded "Progressive Era" begin. Some historians, including Elisabeth Israels Perry and Rebecca Edwards (one of the authors of this textbook), have identified themes that give us a different perspective on the late-nineteenth-century United States.

ELISABETH ISRAELS PERRY

SOURCE: Elisabeth Israels Perry, "Men Are from the Gilded Age, Women Are from the Progressive Era," *Journal of the Gilded Age and Progressive Era* 1, no. 1 (January 2002): 43.

"When *was* the Progressive Era exactly?" my students ask. Roughly during the first two decades of the twentieth century, I tell them. . . . Some historians still use 1900 as a starting date, although more recently 1890 has become popular. . . . From the perspective of women progressives, however, these boundaries need to be much more fluid. . . . The women who founded social settlements in the 1880s, along with the temperance and suffrage campaigners, comprise a group of American citizens active in conceptualizing progressive reform long before the presumed dawn of progressivism.

REBECCA EDWARDS

SOURCE: Rebecca Edwards, *New Spirits: Americans in the "Gilded Age," 1865–1905*, 3rd ed. (New York: Oxford University Press, 2015), 5–6.

Millions of freedmen, immigrants, students, workers, artists, intellectuals, and reformers believed that post–Civil War America offered a chance to start anew. . . . Many Americans worked energetically between 1865 and 1900 to purify politics, restrict the power of big business, and fight injustice. Those decades witnessed the first march on Washington, the first federal welfare programs, the first elections in which women and black men voted for president, and the first national park in the world. At the same time, problems that plagued the so-called Gilded Age continued and even intensified during the so-called "Progressive Era."

QUESTIONS FOR ANALYSIS

1. How does each of these historians challenge conventional interpretations of the "Gilded Age" and "Progressive Era" as separate periods?
2. Identify one key difference between these two assessments of the Gilded Age and Progressive Era.
3. Based on your reading of Chapters 14 to 19, how would you date and name the post–Civil War decades? Why?

As president, Cleveland showed that he largely did share their views. He vetoed, for example, thousands of bills providing pensions for individual Union veterans. But in 1887, responding to pressure from farmer-labor advocates in the Democratic Party who demanded action to limit corporate power, he signed the Interstate Commerce Act (Chapter 16). At the same time, municipal and state-level initiatives were showing how expanded government could help solve industrial problems. In the 1870s and early 1880s, many states created Bureaus of Labor Statistics to investigate workplace safety and unemployment. Some appointed commissions to oversee key industries, from banking to dairy farming. By later standards, such commissions were underfunded, but even when they lacked legal power, energetic commissioners could serve as public advocates, exposing unsafe practices and generating pressure for further laws.

Republican Activism In 1888, after a decade of divided government, Republicans gained control of both Congress and the White House. They pursued an ambitious agenda they believed would meet the needs of a modernizing nation. In 1890, Congress extended pensions to all Union veterans and yielded to growing public outrage over trusts by passing a law to regulate interstate corporations. Though it proved difficult to enforce and was soon weakened by the Supreme Court, the **Sherman Antitrust Act** (1890) was the first federal attempt to forbid any "combination, in the form of trust or otherwise, or conspiracy, in restraint of trade."

President Benjamin Harrison also sought to protect black voting rights in the South. Warned during his campaign that the issue was politically risky, Harrison vowed that he would not "purchase the presidency by a compact of silence upon this question." He found allies in Congress. Massachusetts representative Henry Cabot Lodge drafted the Federal Elections Bill of 1890, or **Lodge Bill**, proposing that whenever one hundred citizens in any district appealed for intervention, a bipartisan federal board could investigate and seat the rightful winner.

Despite cries of outrage from southern Democrats, who warned that it meant "Negro supremacy," the House passed the measure. But it met resistance in the Senate. Northern classical liberals, who wanted the "best men" to govern through professional expertise, thought it provided too much democracy, while machine bosses feared the threat of federal interference in the cities. Unexpectedly, many western Republicans also opposed the bill — and with the entry of ten new states since 1863, the West had gained enormous clout. Senator William Stewart of Nevada, who had southern family ties, claimed that federal oversight of elections would bring "monarchy or revolution." He and his allies killed the bill by a single vote.

The defeat was a devastating blow to those seeking to defend black voting rights. In the verdict of one furious Republican leader who supported Lodge's proposal, the episode marked the demise of the party of emancipation. "Think of it," he fumed. "Nevada, barely a respectable *county*, furnished two senators to betray the Republican Party and the rights of citizenship."

Other Republican initiatives also proved unpopular — at the polls as well as in Congress. In the Midwest, swing voters reacted against local Republican campaigns to prohibit liquor sales and end state funding for Catholic schools. Blaming high consumer prices on protective tariffs, other voters rejected Republican economic policies. In a major shift in the 1890 election, Democrats captured the House of Representatives. Two years later, by the largest margin in twenty years, voters reelected Democrat Grover Cleveland to the presidency for a nonconsecutive second term. Republican congressmen abandoned any further attempt to enforce fair elections in the South.

Sherman Antitrust Act
Landmark 1890 act that forbade anticompetitive business activities, requiring the federal government to investigate trusts and any companies operating in violation of the act.

Lodge Bill
Also known as the Federal Elections Bill of 1890, a bill proposing that whenever 100 citizens in any district appealed for intervention, a bipartisan federal board could investigate and seat the rightful winner. The defeat of the bill was a blow to those seeking to defend African American voting rights and to ensure full participation in politics.

The Populist Program

As Democrats took power in Washington, they faced rising pressure from rural voters in the South and West who had organized the Farmers' Alliance. Savvy politicians responded quickly. Iowa Democrats, for example, took up some of the farmers' demands, forestalling creation of a separate farmer-labor party in that state. But other politicians listened to Alliance pleas and did nothing. It was a response they came to regret.

Republicans utterly dominated Kansas, a state chock-full of Union veterans and railroad boosters. But politicians there treated the Kansas Farmers' Alliance with contempt. In 1890, the Kansas Alliance joined with the Knights of Labor to create a People's Party. They then stunned the nation by capturing four-fifths of the lower house of the Kansas legislature and most of the state's congressional seats. The victory electrified labor and agrarian radicals nationwide. In July 1892, delegates from these groups met at Omaha, Nebraska, and formally created the national People's Party. Nominating former Union general and Greenback-Labor leader James B. Weaver for president, the Populists, as they became known, captured a million votes in November. They returned to Washington with three representatives in the U.S. Senate and eleven in the House (Map 19.2). By 1896 they would double those totals — still only a sliver of congressional offices, but enough to make them one of the most successful insurgent parties in U.S. history.

In recognizing an "irrepressible conflict between capital and labor," Populists split from the mainstream parties, calling for stronger government to protect ordinary Americans. Their **Omaha Platform** called for public ownership of railroad and telegraph systems, protection of land from monopoly and foreign ownership, a

Omaha Platform
An 1892 statement by the Populists calling for stronger government to protect ordinary Americans.

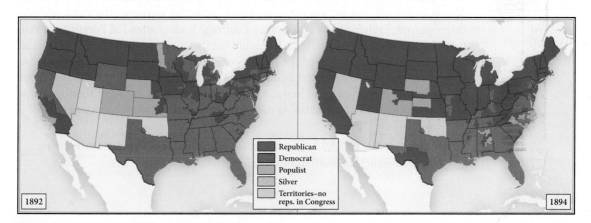

MAP 19.2 House of Representatives Elected in 1892 and 1894
Americans focus intensive effort and attention on presidential elections, but midterm congressional elections can be key turning points, as well. In response to the severe economic depression that began in 1893, American voters turned sharply away from the Democrats and toward the Republicans. That dramatic shift was first obvious not in 1896, with the election of President William McKinley, but in the midterm election that transformed Congress. These maps show the number of Democrats, Republicans, and Populists in the House of Representatives after the elections of 1892 (left) and 1894 (right). Where did Republicans make the biggest gains? How would the parties' strength in Congress have differed if Southern Populists in states such as Alabama, Arkansas, and Georgia had not been defeated through fraud?

federal income tax on the rich, and a looser monetary policy to help borrowers. Some Populist allies went further to make their point: in New Mexico, the Gorras Blancas, a vigilante group of small-scale Mexican American farmers, protested exploitative railroads and "land grabbers" by intimidating railroad workers and cutting fences on large Anglo farms.

Populist leaders represented a grassroots uprising of ordinary farmers, and some won colorful nicknames. After a devastating debate triumph, James H. Davis of Texas became known as "Cyclone." Mary E. Lease was derided as "Yellin' Mary Ellen"; her fellow Kansan Jerry Simpson was called "Sockless Jerry" after he ridiculed a wealthy opponent for wearing "fine silk hosiery," boasting that he himself wore no socks at all. The national press, based in northeastern cities, ridiculed such "hayseed politicians," but farmers insisted on being taken seriously. In the run-up to one election, a Populist writer encouraged party members to sing these lyrics to the tune of an old gospel hymn:

> I once was a tool of oppression,
>   As green as a sucker could be
> And monopolies banded together
>   To beat a poor hayseed like me. . . .
> But now I've roused up a little,
>   And their greed and corruption I see,
> And the ticket we vote next November
>   Will be made up of hayseeds like me.

Driven by farmers' votes, the People's Party had mixed success in attracting other constituencies. Its labor planks won support among Alabama steelworkers and Rocky Mountain miners, but not among many other industrial workers, who stuck with the major parties. Prohibitionist and women's suffrage leaders attended Populist conventions, hoping their issues would be taken up, but they were disappointed. The legacies of the Civil War also hampered the party. Southern Democrats warned that Populists were really Radical Republicans in disguise, while northeastern Republicans claimed the southern "Pops" were ex-Confederates plotting another round of treason. Amid these heated debates, the political system suddenly confronted an economic crisis.

> **IN YOUR OWN WORDS** How did the political goals of Populists differ from those of Democrats and Republicans?

The Political Earthquakes of the 1890s

In 1893, a severe economic depression hit the United States. Though it was a global shock, and the agriculture sector had already lagged for years, Republicans blamed Grover Cleveland, who had just reentered the White House. "On every hand can be seen evidences of Democratic times," declared one Republican. "The deserted farm, the silent factory."

Apparently receptive to such appeals, voters outside the South abandoned the Democrats in 1894 and 1896. Republicans, promising prosperity, gained control of the

White House and both chambers of Congress for the next sixteen years. This development created both opportunities and challenges for progressive reformers. A different pattern emerged in the South: Democrats deployed fraud, violence, and race-based appeals for white solidarity to defeat the Populist revolt.

Depression and Reaction

When Cleveland took the oath of office in March 1893, hard times were prompting European investors to pull money out of the United States; farm foreclosures and railroad bankruptcies signaled economic trouble. A few weeks later, a Pennsylvania railroad went bankrupt, followed by several other companies. Investors panicked; the stock market crashed. By July, major banks had drained their reserves and "suspended" withdrawals, unable to give depositors access to their money. By year's end, five hundred banks and thousands of other businesses had gone under. "Boston," one man remembered, "grew suddenly old, haggard, and thin." The unemployment rate in industrial cities soared above 20 percent.

For Americans who had lived through the terrible 1870s, conditions looked grimly familiar. Even fresher in the public mind were recent labor uprisings, including the 1886 Haymarket violence and the 1892 showdown at Homestead — followed, during the depression's first year, by a massive Pennsylvania coal strike and a Pullman railroad boycott that ended with bloody clashes between angry crowds and the U.S. Army. Prosperous Americans, fearful of Populism, were even more terrified that workers would embrace socialism or Marxism. Reminding Americans of upheavals such as the Paris Commune of 1871 and its bloody aftermath, conservative commentators of the 1890s launched America's first "Red Scare" — a precursor to similar episodes of hysteria in the 1920s and 1950s.

In the summer of 1894, a further protest jolted affluent Americans. Radical businessman Jacob Coxey of Ohio proposed that the U.S. government hire the unemployed to fix America's roads. In 1894, he organized hundreds of jobless men — nicknamed Coxey's Army — to march peacefully to Washington and appeal for the program. Though public employment of the kind Coxey proposed would become central to the New Deal in the 1930s, many Americans in the 1890s viewed Coxey as a dangerous extremist. Public alarm grew when more protesters, inspired by Coxey, started out from Los Angeles, Seattle, and other cities. As they marched east, these men found warm support and offers of aid in Populist-leaning cities and towns. In other places, police and property owners drove marchers away at gunpoint. Coxey was stunned by what happened when he reached Capitol Hill: he was jailed for trespassing on the grass. Some of his men, arrested for vagrancy, ended up in Maryland chain gangs. The rest went home hungry.

As this response suggested, President Grover Cleveland's administration was increasingly out of step with rural and working-class demands. Any president would have been hard-pressed to cope with the depression, but Cleveland was particularly inept. He steadfastly resisted pressure to loosen the money supply by expanding federal coinage to include silver as well as gold. Advocates of this **free silver** policy ("free" because, under this plan, the U.S. Mint would not charge a fee for minting silver coins) believed the policy would encourage borrowing and stimulate industry. But Cleveland clung to the gold standard. However dire things became, he believed, the money supply must remain tied to the nation's reserves of gold.

free silver
A policy of loosening the money supply by expanding federal coinage to include silver as well as gold. Advocates of the policy thought it would encourage borrowing and stimulate industry, but the defeat of Democratic presidential candidate William Jennings Bryan ended the "free silver" movement and gave Republicans power to retain the gold standard.

As the 1894 midterm elections loomed, Democratic candidates tried to distance themselves from the president. But on election day, large numbers of voters chose Republicans, who promised to support business, put down social unrest, and bring back prosperity. Western voters turned many Populists out of office. In the next congressional session, Republicans controlled the House by a margin of 245 to 105 (see Map 19.2).

Democrats and the "Solid South"

In the South, the only region where Democrats gained strength in the 1890s, the People's Party lost ground for distinctive reasons. After the end of Reconstruction, African Americans in most states had continued to vote in significant numbers. As long as Democrats competed for (and sometimes bought) black votes, the possibility remained that other parties could win them away. Populists proposed new measures to help farmers and wage earners — an appealing message for poverty-stricken people of both races. Some white Populists went out of their way to build cross-racial ties. "The accident of color can make no difference in the interest of farmers, croppers, and laborers," argued Georgia Populist Tom Watson. "You are kept apart that you may be separately fleeced of your earnings."

Such appeals threatened the foundations of southern politics. Democrats struck back, calling themselves the "white man's party" and denouncing Populists for advocating "Negro rule." From Georgia to Texas, many poor white farmers, tenants, and wage earners ignored such appeals and continued to support the Populists in large numbers. Democrats found they could put down the Populist threat only through fraud and violence. After using such tactics, Pitchfork Ben Tillman of South Carolina openly bragged that he and other southern whites had "done our level best" to block "every last" black vote. "We stuffed ballot boxes," he said in 1900. "We shot them. We are not ashamed of it." "We had to do it," a Georgia Democrat later argued. "Those damned Populists would have ruined the country."

Having suppressed the political revolt, Democrats looked for new ways to enforce white supremacy. In 1890, a constitutional convention in Mississippi had adopted a key innovation: an "understanding clause" that required would-be voters to interpret

Lynching in Texas Lynchings peaked between 1890 and 1910; while most common in the South, they occurred in almost every state, from Oregon to Minnesota to New York. After many lynchings — such as this one in the town of Center, Texas, in 1920 — crowds posed to have their pictures taken. Commercial photographers often, as in this case, produced photographic postcards to sell as souvenirs. What do we make of these gruesome rituals? Who is in the crowd, and who is not? What do we learn from the fact that this group of white men, some of whom may have been responsible for the lynching, felt comfortable having their photographs recorded with the body? The victim in this photograph, a young man named Lige Daniels, was seized from the local jail by a mob that broke down the prison door to kidnap and kill him. The inscription on the back of the postcard includes information about the killing, along with the instructions "Give this to Bud From Aunt Myrtle." Picture Research Consultants & Archives.

parts of the state constitution, with local Democratic officials deciding who met the standard. After the Populist uprising, such measures spread to other southern states. Louisiana's grandfather clause, which denied the ballot to any man whose grandfather had been unable to vote in slavery days, was struck down by the U.S. Supreme Court. But in **Williams v. Mississippi** (1898), the Court allowed poll taxes and literacy tests to stand. By 1908, every southern state had adopted such measures.

Williams v. Mississippi
An 1898 Supreme Court ruling that allowed states to impose poll taxes and literacy tests. By 1908, every southern state had adopted such measures.

The impact of disfranchisement can hardly be overstated (Map 19.3). Across the South, voter turnout plunged, from above 70 percent to 34 percent or even lower. Not only blacks but also many poor whites ceased to vote. Since Democrats faced virtually no opposition, action shifted to the "white primaries," where Democratic candidates competed for nominations. Some former Populists joined the Democrats in openly advocating white supremacy. The racial climate hardened. Segregation laws proliferated. Lynchings of African Americans increasingly occurred in broad daylight, with crowds of thousands gathered to watch.

The convict lease system, which had begun to take hold during Reconstruction, also expanded. Blacks received harsh sentences for crimes such as "vagrancy," often when they were traveling to find work or if they could not produce a current employment contract. By the 1890s, Alabama depended on convict leasing for 6 percent of its total revenue. Prisoners were overwhelmingly black: a 1908 report showed that almost 90 percent of Georgia's leased convicts were black; out of a white population of 1.4 million, only 322 were in prison. Calling attention to the torture and deaths of prisoners, as well as the damaging economic effect of their unpaid labor, reformers, labor unions, and Populists protested the situation strenuously. But "reforms" simply replaced convict leasing with the chain gang, in which prisoners worked directly for the state on roadbuilding and other projects, under equally cruel conditions. All these developments depended on a political "Solid South" in which Democrats exercised almost complete control.

The impact of the 1890s counter-revolution was dramatically illustrated in Grimes County, a cotton-growing area in east Texas where blacks comprised more than half of the population. African American voters kept the local Republican Party going after Reconstruction and regularly sent black representatives to the Texas legislature. Many local white Populists dismissed Democrats' taunts of "negro supremacy," and a

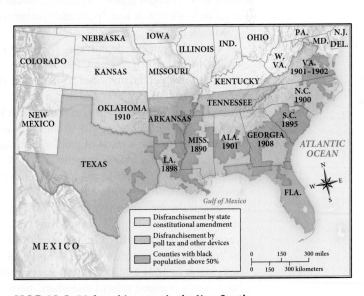

MAP 19.3 Disfranchisement in the New South
In the midst of the Populist challenge to Democratic one-party rule in the South, a movement to deprive blacks of the right to vote spread from Mississippi across the South. By 1910, every state in the region except Tennessee, Arkansas, Texas, and Florida had made constitutional changes designed to prevent blacks from voting, and these four states accomplished much the same result through poll taxes and other exclusionary methods. For the next half century, the political process in the South would be for whites only.

Populist-Republican coalition swept the county elections in 1896 and 1898. But after their 1898 defeat, Democrats in Grimes County organized a secret brotherhood and forcibly prevented blacks from voting in town elections, shooting two in cold blood. The Populist sheriff proved unable to bring the murderers to justice. Reconstituted in 1900 as the White Man's Party, Democrats carried Grimes County by an overwhelming margin. Gunmen then laid siege to the Populist sheriff's office, killed his brother and a friend, and drove the wounded sheriff out of the county. The White Man's Party ruled Grimes County for the next fifty years.

New National Realities

While their southern racial policies were abhorrent, the national Democrats simultaneously amazed the country in 1896 by embracing parts of the Populists' radical farmer-labor program. They did so in defiance of President Cleveland, whose decisions continued to alienate him from his party's agrarian and labor base. Despite the worsening economic depression, collapsing prices, and a hemorrhage of gold to Europe, the president refused to budge from his defense of the gold standard. With gold reserves dwindling in 1895, he made a secret arrangement with a syndicate of bankers led by J. P. Morgan to arrange purchases to replenish the treasury. Morgan helped maintain America's gold supply — preserving the gold standard — and turned a tidy profit by earning interest on the bonds he provided. Cleveland's deal, once discovered, enraged fellow Democrats. South Carolina governor Ben Tillman vowed to go to Washington and "poke old Grover with a pitchfork," earning the nickname "Pitchfork Ben."

In 1896, amid such outrage, Democrats rejected Cleveland and nominated a young Nebraska congressman, free silver advocate William Jennings Bryan, who passionately defended farmers and workers and attacked the gold standard. "Burn down your cities and leave our farms," Bryan declared in his famous convention speech, "and your cities will spring up again as if by magic; but destroy our farms and the grass will grow in the streets of every city in the country." He ended with a vow: "You shall not crucify mankind on a cross of gold." Cheering delegates endorsed a platform calling for free silver and a federal income tax on the wealthy that would replace tariffs as a source of revenue. Democrats, long defenders of limited government, were moving toward a more activist stance.

Populists, reeling from recent defeats, endorsed Bryan in the campaign, but their power was waning. Populist leader Tom Watson, who wanted a separate program that was more radical than Bryan's, observed that Democrats in 1896 had cast the Populists as "Jonah while they play whale." The People's Party never recovered from its electoral losses in 1894 and from Democrats' ruthless opposition in the South. By 1900, rural voters pursued reform elsewhere, particularly through the new Bryan wing of the Democratic Party.

Meanwhile, horrified Republicans denounced Bryan's platform as anarchistic. Their nominee, the Ohio congressman and tariff advocate William McKinley, chose a brilliant campaign manager, Ohio coal and shipping magnate Marcus Hanna, who orchestrated an unprecedented corporate fund-raising campaign. Under his guidance, the party backed away from moral issues such as prohibition of liquor and reached out to new immigrants. Though the popular vote was closer, McKinley won big: 271 electoral votes to Bryan's 176 (Map 19.4).

Nationwide, as in the South, the realignment of the 1890s prompted new measures to exclude voters. Influenced by classical liberals' denunciations of "unfit voters," many northern states imposed literacy tests and restrictions on immigrant voting. Leaders of both major parties, determined to prevent future Populist-style threats, made it more difficult for new parties to get candidates listed on the ballot. In the wake of such laws, voter turnout declined, and the electorate narrowed in ways that favored the native-born and wealthy.

Antidemocratic restrictions on voting helped, paradoxically, to foster certain democratic innovations. Having excluded or reduced the number of poor, African American, and immigrant voters, elite and middle-class reformers felt more comfortable increasing the power of the voters who remained. Both major parties increasingly turned to the direct primary, asking voters (in most states, registered party members) rather than party leaders to choose nominees. Another measure that enhanced democratic participation was the Seventeenth Amendment to the Constitution (1913), requiring that U.S. senators be chosen not by state legislatures, but by popular vote. Though many states had adopted the practice well before 1913, southern states had resisted, since Democrats feared that it might give more power to their political opponents. After disfranchisement, such objections faded and the measure passed. Thus disfranchisement enhanced the power of remaining voters in multiple, complicated ways.

At the same time, the Supreme Court proved hostile to many proposed reforms. In 1895, for example, it struck down a recently adopted federal income tax on the wealthy. The Court ruled that unless this tax was calculated on a per-state basis, rather than by the wealth of individuals, it could not be levied without a constitutional amendment. It took progressives nineteen years to achieve that goal.

Labor organizations also suffered in the new political regime, as federal courts invalidated many

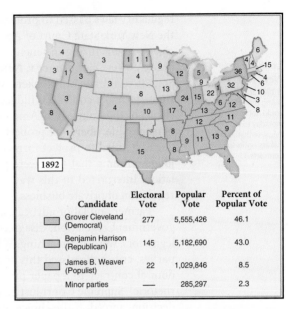

Candidate	Electoral Vote	Popular Vote	Percent of Popular Vote
Grover Cleveland (Democrat)	277	5,555,426	46.1
Benjamin Harrison (Republican)	145	5,182,690	43.0
James B. Weaver (Populist)	22	1,029,846	8.5
Minor parties	—	285,297	2.3

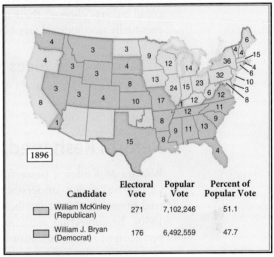

Candidate	Electoral Vote	Popular Vote	Percent of Popular Vote
William McKinley (Republican)	271	7,102,246	51.1
William J. Bryan (Democrat)	176	6,492,559	47.7

MAP 19.4 The Presidential Elections of 1892 and 1896

In the 1890s, the age of political stalemate came to an end. Compare the 1892 map with Map 19.1 (p. 617) and note especially Cleveland's breakthrough in the normally Republican states of the Upper Midwest. In 1896, the pendulum swung in the opposite direction, with McKinley's consolidation of Republican control over the Northeast and Midwest far overbalancing the Democratic advances in the thinly populated western states. The 1896 election marked the beginning of sixteen years of Republican dominance in national politics.

Lochner v. New York
A 1905 Supreme Court ruling that New York State could not limit bakers' workday to ten hours because that violated bakers' rights to make contracts.

regulatory laws passed to protect workers. As early as 1882, in the case of *In re Jacobs*, the New York State Court of Appeals struck down a public-health law that prohibited cigar manufacturing in tenements, arguing that such regulation exceeded the state's police powers. In ***Lochner v. New York*** (1905), the U.S. Supreme Court told New York State it could not limit bakers' workdays to ten hours because that violated bakers' rights to make contracts. Judges found support for such rulings in the due process clause of the Fourteenth Amendment, which prohibited states from depriving "any person of life, liberty, or property, without due process of law." Though the clause had been intended to protect former slaves, courts used it to shield contract rights, with judges arguing that they were protecting workers' freedom *from* government regulation. Interpreted in this way, the Fourteenth Amendment was a major obstacle to regulation of private business.

Farmer and labor advocates, along with urban progressives who called for more government regulation, disagreed with such rulings. They believed judges, not state legislators, were overreaching. While courts treated employers and employees as equal parties, critics dismissed this as a legal fiction. "Modern industry has reduced 'freedom of contract' to a paper privilege," declared one labor advocate, "a mere figure of rhetoric." Supreme Court justice Oliver Wendell Holmes Jr., dissenting in the *Lochner* decision, agreed. If the choice was between working and starving, he observed, how could bakers "choose" their hours of work? Holmes's view, known as legal realism, eventually won judicial favor, but only after years of progressive and labor activism.

> **IN YOUR OWN WORDS** How did the depression of the 1890s impact federal politics and policy?

Reform Reshaped, 1901–1912

William McKinley, a powerful presence in the White House, was no reformer. His victory was widely understood as a triumph for business and especially for industrial titans who had contributed heavily to his campaign. But the depression of the 1890s, by subjecting millions to severe hardship, had dramatically illustrated the problems of industrialization. At the same time, the success of McKinley's campaign managers — who spent more than $3.5 million, versus Bryan's $300,000 — raised unsettling questions about corporate power. Once the crisis of the 1890s passed, many middle-class Americans proved ready to embrace progressive ideas. The rise of such ideas was aided by historical chance, when a shocking assassination put a reformer in the White House.

Theodore Roosevelt as President

On September 14, 1901, only six months after William McKinley won his second face-off against Democrat William Jennings Bryan, the president was shot as he attended the Pan-American Exposition in Buffalo, New York. He died eight days later. The murderer, Leon Czolgosz, was influenced by anarchists who had carried out recent assassinations in Europe. Though Czolgosz was American-born, many feared that

McKinley's violent death was another warning of the threat posed by radical immi-grants. As the nation mourned its third murdered president in less than four decades, Vice President Theodore Roosevelt was sworn into office.

Roosevelt, from a prominent family, had chosen an unconventional path. After graduating from Harvard, he plunged into politics, winning a seat as a Republican New York assemblyman. Disillusioned by his party's resistance to reform, he left politics in the mid-1880s and moved to a North Dakota ranch. But his cattle herd was wiped out in the blizzards of 1887. He returned east, winning appointments as a U.S. Civil Service commissioner, head of the New York City Police Commission, and McKinley's assistant secretary of the navy. An energetic presence in all these jobs, Roosevelt gained broad knowledge of the problems America faced at the municipal, state, and federal levels.

After serving in the War of 1898 (Chapter 20), Roosevelt was elected as New York's governor. In this job, he pushed through civil service reform and a tax on corpora-tions. Seeking to neutralize this progressive and rather unpredictable political star, Republican bosses chose Roosevelt as McKinley's running mate in 1900, hoping the vice-presidency would be a political dead end. Instead, they suddenly found Roosevelt in the White House. The new president, who called for vigorous reform, represented a major shift for the Republicans.

Antitrust Legislation Roosevelt blended reform with the needs of private enter-prise, but on occasion he challenged corporations in new ways. During a bitter 1902 coal strike, for example, he threatened to nationalize the big coal companies if their owners refused to negotiate with the miners' union. The owners hastily came to the table. Roosevelt also sought better enforcement of the Interstate Commerce Act and Sherman Antitrust Act. He pushed through the Elkins Act (1903), which prohibited discriminatory railway rates that favored powerful customers. That same year, he cre-ated the Bureau of Corporations, empowered to investigate business practices and bol-ster the Justice Department's capacity to mount antitrust suits. The department had already filed such a suit against the Northern Securities Company, arguing that this combination of northwestern railroads had created a monopoly in violation of the Sherman Antitrust Act. In a landmark decision in 1904, the Supreme Court ordered Northern Securities dissolved.

That year, calling for every American to get what he called a Square Deal, Roosevelt handily defeated Democratic candidate Alton B. Parker. Now president in his own right, Roosevelt stepped up his attack on trusts. He regarded large-scale enterprise as the natural tendency of modern industry, but he hoped to identify and punish "male-factors of great wealth" who abused their power. After much wrangling in Congress, Roosevelt won a major victory with the passage of the **Hepburn Act** (1906), which strengthened the Interstate Commerce Commission, authorizing it to set shipping rates when it found evidence of railroad collusion to fix prices.

At the time Roosevelt acted, trusts had partially protected themselves with the help of two friendly states, New Jersey and Delaware, whose legislatures had loosened regu-lations and invited trusts to incorporate under their new state laws. With its Northern Securities ruling, however, the Supreme Court began to recognize federal authority to dissolve the most egregious monopolies. Roosevelt left a powerful legacy to his

Hepburn Act
A 1906 antitrust law that empowered the federal Interstate Commerce Commission to set railroad shipment rates wherever it believed that railroads were unfairly colluding to set prices.

Standard Oil decision
A 1911 Supreme Court decision that directed the breakup of the Standard Oil Company into smaller companies because its overwhelming market dominance and monopoly power violated antitrust laws.

successor, William Howard Taft. In its **Standard Oil decision** (1911), the Supreme Court agreed with Taft's Justice Department that John D. Rockefeller's massive oil monopoly should be broken up into several competing companies. After this ruling, Taft's attorney general undertook antitrust actions against other giant companies.

Environmental Conservation   Roosevelt was an ardent outdoorsman and hunter. It was after the president went bear hunting in Mississippi in 1902, in fact, that a Russian Jewish immigrant couple in New York began to sell stuffed "Teddy's bears," which became an American childhood tradition. After John Muir gave Roosevelt a tour of Yosemite Valley, the president described the transcendent experience of camping in the open air under the giant sequoias. "The majestic trunks, beautiful in color and in symmetry," he wrote, "rose round us like the pillars of a mightier cathedral than ever was conceived."

Roosevelt translated his love of nature into environmental action. By the end of his presidency, he had issued fifty-one executive orders creating wildlife refuges and signed a number of bills advocated by environmentalists. He also oversaw creation of three national parks, including Colorado's Mesa Verde, the first to "protect the works of man": American Indian archaeological sites. Also notable was his vigorous use of the Antiquities Act, through which he set aside such beautiful sites as Arizona's Grand Canyon and Washington's Mt. Olympus.

Some of Roosevelt's conservation policies, however, had a probusiness bent. He increased the amount of land held in federal forest reserves and turned their management over to the new, independent U.S. Forest Service, created in 1905. But his forestry chief, Gifford Pinchot, insisted on fire suppression to maximize logging potential. In addition, Roosevelt lent support to the **Newlands Reclamation Act** (1902), which had much in common with earlier Republican policies to promote economic development in the West. Under the act, the federal government sold public lands to raise money for irrigation projects that expanded agriculture on arid lands. The law, interestingly, fulfilled one of the demands of the unemployed men who had marched with Coxey's Army.

Newlands Reclamation Act
A 1902 law, supported by President Theodore Roosevelt, that allowed the federal government to sell public lands to raise money for irrigation projects that expanded agriculture on arid lands.

Roosevelt's Legacies   Like the environmental laws enacted during his presidency, Theodore Roosevelt was full of contradictions. An unabashed believer in what he called "Anglo-Saxon" superiority, Roosevelt nonetheless incurred the wrath of white supremacists by inviting Booker T. Washington to dine at the White House. Roosevelt called for elite "best men" to enter politics, but he also defended the dignity of labor.

In 1908, Roosevelt chose to retire, bequeathing the Republican nomination to talented administrator William Howard Taft. Taft portrayed himself as Roosevelt's man, though he maintained a closer relationship than his predecessor with probusiness Republicans in Congress. In 1908, Taft faced off against Democrat William Jennings Bryan, who, eloquent as ever, attacked Republicans as the party of "plutocrats": men who used their wealth to buy political influence. Bryan outdid Taft in urging tougher antitrust and prolabor legislation, but Taft won comfortably.

In the wake of Taft's victory, however, rising pressure for reform began to divide Republicans. Conservatives dug in, while militant progressives within the party thought Roosevelt and his successor had not gone far enough. Reconciling these conflicting forces was a daunting task. For Taft, it spelled disaster. Through various incidents, he found himself on the opposite side of progressive Republicans, who began to call themselves "Insurgents" and to plot their own path.

Diverse Progressive Goals

The revolt of Republican Insurgents signaled the strength of grassroots demands for change. No one described these emerging goals more eloquently than Jane Addams, who famously declared in *Democracy and Social Ethics* (1902), "The cure for the ills of Democracy is more Democracy." It was a poignant statement, given the sharply antidemocratic direction American politics had taken since the 1890s. What, now, should more democracy look like? Various groups of progressives — women, antipoverty reformers, African American advocates — often disagreed about priorities and goals. Some, frustrated by events in the United States, traveled abroad to study inspiring experiments in other nations, hoping to bring ideas home.

States also served as seedbeds of change. Theodore Roosevelt dubbed Wisconsin a "laboratory of democracy" under energetic Republican governor Robert La Follette (1901–1905). La Follette promoted what he called the **Wisconsin Idea** — greater government intervention in the economy, with reliance on experts, particularly progressive economists, for policy recommendations. Like Addams, La Follette combined respect for expertise with commitment to "more Democracy." He won battles to restrict lobbying and to give Wisconsin citizens the right of recall — voting to remove unpopular politicians from office — and referendum — voting directly on a proposed law, rather than leaving it in the hands of legislators. Continuing his career in the U.S. Senate, La Follette, like Roosevelt, advocated increasingly aggressive measures to protect workers and rein in corporate power.

Protecting the Poor The urban settlement movement called attention to poverty in America's industrial cities. In the emerging social sciences, experts argued that unemployment and crowded slums were not caused by laziness and ignorance, as elite Americans had long believed. Instead, as journalist Robert Hunter wrote in his landmark study, *Poverty* (1904), such problems resulted from "miserable and unjust social conditions." Charity work was at best a limited solution. "How vain to waste our energies on single cases of relief," declared one reformer, "when *society* should aim at removing the prolific sources of all the woe."

By the early twentieth century, reformers placed particular emphasis on labor conditions for women and children. The **National Child Labor Committee**, created in 1907, hired photographer Lewis Hine to record brutal conditions in mines and mills where children worked. (See one of Hine's photographs on p. 542 in Chapter 16.) Impressed by the committee's investigations, Theodore Roosevelt sponsored the first White House Conference on Dependent Children in 1909, bringing national attention to child welfare issues. In 1912, momentum from the conference resulted in creation of the Children's Bureau in the U.S. Labor Department.

Those seeking to protect working-class women scored a major triumph in 1908 with the Supreme Court's decision in *Muller v. Oregon*, which upheld an Oregon law limiting women's workday to ten hours. Given the Court's ruling three years earlier in *Lochner v. New York*, it was a stunning victory. To win the case, the National Consumers' League (Chapter 18) recruited Louis Brandeis, a son of Jewish immigrants who was

Wisconsin Idea
A policy promoted by Republican governor Robert La Follette of Wisconsin for greater government intervention in the economy, with reliance on experts, particularly progressive economists, for policy recommendations.

National Child Labor Committee
A reform organization that worked (unsuccessfully) to win a federal law banning child labor. The NCLC hired photographer Lewis Hine to record brutal conditions in mines and mills where thousands of children worked.

Muller v. Oregon
A 1908 Supreme Court case that upheld an Oregon law limiting women's workday to ten hours, based on the need to protect women's health for motherhood. *Muller* complicated the earlier decision in *Lochner v. New York*, laying out grounds on which states could intervene to protect workers. It divided women's rights activists, however, because some saw its provisions as discriminatory.

To see a longer excerpt from the Supreme Court majority opinion in *Muller v. Oregon*, along with other primary sources from this period, see **Sources for America's History**.

widely known as "the people's lawyer" for his eagerness to take on vested interests. Brandeis's legal brief in the *Muller* case devoted only two pages to the constitutional issue of state police powers. Instead, Brandeis rested his arguments on data gathered by the NCL describing the toll that long work hours took on women's health. The "Brandeis brief" cleared the way for use of social science research in court decisions. Sanctioning a more expansive role for state governments, the *Muller* decision encouraged women's organizations to lobby for further reforms. Their achievements included the first law providing public assistance for single mothers with dependent children (Illinois, 1911) and the first minimum wage law for women (Massachusetts, 1912).

Muller had drawbacks, however. Though men as well as women suffered from long work hours, the *Muller* case did not protect men. Brandeis's brief treated all women as potential mothers, focusing on the state's interest in protecting future children. Brandeis and his allies hoped this would open the door to broader regulation of working hours. The Supreme Court, however, seized on motherhood as the key issue, asserting that the female worker, because of her maternal function, was "in a class by herself, and legislation for her protection may be sustained, even when like legislation is not necessary for men." This conclusion dismayed labor advocates and divided female reformers for decades afterward.

Male workers did benefit, however, from new workmen's compensation measures. Between 1910 and 1917, all the industrial states enacted insurance laws covering on-the-job accidents, so workers' families would not starve if a breadwinner was injured or killed. Some states also experimented with so-called **mothers' pensions**, providing state assistance after a breadwinner's desertion or death. Mothers, however, were subjected to home visits to determine whether they "deserved" government aid; injured workmen were not judged on this basis, a pattern of gender discrimination that reflected the broader impulse to protect women, while also holding them to different standards than men. Mothers' pensions reached relatively small numbers of women, but they laid foundations for the national program Aid to Families with Dependent Children, an important component of the Social Security Act of 1935.

While federalism gave the states considerable freedom to innovate, it hampered national reforms. In some states, for example, opponents of child labor won laws barring young children from factory work and strictly regulating hours and conditions for older children's labor. In the South, however, and in coal-mining states like Pennsylvania, companies fiercely resisted such laws — as did many working-class parents who relied on children's income to keep the family fed. A proposed U.S. constitutional amendment to abolish child labor never won ratification; only four states passed it. Tens of thousands of children continued to work in low-wage jobs, especially in the South. The same decentralized power that permitted innovation in Wisconsin hampered the creation of national minimum standards for pay and job safety.

mothers' pensions
Progressive Era government support provided to mothers whose husbands had died, been disabled, or abandoned the family. Recipients had to meet standards of "respectability" defined by middle-class home visitors, but those who met approval got help in raising their young children.

talented tenth
A term used by Harvard-educated sociologist W. E. B. Du Bois for the top 10 percent of educated African Americans, whom he called on to develop new strategies to advocate for civil rights.

The Birth of Modern Civil Rights Reeling from disfranchisement and the sanction of racial segregation in the Supreme Court's 1896 *Plessy v. Ferguson* decision (Chapter 17), African American leaders faced distinctive challenges. Given the obvious deterioration of African American rights, a new generation of black leaders proposed bolder approaches than those popularized earlier by Booker T. Washington. Harvard-educated sociologist W. E. B. Du Bois called for a **talented tenth** of educated blacks to develop new strategies. "The policy of compromise has failed," declared William Monroe Trotter, pugnacious editor of the *Boston Guardian*. "The policy of resistance and aggression deserves a trial."

In 1905, Du Bois and Trotter called a meeting at Niagara Falls — on the Canadian side, because no hotel on the U.S. side would admit blacks. The resulting Niagara Principles called for full voting rights; an end to segregation; equal treatment in the justice system; and equal opportunity in education, jobs, health care, and military service. These principles, based on African American pride and an uncompromising demand for full equality, guided the civil rights movement throughout the twentieth century.

In 1908, a bloody race riot broke out in Springfield, Illinois. Appalled by the white mob's violence in the hometown of Abraham Lincoln, New York settlement worker Mary White Ovington called together a group of sympathetic progressives to formulate a response. Their meeting led in 1909 to creation of the **National Association for the Advancement of Colored People (NAACP)**. Most leaders of the Niagara Movement soon joined; W. E. B. Du Bois became editor of the NAACP journal, *The Crisis*. The fledgling group found allies in many African American women's clubs and churches. It also cooperated with the National Urban League (1911), a union of agencies that assisted black migrants in the North. Over the coming decades, these groups grew into a powerful force for racial justice.

Niagara Movement Leaders This superimposed image from 1905 shows some of the founders of the Niagara Movement in front of the famous waterfall near their meeting place. The men depicted came from Massachusetts, Minnesota, Kansas, Illinois, New York, Washington, D.C., and Georgia. W. E. B. DuBois, wearing a white hat and bow tie, is second from right in the middle row. The group's efforts eventually led to creation of the National Association for the Advancement of Colored People. What factors might have led Niagara leaders to include only men (and one boy, Norris B. Herndon, son of Alonzo F. Herndon of Georgia) in the photograph, though women played supportive roles in the Niagara meeting? How might we account for the dearth of participants from the South, where the majority of the nation's African American population lived? Library of Congress.

The Problem of Labor Samuel Gompers and other leaders of the nation's dominant union, the American Federation of Labor, were slow to ally with progressives. They had long believed workers should improve their situation through strikes and direct negotiation with employers, not through politics. But by the 1910s, as progressive reformers came forward with solutions, labor leaders in state after state began to press for political action.

The nation also confronted a daring wave of radical labor militancy. In 1905, the Western Federation of Miners (WFM), led by fiery leaders such as William "Big Bill" Haywood, helped create a new movement, the **Industrial Workers of the World** (IWW). The Wobblies, as they were called, fervently supported the Marxist class struggle. As syndicalists, they believed that by resisting in the workplace and ultimately launching a general strike, workers could overthrow capitalism. A new society would emerge, run directly by workers. At its height, around 1916, the IWW had about 100,000 members. Though divided by internal conflicts, the group helped spark a number of local protests

National Association for the Advancement of Colored People (NAACP)

An organization founded in 1909 by leading African American reformers and white allies as a vehicle for advocating equal rights for African Americans, especially through the courts.

Industrial Workers of the World

An umbrella union and radical political group founded in 1905, dedicated to organizing unskilled workers to oppose capitalism. Nicknamed the Wobblies, it advocated direct action by workers, including sabotage and general strikes.

JUNE, 1914   10 CENTS

IN THIS ISSUE
CLASS WAR IN COLORADO—Max Eastman
WHAT ABOUT MEXICO?—John Reed

The Ludlow Massacre, 1914 Like his drawings of Triangle Shirtwaist fire victims in New York (see p. 611), this cover illustration for the popular socialist magazine *The Masses* demonstrates John Sloan's outrage at social injustice in progressive America. The drawing memorializes a tragic episode during a coal miners' strike at Ludlow, Colorado — the asphyxiation of women and children when vigilantes torched the tent city of evicted miners — and the aftermath, an armed revolt by enraged miners. Picture Research Consultants & Archives.

New Nationalism
In a 1910 speech, Theodore Roosevelt called for a "New Nationalism" that promoted government intervention to enhance public welfare, including a federal child labor law, more recognition of labor rights, a national minimum wage for women, women's suffrage, and curbs on the power of federal courts to stop reform.

during the 1910s, including strikes of rail car builders in Pennsylvania, textile operatives in Massachusetts, rubber workers in Ohio, and miners in Minnesota.

Meanwhile, after midnight on October 1, 1910, an explosion ripped through the *Los Angeles Times* headquarters, killing twenty employees and wrecking the building. It turned out that John J. McNamara, a high official of the American Federation of Labor's Bridge and Structural Iron Workers Union, had planned the bombing against the fiercely antiunion *Times*. McNamara's brother and another union member had carried out the attack. The bombing created a sensation, as did the terrible Triangle Shirtwaist fire (Chapter 18) and the IWW's high-profile strikes. What should be done? As the election of 1912 approached, labor issues moved high on the nation's agenda.

The Election of 1912

Retirement did not sit comfortably with Theodore Roosevelt. Returning from a yearlong safari in Africa in 1910 and finding Taft wrangling with the Insurgents, Roosevelt itched to jump in. In a speech in Osawatomie, Kansas, in August 1910, he called for a **New Nationalism**. In modern America, he argued, private property had to be controlled "to whatever degree the public welfare may require it." He proposed a federal child labor law, more recognition of labor rights, and a national minimum wage for women. Pressed by friends like Jane Addams, Roosevelt also endorsed women's suffrage. Most radical was his attack on the legal system. Insisting that courts blocked reform, Roosevelt proposed sharp curbs on their powers.

Early in 1912, Roosevelt announced himself as a Republican candidate for president. A battle within the party ensued. Roosevelt won most states that held primary elections, but Taft controlled party caucuses elsewhere. Dominated by regulars, the Republican convention chose Taft. Roosevelt then led his followers into what became known as the Progressive Party, offering his New Nationalism directly to the people. Though Jane Addams harbored private doubts (especially about Roosevelt's mania for battleships), she seconded his nomination, calling the Progressive Party "the American exponent of a world-wide movement for juster social conditions." In a nod to Roosevelt's combative stance, party followers called themselves "Bull Mooses."

Roosevelt was not the only rebel on the ballot: the major parties also faced a challenge from charismatic socialist Eugene V. Debs. In the 1890s, Debs had founded the American Railway Union (ARU), a broad-based group that included both skilled and unskilled workers. In 1894, amid the upheavals of depression and popular protest, the ARU had boycotted luxury Pullman sleeping cars, in support of a strike by workers at the Pullman Company. Railroad managers, claiming the strike obstructed the U.S. mail, persuaded Grover Cleveland's administration to intervene against the union. The strike failed, and Debs served time in prison along with other ARU leaders. The experience radicalized him, and in 1901 he launched the Socialist Party of America. Debs translated socialism into an American idiom, emphasizing the democratic process as a means to defeat capitalism. By the early 1910s, his party had secured a minor but persistent role in politics. Both the Progressive and Socialist parties drew strength from the West, a region with vigorous urban reform movements and a legacy of farmer-labor activism.

Watching the rise of the Progressives and Socialists, Democrats were keen to build on dramatic gains they had made in the 1910 midterm election. Among their younger leaders was Virginia-born Woodrow Wilson, who as New Jersey's governor had compiled an impressive reform record, including passage of a direct primary, workers' compensation, and utility regulation. In 1912, he won the Democrats' nomination. Wilson possessed, to a fault, the moral certainty that characterized many elite progressives. He had much in common with Roosevelt. "The old time of individual competition is probably gone by," he admitted, agreeing for more federal measures to restrict big business. But his goals were less sweeping than Roosevelt's, and only gradually did he hammer out a reform program, calling it the New Freedom. "If America is not to have free enterprise," Wilson warned, "then she can have freedom of no sort whatever." He claimed Roosevelt's program represented collectivism, whereas the New Freedom would preserve political and economic liberty.

With four candidates in the field — Taft, Roosevelt, Wilson, and Debs — the 1912 campaign generated intense excitement. Democrats continued to have an enormous blind spot: their opposition to African American rights. But Republicans, despite plentiful opportunities, had also conspicuously failed to end segregation or pass antilynching laws. Though African American leaders had high hopes for the Progressive Party, they were crushed when the new party refused to seat southern black delegates or take a stand for racial equality. W. E. B. Du Bois considered voting for Debs, calling the Socialists the only party "which openly recognized Negro manhood." But he ultimately endorsed Wilson. Across the North, in a startling shift, thousands of African American men and women worked and voted for Wilson, hoping Democrats' reform energy would benefit Americans across racial lines. The change helped lay the foundations for Democrats' New Deal coalition of the 1930s.

Despite the intense campaign, Republicans' division between Taft and Roosevelt made the result fairly easy to predict. Wilson won, though he

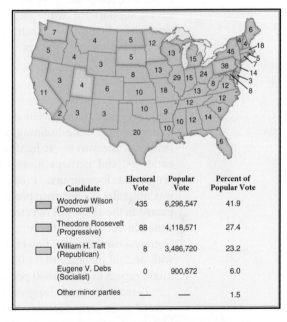

Candidate	Electoral Vote	Popular Vote	Percent of Popular Vote
Woodrow Wilson (Democrat)	435	6,296,547	41.9
Theodore Roosevelt (Progressive)	88	4,118,571	27.4
William H. Taft (Republican)	8	3,486,720	23.2
Eugene V. Debs (Socialist)	0	900,672	6.0
Other minor parties	—	—	1.5

MAP 19.5 The Presidential Election of 1912
The 1912 election reveals why the two-party system is so strongly rooted in American politics — especially in presidential elections. The Democrats, though a minority party, won an electoral landslide because the Republicans divided their vote between Roosevelt and Taft. This result indicates what is at stake when major parties splinter. The Socialist Party candidate, Eugene V. Debs, despite a record vote of 900,000, received no electoral votes.

received only 42 percent of the popular vote and almost certainly would have lost if Roosevelt had not been in the race (Map 19.5). In comparison with Roosevelt and Debs, Wilson appeared to be a rather old-fashioned choice. But with labor protests cresting and progressives gaining support, Wilson faced intense pressure to act.

IN YOUR OWN WORDS   What factors transformed national politics between 1900 and 1912?

Wilson and the New Freedom, 1913–1917

In his inaugural address, Wilson acknowledged that industrialization had precipitated a crisis. "There can be no equality of opportunity," he said, "if men and women and children be not shielded . . . from the consequences of great industrial and social processes which they cannot alter, control, or singly cope with." Wilson was a Democrat, and labor interests and farmers — some previously radicalized in the People's Party — were important components of his base. In the South, many of those voters also upheld strong support for white supremacy. Despite many northern African Americans' support for Wilson, his administration did little for those constituents. But he undertook bold economic reforms.

Economic Reforms

In an era of rising corporate power, many Democrats believed workers needed stronger government to intervene on their behalf, and they began to transform themselves into a modern, state-building party. The Wilson administration achieved a series of landmark measures — at least as significant as those enacted during earlier administrations, and perhaps more so (Table 19.1). The most enduring was the federal progressive income tax. "Progressive," by this definition, referred to the fact that it was not a flat tax but rose progressively toward the top of the income scale. The tax, passed in the 1890s but rejected by the Supreme Court, was reenacted as the Sixteenth Amendment to the Constitution, ratified by the states in February 1913. The next year, Congress used the new power to enact an income tax of 1 to 7 percent on Americans with annual incomes of $4,000 or more. At a time when white male wageworkers might expect to make $800 per year, the tax affected less than 5 percent of households.

Three years later, Congress followed this with an inheritance tax. These measures created an entirely new way to fund the federal government, replacing Republicans' high tariff as the chief source of revenue. Over subsequent decades, especially between the 1930s and the 1970s, the income tax system markedly reduced America's extremes of wealth and poverty.

Wilson also reorganized the financial system to address the absence of a central bank. At the time, the main function of national central banks was to back up commercial banks in case they could not meet their obligations. In the United States, the great private banks of New York (such as J. P. Morgan's) assumed this role; if they weakened, the entire system could collapse. This had nearly happened in 1907, when

TABLE 19.1

Major Federal Progressive Measures, 1883–1921

Before 1900

Pendleton Civil Service Act (1883)

Hatch Act (1887; Chapter 16)

Interstate Commerce Act (1887; Chapter 16)

Sherman Antitrust Act (1890)

Federal income tax (1894; struck down by Supreme Court, 1895)

During Theodore Roosevelt's Presidency, 1901–1909

Newlands Reclamation Act for federal irrigation (1902)

Elkins Act (1903)

First National Wildlife Refuge (1903; Chapter 17)

Bureau of Corporations created to aid Justice Department antitrust work (1903)

U.S. Forest Service created (1905)

Antiquities Act (1906; Chapter 17)

Pure Food and Drug Act (1906; Chapter 18)

Hepburn Act (1906)

First White House Conference on Dependent Children (1909)

During William Howard Taft's Presidency, 1909–1913

Mann Act preventing interstate prostitution (1910; Chapter 18)

Children's Bureau created in the U.S. Labor Department (1912)

U.S. Commission on Industrial Relations appointed (1912)

During Woodrow Wilson's Presidency, 1913–1920

Sixteenth Amendment to the Constitution; federal income tax (1913)

Seventeenth Amendment to the Constitution; direct election of U.S. senators (1913)

Federal Reserve Act (1913)

Clayton Antitrust Act (1914)

Seamen's Act (1915)

Workmen's Compensation Act (1916)

Adamson Eight-Hour Act (1916)

National Park Service created (1916; Chapter 17)

Eighteenth Amendment to the Constitution; prohibition of liquor (1920; Chapter 21)

Nineteenth Amendment to the Constitution; women's suffrage (1920; Chapter 20)

Wilson Chases Big Business, 1913–1914 Robert Carter, cartoonist for the *New York Sun*, drew on images of earlier president Theodore Roosevelt carrying a "big stick" in foreign policy, to show Woodrow Wilson's domestic policy toward big business. Wilson, a former schoolteacher, carries a "big ruler" instead of a big stick. Backed by Democratic working-class and agrarian interests, Wilson found himself forced as president to fight corporate monopolies and extend new protections for labor. The Granger Collection, New York.

Federal Reserve Act
The central bank system of the United States, created in 1913. The Federal Reserve helps set the money supply level, thus influencing the rate of growth of the U.S. economy, and seeks to ensure the stability of the U.S. monetary system.

the Knickerbocker Trust Company failed, precipitating a panic. The **Federal Reserve Act** (1913) gave the nation a banking system more resistant to such crises. It created twelve district reserve banks funded and controlled by their member banks, with a central Federal Reserve Board to impose regulation. The Federal Reserve could issue currency — paper money based on assets held in the system — and set the interest rate that district reserve banks charged to their members. It thereby regulated the flow of credit to the general public. The act strengthened the banking system and, to a modest degree, discouraged risky speculation on Wall Street.

Wilson and the Democratic Congress turned next to the trusts. In doing so, Wilson relied heavily on Louis D. Brandeis, the celebrated people's lawyer. Brandeis denied that monopolies were efficient. On the contrary, he believed the best source of efficiency was vigorous competition in a free market. The trick was to prevent trusts from unfairly using their power to curb such competition. In the **Clayton Antitrust Act** (1914), which amended the Sherman Act, the definition of illegal practices was left flexible, subject to the test of whether an action "substantially lessen[ed] competition." The new Federal Trade Commission received broad powers to decide what was fair, investigating companies and issuing "cease and desist" orders against anticompetitive practices.

Labor issues, meanwhile, received attention from a blue-ribbon U.S. Commission on Industrial Relations, appointed near the end of Taft's presidency and charged with investigating the conditions of labor. In its 1913 report, the commission summed up the impact of industrialization on low-skilled workers. Many earned $10 or less a week and endured regular episodes of unemployment; some faced long-term poverty and hardship. Workers held "an almost universal conviction" that they were "denied justice." The commission concluded that a major cause of industrial violence was the ruthless antiunionism of American employers. In its key recommendation, the report called for federal laws protecting workers' right to organize and engage in collective bargaining. Though such laws were, in 1915, too radical to win passage, the commission helped set a new national agenda that would come to fruition in the 1930s.

Guided by the commission's revelations, President Wilson warmed up to labor. In 1915 and 1916, he championed a host of bills to benefit American workers. They included the Adamson Act, which established an eight-hour day for railroad workers; the Seamen's Act, which eliminated age-old abuses of merchant sailors; and a workmen's compensation law for federal employees. Wilson, despite initial modest goals, presided over a major expansion of federal authority, perhaps the most significant since Reconstruction. The continued growth of U.S. government offices during Wilson's term reflected a reality that transcended party lines: corporations had grown in size and power, and Americans increasingly wanted federal authority to grow, too.

Wilson's reforms did not extend to the African Americans who had supported him in 1912. In fact, the president rolled back certain Republican policies, such as selected appointments of black postmasters. "I tried to help elect Wilson," W. E. B. Du Bois reflected gloomily, but "under Wilson came the worst attempt at Jim Crow legislation and discrimination in civil service that we had experienced since the Civil War." Wilson famously praised the film *Birth of a Nation* (1915), which depicted the Reconstruction-era Ku Klux Klan in heroic terms. In this way, Democratic control of the White House helped set the tone for the Klan's return in the 1920s.

Progressive Legacies

In the industrial era, millions of Americans decided that their political system needed to adjust to new conditions. Whatever their specific goals — and whether they were rural, working-class, or middle-class — reformers faced fierce opposition from powerful business interests. When they managed to win key regulatory laws, they often found these struck down by hostile courts and were forced to try again by different means. Thus the Progressive Era in the United States should be understood partly

Clayton Antitrust Act
A 1914 law that strengthened federal definitions of "monopoly" and gave more power to the Justice Department to pursue antitrust cases; it also specified that labor unions could not generally be prosecuted for "restraint of trade," ensuring that antitrust laws would apply to corporations rather than unions.

AMERICA IN GLOBAL CONTEXT

Economic Output and Government Social Spending, 1913

This graph shows social spending—expenditures at all levels of government for health, housing, and assistance to the elderly and the poor—in thirteen industrialized nations in 1913. The horizontal axis shows the size of each nation's economy, measured by gross domestic product (GDP). The vertical axis estimates percentage of GDP devoted to social spending.

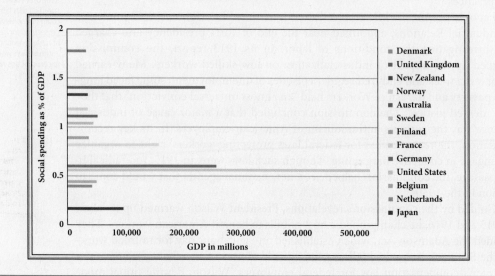

QUESTIONS FOR ANALYSIS

1. What similarities and differences does the graph show, in the size of each nation's economy and the amount of its spending on public social welfare?
2. Based on your reading of this textbook, what factors accounted for the United States's position on the graph?

by its limitations. Elitism and racial prejudice, embodied in new voting restrictions, limited working-class power at the polls; African Americans, their plight ignored by most white reformers, faced segregation and violence. Divided power in a federalist system blocked passage of uniform national policies on such key issues as child labor. Key social welfare programs that became popular in Europe during these decades, including national health insurance and old-age pensions, scarcely made it onto the American agenda until the 1930s (America in Global Context).

An international perspective suggests several reasons for American resistance to such programs. Business interests in the United States were exceptionally successful and powerful, flush with recent expansion. At the time, also, voters in countries with older, more native-born populations tended to support government regulation and welfare spending to a greater extent than their counterparts in countries with younger populations and large numbers of immigrants. Younger voters, understandably, seem to have been less concerned than older voters about health insurance and old-age security. Divisions in the American working class also played a role. Black, immigrant, and native-born white laborers often viewed one another as enemies or strangers rather than as members of a single class with common interests. This helps explain why the Socialist Party drew, at peak, less than 6 percent of the U.S. vote at a time when its counterparts in Finland, Germany, and France drew 40 percent or more. Lack of pressure from a strong, self-conscious workingmen's party contributed to more limited results in the United States.

But it would be wrong to underestimate progressive achievements. Over several decades, in this period, more and more prosperous Americans began to support stronger economic regulations. Even the most cautious, elite progressives recognized that the United States had entered a new era. Multinational corporations overshadowed small businesses; in vast cities, old support systems based on village and kinship melted away. Outdated political institutions — from the spoils system to urban machines — would no longer do. Walter Lippmann, founding editor of the progressive magazine *New Republic*, observed in 1914 that Americans had "no precedents to guide us, no wisdom that wasn't made for a simpler age." Progressives created new wisdom. By 1917, they had drawn blueprints for a modern American state, one whose powers more suited the needs of an industrial era.

IN YOUR OWN WORDS What caused Woodrow Wilson to become a reformer once he entered the White House?

Summary

The Progressive Era emerged from the political turmoil of the 1880s and 1890s. In the 1880s, despite the limits imposed by close elections, federal and state governments managed to achieve important administrative and economic reforms. After 1888, Republican leaders undertook more sweeping efforts, including the Sherman Antitrust Act, but failed in a quest to protect black voting rights. In the South and West, the People's Party called for much stronger government intervention in the economy, but its radical program drew bitter Republican and Democratic resistance.

The depression of the 1890s brought a wave of reaction. Labor unrest threw the nation into crisis, and Cleveland's intransigence over the gold standard cost the Democrats dearly in the 1894 and 1896 elections. While Republicans took over the federal government, southern Democrats restricted voting rights in the Solid South. Federal courts struck down regulatory laws and supported southern racial discrimination.

After McKinley's assassination, Roosevelt launched a program that balanced reform and private enterprise. At both the federal and state levels, progressive reformers made extensive use of elite expertise. At the grassroots, black reformers battled racial discrimination, women reformers worked on issues ranging from public health to women's working conditions, and labor activists tried to address the problems that fueled persistent labor unrest. The election of 1912 split the Republicans, giving victory to Woodrow Wilson, who launched a Democratic program of economic and labor reform. Despite the limits of the Progressive Era, the reforms of this period laid the foundation for a modern American state.

CHAPTER 19 REVIEW

TERMS TO KNOW   *Identify and explain the significance of each term below.*

Key Concepts and Events

Pendleton Act (p. 620)

Sherman Antitrust Act (p. 622)

Lodge Bill (p. 622)

Omaha Platform (p. 623)

free silver (p. 625)

Williams v. Mississippi (p. 627)

Lochner v. New York (p. 630)

Hepburn Act (p. 631)

Standard Oil decision (p. 632)

Newlands Reclamation Act (p. 632)

Wisconsin Idea (p. 633)

National Child Labor Committee (p. 633)

Muller v. Oregon (p. 633)

mothers' pensions (p. 634)

talented tenth (p. 634)

National Association for the Advancement of Colored People (NAACP) (p. 635)

Industrial Workers of the World (p. 635)

New Nationalism (p. 636)

Federal Reserve Act (p. 640)

Clayton Antitrust Act (p. 641)

Key People

Mary E. Lease (p. 624)

William Jennings Bryan (p. 628)

Theodore Roosevelt (p. 631)

Robert La Follette (p. 633)

Louis Brandeis (p. 633)

W. E. B. Du Bois (p. 634)

Eugene V. Debs (p. 636)

REVIEW QUESTIONS   *Answer these questions to demonstrate your understanding of the chapter's main ideas.*

1. How did the political goals of Populists differ from those of Democrats and Republicans?

2. How did the depression of the 1890s impact federal politics and policy?

3. What factors transformed national politics between 1900 and 1912?

4. What caused Woodrow Wilson to become a reformer once he entered the White House?

5. Look at the events on the thematic timeline on pages 526–527. Historians often call the later decades of this period (1890 to 1920) the Progressive Era. Given the limitations and new problems that emerged during this time, as well as the achievements of progressive policymaking, do you think the name is warranted? What other names might we suggest for this era?

1. Returning to Chapter 16, review the strategies and goals of the labor and agrarian organizations that flourished in the 1870s and 1880s. The People's Party embodied many of those ideas. Imagine that you are a journalist interviewing a former People's Party leader in 1917. To what extent might he or she have said that progressives had, after 1900, fulfilled the agrarian-labor agenda? To what extent might he or she criticize progressives for failing to achieve important reforms? What do you conclude from this about the similarities and differences of populism and progressivism?

2. Compare the economic policies implemented by Republicans during the Civil War (Chapters 13 and 15) with the policies adopted in the Progressive Era. What were the main goals of legislators and presidents in each period? In what ways did those goals overlap? To what extent did progressive leaders seek to remedy limitations or problems that emerged as a result of the Civil War–era legislation?

KEY TURNING POINTS   *Refer to the chapter chronology on page 616 for help in answering the questions below.*

Theodore Roosevelt and Woodrow Wilson both became president under unusual circumstances: Roosevelt after the assassination of William McKinley, and Wilson in a four-way race, in which the candidate of the previously dominant Republican Party came in third. How important was each man's arrival in the White House, based on events that occurred during their presidencies? Which events might have happened anyway, even if Roosevelt and Wilson had not served as chief executive? What does this suggest about the significance of the presidency during the Progressive Era?

7

PART

Domestic and Global Challenges

1890–1945

What should be the role of the United States in the world, and what is the proper relationship between government and society? If these seem like monumental questions, they are indeed. In Part 7, we show how these two pressing questions came to the fore in a tumultuous period of global warfare and domestic strife and reform. Globally, the United States expanded its empire overseas and fought on the winning side in two world wars. Domestically, the reform impulse retreated during and immediately after World War I but surged back to the center of national life during the crisis of the Great Depression, when Americans once more debated the responsibilities and limits of their government.

As the chapters in this part show, on the world stage the United States acted both in calculated self-interest and to protect democratic nations and institutions. By acquiring the Philippines, Hawaii, Guam, and Puerto Rico, the United States behaved as a traditional empire, securing important strategic assets and protecting American investments abroad. In joining its European allies in the two world wars, the United States embraced a broad international partnership against the threat of autocracy and fascism. In his famous speech in 1918 outlining his Fourteen Points for international peace, made amid the horrors of World War I, President Woodrow Wilson argued that as responsible global citizens Americans "cannot be separated in interest or divided in purpose."

Fifteen years later, President Franklin Delano Roosevelt made a similar call for solidarity during the Great Depression. "We face the arduous days that lie before us," he said, "in the warm courage of national unity." During the crises of the depression and World War II, American voters called for—and got—what Roosevelt called "action and action now." We conclude Part 7 in 1945, when the United States emerged from World War II with unprecedented global power and the federal government with a broad mandate for sustaining the new welfare state, a major turning point in modern American history. ▶

America's Rise to World Power

The United States became a major international power beginning in the 1890s, first in the Western Hemisphere and by the 1940s across the world, renewing debates at home about America's global role. After the War of 1898, the United States claimed overseas colonies and asserted control over the Caribbean basin. And although President Wilson attempted to maintain neutrality at the start of World War I, trade ties and old alliances drew America into the conflict on the Allied side. Wilson sought to influence the peace, but Allied leaders ignored his proposals and the Senate rejected the Treaty of Versailles. By war's end, the U.S. position on the world stage remained uncertain.

The 1920s was an era of dollar diplomacy and U.S. business expansion abroad. In the 1930s, faced with isolationist sentiment at home and the rise of fascist powers in Europe and Japan, the Roosevelt administration steered a middle course. In the late 1930s, it began to send aid to its traditional ally Great Britain without committing U.S. forces to the conflict. When the United States entered World War II in 1941, it did so as part of an alliance with both England and the Soviet Union against Germany, Japan, and Italy. The United States emerged from the war as the dominant global power.

Modernity and Its Discontents

World War I had a powerful domestic impact in the United States, producing a sharp right turn in the postwar years. A Red Scare, rollback of labor and immigrant rights, race riots against African Americans, and a resurgent nationwide Ku Klux Klan marked the political scene between 1919 and the late 1920s. A full-blown modern consumer culture also emerged in the decade as radio, automobiles, and Hollywood movies transformed leisure pastimes. Prosperity did not prevent conflict over an emerging secular, diverse, and modern society, however, as Americans battled over immigration, race, and religion in the 1920s.

During the Great Depression, the U.S. government deported hundreds of thousands of people of Mexican descent, including American citizens. During World War II, the government temporarily imprisoned Japanese Americans in a mass relocation policy, turned away most Jewish refugees fleeing Hitler, and segregated African Americans in a Jim Crow military. Yet many Americans celebrated the New Deal and the war effort as evidence of what a united country could accomplish. These events, too, represented battles over what a diverse, modern nation would look like.

Creation of the Welfare State

Republican policymakers of the 1920s believed in hands-off government. Their policies likely helped trigger the Great Depression and deepened its impact after it arrived. President Franklin Roosevelt's New Deal programs (1933–1938) expanded federal responsibility for the welfare of ordinary citizens, breaking dramatically with the *laissez faire* individualism of the previous decade. Though the New Deal faced considerable challenges on the political right—especially from business and corporate leaders and a hostile Supreme Court—the popularity of its programs, such as Social Security, established a broad consensus that the United States needed a modern welfare state to regulate the economy and provide a basic safety net for the nation's citizens.

During World War II, the welfare state became a "warfare state," and Congress gave the president broad powers to fight the war abroad and reorganize the economy at home. Under the government-directed wartime economy, business boomed and productivity grew, but other policies, such as the internment of Japanese immigrants and Japanese Americans, violated fragile civil liberties, leaving a mixed legacy.

Domestic and Global Challenges 1890–1945

Library of Congress.

Thematic Understanding:

This timeline arranges some of the important events of this period into seven themes. Consider the entries under each theme. What connections do you see between events on the world stage and developments within the United States? What impact did World War I, the Great Depression, and World War II appear to have on American politics, society, and culture?

	AMERICAN AND NATIONAL IDENTITY	POLITICS AND POWER	WORK, EXCHANGE, AND TECHNOLOGY
1890	• "American exceptionalism" and rise of imperialism • Alfred Mahan, *The Influence of Sea Power upon History* (1890)	• Republicans sweep congressional elections after severe depression (1894) • Republican William McKinley elected president (1896)	• Depression of 1890s increases pressure to secure foreign markets
1900	• *Insular Cases* establish noncitizenship status for new territories (1901) • California, Washington, and Hawaii limit rights for Asian immigrants	• McKinley reelected on pro-imperialist platform (1900) • McKinley assassinated; Theodore Roosevelt becomes president (1901)	• Root-Takahira Agreement affirms free oceanic commerce (1908) • Ford Motor Company introduces Model T
1910	• New Ku Klux Klan founded (1915) • Post–World War I race riots • Wartime pressure for "100 percent loyalty"; dissent suppressed	• Woodrow Wilson elected president (1912) • Red Scare (1919) • Wilson issues Fourteen Points (1919)	• Assembly-line production of automobiles begins • U.S. Army Corps employs tens of thousands of workers to build Panama Canal
1920	• Harlem Renaissance artists emphasize black pride • National Origins Act limits immigration (1924)	• Nineteenth Amendment grants women's suffrage (1920) • Prohibition (1920–1933)	• Economic prosperity (1922–1929) • Rise of automobile loans and consumer credit
1930	• Bonus Army (1932) • Indian Reorganization Act (1934) • Social Security created (1935)	• Franklin Roosevelt elected president (1932) • First New Deal (1933) • Second New Deal (1935)	• Great Depression (1929–1941) • Rise of CIO and organized labor
1940	• Internment of Japanese Americans (1942) • Segregation in armed services until 1948	• Roosevelt elected to fourth term (1944) • Roosevelt dies and Harry Truman becomes president (1945)	• War spending ends depression • Married women take war jobs

CULTURE AND SOCIETY	MIGRATION AND SETTLEMENT	GEOGRAPHY AND THE ENVIRONMENT	AMERICA IN THE WORLD
1890 • "Remember the *Maine*" campaign fuels surge in nationalism	• Josiah Strong encourages overseas Christian missionaries	• Americans debate overseas expansion and empire • Teller Amendment (1898)	• U.S. wins War of 1898 against Spain; claims Hawaii, Puerto Rico, Guam, and Philippines
1900 • Social Darwinism used to justify U.S. imperialism (1898–1910s)	• Rising immigration from Southern and Eastern Europe • Gentleman's agreement bars Japanese immigration (1907)	• Congress authorizes funds to purchase land in Colombia for future canal	• Platt Amendment (1902) • Roosevelt Corollary to Monroe Doctrine (1904) • U.S. helps crush Boxer Rebellion in China (1900)
1910 • Moviemaking industry moves to southern California • Radio Corporation of America created (1919)	• African American Great Migration to northern cities • St. Louis (1917) and Chicago (1919) race riots	• Panama Canal construction • Panama Canal opens (1914) and links Atlantic and Pacific Oceans	• Wilson intervenes in Mexico (1914) • United States enters World War I (1917)
1920 • Rise of Hollywood • Harlem Renaissance • Popularity of jazz music • Scopes trial (1925)	• Rise of nativism • National Origins Act (1924) imposes immigration restriction	• Suburban housing boom • First suburban shopping center opens outside Kansas City, Missouri (1924)	• Heyday of "dollar diplomacy" • U.S. occupation of Haiti and other Caribbean and Central American nations
1930 • Documentary impulse in arts • WPA assists artists • Federal Writers' Project established (1935)	• Migrants ("Okies") leave drought-struck Midwest for California • U.S. deports Mexican immigrants and Mexican Americans	• "Dust Bowl" drought strikes Midwest (1930–1941) • Works Progress Administration builds parks, zoos, trails (1935–1943)	• Rise of European fascist powers • Japan invades China (1937)
1940 • Film industry aids war effort	• War production leads to migration to California and major cities • Bracero program increases immigration from Mexico	• Temporary encampments isolate Japanese and Japanese Americans in inland states (1942)	• United States enters World War II (1941) • Atomic bombing of Japan and end of World War II (1945) • United Nations founded (1945)

An Emerging World Power
1890–1918

Accepting the Democratic presidential nomination in 1900, William Jennings Bryan delivered a famous speech denouncing U.S. military occupations overseas. "God Himself," Bryan declared, "placed in every human heart the love of liberty. . . . He never made a race of people so low in the scale of civilization or intelligence that it would welcome a foreign master." At the time, Republican president William McKinley was leading an ambitious and popular plan of overseas expansion. The United States had asserted control over the Caribbean, claimed Hawaii, and sought to annex the Philippines. Bryan failed to convince a majority of voters that imperialism — the exercise of military, political, and economic power overseas — was the wrong direction. He lost the election by a landslide.

By the 1910s, however, American enthusiasm for overseas involvement cooled. Despite efforts to stay neutral, the United States got caught up in the global catastrophe of World War I, which killed 8 million combatants, including over 50,000 U.S. soldiers. By the war's end, European powers' grip on their colonial empires was weakening. The United States also ceased acquiring overseas territories and pursued a different path. It did so in part because the war brought dramatic changes at home, leaving Americans a postwar legacy of economic upheaval and political disillusionment.

President Woodrow Wilson, who in 1913 appointed Bryan as his secretary of state, tried to steer a middle course between revolutionary socialism and European-style imperialism. In Wilson's phrase, America would "make the world safe for democracy" while unapologetically working to advance U.S. economic interests. The U.S. Senate, however, rejected the 1919 Treaty of Versailles and with it Wilson's vision, leaving the nation's foreign policy in doubt. Should the United States try to promote democracy abroad? If so, how? To what degree should the federal government seek to promote American business interests? Under what conditions was overseas military action justified? When, on the contrary, did it impinge on others' sovereignty, endanger U.S. soldiers, and invite disaster? Today's debates over foreign policy still center to a large degree on questions that Americans debated in the era of McKinley, Bryan, and Wilson, when the nation first asserted itself as a major world power.

IDENTIFY THE BIG IDEA

As the United States became a major power on the world stage, what ideas and interests did policymakers promote in international affairs?

The Great White Fleet   The U.S. Navy's newest battle fleet, nicknamed the "Great White Fleet" and celebrated proudly by President Theodore Roosevelt, took a world tour between 1907 and 1909, demonstrating to the world that the U.S. now had naval power rivaling Britain and Germany. Here, the USS *Connecticut* leads the fleet of sixteen battleships on its way out of Hampton Roads, Virginia, at the start of the voyage. By 1900, global economic and military power brought the United States new prestige — and new problems. Bettmann/Getty Images.

As you read, ask yourself why this chapter begins and ends with these dates and then identify the links among related events.

1886	▶ United States begins building modern battleships
1892	▶ U.S.-backed planters overthrow Hawaii's Queen Liliuokalani
1895	▶ United States arbitrates border dispute between Britain and Venezuela ▶ Guerrilla war against Spanish rule begins in Cuba
1898	▶ War between United States and Spain ▶ United States annexes Hawaii, Puerto Rico, and Guam
1899–1902	▶ U.S.-Philippine War, ending in U.S. occupation of Philippines ▶ United States pursues open door policy in China
1900	▶ United States helps suppress nationalist rebellion in China ("Boxer Rebellion")
1901	▶ Hay-Pauncefote Treaty
1902	▶ Platt Amendment gives United States exclusive role in Cuba
1903	▶ United States recognizes Panama's independence from Colombia

1905	▶ Russo-Japanese War; Roosevelt mediates peace
1908	▶ Root-Takahira Agreement
1914	▶ Panama Canal opens ▶ U.S. military action in Veracruz, Mexico ▶ World War I begins in Europe
1916	▶ Jones Act commits United States to future Philippine independence
1917	▶ United States declares war on Germany and its allies, creates new agencies to mobilize economy and promote national unity ▶ Espionage Act
1918	▶ Sedition Act ▶ World War I ends ▶ Beginning of two-year influenza pandemic that kills 50 million people worldwide
1919	▶ *Schenck v. United States* and *Abrams v. United States* ▶ Wilson promotes Fourteen Points at Paris Peace Conference ▶ Senate rejects the Treaty of Versailles
1920	▶ Nineteenth Amendment grants women suffrage

From Expansion to Imperialism

Historians used to describe turn-of-the-twentieth-century U.S. imperialism as something new and unprecedented. Now they stress continuities between foreign policy in this era and the nation's earlier, relentless expansion across North America. Wars against Native peoples had occurred almost continuously since the country's founding; in the 1840s, the United States had annexed a third of Mexico. The United States never administered a large colonial empire, as did European powers like Spain, England, and Germany, partly because it had a plentiful supply of natural resources in the American West. But policymakers undertook a determined quest for global markets. Events in the 1890s opened opportunities to pursue this goal in new ways.

Foundations of Empire

American empire builders around 1900 fulfilled a vision laid out earlier by William Seward, secretary of state under presidents Abraham Lincoln and Andrew Johnson, who saw access to global markets as the key to power (Chapter 15). Seward's ideas had won only limited support at the time, but the severe economic depression of the 1890s brought Republicans into power and Seward's ideas back into vogue. Confronting high unemployment and mass protests, policymakers feared American workers would embrace socialism or Marxism. The alternative, they believed, was to create jobs and prosperity at home by selling U.S. products in overseas markets.

Intellectual trends also favored imperialism. As early as 1885, in his popular book *Our Country*, Congregationalist minister Josiah Strong urged Protestants to proselytize overseas. He predicted that the American "Anglo-Saxon race," which represented "the largest liberty, the purest Christianity, the highest civilization," would "spread itself over the earth." Such arguments were grounded in **American exceptionalism**, the idea that the United States had a unique destiny to foster democracy and civilization.

As Strong's exhortation suggested, imperialists also drew on the popular racial theory that people of "Anglo-Saxon" descent — English and often German — were superior to all others. "Anglo-Saxon" rule over foreign people of color made sense in an era when, at home, the United States denied most American Indians and Asian immigrants citizenship and southern states disfranchised blacks. Imperialists argued that "free land" on the western frontier was dwindling, and thus new outlets needed to be found for American energy and enterprise. Responding to critics of U.S. occupation of the Philippines, Theodore Roosevelt scoffed: if Filipinos should control their own islands, he declared, then America was "morally bound to return Arizona to the Apaches."

Imperialists also justified their views through racialized Social Darwinism (Chapter 17). Josiah Strong, for example, predicted that with the globe fully occupied, a "competition of races" would ensue, with victory based on "survival of the fittest." Fear of ruthless competition drove the United States, like European nations, to invest in the latest weapons. Policymakers saw that European powers were amassing steel-plated battleships and carving up Africa and Asia among themselves. In his book *The Influence of Sea Power upon History* (1890), U.S. naval officer Alfred Mahan urged the United States to enter the fray, observing that naval power had been essential to past empires. As early as 1886, Congress ordered construction of two steel-hulled battle-ships, the USS *Texas* and USS *Maine*; in 1890, it appropriated funds for three more, a program that expanded over the next two decades.

During Grover Cleveland's second term (1893–1897), his secretary of state, Richard Olney, turned to direct confrontation. He warned Europe to stay away from Latin America, which he saw as the United States's rightful sphere of influence. Without consulting the nation of Venezuela, Olney suddenly demanded in 1895 that Britain resolve a long-standing border dispute between Venezuela and Britain's neighboring colony, British Guiana. Invoking the Monroe Doctrine, which stated that the Western Hemisphere was off-limits to further European colonization, Olney warned that the United States would brook no challenge to its interests. Startled, Britain agreed to arbitrate. U.S. power was on the rise.

American exceptionalism
The idea that the United States has a unique destiny to foster democracy and civilization on the world stage.

The War of 1898

Events in the Caribbean presented the United States with far greater opportunities. In 1895, Cuban patriots mounted a major guerrilla war against Spain, which had lost most of its other New World territories. The Spanish commander responded by rounding up Cuban civilians into concentration camps, where as many as 200,000 died of starvation, exposure, or dysentery. In the United States, "yellow journalists" such as William Randolph Hearst turned their plight into a cause célèbre. Hearst's coverage of Spanish atrocities fed a surge of nationalism, especially among those who feared that industrialization was causing American men to lose physical strength and valor. The government should not pass up this opportunity, said Indiana senator Albert Beveridge, to "manufacture manhood." Congress called for Cuban independence.

President Cleveland had no interest in supporting the Cuban rebellion but worried over Spain's failure to end it. The war disrupted trade and damaged American-owned sugar plantations on the island. Moreover, an unstable Cuba was incompatible with U.S. strategic interests, including a proposed canal whose Caribbean approaches had to be safeguarded. Taking office in 1897, President William McKinley took a tough stance. In September, a U.S. diplomat informed Spain that it must ensure an "early and certain peace" or the United States would step in. At first, this hard line seemed to work: Spain's conservative regime fell, and a liberal government, taking office in October 1897, offered Cuba limited self-rule. But Spanish loyalists in Havana rioted against this proposal, while Cuban rebels held out for full independence.

In February 1898, Hearst's *New York Journal* published a private letter in which a Spanish minister to the United States belittled McKinley. The minister, Dupuy de Lôme, resigned, but exposure of the de Lôme letter intensified Americans' indignation toward Spain. The next week brought shocking news: the U.S. battle cruiser *Maine* had exploded and sunk in Havana harbor, with 260 seamen lost. "Whole Country Thrills with the War Fever," proclaimed the *New York Journal*. "Remember the *Maine*" became a national chant. Popular passions were now a major factor in the march toward war.

McKinley assumed the sinking of the *Maine* had been accidental. Improbably, though, a naval board of inquiry blamed an underwater mine, fueling public outrage. (Later investigators disagreed: the more likely cause was a faulty ship design that placed explosive munitions too close to coal bunkers, which were prone to fire.) No evidence linked Spain to the purported mine, but if a mine sank the *Maine*, then Spain was responsible for not protecting the ship.

Business leaders became impatient, believing war was preferable to an unending Cuban crisis. On March 27, McKinley cabled an ultimatum to Madrid: an immediate ceasefire in Cuba for six months and, with the United States mediating, peace negotiations with the rebels. Spain, while desperate to avoid war, balked at the added demand that mediation must result in Cuban independence. On April 11, McKinley asked Congress for authority to intervene in Cuba "in the name of civilization, [and] in behalf of endangered American interests."

Historians long referred to the ensuing fight as the Spanish-American War, but because that name ignores the central role of Cuban revolutionaries, many historians now call the three-way conflict the War of 1898. Though Americans widely admired Cubans' aspirations for freedom, the McKinley administration defeated a congressional attempt to recognize the rebel government. In response, Senator Henry M. Teller of Colorado added an amendment to the war bill disclaiming any intention by the United States to occupy Cuba. The **Teller Amendment** reassured Americans that their country would uphold democracy abroad as well as at home. McKinley's expectations differed. He wrote privately, "We must keep all we get; when the war is over we must keep what we want."

On April 24, 1898, Spain declared war on the United States. The news provoked full-blown war fever. Across the country, young men enlisted for the fight. Theodore

Teller Amendment
An amendment to the 1898 U.S. declaration of war against Spain disclaiming any intention by the United States to occupy Cuba. The amendment assured the public that the United States would uphold democracy abroad as well as at home.

Roosevelt, serving in the War Department, resigned to become lieutenant colonel of a cavalry regiment. Recruits poured into makeshift bases around Tampa, Florida, where confusion reigned. Rifles failed to arrive; food was bad, sanitation worse. No provision had been made for getting troops to Cuba, so the government hastily collected a fleet of yachts and commercial boats. Fortunately, the regular army was a disciplined, professional force; its 28,000 seasoned troops provided a nucleus for 200,000 volunteers. The navy was in better shape: Spain had nothing to match America's seven battleships and armored cruisers. The Spanish admiral bitterly predicted that his fleet would "like Don Quixote go out to fight windmills and come back with a broken head."

The first, decisive military engagement took place in the Pacific. This was the handiwork of Theodore Roosevelt, who, in his government post, had gotten the intrepid Commodore George Dewey appointed commander of the Pacific fleet. In the event of war, Dewey had instructions to sail immediately for the Spanish-owned Philippines. When war was declared, Roosevelt confronted his surprised superior and pressured him into validating Dewey's instructions. On May 1, 1898, American ships cornered the Spanish fleet in Manila Bay and destroyed it. Manila, the Philippine capital, fell on August 13. "We must on no account let the [Philippines] go," declared Senator Henry Cabot Lodge. McKinley agreed. The United States now had a major foothold in the western Pacific.

Dewey's victory directed policymakers' attention to Hawaii. Nominally independent, these islands had long been subject to U.S. influence, including a horde of resident American sugarcane planters. An 1876 treaty between the United States and the island's monarch gave Hawaiian sugar free access to the American market, without tariff payments, and Hawaii pledged to sign no such agreement with any other power. When this treaty was renewed in 1887, Hawaii also granted a long-coveted lease for a U.S. naval base at Pearl Harbor. Four years later, succeeding her brother as Hawaii's monarch, Queen Liliuokalani made known her frustration with these treaties. In response, an Annexation Club of U.S.-backed planters organized secretly and in 1892, with the help of U.S. Marines, overthrew the queen. They then negotiated a treaty of annexation, but Grover Cleveland rejected it when he entered office in 1893. Cleveland declared that it would violate America's "unbroken tradition" against acquiring territory overseas.

Dewey's victory in Manila, however, delivered what the planters wanted: Hawaii acquired strategic value as a halfway station to the Philippines. In July 1898, Congress voted for annexation, over the protests of Hawaii's deposed queen. "Oh, honest Americans," she pleaded, "as Christians hear me for my down-trodden people! Their form of government is as dear to them as yours is precious to you. Quite as warmly as you love your country, so they love theirs." But to the great powers, Hawaii was not a country. One congressman dismissed Hawaii's monarchy as "absurd, grotesque, tottering"; the "Aryan race," he declared, would "rescue" the islands from it.

Further U.S. annexations took on their own logic. The navy pressed for another coaling base in the central Pacific; that meant Guam, a Spanish island in the Marianas. A strategic base was needed in the Caribbean; that meant Puerto Rico. By early summer, before U.S. troops had fired a shot in Cuba, McKinley's broader war aims were crystallizing.

In Cuba, Spanish forces were depleted by the long guerrilla war. Though poorly trained and equipped, American forces had the advantages of a demoralized foe and

📖 To see a longer excerpt from Queen Liliuokalani's appeal, along with other primary sources from this period, see *Sources for America's History*.

knowledgeable Cuban allies. The main battle occurred on July 1 at San Juan Hill, near Santiago, where the Spanish fleet was anchored. Roosevelt's Rough Riders took the lead, but four African American regiments bore the brunt of the fighting. Observers credited much of the victory to the "superb gallantry" of these soldiers. Spanish troops retreated to a well-fortified second line, but U.S. forces were spared the test of a second assault. On July 3, the Spanish fleet in Santiago harbor tried a desperate run through the American blockade and was destroyed. Days later, Spanish forces surrendered. American combat casualties had been few; most U.S. soldiers' deaths had resulted from malaria and yellow fever.

Spoils of War

The United States and Spain quickly signed a preliminary peace agreement in which Spain agreed to liberate Cuba and cede Puerto Rico and Guam to the United States. But what would happen to the Philippines, an immense archipelago that lay more than 5,000 miles from California? Initially, the United States aimed to keep only Manila, because of its fine harbor. Manila was not defensible, however, without the whole island of Luzon, on which it sat. After deliberating, McKinley found a justification for annexing all of the Philippines. He decided that "we could not leave [the Filipinos] to themselves — they were unfit for self-rule."

This declaration provoked heated debate. Under the Constitution, as Republican senator George F. Hoar argued, "no power is given to the Federal Government to acquire territory to be held and governed permanently as colonies" or "to conquer alien people and hold them in subjugation." Leading citizens and peace advocates, including Jane Addams and Mark Twain, enlisted in the anti-imperialist cause. Steel king Andrew Carnegie offered $20 million to purchase Philippine independence. Labor leader Samuel Gompers warned union members about the threat of competition from low-wage Filipino immigrants. Anti-imperialists, however, were a diverse lot. Some argued that Filipinos were perfectly capable of self-rule; others warned about the dangers of annexing eight million Filipinos of an "inferior race." "No matter whether they are fit to govern themselves or not," declared a Missouri congressman, "they are not fit to govern us."

Beginning in late 1898, anti-imperialist leagues sprang up around the country, but they never sparked a mass movement. On the contrary, McKinley's "splendid little war" proved immensely popular. Confronted with that reality, Democrats waffled. Their standard-bearer, William Jennings Bryan, decided not to stake Democrats' future on opposition to a policy that he believed to be irreversible. He threw his party into turmoil by declaring last-minute support for McKinley's proposed treaty. Having met military defeat, Spanish representatives had little choice. In the Treaty of Paris, Spain ceded the Philippines to the United States for $20 million.

Annexation was not as simple as U.S. policymakers had expected. On February 4, 1899, two days before the Senate ratified the treaty, fighting broke out between American and Filipino patrols on the edge of Manila. Confronted by annexation, rebel leader Emilio Aguinaldo asserted his nation's independence and turned his guns on occupying American forces. Though Aguinaldo found it difficult to organize a mass-based resistance movement, the ensuing conflict between Filipino nationalists

Philippine Exhibition at the St. Louis World's Fair, 1904 Anthropological displays were
a popular feature of World's Fairs — scientific in purpose, but giving American and European tourists
an opportunity to contrast their civilization, as they saw it, with various degrees of "barbarism" and
"savagery." The Philippine Reservation in St. Louis was particularly controversial because it featured an
array of peoples — many westernized, others traditionally tribal — from the United States' latest imperial
possession. Here, Igorrote dancers rest after a performance. Some participants in such displays were lured
with false promises of wealth and rapid return to their homelands; when promoters went bankrupt, some
performers were stranded in the United States and never returned to their families and communities. Library
of Congress.

and U.S. troops far exceeded in length and ferocity the war just concluded with Spain.
Fighting tenacious guerrillas, the U.S. Army resorted to the same tactics Spain had
employed in Cuba: burning crops and villages and rounding up civilians. Atrocities
became commonplace on both sides. In three years of warfare, 4,200 Americans and
an estimated 200,000 Filipinos died; many of the latter were dislocated civilians, particularly children, who succumbed to malnutrition and disease.

McKinley's convincing victory over William Jennings Bryan in 1900 suggested
popular satisfaction with America's overseas adventures, even in the face of dogged
Filipino resistance to U.S. rule. The fighting ended in 1902, and William Howard
Taft, appointed as governor-general of the Philippines, sought to make the territory
a model of roadbuilding and sanitary engineering. Yet misgivings lingered as
Americans confronted the brutality of the war. Philosopher William James noted that
the United States had destroyed "these islanders by the thousands, their villages and

cities. . . . Could there be any more damning indictment of that whole bloated ideal termed 'modern civilization'?"

Constitutional issues also remained unresolved. The treaty, while guaranteeing freedom of religion to inhabitants of ceded Spanish territories, withheld any promise of citizenship. It was up to Congress to decide Filipinos' "civil rights and political status." In 1901, the Supreme Court upheld this provision in a set of decisions known as the ***Insular Cases***. The Constitution, declared the Court, did not automatically extend citizenship to people in acquired territories; Congress could decide. Puerto Rico, Guam, and the Philippines were thus marked as colonies, not future states.

The next year, as a condition for withdrawing from Cuba, the United States forced the newly independent island to accept a proviso in its constitution called the **Platt Amendment** (1902). This blocked Cuba from making a treaty with any country except the United States and gave the United States the right to intervene in Cuban affairs if it saw fit. Cuba also granted the United States a lease on Guantánamo Bay (still in effect), where the U.S. Navy built a large base. Cubans' hard-fought independence was limited; so was that of Filipinos. Eventually, the Jones Act of 1916 committed the United States to Philippine independence but set no date. (The Philippines at last achieved independence in 1946.) Though the war's carnage had rubbed off some of the moralizing gloss, America's global aspirations remained intact.

Insular Cases
A set of Supreme Court rulings in 1901 that declared that the U.S. Constitution did not automatically extend citizenship to people in acquired territories; only Congress could decide whether to grant citizenship.

Platt Amendment
A 1902 amendment to the Cuban constitution that blocked Cuba from making a treaty with any country except the United States and gave the United States the right to intervene in Cuban affairs. The amendment was a condition for U.S. withdrawal from the newly independent island.

> **IN YOUR OWN WORDS** Explain the steps by which the late-nineteenth-century U.S. government began to exert military influence in different regions of the world.

A Power Among Powers

No one appreciated America's emerging influence more than the man who, after William McKinley's assassination, became president in 1901. Theodore Roosevelt was an avid student of world affairs who called on "the civilized and orderly powers to insist on the proper policing of the world." He meant, in part, directing the affairs of "backward peoples." For Roosevelt, imperialism went hand in hand with domestic progressivism. He argued that a strong federal government, asserting itself both at home and abroad, would enhance economic stability and political order. Overseas, Roosevelt sought to arbitrate disputes and maintain a global balance of power, but he also asserted U.S. interests.

The Open Door in Asia

"open door" policy
A claim put forth by U.S. Secretary of State John Hay that all nations seeking to do business in China should have equal trade access.

U.S. officials and business leaders had a burning interest in East Asian markets, but they were entering a crowded field (Map 20.1). In the late 1890s, following Japan's victory in the Sino-Japanese War of 1894–1895, Japan, Russia, Germany, France, and Britain divided coastal China into spheres of influence. Fearful of being shut out, U.S. Secretary of State John Hay sent these powers a note in 1899, claiming the right of equal trade access — an **"open door" policy** — for all nations seeking to do business in China. The United States lacked leverage in Asia, and Hay's note elicited only noncommittal responses. But he chose to interpret this as acceptance of his position.

MAP 20.1 The Great Powers in East Asia, 1898–1910

European powers established dominance over China by way of "treaty ports," where the powers based their naval forces, and through "spheres of influence" that extended from the ports into the hinterland. This map reveals why the United States had a weak hand: it lacked a presence on this colonized terrain. An uprising of Chinese nationalists in 1900 gave the United States a chance to insert itself on the Chinese mainland by sending an American expeditionary force. American diplomats made the most of the opportunity to defend U.S. commercial interests in China. As noted in the key, all place names in this map are those in use in 1910: Modern *Beijing*, for example, is shown as *Peking*.

When a secret society of Chinese nationalists, known outside China as "Boxers" because of their pugnacious political stance, rebelled against foreign occupation in 1900, the United States sent 5,000 troops to join a multinational campaign to break the nationalists' siege of European offices in Beijing. Hay took this opportunity to assert a second open door principle: China must be preserved as a "territorial and administrative entity." As long as the legal fiction of an independent China survived, Americans could claim equal access to its market.

European and American plans were, however, unsettled by Japan's emergence as East Asia's dominant power. A decade after its victory over China, Japan responded to Russia's bids for control of both Korea and Manchuria, in northern China, by attacking

Russia's fleet at its leased Chinese port. In a series of brilliant victories, the Japanese smashed the Russian forces. Westerners were shocked: for the first time, a European power had been defeated by a non-Western nation. Conveying both admiration and alarm, American cartoonists sketched Japan as a martial artist knocking down the Russian giant. Roosevelt mediated a settlement to the war in 1905, receiving for his efforts the first Nobel Peace Prize awarded to an American.

Though he was contemptuous of other Asians, Roosevelt respected the Japanese, whom he called "a wonderful and civilized people." More important, he understood Japan's rising military might and aligned himself with the mighty. The United States approved Japan's "protectorate" over Korea in 1905 and, six years later, its seizure of full control. With Japan asserting harsh authority over Manchuria, energetic Chinese diplomat Yüan Shih-k'ai tried to encourage the United States to intervene. But Roosevelt reviewed America's weak position in the Pacific and declined. He conceded that Japan had "a paramount interest in what surrounds the Yellow Sea." In 1908, the United States and Japan signed the **Root-Takahira Agreement**, confirming principles of free oceanic commerce and recognizing Japan's authority over Manchuria.

Root-Takahira Agreement
A 1908 agreement between the United States and Japan confirming principles of free oceanic commerce and recognizing Japan's authority over Manchuria.

William Howard Taft entered the White House in 1909 convinced that the United States had been shortchanged in Asia. He pressed for a larger role for American investors, especially in Chinese railroad construction. Eager to promote U.S. business interests abroad, he hoped that infusions of American capital would offset Japanese power. When the Chinese Revolution of 1911 toppled the Manchu dynasty, Taft supported the victorious Nationalists, who wanted to modernize their country and liberate it from Japanese domination. The United States had entangled itself in China and entered a long-term rivalry with Japan for power in the Pacific, a competition that would culminate thirty years later in World War II.

The United States and Latin America

Roosevelt famously argued that the United States should "speak softly and carry a big stick." By "big stick," he meant naval power, and rapid access to two oceans required a canal. European powers conceded the United States's "paramount interest" in the Caribbean. Freed by Britain's surrender of canal-building rights in the Hay-Pauncefote Treaty (1901), Roosevelt persuaded Congress to authorize $10 million, plus future payments of $250,000 per year, to purchase from Colombia a six-mile strip of land across Panama, a Colombian province.

Furious when Colombia rejected this proposal, Roosevelt contemplated outright seizure of Panama but settled on a more roundabout solution. Panamanians, long separated from Colombia by remote jungle, chafed under Colombian rule. The United States lent covert assistance to an independence movement, triggering a bloodless revolution. On November 6, 1903, the United States recognized the new nation of Panama; two weeks later, it obtained a perpetually renewable lease on a canal zone. Roosevelt never regretted the venture, though in 1922 the United States paid Colombia $25 million as a kind of conscience money.

To build the canal, the U.S. Army Corps of Engineers hired 60,000 laborers, who came from many countries to clear vast swamps, excavate 240 million cubic yards of earth, and construct a series of immense locks. The project, a major engineering feat, took eight years and cost thousands of lives among the workers who built it. Opened in 1914, the **Panama Canal** gave the United States a commanding position in the Western Hemisphere.

Meanwhile, arguing that instability invited European intervention, Roosevelt announced in 1904 that the United States would police all of the Caribbean (Map 20.2). This so-called **Roosevelt Corollary** to the Monroe Doctrine actually turned that doctrine upside down: instead of guaranteeing that the United States would protect its neighbors from Europe and help preserve their independence, it asserted the United States's unrestricted right to regulate Caribbean affairs. The Roosevelt Corollary was not a treaty but a unilateral declaration sanctioned only by America's military and economic might. Citing it, the United States intervened regularly in Caribbean and Central American nations over the next three decades.

Entering office in 1913, Democratic president Woodrow Wilson criticized his predecessors' foreign policy. He pledged that the United States would "never again seek one additional foot of territory by conquest." This stance appealed to anti-imperialists in the Democratic base, including longtime supporters of William Jennings Bryan. But the new president soon showed that, when American interests called for it, his actions were not so different from those of Roosevelt and Taft.

Since the 1870s, Mexican dictator Porfirio Díaz had created a friendly climate for American companies that purchased Mexican plantations, mines, and oil fields. By the early 1900s, however, Díaz feared the extraordinary power of these foreign interests and began to nationalize — reclaim — key resources. American investors who

Panama Canal

A canal across the Isthmus of Panama connecting trade between the Atlantic and Pacific oceans. Built by the U.S. Army Corps of Engineers and opened in 1914, the canal gave U.S. naval vessels quick access to the Pacific and provided the United States with a commanding position in the Western Hemisphere.

Roosevelt Corollary

The 1904 assertion by President Theodore Roosevelt that the United States would act as a "policeman" in the Caribbean region and intervene in the affairs of nations that were guilty of "wrongdoing or impotence" in order to protect U.S. interests in Latin America.

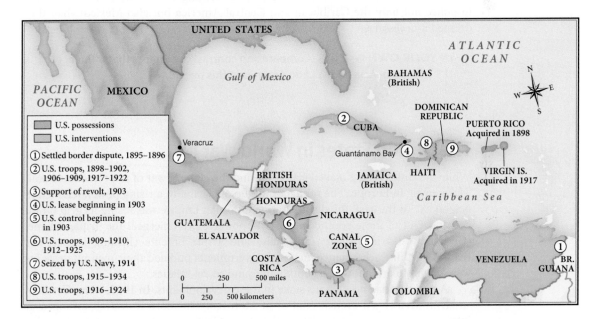

MAP 20.2 Policeman of the Caribbean

After the War of 1898, the United States vigorously asserted its interest in the affairs of its neighbors to the south. As the record of interventions shows, the United States truly became the "policeman" of the Caribbean and Central America.

faced the loss of Mexican holdings began to back Francisco Madero, an advocate of constitutional government who was friendly to U.S. interests. In 1911, Madero forced Díaz to resign and proclaimed himself president. Thousands of poor Mexicans took this opportunity to mobilize rural armies and demand more radical change. Madero's position was weak, and several strongmen sought to overthrow him; in 1913, he was deposed and murdered by a leading general. Immediately, several other military men vied for control.

Wilson, fearing that the unrest threatened U.S. interests, decided to intervene in the emerging Mexican Revolution. On the pretext of a minor insult to the navy, he ordered U.S. occupation of the port of Veracruz on April 21, 1914, at the cost of 19 American and 126 Mexican lives. Though the intervention helped Venustiano Carranza, the revolutionary leader whom Wilson most favored, Carranza protested it as illegitimate meddling in Mexican affairs. Carranza's forces, after nearly engaging the Americans themselves, entered Mexico City in triumph a few months later. Though Wilson had supported this outcome, his interference caused lasting mistrust.

Carranza's victory did not subdue revolutionary activity in Mexico. In 1916, General Francisco "Pancho" Villa—a thug to his enemies, but a heroic Robin Hood to many poor Mexicans—crossed the U.S.-Mexico border, killing sixteen American civilians and raiding the town of Columbus, New Mexico. Wilson sent 11,000 troops to pursue Villa, a force that soon resembled an army of occupation in northern Mexico. Mexican public opinion demanded withdrawal as armed clashes broke out between U.S. and Mexican troops. At the brink of war, both governments backed off and U.S. forces departed. But policymakers in Washington had shown their intention to police not only the Caribbean and Central America but also Mexico when they deemed it necessary.

> **IN YOUR OWN WORDS** Compare and contrast the factors that influenced U.S. actions in Asia and in Latin America in this period.

The United States in World War I

While the United States staked claims around the globe, a war of unprecedented scale was brewing in Europe. The military buildup of Germany, a rising power, terrified its neighbors. To the east, the disintegrating Ottoman Empire was losing its grip on the Balkans. Out of these conflicts, two rival power blocs emerged: the Triple Alliance (Germany, Austria-Hungary, and Italy) and Triple Entente (Britain, France, and Russia). Within each alliance, national governments pursued their own interests but were bound to one another by both public and secret treaties.

Americans had no obvious stake in these developments. In 1905, when Germany suddenly challenged French control of Morocco, Theodore Roosevelt arranged an international conference to defuse the crisis. Germany got a few concessions, but France—with British backing—retained Morocco. Accomplished in the same year that Roosevelt brokered peace between Russia and Japan, the conference seemed another diplomatic triumph. One U.S. official boasted that America had kept peace by "the power of our detachment." It was not to last.

From Neutrality to War

The spark that ignited World War I came in the Balkans, where Austria-Hungary and Russia competed for control. Austria's 1908 seizure of Ottoman provinces, including Bosnia, angered the nearby Slavic nation of Serbia and its ally, Russia. Serbian revolutionaries recruited Bosnian Slavs to resist Austrian rule. In June 1914, in the city of Sarajevo, university student Gavrilo Princip assassinated Archduke Franz Ferdinand, heir to the Austro-Hungarian throne.

Like dominos falling, the system of European alliances pushed all the powers into war. Austria-Hungary blamed Serbia for the assassination and declared war on July 28. Russia, tied by secret treaty to Serbia, mobilized against Austria-Hungary. This prompted Germany to declare war on Russia and its ally France. As a preparation for attacking France, Germany launched a brutal invasion of the neutral country of Belgium, which caused Great Britain to declare war on Germany. Within a week, most of Europe was at war, with the major Allies — Great Britain, France, and Russia — confronting the Central Powers of Germany and Austria-Hungary. Two military zones emerged. On the Western Front, Germany battled the British and French; on the Eastern Front, Germany and Austria-Hungary fought Russia. Because most of the warring nations held colonial empires, the conflict soon spread to the Middle East, Africa, and Asia.

The so-called Great War wreaked terrible devastation. New technology, some of it devised in the United States, made warfare deadlier than ever before. Every soldier carried a long-range, high-velocity rifle that could hit a target at 1,000 yards — a vast technical advancement over the 300-yard range of rifles used in the U.S. Civil War. The machine gun was even more lethal. Its American-born inventor, Hiram Maxim, had moved to Britain in the 1880s to follow a friend's advice: "If you want to make your fortune, invent something which will allow those fool Europeans to kill each other more quickly." Elaborate trenches, familiar from the Civil War era, were now enhanced with barbed wire to protect soldiers in defensive positions. Once advancing Germans ran into French fortifications, they stalled. Across a swath of Belgium and northeastern France, millions of soldiers on both sides hunkered down in fortified trenches. During 1916, repeatedly trying to break through French lines at Verdun, Germans suffered 450,000 casualties. The French fared even worse, with 550,000 dead or wounded. It was all to no avail. From 1914 to 1918, the Western Front barely moved.

At the war's outbreak, President Wilson called on Americans to be "neutral in fact as well as in name." If the United States remained out of the conflict, Wilson reasoned, he could influence the postwar settlement, much as Theodore Roosevelt had done after previous conflicts. Even if Wilson had wished to, it would have been nearly impossible in 1914 to unite Americans behind the Allies. Many Irish immigrants viewed Britain as an enemy — based on its continued occupation of Ireland — while millions of German Americans maintained ties to their homeland. Progressive-minded Republicans, such as Senator Robert La Follette of Wisconsin, vehemently opposed taking sides in a European fight, as did socialists, who condemned the war as a conflict among greedy capitalist empires. Two giants of American industry, Andrew Carnegie and Henry Ford, opposed the war. In December 1915, Ford sent a hundred men and women to Europe on a "peace ship" to urge an end to the war. "It would be folly," declared the *New York Sun*, "for the country to sacrifice itself to . . . the clash of ancient hatreds which is urging the Old World to destruction."

The Struggle to Remain Neutral The United States, wishing to trade with all the warring nations, might have remained neutral if Britain had not held commanding power at sea. In September 1914, the British imposed a naval blockade on the Central Powers to cut off vital supplies of food and military equipment. Though the Wilson administration protested this infringement of the rights of neutral carriers, commerce with the Allies more than made up for the economic loss. Trade with Britain and France grew fourfold over the next two years, to $3.2 billion in 1916; by 1917, U.S. banks had lent the Allies $2.5 billion. In contrast, American trade and loans to Germany stood then at a mere $56 million. This imbalance undercut U.S. neutrality. If Germany won and Britain and France defaulted on their debts, American companies would suffer catastrophic losses.

To challenge the British navy, Germany launched a devastating new weapon, the U-boat (short for *Unterseeboot*, "undersea boat," or submarine). In April 1915, Germany issued a warning that all ships flying flags of Britain or its allies were liable to destruction. A few weeks later, a U-boat torpedoed the British luxury liner *Lusitania* off the coast of Ireland, killing 1,198 people, including 128 Americans. The attack on the passenger ship (which was later revealed to have been carrying munitions) incensed Americans. The following year, in an agreement known as the Sussex pledge, Germany agreed not to target passenger liners or merchant ships unless an inspection showed the latter carried weapons. But the *Lusitania* sinking prompted Wilson to reconsider his options. After quietly trying to mediate in Europe but finding neither side interested in peace, he endorsed a $1 billion U.S. military buildup.

American public opinion still ran strongly against entering the war, a fact that shaped the election of 1916. Republicans rejected the belligerently prowar Theodore Roosevelt in favor of Supreme Court justice Charles Evans Hughes, a progressive former governor of New York. Democrats renominated Wilson, who campaigned on his domestic record and as the president who "kept us out of war." Wilson eked out a narrow victory; winning California by a mere 4,000 votes, he secured a slim majority in the electoral college.

America Enters the War Despite Wilson's campaign slogan, events pushed him toward war. In February 1917, Germany resumed unrestricted submarine warfare, a decision dictated by the impasse on the Western Front. In response, Wilson broke off diplomatic relations with Germany. A few weeks later, newspapers published an intercepted dispatch from German foreign secretary Arthur Zimmermann to his minister in Mexico. The **Zimmermann telegram** urged Mexico to join the Central Powers, promising that if the United States entered the war, Germany would help Mexico recover "the lost territory of Texas, New Mexico, and Arizona." With Pancho Villa's border raids still fresh in Americans' minds, this threat jolted public opinion. Meanwhile, German U-boats attacked U.S. ships without warning, sinking three on March 18 alone.

On April 2, 1917, Wilson asked Congress for a declaration of war. He argued that Germany had trampled on American rights and imperiled U.S. trade and citizens' lives. "We desire no conquest," Wilson declared, "no material compensation for the sacrifices we shall freely make." Reflecting his progressive idealism, Wilson promised that American involvement would make the world "safe for democracy." On April 6,

Zimmermann telegram
A 1917 intercepted dispatch in which German foreign secretary Arthur Zimmermann urged Mexico to join the Central Powers and promised that if the United States entered the war, Germany would help Mexico recover Texas, New Mexico, and Arizona. Published by American newspapers, the telegram outraged the American public and helped precipitate the move toward U.S. entry in the war on the Allied side.

the United States declared war on Germany. Reflecting the nation's divided views, the vote was far from unanimous. Six senators and fifty members of the House voted against entry, including Representative Jeannette Rankin of Montana, the first woman elected to Congress. "You can no more win a war than you can win an earthquake," Rankin said. "I want to stand by my country, but I cannot vote for war."

"Over There"

To Americans, Europe seemed a great distance away. Many assumed the United States would simply provide munitions and economic aid. "Good Lord," exclaimed one U.S. senator to a Wilson administration official, "you're not going to send soldiers over there, are you?" But when General John J. Pershing asked how the United States could best support the Allies, the French commander put it bluntly: "Men, men, and more men." Amid war fever, thousands of young men prepared to go "over there," in the words of George M. Cohan's popular song: "Make your Daddy glad to have had such a lad. / Tell your sweetheart not to pine, / To be proud her boy's in line."

Americans Join the War In 1917, the U.S. Army numbered fewer than 200,000 soldiers; needing more men, Congress instituted a military draft in May 1917. In contrast to the Civil War, when resistance was common, conscription went smoothly, partly because local, civilian-run draft boards played a central role in the new system. Still, draft registration demonstrated government's increasing power over ordinary citizens. On a single day—June 5, 1917—more than 9.5 million men between the ages of twenty-one and thirty registered at local voting precincts for possible military service.

President Wilson chose General Pershing to head the American Expeditionary Force (AEF), which had to be trained, outfitted, and carried across the submarine-plagued Atlantic. This required safer shipping. When the United States entered the war, German U-boats were sinking 900,000 tons of Allied ships each month. By sending merchant and troop ships in armed convoys, the U.S. Navy cut that monthly rate to 400,000 tons by the end of 1917. With trench warfare grinding on, Allied commanders pleaded for American soldiers to fill their depleted units, but Pershing waited until the AEF reached full strength. As late as May 1918, the brunt of the fighting fell to the French and British.

The Allies' burden increased when the Eastern Front collapsed following the Bolshevik (Communist) Revolution in Russia in November 1917. To consolidate power at home, the new Bolshevik government, led by Vladimir Lenin, sought peace with the Central Powers. In a 1918 treaty, Russia surrendered its claims over vast parts of its territories in exchange for peace. Released from war against Germany, the Bolsheviks turned their attention to a civil war at home. Terrified by communism, Japan and several Allied countries, including the United States, later sent troops to fight the Bolsheviks and aid forces loyal to the deposed tsar. But after a four-year civil war, Lenin's forces established full control over Russia and reclaimed Ukraine and other former possessions.

Peace with Russia freed Germany to launch a major offensive on the Western Front. By May 1918, German troops had advanced to within 50 miles of Paris. Pershing at last committed about 60,000 U.S. soldiers to support the French defense. With American soldiers engaged in massive numbers, Allied forces brought the Germans to a halt in July; by September, they forced a retreat. Pershing then pitted more than one million American soldiers against an outnumbered and exhausted German army in the Argonne forest. By early November, this attack broke German defenses at a crucial rail hub, Sedan. The cost was high: 26,000 Americans killed and 95,000 wounded (Map 20.3). But the flood of U.S. troops and supplies determined the outcome. Recognizing inevitable defeat and facing popular uprisings at home, Germany signed an armistice on November 11, 1918. The Great War was over.

The American Fighting Force By the end of World War I, almost 4 million American men — popularly known as "doughboys" — wore U.S. uniforms, as did several thousand female nurses. The recruits reflected America's heterogeneity: one-fifth had been born outside the United States, and soldiers spoke forty-nine different languages. Though ethnic diversity worried some observers, most predicted that military service would promote Americanization.

Over 400,000 African American men enlisted, accounting for 13 percent of the armed forces. Their wartime experiences were often grim: serving in segregated units,

MAP 20.3 U.S. Participation on the Western Front, 1918
When American troops reached the European front in significant numbers in 1918, the Allies and Central Powers had been fighting a deadly war of attrition for almost four years. The influx of American troops and supplies helped break the stalemate. Successful offensive maneuvers by the American Expeditionary Force included those at Belleau Wood and Château-Thierry and the Meuse-Argonne campaign.

they were given the most menial tasks. Racial discrimination hampered military efficiency and provoked violence at several camps. The worst incident occurred in August 1917, when, after suffering a string of racial attacks, black members of the 24th Infantry's Third Battalion rioted in Houston, killing 15 white civilians and police officers. The army tried 118 of the soldiers in military courts for mutiny and riot, hanged 19, and sentenced 63 to life in prison.

Unlike African Americans, American Indians served in integrated combat units. Racial stereotypes about Native Americans' prowess as warriors enhanced their military reputations, but it also prompted officers to assign them hazardous duties as scouts and snipers. About 13,000, or 25 percent, of the adult male American Indian population served during the war; roughly 5 percent died, compared to 2 percent for the military as a whole.

Most American soldiers escaped the horrors of sustained trench warfare. Still, during the brief period of U.S. participation, over 50,000 servicemen died in action; another 63,000 died from disease, mainly the devastating influenza pandemic that began early in 1918 and, over the next two years, killed 50 million people worldwide. The nation's military deaths, though substantial, were only a tenth as many as the 500,000 American civilians who died of this terrible epidemic — not to mention the staggering losses of Europeans in the war (America in Global Context).

War on the Home Front

In the United States, opponents of the war were a minority. Helping the Allies triggered an economic boom that benefitted farmers and working people. Many progressives also supported the war, hoping Wilson's ideals and wartime patriotism would renew Americans' attention to reform. But the war bitterly disappointed them. Rather than enhancing democracy, it chilled the political climate as government agencies tried to enforce "100 percent loyalty."

Mobilizing the Economy   American businesses made big bucks from World War I. As grain, weapons, and manufactured goods flowed to Britain and France, the United States became a creditor nation. Moreover, as the war drained British financial reserves, U.S. banks provided capital for investments around the globe.

Government powers expanded during wartime, with new federal agencies overseeing almost every part of the economy. The **War Industries Board** (WIB), established in July 1917, directed military production. After a fumbling start that showed the limits of voluntarism, the Wilson administration reorganized the board and placed Bernard Baruch, a Wall Street financier and superb administrator, at its head. Under his direction, the WIB allocated scarce resources among industries, ordered factories to convert to war production, set prices, and standardized procedures. Though he could compel compliance, Baruch preferred to win voluntary cooperation. A man of immense charm, he usually succeeded — helped by the lucrative military contracts at his disposal. Despite higher taxes, corporate profits soared, as military production sustained a boom that continued until 1920.

Some federal agencies took dramatic measures. The **National War Labor Board** (NWLB), formed in April 1918, established an eight-hour day for war workers with time-and-a-half pay for overtime, and it endorsed equal pay for women. In return for

War Industries Board
A federal board established in July 1917 to direct military production, including allocation of resources, conversion of factories to war production, and setting of prices.

National War Labor Board
A federal agency founded in 1918 that established an eight-hour day for war workers (with time-and-a-half pay for overtime), endorsed equal pay for women, and supported workers' right to organize.

The Human Cost of World War I

The United States played a crucial role in financing World War I. In its war-related expenditures, totaling $22.6 billion, the United States ranked fourth among all nations that participated, ranking behind only Germany ($37.7 billion), Britain ($35.3 billion), and France ($24.3 billion). In human terms, however, the U.S. role was different. Note that the figures below for military casualties are rough estimates. Civilian casualties are even more uncertain: the exact number of Russians, Italians, Romanians, Serbians, and others who died will never be known.

TABLE 20.1

World War I Casualties			
Country	Total Population	Military Killed or Missing	Total Civilian Deaths
Germany	67,000,000	2,037,000	700,000
Russia	167,000,000	1,800,000	2,000,000
France	39,000,000	1,385,300	40,000
Austria-Hungary	49,900,000	1,016,200	unknown
United Kingdom	46,400,000	702,410	1,386
Italy	35,000,000	462,400	unknown
Turkey	21,300,000	236,000	2,000,000*
Romania	7,510,000	219,800	265,000–500,000
Serbia	5,000,000	127,500	600,000
Bulgaria	5,500,000	77,450	275,000
India	316,000,000	62,060	negligible
Canada	7,400,000	58,990	negligible
Australia	4,872,000	53,560	negligible
United States	92,000,000	51,822	negligible

*Mostly Armenians

QUESTIONS FOR ANALYSIS

1. What does this data suggest about the comparative role of the United States in World War I? The experience of its soldiers? The war's impact on civilians in each nation?

2. Which other countries made contributions similar to that of the United States, and why?

Selling Liberty Bonds: Two Appeals   Once the United States entered the Great War, government officials sought to enlist all Americans in the battle against the Central Powers. They carefully crafted patriotic advertising campaigns that urged Americans to buy bonds, conserve food, enlist in the military, and support the war effort in many other ways. One of these posters appeals to recent immigrants, reminding them of their debt to American Liberty. The other shows the overtly anti-German prejudices of many war appeals: it depicts the "Hun," a slur for a German soldier, with bloody hands and bayonet.   Library of Congress.

a no-strike pledge, the NWLB also supported workers' right to organize — a major achievement for the labor movement. The Fuel Administration, meanwhile, introduced daylight saving time to conserve coal and oil. In December 1917, the Railroad Administration seized control of the nation's hodgepodge of private railroads, seeking to facilitate rapid movement of troops and equipment — an experiment that had, at best, mixed results.

Perhaps the most successful wartime agency was the Food Administration, created in August 1917 and led by engineer Herbert Hoover. With the slogan "Food will win the war," Hoover convinced farmers to nearly double their acreage of grain. This increase allowed a threefold rise in food exports to Europe. Among citizens, the Food Administration mobilized a "spirit of self-denial" rather than mandatory rationing. Female volunteers went from door to door to persuade housekeepers to observe "Wheatless" Mondays and "Porkless" Thursdays. Hoover, a Republican, emerged from the war as one of the nation's most admired public figures.

Promoting National Unity Suppressing wartime dissent became a near obsession for President Wilson. In April 1917, Wilson formed the Committee on Public Information (CPI), a government propaganda agency headed by journalist George Creel. Professing lofty goals — educating citizens about democracy, assimilating immigrants, and ending the isolation of rural life — the committee set out to mold Americans into "one white-hot mass" of war patriotism. The CPI touched the lives of nearly all civilians. It distributed seventy-five million pieces of literature and enlisted thousands of volunteers — **Four-Minute Men** — to deliver short prowar speeches at movie theaters.

Four-Minute Men
Name given to thousands of volunteers enlisted by the Committee on Public Information to deliver short prowar speeches at movie theaters to galvanize public support for the war. Their work, as part of the broader objectives of the CPI, helped create a political climate intolerant of dissent.

The CPI also pressured immigrant groups to become "One Hundred Percent Americans." German Americans bore the brunt of this campaign (Thinking Like a Historian). With posters exhorting citizens to root out German spies, a spirit of conformity pervaded the home front. A quasi-vigilante group, the American Protective League, mobilized about 250,000 "agents," furnished them with badges issued by the Justice Department, and trained them to spy on neighbors and coworkers. In 1918, members of the league led violent raids against draft evaders and peace activists. Government propaganda helped rouse a nativist hysteria that lingered into the 1920s.

Sedition Act of 1918
Wartime law that prohibited any words or behavior that might promote resistance to the United States or help in the cause of its enemies.

Congress also passed new laws to curb dissent. Among them was the **Sedition Act of 1918**, which prohibited any words or behavior that might "incite, provoke, or encourage resistance to the United States, or promote the cause of its enemies." Because this and an earlier Espionage Act (1917) defined treason loosely, they led to the conviction of more than a thousand people. The Justice Department prosecuted members of the Industrial Workers of the World, whose opposition to militarism threatened to disrupt war production of lumber and copper. When a Quaker pacifist teacher in New York City refused to teach a prowar curriculum, she was fired. Socialist Party leader Eugene V. Debs was sentenced to ten years in jail for the crime of arguing that wealthy capitalists had started the conflict and were forcing workers to fight.

Federal courts mostly supported the acts. In *Schenck v. United States* (1919), the Supreme Court upheld the conviction of a socialist who was jailed for circulating pamphlets that urged army draftees to resist induction. The justices followed this with a similar decision in *Abrams v. United States* (1919), ruling that authorities could prosecute speech they believed to pose "a clear and present danger to the safety of the country." In an important dissent, however, Justices Oliver Wendell Holmes Jr. and Louis Brandeis objected to the *Abrams* decision. Holmes's probing questions about the definition of "clear and present danger" helped launch twentieth-century legal battles over free speech and civil liberties.

Great Migrations World War I created tremendous economic opportunities at home. Jobs in war industries drew thousands of people to the cities. With so many men in uniform, jobs in heavy industry opened for the first time to African Americans, accelerating the pace of black migration from South to North. During World War I, more than 400,000 African Americans moved to such cities as St. Louis, Chicago, New York, and Detroit, in what became known as the **Great Migration**. The rewards were great, and taking war jobs could be a source of patriotic pride. "If it hadn't been for the negro," a Carnegie Steel manager later recalled, "we could hardly have carried on our operations."

Great Migration
The migration of over 400,000 African Americans from the rural South to the industrial cities of the North during and after World War I.

Blacks in the North encountered discrimination in jobs, housing, and education. But in the first flush of opportunity, most celebrated their escape from the repressive racism and poverty of the South. "It is a matter of a dollar with me and I feel that God made the path and I am walking therein," one woman reported to her sister back home. "Tell your husband work is plentiful here." "I just begin to feel like a man," wrote another migrant to a friend in Mississippi. "My children are going to the same school with the whites. . . . Will vote the next election and there isn't any 'yes sir' and 'no sir'—it's all yes and no and Sam and Bill."

Wartime labor shortages prompted Mexican Americans in the Southwest to leave farmwork for urban industrial jobs. Continued political instability in Mexico, combined with increased demand for farmworkers in the United States, also encouraged more Mexicans to move across the border. Between 1917 and 1920, at least 100,000 Mexicans entered the United States; despite discrimination, large numbers stayed. If asked why, many might have echoed the words of an African American man who left New Orleans for Chicago: they were going "north for a better chance." The same was true for Puerto Ricans such as Jésus Colón, who also confronted racism. "I came to New York to poor pay, long hours, terrible working conditions, discrimination even in the slums and in the poor paying factories," Colón recalled, "where the bosses very dexterously pitted Italians against Puerto Ricans and Puerto Ricans against American Negroes and Jews."

Women were the largest group to take advantage of wartime job opportunities. About 1 million women joined the paid labor force for the first time, while another 8 million gave up low-wage service jobs for higher-paying industrial work. Americans soon got used to the sight of female streetcar conductors, train engineers, and defense workers. Though most people expected these jobs to return to men in peacetime, the war created a new comfort level with women's employment outside the home—and with women's suffrage.

The Great Migration: Union Station, Jacksonville, Florida This photograph from 1921 shows a familiar sight across the South, especially after 1917 and 1918, when wartime jobs in Northern cities offered new opportunities for African Americans seeking to escape the Jim Crow South. Northern manufacturers, facing severe wartime labor shortages, sent labor agents to the South to recruit workers. These agents often arranged loans to pay for train fare and other travel expenses; once laborers were settled and employed in the North, they repaid the loans from their wages. In a typical pattern, some of the travelers in this photograph may have previously moved from rural parts of Florida to Jacksonville, before making the leap to the urban North. Photo by Woodward, courtesy of the State Archives of Florida.

Women's Voting Rights The National American Woman Suffrage Association (NAWSA) threw the support of its 2 million members wholeheartedly into the war effort. Its president, Carrie Chapman Catt, declared that women had to prove their patriotism to win the ballot. NAWSA members in thousands of communities promoted food conservation and distributed emergency relief through organizations such as the Red Cross.

Alice Paul and the **National Woman's Party** (NWP) took a more confrontational approach. Paul was a Quaker who had worked in the settlement movement and earned a PhD in political science. Finding as a NAWSA lobbyist that congressmen dismissed

National Woman's Party
A political party founded in 1916 that fought for an Equal Rights Amendment to the U.S. Constitution in the early twentieth century.

German Americans in World War I

Before 1917, Americans expressed diverse opinions about the war in Europe. After the United States joined the Allies, however, German Americans' loyalty became suspect. German immigrant men who were not U.S. citizens were required to register as "alien enemies," and government propaganda fueled fear of alleged German spies. In April 1918 in Collinsville, Illinois, a German-born socialist named Robert Prager—who had sought U.S. citizenship and tried to enlist in the navy—was lynched by drunken miners. The documents below shed light on German Americans' wartime experiences.

1. Advertisement, *Fatherland*, 1915. *This ad appeared in a political journal for German Americans. The translation of the songs offered on this recording are "Germany, Germany Above All" and "Precious Homeland."*

Patriotic German Music on Columbia Double-Disc Records

E2039	Deutschland, Deutschland über alles. . . .
10 in. — 75¢	Teure Heimat. . . .

COLUMBIA GRAMOPHONE COMPANY . . . DEALERS EVERYWHERE.

2. C. J. Hexamer, speech, Milwaukee, 1915. *This address by a German American community leader was widely cited during a 1918 investigation by the Senate Judiciary Committee.*

Whoever casts his Germanism from him like an old glove, is not worthy to be spit upon. . . . We have long suffered the preachment that "you Germans must allow yourselves to be assimilated, you must merge more in the American people;" but no one will ever find us prepared to step down to a lesser culture. No, we have made it our aim to elevate the others to us. . . . Be strong, and German. Remember, you German pioneers, that we are giving to this people the best the earth affords, the benefits of Germanic *kultur*.

3. Sign in a Chicago park, 1917.

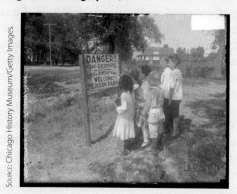

SOURCE: Chicago History Museum/Getty Images.

4. "Lager Uber Alles" cartoon, 1918. *This cartoon was part of an Ohio Anti-Saloon League referendum campaign to prohibit liquor sales. Ohio voters had rejected such a measure in 1915 and 1917, but in 1918 a majority voted for prohibition. Many U.S. breweries, such as Anheuser-Busch and Pabst, were owned by German Americans. "Hun" was an epithet for Germans; "Lager (Beer) Uber Alles" refers to the German national anthem cited in source 1.*

SOURCE: Courtesy of The Ohio State University Department of History.

5. James W. Gerard, radio address, 1917. *Gerard was U.S. ambassador to Great Britain.*

The great majority of American citizens of German descent have, in this great crisis in our history, shown themselves splendidly loyal to our flag. Everyone has a right to sympathize with any warring nation. But now that we are in the war there are only two sides, and the time has come when every citizen must declare himself American — or traitor!

. . . The Foreign Minister of Germany once said to me ". . . we have in your country 500,000 German reservists who will rise in arms against your government if you dare to make a move against Germany." Well, I told him that that might be so, but that we had 500,001 lampposts in this country, and that that was where the reservists would be hanging the day after they tried to rise. And if there are any German-Americans here who are so ungrateful for all the benefits they have received that they are still for the Kaiser, there is only one thing to do with them. And that is to hog-tie them, give them back the wooden shoes and the rags they landed in, and ship them back. . . . There is no animal that bites and kicks and squeals . . . equal to a fat German-American, if you commenced to tie him up and told him that he was on his way back to the Kaiser.

6. Actions by New York *liederkranz* reported in *New Orleans Times-Picayune*, May 16, 1918. *Liederkranz, or singing societies, played a vital role in German immigrant communities. Before World War I the city of Wheeling, West Virginia, counted eleven such societies, with names like Harmonie, Germania, and Mozart. By 1918 most liederkranz had vanished. New York City's was one of the few that did not.*

Members of the [New York] Liederkranz, an organization founded seventy-one years ago by Germans . . . met tonight and placed on record their unqualified Americanism.

. . . They declared English the official language of the organization, and for the first time in years the sound of an enemy tongue will not be heard in the club's halls. Likewise they reiterated their offer to turn the buildings over to the government as a hospital if it were necessary.

7. Lola Gamble Clyde, 1976 interview on life in Idaho during World War I. *In the 1970s, historians interviewed residents of rural Latah County, Idaho, about their experiences in World War I. Frank Brocke, a farmer, recalled that neighbors on their joint telephone line would slam down the phone when his mother or sister spoke German. "We had to be so careful," he said.*

I remember when they smashed out store windows at Uniontown that said [sauer] kraut. . . . Nobody would eat kraut. Throw the Kraut out, they were Germans. . . . Even the great Williamson store, he went in and gathered up everything that was made in Germany, and had a big bonfire out in the middle of the street, you know. Although he had many good German friends all over the county that had helped make him rich. . . . And if it was a German name — we'll just change our name. . . . There were some [German American] boys that got draft deferments. . . . Some of them said that their fathers were sick and dying, and their father had so much land they had to stay home and farm it for them. . . . [Local men] tarred and feathered some of them. Some of them as old men dying still resented and remembered.

Sources: (1) Frederick C. Luebke, *Bonds of Loyalty: German Americans and World War I* (Dekalb: Northern Illinois University Press, 1974), 109; (2) *Hearings Before the Subcommittee on the Judiciary, United States Senate, 65th Congress, Second Session* (Washington, DC: Government Printing Office, 1918), 300; (5) Gerard speech, transcript and recording, at Library of Congress American Memory: memory.loc.gov/ammem/nfhtml/nforSpeakers01.html; (6) *New Orleans Times-Picayune*, May 16, 1918; (7) Oral histories of Idaho residents at GMU History Matters, historymatters.gmu.edu/d/2/. Excerpt courtesy of Latah County Historical Society.

ANALYZING THE EVIDENCE

1. How did conditions change for German Americans between 1915 and 1918?

2. According to these sources, what aspects of German American culture did other Americans find threatening? What forms did anti-German hostility take?

3. Compare the sources that offer a German American perspective (sources 1, 2, 6, and 7) to those that represent a threat to German Americans' way of life (3, 4, 5). How did German Americans respond to growing anti-German sentiment in this period?

PUTTING IT ALL TOGETHER

World War I heightened anxieties about who was a "true" American. What groups were singled out in particular and why? What continuities do you see between these fears over "hyphenated" identities and controversies in earlier eras of U.S. history? Today?

her, Paul founded the NWP in 1916. Inspired by militant British suffragists, the group began in July 1917 to picket the White House. Standing silently with their banners, Paul and other NWP activists faced arrest for obstructing traffic and were sentenced to seven months in jail. They protested by going on a hunger strike, which prison authorities met with forced feeding. Public shock at the women's treatment drew attention to the suffrage cause.

Impressed by NAWSA's patriotism and worried by the NWP's militancy, the anti-suffrage Wilson reversed his position. In January 1918, he urged support for woman suffrage as a "war measure." The constitutional amendment quickly passed the House of Representatives; it took eighteen months to get through the Senate and another year to win ratification by the states. On August 26, 1920, when Tennessee voted for ratification, the Nineteenth Amendment became law. The state thus joined Texas as one of two ex-Confederate states to ratify it. In most parts of the South, the measure meant that *white* women began to vote: in this Jim Crow era, African American women's voting rights remained restricted along with men's.

In explaining suffragists' victory, historians have debated the relative effectiveness of Catt's patriotic strategy and Paul's militant protests. Both played a role in persuading Wilson and Congress to act, but neither might have worked without the extraordinary impact of the Great War. Across the globe, before 1914, the only places where women had full suffrage were New Zealand, Australia, Finland, and Norway. After World War I, many nations moved to enfranchise women. The new Soviet Union acted first, in 1917, with Great Britain and Canada following in 1918; by 1920, the measure had passed in Germany, Austria, Poland, Czechoslovakia, and Hungary as well as the United States. (Major exceptions were France and Italy, where women did not gain voting rights until after World War II, and Switzerland, which held out until 1971.) Thus, while World War I introduced modern horrors on the battlefield — machine guns and poison gas — it brought some positive results at home: economic opportunity and women's political participation.

> **IN YOUR OWN WORDS** What changes did U.S. participation in World War I bring about on the home front?

Catastrophe at Versailles

Fourteen Points
Principles for a new world order proposed in 1919 by President Woodrow Wilson as a basis for peace negotiations at Versailles. Among them were open diplomacy, freedom of the seas, free trade, territorial integrity, arms reduction, national self-determination, and creation of the League of Nations.

The idealistic Wilson argued that no victor should be declared after World War I: only "peace among equals" could last. Having won at an incredible price, Britain and France showed zero interest in such a plan. But the devastation wrought by the war created popular pressure for a just and enduring outcome. At the peace conference held at Versailles, near Paris, in 1919, Wilson scored a diplomatic victory when the Allies chose to base the talks on his **Fourteen Points**, a blueprint for peace that he had presented a year earlier in a speech to Congress.

Wilson's Points embodied an important strand in progressivism. They called for open diplomacy; "absolute freedom of navigation upon the seas"; arms reduction; removal of trade barriers; and national self-determination for peoples in the Austro-Hungarian, Russian, and German empires. Essential to Wilson's vision was the creation of an international regulatory body — eventually called the **League of Nations** — that would guarantee each country's "independence and territorial integrity." The League would mediate disputes, supervise arms reduction, and — according to its crucial Article X — curb aggressor nations through collective military action. Wilson hoped the League would "end all wars." But his ideals had marked limits, and in negotiations he confronted harsh realities (Interpretations).

The Fate of Wilson's Ideas

The peace conference included ten thousand representatives from around the globe, but leaders of France, Britain, and the United States dominated the proceedings. When the Japanese delegation proposed a declaration for equal treatment of all races, the Allies rejected it. Similarly, the Allies ignored a global Pan-African Congress, organized by W. E. B. Du Bois and other black leaders; they snubbed Arab representatives who had been military allies during the war. Even Italy's prime minister — included among the influential "Big Four" because in 1915 Italy had switched to the Allied side — withdrew from the conference, aggrieved at the way British and French leaders marginalized him. The Allies excluded two key players: Russia, because they distrusted its communist leaders, and Germany, because they planned to dictate terms to their defeated foe. For Wilson's "peace among equals," it was a terrible start.

Prime Minister David Lloyd George of Britain and Premier Georges Clemenceau of France imposed harsh punishments on Germany. Unbeknownst to others at the time, they had already made secret agreements to divide up Germany's African colonies and take them as spoils of war. At Versailles, they also forced the defeated nation to pay $33 billion in reparations and surrender coal supplies, merchant ships, valuable patents, and even territory along the French border. These terms caused keen resentment and economic hardship in Germany, and over the following two decades they helped lead to World War II.

Given these conditions, it is remarkable that Wilson influenced the **Treaty of Versailles** as much as he did. He intervened repeatedly to soften conditions imposed on Germany. In accordance with the Fourteen Points, he worked with the other Allies to fashion nine new nations, stretching from the Baltic to the Mediterranean (Map 20.4 and Map 20.5). These were intended as a buffer to protect Western Europe from communist Russia; the plan also embodied Wilson's principle of self-determination for European states. Elsewhere in the world, the Allies dismantled their enemies' empires but did not create independent nations, keeping colonized people subordinate to European power. France, for example, refused to give up its long-standing occupation of Indochina; Clemenceau's snub of future Vietnamese leader Ho Chi Minh, who sought representation at Versailles, had grave long-term consequences for both France and the United States.

The establishment of a British mandate in Palestine (now Israel) also proved crucial. During the war, British foreign secretary Sir Arthur Balfour had stated that his country would work to establish there a "national home for the Jewish people," with the condition that "nothing shall be done which may prejudice the civil and religious rights of existing non-Jewish communities in Palestine." Under the British mandate, thousands of Jews moved to Palestine and purchased land, in some cases evicting Palestinian tenants. As early as 1920, riots erupted between Jews and Palestinians — a situation that, even before World War II, escalated beyond British control.

League of Nations
The international organization bringing together world governments to prevent future hostilities, proposed by President Woodrow Wilson in the aftermath of World War I. Although the League of Nations did form, the United States never became a member state.

Treaty of Versailles
The 1919 treaty that ended World War I. The agreement redrew the map of the world, assigned Germany sole responsibility for the war, and saddled it with a debt of $33 billion in war damages. Its long-term impact around the globe — including the creation of British and French imperial "mandates" — was catastrophic.

MAP 20.4 AND MAP 20.5 Europe and the Middle East Before and After World War I
World War I and its aftermath dramatically altered the landscape of Europe and the Middle East. Before the war, the most powerful nations belonged to two alliances: the Central Powers (Germany, Austria-Hungary, and Italy) and the Entente (Great Britain, France, and Russia). The latter's victory, along with the 1917 communist revolution in Russia, dramatically reshaped power relations. Collapse of the German, Austro-Hungarian, and Russian empires allowed reconstitution of Poland and creation of a string of new states along the Baltic Sea and in Eastern Europe, based on the principle of national (ethnic) self-determination. The demise of the Ottoman Empire prompted creation of four quasi-independent territories, or "mandates": Iraq, Syria, Lebanon, and Palestine. The League of Nations stipulated that their affairs would be supervised by one of the victorious Allied powers.

The Versailles treaty thus created conditions for horrific future bloodshed, and it must be judged one of history's great catastrophes. Balfour astutely described Clemenceau, Lloyd George, and Wilson as "all-powerful, all-ignorant men, sitting there and carving up continents." Wilson, however, remained optimistic as he returned home, even though his health was beginning to fail. The president hoped the new League of Nations, authorized by the treaty, would moderate the settlement and secure peaceful resolutions of other disputes. For this to occur, U.S. participation was crucial.

Congress Rejects the Treaty

The outlook for U.S. ratification was not promising. Though major opinion makers and religious denominations supported the treaty, openly hostile Republicans held a majority in the Senate. One group, called the "irreconcilables," consisted of western progressive Republicans such as Hiram Johnson of California and Robert La Follette of Wisconsin, who opposed U.S. involvement in European affairs. Another group, led by Senator Henry Cabot Lodge of Massachusetts, worried that Article X—the provision for collective security—would prevent the United States from pursuing an independent foreign policy. Was the nation, Lodge asked, "willing to have the youth

Was Wilson's Internationalism Successful?

President Woodrow Wilson won a hard-fought reelection in 1916 by maintaining American neutrality in the Great War then raging across Europe. Only a month after his second inauguration, however, he reluctantly abandoned his policy of "armed neutrality" after Germany resumed its unrestricted submarine warfare and sunk American ships.

In asking Congress for a declaration of war, Wilson envisioned a future peace based on the principles of democracy, the collective security of nations, and a system of international law to avert future wars. A League of Nations was at the center of his postwar vision, which he announced in his January 1918 "Fourteen Points" speech. But a number of factors frustrated Wilson's plans, with the result that the Republican-controlled Congress rejected the treaty Wilson had negotiated. Historians John Milton Cooper Jr. and Elizabeth McKillen offer contrasting views of Wilson's internationalism and the League of Nations proposal.

JOHN MILTON COOPER JR.

SOURCE: John Milton Cooper Jr., *Woodrow Wilson: A Biography* (New York: Alfred A. Knopf, 2009), 474–475.

[T]he substance of the Draft Covenant . . . [included the] guarantee of independence and territorial integrity . . . and asserted the right of the League of Nations to concern itself about "war or threat of war" anywhere in the world. Articles XII through XV established procedures for mediation and arbitration and called for a "Permanent Court of International Justice." Article XVI laid down the League's authority to impose economic boycotts and recommend the use of force. . . . [A]ll these features of Wilson's . . . were in the Draft Covenant. . . . It was a remarkable achievement, and the lion's share of the credit belonged to Wilson.

ELIZABETH MCKILLEN

SOURCE: Elizabeth McKillen, *Making the World Safe for Workers: Labor, the Left and Wilsonian Internationalism* (Urbana: University of Illinois Press, 2013), 243–244.

The U.S. and transnational labor and Left debate over the Versailles Treaty, League [of Nations] and ILO [International Labor Organization] exposed fundamental contradictions in Wilsonian internationalism. . . . [F]rom the perspective of Left activists, a League comprised of the same government elites who had caused World War I was unlikely to fundamentally alter the imperial status quo in ways that would advance the interests of the world's workers or ensure future peace and prosperity. . . . Socialist and labor activists unmasked the Wilson administration's tendencies toward . . . the belief that other nations could be immeasurably improved by reshaping them in an American mold.

QUESTIONS FOR ANALYSIS

1. How do these historians differ in their assessment of Wilson's internationalism?
2. To what extent do these historians see the League of Nations as a solution to the international problems Wilson observed?
3. From these excerpts and the relevant sections of the chapter, identify at least two reasons why Wilson failed to win ratification of the Treaty of Versailles.

of America ordered to war" by an international body? Wilson refused to accept any amendments, especially to placate Lodge, a hated rival. "I shall consent to nothing," the president told the French ambassador. "The Senate must take its medicine."

To mobilize support, Wilson embarked on an exhausting speaking tour. His impassioned defense of the League of Nations brought audiences to tears, but the strain proved too much for the president. While visiting Colorado in September 1919, Wilson collapsed. A week later, back in Washington, he suffered a stroke that left one side of his body paralyzed. Wilson still urged Democratic senators to reject all Republican amendments. When the treaty came up for a vote in November 1919, it failed to win the required two-thirds majority. A second attempt, in March 1920, fell seven votes short.

The treaty was dead, and so was Wilson's leadership. The president never fully recovered from his stroke. During the last eighteen months of his administration, the government drifted as Wilson's physician, his wife, and various cabinet heads secretly took charge. The United States never ratified the Versailles treaty or joined the League of Nations. In turn, the League was weak. When Wilson died in 1924, his dream of a just and peaceful international order lay in ruins.

The impact of World War I can hardly be overstated. Despite bids for power by Britain and France, Europe's hold on its colonial empires never recovered. The United States, now a major world power, appeared to turn its back on the world when it rejected the Versailles treaty. But in laying claim to Hawaii and the Philippines, asserting power in Latin America, and intervening in Asia, the United States had entangled itself deeply in global politics. By 1918, the nation had gained too much diplomatic clout — and was too dependent on overseas trade — for isolation to be a realistic long-term option.

On the home front, the effects of World War I were no less dramatic. Wartime jobs and prosperity ushered in an era of exuberant consumerism, while the achievements of women's voting rights seemed to presage a new progressive era. But as peace returned, it became clear that the war had not advanced reform. Rather than embracing government activism, Americans of the 1920s proved eager to relinquish it.

> **IN YOUR OWN WORDS**   What arguments did U.S. political leaders make for and against ratification of the Versailles treaty?

Summary

Between 1877 and 1918, the United States rose as a major economic and military power. Justifications for overseas expansion emphasized access to global markets, the importance of sea power, and the need to police international misconduct and trade. These justifications shaped U.S. policy toward European powers in Latin America, and victory in the War of 1898 enabled the United States to take control of former Spanish colonies in the Caribbean and Pacific. Victory, however, also led to bloody conflict in the Philippines as the United States struggled to suppress Filipino resistance to American rule.

After 1899, the United States aggressively asserted its interests in Asia and Latin America. In China, the United States used the so-called Boxer Rebellion to make good its claim to an "open door" to Chinese markets. Later, President Theodore Roosevelt strengthened relations with Japan, and his successor, William Howard Taft, supported U.S. business interests in China. In the Caribbean, the United States constructed the Panama Canal and regularly exercised the right, claimed under the Roosevelt Corollary, to intervene in the affairs of states in the region. President Woodrow Wilson publicly disparaged the imperialism of his predecessors but repeatedly used the U.S. military to "police" Mexico.

At the outbreak of World War I, the United States asserted neutrality, but its economic ties to the Allies rapidly undercut that claim. In 1917, German submarine attacks drew the United States into the war on the side of Britain and France. Involvement in the war profoundly transformed the economy, politics, and society of the nation, resulting in an economic boom, mass migrations of workers to industrial centers, and the achievement of national voting rights. At the Paris Peace Conference, Wilson attempted to implement his Fourteen Points. However, the designs of the Allies in Europe undermined the Treaty of Versailles, while Republican resistance at home prevented ratification of the treaty. Although Wilson's dream of a just international order failed, the United States had taken its place as a major world power.

CHAPTER 20 REVIEW

TERMS TO KNOW   *Identify and explain the significance of each term below.*

Key Concepts and Events

American exceptionalism (p. 653)	Root-Takahira Agreement (p. 660)	War Industries Board (p. 667)	Great Migration (p. 670)
Teller Amendment (p. 654)	Panama Canal (p. 661)	National War Labor Board (p. 667)	National Woman's Party (p. 671)
Insular Cases (p. 658)	Roosevelt Corollary (p. 661)	Four-Minute Men (p. 670)	Fourteen Points (p. 674)
Platt Amendment (p. 658)	Zimmermann telegram (p. 664)	Sedition Act of 1918 (p. 670)	League of Nations (p. 675)
"open door" policy (p. 658)			Treaty of Versailles (p. 675)

Key People

Theodore Roosevelt (p. 653)	Queen Liliuokalani (p. 665)	Woodrow Wilson (p. 661)	Herbert Hoover (p. 669)
Alfred Mahan (p. 653)	Emilio Aguinaldo (p. 656)	Porfirio Díaz (p. 661)	Alice Paul (p. 671)

REVIEW QUESTIONS   *Answer these questions to demonstrate your understanding of the chapter's main ideas.*

1. Explain the steps by which the late-nineteenth-century U.S. government began to exert military influence in different regions of the world.

2. Compare and contrast the factors that influenced U.S. actions in Asia and in Latin America in this period.

3. What changes did U.S. participation in World War I bring about on the home front?

4. What arguments did U.S. political leaders make for and against ratification of the Versailles treaty?

5. Review the events listed under "America in the World" on the thematic timeline on page 649. By the end of World War I, what influence did the United States exercise in European affairs and in the Caribbean, Latin America, the Pacific, and China? How, and to what extent, had its power in each region expanded over the previous four decades? Compare and contrast the role of the United States to the roles of other powers in each region.

MAKING CONNECTIONS   *Recognize the larger developments and continuities within and across chapters.*

1. Read again the documents from "Representing Indians" in Chapter 15 (Thinking Like a Historian, pp. 514–515). In what ways might ideas about Native Americans have informed attitudes toward Hawaiians, Filipinos, and other people of color overseas? How might this explain which peoples Woodrow Wilson included and excluded in his ideal of "national self-determination"? Write a short essay in which you explain how Americans' policies and attitudes toward Native peoples within North America shaped U.S. foreign policy between 1898 and 1918.

2. Review the images on pages 669, 671, and 672. What do they tell us about the opportunities and risks that World War I posed for different groups of Americans? What constraints might young men and women of different ethnic backgrounds have faced, and what factors might they have considered, when deciding what wartime activities to pursue?

KEY TURNING POINTS   *Refer to the chapter chronology on page 652 for help in answering the question below.*

Identify at least five events from the chapter chronology that demonstrate the rising global power of the United States. Compare their consequences. How might an observer from another country have interpreted the United States's actions in each case?

21

CHAPTER

Unsettled Prosperity: From War to Depression
1919–1932

For the United States, World War I was neither the ghastly and devastating experience that it was for Europe nor the profoundly disillusioning one it was in many other parts of the world. Yet the war years marked a crucial historical divide for Americans, and the country entered a distinctly new era after 1919. Progressivism flagged and gave way to a business-centered philosophy of government. The manufacturing economy surged and delivered a cornucopia of consumer goods to a growing middle class. In the halls of government and in the streets, Americans clashed over what a pluralist, modern society should look like — who got to define what it meant to be "American"? In the complex and turbulent years between World War I and the coming of a new era of reform in 1933, these were the defining themes: limited government, consumerism, and cultural warfare.

In this decade and a half, economic growth and cultural conflict revealed patterns in American life that would hold for the remainder of the twentieth century. The nation had become urban. Mass media and Hollywood shaped popular culture. The automobile became an affordable mass commodity, even a necessity, changing forever the way people lived. Many Americans celebrated the dawning of what they called a "new era," defined by freer individual lifestyles, convenient consumer technologies, and "modern" ways of thinking. Others saw this emerging modernity as a threat to their own social and cultural influence. Groups of native-born, Protestant Americans, for instance, battled with immigrants to define the meaning of race, religion, and national belonging. Many white Americans lashed out at black Americans — in often deadly ways — over economic opportunity. And Catholic, Protestant, Jewish, and secular Americans clashed over everything from the prohibition of alcohol to the teaching of evolution.

By the end of the 1920s, political and cultural divides had hardened, and economic abundance proved short-lived, as the nation slid from consumer boom to Great Depression bust in 1929. The United States had grown more affluent, but it was an unsettled affluence. If the question in the decades of populist and progressive insurgent movements had been "whose government?" in the 1920s the question took on a broader cast: "whose country?"

> ## IDENTIFY THE BIG IDEA
>
> **What conflicts in culture and politics arose in the 1920s, and how did economic developments in that decade help cause the Great Depression?**

Celebrating the Fourth of July, 1926 This *Life* magazine cover celebrates two famous symbols of the 1920s: jazz music and the "flapper," in her droopy leggings and scandalously short skirt, who loves to dance to its rhythms. The flags at the top record the latest slang expressions, including "so's your old man" and "step on it" ("it" being the accelerator of an automobile, in a decade when cars were America's hottest commodity). Americans embraced new and exuberant forms of consumption and material well being in the 1920s, but in an age of alcohol prohibition and the rise of the Ku Klux Klan, they also fought with one another over deeply held beliefs and values. Picture Research Consultants & Archives.

CHAPTER CHRONOLOGY

As you read, ask yourself why this chapter begins and ends with these dates and identify the links among related events.

1915	▶ New Ku Klux Klan founded ▶ United States occupies Haiti	**1923**	▶ President Harding dies ▶ Calvin Coolidge assumes presidency ▶ Race riot in Rosewood, Florida ▶ Teapot Dome scandal ▶ Equal Rights Amendment first introduced in Congress
1916	▶ United States occupies Dominican Republic		
1917	▶ Race riot in East St. Louis, Illinois		
1919	▶ Race riot in Chicago ▶ Boston police strike ▶ Palmer raids	**1924**	▶ National Origins Act ▶ Coolidge wins presidential election against Democrats and La Follette's Progressive Party ▶ First suburban shopping center opens outside Kansas City, Missouri
1920	▶ Height of Red Scare ▶ Eighteenth Amendment (prohibition) takes effect ▶ Warren Harding wins presidency		
		1925	▶ Scopes "monkey trial" ▶ Alain Locke's *The New Negro*
1921	▶ Race riot in Tulsa, Oklahoma ▶ Sheppard-Towner Federal Maternity and Infancy Act	**1927**	▶ Sacco and Vanzetti executed
		1928	▶ Herbert Hoover wins presidency
		1929	▶ Stock market crashes precipitate Great Depression

Resurgent Conservatism

World War I brought an end to the long period of reform stretching from the 1880s to the 1910s (Chapter 19). A resurgent political conservatism emerged in the war's aftermath. Progressivism survived, but limited government was the dominant motif of national political life from 1919 to the election of Franklin D. Roosevelt in 1932. In place of progressives' call for economic regulation, business priorities now came to the fore. President Calvin Coolidge declared, "The man who builds a factory builds a temple. The man who works there worships there." The same theme prevailed in continued U.S. foreign policy: American business needs were the top priority. The single year of 1919 set the tone for this resurgent conservatism. An antiradical Red Scare, a massive strike wave, and white violence against African Americans together roiled the country and slowed the pace of social change.

The Red Scare

The war effort, overseen by a Democratic administration sympathetic to organized labor, had increased the size and power of labor unions. Membership in the American Federation of Labor (AFL) grew by a third during World War I, reaching more than 3 million by war's end. Workers' expectations also rose as the war economy brought higher pay and better working conditions. To extend these gains, in the first year after the armistice, 1919, more than 4 million wage laborers — one in every five — went on strike, a proportion never since equaled. A walkout of shipyard workers in Seattle sparked a general strike that shut down the entire city. Another strike disrupted the steel industry, as 350,000 workers demanded union recognition and an end to twelve-hour

Red Scare
A term for anticommunist hysteria that swept the United States, first after World War I, and led to a series of government raids on alleged subversives and a suppression of civil liberties.

shifts. Most strikes were about basic economic issues — pay and hours — rather than revolution, but the bold exercise of worker power fueled dire warnings of rising radicalism from labor's opponents.

That same year, when the Soviet Union's new Bolshevik leaders founded the Third International with the intent to foster revolutions abroad, some Americans raised fears that the U.S. harbored dangerous radicals. Wartime hatred of Germans was replaced by hostility toward Bolsheviks (labeled "Reds," after the color of communist flags). In a telling example, Ole Hanson, Seattle's mayor during the general strike, wrote a book called *Americanism Versus Bolshevism* and toured the country lecturing about the threat of revolution. Under the banner of "one hundred percent Americanism," groups such as the newly formed American Legion decried socialists, communists, and the Industrial Workers of the World (IWW) as un-American. Ironically, American communists remained few in number and had little political influence. Of the 63 million adults in the United States in 1920, no more than 13,000 belonged to either the fledgling U.S. Communist Party or the Communist Labor Party.

The strike wave combined with anti-Bolshevism to create fertile conditions for repression. When alert postal workers discovered thirty-four mail bombs addressed to government officials in April 1919, and in June a bomb detonated outside the Washington town house of Attorney General A. Mitchell Palmer, the repression came. Palmer escaped unharmed, but he used the incident to fan public fears, precipitating a convulsive **Red Scare**. He set up an antiradicalism division in the Justice Department and appointed his assistant J. Edgar Hoover to direct it; in 1935, it became the Federal Bureau of Investigation (FBI). In November, Palmer's agents stormed the headquarters of radical organizations. The dragnet captured thousands of immigrants who had committed no crimes but who held anarchist or revolutionary beliefs. Lacking the protection of U.S. citizenship, many were deported without indictment or trial. The **Palmer raids** peaked on a notorious night in January 1920, when federal agents invaded homes and meeting halls, arrested six thousand citizens and aliens (immigrants without U.S. citizenship), and denied the prisoners access to legal counsel.

The Red Scare's fusion of antiradicalism and anti-immigrant sentiment had dire consequences in the case of Sacco and Vanzetti. In May 1920, at the height of the Red Scare, police arrested Nicola Sacco, a shoemaker, and Bartolomeo Vanzetti,

When it sticks its head out, soak it.

Fear of "Bolshevism," 1919 This cartoon from the *Cleveland Plain Dealer* in Cleveland, Ohio, reflects nationwide panic over the general strike by 110 unions that paralyzed Seattle in February 1919. Opponents of radical labor unrest had a deeper fear: the Bolshevik Revolution in Russia, resulting in creation of the USSR, had brought into existence the world's first enduring communist state. By crushing unions in Seattle with a club of "Law and Order," this image suggests that Uncle Sam could beat back the global communist threat. This aspect of the 1919 Red Scare prefigured, at an early date, the anxieties of the Cold War era. Ohio Historical Society Red Dawn RD8A.

Palmer raids
A series of raids led by Attorney General A. Mitchell Palmer on radical organizations that peaked in January 1920, when federal agents arrested six thousand citizens and aliens and denied them access to legal counsel.

a fish peddler, for the murder of two men during a robbery of a shoe company in South Braintree, Massachusetts. Sacco and Vanzetti were Italian immigrants and self-proclaimed anarchists who had evaded the draft. Convicted of the murders, Sacco and Vanzetti sat in jail for six years while supporters appealed their verdicts. In 1927, Judge Webster Thayer denied a motion for a new trial and sentenced them to death. Scholars still debate their guilt or innocence. But the case was clearly biased by prosecutors' emphasis on their ties to radical groups and perhaps on their foreign birth. The execution of Sacco and Vanzetti was one of the ugly scars left by the hostilities of the Red Scare.

Racial Backlash

Other forms of repression escalated during and after World War I. The Great Migration drew hundreds of thousands of African Americans from the South to northern and midwestern industrial cities, where they secured wartime jobs and found they could vote and use their new economic clout to build community institutions and work for racial justice. The arrival of these southern migrants during the war deepened existing racial tensions, as African Americans competed with whites — including recent immigrants from Europe — for jobs and scarce housing.

Racism turned such conflicts into violent confrontations during the war. One of the deadliest riots in American history occurred in 1917 in East St. Louis, Illinois, where rampaging whites burned more than 300 black homes and murdered between 50 and 150 black men, women, and children (the exact death toll remains unknown). "This is a crime against the laws of humanity," said Marcus Garvey, the influential black leader of the Universal Negro Improvement Association.

Tensions also increased after the war because African Americans emerged from the conflict determined to achieve citizenship rights. Millions had loyally supported the war effort, and 370,000 had served in uniform. Returning veterans, empowered by their military service, often refused to accept second-class treatment at the hands of whites, whether North or South. The black man, one observer wrote, "realized that he was part and parcel of the great army of democracy. . . . With this realization came the consciousness of pride in himself as a man, and an American citizen."

These developments sparked white violence. In what became known as **Red Summer** because of bloody battles in more than twenty-four cities, Chicago endured five days of rioting in July 1919 after white youths stoned a black teenager to death on a Lake Michigan beach. By September, the national death toll from racial violence that year reached 120. There were also 78 lynchings in 1919, up from 48 in 1917. That number included several murders of returning black soldiers in uniform.

Attacks on African Americans continued after 1919. The oil boomtown of Tulsa, Oklahoma, was the site of a horrific incident in June 1921. Sensational, false reports of an alleged rape helped incite white mobs who resented growing black prosperity. Anger focused on the 8,000 residents of Tulsa's prosperous Greenwood district, locally known as "the black Wall Street." The mobs — helped by National Guardsmen, who arrested African Americans who resisted — burned thirty-five blocks of Greenwood and killed several dozen people. The city's leading paper acknowledged that "semi-organized bands of white men systematically applied the torch, while others shot on sight men of color." It took a decade for black residents to rebuild Greenwood. And

Red Summer
The summer and fall of 1919, in which antiblack riots by white Americans in more than two dozen cities led to hundreds of deaths. So named because of the bloody clashes. The worst occurred in Chicago, in which 38 people were killed (23 blacks, 15 whites), 537 injured, and 1,000 black families made homeless.

in the January 1923 Rosewood Massacre, mobs of furious whites in a small Florida town torched houses and hunted down African Americans, killing at least six. Police and state authorities refused to intervene, and the town of Rosewood vanished from the map.

The Business of America

African Americans were not the only ones who faced challenges to their hard-won gains. So did labor unions. Following the strike wave of 1919, business leaders and their political allies fought back against organized labor, which entered a decade of decline. Across the country, employers advocated what they called the **American Plan** of employment — refusing to negotiate with unions. Facing a strike of Boston's police force, Massachusetts governor Calvin Coolidge illustrated this defiant approach by declaring, "There is no right to strike against the public safety by anybody, anywhere, anytime." A majority of the public supported the governor, and Republicans rewarded Coolidge by nominating him for the vice-presidency in 1920.

Decisions by the Supreme Court were an additional factor in organized labor's decline. In *Coronado Coal Company v. United Mine Workers of America* (1925), the Court ruled that a striking union could be penalized for illegal restraint of trade. Such decisions, along with the aggressive antiunion campaigns under the American Plan, caused membership in labor unions to fall from 5.1 million in 1920 to 3.6 million in 1929 — just 10 percent of the nonagricultural workforce. Labor's long-sought goal of organizing the nation's workforce retreated further from realization.

In place of unions, the 1920s marked the heyday of **welfare capitalism**, a system of labor relations that stressed a company's responsibility for its employees' well-being. Employers hoped this would build a loyal workforce and head off labor unrest. Automaker Henry Ford, among others, pioneered this system before World War I, famously paying $5 a day. Ford also offered a profit-sharing plan to employees who met the standards of its Sociological Department, which investigated to ensure that workers' private lives met the company's moral standards. At a time when government unemployment compensation and Social Security did not exist, General Electric and U.S. Steel provided health insurance and old-age pensions. Other employers built athletic facilities and selectively offered paid vacations. Such plans covered only about 5 percent of the industrial workforce, however, and when faced with new financial pressures in the late 1920s, even Henry Ford cut back his $5 day. In the tangible benefits it offered workers, welfare capitalism had distinct limitations.

Dollar Diplomacy   American business interests shaped foreign affairs as well. The thrust of U.S. foreign policy after World War I continued to be in Latin America. There, under a policy initiated by Taft and continued under Wilson, presidents worked to advance U.S. business interests, especially by encouraging private banks to make foreign loans. Policymakers hoped loans would stimulate growth and increase demand for U.S. products in developing markets. Bankers, for their part, wanted government guarantees of repayment in countries they perceived as weak or unstable.

Officials provided such assurance. In 1922, for example, when American banks offered an immense loan to Bolivia (at a hefty profit), State Department officials pressured the South American nation to accept it. A similar arrangement was reached with

American Plan
Strategy by American business in the 1920s to keep workplaces free of unions, which included refusing to negotiate with trade unions and requiring workers to sign contracts (known as "yellow dog" contracts) pledging not to join a union.

welfare capitalism
A system of labor relations that stressed management's responsibility for employees' well-being.

El Salvador's government in 1923. In other cases, the United States intervened militarily, often to force repayment of debt. To implement such policies, the U.S. Marines occupied Nicaragua almost continuously from 1912 to 1933, the Dominican Republic from 1916 to 1924, and Haiti from 1915 to 1934. White Americans viewed these nations through demeaning racial stereotypes. They regarded Haitians as primitive savages or childlike people who needed U.S. guidance and supervision. One commander testified that his troops saw themselves as "trustees of a huge estate that belonged to minors. . . . The Haitians were our wards."

dollar diplomacy
Policy emphasizing the connection between America's economic and political interests overseas. Business would gain from diplomatic efforts on its behalf, while the strengthened American economic presence overseas would give added leverage to American diplomacy.

At home, critics denounced loan guarantees and military interventions as **dollar diplomacy**. The term was coined in 1924 by Samuel Guy Inman, a Disciples of Christ missionary who toured U.S.-occupied Haiti and the Dominican Republic. "The United States," Inman declared, "cannot go on destroying with impunity the sovereignty of other peoples, however weak." African American leaders also denounced the Haitian occupation. On behalf of the International Council of Women of the Darker Races and the Women's International League for Peace and Freedom, a delegation conducted a fact-finding tour of Haiti in 1926. Their report exposed, among other things, the sexual exploitation of Haitian women by U.S. soldiers.

Inman and other critics put dollar diplomacy on the defensive by the late 1920s. The poor results spoke for themselves. Loans got repaid, securing bankers' profits, but the proceeds often ended up in the pockets of local elites; U.S. policies failed to build broad-based prosperity overseas. Military intervention had even worse results. In Haiti, for example, the marines crushed peasant protests and helped the Haitian elite consolidate power. U.S. occupation thus contributed to the harsh dictatorships that Haitians endured through the rest of the twentieth century. President Franklin Roosevelt initiated the "Good Neighbor" policy with respect to Latin America in 1933 in an effort to reverse these ill effects.

Dollar diplomacy guided U.S. interests in Latin America, but behind the scenes many diplomats considered East Asia more critical to long-term American foreign policy. To ease growing tensions there, the United States signed a major treaty in 1922, known as the Four Powers Act, with Japan, Great Britain, and France, limiting naval strength in the Pacific. A diplomatic triumph for President Harding, the treaty failed to address underlying East-West international rivalries because it reinforced European and American naval superiority over Japan. That island nation would gradually come to see the United States, not the traditional European powers, as its principal adversary for dominance in Asia.

Politics of Normalcy

The postwar conservative turn was particularly evident in national politics. With President Woodrow Wilson ailing from a stroke, in 1920 Democrats nominated Ohio governor James M. Cox for president, on a platform calling for U.S. participation in the League of Nations and continuation of Wilson's progressivism. Republicans, led by their probusiness wing, tapped genial Ohio senator Warren G. Harding. In a dig at Wilson's idealism, Harding promised "not nostrums but normalcy." On election day, he won in a landslide, beginning an era of Republican political dominance that lasted until 1932.

Harding's most energetic appointee was Secretary of Commerce Herbert Hoover, well known as head of the wartime Food Administration. Under Hoover's direction, the Commerce Department helped create two thousand trade associations representing companies in almost every major industry. Government officials worked closely with the associations, providing statistical research, suggesting industry-wide standards, and promoting stable prices and wages. Hoover hoped that through voluntary business cooperation with government — an **associated state** — he could achieve what progressives had sought through governmental regulation.

Other changes were afoot in Washington, D.C. The practice of lobbying Congress was a long-standing tradition among businesses, trade unions, and other organized interests. That practice grew in scale and became more formal and systematic in the 1920s. Noting the change, one observer joked that "the lobbyists were so thick they were constantly falling over one another." Hundreds of groups set up offices to lobby members of Congress—from religious and civic organizations to the Anti-Saloon League— but business took the lead. The National Association of Manufacturers, the Chamber of Commerce, and public utilities (water and electric companies), among many other business organizations, assumed an ever-larger role in the legislative process.

More malign links between government and corporate interests were soon revealed. When President Harding died suddenly of a heart attack in August 1923, evidence was just emerging that parts of his administration were riddled with corruption. The worst scandal concerned secret leasing of government oil reserves in **Teapot Dome**, Wyoming, and Elk Hills, California, to private companies. Secretary of the Interior Albert Fall was eventually convicted of taking over $300,000 in bribes and became the first cabinet officer in U.S. history to serve a prison sentence.

Vice President Calvin Coolidge became president upon Harding's death. He maintained Republican dominance, calling for limited government and tax cuts for business while campaigning for election in his own right in 1924. Rural and urban Democrats, deeply divided over such issues as prohibition and immigration restriction, deadlocked at their national convention; after 102 ballots, delegates finally nominated John W. Davis, a Wall Street lawyer. Coolidge easily defeated Davis and staved off a challenge from Senator Robert M. La Follette of Wisconsin, who tried to resuscitate the Progressive Party. The 1924 Progressive platform called for stronger government regulation at home and international efforts to reduce weapons production and prevent war. "Free men of every generation," La Follette had once declared in a speech, "must combat the renewed efforts of organized force and greed." In the end, Coolidge received 15.7 million votes to Davis's 8.4 million and La Follette's 4.9 million.

As the progressive reform ethos faded and a conservative impulse grew stronger, the formative period between 1919 and 1932 revealed important tendencies in national political life. Antiradicalism became more pervasive. Business and government became more cooperative. Lobbying surged as a feature of the legislative process. Each development would remain important throughout the remainder of the twentieth century.

associated state
A system of voluntary business cooperation with government. The Commerce Department helped create two thousand trade associations representing companies in almost every major industry.

Teapot Dome
Nickname for scandal in which Interior Secretary Albert Fall accepted $300,000 in bribes for leasing oil reserves on public land in Teapot Dome, Wyoming. It was part of a larger pattern of corruption that marred Warren G. Harding's presidency.

To see a longer excerpt of the Progressive Party platform, along with other primary sources from this period, see **Sources for America's History**.

IN YOUR OWN WORDS   How and why did the United States take a conservative turn in the 1920s?

Making a Modern Consumer Economy

Spurred by rapid expansion during the war, and benefitting from earlier innovations in mass production such as the assembly line, American business thrived in the 1920s. Corporations expanded more and more into overseas markets, while at home a truly national consumer culture — emphasizing convenience, leisure, and fun — took shape. The years between 1922 and 1929 mark a crucial turning point in the emergence of a mass consumer economy in the United States.

Postwar Abundance

Productivity proved to be the key. Manufacturing efficiencies accumulated since the turn of the century — the assembly line, mechanization, electrification — made possible enormous increases in productivity. If an American worker who made 6 toasters a day in 1920 fell asleep and woke up in 1929, she or he could now make 10 toasters a day — an incredible 66 percent more. Also, national per capita income rose an impressive 24 percent in that period. Productivity gains and rising incomes, especially among the middle class, meant an explosion of consumer goods. From toasters and radios to telephones, vacuum cleaners, and automobiles, a vast array of consumer products became more affordable. Americans bought them in droves, spurring an economic boom that lasted until the onset of the Great Depression in 1929.

Large-scale corporations continued to replace small business in many sectors of the economy. By 1929, through successive waves of consolidation, the two hundred largest businesses had come to control almost half of the country's nonbanking corporate wealth. The greatest number of mergers occurred in rising industries such as chemicals (with DuPont in the lead) and electrical appliances (General Electric), as well as among Wall Street banks. Aided by Washington's dollar diplomats, U.S. companies exercised growing global power. Seeking cheaper livestock, giant American meatpackers opened plants in Argentina; the United Fruit Company developed plantations in Costa Rica, Honduras, and Guatemala; General Electric set up production facilities in Latin America, Asia, and Australia.

Despite the boom, the U.S. economy had areas of significant weakness throughout the 1920s. Agriculture, which still employed one-fourth of all American workers, never fully recovered from the postwar recession. Once Europe's economy revived, its farmers flooded world markets with grain and other farm products, causing agricultural prices to fall. Other industries, including coal and textiles, languished for similar reasons. As a consequence, many rural Americans shared little of the decade's prosperity. The bottom 40 percent of American families earned an average annual income of only $725 (about $10,000 today). Many, especially rural tenants and sharecroppers, languished in poverty and malnutrition.

Consumer Culture

In middle-class homes, Americans of the 1920s embraced a consumer ethos. They sat down to a breakfast of Kellogg's corn flakes before getting into Ford Model T's to work or shop at Safeway. On weekends, they might head to the local theater to see the newest Charlie Chaplin film. By 1929, electric refrigerators and vacuum cleaners came into use in affluent homes; 40 percent of American households owned a radio.

The advertising industry reached new levels of ambition, entering what one historian calls the era of the "aggressive hard sell." The 1920s gave birth, for example, to fashion modeling and style consulting. "Sell them their dreams," one radio announcer urged advertisers in 1923. "People don't buy things to have things. . . . They buy hope — hope of what your merchandise will do for them."

Many poor and affluent families shared one thing in common: they stretched their incomes, small or large, through new forms of borrowing such as auto loans and installment plans. "Buy now, pay later," said the ads, and millions did. Anyone, no matter how rich, could get into debt, but **consumer credit** was particularly perilous for those living on the economic margins. In Chicago, one Lithuanian man described his neighbor's situation: "She ain't got no money. Sure she buys on credit, clothes for the children and everything." Such borrowing brought consumer merchandise within reach of more and more Americans, but the accumulated debt also turned out to be a factor in the bust of 1929.

consumer credit
New forms of borrowing, such as auto loans and installment plans, that flourished in the 1920s but helped trigger the Great Depression.

Hollywood Movies became a centerpiece of consumer culture. In the 1910s, the moviemaking industry had begun relocating to southern California to take advantage of cheap land, sunshine, and varied scenery within easy reach. The large studios — United Artists, Paramount, and Metro-Goldwyn-Mayer — were run mainly by Eastern European Jewish immigrants like Adolph Zukor, who arrived from Hungary in the 1880s. Starting with fur sales, Zukor and a partner then set up five-cent theaters in Manhattan. "I spent a good deal of time watching the faces of the audience," Zukor recalled. "With a little experience I could see, hear, and 'feel' the reaction to each melodrama and comedy." Founding Paramount Pictures, Zukor signed emerging stars and produced successful feature-length films.

By 1920, **Hollywood** reigned as the world's movie capital, producing nearly 90 percent of all films. Large, ornate movie palaces attracted both middle-class and working-class audiences. Idols such as Rudolph Valentino, Mary Pickford, and Douglas Fairbanks set national trends in style. Thousands of young women followed the lead of actress Clara Bow, Hollywood's famous **flapper**, who flaunted her boyish figure. Decked out in knee-length skirts, flappers shocked the older generation by smoking and wearing makeup. They represented only a tiny minority of women, but thanks to the movies and advertising, flappers became influential symbols of women's sexual and social emancipation. In cities, young immigrant women eagerly bought makeup and the latest flapper fashions. Jazz stars helped popularize the style among working-class African Americans. Mexican American teenagers joined the trend in major cities such as San Antonio and Los Angeles.

Hollywood
The city in southern California that became synonymous with the American movie industry in the 1920s.

flapper
A young woman of the 1920s who defied conventional standards of conduct by wearing short skirts and makeup, freely spending the money she earned on the latest fashions, dancing to jazz, and flaunting her liberated lifestyle.

Politicians quickly grasped the publicity value of American radio and film to foreign relations. In 1919, with government support, General Electric spearheaded the creation of Radio Corporation of America (RCA) to expand U.S. presence in foreign radio markets. RCA — which had a federal appointee on its board of directors — emerged as a major provider of radio transmission in Latin America and East Asia. Meanwhile, by 1925, American films made up 95 percent of the movies screened in Britain, 80 percent in Latin America, and 70 percent in France (America in Global Context). The United States was experimenting with what historians call **soft power** — the exercise of popular cultural influence — as radio and film exported the American standard of consumption to the world.

soft power
The exercise of popular cultural influence abroad, as American radio and movies became popular around the world in the 1920s, transmitting American cultural ideals overseas.

Hollywood in Europe

European film studios struggled after World War I to reach audiences who had fallen in love with American movies. Working-class Europeans, in particular, preferred Hollywood's offerings to the films produced in Europe. In this 1928 article from a cinematography journal, German expressionist filmmaker Erich Pommer suggested new strategies for expanding an audience for European films. Expressionists, influenced by romanticism and modernism, explored dark themes such as spiritual crisis and insanity. (A famous example of expressionist painting is Edvard Munch's *The Scream*.) Pommer worked for American studios and later fled to the United States after the rise of Hitler.

The towering importance of the American motion picture on the world's markets cannot be safely explained by the unlimited financial resources at the disposal of the American producers. . . . Its main reason is the mentality of the American picture, which, notwithstanding all attacks and claims to the contrary, apparently comes nearest to the taste of international cinema audiences.

. . . The specific and unique element of the American film is the fact of its being absolutely uncomplicated. Being what is called "naïve" it knows no problems. . . .

Universal Appeal. It is really preferable to have a picture too light rather than too heavy, because in the latter case there is a danger that the public will not understand the story. This is the worst thing that can happen with a picture. . . .

Spectacular Appeal. The international appeal of a picture has its foundation in a story. It is totally independent of the capital invested and of the splendor and luxury used in its production. The fact that in most cases the supers and monumental pictures have proved to be such international successes, does not disprove this claim. Such productions always have a simple story of universal appeal, because it is simply impossible to use spiritual thoughts and impressions of the soul in a picture deluxe. The splendour in such production is not merely created for decoration — it is its outstanding purpose. . . . But splendour means show, and a show is always and everywhere easy to understand. . . .

Source: Excerpt from "The International Picture: A Lesson on Simplicity," by Erich Pommer, from *"Film Europe" and "Film America": Cinema, Commerce and Cultural Exchange 1920–1939*, edited by Andrew Higson and Richard Maltby, 1999, ISBN: 978-0-85989-546-0. Used by permission of Exeter University Press.

QUESTIONS FOR ANALYSIS

1. How does Pommer characterize the attraction of popular American films for European audiences? What does he mean when he calls those films "naïve"?

2. How does Pommer propose to produce German films that will compete with Hollywood? What constraints and challenges did he face?

The Automobile and Suburbanization

No possession proved more popular than the automobile, a showpiece of modern consumer capitalism that revolutionized American life. The Ford Motor Company introduced the first widely affordable automobile, the Model T, in 1908, but the industry experienced its most dramatic growth in the 1920s. Car sales played a major role in the decade's economic boom: in one year, 1929, Americans spent $2.58 billion on automobiles. By the end of the decade, they owned 26 million cars — about 80 percent of the world's automobiles — or an average of one for every five people (it was one for every forty in France). The number of cars on American roads tripled in ten years.

The auto industry's exuberant expansion rippled through the economy. It stimulated steel, petroleum, chemical, rubber, and glass production and, directly or indirectly, created 3.7 million jobs. Highway construction became a billion-dollar-a-year enterprise, financed by federal subsidies and state gasoline taxes. Car ownership spurred urban sprawl and, in 1924, the first suburban shopping center: Country Club Plaza outside Kansas City, Missouri. But cars were expensive, and most Americans bought them on credit. Alfred Sloan, the president of General Motors and Henry Ford's primary competitor, founded the first national consumer credit agency to help Americans buy more Chevrolets. Other car companies followed. Amid the boom of the 1920s, few worried whether purchasing such expensive items on credit was a good idea. When asked why her family purchased a car before installing indoor plumbing, one woman replied simply, "Why, you can't go to town in a bathtub."

Cars changed the way Americans spent their leisure time, as proud drivers took their machines on the road. An infrastructure of gas stations, motels, and drive-in restaurants soon catered to drivers. Railroad travel faltered. The American Automobile Association, founded in 1902, estimated that by 1929 almost a third of the population took vacations by car. "I had a few days after I got my wheat cut," reported one Kansas farmer, "so I just loaded my family . . . and lit out." An elite Californian complained that automobile travel was no longer "aristocratic." "The clerks and their wives and sweethearts," observed a reporter, "driving through the Wisconsin lake country, camping at Niagara, scattering tin cans and pop bottles over the Rockies, made those places taboo for bankers."

Rising middle-class incomes, new forms of borrowing, and the automobile combined powerfully in the 1920s to produce a major suburban housing boom. Cars were key. The nineteenth-century "streetcar suburbs" allowed the nation's affluent to live outside central cities, but in communities narrowly built along the tracks. After World War I, automobile suburbs grew like the crabgrass of suburban lawns—fast and everywhere. "Cities are spreading out," *National Geographic* announced in a 1923 special feature. Long Island's Nassau County, a major suburb of New York City, tripled in population, and the fifteen fastest-growing towns in Connecticut were all suburbs.

Spreading out happened everywhere — from New York to Chicago, St. Louis to Seattle — but the growth of Los Angeles epitomized the new role of automobiles in American cities. Housing subdivisions opened monthly across a vast expanse of southern California, and the automobile gave birth to an explosive metropolis. Its population more than doubled in the 1920s alone, and Los Angeles went from the tenth largest American city to the fifth in just ten years. Southern California became

Automobiles Michigan Boulevard in Chicago in 1930. In a single generation, automobiles transformed American cities and the countryside alike. As more and more Americans made cars their primary form of transportation, auto travel created a booming business in gas stations, roadside motels, campgrounds, and sightseeing destinations. But cars also choked city streets that were once the province of horse-drawn carriages and electric trains. Cities needed new roads, traffic signs, and rules governing traffic, and the booming automobile industry stimulated highway construction across the country. The automobile was a technology but also a consumer item that changed virtually every aspect of American life. ullstein bild/Getty Images.

identified with what historians call "automobility," and Los Angeles led the way in defining American car culture.

> **IN YOUR OWN WORDS** What were the primary characteristics of the American economy in the 1920s?

The Politics and Culture of a Diversifying Nation

At the dawn of the 1920s, public life in the United States had grown immeasurably more diverse. Women could now vote. More than 24 million immigrants—hailing primarily from Europe but also from Latin America and East Asia—called the country home. They spoke different languages, practiced a variety of religions, and followed unique cultural traditions (Interpretations). The Great Migration brought more than

How Did Immigrants Experience America at the Turn of the Century?

From the half century between the Civil War and World War I, more than 24 million people migrated to the United States. Many of these people came from Europe, but others left Asia, Latin America, and Africa in search of better opportunities or refuge in the United States. This turn-of-the-century migration included people from regions of southern and central Europe who had not previously come to the United States in such large numbers. Their presence in America's urban centers changed those places, but those immigrants were also changed. The extent to which migration from the Old to the New World affected these millions of people has, however, been a topic of debate among historians.

Oscar Handlin's classic history of the immigrant experience, *The Uprooted* (1951), defined the way historians thought about the topic for a generation. John Bodnar, writing three decades later, offered a different interpretation in *The Transplanted*. To what extent do the titles of their books hint at the argument each makes?

OSCAR HANDLIN

SOURCE: Oscar Handlin, *The Uprooted: The Epic Story of the Great Migrations That Made the American People* (New York: Grosset & Dunlap, 1951), 144.

Settlement in America had snipped the continuity of the immigrants' work and ideas, of their religious life . . . newcomers pushed their roots into many different soils. Along the city's unyielding asphalt streets, beside the rutted roads of mill or mining towns, amidst the exciting prairie acres, they established the homes of the New World. But . . . nowhere could they transplant the European village. . . . The pressure of that strangeness exerted a deep influence upon the character of resettlement, upon the usual forms of behavior, and upon the modes of communal action that emerged as the immigrants became Americans. . . . The old conditions of living could not survive in the new conditions of space.

JOHN BODNAR

SOURCE: John Bodnar, *The Transplanted: A History of Immigrants in Urban America* (Bloomington: Indiana University Press, 1985), 83–84.

Kin and friends were free to assist each other in entering America by providing access to jobs and homes and supplying important information of labor market conditions. New arrivals were adept at determining where they might enter a very large economy. The immigrant family economy survived and flourished among most newcomers in industrial America because new economic structures actually reinforced traditional ways of ordering life. . . . [I]ndividual inclinations were muted and the household . . . superseded all other goals and objectives. . . . Members of nearly all groups received indoctrination in the need to remain loyal to the familial and household unit. . . . [I]n the movement to a capitalist world and in the initial decades of settlement, familial and communal networks abounded.

QUESTIONS FOR ANALYSIS

1. How does Handlin's argument about immigrants as "uprooted" people differ from Bodnar's description of them as "transplanted"?

2. According to each author, what role did family and community play in the immigrant experience?

3. Which point of view — Handlin's or Bodnar's — is better supported by the chapter narrative? Give specific examples to support your argument.

one million African Americans from all parts of the South to northern cities such as Chicago, New York, and Philadelphia. Cities grew at the expense of rural areas. Such dramatic changes led to social tensions and pronounced conflict over how the nation would be defined.

Women in a New Age

At the start of the 1920s, many progressives hoped the attainment of women's voting rights would offer new leverage to tackle poverty. They created organizations like the Women's Joint Congressional Committee, a Washington-based advocacy group. The committee's greatest accomplishment was the first federally funded health-care legislation, the **Sheppard-Towner Federal Maternity and Infancy Act** (1921). Sheppard-Towner provided federal funds for medical clinics, prenatal education programs, and visiting nurses, improving health care for the poor and significantly lowering infant mortality rates. It also marked the first time that Congress designated federal funds for the states to encourage them to administer a social-welfare program. But other reforms stalled, and the decade proved not to be a watershed of welfare legislation.

Sheppard-Towner Federal Maternity and Infancy Act
The first federally funded health-care legislation that provided federal funds for medical clinics, prenatal education programs, and visiting nurses.

Other activist women focused on securing legal equality with men. In 1923, Alice Paul, founder of the National Woman's Party, persuaded congressional allies to consider an Equal Rights Amendment (ERA) to the U.S. Constitution. It stated simply that "men and women shall have equal rights throughout the United States." Advocates were hopeful; Wisconsin had passed a similar law two years earlier, and it helped women fight gender discrimination. But opponents pointed out that the ERA would threaten recent labor laws that protected women from workplace abuses. Such laws recognized women's vulnerable place in a heavily sex-segregated labor market. Would a theoretical statement of "equality" help poor and working women more than existing protections did? This question divided women's rights advocates. Introduced repeatedly in Congress over the next five decades, the ERA was debated again and again until the bitter ratification struggle of the 1970s (Chapter 28).

African American Women   African American women had distinct priorities. Groups such as the National Association of Colored Women (NACW) fought for suffrage in the 1910s, just as white women had. But the constitutional right of black women to vote was meaningless in the South, where disfranchisement was law. Black women sought racial, not just gender, equality. When Addie Hunton, field secretary of the National Association for the Advancement of Colored People, and sixty black women from the NACW urged the National Woman's Party to take up their cause, Paul refused, declaring disfranchisement to be a racial not a gender injustice. Hunton countered that "five million women in the United States cannot be denied their rights without all women of the United States feeling the effect of that denial. No women are free until all women are free."

Other challenges remained. Women proved to be effective lobbyists for a variety of causes, but the Republican and Democratic parties endured as largely male domains. Finding that women did not vote as a bloc, politicians in both parties began to accord their votes less weight. New reforms failed to gain support, and others were rolled back. Many congressmen, for example, had supported the Sheppard-Towner Act because they feared the voting power of women, but Congress ended the program in the late 1920s.

New Woman Magazines, advertisements, and Hollywood movies crafted an idealized image of the American "new woman" in the 1920s. She had thrown off Victorian modesty and claimed a place for herself alongside men in a new culture of consumption and fun. Such images, used primarily to sell products to the middle class, exaggerated reality. But that did not mean women's lives remained unchanged. The nineteenth-century notion of separate spheres for men and women had eroded considerably by 1930. More women attended college than ever before. Female athletes such as the golfer Glenna Collett, adventurers such as the celebrated pilot Amelia Earhart, and performers such as the brilliant jazz singer Josephine Baker carved out new, more liberated roles for women in public life.

Social change takes time, however, and for the majority of American women in the 1920s ordinary life was far less glamorous. In some professions, such as medicine, women actually declined as a percentage of the workforce: only 3 percent of lawyers and 4 percent of physicians were women in the decade. Women's wages lagged far behind those of men, and women remained confined to strictly gendered occupations: sales clerks in the new department stores, secretaries in the growing corporate world, and low-paid assembly-line workers in industry, alongside their traditional roles as domestic servants. African American and Latino women could not even get jobs as clerks and secretaries. Thus although American women in this era, especially the young, left behind the Victorian prescriptions of feminine modesty and confinement to a female-only separate sphere, they had yet to fully transform women's second-class standing.

Culture Wars

By 1929, ninety-three U.S. cities had populations of more than 100,000. New York City's population exceeded 7 million; Los Angeles's had exploded to 1.2 million. The 1920 census marked the first time there were more urban than rural Americans. The lives and beliefs of urban Americans, however, often differed dramatically from those in small towns and farming areas. One sharp critic, the writer Sinclair Lewis, wrote three satirical novels—*Main Street* (1920), *Babbitt* (1922), and *Elmer Gantry* (1927)—that mocked small-town life for its religiosity and, as Lewis saw it, hypocrisy and lack of sophistication.

In a decade of conflict between traditional and modern worldviews, the urban-rural split embodied by Lewis represented one line of conflict among many. Others that came to the fore included Protestant versus Catholic and Jewish; religious versus secular; native born versus immigrant; and white versus black. A series of cultural battles in the 1920s revealed a stark conflict over the kinds of values, beliefs, and even people deemed "American."

Prohibition Rural and native-born Protestants started the decade with the achievement of a longtime goal: national prohibition of liquor (Chapter 17). The two principal antialcohol organizations, the Woman's Christian Temperance Union and the Anti-Saloon League, had long hailed temperance as good for health and Christian virtue. In the 1910s, some progressives joined the campaign, convinced that alcohol kept immigrant workers in poverty and the saloon was a source of political corruption. World War I, too, spurred the cause. Mobilizing the economy for war, Congress limited brewers' and distillers' use of barley and other scarce grains, causing consumption to decline. Moreover, anti-German hysteria identified the many German breweries in American cities, like Pabst and Anheuser-Busch, with the wartime enemy. The decades-long prohibition campaign culminated with Congress's passage of the **Eighteenth Amendment** in 1917. Ratified over the next two years by nearly every state and taking effect in January 1920, the amendment prohibited "manufacture, sale, or transportation of intoxicating liquors" anywhere in the United States. It was enforced by the federal government under the 1920 **Volstead Act**.

Defenders of prohibition, especially native-born Protestants in small towns, celebrated prohibition as a victory over sin and vice. In urban areas, though, thousands flagrantly ignored the law, many mocking prohibition as old-fashioned Puritanism. Patrons flocked to urban speakeasies, or illegal drinking sites, which flourished in almost every major city; one raid on a Chicago speakeasy yielded 200,000 gallons of alcohol. Profits from the secret clubs enriched notorious gangsters such as Chicago's Al Capone and New York's Jack Diamond. Immigrants saw prohibition as an attack on the working-class saloon and also resisted the ban, but as the price of alcohol soared on the illegal market it often proved out of reach for the laboring classes. Prohibition's most ardent supporters were native-born, small-town Protestants, and its greatest opponents were middle-class urbanites and immigrants.

The national ban on alcohol was a prolonged social experiment that fizzled. Alcohol consumption declined in 1921 and 1922 but then began climbing again—though it did not reach pre-1920 levels until after repeal in 1933. Among the middle class, which could afford higher prices, alcohol consumption declined hardly at all in these years. The fact that only the *sale* and not the *possession* of alcohol was illegal made prohibition exceedingly difficult to enforce. And yet the Eighteenth Amendment's most important legacy might well have been the growing influence of the Federal Bureau of Investigation (FBI), the federal agency tasked with enforcing the Volstead Act. Under the shrewd direction of J. Edgar Hoover, the FBI used the Red Scare and prohibition to increase its resources, enlarge its investigative domain, and become a fixture of federal police power. Difficult to enforce, associated with organized crime, and increasingly politically unpopular, prohibition was repealed in 1933.

Evolution in the Schools In another episode of the clash between modern and traditionalist worldviews, controversy erupted as fundamentalist Protestants sought to mandate school curricula based on the biblical account of creation. In 1925, Tennessee's legislature outlawed the teaching of "any theory that denies the story of the Divine creation of man as taught in the Bible, [and teaches] instead that man has descended from a lower order of animals." The **American Civil Liberties Union** (ACLU), formed during the Red Scare to protect free speech rights, challenged the law's constitutionality. The ACLU intervened in the trial of John T. Scopes, a high school biology teacher who taught the theory of evolution to his class and faced a jail sentence for doing so. The case attracted national attention because Clarence Darrow, a famous criminal lawyer, defended Scopes, while William Jennings Bryan, the three-time Democratic presidential candidate, spoke for the prosecution.

Journalists dubbed the **Scopes trial** "the monkey trial." This label referred both to Darwin's argument that human beings and other primates share a common ancestor

---

Eighteenth Amendment
The ban on the manufacture and sale of alcohol that went into effect in January 1920. Also called "prohibition," the amendment was repealed in 1933.

Volstead Act
Officially the National Prohibition Act, passed by Congress in 1920 to enforce the provisions of the Eighteenth Amendment banning the sale of alcohol.

American Civil Liberties Union
An organization formed during the Red Scare to protect free speech rights.

Scopes trial
The 1925 trial of John Scopes, a biology teacher in Dayton, Tennessee, for violating his state's ban on teaching evolution. The trial created a nationwide media frenzy and came to be seen as a showdown between urban and rural values.

and to the circus atmosphere at the trial, which was broadcast live over a Chicago radio station. (Proving that urbanites had their own prejudices, acerbic critic H. L. Mencken dismissed antievolutionists as "gaping primates of the upland valleys," implying that they had not evolved.) The jury took only eight minutes to deliver its verdict: guilty. Though the Tennessee Supreme Court later overturned Scopes's conviction, the law remained on the books for more than thirty years.

Nativism   Some native-born Protestants pointed to immigration as the primary cause of what they saw as America's moral decline. A nation of 105 million people had added more than 24 million immigrants over the previous four decades; the newcomers included many Catholics and Jews from Southern and Eastern Europe, whom one Maryland congressman referred to as "indigestible lumps" in the "national stomach." Such attitudes recalled hostility toward Irish and Germans in the 1840s and 1850s. In this case, they fueled a momentous shift in immigration policy.

"America must be kept American," President Coolidge declared in 1924. Congress had banned Chinese immigration in 1882, and Theodore Roosevelt had negotiated a so-called gentleman's agreement that limited Japanese immigration in 1907. Now nativists charged that there were also too many European arrivals, some of whom, they claimed, undermined Protestantism and imported anarchism, socialism, and other radical doctrines. Responding to this pressure, Congress passed emergency immigration restrictions in 1921 and a permanent measure three years later. The **National Origins Act** (1924) used backdated census data to establish a baseline: in the future, annual immigration from each country could not exceed 2 percent of that nationality's percentage of the U.S. population as it had stood in 1890. Since only small numbers of Italians, Greeks, Poles, Russians, and other Southern and Eastern European immigrants had arrived before 1890, the law drastically limited immigration from those places. In 1929, Congress imposed even more restrictive quotas, setting a cap of 150,000 immigrants per year from Europe and continuing to ban most immigrants from Asia.

The new law, however, permitted unrestricted immigration from the Western Hemisphere. As a result, Latin Americans arrived in increasing numbers, finding jobs that had gone to other immigrants before exclusion. More than 1 million Mexicans entered the United States between 1900 and 1930, including many fleeing the instability caused by the Mexican Revolution. Nativists lobbied Congress to cut this flow; so did labor leaders, who argued that impoverished migrants lowered wages for other American workers. But Congress heeded the pleas of employers, especially farmers in Texas and California, who wanted cheap labor.

Other anti-immigrant measures emerged at the state level. In 1913, by an overwhelming majority, California's legislature had passed a law declaring that "aliens ineligible to citizenship" could not own "real property." The aim was to prevent Asians, especially Japanese immigrants, from owning land, though some had lived in the state for decades and built up prosperous farms. In the wake of World War I, California tightened these laws, making it increasingly difficult for Asian families to establish themselves. California, Washington, and Hawaii also severely restricted any school that taught Japanese language, history, or culture. Denied both citizenship and land rights, Japanese Americans would be in a vulnerable position at the outbreak of World War II, when anti-Japanese hysteria swept the United States.

National Origins Act
A 1924 law limiting annual immigration from each country to no more than 2 percent of that nationality's percentage of the U.S. population as it had stood in 1890. The law severely limited immigration, especially from Southern and Eastern Europe.

Ku Klux Klan
Secret society that first undertook violence against African Americans in the South after the Civil War but was reborn in 1915 to fight the perceived threats posed by African Americans, immigrants, radicals, feminists, Catholics, and Jews.

The National Klan The 1920s brought a nationwide resurgence of the **Ku Klux Klan** (KKK), the white supremacist group formed in the post–Civil War South. Soon after the premiere of *Birth of a Nation* (1915), a popular film glorifying the Reconstruction-era Klan, a group of southerners gathered on Georgia's Stone Mountain to revive the organization. With its blunt motto, "Native, white, Protestant supremacy," the Klan recruited supporters across the country (Thinking Like a Historian). KKK members did not limit their harassment to African Americans but targeted immigrants, Catholics, and Jews as well, with physical intimidation, arson, and economic boycotts.

At the height of its influence in the early 1920s, the Klan counted more than 3 million members and wielded considerable political clout, particularly at the local level. A typical example was the small town of Monticello, Arkansas, where in the first half of the decade the mayor, city marshall, half the city council, the sheriff, the county clerk, tax assessor, and treasurer, and eleven of fifteen male teachers were all Klan members. From small-town mayors to President Woodrow Wilson, who effusively praised *Birth of a Nation*, the Klan enjoyed broad support among native-born white Protestant Americans for a decade. Klan activism lent a menacing cast to political issues, as its members defined "one hundred percent Americanism" to include white racial purity, Protestantism, prohibition of alcohol, conservative sexual mores, and immigration restriction—the Klan avidly supported both the Eighteenth Amendment and the Immigration Act of 1924.

The Klan declined rapidly after 1925, but its rise was part of an ugly trend that began before World War I and extended into subsequent decades. The rise of the national Klan helped prepare the way for white supremacist movements of the 1930s, such as the Los Angeles–based Silver Legion, a fringe paramilitary group aligned with Hitler's Nazis. Far more influential were major figures such as industrialist Henry Ford, whose *Dearborn Independent* railed against immigrants and warned that members of "the proud Gentile race" must arm themselves against a Jewish conspiracy aimed at world domination. Challenged by critics, Ford issued an apology in 1927 and admitted that his allegations had been based on "gross forgeries." But with his paper's editorials widely circulated by the Klan and other groups, considerable long-term damage had been done.

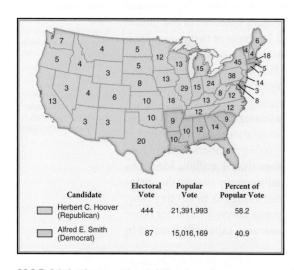

Candidate	Electoral Vote	Popular Vote	Percent of Popular Vote
Herbert C. Hoover (Republican)	444	21,391,993	58.2
Alfred E. Smith (Democrat)	87	15,016,169	40.9

MAP 21.1 The Presidential Election of 1928
Historians still debate the extent to which 1928 was a critical election—an election that produced a significant realignment in voting behavior. Although Republican Herbert Hoover swept the popular and the electoral votes, Democrat Alfred E. Smith won majorities not only in the South, his party's traditional stronghold, but also in Rhode Island, Massachusetts, and (although it is not evident on this map) all of the large cities of the North and Midwest. In subsequent elections, the Democrats won even more votes among African Americans and European ethnic groups and, until 1980, were the nation's dominant political party.

The Election of 1928 Conflicts over race, religion, and ethnicity created the climate for a stormy presidential election in 1928. Democrats had traditionally drawn strength from white voters in the South and immigrants in the North: groups that divided over prohibition, immigration restriction, and the Klan. By 1928, the northern urban wing gained firm control. Democrats nominated Governor Al Smith of New York, the first presidential candidate to reflect the aspirations of the urban working class. A grandson of Irish peasants, Smith had risen through New York City's Democratic machine to become a dynamic reformer. But he offended many small-town and rural Americans with his heavy New York accent and brown derby hat, which highlighted his ethnic working-class origins. Middle-class reformers questioned his ties to Tammany Hall; temperance advocates opposed him as a "wet." But the governor's greatest handicap was his religion. Although Smith insisted that his Catholic beliefs would not affect his duties as president, many Protestants opposed him. "No Governor can kiss the papal ring and get within gunshot of the White House," vowed one Methodist bishop.

Smith proved no match for the Republican nominee, Secretary of Commerce Herbert Hoover, who embodied the technological promise of the modern age. An organizational genius and a dedicated public servant, Hoover won fame during World War I for successfully managing huge food relief and refugee projects before energizing and reorganizing the Treasury Department as secretary of commerce under President Harding. Riding on eight years of Republican prosperity, Hoover credited business with the country's rising affluence and embraced, updated for a more technocratic age, the American tradition of individualism. He won overwhelmingly, with 444 electoral votes to Smith's 87 (Map 21.1). Because many southern Protestants refused to vote for a Catholic, Hoover carried five ex-Confederate states, breaking the Democratic "Solid South" for the first time since Reconstruction. Smith, though, carried industrialized Massachusetts and Rhode Island as well as the nation's twelve largest cities, suggesting that urban voters were moving into the Democrats' camp.

The Harlem Renaissance

Amidst these clashes over religion, morality, and Americanism, black artists and intellectuals claimed a voice for themselves. They questioned long-standing assumptions about civilization, progress, and the alleged superiority of Western cultures over so-called primitive people. Based in New York City, where the Great Migration had tripled the black population in the decade after 1910 (Map 21.2), a vibrant new black cultural movement took

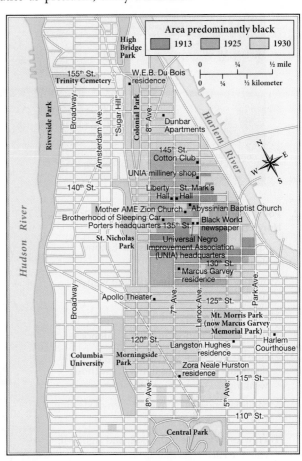

MAP 21.2 Harlem, 1913–1930

African Americans had lived in New York City since its founding in 1624 as part of the Dutch settlement of New Amsterdam. A small number lived in Harlem, in the northern part of Manhattan Island until the early 1900s. Then in 1904, a subway line connecting 145th Street in Harlem to lower Manhattan and Brooklyn opened, and black tenants and homeowners began to come in larger numbers. During and after World War I, large numbers of southern migrants joined established black families there, bringing with them the food, music, and folkways of the South, and Harlem increasingly became a center of black life in New York City. By 1930, 165,000 African Americans, almost 75 percent of Manhattan's black population, were concentrated in Harlem.

Who Joined the Ku Klux Klan?

Asked why a person would join the Klan, you might cite racism and religious bigotry. But the story is complicated: many whites with strong prejudices did not join the Klan in the 1920s, while others did. Why?

1. **Klan wedding in Washington, D.C., 1925.**

Source: FPG/Getty Images.

2. **Poem read at a meeting of KKK Grand Dragons, North Carolina, 1923.**

God Give Us Men! The Invisible Empire demands strong

Minds, great hearts, true faith and ready hands . . .

Men who possess opinions and a will;

Men who have honor; men who will not lie;

Men who can stand before a demagogue and damn his treacherous flattering without winking! . . .

Men of dependable character; men of sterling worth;

Then wrongs will be redressed, and right will rule the earth.

3. **"95% of Bootleggers Jews," editorial, *Dearborn Independent*, Michigan, 1922.**

Violation and evasion of the Prohibition laws has had a deep Jewish complexion from the very beginning. . . . This does not mean, of course, that every bootlegger is a Jew. Unless you live in Chicago, New York or other large cities, an actual meeting with the Jew in this minor capacity will not be frequent. The Jew is the possessor of the wholesale stocks; . . . But

notwithstanding all this carefulness, the bulk of the arrests made in the United States have been among Jews. . . . The maintenance of *the idea of drink* in the minds of the people is due to Jewish propaganda. . . . *The idea of drink* will be maintained by means of the Jewish stage, Jewish jazz, and the Jewish comics, until somebody comes down hard upon it.

4. **Report on a Klan gathering in Birmingham, Alabama, 1923.**

Edgewood Park was crowded by noon. Klansmen and their wives and families enjoyed a great barbecue, went swimming, dancing, and picnicking. There were airplane stunts during the day with band concerts thrown in for good measure. At night there was a wonderful display of fireworks following the initiation and the address of the Imperial Wizard.

5. **Klansmen in Buffalo, New York, 1924.** *Data based on historical research into a Klan membership list of almost 2,000 men in the Buffalo area.*

TABLE 21.1

Klansmen in Buffalo, New York, 1924		
Occupational Group	Percentage of KKK Members	Percentage of Total Native White Male Workers in Buffalo
Professional (predominantly clergy, doctors, engineers, pharmacists)	6.1	4.7
Business (small businessmen, managers, inspectors, accountants)	18.5	10.4
Low nonmanual (salesmen, clerks, foremen)	27.7	22.6

Occupational Group	Percentage of KKK Members	Percentage of Total Native White Male Workers in Buffalo
Skilled (machinists, electricians, railroad engineers, construction trades)	30.6	25.3
Semiskilled and service (factory and rail workers, deliverymen, policemen, repairmen)	16.4	30.2
Unskilled (laborers, gardeners)	0.5	14.5

6. **Interviews conducted in the 1980s with Indiana Klanswomen about Klan life in the 1920s.** *Seeking truthful accounts, the interviewer allowed the women to remain anonymous.*

Anonymous

For [the Klan] to say, we want to get rid of the niggers, we want to get rid of the Catholics, it didn't mean a thing to us. . . . I can remember quite well the stories that you hear sitting on the porch. . . . They'd talk about religion, and they'd talk about Catholics. . . . The Catholics were considered horrible people. . . .

Anonymous

Kelly had a grocery store. Well, it hurt their business terribly because people wouldn't go in there, because the Klan would tell you not to. . . . If you had a empty house . . . , why you were told not to rent it to a Catholic.

Some Klan leader said that the Pope was coming to take over the country, and he said he might be on the next train that went through North Manchester. You know, just trying to make it specific. So, about a thousand people went out to the train station and stopped the train. It only had . . . one passenger on it. They took him off, and he finally convinced them that he wasn't the Pope. He was a carpet salesman. And so they put him on the next train and he went on to Chicago.

7. **Editorial by National Imperial Wizard Hiram Wesley Evans in the KKK periodical *Dawn: A Journal for True American Patriots*, November 10, 1923.**

Humanity has become a commodity. For mercenary motives, our importers of it want the most inferior grade. Industry desires cheap labor. Therefore, we have had this recent flood of 5 and 10-cent citizenship. Take any map which shows the concentration of the South and Eastern European type of immigrant and you will see [that] wherever manufacturing and mining and lumbering predominate, there the hordes of unskilled labor have overwhelmingly been assembled. . . .

The present and recent flood of inferior foreigners has vastly increased our illiteracy, vitally lowered the health level and visibly menaced America by inheritable mental and moral deficiencies. . . . [Farms are] the only legitimate and justifiable excuse for cheap labor, yet that class is moving irresistibly cityward to swell the slums and multiply immorality. For example, throughout the south the colored race . . . is migrating to the North — not to its rural districts, but to its industrial centers.

8. **"Program for America," in the KKK newspaper *American Standard*, April 15, 1925.**

- Laws to require the reading of the Holy Bible in every American public school.
- Recognition of the fact . . . that Romanism is working here to undermine Americanism. . . . Since Roman Catholics give first allegiance to an alien political potentate, the pope . . . their claim to citizenship, to the ballot, and to public office in this Protestant country is illegitimate, and must be forbidden by law. . . .
- A law to destroy the alien influence of the foreign language press [by] requiring that the English language be used exclusively.
- . . . Recognition of the tendency toward moral disintegration, resulting from the activities . . . of the anti-Christian Jews, in our theaters, our motion pictures, and in American business circles; the discontinuance of these

anti-Christian activities, and the exclusion of Jews of this character from America.

- The return of the Negroes to their homeland of Africa, under the protection and with the help of the United States Government.
- Strict adherence to the Constitution of the United States, including the Prohibition Amendment, by every citizen.

SOURCES: (2) Kelly J. Baker, *Gospel According to the Klan* (Lawrence: University Press of Kansas, 2011), 119; (3) *Dearborn Independent* editorial reprinted in *Aspects of Jewish Power in the United States* (Dearborn, MI: Dearborn Publishing, 1922), 34–40; (4) Rory McVeigh, *The Rise of the Ku Klux Klan* (Minneapolis: University of Minnesota Press, 2009), 150; (5) Shawn Lay, *Hooded Knights on the Niagara* (New York: New York University Press, 1995), chapter 4 (esp. 87); (6) Kathleen M. Blee, *Women in the Klan* (Berkeley and Los Angeles: University of California Press, 1991), 78–79, 149–151; (7) McVeigh, 64–65; (8) *American Standard*, April 15, 1925, 172.

ANALYZING THE EVIDENCE

1. Based on the documents above, identify factors that made the KKK appealing to some Americans in the 1920s.

2. Which groups in source 5 were over- and underrepresented in the Klan? The same historian found that at least 34 percent of local Klan members were German American. Review the Thinking Like a Historian feature in Chapter 20, pages 672–673. Why might Germans have been especially likely to join the Klan in this period?

3. What are the advantages and limitations of source 6?

4. Imagine that Republican president Calvin Coolidge had set up a federal agency to discourage KKK activity (an action he did NOT take). He put you in charge of the effort and gave you a generous budget. How would you have spent the funds? Explain why you believe your strategy might have been effective.

PUTTING IT ALL TOGETHER

Using your knowledge of Chapter 21, and drawing on evidence from the documents above, write a brief essay explaining how the rise of the KKK in the 1920s reflected larger patterns in American society and politics.

---

shape. Harlem stood as "the symbol of liberty and the Promised Land to Negroes everywhere," as one minister put it. Talented African Americans flocked to the district, where they created bold new art forms and asserted ties to Africa.

Black Writers and Artists Poet Langston Hughes captured the upbeat spirit of the **Harlem Renaissance** when he asserted, "I am a Negro — and beautiful." Other writers and artists also championed race pride. Claude McKay and Jean Toomer represented in fiction what philosopher Alain Locke called, in an influential 1925 book, the "New Negro." Painter Jacob Lawrence, who had grown up in crowded tenement districts of the urban North, used bold shapes and vivid colors to portray the daily life, aspirations, and suppressed anger of African Americans.

Harlem Renaissance
A flourishing of African American artists, writers, intellectuals, and social leaders in the 1920s, centered in the neighborhoods of Harlem, New York City.

No one embodied the energy and optimism of the Harlem Renaissance more than Zora Neale Hurston. Born in the prosperous black community of Eatonville, Florida, Hurston had been surrounded as a child by examples of achievement, though she struggled later with poverty and isolation. In contrast to some other black thinkers, Hurston believed African American culture could be understood without heavy emphasis on the impact of white oppression. After enrolling at Barnard College and studying with anthropologist Franz Boas, Hurston traveled through the South and the Caribbean for a decade, documenting folklore, songs, and religious beliefs. She incorporated this material into her short stories and novels, celebrating the humor and spiritual strength of ordinary black men and women. Like other work of the Harlem Renaissance, Hurston's stories and novels sought to articulate what it meant, as black intellectual W. E. B. Du Bois wrote, "to be both a Negro and an American."

Jazz   To millions of Americans, the most famous product of the Harlem Renaissance was **jazz**. Though the origins of the word are unclear, many historians believe it was a slang term for sex — an etymology that makes sense, given the music's early association with urban vice districts. As a musical form, jazz coalesced in New Orleans and other parts of the South before World War I. Borrowing from blues, ragtime, and other popular forms, jazz musicians developed an ensemble style in which performers, keeping a rapid ragtime beat, improvised around a basic melodic line. The majority of early jazz musicians were black, but white performers, some of whom had more formal training, injected elements of European concert music.

In the 1920s, as jazz spread nationwide, musicians developed its signature mode, the improvised solo. The key figure in this development was trumpeter Louis Armstrong. A native of New Orleans, Armstrong learned his craft playing in the saloons and brothels of the city's vice district. Like tens of thousands of other African Americans, he moved north, settling in Chicago in 1922. Armstrong showed an inexhaustible capacity for melodic invention, and his dazzling solos inspired other musicians. By the late 1920s, soloists became the celebrities of jazz, thrilling audiences with their improvisational skill.

As jazz spread, it followed the routes of the Great Migration from the South to northern and midwestern cities, where it met consumers primed to receive it. Most cities had plentiful dance halls where jazz could be featured. Radio also helped popularize jazz, with the emerging record industry marketing the latest tunes. As white listeners flocked to ballrooms and clubs to hear Duke Ellington and other stars, Harlem became the hub of this commercially lucrative jazz. Those who hailed "primitive" black music, however, rarely suspended their racial condescension: visiting a mixed-race club became known as "slumming."

The recording industry soon developed so-called race records specifically aimed at urban working-class African Americans. The breakthrough came in 1920, when Otto K. E. Heinemann, a producer who sold immigrant records in Yiddish, Swedish, and other languages, recorded singer Mamie Smith performing "Crazy Blues." This smash hit prompted big recording labels like Columbia and Paramount to copy Heinemann's approach. Yet, while its marketing reflected the segregation of American society, jazz brought black music to the center stage of American culture. It became the era's signature music, so much so that novelist F. Scott Fitzgerald dubbed the 1920s the "Jazz Age."

Marcus Garvey and the UNIA   Harlem's creative energy generated broad political aspirations. The Harlem-based **Universal Negro Improvement Association** (UNIA), led by charismatic Jamaican-born Marcus Garvey, arose in the 1920s to mobilize African American workers and champion black nationalism. Garvey urged followers to move to Africa, arguing that people of African descent would never be treated justly in white-run countries.

The UNIA soon claimed 4 million followers, including many recent migrants to northern cities. It published a newspaper, *Negro World*, and solicited funds for the

jazz
Unique American musical form that arose in New Orleans and other parts of the South before World War I. Jazz musicians developed an ensemble improvisational style.

Universal Negro Improvement Association
A Harlem-based group, led by charismatic, Jamaican-born Marcus Garvey, that arose in the 1920s to mobilize African American workers and champion black separatism.

Archibald Motley, *Blues,* 1929   Painter Archibald Motley (1891–1981) was born in New Orleans but arrived in Chicago as a small child, when his family—like thousands of other African Americans—moved north in search of opportunity. Motley was able to study at the Art Institute of Chicago and by the 1920s also showed his work in New York City. Many of his paintings depicted life in the predominantly African American neighborhood on Chicago's South Side that was widely known as the Black Belt. This piece, *Blues*, was painted when Motley was living in Paris. It shows the powerful impact jazz had on European listeners.   Private Collection/© Valerie Gerrard Browne/Chicago History Museum/Bridgeman Images.

Black Star steamship company, which Garvey created as an enterprise that would foster trade with the West Indies and carry black Americans to Africa. But the UNIA declined as quickly as it had risen. In 1925, Garvey was imprisoned for mail fraud because of his solicitations for the Black Star Line. President Coolidge commuted his sentence but ordered his deportation to Jamaica. Without Garvey's leadership, the movement collapsed.

However, the UNIA left a legacy of activism, especially among the working class. Garvey and his followers represented an emerging **pan-Africanism**. They argued that people of African descent, in all parts of the world, had a common destiny and should cooperate in political action. Several developments contributed to this ideal: black men's military service in Europe during World War I, the Pan-African Congress that had sought representation at the Versailles treaty table, and protests against U.S. occupation of Haiti. One African American historian wrote in 1927, "The grandiose

pan-Africanism
The idea that people of African descent, in all parts of the world, have a common heritage and destiny and should cooperate in political action.

schemes of Marcus Garvey gave to the race a consciousness such as it had never possessed before. The dream of a united Africa, not less than a trip to France, challenged the imagination."

IN YOUR OWN WORDS What were the main causes of cultural conflict in the 1920s?

The Coming of the Great Depression

By 1927, strains on the economy showed that the mass consumer society that had emerged after World War I was in trouble. Americans of all sorts were overleveraged—that is, sinking in debt. Consumer lending had become the tenth largest business in the country, topping $7 billion that year. Millions of farmers were, like their nineteenth-century forebears, trapped in an annual cycle of debt. Increasing numbers of Americans bought into the stock market, often with borrowed money ("on margin") and usually with unrealistic expectations. An investor might, for example, spend $20 of his own money and borrow $80 to buy a $100 share of stock, expecting to pay back the loan as the stock rose quickly in value. This worked as long as the economy grew and the stock market climbed.

But those conditions did not last. Americans who worried over the rapid economic growth and easy credit that fueled the Roaring Twenties proved right: the "Roar" ended in the Great Depression. Taking into account the recession of 1921, the economic boom lasted only a brief seven years, from 1922 to 1929.

From Boom to Bust

When the stock market fell, in a series of plunges between October 25 and November 13, 1929, few onlookers understood the magnitude of the crisis. Cyclical downturns had been a familiar part of the industrializing economy since the panic of the 1830s; they tended to follow periods of rapid growth and speculation. The market rose again in late 1929 and early 1930, and while a great deal of money had been lost, most Americans hoped the aftermath of the crash would be brief. In fact, the nation had entered the Great Depression, the most severe economic downturn to that point in the nation's history. Over the next four years, industrial production fell 37 percent. Construction plunged 78 percent. Prices for crops and other raw materials, already low, fell by half. By 1932, unemployment had reached a staggering 24 percent (Figure 21.1).

A precipitous drop in consumer spending deepened the crisis. Facing hard times and unemployment, Americans cut back dramatically, creating a vicious cycle of falling demand and forfeited loans. If buying homes, cars, and appliances on credit seemed like a good deal in 1925, by 1930 the deal turned sour. That year, several major banks went under, victims of overextended credit and reckless management. The following year, as industrial production slowed, a much larger wave of bank failures occurred, causing an even greater shock. Since the government did not insure bank deposits, accounts in failed banks simply vanished. Some people who had had steady jobs and comfortable savings found themselves broke and out of work.

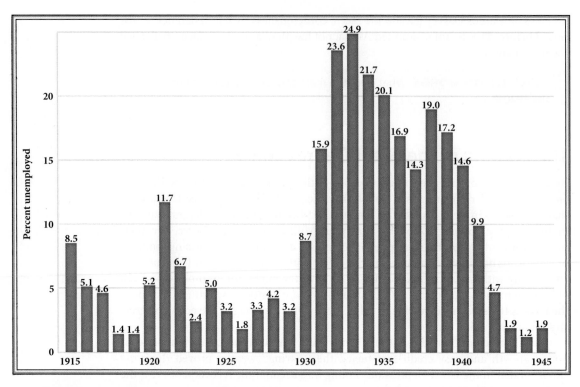

FIGURE 21.1 Unemployment, 1915–1945

During the 1920s, business prosperity and low rates of immigration resulted in historically low unemployment levels. The Great Depression threw millions of people out of work; by 1933, one in four American workers was unemployed, and the rate remained high until 1941, when the nation mobilized for World War II.

Early Depression Years

Not all Americans were devastated by the depression; the middle class did not disappear and the rich lived in accustomed luxury. But incomes plummeted even among workers who kept their jobs. Salt Lake City went bankrupt in 1931. Barter systems developed, as barbers traded haircuts for onions and potatoes and laborers worked for payment in eggs or pork. "We do not dare to use even a little soap," reported one jobless Oregonian, "when it will pay for an extra egg, a few more carrots for our children." "I would be only too glad to dig ditches to keep my family from going hungry," wrote a North Carolina man.

Where did desperate people turn for aid? Their first hope lay in private charity, especially churches and synagogues. But by the winter of 1931, these institutions were overwhelmed, unable to keep pace with the extraordinary need. Only eight states provided even minimal unemployment insurance. There was no public support for the elderly, statistically among the poorest citizens. Few Americans had any retirement savings, and many who had saved watched their accounts erased by failing banks.

Even those who were not wiped out had to adapt to depression conditions. Couples delayed marriage and reduced the number of children they conceived. As a result, the marriage rate fell to a historical low, and by 1933 the birthrate dropped from 97 births per 1,000 women to 75. Often the responsibility for birth control fell to women. It was "one of the worst problems of women whose husbands were out of work," a Californian told a reporter. Campaigns against hiring married women were common, on the theory that available jobs should go to male breadwinners. Three-quarters of the nation's school districts banned married women from working as teachers — ignoring the fact that many husbands were less able to earn than ever before. Despite restrictions, female employment increased, as women expanded their financial contributions to their families in hard times.

Minnesota Potato Farmers The prosperity and consumer pleasures of the 1920s hardly extended to all Americans. This Minnesota family had horses, not a tractor; many of the women's clothes were probably made by hand. Rural and working-class Americans, who often struggled in the 1920s, found conditions even harsher after 1929. On the other hand, farmers had resources to fall back on that city folks did not: they could grow their own food, and they had long experience in "making do." Minnesota Historical Society.

The depression crossed regional boundaries, though its severity varied from place to place. Bank failures clustered heavily in the Midwest and plains, while areas dependent on timber, mining, and other extractive industries suffered catastrophic declines. Although southern states endured less unemployment because of their smaller manufacturing base, farm wages plunged. In many parts of the country, unemployment rates among black men stood at double that of white men; joblessness among African American women was triple that of white women.

By 1932, comprehending the magnitude of the crisis, Americans went to the ballot box and decisively rejected the probusiness, antiregulatory policies of the 1920s. A few years earlier, with business booming, politics had been so placid that people chuckled when President Coolidge disappeared on extended fishing trips. Now, Americans wanted bold action in Washington. Faced with the cataclysm of the Great Depression, Americans would transform their government and create a modern welfare state.

IN YOUR OWN WORDS What domestic economic factors helped cause the Great Depression?

Summary

Involvement in World War I strengthened the United States economically and diplomatically, but it left the nation profoundly unsettled. Racial tensions exploded after the war as African Americans pursued new opportunities and asserted their rights. Meanwhile, labor unrest grew as employers cut wages and sought to break unions, while anxieties over radicalism and immigration prompted a nationwide Red Scare.

The politics of the 1920s brought a backlash against prewar progressivism and a series of clashes over religion, morality, and national belonging. The agenda of women reformers met very limited success. Republican administrations pursued probusiness "normalcy" at home and "dollar diplomacy" abroad. Prohibition and the Scopes trial demonstrated the influence religion could exert on public policy, while rising nativism fueled a resurgent Ku Klux Klan and led to sweeping new restrictions on immigration. Meanwhile, black artists and intellectuals of the Harlem Renaissance, including many inspired by pan-African ideas, explored the complexities of African American life.

Business thrived and a booming consumer culture, exemplified by the radio, the automobile, and Hollywood films, created new forms of leisure, influencing daily life and challenging older sexual norms. However, the risky speculation and easy credit of the 1920s undermined the foundations of the economy. After the 1929 crash, these factors, along with a range of interconnected global conditions to be discussed in Chapter 22, plunged the United States into the Great Depression.

CHAPTER 21 REVIEW

TERMS TO KNOW   *Identify and explain the significance of each term below.*

Key Concepts and Events

Red Scare (p. 685)	consumer credit (p. 691)	Volstead Act (p. 698)	jazz (p. 705)
Palmer raids (p. 685)	Hollywood (p. 691)	American Civil Liberties Union (p. 698)	Universal Negro Improvement Association (p. 705)
Red Summer (p. 686)	flapper (p. 691)		
American Plan (p. 687)	soft power (p. 691)	Scopes trial (p. 698)	
welfare capitalism (p. 687)	Sheppard-Towner Federal Maternity and Infancy Act (p. 696)	National Origins Act (p. 699)	pan-Africanism (p. 706)
dollar diplomacy (p. 688)		Ku Klux Klan (p. 700)	
associated state (p. 689)	Eighteenth Amendment (p. 698)	Harlem Renaissance (p. 704)	
Teapot Dome (p. 689)			

Key People

Nicola Sacco and Bartolomeo Vanzetti (p. 685)	Henry Ford (p. 687)	Zora Neale Hurston (p. 704)	Louis Armstrong (p. 705)
	Adolph Zukor (p. 691)		Marcus Garvey (p. 705)

REVIEW QUESTIONS   *Answer these questions to demonstrate your understanding of the chapter's main ideas.*

1. How and why did the United States take a conservative turn in the 1920s?

2. What were the primary characteristics of the American economy in the 1920s?

3. What caused the cultural conflict of the 1920s?

4. What domestic and global factors helped cause the Great Depression?

5. Between 1917 and 1945, the "Roaring Twenties" were the only years when the United States did not face a major economic or international crisis. Review the categories of "America in the World," "Politics and Power," and "American and National Identity" on the thematic timeline on pages 648–649. In what ways do they suggest that the prosperous 1920s were a politically distinctive era? What continuities do you see in politics and foreign policy?

MAKING CONNECTIONS   *Recognize the larger developments and continuities within and across chapters.*

1. The Ku Klux Klan of the Reconstruction era (Chapter 14) emerged in a specific political and social context; while the Klan of the 1920s built on its predecessor, its goals and scope were different. Using material from Chapters 14 and 21, imagine that you are investigating a series of Klan meetings in each era (1870s and 1920s). Where would you conduct your investigation? How might you explain, to the public, the Klan's membership and activities? How would you compare the two Klans?

2. Along what lines did Americans find themselves divided in the 1920s? How were those conflicts expressed in politics? In culture and intellectual life?

3. What factors contributed to the economic boom of the 1920s and the crash that followed?

KEY TURNING POINTS   *Refer to the chapter chronology on page 684 for help in answering the questions below.*

American politics underwent two shifts in the period covered in this chapter: one in the aftermath of World War I, and another in 1932. What caused each turning point? What factors in American society, economics, and culture help explain each moment of political change?

22

CHAPTER

Managing the Great Depression, Forging the New Deal
1929–1938

In his inaugural address in March 1933, President Franklin Delano Roosevelt did not hide the country's precarious condition. "A host of unemployed citizens face the grim problem of existence," he said, "and an equally great number toil with little return. Only a foolish optimist can deny the dark realities of the moment." Roosevelt, his demeanor sincere and purposeful, saw both despair and determination in the nation's citizens. "This nation asks for action, and action now." From Congress he would request "broad Executive power to wage a war against the emergency, as great as the power that would be given to me if we were in fact invaded by a foreign foe." With these words, Roosevelt launched a program of federal activism — which he called the New Deal — that would change the nature of American government.

> ### IDENTIFY THE BIG IDEA
>
> **What new roles did the American government take on during the New Deal, and how did these roles shape the economy and society?**

The New Deal represented a new form of liberalism, a fresh interpretation of the ideology of individual rights that had long shaped the character of American society and politics. Classical nineteenth-century liberals believed that, to protect those rights, government should be small and relatively weak. However, the progressives of the early twentieth century believed individual freedom and opportunity were best safeguarded by strengthening state and federal control over large businesses and monopolies. New Deal activists went much further: their social-welfare liberalism expanded individual rights to include economic security. Beginning in the 1930s and continuing through the 1960s, they increased the responsibility of the national government for the welfare of ordinary citizens. Their efforts did not go unchallenged. Conservative critics of the New Deal charged that its "big government" programs were paternalistic and dangerous, undermining individual responsibility and constraining personal freedom. This division between the advocates and the critics of the New Deal shaped American politics for the next half century.

Before Roosevelt was elected president, between the onset of the depression in 1929 and November 1932, the "dark realities of the moment" wore down American society. Rising unemployment, shuttered businesses, failing banks, and home foreclosures tore at the nation's social fabric. As crisis piled upon crisis and the federal government's initiatives under President Hoover proved ineffectual, Americans had to reconsider more than the role of government in economic life: they had to rethink many of the principles of individualism and free enterprise that had guided so much of the nation's history.

ILLINIOS
NATIONAL YOUTH ADMINISTRATION

GIRLS – ARE YOU INTERESTED IN A JOB?
FIND OUT WHAT AN OCCUPATION HAS TO OFFER YOU IN
PAY-EMPLOYMENT-SECURITY AND PROMOTION
FREE CLASSES

The New Deal This Federal Arts Project poster from 1936 captured the spirit of the New Deal under President Franklin Roosevelt. Produced for the Illinois branch of the National Youth Administration, one of the many New Deal agencies of the decade, the poster demonstrates the goal of getting Americans working again. Roosevelt and other "New Dealers" hoped to decrease unemployment, raise people's spirits, and point to a brighter future in the midst of the Great Depression. Library of Congress.

As you read, ask yourself why this chapter begins and ends with these dates and identify the links among related events.

1929	▶ Stock market crash
1930	▶ Smoot-Hawley Tariff
1931–1937	▶ Scottsboro case: trials and appeals
1932	▶ Bonus Army marches on Washington, D.C. (May–July)
	▶ Franklin Delano Roosevelt elected president (November)
1933	▶ FDR's inaugural address and first fireside chats
	▶ Emergency Banking Act launches the Hundred Days
	▶ FDR takes United States off the gold standard
	▶ Civilian Conservation Corps (CCC) created
	▶ Agricultural Adjustment Act (AAA)
	▶ National Industrial Recovery Act (NIRA)
	▶ Tennessee Valley Authority (TVA) established
	▶ Townsend Clubs promote Old Age Revolving Pension Plan
1934	▶ Securities and Exchange Commission (SEC) created
	▶ Southern Tenant Farmers Union (STFU) founded
	▶ Indian Reorganization Act
	▶ Senator Huey Long promotes Share Our Wealth Society

1935	▶ Supreme Court voids NIRA in *Schechter v. United States*
	▶ National Labor Relations (Wagner) Act
	▶ Social Security Act creates old-age pension system
	▶ Works Progress Administration (WPA) created
	▶ Rural Electrification Administration (REA) established
	▶ Supreme Court voids Agricultural Adjustment Act
	▶ Congress of Industrial Organizations (CIO) formed
1936	▶ Landslide reelection of FDR marks peak of New Deal
1937	▶ FDR's Supreme Court plan fails
1937–1938	▶ "Roosevelt recession" raises unemployment
1938	▶ Fair Labor Standards Act

Early Responses to the Depression, 1929–1932

The American economy collapsed between 1929 and 1932, by virtually any measurement. U.S. gross domestic product fell almost by half, from $103 billion to $58 billion. Consumption dropped by 18 percent, construction by 78 percent, and private investment by 88 percent. Nearly 9,000 banks closed their doors, and 100,000 businesses failed. Corporate profits fell from $10 billion to $1 billion. Unemployment rose to 25 percent. Fifteen million people were out of work by 1933. "Hoover made a souphound outa me!" sang jobless harvest hands in the Southwest.

The depression respected no national boundaries. Germany had preceded the United States into economic contraction in 1928, and its economy, burdened by heavy World War I reparations payments, was brought to its knees by 1929. France, Britain, Argentina, Brazil, Poland, and Canada were hard hit as well. Recovery proved difficult because the international gold standard constrained economic policymaking. The United States and most European nations had tied the value of their currencies to the price of gold, and the amount of gold held in reserves, since the late nineteenth century. This system had worked fairly well for a few decades, but it was vulnerable during economic downturns, when large financiers withdrew their investments and demanded gold payments. The gold standard rendered the

*To see a longer excerpt of Roosevelt's inaugural address, mentioned in the chapter introduction, along with other primary sources from this period, see **Sources for America's History**.*

international monetary system inflexible at precisely the moment when maximum flexibility was needed.

Enter Herbert Hoover

President Herbert Hoover and Congress responded to the downturn by drawing on two influential American traditions. The first was the belief that economic outcomes were the product of individual character: people's fate was in their own hands, and success went to those who deserved it. The second tradition held that through voluntary action, the business community could right itself and recover from economic downturns without relying on government assistance or, worse, submitting to government regulation. Following these principles, Hoover asked Americans to tighten their belts and work hard. After the stock market crash, he cut federal taxes in an attempt to boost private spending and corporate investment. "Any lack of confidence in the economic future or the strength of business in the United States is foolish," Hoover assured the country in late 1929. Treasury secretary Andrew Mellon suggested that the downturn would help Americans "work harder" and "live a more moral life."

While many factors caused the Great Depression, Hoover's adherence to the gold standard was a major reason for its length and severity in the United States. Faced with economic catastrophe, both Britain and Germany abandoned the gold standard in 1931; when they did so, their economies recovered modestly. But the Hoover administration feared that such a move would weaken the value of the dollar. In reality, an inflexible money supply discouraged investment and therefore prevented growth. The Roosevelt administration would ultimately remove the United States from the burdens of the gold standard in 1933. By that time, however, the crisis had achieved catastrophic dimensions. Billions had been lost in business and bank failures, and the economy had stalled completely.

Along with adherence to the gold standard, Hoover and many congressional Republicans believed in another piece of economic orthodoxy that had protected American manufacturing in good economic times but that proved damaging during the downturn: high tariffs (taxes on imported goods designed to stimulate American manufacturing). In 1930, Republicans enacted the **Smoot-Hawley Tariff**. Despite receiving a letter from more than a thousand economists urging him to veto it, Hoover approved the legislation. What served American interests in earlier eras now undermined them. Smoot-Hawley triggered retaliatory tariffs in other countries, which further hindered global trade and worsened economic contraction throughout the industrialized world.

The president recognized that individual initiative, business voluntarism, and high tariffs might not be enough, given the depth of the crisis, so he proposed government action as well. He called on state and local governments to provide jobs by investing in public projects. And in 1931, he secured an unprecedented increase of $700 million in federal spending for public works. Hoover's most innovative program was the Reconstruction Finance Corporation (RFC), which provided federal loans to railroads, banks, and other businesses. But the RFC lent money too cautiously, and by the end of 1932 it had loaned out only 20 percent of its $1.5 billion in funds. Like most

Smoot-Hawley Tariff
A high tariff enacted in 1930 during the Great Depression. By taxing imported goods, Congress hoped to stimulate American manufacturing, but the tariff triggered retaliatory tariffs in other countries, which further hindered global trade and led to greater economic contraction.

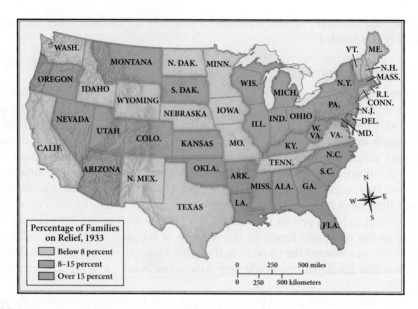

MAP 22.1 The Great Depression: Families on Relief

Although the Great Depression was a nationwide crisis, some regions were hit harder than others. Economic hardship was widespread in the agricultural South, the rural Appalachian states, and the industrial states of the Northeast and Midwest. As the depression worsened in 1931 and 1932, local and state governments, as well as charitable organizations, could not keep up with the demand for relief. After Franklin D. Roosevelt assumed the presidency in 1933, the national government began a massive program of aid through the Federal Emergency Relief Administration (FERA).

federal initiatives under Hoover, the RFC was not nearly aggressive enough given the severity of the depression.

Few chief executives could have survived the downward economic spiral of 1929–1932, but Hoover's reluctance to break with the philosophy of limited government and his insistence that recovery was just around the corner contributed to his unpopularity. By 1932, Americans perceived Hoover as insensitive to the depth of economic suffering. The nation had come a long way since the depressions of the 1870s and 1890s, when no one except the most radical figures, such as Jacob Coxey, called for direct federal aid to the unemployed (Chapter 19). Compared with previous chief executives — and in contrast to his popular image as a "do-nothing" president — Hoover had responded to the national emergency with unprecedented government action. But the nation's needs were even more unprecedented, and Hoover's programs failed to meet them (Map 22.1).

Rising Discontent

As the depression deepened, the American vocabulary now included the terms *Hoovervilles* (shantytowns where people lived in packing crates) and *Hoover blankets* (newspapers). Bankrupt farmers banded together to resist the bank agents and sheriffs who tried to evict them from their land. To protest low prices for their goods, in the spring of 1932 thousands of midwestern farmers joined the Farmers' Holiday Association, which cut off supplies to urban areas by barricading roads and dumping milk, vegetables, and other foodstuffs onto the roadways. Agricultural prices were so

Hooverville The depression cast hundreds of thousands of Americans out of their homes. Most found shelter with relatives, but those with little choice had to make do as they could. Encampments such as this one south of downtown Seattle, Washington — places where the homeless crafted makeshift lodging out of whatever materials were at hand — became known as Hoovervilles. The name reflected Americans' attitudes toward President Hoover, whose popularity plummeted as the depression deepened. AP Photo.

low that the group advocated a government-supported farm program — drawing on Populist ideas from the 1890s (Chapter 19).

In the industrial sector, layoffs and wage cuts led to violent strikes. When coal miners in Harlan County, Kentucky, went on strike over a 10 percent wage cut in 1931, the mine owners called in the state's National Guard, which crushed the union. A 1932 confrontation between workers and security forces at the Ford Motor Company's giant River Rouge factory outside Detroit left five workers dead and fifty with serious injuries. A news photographer had his camera shot from his hands, and fifteen policemen were beaten. Whether on farms or in factories, those who produced the nation's food and goods had begun to agitate, protest, and organize in the face of mounting economic troubles.

Veterans staged the most publicized — and most tragic — protest. In the summer of 1932, the **Bonus Army**, a determined group of between fifteen thousand and twenty thousand unemployed World War I veterans, piled into cars, hitchhiked, and even walked to Washington to demand immediate payment of pension awards that were due to be paid in 1945. "We were heroes in 1917, but we're bums now," one veteran complained bitterly. While their leaders unsuccessfully lobbied Congress, the Bonus Army set up camps near the Capitol building. Hoover deployed regular army

Bonus Army
A group of fifteen thousand to twenty thousand unemployed World War I veterans who set up camps near the Capitol building in 1932 to demand immediate payment of pension awards due to be paid in 1945.

troops under the command of General Douglas MacArthur, who forcefully evicted the marchers and burned their encampment to the ground. When newsreel footage showing the U.S. Army attacking and injuring veterans reached movie theaters across the nation, Hoover's popularity plunged even further. In another measure of how the country had changed since the 1890s, what Americans had applauded when done to Coxey in 1894 was condemned in 1932.

The 1932 Election

Amidst rising discontent as the 1932 election approached, most Americans believed that something altogether new had to be tried — whatever that might be. The Republicans, reluctant to dump an incumbent president, unenthusiastically renominated Hoover. The Democrats turned to New York governor Franklin Delano Roosevelt, whose state had initiated innovative relief and unemployment programs.

Roosevelt, born into a wealthy New York family, was a distant cousin to former president Theodore Roosevelt, whose career he emulated. After attending Harvard College and Columbia University, Franklin Roosevelt served as assistant secretary of the navy during World War I (as Theodore Roosevelt had done before the War of 1898). Then, in 1921, a crippling attack of polio left both of his legs permanently paralyzed. Supported by his wife, Eleanor, he slowly returned to public life and campaigned successfully for the governorship of New York in 1928 and again in 1930. Running for the presidency in 1932, Roosevelt pledged vigorous action but gave no indication what that action might be, arguing simply that "the country needs and, unless I mistake its temper, the country demands bold, persistent experimentation." He won easily, receiving 22.8 million votes to Hoover's 15.7 million.

Elected in November, Roosevelt would not begin his presidency until March 1933. (The Twentieth Amendment, ratified in 1933, set subsequent inaugurations for January 20.) Meanwhile, Americans suffered through the worst winter of the depression. Unemployment continued to climb nationwide. In a measure of the depth of woe, in three major industrial cities in Ohio, the jobless rate shot to staggering levels: 50 percent in Cleveland, 60 percent in Akron, and 80 percent in Toledo. Private charities and public relief agencies reached only a fraction of the needy. The nation's banking system was so close to collapse that many state governors closed banks temporarily to avoid further withdrawals. Several states were approaching bankruptcy, their tax revenues too low to pay for basic services. By March 1933, the nation had hit rock bottom.

> **IN YOUR OWN WORDS** How did Americans, from ordinary citizens to political leaders, respond to the Great Depression?

The New Deal Arrives, 1933–1935

The ideological differences between Herbert Hoover and Franklin Roosevelt were not vast. Both leaders wished to maintain the nation's economic institutions and preserve its social structure, to save capitalism while easing its worst downturns. Both believed in a balanced government budget and extolled the values of hard work, cooperation, and sacrifice. But Roosevelt's personal charm, political savvy, and willingness to experiment made him far more effective and popular than Hoover. Most Americans felt a kinship with their new president, calling him simply FDR. His New Deal would put people to work and restore hope in the nation's future.

Roosevelt and the First Hundred Days

A wealthy patrician, Roosevelt was an unlikely figure to inspire millions of ordinary Americans. But his close rapport with the American people was critical to his political success. More than 450,000 letters poured into the White House in the week after his inauguration. The president's masterful use of the new medium of radio, especially his evening radio addresses to the American public known as **fireside chats**, made him an intimate presence in people's lives. Thousands of citizens felt a personal relationship with FDR, saying, "He gave me a job" or "He saved my home."

Citing the national economic emergency, Roosevelt further expanded the presidential powers that Theodore Roosevelt and Woodrow Wilson had increased previously. To draft legislation and policy, he relied heavily on financier Bernard Baruch and a "Brains Trust" of professors from Columbia, Harvard, and other leading universities. Roosevelt also turned to his talented cabinet, which included Harold L. Ickes, secretary of the interior; Frances Perkins at the Labor Department; Henry A. Wallace at Agriculture; and Henry Morgenthau Jr., secretary of the treasury. These intellectuals and administrators attracted hundreds of highly qualified recruits to Washington. Inspired by New Deal idealism, many of them would devote their lives to public service and the principles of social-welfare liberalism.

Roosevelt could have done little, however, without a sympathetic Congress. The 1932 election had swept Democratic majorities into both the House and Senate, giving the new president the lawmaking allies he needed. The first months of FDR's administration produced a whirlwind of activity on Capitol Hill. In a legendary session, known as the **Hundred Days**, Congress enacted fifteen major bills that focused primarily on four problems: banking failures, agricultural overproduction, the business slump, and soaring unemployment. Derided by some as an "alphabet soup" because of their many abbreviations (CCC, WPA, AAA, etc.), the new policies and agencies represented the emergence of a new American state.

Banking Reform   The collapsing banking system hobbled the entire economy, curtailing consumer spending and business investment. Widespread bank failures had reduced the savings of nearly nine million families, and panicked account holders raced to withdraw their funds. On March 5, 1933, the day after his inauguration, FDR declared a national "bank holiday" — closing all the banks — and called Congress into special session. Four days later, Congress passed the Emergency Banking Act, which permitted banks to reopen if a Treasury Department inspection showed they had sufficient cash reserves.

In his first Sunday night fireside chat, to a radio audience of sixty million, the president reassured citizens that their money was safe. When the banks reopened on March 13, calm prevailed and deposits exceeded withdrawals, restoring stability to the nation's basic financial institutions. "Capitalism was saved in eight days," quipped Roosevelt's advisor Raymond Moley. Four thousand banks had failed in the months

fireside chats
A series of informal radio addresses Franklin Roosevelt made to the nation in which he explained New Deal initiatives.

Hundred Days
A legendary session during the first few months of Franklin Roosevelt's administration in which Congress enacted fifteen major bills that focused primarily on four problems: banking failures, agricultural overproduction, the business slump, and soaring unemployment.

Glass-Steagall Act

A 1933 law that created the Federal Deposit Insurance Corporation (FDIC), which insured deposits up to $2,500 (and now up to $250,000). The act also prohibited banks from making risky, unsecured investments with customers' deposits.

prior to Roosevelt's inauguration; only sixty-one closed their doors in all of 1934. A second banking law, the **Glass-Steagall Act**, further restored public confidence by creating the Federal Deposit Insurance Corporation (FDIC), which insured deposits up to $2,500 (and now insures them up to $250,000). The act also prohibited banks from making risky, unsecured investments with the deposits of ordinary people. And in a profoundly important economic and symbolic gesture, Roosevelt removed the U.S. Treasury from the gold standard in June 1933, which allowed the Federal Reserve to lower interest rates; since 1931, it had been raising rates, which had only deepened the downturn.

Agriculture and Manufacturing

Agriculture and Manufacturing   Roosevelt and the New Deal Congress next turned to agriculture and manufacturing. In those sectors, a seeming paradox was evident: the depression led to overproduction in agriculture and underproduction in manufacturing. Reversing both problematic trends was critical. The **Agricultural Adjustment Act** (AAA) began direct governmental regulation of the farm economy for the first time. To solve the problem of overproduction, which lowered prices, the AAA provided cash subsidies to farmers who cut production of seven major commodities: wheat, cotton, corn, hogs, rice, tobacco, and dairy products. Policymakers hoped that farm prices would rise as production fell.

Agricultural Adjustment Act

New Deal legislation passed in May 1933 that aimed at cutting agricultural production to raise crop prices and thus farmers' income.

By dumping cash in farmers' hands, the AAA briefly stabilized the farm economy. But the act's benefits were not evenly distributed. Subsidies went primarily to the owners of large and medium-sized farms, who often cut production by reducing the amount of land they rented to tenants and sharecroppers. In Mississippi, one plantation owner received $26,000 from the federal government, while thousands of black sharecroppers living in the same county received only a few dollars in relief payments.

In manufacturing, the New Deal attacked declining production with the National Industrial Recovery Act. A new government agency, the **National Recovery Administration** (NRA), set up separate self-governing private associations in six hundred industries. Each industry—ranging from large corporations producing coal, cotton textiles, and steel to small businesses making pet food and costume jewelry—regulated itself by agreeing on prices and production quotas.

National Recovery Administration

Federal agency established in June 1933 to promote industrial recovery during the Great Depression. It encouraged industrialists to voluntarily adopt codes that defined fair working conditions, set prices, and minimized competition.

The AAA and the NRA were designed to rescue the nation's productive industries and stabilize the economy. The measures had positive effects in some regions, but most historians agree that, overall, they did little to end the depression.

Unemployment Relief

Unemployment Relief   The Roosevelt administration next addressed the massive unemployment problem. By 1933, local governments and private charities had exhausted their resources and were looking to Washington for assistance. Although Roosevelt wanted to avoid a budget deficit, he asked Congress to provide relief for millions of unemployed Americans. In May, Congress established the Federal Emergency Relief Administration (FERA). Directed by Harry Hopkins, a hard-driving social worker from New York, the FERA provided federal funds for state relief programs.

Roosevelt and Hopkins had strong reservations about the "dole," the nickname for government welfare payments. As Hopkins put it, "I don't think anybody can go year after year, month after month, accepting relief without affecting his character."

To support the traditional values of individualism, the New Deal put people to work. Early in 1933, Congress established the **Public Works Administration** (PWA), a construction program, and several months later, Roosevelt created the Civil Works Administration (CWA) and named Hopkins its head. At its peak in 1934, the CWA provided jobs for 4 million Americans, repairing bridges, building highways, and constructing public buildings. A stopgap measure to get the country through the winter of 1933–1934, the CWA lapsed in the spring, when Republican opposition compelled New Dealers to abandon it. A longer-term program, the **Civilian Conservation Corps** (CCC), mobilized 250,000 young men to do reforestation and conservation work. Over the course of the 1930s, the "CCC boys" built thousands of bridges, roads, trails, and other structures in state and national parks, bolstering the national infrastructure (Map 22.2).

Housing Crisis Millions of Americans also faced the devastating prospect of losing their homes. The economic expansion of the 1920s had produced the largest inflationary housing bubble in American history to that point, a scenario in which home prices

Public Works Administration
A New Deal construction program established by Congress in 1933. Designed to put people back to work, the PWA built the Boulder Dam (renamed Hoover Dam) and Grand Coulee Dam, among other large public works projects.

Civilian Conservation Corps
Federal relief program that provided jobs to millions of unemployed young men who built thousands of bridges, roads, trails, and other structures in state and national parks, bolstering the national infrastructure.

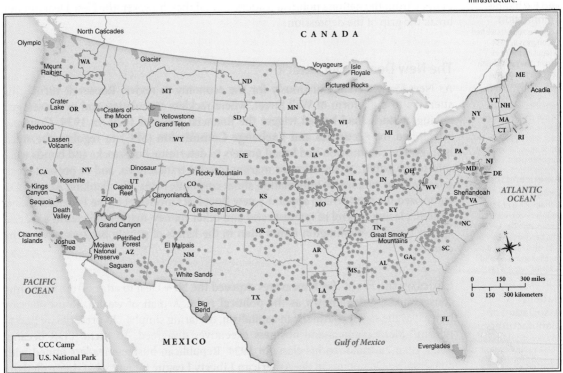

MAP 22.2 Civilian Conservation Corps Camps
The Civilian Conservation Corps (CCC) gave hope to unemployed young men during the Great Depression. The first camp opened in Big Meadows, Virginia, in July 1933, and by the end of the decade CCC camps had appeared across the length of the country, located in rural, mountainous, and forested regions alike. Young men constructed bridges and roads, built hiking trails, erected public campgrounds, and performed other improvements. By the early 1940s, the CCC had planted three billion trees, among its many other contributions to the national infrastructure.

rose rapidly, fueled by widespread borrowing. In the early 1930s, home prices collapsed, banks closed, and the jobless could not afford mortgage payments. More than half a million Americans lost their homes between 1930 and 1932. In response, Congress created the Home Owners Loan Corporation (HOLC) to refinance home mortgages. In just two years, the HOLC helped more than a million Americans retain their homes. The Federal Housing Act of 1934 would extend this program under a new agency, the **Federal Housing Administration** (FHA). Together, the HOLC, the FHA, and the subsequent Housing Act of 1937 permanently changed the mortgage system and set the foundation for the broad expansion of home ownership in the post–World War II decades (Chapter 24).

When an exhausted Congress recessed in June 1933, at the end of the Hundred Days, it had enacted Roosevelt's agenda: banking reform, recovery programs for agriculture and industry, public works, and unemployment relief. Few presidents had won the passage of so many measures in so short a time. The new federal agencies were far from perfect and had their critics on both the radical left and the conservative right. But the vigorous actions taken by Roosevelt and Congress had halted the downward economic spiral of the Hoover years, stabilized the financial sector, and sent a message of hope from the nation's political leaders. For all that, however, the New Deal did not break the grip of the depression.

The New Deal Under Attack

As New Dealers waited anxiously for the economy to revive, Roosevelt turned his attention to the reform of Wall Street, where reckless speculation and overleveraged buying of stocks had helped trigger the financial panic of 1929. In 1934, Congress established the **Securities and Exchange Commission** (SEC) to regulate the stock market. The commission had broad powers to determine how stocks and bonds were sold to the public, to set rules for margin (credit) transactions, and to prevent stock sales by those with inside information about corporate plans. The Banking Act of 1935 authorized the president to appoint a new Board of Governors of the Federal Reserve System, placing control of interest rates and other money-market policies in a federal agency based in Washington rather than in the hands of private bankers around the country.

Critics on the Right Such measures exposed the New Deal to attack from economic conservatives — also known as the political right. A man of wealth, Roosevelt saw himself as the savior of American capitalism, declaring simply, "To preserve we had to reform." Many bankers and business executives disagreed. To them, FDR became "That Man," a traitor to his class. In 1934, Republican business leaders joined with conservative Democrats in the **American Liberty League** to fight what they called the "reckless spending" and "socialist" reforms of the New Deal. Herbert Hoover condemned the NRA as "tyranny, not liberalism."

The **National Association of Manufacturers** (NAM) was a more lasting opponent of the New Deal — its influence stretched far into the post–World War II decades. Sparked by a new generation of corporate leaders who launched a probusiness

---

Federal Housing Administration
An agency established by the Federal Housing Act of 1934 that refinanced home mortgages for mortgage holders facing possible foreclosure.

Securities and Exchange Commission
A commission established by Congress in 1934 to regulate the stock market. The commission had broad powers to determine how stocks and bonds were sold to the public, to set rules for margin (credit) transactions, and to prevent stock sales by those with inside information about corporate plans.

American Liberty League
A group of Republican business leaders and conservative Democrats who banded together to fight what they called the "reckless spending" and "socialist" reforms of the New Deal.

National Association of Manufacturers
An association of industrialists and business leaders opposed to government regulation. In the era of the New Deal, the group promoted free enterprise and capitalism through a publicity campaign of radio programs, motion pictures, billboards, and direct mail.

publicity campaign to "serve the purposes of business salvation," the NAM promoted free enterprise and unfettered capitalism. In response to what many conservatives perceived as Roosevelt's antibusiness policies, the NAM produced radio programs, motion pictures, billboards, and direct mail campaigns carrying its message. After World War II, the NAM emerged as a staunch critic of liberalism and forged alliances with influential conservative politicians such as Barry Goldwater and Ronald Reagan.

Based on conservative legal doctrine dating to the late nineteenth century, the Supreme Court repudiated several cornerstones of the early New Deal. In May 1935, in *Schechter v. United States*, the Court unanimously ruled the National Industrial Recovery Act unconstitutional because it delegated Congress's lawmaking power to the executive branch and extended federal authority to intrastate (in contrast to interstate) commerce. Roosevelt protested but watched helplessly as the Court struck down more New Deal legislation: the Agricultural Adjustment Act, the Railroad Retirement Act, and a debt-relief law known as the Frazier-Lemke Act.

Critics on the Populist Left   If business leaders and the Supreme Court thought that the New Deal had gone too far, other Americans believed it had not gone far enough. Among these were public figures who, in the tradition of American populism, sought to place government on the side of ordinary citizens against corporations and the wealthy. Francis Townsend, a doctor from Long Beach, California, spoke for the nation's elderly, most of whom had no pensions and feared poverty. In 1933, Townsend proposed the Old Age Revolving Pension Plan, which would give $200 a month (about $3,600 today) to citizens over the age of sixty. To receive payments, the elderly would have to retire and open their positions to younger workers. Townsend Clubs sprang up across the country in support of the **Townsend Plan**, mobilizing mass support for old-age pensions.

The most direct political threat to Roosevelt came from Louisiana senator Huey Long. As the Democratic governor of Louisiana from 1928 to 1932, the flamboyant Long had achieved stunning popularity. He increased taxes on corporations, lowered the utility bills of consumers, and built new highways, hospitals, and schools. To push through these measures, Long seized almost dictatorial control of the state government. A U.S. senator by 1934, Long broke with the New Deal and, like Townsend, established a national movement. According to his Share Our Wealth Society, inequalities in the distribution of wealth prohibited millions of ordinary families from buying the goods that kept factories humming. Long's society advocated a tax of 100 percent on all income over $1 million and on all inheritances over $5 million. He hoped that this populist program would carry him into the White House. Roosevelt himself feared that Long and Townsend, along with the popular "Radio Priest," Father Charles Coughlin, might join forces to form a third party. He had to respond or risk the political unity of the country's liberal forces (Map 22.3).

Townsend Plan
A plan proposed by Francis Townsend in 1933 that would give $200 a month (about $3,600 today) to citizens over the age of sixty. Townsend Clubs sprang up across the country in support of the plan, mobilizing mass support for old-age pensions.

IN YOUR OWN WORDS   What were the major components of the Hundred Days, and what was their purpose?

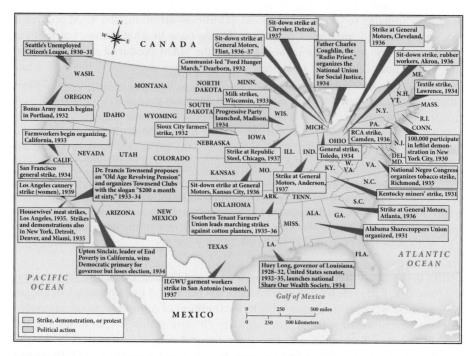

MAP 22.3 **Popular Protest in the Great Depression, 1933–1939**

The depression forced Americans to look closely at their society, and many of them did not like what they saw. Some citizens expressed their discontent through popular movements, and this map suggests the geography of discontent. The industrial Midwest witnessed union movements, strikes, and "Radio Priest" Charles Coughlin's demands for social reform. Simultaneously, farmers' movements — tenants in the South, smallholders in the agricultural Midwest — engaged in strikes and dumping campaigns and rallied behind the ideas of progressives in Wisconsin and Huey Long in the South. Protests took diverse forms in California, which was home to strikes by farmworkers, women, and — in San Francisco — all wageworkers. The West was also the seedbed of two important reform proposals: Upton Sinclair's End Poverty in California (EPIC) movement and Francis Townsend's Old Age Revolving Pension clubs.

The Second New Deal and the Redefining of Liberalism, 1935–1938

As attacks on the New Deal proliferated, Roosevelt and his advisors moved politically to the left. Historians have labeled this shift in policy the Second New Deal. Roosevelt now openly criticized the "money classes," proudly stating, "We have earned the hatred of entrenched greed." He also decisively countered the rising popularity of Townsend, Long, and Coughlin by adopting parts of their programs. The administration's Revenue Act of 1935 proposed a substantial tax increase on corporate profits and higher income and estate taxes on the wealthy. When conservatives attacked this legislation as an attempt to "soak the rich," Congress moderated its taxation rates. But FDR was satisfied. He had met the Share Our Wealth Society's proposal with a tax plan of his own.

The Welfare State Comes into Being

The Revenue Act symbolized the administration's new outlook. Unlike the First New Deal, which focused on economic recovery, the Second New Deal emphasized social justice and the creation of a safety net: the use of the federal government to assist working people and to provide economic security for the old, the disabled, and the unemployed. The resulting **welfare state** — a term applied to industrial democracies that adopted various government-guaranteed social-welfare programs — fundamentally changed American society.

The Wagner Act and Social Security The first beneficiary of Roosevelt's Second New Deal was the labor movement. Section 7(a) of the National Industrial Recovery Act (NIRA) had given workers the right to organize unions, producing a dramatic growth in rank-and-file militancy and leading to a strike wave in 1934. When the Supreme Court voided the NIRA in 1935, labor unions called for new legislation that would allow workers to organize and bargain collectively with employers. Named for its sponsor, Senator Robert F. Wagner of New York, the **Wagner Act** (1935) established the right of industrial workers to join unions. The act outlawed many practices that employers had used to suppress unions, such as firing workers for organizing activities. A new federal agency, the National Labor Relations Board (NLRB), had the authority to protect workers from employer coercion and would guarantee collective bargaining.

A second initiative, the **Social Security Act** of 1935, had an equally widespread impact. Other industrialized societies, such as Germany and Britain, had created national old-age pension systems at the turn of the century, but American reformers had failed to secure a similar program. The Townsend and Long movements now pressed Roosevelt to act, giving political leverage to pension proponents within the administration. Children's welfare advocates, concerned about the fate of fatherless families, also pressured the president. The resulting Social Security Act had three main provisions: old-age pensions for workers; a joint federal-state system of compensation for unemployed workers; and a program of payments to widowed mothers and the blind, deaf, and disabled. Roosevelt, however, limited the reach of the legislation. Knowing that compulsory pension and unemployment legislation alone would be controversial, he dropped a provision for national health insurance, fearing it would doom the entire bill.

The Social Security Act was a milestone in the creation of an American welfare state. Never before had the federal government assumed such responsibility for the well-being of so many citizens. Social Security, as old-age pensions were known, became one of the most popular government programs in American history. On the other hand, the assistance program for widows and children known as Aid to Dependent Children (ADC) became one of its most controversial measures. ADC covered only 700,000 youngsters in 1939; by 1994, its successor, Aid to Families with Dependent Children (AFDC), enrolled 14.1 million Americans. A minor program during the New Deal, AFDC grew enormously in the 1960s and remained an often maligned cornerstone of the welfare state until it was eliminated under President Bill Clinton in 1996.

welfare state
A term applied to industrial democracies that adopt various government-guaranteed social-welfare programs. The creation of Social Security and other measures of the Second New Deal fundamentally changed American society and established a national welfare state for the first time.

Wagner Act
A 1935 act that upheld the right of industrial workers to join unions and established the National Labor Relations Board (NLRB), a federal agency with the authority to protect workers from employer coercion and to guarantee collective bargaining.

Social Security Act
A 1935 act with three main provisions: old-age pensions for workers; a joint federal-state system of compensation for unemployed workers; and a program of payments to widowed mothers and the blind, deaf, and disabled.

**classical
liberalism**
The political ideology of individual liberty, private property, a competitive market economy, free trade, and limited government. The ideal is a *laissez faire* or "let alone" policy, in which government does the least possible, particularly in reference to economic policies such as tariffs and incentives for industrial development. Attacking corruption and defending private property, late-nineteenth-century liberals generally called for elite governance and questioned the advisability of full democratic participation.

New Deal Liberalism   The Second New Deal created what historians call New Deal liberalism. **Classical liberalism** held individual liberty to be the foundation of a democratic society, and the word *liberal* had traditionally denoted support for free-market policies and weak government. Roosevelt and his advisors, along with intellectuals such as British economist John Maynard Keynes, disagreed. They countered that, to preserve individual liberty, government must assist the needy and guarantee the basic welfare of citizens. This liberal welfare state was opposed by inheritors of the nineteenth-century ideology of *laissez faire* capitalism, who gradually became known as conservatives. These two visions of liberty and government — with liberals on one side and conservatives on the other — would shape American politics for the remainder of the twentieth century.

From Reform to Stalemate

Roosevelt's first term had seen an extraordinary expansion of the federal state. The great burst of government action between 1933 and 1935 was unequaled in the nation's history, though Congress and President Lyndon Johnson nearly matched it in 1965 and 1966 (Chapter 27). Roosevelt's second term, however, was characterized by a series of political entanglements and economic bad news that stifled further reform.

**Works Progress
Administration**
Federal New Deal program established in 1935 that provided government-funded public works jobs to millions of unemployed Americans during the Great Depression in areas ranging from construction to the arts.

The 1936 Election   FDR was never enthusiastic about public relief programs. But with the election of 1936 on the horizon and 10 million Americans still out of work, he won funding for the **Works Progress Administration** (WPA). Under the energetic direction of Harry Hopkins, the WPA employed 8.5 million Americans between 1935, when it was established, and 1943. The agency's workers constructed or repaired 651,087 miles of road, 124,087 bridges, 125,110 public buildings, 8,192 parks, and 853 airports. The WPA was an extravagant operation by 1930s standards, yet it reached only about one-third of the nation's unemployed.

As the 1936 election approached, new voters joined the Democratic Party. Many had personally benefitted from New Deal programs such as the WPA or knew people who had (Table 22.1). One was Jack Reagan, a down-on-his-luck shoe salesman (and the father of future president Ronald Reagan), who took a job as a federal relief administrator in Dixon, Illinois, and became a strong supporter of the New Deal. In addition to voters such as Reagan, Roosevelt could count on a powerful coalition of organized labor, midwestern farmers, white ethnic groups, northern African Americans, and middle-class families concerned about unemployment and old-age security. He also commanded the support of intellectuals and progressive Republicans. With difficulty, the Democrats held on to the votes of their white southern constituency as well.

Republicans recognized that the New Deal was too popular to oppose directly, so they chose as their candidate the progressive governor of Kansas, Alfred M. Landon. Landon accepted the legitimacy of many New Deal programs but criticized their inefficiency and expense. He also pointed to authoritarian regimes in Italy and Germany and hinted that FDR harbored similar dictatorial ambitions. These charges fell on deaf ears. Roosevelt's victory in 1936 was one of the most lopsided in American history. The assassination of Huey Long by a Louisiana political rival in September 1935 had eliminated the threat of a serious third-party challenge. Roosevelt received 60 percent of the popular vote and carried every state except Maine and Vermont. The *New Republic*, a liberal publication, boasted that "it was the greatest revolution in our political history."

TABLE 22.1

Major New Deal Legislation

Agriculture

1933	Agricultural Adjustment Act (AAA)
1935	Resettlement Administration (RA) Rural Electrification Administration (REA)
1937	Farm Security Administration (FSA)
1938	Agricultural Adjustment Act of 1938

Finance and Industry

1933	Emergency Banking Act Glass-Steagall Act (created the FDIC) National Industrial Recovery Act (NIRA)
1934	Securities and Exchange Commission (SEC)
1935	Banking Act of 1935 Revenue Act (wealth tax)

Conservation and the Environment

1933	Tennessee Valley Authority (TVA) Civilian Conservation Corps (CCC) Soil Conservation and Domestic Allotment Act

Labor and Social Welfare

1933	Section 7(a) of NIRA
1935	National Labor Relations Act (Wagner Act) National Labor Relations Board (NLRB) Social Security Act
1937	National Housing Act
1938	Fair Labor Standards Act (FLSA)

Relief and Reconstruction

1933	Federal Emergency Relief Administration (FERA) Civil Works Administration (CWA) Public Works Administration (PWA)
1935	Works Progress Administration (WPA) National Youth Administration (NYA)

"I see one-third of a nation ill-housed, ill-clad, ill-nourished," the president declared in his second inaugural address in January 1937, pointing to the depression's persistent social costs. But any hopes that FDR had for expanding the liberal welfare state were quickly dashed. Within a year, staunch opposition to Roosevelt's initiatives arose in Congress, and a sharp recession undermined confidence in his economic leadership.

Court Battle and Economic Recession Roosevelt's first setback in 1937 came when he surprised the nation by seeking fundamental changes to the Supreme Court. In 1935, the Court had struck down a series of New Deal measures by the narrow margin of 5 to 4. With the Wagner Act, the Tennessee Valley Authority, and Social Security all slated to come before the Court, the future of the New Deal rested in the hands of a few elderly, conservative-minded judges. To diminish their influence, the president proposed adding a new justice to the Court for every member over the age of seventy, a scheme that would have brought six new judges to the bench at the time the legislation was proposed. Roosevelt's opponents protested that he was trying to "pack" the Court. After a bitter, months-long debate, Congress rejected this blatant attempt to alter the judiciary to the president's advantage.

If Roosevelt lost the battle, he went on to win the war. Swayed in part by the president's overwhelming electoral victory in the 1936 election, the Court upheld the Wagner and Social Security Acts. Moreover, a series of timely resignations allowed Roosevelt to reshape the Supreme Court after all. His new appointees — who included the liberal-leaning and generally pro–New Deal Hugo Black, Felix Frankfurter, and William O. Douglas — viewed the Constitution as a "living document" that had to be interpreted in the light of present conditions.

Roosevelt recession

A recession from 1937 to 1938 that occurred after President Roosevelt cut the federal budget.

Keynesian economics

The theory, developed by British economist John Maynard Keynes in the 1930s, that purposeful government intervention in the economy (through lowering or raising taxes, interest rates, and government spending) can affect the level of overall economic activity and thereby prevent severe depressions and runaway inflation.

Fair Labor Standards Act

One of the final major laws of the New Deal, it outlawed child labor, made the 40-hour workweek standard (and mandated overtime pay), and established a national minimum wage.

The so-called **Roosevelt recession** of 1937–1938 dealt another blow to the president. From 1933 to 1937, gross domestic product had grown at a yearly rate of about 10 percent, bringing industrial output back to 1929 levels. Unemployment had declined from 25 percent to 14 percent. "The emergency has passed," declared Senator James F. Byrnes of South Carolina. Acting on this assumption, Roosevelt slashed the federal budget. Following the president's lead, Congress cut the WPA's funding in half, causing layoffs of about 1.5 million workers, and the Federal Reserve, fearing inflation, raised interest rates. These measures halted recovery. The stock market dropped sharply, and unemployment jumped to 19 percent. Quickly reversing course, Roosevelt began once again to spend his way out of the recession by boosting funding for the WPA and resuming public works projects.

Although improvised, this spending program accorded with the theories of John Maynard Keynes, a visionary British economist. Keynes transformed economic thinking in capitalist societies in the 1920s by arguing that government intervention could smooth out the highs and lows of the business cycle through deficit spending and the manipulation of interest rates, which determined the money supply. This view was sharply criticized by Republicans and conservative Democrats in the 1930s, who opposed government management of the economy. But **Keynesian economics** gradually won wider acceptance as World War II defense spending finally ended the Great Depression.

In the midst of boosting WPA spending, Roosevelt achieved a final legislative victory for the New Deal. In 1938, Congress passed the **Fair Labor Standards Act**, which outlawed child labor, made the 40-hour workweek the national standard, mandated overtime pay, and established a federal minimum wage. FDR considered it nearly as important as the Social Security Act because of its implications for how Americans worked and what they earned. But it would be the last major reform of his presidency.

A reformer rather than a revolutionary, Roosevelt had preserved capitalism and liberal individualism — even as he transformed them in significant ways (Interpretations). But the president stopped well short of more radical measures, such as the seizure of private property, that some world leaders considered (America in Global Context). At the same time, conservatives had reclaimed a measure of power in Congress, and those who believed the New Deal had created an intrusive federal bureaucracy kept reform in check after 1938. Throughout Roosevelt's second term, a conservative coalition of southern Democrats, rural Republicans, and industrial interests in both parties worked to block or impede social legislation. By 1938, the era of change was over.

> **IN YOUR OWN WORDS** How did the Second New Deal reshape American government, and what political differences did it highlight?

The New Deal and American Society

Whatever its limits, the New Deal had a tremendous impact on American society. Its ideology of social-welfare liberalism fundamentally altered Americans' relationship to their government and provided assistance to a wide range of ordinary people: the unemployed, the elderly, workers, and the poor. In doing so, New Dealers created a sizable federal bureaucracy: the number of civilian federal employees increased by 80 percent between 1929 and 1940, reaching a total of 1 million. The expenditures — and deficits — of the federal government grew at an even faster rate. In 1930, the Hoover administration spent $3.1 billion and had a surplus of almost $1 billion; in 1939, New Dealers expended $9.4 billion and ran a deficit of nearly $3 billion (still small by later standards). But the New Deal represented more than figures on a balance sheet. Across the country, it inspired new visions of democracy among ordinary citizens (Thinking Like a Historian).

A People's Democracy

In 1939, writer John La Touche and musician Earl Robinson produced the patriotic song "Ballad for Americans." The lyrics called for uniting "everybody who's nobody . . . Irish, Negro, Jewish, Italian, French, and English, Spanish, Russian, Chinese, Polish, Scotch, Hungarian, Litvak, Swedish, Finnish, Canadian, Greek, and Turk, and Czech and double Czech American." The song captured the democratic aspirations that the New Deal had awakened. Millions of ordinary people believed that the nation could, and should, become more egalitarian, and Americans from all walks of life seized the chance to work toward that goal.

Organized Labor Demoralized and shrinking during the 1920s, labor unions increased their numbers and clout during the New Deal, thanks to the Wagner Act. "The era of privilege and predatory individuals is over," the fiery and outspoken labor

Was the New Deal a Reform or a Revolution?

The 1930s Great Depression left a deep imprint on the lives of the millions of Americans who suffered the economic consequences of financial collapse. The familiar images of farm foreclosures, soup lines, and dusty migrants heading west with only a fading faith in the future to keep them moving tell a story of personal and national despair. Many of these disheartened Americans brightened at the 1932 election of President Franklin Roosevelt, whose New Deal programs gave them hope that, as his campaign said, "happy days are here again."

Happier days dawned for some, but not for others. The New Deal did not solve every problem. Commentators at the time and historians ever since have tried to understand exactly what the New Deal accomplished. Did Roosevelt's New Deal reform the relationship between the federal government and the economy, or revolutionize it? Two historians, Carl Degler and Alan Brinkley, pick up this theme and offer competing interpretations of the New Deal and its legacy.

CARL N. DEGLER

Source: Carl N. Degler, *Out of Our Past: The Forces That Shaped Modern America* (New York: Harper & Row, 1959), 414–415.

[T]he guarantor state . . . under the New Deal was . . . a vigorous and dynamic force in the society, energizing and . . . supplanting private enterprise when the general welfare required it. . . . When social and economic problems . . . were ignored or shirked by private enterprise, then the federal government undertook to do the job. [If] private enterprise failed to provide adequate and sufficient housing for a minimum standard of welfare for the people, then the government would build houses. . . . Few areas of American life were beyond the touch of the experimenting fingers of the New Deal. . . . The New Deal Revolution has become so much a part of the American Way that no political party which aspires to high office dares now to repudiate it.

ALAN BRINKLEY

Source: Alan Brinkley, *The End of Reform: New Deal Liberalism in Recession and War* (New York: Alfred A. Knopf, 1995), 6–7.

The critique of modern capitalism that had been so important in the early 1930s . . . was largely gone. . . . In its place was a set of liberal ideas essentially reconciled to the existing structure of the economy and committed to using the state to compensate for capitalism's inevitable flaws. . . . When liberals spoke now of government's responsibility to protect the health of the industrial world, they defined that responsibility less as a commitment to restructure the economy than as an effort to stabilize it and help it to grow. They were no longer much concerned about controlling or punishing "plutocrats" and "economic royalists," an impulse central to New Deal rhetoric in the mid-1930s. Instead, they spoke of their commitment to providing a healthy environment in which the corporate world could flourish and in which the economy could sustain "full employment."

QUESTIONS FOR ANALYSIS

1. Identify the major difference in the interpretations of the New Deal offered by Degler and Brinkley.
2. What does each historian see as the impact of New Deal policies on America's system of capitalism and private enterprise?
3. What two pieces of evidence from the chapter can you identify to make an argument for or against the revolutionary impact of the New Deal?

Economic Nationalism in the United States and Mexico

President Franklin Roosevelt's New Deal sought to regulate the economy and provide a degree of economic security to American citizens while maintaining the structures of capitalism. In Mexico, President Lázaro Cárdenas (1934–1940) also hoped to achieve economic security for his country's citizens, but he took different steps than Roosevelt. His most famous action was to *nationalize* the oil industry — that is, the government took ownership of the industry away from private companies, most of which were based in Europe and the United States. In what follows, compare how each leader describes his new policies.

FRANKLIN ROOSEVELT

"Annual Message to Congress," 1936

SOURCE: Deborah Kalb, Gerhard D. Peters, and John Turner Woolley, eds., *State of the Union: Presidential Rhetoric from Woodrow Wilson to George W. Bush* (Washington, D.C.: CQ Press, 2007), 267.

In March, 1933, I appealed to the Congress of the United States and to the people of the United States in a new effort to restore power to those to whom it rightfully belonged. The response to that appeal resulted in the writing of a new chapter in the history of popular government. You, the members of the Legislative branch, and I, the Executive, contended for and established a new relationship between Government and people.

What were the terms of that new relationship? They were an appeal from the clamor of many private and selfish interests, yes, an appeal from the clamor of partisan interest, to the ideal of the public interest. Government became the representative and the trustee of the public interest. Our aim was to build upon essentially democratic institutions, seeking all the while the adjustment of burdens, the help of the needy, the protection of the weak, the liberation of the exploited and the genuine protection of the people's property. . . .

To be sure, in so doing, we have invited battle. We have earned the hatred of entrenched greed.

LÁZARO CÁRDENAS

"Speech to the Nation," 1938

SOURCE: Nora E. Jaffary, Edward Osowski, and Susie S. Porter, eds., *Mexican History: A Primary Source Reader* (Boulder, CO: Westview Press, 2010), 348–349.

It has been repeated *ad nauseam* that the oil industry has brought additional capital for the development and progress of the country. This assertion is an exaggeration. For many years throughout the major period of their existence, oil companies have enjoyed great privileges for development and expansion, including customs and tax exemptions and innumerable prerogatives; it is these factors of special privilege, together with the prodigious productivity of the oil deposits granted them by the Nation often against public will and law, that represent almost the total amount of this so-called capital.

Potential wealth of the Nation; miserably underpaid Native labor; tax exemptions; economic privileges; governmental tolerance — these are the factors of the boom of the Mexican oil industry.

. . . it was therefore necessary to adopt a definite and legal measure to end this permanent state of affairs in which the country sees its industrial progress held back by those who hold in their hands the power to erect obstacles as well as the motive power of all activity and who, instead of using it to high and worthy purposes, abuse their economic strength to the point of jeopardizing the very life of a Nation endeavoring to bring about the elevation of its people through its own laws, its own resources, and the free management of its own destinies.

QUESTIONS FOR ANALYSIS

1. What does Roosevelt mean by "a new relationship between Government and people"?
2. What were the "economic privileges" that Cárdenas opposes? How did his goal differ from Roosevelt's?

The New Deal and Public Works

More than half a dozen New Deal programs were devoted to building up the physical and cultural infrastructure of the country. The former included roads, bridges, dams, trails, and national parks. The latter included artwork, murals, plays, and other forms of literary expression. Examine the following documents and use them collectively to analyze the New Deal's relationship to infrastructure, art, culture, and politics.

1. **Harold L. Ickes, secretary of the interior, *The New Democracy*, 1934.**

   Our Government is no longer a laissez-faire Government, exercising traditional and more or less impersonal powers. There exists in Washington a sense of responsibility for the health, safety, and well-being of the people. . . . I believe that we are at the dawn of a day when the average man, woman, and child in the United States will have an opportunity for a happier and richer life. And it is just and desirable that this should be so. . . . We are not here merely to endure a purgatorial existence in anticipation of a beatific eternity after the grave closes on us. We are here with hopes and aspirations and legitimate desires that we are entitled to have satisfied to at least a reasonable degree. Nor will such a social program as we are discussing cause a strain on our economic system.

2. **Herbert Johnson cartoon, *Saturday Evening Post*, 1935.**

   SOURCE: The Granger Collection, New York.

3. **Federal Writers' Project interview with a WPA draftsman, Newburyport, Massachusetts, June 25, 1939.**

   One reason people here don't like the WPA is because they don't understand it's not all bums and drunks and aliens! Nobody ever explains to them that they'd never have had the new High School they're so [. . .] proud of if it hadn't been for the WPA. They don't stop to figure that new brick sidewalks wouldn't be there, the shade trees wouldn't be all dressed up to look at along High Street and all around town, if it weren't for WPA projects. To most in this town, and I guess it's not much different in this, than any other New England place, WPA's just a racket, set up to give a bunch of loafers and drunks steady pay to indulge in their vices! They don't stop to consider that on WPA are men and women who have traveled places and seen things, been educated and found their jobs folded up and nothing to replace them with.

4. **Ben Shahn, WPA mural, 1938.** *This is part of a three-panel mural commissioned by the Works Progress Administration (WPA) and painted at a public school in Roosevelt, New Jersey, by the well-known artist Ben Shahn.*

   SOURCE: Picture Research Consultants & Archives.

5. David E. Lilienthal, *TVA: Democracy on the March*, 1944. *Written by the former chairman of the Tennessee Valley Authority.*

I believe men may learn to work in harmony with the forces of nature, neither despoiling what God has given nor helpless to put them to use. I believe in the great potentialities for well-being of the machine and technology and science; and though they do hold a real threat of enslavement and frustration for the human spirit, I believe those dangers can be averted. I believe that through the practice of democracy the world of technology holds out the greatest opportunity in all history for the development of the individual, according to his own talents, aspirations, and willingness to carry the responsibilities of a free man. . . .

Such are the things that have happened in the Tennessee Valley. Here men and science and organizational skills applied to the resources of waters, land, forests, and minerals have yielded great benefits for the people. And it is just such fruits of technology and resources that people all over the world will, more and more, demand for themselves. That people believe these things can be theirs — this it is that constitutes the real revolution of our time, the dominant political fact of the generation that lies ahead.

SOURCES: (1) Harold L. Ickes, *The New Democracy* (New York: W. W. Norton & Company Inc., 1934), 60–61; (3) Federal Writers' Project Life Histories, Library of Congress, lcweb2.loc.gov/ammem/wpaintro/wpahome. html; (5) David E. Lilienthal, *TVA: Democracy on the March* (New York: Harper & Row Publishers, 1944), xxii, 3.

ANALYZING THE EVIDENCE

1. What sorts of reasons do the authors of sources 1 and 5 give for supporting New Deal programs? What does the "good life" look like in their view, and how is it connected to the New Deal?

2. What do sources 2 and 3 suggest about possible opposition to New Deal programs? What sorts of public burdens do New Deal opponents envision?

3. Consider source 4. What can we learn from a mural about the spirit of the New Deal? Identity specific elements of the mural and think about what they might signify about the society the muralist envisioned. What kind of faith in the federal government does the mural reveal?

PUTTING IT ALL TOGETHER

Using evidence from the sources in this feature, alongside material from the chapter and from your knowledge of the period, write an essay in which you analyze Americans' attitudes toward New Deal public works projects. If they were positive or optimistic, what was the basis of their optimism? If they were critical, what was the basis of their criticism? From these sources, can you identify a governing spirit of New Deal reform?

---

leader John L. Lewis declared. By the end of the decade, the number of unionized workers had more than doubled to an unprecedented 23 percent of the nonagricultural workforce. A new union movement, led by the Congress of Industrial Organizations (CIO), promoted "industrial unionism" — organizing all the workers in an industry, from skilled machinists to unskilled janitors, into a single union. The American Federation of Labor (AFL), representing the other major group of unions, favored organizing workers on a craft-by-craft basis. Both federations dramatically increased their membership in the second half of the 1930s.

Labor's new vitality translated into political action and a long-lasting alliance with the Democratic Party. The CIO backed Democratic candidates in 1936, and its political action committee became a major Democratically during the 1940s. These successes were real but limited. Unions never enrolled a majority of American wageworkers, and antiunion employer groups such as the National Association of Manufacturers and the Chamber of Commerce remained powerful forces in American business life. After a decade of gains, organized labor remained an important, but still secondary, force in American industry.

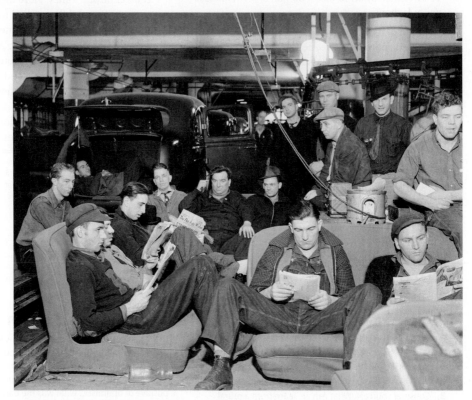

United Auto Workers Strike Trade unions were among the most active and vocal organizations of the 1930s. Organized labor led a number of major strikes between 1934 and 1937 in various industries. None was more important to the future of trade unions than the sit-down strikes at major automobile plants, including General Motors and Chevrolet in Flint, Michigan, in 1936 and 1937. These strikes, in which workers stopped the assembly lines but refused to leave the factories, compelled GM to recognize the United Auto Workers (UAW), which became one of the strongest trade unions in American history. Bettmann/Getty Images.

Women and the New Deal Because policymakers saw the depression primarily as a crisis of male breadwinners, the New Deal did not directly challenge gender inequities. New Deal measures generally enhanced women's welfare, but few addressed their specific needs and concerns. However, Roosevelt welcomed women into the ranks of government in greater numbers than any previous president. Frances Perkins, the first woman named to a cabinet post, served as secretary of labor throughout Roosevelt's presidency. Josephine Roche was FDR's assistant secretary of the treasury, and the president appointed female ambassadors and the first women to the U.S. Court of Appeals. While still relatively few, female appointees often worked to open up other opportunities in government for other talented women.

The most prominent woman in American politics was the president's wife, Eleanor Roosevelt. In the 1920s, she had worked to expand positions for women in political parties, labor unions, and education. A tireless advocate for women's rights, during her years in the White House Mrs. Roosevelt emerged as an independent public figure and the most influential First Lady in the nation's history. Descending into coal mines to view working conditions, meeting with African Americans seeking antilynching laws, and talking to people on breadlines, she became the conscience of the New Deal, pushing her husband to do more for the disadvantaged. "I sometimes acted as a spur," Mrs. Roosevelt later reflected, "even though the spurring was not always wanted or welcome."

Without the intervention of Eleanor Roosevelt, Frances Perkins, and other prominent women, New Deal policymakers would have largely ignored the needs of women. A fourth of the National Recovery Act's employment rules set a lower minimum wage for women than for men performing the same jobs, and only 7 percent of the workers hired by the Civil Works Administration were female. The Civilian Conservation Corps excluded women entirely. Women fared better under the Works Progress Administration; at its peak, 440,000 women were on the payroll. Most Americans agreed with such policies. When Gallup pollsters in 1936 asked people whether wives should work outside the home when their husbands had jobs, 82 percent said no. Such sentiment reflected a persistent belief in women's subordinate status in American economic life.

African Americans and the New Deal Across the nation, but especially in the South, African Americans held the lowest-paying jobs and faced harsh social and political discrimination. Though FDR did not fundamentally change this fact, he was the most popular president among African Americans since Abraham Lincoln. African Americans held 18 percent of WPA jobs, although they constituted 10 percent of the population. The Resettlement Administration, established in 1935 to help small farmers and tenants buy land, actively protected the rights of black tenant farmers. Black involvement in the New Deal, however, could not undo centuries of racial subordination, nor could it change the disproportionate power of segregationist southern whites in the Democratic Party.

Nevertheless, black Americans received significant benefits from New Deal relief programs and believed that the White House cared about their plight, which caused a momentous shift in their political allegiance. Since the Civil War, black voters had staunchly supported the Republican Party, the party of Lincoln, who was known as the Great Emancipator. Even in the depression year of 1932, they overwhelmingly supported Republican candidates. But in 1936, as part of the tidal wave of national support for FDR, northern African Americans gave Roosevelt 71 percent of their votes and have remained solidly Democratic ever since.

African Americans supported the New Deal partly because the Roosevelt administration appointed a number of black people to federal office, and an informal "black cabinet" of prominent black intellectuals advised New Deal agencies. Among the most important appointees was Mary McLeod Bethune. Born in 1875 in South Carolina to former slaves, Bethune founded Bethune-Cookman College and served during the 1920s as president of the National Association of Colored Women. She joined the New Deal in 1935, confiding to a friend that she "believed in the democratic and humane program" of FDR. Americans, Bethune observed, had to become "accustomed to seeing Negroes in high places." Bethune had access to the White House and pushed continually for New Deal programs to help African Americans.

But the New Deal was limited in its approach to race. Roosevelt did not go further in support of black rights, because of both his own racial conservatism and his need for the votes of the white southern Democrats in Congress — including powerful southern senators, many of whom held influential committee posts in Congress. Most New Deal programs reflected prevailing racial attitudes. Civilian Conservation Corps camps segregated blacks, and most NRA rules did not protect black workers from discrimination. Both Social Security and the Wagner Act explicitly excluded the domestic and agricultural jobs held by most African Americans in the 1930s. Roosevelt also refused to support legislation making lynching a federal crime, which was one of the most pressing demands of African Americans in the 1930s. Between 1882 and 1930, more than 2,500 African Americans were lynched by white mobs in the southern states, which means that statistically, one man, woman, or child was murdered every week for fifty years. But despite pleas from black leaders, and from Mrs. Roosevelt herself, FDR feared that southern white Democrats would block his other reforms in retaliation for such legislation.

If lynching embodied southern lawlessness, southern law was often not much better. In an infamous 1931 case in Scottsboro, Alabama, nine young black men were

African Americans and the New Deal A Federal Theater Project production of *Battle Hymn* in New York City in the mid-1930s. *Battle Hymn* dramatized the life of the radical abolitionist John Brown, who led a bloody and ill-fated insurrection against slavery in 1859. The New Deal's record of improving the lives of African Americans was mixed, but many artists, writers, and playwrights, such as those behind *Battle Hymn*, wrote about racial injustice alongside economic injustice during the Great Depression. New Deal programs like the Federal Theater Project fostered socially conscious artistic expression in which the improvement of society was an explicit objective. FDR Library.

accused of rape by two white women hitching a ride on a freight train. The women's stories contained many inconsistencies, but within weeks a white jury had convicted all nine defendants; eight received the death sentence. After the U.S. Supreme Court overturned the sentences because the defendants had been denied adequate legal counsel, five of the men were again convicted and sentenced to long prison terms. Across the country, the Scottsboro Boys, as they were known, inspired solidarity within African American communities. Among whites, the Communist Party took the lead in publicizing the case — and was one of the only white organizations to do so — helping to support the Scottsboro Defense Committee, which raised money for legal efforts on the defendants' behalf.

In southern agriculture, where many sharecroppers were black while landowners and government administrators were white, the Agricultural Adjustment Act hurt rather than helped the poorest African Americans. White landowners collected government subsidy checks but refused to distribute payments to their sharecroppers. Such practices forced 200,000 black families off the land. Some black farmers tried to protect themselves by joining the Southern Tenant Farmers Union (STFU), a biracial organization founded in 1934. "The same chain that holds you holds my people, too," an elderly black farmer reminded his white neighbors. But landowners had such economic power and such support from local sheriffs that the STFU could do little.

A generation of African American leaders came of age inspired by the New Deal's democratic promise. But it remained just a promise. From the outset, New Dealers wrestled with potentially fatal racial politics. Roosevelt and the Democratic Party depended heavily on white voters in the South, who wished to maintain racial segregation and white supremacy. But many Democrats in the North and West — centers of New Deal liberalism — would come to oppose racial discrimination. This meant, ironically, that the nation's most liberal political forces and some of its most conservative political forces existed side by side in the same political party. Another thirty years would pass before black Americans would gain an opportunity to reform U.S. racial laws and practices.

Indian Policy New Deal reformers seized the opportunity to implement their vision for the future of Native Americans, with mixed results. Indian peoples had long been one of the nation's most disadvantaged and powerless groups. In 1934, the average individual Indian income was only $48 per year, and the Native American unemployment rate was three times the national average. The plight of Native Americans won the attention of the progressive commissioner of the Bureau of Indian Affairs (BIA), John Collier, a critic of past BIA practices. Collier understood what Native Americans had long known: that the government's decades-long policy of forced assimilation, prohibition of Indian religions, and confiscation of Indian lands had left most tribes poor, isolated, and without basic self-determination.

Collier helped to write and push through Congress the **Indian Reorganization Act** of 1934, sometimes called the Indian New Deal. On the positive side, the law reversed the Dawes Act of 1887 (Chapter 15) by promoting Indian self-government through formal constitutions and democratically elected tribal councils. A majority of Indian peoples — some 181 tribes — accepted the reorganization policy, but 77 declined to participate, primarily because they preferred the traditional way of making

Indian Reorganization Act
A 1934 law that reversed the Dawes Act of 1887. Through the law, Indians won a greater degree of religious freedom, and tribal governments regained their status as semisovereign dependent nations.

decisions by consensus rather than by majority vote. Through the new law, Indians won a degree of religious freedom, and tribal governments regained their status as semisovereign dependent nations. When the latter policy was upheld by the courts, Indian people gained a measure of leverage that would have major implications for Native rights in the second half of the twentieth century.

Like so many other federal Indian policies, however, the "Indian New Deal" was a mixed blessing. For some peoples, the act imposed a model of self-government that proved incompatible with tribal traditions and languages. The Papagos of southern Arizona, for instance, had no words for *budget* or *representative*, and they made no linguistic distinctions among *law*, *rule*, *charter*, and *constitution*. In another case, the nation's largest tribe, the Navajos, rejected the BIA's new policy, largely because the government was simultaneously reducing Navajo livestock to make room for the Boulder Dam project. In theory, the new policy gave Indians a much greater degree of self-determination. In practice, however, although some tribes did benefit, the BIA and Congress continued to interfere in internal Indian affairs and retained financial control over reservation governments.

Struggles in the West   By the 1920s, agriculture in California had become a big business — intensive, diversified, and export-oriented. Large-scale corporate-owned farms produced specialty crops — lettuce, tomatoes, peaches, grapes, and cotton — whose staggered harvests allowed the use of transient laborers. Thousands of workers, immigrants from Mexico and Asia and white migrants from the midwestern states, trooped from farm to farm and from crop to crop during the long picking season. Some migrants settled in the rapidly growing cities along the West Coast, especially the sprawling metropolis of Los Angeles. Under both Hoover and FDR, the federal government promoted the "repatriation" of Mexican citizens — their deportation to Mexico. Between 1929 and 1937, approximately half a million people of Mexican descent were deported. But historians estimate that more than 60 percent of these were legal U.S. citizens, making the government's actions constitutionally questionable.

Despite the deportations, many Mexican Americans benefitted from the New Deal and generally held Roosevelt and the Democratic Party in high regard. People of Mexican descent, like other Americans, took jobs with the WPA and the CCC, or received relief in the worst years of the depression. The National Youth Administration (NYA), which employed young people from families on relief and sponsored a variety of school programs, was especially important among Mexican Americans in southwestern cities. Even though New Deal programs did not fundamentally improve the migrant farm labor system under which so many people of Mexican descent labored, the New Deal coalition attracted Mexican Americans in large numbers because of the Democrats' commitment to ordinary people. "Franklin D. Roosevelt's name was the spark that started thousands of Spanish-speaking persons to the polls," noted one Los Angeles activist.

Men and women of Asian descent — mostly from China, Japan, and the Philippines — formed a small minority of the American population but were a significant presence in some West Coast cities. Immigrants from Japan and China had long faced discrimination. A 1913 California law prohibited them from owning land. Japanese farmers, who specialized in fruit and vegetable crops, circumvented this restriction by putting land titles in the names of their American-born children. As the depression cut farm prices and racial discrimination excluded young Japanese Americans from nonfarm jobs, about 20 percent of the immigrants returned to Japan.

Chinese Americans were less prosperous than their Japanese American counterparts. Only 3 percent of Chinese Americans worked in professional and technical positions, and discrimination barred them from most industrial jobs. In San Francisco, the majority of Chinese worked in small businesses: restaurants, laundries, and firms that imported textiles and ceramics. During the depression, they turned for assistance to Chinese social organizations such as *huiguan* (district associations) and to the city government; in 1931, about one-sixth of San Francisco's Chinese population was receiving public aid. But few Chinese benefitted from the New Deal. Until the repeal of the Exclusion Act in 1943, Chinese immigrants were classified as "aliens ineligible for citizenship" and therefore were excluded from most federal programs.

Because Filipino immigrants came from a U.S. territory, they were not affected by the ban on Asian immigration enacted in 1924. During the 1920s, their numbers swelled to about 50,000, many of whom worked as laborers on large corporate-owned farms. As the depression cut wages, Filipino immigration slowed to a trickle, and it was virtually cut off by the **Tydings-McDuffie Act** of 1934. The act granted independence to the Philippines (which since 1898 had been an American colony), classified all Filipinos in the United States as aliens, and restricted immigration from the Philippines to fifty people per year.

Reshaping the Environment

Attention to natural resources was a consistent theme of the New Deal, and the shaping of the landscape was among its most visible legacies. Franklin Roosevelt and Interior Secretary Harold Ickes saw themselves as conservationists in the tradition of FDR's cousin, Theodore Roosevelt. In an era before environmentalism, FDR practiced what he called the "gospel of conservation." The president cared primarily about making the land — and other natural resources, such as trees and water — better serve human needs. National policy stressed scientific land management and ecological balance. Under Roosevelt, the federal government both responded to environmental crises and reshaped the use of natural resources, especially water, in the United States.

The Dust Bowl Among the most hard-pressed citizens during the depression were farmers fleeing the "**dust bowl**" of the Great Plains. Between 1930 and 1941, a severe drought afflicted the semiarid states of Oklahoma, Texas, New Mexico, Colorado, Arkansas, and Kansas. Farmers in these areas had stripped the land of its native vegetation, which destroyed the delicate ecology of the plains. To grow wheat and other crops, they had pushed agriculture beyond the natural limits of the soil, making their land vulnerable, in times of drought, to wind erosion of the topsoil (Map 22.4). When the winds came, huge clouds of thick dust rolled over the land, turning the day into night. This ecological disaster prompted a mass exodus. At least 350,000 "Okies" (so called whether or not they were from Oklahoma) loaded their belongings into cars and trucks and headed to California. John Steinbeck's novel *The Grapes of Wrath* (1939) immortalized them, and New Deal photographer Dorothea Lange's haunting images of California migrant camps made them the public face of the depression's human toll.

Tydings-McDuffie Act
A 1934 law that provided for the independence of the Philippines, after a ten-year transition period. Though it granted Philippine independence, its origins were nativist, because the law's proponents wished to classify Filipinos as "alien" and reduce their immigration to the United States.

dust bowl
An area including the semiarid states of Oklahoma, Texas, New Mexico, Colorado, Arkansas, and Kansas that experienced a severe drought and large dust storms from 1930 to 1941.

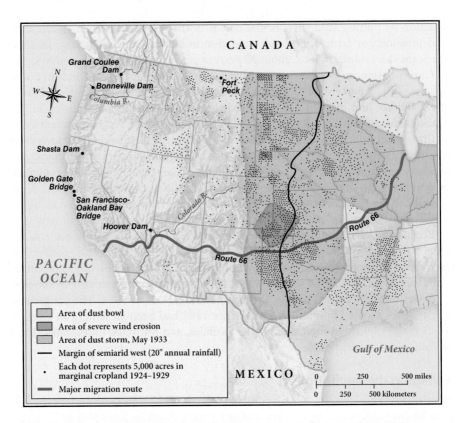

MAP 22.4 The Dust Bowl and Federal Building Projects in the West, 1930–1941
A U.S. Weather Bureau scientist called the drought of the 1930s "the worst in the climatological history of the country." Conditions were especially severe in the southern plains, where farming on marginal land threatened the environment even before the drought struck. As farm families migrated west on U.S. Route 66, the federal government began a series of massive building projects that provided flood control, irrigation, electric power, and transportation facilities to residents of the states of the Far West.

Roosevelt and Ickes believed that poor land practices made for poor people. Under their direction, government agencies tackled the dust bowl's human causes. Agents from the newly created Soil Conservation Service, for instance, taught farmers to prevent soil erosion by tilling hillsides along the contours of the land. They also encouraged (and sometimes paid) farmers to take certain commercial crops out of production and plant soil-preserving grasses instead. One of the U.S. Forest Service's most widely publicized programs was the Shelterbelts, the planting of 220 million trees running north along the 99th meridian from Abilene, Texas, to the Canadian border. Planted as a windbreak, the trees also prevented soil erosion. A variety of government agencies, from the CCC to the U.S. Department of Agriculture, lent their expertise to establishing sound farming practices in the plains.

Tennessee Valley Authority

An agency funded by Congress in 1933 that integrated flood control, reforestation, electricity generation, and agricultural and industrial development in the Tennessee Valley area.

Tennessee Valley Authority The most extensive New Deal environmental undertaking was the **Tennessee Valley Authority** (TVA), which Roosevelt saw as the first step in modernizing the South. Funded by Congress in 1933, the TVA integrated flood control, reforestation, electricity generation, and agricultural and industrial development. The dams and their hydroelectric plants provided cheap electric power for homes and factories as well as ample recreational opportunities for the valley's residents. The massive project won praise around the world (Map 22.5).

The TVA was an integral part of the Roosevelt administration's effort to keep farmers on the land by enhancing the quality of rural life. The **Rural Electrification Administration** (REA), established in 1935, was also central to that goal. Fewer than one-tenth of the nation's 6.8 million farms had electricity. The REA addressed this problem by promoting nonprofit farm cooperatives that offered loans to farmers to install power lines. By 1940, 40 percent of the nation's farms had electricity; a decade later, 90 percent did. Electricity brought relief from the drudgery and isolation of farm life. Electric irons, vacuum cleaners, and washing machines eased women's burdens, and radios brightened the lives of the entire family. Along with the automobile and the movies, electricity broke down the barriers between urban and rural life.

Rural Electrification Administration
An agency established in 1935 to promote nonprofit farm cooperatives that offered loans to farmers to install power lines.

Grand Coulee As the nation's least populated but fastest-growing region, the West benefitted enormously from the New Deal's attention to the environment. With the largest number of state and federal parks in the country, the West gained countless trails, bridges, cabins, and other recreational facilities, laying the groundwork for the post–World War II expansion of western tourism. On the Colorado River, Boulder

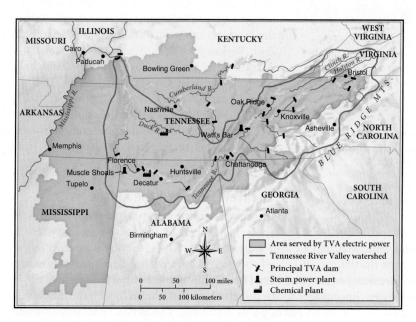

MAP 22.5 The Tennessee Valley Authority, 1933–1952
The Tennessee Valley Authority was one of the New Deal's most far-reaching environmental projects. Between 1933 and 1952, the TVA built twenty dams and improved five others, taming the flood-prone Tennessee River and its main tributaries. The cheap hydroelectric power generated by the dams brought electricity to industries as well as hundreds of thousands of area residents, and artificial lakes provided extensive recreational facilities. Widely praised at the time, the TVA came under attack in the 1970s for its practice of strip mining and the pollution caused by its power plants and chemical factories.

Grand Coulee Dam This extraordinary photo from a *Life* magazine essay shows workers hitching a ride on a 13-ton conduit as it is lowered into place on the Grand Coulee Dam in Washington State. Dozens of dams were constructed across the country under the auspices of various New Deal programs, but none were more majestic than two in the West: Boulder Dam (renamed Hoover Dam in 1947) and Grand Coulee. Built to harness the awesome power of the Columbia River as it rushed to the Pacific, Grand Coulee would ultimately provide electric power to Seattle, Portland, and other West Coast cities and new irrigation waters for Washington's apple and cherry orchards, among many other crops. Library of Congress.

Dam (later renamed Hoover Dam) was completed in 1935 with Public Works Administration funds; the dam generated power for the region's growing cities such as Las Vegas, Los Angeles, and Phoenix.

The largest project in the West, however, took shape in an obscure corner of Washington State, where the PWA and the Bureau of Reclamation built the Grand Coulee Dam on the Columbia River. When it was completed in 1941, Grand Coulee was the largest electricity-producing structure in the world, and its 150-mile lake provided irrigation for the state's major crops: apples, cherries, pears, potatoes, and wheat. Inspired by the dam and the modernizing spirit of the New Deal, folk singer Woody Guthrie wrote a song about the Columbia. "Your power is turning our darkness to dawn," he sang, "so roll on, Columbia, roll on!"

New Deal projects that enhanced people's enjoyment of the natural environment can be seen today throughout the country. CCC and WPA workers built the famous Blue Ridge Parkway, which connects the Shenandoah National Park in Virginia with the Great Smoky Mountains National Park in North Carolina. In the West, government workers built the San Francisco Zoo, Berkeley's Tilden Park, and the canals of San Antonio. The Civilian Conservation Corps helped to complete the East Coast's Appalachian Trail and the West Coast's Pacific Crest Trail through the Sierra Nevada. In state parks across the country, cabins, shelters, picnic areas, lodges, and observation towers stand as monuments to the New Deal ethos of recreation coexisting with nature.

The New Deal and the Arts

In response to the Great Depression, many American writers and artists redefined their relationship to society. Never had there been a decade, critic Malcolm Cowley suggested in 1939, "when literary events followed so closely on the flying coat-tails of social events." New Deal administrators encouraged artists to create projects that would be of interest to the entire community, not just the cultured elite. Encouraged by the popular New Deal slogan "art for the millions," artists painted murals in hundreds of public buildings. The WPA's Federal Art Project gave work to many young artists who would become the twentieth century's leading painters, muralists, and sculptors. Jackson Pollock, Alice Neel, Willem de Kooning, and Louise Nevelson all received support. The Federal Music Project and **Federal Writers' Project** (FWP) employed 15,000 musicians and 5,000 writers, respectively. Among the latter were Saul Bellow, Ralph Ellison, and John Cheever, who became great American writers. The FWP also collected oral histories, including two thousand narratives by former slaves. The black folklorist and novelist Zora Neale Hurston finished three novels while in the Florida FWP, among them her best-known work, *Their Eyes Were Watching God* (1937). Richard Wright won the 1938 *Story* magazine prize for the best tale by a WPA writer and went on to complete *Native Son* (1940), a searing novel about white racism. Similarly, the Federal Theatre Project (FTP) nurtured such talented directors, actors, and playwrights as Orson Welles, John Huston, and Arthur Miller.

The Legacies of the New Deal

The New Deal addressed the Great Depression by restoring hope and promising security. FDR and Congress created a powerful social-welfare state that took unprecedented responsibility for the well-being of American citizens. During the 1930s, millions of people began to pay taxes directly to the Social Security Administration, and more than one-third of the population received direct government assistance from federal programs. New legislation regulated the stock market, reformed the Federal Reserve System, and subjected business corporations to federal regulation. The New Deal's pattern of government involvement in social life would persist for the rest of the twentieth century. In the 1960s, Lyndon Johnson and the "Great Society" Congress dramatically expanded social-welfare programs — by creating Medicare and Medicaid, for instance — most of which remained intact in the wake of the "Reagan Revolution" of the 1980s (Chapter 29).

Like all other major social transformations, the New Deal was criticized both by those who thought it did too much and by those who believed it did too little. Conservatives, who prioritized limited government and individual freedom, pointed out that the New Deal state intruded deeply into the personal and financial lives of citizens and the affairs of business. Conversely, advocates of social-welfare liberalism complained that the New Deal's safety net had too many holes: no national health-care system, welfare programs that excluded domestic workers and farm laborers, and state governments that often limited the benefits distributed under New Deal programs.

Whatever the merits of its critics, the New Deal unquestionably transformed the American political landscape. From 1896 to 1932, the Republican Party had commanded the votes of a majority of Americans. That changed as Franklin Roosevelt's magnetic personality and innovative programs brought millions of voters into the Democratic fold. Democratic recruits included first- and second-generation immigrants from southern and central Europe — Italians, Poles, Russians, and Slavs, among others, most of them Catholic or Jewish — as well as African American migrants to northern cities. Organized labor aligned itself with a Democratic administration that had recognized unions as a legitimate force in modern industrial life. The elderly and the unemployed, assisted by the Social Security Act, likewise supported FDR. This New Deal coalition of ethnic groups, city dwellers, organized labor, African Americans, and a cross section of the middle class formed the nucleus of the northern Democratic Party and supported additional liberal reforms in the decades to come.

Federal Writers' Project
A program under the Works Progress Administration (WPA) from 1935 to 1939 in which historians, teachers, editors, novelists, poets, and playwrights were employed by the federal government to produce a variety of materials — this included, for example, interviews with hundreds of former slaves; a major survey of American foodways; and state-by-state guidebooks to history, geography, and culture.

IN YOUR OWN WORDS In what ways did the New Deal promote change in American society? In what ways did it not?

Summary

We have seen how Franklin Delano Roosevelt's First New Deal focused on stimulating recovery, providing relief to the unemployed, and regulating banks and other financial institutions. The Second New Deal was different. Influenced by the persistence of the depression and the growing popularity of Huey Long's Share Our Wealth proposals, Roosevelt promoted social-welfare legislation that provided Americans with economic security.

We also explored the impact of the New Deal on various groups of citizens, especially African Americans, women, and unionized workers. Our survey paid particular attention to the lives of the Mexicans, Asians, and Okies who worked in the farms and factories of California. Because of New Deal assistance, the members of those groups gravitated toward the Democratic Party. The party's coalition of ethnic workers, African Americans, farmers, parts of the middle classes, and white southerners gave FDR and other Democrats a landslide victory in 1936.

Finally, we examined the accomplishments of the New Deal. In 1933, New Deal programs resolved the banking crisis while preserving capitalist institutions. Subsequently, these programs expanded the federal government and, through the Social Security system, farm subsidy programs, and public works projects, launched federal policies that were important to nearly every American. Great dams and electricity projects sponsored by the Tennessee Valley Authority, the Works Progress Administration in the West, and the Rural Electrification Administration permanently improved the quality of life for the nation's citizens.

CHAPTER 22 REVIEW

TERMS TO KNOW   *Identify and explain the significance of each term below.*

Key Concepts and Events

Smoot-Hawley Tariff (p. 715)

Bonus Army (p. 717)

fireside chats (p. 719)

Hundred Days (p. 719)

Glass-Steagall Act (p. 720)

Agricultural Adjustment Act (p. 720)

National Recovery Administration (p. 720)

Public Works Administration (p. 721)

Civilian Conservation Corps (p. 721)

Federal Housing Administration (p. 722)

Securities and Exchange Commission (p. 722)

American Liberty League (p. 722)

National Association of Manufacturers (p. 722)

Townsend Plan (p. 723)

welfare state (p. 725)

Wagner Act (p. 725)

Social Security Act (p. 725)

classical liberalism (p. 726)

Works Progress Administration (p. 726)

Roosevelt recession (p. 728)

Keynesian economics (p. 728)

Fair Labor Standards Act (p. 728)

Indian Reorganization Act (p. 737)

Tydings-McDuffie Act (p. 739)

dust bowl (p. 739)

Tennessee Valley Authority (p. 740)

Rural Electrification Administration (p. 741)

Federal Writers' Project (p. 742)

Key People

Herbert Hoover (p. 715)   Huey Long (p. 723)   Eleanor Roosevelt (p. 734)   John Collier (p. 737)

Franklin Delano Roosevelt   Frances Perkins   Mary McLeod Bethune
(p. 718)   (p. 734)   (p. 735)

REVIEW QUESTIONS *Answer these questions to demonstrate your understanding of the chapter's main ideas.*

1. How did Americans, from ordinary citizens to political leaders, respond to the Great Depression?

2. What were the major components of the Hundred Days, and what was their purpose?

3. How did the Second New Deal reshape American government, and what political differences did it highlight?

4. In what ways did the New Deal promote change in American society? In what ways did it not?

5. Review the events listed under "American and National Identity," "Politics and Power," and "Culture and Society" on the thematic timeline on pages 648–649. Some historians have seen the New Deal as a natural evolution of progressive reforms from earlier in the century. Others have argued that it represented a revolution in social values and government institutions. Do you view the New Deal as an extension of progressivism, or a radical break with the past? Provide evidence for your argument.

MAKING CONNECTIONS *Recognize the larger developments and continuities within and across chapters.*

1. People often view the New Deal as a set of government programs and policies enacted by President Roosevelt and Congress. In this version, change comes from above. Yet there is also evidence that ordinary Americans played an important role in inspiring and championing aspects of the New Deal. Find several specific examples of this, and think about the possible connections between the struggles, protests, and actions of ordinary people and the programs of the New Deal.

2. How did the lives of women, workers, and historically underrepresented racial and ethnic groups change during the Great Depression? What role did the New Deal play in helping those groups of Americans?

KEY TURNING POINTS *Refer to the chapter chronology on page 714 for help in answering the question below.*

Identify two critical turning points between 1934 and 1937 when the New Deal faced specific challenges.

23

CHAPTER

The World at War
1937–1945

The Second World War was the defining international event of the twentieth century. Battles raged across three continents and all of the world's oceans. It killed between 50 and 80 million people and wounded hundreds of millions more. When it was over, the industrial economies and much of the infrastructure of Europe and East Asia lay in ruins. Waged with both technologically advanced weapons and massive armies, the war involved every industrialized power in Europe, North America, and Asia, as well as dozens of other nations, many of them colonies of the industrialized countries.

IDENTIFY THE BIG IDEA

How did World War II transform the United States domestically and change its relationship with the world?

The military conflict began on two continents: in Asia with Japan's 1937 invasion of China across the Sea of Japan, and in Europe with the 1939 blitzkrieg (lightning war) by Germany against Poland. It ended in 1945 after American planes dropped two atomic bombs, the product of stunning yet ominous scientific breakthroughs, on the Japanese cities of Hiroshima and Nagasaki. In between these demonstrations of technological prowess and devastating power, huge armies confronted and destroyed one another in the fields of France, the forests and steppes of Russia, the river valleys of China, the volcanic islands of the Pacific, and the deserts of North Africa.

"Armed defense of democratic existence is now being gallantly waged in four continents," President Franklin Delano Roosevelt told the nation in January 1941. After remaining neutral for several years, the United States would commit to that "armed defense." Both FDR and British prime minister Winston Churchill came to see the war as a defense of democratic values from the threat posed by German, Italian, and Japanese fascism. For them, the brutal conflict was the "good war." When the grim reality of the Jewish Holocaust came to light, U.S. participation in the war seemed even more just. But as much as it represented a struggle between democracy and fascism, it was also inescapably a war to maintain British, French, and Dutch control of colonies in Africa, India, the Middle East, and Southeast Asia. By 1945, democracy in the industrialized world had been preserved, and a new alliance between Western Europe and the United States had taken hold; the future of the vast European colonial empires, however, remained unresolved.

On the U.S. domestic front, World War II ended the Great Depression, hastened profound social changes, and expanded the scope and authority of the federal government. Racial politics and gender roles shifted under the weight of wartime migration and labor shortages. The pace of urbanization increased as millions of Americans uprooted themselves and moved hundreds or thousands of miles to join the military or to take a war job. A stronger, more robust federal government, the product of a long, hard-fought war, would remain in place to fight an even longer, more expensive, and potentially more dangerous Cold War in the ensuing years. These developments, which accelerated transformations already under way, would have repercussions far into the postwar decades.

Black Pilots in Tuskegee, Alabama World War II was a "total war," fought on three continents by hundreds of millions of people and massive national armies. Though a late arrival to the conflict, the United States played a critical role in defeating the Axis powers. Here, African American pilots in Tuskegee, Alabama, read a map in preparation for a training flight. Afro American Newspapers/Gado/Getty Images.

As you read, ask yourself why this chapter begins and ends with these dates and identify the links among related events.

1933	▶ Adolf Hitler becomes chancellor of Germany
1935	▶ Italy invades Ethiopia
1935–1939	▶ U.S. Neutrality Acts
1936	▶ Germany reoccupies Rhineland demilitarized zone ▶ Rome-Berlin Axis established
1937	▶ Japan invades China
1938	▶ Munich Conference
1939	▶ German-Soviet nonaggression pact ▶ Germany invades Poland ▶ Britain and France declare war on Germany
1940	▶ Germany, Italy, and Japan form alliance
1941	▶ Germany invades Soviet Union ▶ Lend-Lease Act and Atlantic Charter established ▶ Japanese attack Pearl Harbor (December 7)

1942	▶ Executive Order 9066 imprisons Japanese and Japanese Americans ▶ Battles of Coral Sea and Midway halt Japanese advance
1942–1945	▶ Rationing of scarce goods
1943	▶ Race riots in Detroit and Los Angeles
1944	▶ D-Day: Allied landing in France (June 6)
1945	▶ Yalta Conference (February) ▶ Germany surrenders (May 7) ▶ United Nations founded ▶ Potsdam Conference (July–August) ▶ United States drops atomic bombs on Hiroshima and Nagasaki (August 6 and 9) ▶ Japan surrenders (August 10)

The Road to War

The Great Depression disrupted economic life around the world and led to the collapse of traditional political institutions. In response, an antidemocratic movement known as fascism, which had originated in Italy during the 1920s, developed in Germany, Spain, and Japan. By the mid-1930s, these nations had instituted authoritarian, militaristic governments led by powerful dictators: Benito Mussolini in Italy, Adolf Hitler in Nazi Germany, Francisco Franco in Spain, and, after 1940, Hideki Tojo in Japan. As early as 1936, President Roosevelt warned that other nations had "sold their heritage of freedom" and urged Americans to work for "the survival of democracy" both at home and abroad. Constrained by strong isolationist sentiment, by 1940 FDR was cautiously leading the nation toward war against the fascist powers.

The Rise of Fascism

World War II had its roots in the settlement of World War I. Germany struggled under the harsh terms of the Treaty of Versailles, and Japan and Italy had their desire for overseas empires thwarted by the treaty makers. Faced with the expansive ambitions and nationalist resentments of those countries, the League of Nations, the collective security system established at Versailles, proved unable to maintain the existing international order.

Fascism, as instituted in Germany by Hitler, combined a centralized, authoritarian state, a doctrine of Aryan racial supremacy, and fervent nationalism in a call for the spiritual reawakening of the German people. Fascist leaders worldwide disparaged

fascism
An authoritarian system of government characterized by dictatorial rule, extreme nationalism, disdain for civil society, and a conviction that imperialism and warfare are the principal means by which nations attain greatness. The United States went to war against fascism when it faced Nazi Germany under Adolf Hitler and Italy under Benito Mussolini during World War II.

parliamentary government, independent labor movements, and individual rights. They opposed both the economic collectivism of the Soviet Union — where, in theory, the state managed the economy to ensure social equality — and the competitive capitalist economies of the United States and Western Europe. Fascist movements arose around the world in the 1930s but managed to achieve power in only a handful of countries. Those countries were at the center of global war making in that decade.

Japan and Italy The first challenge came from Japan. To become an industrial power, Japan required raw materials and overseas markets. Like the Western European powers and the United States before it, Japan embraced an expansionary foreign policy in pursuit of colonial possessions and overseas influence. In 1931, its troops occupied Manchuria, an industrialized province in northern China, and in 1937 the Japanese launched a full-scale invasion of China. In both instances, the League of Nations condemned Japan's actions but did nothing to stop them.

Japan's defiance of the League encouraged a fascist leader half a world away: Italy's Benito Mussolini, who had come to power in 1922. Il Duce (The Leader), as Mussolini was known, had long denounced the Versailles treaty, which denied Italy's colonial claims in Africa and the Middle East after World War I. As in Japan, the Italian fascists desired overseas colonies for raw materials, markets, and national prestige. In 1935, Mussolini invaded Ethiopia, one of the few remaining independent countries in Africa. Ethiopian emperor Haile Selassie appealed to the League of Nations, but the League's verbal condemnation and limited sanctions, its only real leverage, did not stop Italy from taking control of Ethiopia in 1936.

Hitler's Germany Germany, however, posed the gravest threat to the existing world order. Huge World War I reparation payments, economic depression, fear of communism, labor unrest, and rising unemployment fueled the ascent of Adolf Hitler and his **National Socialist (Nazi) Party**. When Hitler became chancellor of Germany in 1933, the Reichstag (the German legislature) granted him dictatorial powers to deal with the economic crisis. Hitler promptly outlawed other political parties, arrested many of his political rivals, and declared himself führer (leader). Under Nazi control, the Reichstag invested all legislative power in Hitler's hands.

Hitler's goal was nothing short of European domination and world power, as he had made clear in his 1925 book *Mein Kampf* (*My Struggle*). The book outlined his plans to overturn the territorial settlements of the Versailles treaty, unite Germans living throughout central Europe in a great German fatherland, and annex large areas of Eastern Europe. The "inferior races" who lived in these regions — Jews, Gypsies, and Slavs — would be removed or subordinated to the German "master race." These territories would provide Germany with what Hitler called "lebensraum" (living space) — a new region of settlement and farming and a source of natural resources. A virulent anti-Semite, Hitler had long blamed Jews for Germany's problems. Once in power, he began a sustained and brutal persecution of Jews, which expanded into a campaign of extermination in the early 1940s.

In 1935, Hitler began to rearm Germany, in violation of the Versailles treaty. No nation stopped him. In 1936, he sent troops into the Rhineland, a demilitarized zone under the terms of Versailles. Again, France and Britain took no action. Later that year,

National Socialist (Nazi) Party
German political party led by Adolf Hitler, who became chancellor of Germany in 1933. The party's ascent was fueled by huge World War I reparation payments, economic depression, fear of communism, labor unrest, and rising unemployment.

Rome-Berlin Axis
A political and military alliance formed in 1936 between German dictator Adolf Hitler and the Italian dictator Benito Mussolini.

Hitler and Mussolini formed the **Rome-Berlin Axis**, a political and military alliance between the two fascist nations. Also in 1936, Germany signed a pact to create a military alliance with Japan against the Soviet Union. With these alliances in place, and with France and Great Britain reluctant to oppose him, Hitler had seized the military advantage in Europe by 1937.

War Approaches

As Hitler pushed his initiatives in Europe, which was as deeply mired in economic depression as the United States, the Roosevelt administration faced widespread isolationist sentiment among Americans. In part, this desire to avoid European entanglements reflected disillusion with American participation in World War I. In 1934, Gerald P. Nye, a progressive Republican senator from North Dakota, launched an investigation into the profits of munitions makers during that war. Nye's committee alleged that arms manufacturers (popularly labeled "merchants of death") had maneuvered President Wilson into World War I.

Neutrality Acts
Legislation, totaling four major acts of Congress, that sought to avoid entanglement in foreign wars while protecting trade. The 1935 Neutrality Act imposed an embargo on selling arms to warring countries and declared that Americans traveling on the ships of belligerent nations did so at their own risk, but subsequent acts in 1936, 1937 and 1939 gradually increased the capacity of Americans to aid the Allies by permitting the sale of first nonmilitary and eventually military goods on a "cash and carry" basis (meaning that U.S. ships would not be used for transportation).

Although Nye's committee failed to prove its charge against weapon makers, its factual findings prompted an isolationist-minded Congress to pass a series of acts to prevent the nation from being drawn into another overseas war. The **Neutrality Act of 1935** imposed an embargo on selling arms to warring countries and declared that Americans traveling on the ships of belligerent nations did so at their own risk. In two subsequent Neutrality Acts, Congress banned loans to belligerents (1936), and then, in 1937, imposed a "cash-and-carry" requirement: if a warring country wanted to purchase nonmilitary goods from the United States, it had to pay cash and carry them in its own ships, keeping the United States out of potentially dangerous naval warfare (a fourth Neutrality Act, in 1939, permitted military goods to be purchased under the same terms).

Americans for the most part had little enthusiasm for war, and a wide variety of groups and individuals espoused isolationism. Many isolationists looked to Republican Ohio senator Robert Taft, who distrusted both Roosevelt and European nations with equal conviction, or to the aviator hero Charles A. Lindbergh, who delivered impassioned speeches against intervention in Europe. Some isolationists, such as the conservative National Legion of Mothers of America, combined anticommunism, Christian morality, and even anti-Semitism. Isolationists were primarily conservatives, but a contingent of progressives (or liberals) opposed America's involvement in the war on pacifist or moral grounds. Whatever their philosophies, ardent isolationists forced Roosevelt to approach the brewing war cautiously.

Popular Front
A small but vocal group of Americans who pushed for greater U.S. involvement in Europe. American Communist Party members, African American civil rights activists, and trade unionists, among other members of the Popular Front coalition, encouraged Roosevelt to take a stronger stand against European fascism.

The Popular Front Other Americans responded to the rise of European fascism by advocating U.S. intervention. Some of the most prominent Americans pushing for greater involvement in Europe, even if it meant war, were affiliated with the **Popular Front**. Wary of German and Japanese aggression, the Soviet Union instructed Communists in Western Europe and the United States to join with liberals in a broad coalition opposing fascism. In the United States, the Popular Front drew from a wide range of social groups, including the American Communist Party (which had increased its membership to between fifty and seventy thousand), African American civil rights activists, trade unionists, left-wing writers and intellectuals, and even a few New Deal administrators. Many supporters in the United States grew uneasy with the Popular

Front because of the brutal political repression in the Soviet Union under Joseph Stalin. Nevertheless, Popular Front activists were among a small but vocal group of Americans encouraging Roosevelt to take a stronger stand against European fascism.

The Failure of Appeasement Encouraged by the weak worldwide response to the invasions of China, Ethiopia, and the Rhineland, and emboldened by British and French neutrality during the Spanish Civil War, Hitler grew more aggressive in 1938. He sent troops to annex German-speaking Austria while making clear his intention to seize part of Czechoslovakia. Because Czechoslovakia had an alliance with France, war seemed imminent. But at the **Munich Conference** in September 1938, Britain and France capitulated, agreeing to let Germany annex the Sudetenland — a German-speaking border area of Czechoslovakia — in return for Hitler's pledge to seek no more territory. The agreement, declared British prime minister Neville Chamberlain, guaranteed "peace for our time." Hitler drew a different conclusion, telling his generals: "Our enemies are small fry. I saw them in Munich."

Within six months, Hitler's forces had overrun the rest of Czechoslovakia and were threatening to march into Poland. Realizing that their policy of appeasement — capitulating to Hitler's demands — had been disastrous, Britain and France warned Hitler that further aggression meant war. Then, in August 1939, Hitler and Stalin shocked the world by signing a mutual nonaggression pact. For Hitler, this pact was crucial, as it meant that Germany would not have to wage a two-front war against Britain and France in the west and the Soviet Union in the east. On September 1, 1939, Hitler launched a blitzkrieg against Poland. Two days later, Britain and France declared war on Germany. World War II had officially begun.

Two days after the European war started, the United States declared its neutrality. But President Roosevelt made no secret of his sympathies. When war broke out in 1914, Woodrow Wilson had told Americans to be neutral "in thought as well as in action." FDR, by contrast, now said: "This nation will remain a neutral nation, but I cannot ask that every American remain neutral in thought as well." The overwhelming majority of Americans — some 84 percent, according to a poll in 1939 — supported Britain and France rather than Germany, but most wanted America to avoid another European war.

At first, the need for U.S. intervention seemed remote. After Germany conquered Poland in September 1939, calm settled over Europe. Then, on April 9, 1940, German forces invaded Denmark and Norway. In May, the Netherlands, Belgium, and Luxembourg fell to the swift German army. The final shock came in mid-June, when France too surrendered. Britain now stood alone against Hitler's plans for domination of Europe.

Isolationists and Interventionists What *Time* magazine would later call America's "thousand-step road to war" had already begun. After a bitter battle in Congress in 1939, Roosevelt won a change in the neutrality laws to allow the Allies to buy arms as well as nonmilitary goods on a cash-and-carry basis. Interventionists, led by journalist William Allen White and his **Committee to Defend America by Aiding the Allies**, became increasingly vocal in 1940 as war escalated in Europe. In response, isolationists formed the **America First Committee** (AFC), with well-respected figures such as Lindbergh and Senator Nye urging the nation to stay out of the war. The AFC held rallies across the United States, and its posters, brochures, and broadsides warning

Munich Conference
A conference in Munich held in September 1938 during which Britain and France agreed to allow Germany to annex the Sudetenland — a German-speaking border area of Czechoslovakia — in return for Hitler's pledge to seek no more territory.

Committee to Defend America by Aiding the Allies
A group of interventionists who believed in engaging with, rather than withdrawing from, international developments. Interventionists became increasingly vocal in 1940 as war escalated in Europe.

America First Committee
A committee organized by isolationists in 1940 to oppose the entrance of the United States into World War II. The membership of the committee included senators, journalists, and publishers and such well-respected figures as the aviator Charles Lindbergh.

against American involvement in Europe suffused many parts of the country, especially the Midwest.

Because of the America Firsters' efforts, Roosevelt proceeded cautiously in 1940 as he moved the United States closer to involvement. The president did not want war, but he believed that most Americans "greatly underestimate the serious implications to our own future," as he confided to White. In May, Roosevelt created the National Defense Advisory Commission and brought two prominent Republicans, Henry Stimson and Frank Knox, into his cabinet as secretaries of war and the navy, respectively. During the summer, the president traded fifty World War I destroyers to Great Britain in exchange for the right to build military bases on British possessions in the Atlantic, circumventing neutrality laws by using an executive order to complete the deal. In October 1940, a bipartisan vote in Congress approved a large increase in defense spending and instituted the first peacetime draft in American history. "We must be the great arsenal of democracy," FDR declared.

As the war in Europe and the Pacific expanded, the United States was preparing for the 1940 presidential election. The crisis had convinced Roosevelt to seek an unprecedented third term. The Republicans nominated Wendell Willkie of Indiana, a former Democrat who supported many New Deal policies. The two parties' platforms differed only slightly. Both pledged aid to the Allies, and both candidates promised not to "send an American boy into the shambles of a European war," as Willkie put it. Willkie's spirited campaign resulted in a closer election than that of 1932 or 1936. Nonetheless, Roosevelt won 55 percent of the popular vote.

Having been reelected, Roosevelt now undertook to persuade Congress to increase aid to Britain, whose survival he viewed as key to American security. In January 1941, he delivered one of the most important speeches of his career. Defining "four essential human freedoms"—freedom of speech, freedom of religion, freedom from want, and freedom from fear—Roosevelt cast the war as a noble defense of democratic societies. He then linked the fate of democracy in Western Europe with the new welfare state at home. Sounding a decidedly New Deal note, Roosevelt pledged to end "special privileges for the few" and to preserve "civil liberties for all." Like President Wilson's speech championing national self-determination at the close of World War I, Roosevelt's "**Four Freedoms**" speech outlined a liberal international order with appeal well beyond its intended European and American audiences.

Two months later, in March 1941, with Britain no longer able to pay cash for arms, Roosevelt persuaded Congress to pass the **Lend-Lease Act**. The legislation authorized the president to "lease, lend, or otherwise dispose of" arms and equipment to Britain or any other country whose defense was considered vital to the security of the United States. When Hitler abandoned his nonaggression pact with Stalin and invaded the Soviet Union in June 1941, the United States extended lend-lease to the Soviets. The implementation of lend-lease marked the unofficial entrance of the United States into the European war.

Roosevelt underlined his support for the Allied cause by meeting in August 1941 with British prime minister Winston Churchill (who had succeeded Chamberlain in 1940). Their joint press release, which became known as the **Atlantic Charter**, provided the ideological foundation of the Western cause. Drawing from Wilson's Fourteen Points and Roosevelt's Four Freedoms, the charter called for economic cooperation, national self-determination, and guarantees of political stability after the

Four Freedoms
Identified by President Franklin D. Roosevelt as the most basic human rights: freedom of speech, freedom of religion, freedom from want, and freedom from fear. The president used these ideas of freedom to justify support for England during World War II, which in turn pulled the United States into the war.

Lend-Lease Act
Legislation in 1941 that enabled Britain to obtain arms from the United States without cash but with the promise to reimburse the United States when the war ended. The act reflected Roosevelt's desire to assist the British in any way possible, short of war.

Atlantic Charter
A press release by President Roosevelt and British prime minister Winston Churchill in August 1941 calling for economic cooperation, national self-determination, and guarantees of political stability after the war.

war to ensure "that all men in all the lands may live out their lives in freedom from fear and want." It would become the basis for a new American-led transatlantic alliance after the war's conclusion. Its promise of national self-determination, however, set up potential conflict in Asia and Africa, where European powers would be reluctant to abandon their colonial holdings.

In the fall of 1941, the reality of U.S. involvement in the war drew closer. By September, Nazi U-boats and the American navy were exchanging fire in the Atlantic. With isolationists still a potent force, Roosevelt hesitated to declare war and insisted that the United States would defend itself only against a direct attack. But behind the scenes, the president and his close advisors considered war inevitable.

> To see a longer excerpt of the "Four Freedoms" speech, along with other primary sources from this period, see *Sources for America's History*.

The Attack on Pearl Harbor

The crucial provocation came not from Germany but from Japan. After Japan invaded China in 1937, Roosevelt had denounced "the present reign of terror and international lawlessness" and suggested that aggressors be "quarantined" by peaceful nations. Despite such rhetoric, the United States refused to intervene later that year when Japanese troops sacked the city of Nanjing, massacred 300,000 Chinese residents, and raped thousands of women.

With China weakened as a counterweight, Japan's military and imperial ambitions expanded. In 1940, General Hideki Tojo became war minister. After concluding a formal military alliance with Germany and Italy that year, Tojo dispatched Japanese troops to occupy the northern part of the French colony of Indochina (present-day Vietnam, Cambodia, and Laos). Tojo's goal, supported by Emperor Hirohito, was to create a "Greater East Asia Co-Prosperity Sphere" under Japan's control, stretching from the Korean Peninsula south to Indonesia. Like Germany and Italy, Japan sought to match the overseas empires of Britain, France, Holland, and the United States.

When Japanese troops staged a full-scale invasion of Indochina in July 1941, Roosevelt froze Japanese assets in the United States and stopped all trade with Japan. This included vital oil shipments that accounted for almost 80 percent of Japanese consumption. In October 1941, General Tojo became prime minister and accelerated secret preparations for war against the United States. By November, American military intelligence knew that Japan was planning an attack but did not know where it would occur.

Early on Sunday morning, December 7, 1941, Japanese bombers attacked **Pearl Harbor** in Hawaii, killing more than 2,400 Americans. They destroyed or heavily damaged eight battleships, three cruisers, three destroyers, and almost two hundred airplanes. Although the assault was devastating, it united the American people. Calling December 7th "a date which will live in infamy," President Roosevelt asked Congress for a declaration of war against Japan. The Senate voted unanimously for war, and the House concurred by a vote of 388 to 1. The lone dissenter was Jeannette Rankin of Montana, a committed pacifist — she also voted against entry into World War I — and the first female member of Congress. Three days later, Germany and Italy declared war on the United States, which in turn declared war on the Axis powers. The long shadows of two wars, one in Europe and one in Asia, had at long last converged over the United States.

Pearl Harbor
A naval base in Pearl Harbor, Hawaii, that was attacked by Japanese bombers on December 7, 1941; more than 2,400 Americans were killed. The following day, President Roosevelt asked Congress for a declaration of war against Japan.

> **IN YOUR OWN WORDS** Explain the steps by which the United States became involved in World War II.

Pearl Harbor, December 7, 1941 On the morning of December 7, 1941, a surprise Japanese attack on the U.S. naval fleet in Pearl Harbor (Hawaii Territory) produced destruction and chaos. Having significantly damaged American forces in the Pacific, Japan quickly overtook virtually all of Southeast Asia. But within sixteen months, the United States had turned the tide and begun to drive the Japanese back toward their home islands. National Archives photo no. 12009098.

Organizing for a Global War

The task of fighting on a global scale dramatically increased the power of the federal government. Shifting from civilian to military production, raising an army, and assembling the necessary workforce required a massive expansion in government authority. When Congress passed the **War Powers Act** in December 1941, it gave President Roosevelt unprecedented control over all aspects of the war effort. Necessary to fight the war, this act marked the beginning of what some historians call the imperial presidency: the far-reaching use (and sometimes abuse) of executive authority during the second half of the twentieth century.

War Powers Act
The 1941 law that gave President Roosevelt unprecedented control over all aspects of the war effort during World War II.

Financing the War

Defense mobilization, not the New Deal of the 1930s, ended the Great Depression. Between 1940 and 1945, the annual gross national product doubled, and after-tax profits of American businesses nearly doubled (America in Global Context). Federal spending on war production powered this advance. By late 1943, two-thirds of the economy was directly involved in the war effort, and war-related production jumped from just 2 percent of GNP to 40 percent. The government paid for these military

The Scales of War: Losses and Gains During World War II

World War II saw an extraordinary loss of life. Worldwide, at least 50 million people perished between 1939 and 1945 from war-related causes. The majority of those who died were civilians, though many millions of soldiers perished in battle as well. For most countries, we have reasonable estimates rather than precise figures. The chart below compares the United States with other major combatants and nations caught in this global struggle.

On the other side of the scale, the war fueled tremendous economic growth, at least in the United States, which was spared the physical devastation of Europe and East Asia. Military production for World War II lifted the United States out of the Great Depression. Gross domestic product (GDP) nearly doubled between 1938 and 1945. Economic production in other combatant nations, as shown in the second figure, grew little if at all.

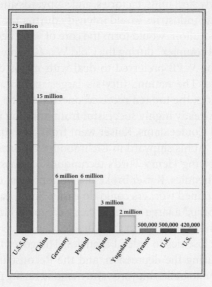

FIGURE 23.1 World War II Military and Civilian Deaths, 1939–1945

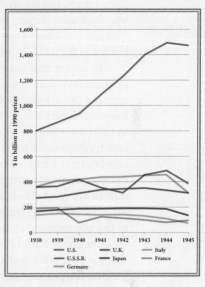

FIGURE 23.2 Gross Domestic Product Rates Worldwide, 1938–1945

SOURCE: GDP data adapted from Mark Harrison, "The Economics of World War II: Six Great Powers" in *International Comparison* (1998), 11. Copyright © 1998 Cambridge University Press. Reprinted by permission of Cambridge University Press.

QUESTIONS FOR ANALYSIS

1. Why did the United States experience so many fewer deaths than other nations? Why were there so many deaths in Eastern Europe and the Soviet Union?

2. Note the relative position of U.S. GDP to other industrial nations in 1938 and in 1945. How were some of the key domestic changes discussed in the chapter, such as rural-urban migration, racial conflict, and women's employment, linked to this economic growth?

3. How might you use these comparisons to add to your understanding of key wartime developments, such as the Holocaust, Stalin's demand for a second front, or the entry of the United States into the war?

Revenue Act
A 1942 act that expanded the number of people paying income taxes from 3.9 million to 42.6 million. These taxes on personal incomes and business profits paid half the cost of World War II.

expenditures by raising taxes and borrowing money. The **Revenue Act** of 1942 expanded the number of people paying income taxes from 3.9 million to 42.6 million. Taxes on personal incomes and business profits paid half the cost of the war. The government borrowed the rest, both from wealthy Americans and from ordinary citizens, who invested in treasury bonds (war bonds).

Financing and coordinating the war effort required far-reaching cooperation between government and private business. The number of civilians employed by the government increased almost fourfold, to 3.8 million — a far higher rate of growth than that during the New Deal. The powerful War Production Board (WPB) awarded defense contracts, allocated scarce resources — such as rubber, copper, and oil — for military uses, and persuaded businesses to convert to military production. For example, it encouraged Ford and General Motors to build tanks rather than cars by granting generous tax advantages for re-equipping existing factories and building new ones. In other instances, the board approved "cost-plus" contracts, which guaranteed corporations a profit and allowed them to keep new steel mills, factories, and shipyards after the war. Such government subsidies of defense industries would intensify during the Cold War and continue to this day. These corporations would form the core of what became known as the nation's "military-industrial complex" during the Cold War (Chapter 24).

To secure maximum production, the WPB preferred to deal with major enterprises rather than with small businesses. The nation's fifty-six largest corporations received three-fourths of the war contracts; the top ten received one-third. The best-known contractor was Henry J. Kaiser. Already highly successful from building roads in California and the Hoover and Grand Coulee dams, Kaiser went from government construction work to navy shipbuilding. At his shipyard in Richmond, California, he revolutionized ship construction by applying Henry Ford's techniques of mass production. To meet wartime production schedules, Kaiser broke the work process down into small, specialized tasks that newly trained workers could do easily. Soon, each of his work crews was building a "Liberty Ship," a large vessel to carry cargo and troops to the war zone, every two weeks. The press dubbed him the Miracle Man.

Central to Kaiser's success were his close ties to federal agencies. The government financed the great dams that he built during the depression, and the Reconstruction Finance Corporation lent him $300 million to build shipyards and manufacturing plants during the war. Working together in this way, American business and government turned out a prodigious supply of military hardware: 86,000 tanks; 296,000 airplanes; 15 million rifles and machine guns; 64,000 landing craft; and 6,500 cargo ships and naval vessels. The American way of war, wrote the Scottish historian D. W. Brogan in 1944, was "mechanized like the American farm and kitchen." America's industrial might, as much as or more than its troops, proved the decisive factor in winning World War II.

Mobilizing the American Fighting Force

The expanding federal bureaucracy also had a human face. To fight the war, the government mobilized tens of millions of soldiers, civilians, and workers — coordinated on a scale unprecedented in U.S. history. During World War II, the armed forces of the United States enlisted more than sixteen million men and women. In no other military conflict have so many American citizens served in the armed services. They came from every region and economic station: black sharecroppers from Alabama; white farmers from the Midwest; the sons and daughters of European, Mexican, and Caribbean immigrants; Native men from Navajo and Choctaw reservations and other tribal communities; women from every state in the nation; even Hollywood celebrities. From urban, rural, and suburban areas, from working-class and middle-class backgrounds — they all served in the military.

In contrast to its otherwise democratic character, the American army segregated the nearly one million African Americans in uniform. The National Association for the Advancement of Colored People (NAACP) and other civil rights groups reprimanded the government, saying, "A Jim Crow army cannot fight for a free world," but the military continued to separate black soldiers and assign them menial duties. The poet Langston Hughes observed the irony: "We are elevator boys, janitors, red caps, maids — a race in uniform." The military uniform, Hughes implied, was not assigned to African Americans so readily. Native Americans and Mexican Americans, on the other hand, were never officially segregated; they rubbed elbows with the sons of European immigrants and native-born soldiers from all regions of the country.

Among the most instrumental soldiers were the Native American "**code talkers**." In the Pacific theater, native Navajo speakers communicated orders to fleet commanders. Japanese intelligence could not decipher the code because it was based on the Navajo language, which fewer than fifty non-Navajos in the world understood. At the battle of Iwo Jima, for instance — one of the war's fiercest — Navajo code talkers, working around the clock, sent and received more than eight hundred messages without error. In the European theater, army commanders used Comanche, Choctaw, and Cherokee speakers to thwart the Nazis and exchange crucial military commands on the battlefield. No Axis nation ever broke these Native American codes.

Approximately 350,000 American women enlisted in the military. About 140,000 served in the Women's Army Corps (WAC), and 100,000 served in the navy's Women Accepted for Volunteer Emergency Service (WAVES). One-third of the nation's registered nurses, almost 75,000 overall, volunteered for military duty. In addition, about 1,000 Women's Airforce Service Pilots (WASPs) ferried planes and supplies in noncombat areas. The armed forces limited the duties assigned to women, however. Female officers could not command men, and WACs and WAVES were barred from combat duty, although nurses of both sexes served close to the front lines, risking capture or death. Most of the jobs that women did in the military — clerical work, communications, and health care — resembled women's jobs in civilian life.

Historians still debate how to characterize the World War II American military. As an army of "citizen-soldiers," it represented a wide stratum of society. Military service gave a generation of men a noble purpose, following a decade of economic depression. And its ethic of patriotism further advanced the children of immigrants into mainstream American life. Yet the military embodied the tensions and contradictions of American society as well. The draft revealed appalling levels of health, fitness, and education among millions of Americans, spurring reformers to call for improved literacy and nutrition. Women's integration into the military was marked by deep anxieties about the threat to "womanhood" allegedly posed by service. The American army was like the nation itself. United in wartime purpose, the military reflected the strengths and weaknesses of a diverse, fractious society.

code talkers
Native American soldiers trained to use native languages to send messages in battle during World War II. Neither the Japanese nor the Germans could decipher the codes used by these Navajo, Comanche, Choctaw, and Cherokee speakers, and the messages they sent gave the Allies great advantage in the battle of Iwo Jima, among many others.

Workers and the War Effort

As millions of working-age citizens joined the military, the nation faced a critical labor shortage. Consequently, many women and African Americans joined the industrial workforce, taking jobs unavailable to them before the conflict. Unions, benefitting from the demand for labor, negotiated higher wages and improved conditions for America's workers. By 1943, with the economy operating at full capacity, the breadlines and double-digit unemployment of the 1930s were a memory.

Rosie the Riveter Government officials and corporate recruiters urged women to take jobs in defense industries, creating a new image of working women. "Longing won't bring him back sooner . . . GET A WAR JOB!" one poster urged, while artist Norman Rockwell's famous "Rosie the Riveter" illustration beckoned to women from the cover of the *Saturday Evening Post*. The government directed its publicity at housewives, but many working women gladly abandoned low-paying "women's jobs" as domestic servants or secretaries for higher-paying work in the defense industry. Suddenly, the nation's factories were full of women working as airplane riveters, ship

Rosie the Riveter Women workers install fixtures and assemblies to a tail fuselage section of a B-17 bomber at the Douglas Aircraft Company plant in Long Beach, California. To entice women to become war workers, the War Manpower Commission created the image of "Rosie the Riveter," later immortalized in posters and by a Norman Rockwell illustration on the cover of the *Saturday Evening Post*. A popular 1942 song celebrating Rosie went: "Rosie's got a boyfriend, Charlie / Charlie, he's a marine / Rosie is protecting Charlie / Working overtime on the riveting machine." Even as women joined the industrial workforce in huge numbers (half a million in the aircraft industry alone), they were understood as fulfilling a nurturing, protective role. Library of Congress.

welders, and drill-press operators. Women made up 36 percent of the labor force in 1945, compared with 24 percent at the beginning of the war. War work did not free women from traditional expectations and limitations, however. Women often faced sexual harassment on the job and usually received lower wages than men did. In ship-yards, women with the most seniority and responsibility earned $6.95 a day, whereas the top men made as much as $22.

Wartime work was thus bittersweet for women, because it combined new oppor-tunities with old constraints. The majority labored in low-wage service jobs. Child care was often unavailable, despite the largest government-sponsored child-care program in history. When the men returned from war, Rosie the Riveter was usually out of a job. Government propaganda now encouraged women back into the home — where, it was implied, their true calling lay in raising families. But many married women refused, or could not afford, to put on aprons and stay home. Women's participation in the paid labor force rebounded by the late 1940s and continued to rise over the rest of the twentieth century, bringing major changes in family life (Chapter 25).

Wartime Civil Rights Among African Americans, a new militancy emerged during the war. Pointing to parallels between anti-Semitism in Germany and racial discrimi-nation in the United States, black leaders waged the Double V campaign: calling for victory over Nazism abroad and racism at home. "This is a war for freedom. Whose freedom?" the renowned black leader W. E. B. Du Bois asked. If it meant "the freedom of Negroes in the Southern United States," Du Bois answered, "my gun is on my shoulder."

Even before Pearl Harbor, black activism was on the rise. In 1940, only 240 of the nation's 100,000 aircraft workers were black, and most of them were janitors. African American leaders demanded that the government require defense contractors to hire more black workers. When the Roosevelt administration took no action, A. Philip Randolph, head of the Brotherhood of Sleeping Car Porters, the largest black labor union in the country, announced plans for a march on Washington in the summer of 1941.

Roosevelt was not a strong supporter of African American equality, but he wanted to avoid public protest and a disruption of the nation's war preparations. So the president made a deal: he issued **Executive Order 8802**, and in June 1941 Randolph canceled the march. The order prohibited "discrimination in the employment of workers in defense industries or government because of race, creed, color, or national origin" and established the Fair Employment Practice Committee (FEPC). Mary McLeod Bethune called the wartime FEPC "a refreshing shower in a thirsty land." This federal commitment to black employment rights was unprecedented but limited: it did not affect segregation in the armed forces, and the FEPC could not enforce compliance with its orders.

Nevertheless, wartime developments laid the groundwork for the civil rights revolution of the 1950s and 1960s. The NAACP grew ninefold, to 450,000 members, by 1945. In Chicago, James Farmer helped to found the Congress of Racial Equality (CORE) in 1942, a group that would become known nationwide in the 1960s for its direct action protests such as sit-ins. The FEPC inspired black organizing against employment discrimination in hundreds of cities and workplaces. Behind this

Executive Order 8802
An order signed by President Roosevelt in 1941 that prohibited "discrimination in the employment of workers in defense industries or gov-ernment because of race, creed, color, or national origin" and established the Fair Employment Practices Commission (FEPC).

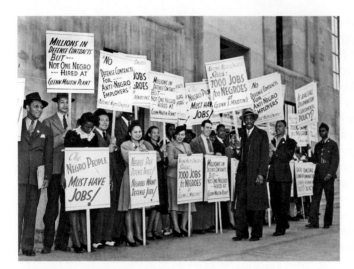

Wartime Civil Rights Fighting fascism abroad while battling racism at home was the approach taken by black communities across the country during World War II. Securing democracy in Europe and Asia while not enjoying it in the United States did not seem just. Jobs were plentiful as the wartime economy hummed along at a fevered pitch. But when employers and unions kept Jim Crow hiring policies in place, African Americans did not hesitate to protest. Here picketers rally for defense jobs outside the Glenn Martin Plant in Omaha, Nebraska, in the early 1940s. Schomburg Center for Research in Black Culture, New York Public Library/Art Resource, NY.

combination of government action and black militancy, the civil rights movement would advance on multiple fronts in the postwar years.

Mexican Americans, too, challenged long-standing practices of discrimination and exclusion. Throughout much of the Southwest, it was still common for signs to read "No Mexicans Allowed," and Mexican American workers were confined to menial, low-paying jobs. Several organizations, including the League of United Latin American Citizens (LULAC) and the Spanish-Speaking People's Congress, pressed the government and private employers to end anti-Mexican discrimination. Mexican American workers themselves, often in Congress of Industrial Organizations (CIO) unions such as the Cannery Workers and Shipyard Workers, also led efforts to enforce the FEPC's equal employment mandate.

Exploitation persisted, however. To meet wartime labor demands, the U.S. government brought tens of thousands of Mexican contract laborers into the United States under the **Bracero Program**. Paid little and treated poorly, the braceros (who took their name from the Spanish *brazo*, "arm") highlighted the oppressive conditions of farm labor in the United States. After the war, the federal government continued to participate in labor exploitation, bringing hundreds of thousands of Mexicans into the country to perform low-wage agricultural work. Future Mexican American civil rights leaders Dolores Huerta and Cesar Chavez began to fight this labor system in the 1950s.

Bracero Program
Officially the Mexican Farm Labor Agreement (signed with Mexico), a federal program that brought hundreds of thousands of Mexican agricultural workers to the United States during and after World War II. The program continued until 1964 and was a major spur of Mexican immigration to the United States.

Organized Labor During the war, unions solidified their position as the most powerful national voice for American workers and extended gains made during the New Deal. By 1945, almost 15 million workers belonged to a union, up from 9 million in 1939. Representatives of the major unions made a no-strike pledge for the duration of the war, and Roosevelt rewarded them by creating the National War Labor Board (NWLB), composed of representatives of labor, management, and the public. The NWLB established wages, hours, and working conditions and had the authority to seize manufacturing plants that did not comply.

Despite these arrangements, unions faced a sometimes hostile Congress. Frustrated with limits on wage increases and the no-strike pledge, in 1943 more than half a million United Mine Workers went out on strike, demanding a higher wage increase than that recommended by the NWLB. Congress responded by passing (over Roosevelt's veto) the Smith-Connally Labor Act of 1943, which allowed the president to prohibit strikes in defense industries and forbade political contributions by unions. Although organized labor would emerge from World War II more powerful than at any time in U.S. history, its business and corporate opponents, too, would emerge from the war with new strength.

Politics in Wartime

In his 1944 State of the Union address, FDR called for a second Bill of Rights, one that would guarantee all Americans access to education and jobs, adequate food and clothing, and decent housing and medical care. Like his Four Freedoms speech, this was a call to extend the New Deal by broadening the rights to individual security and welfare guaranteed by the government. The answer to his call, however, would have to wait for the war's conclusion. Congress created new government benefits only for military veterans, known as GIs (short for "government issue"). The **Servicemen's Readjustment Act** (1944), an extraordinarily influential program popularly known as the "GI Bill of Rights," provided education, job training, medical care, pensions, and home loans for men and women who had served in the armed forces (Chapter 25).

The president's call for social legislation sought to reinvigorate the New Deal political coalition. In the election of 1944, Roosevelt again headed the Democratic ticket. But party leaders, aware of FDR's health problems and fearing that Vice President Henry Wallace's outspoken support for labor and civil rights would alienate moderate voters, dropped him from the ticket. In his place, they chose Senator Harry S. Truman of Missouri, a plain-spoken — some even thought drab — politician with little national experience. The Republicans nominated Governor Thomas E. Dewey of New York. Dewey, who accepted the general principles of welfare-state liberalism domestically and favored internationalism in foreign affairs, attracted some of Roosevelt's supporters. But a majority of voters preferred political continuity, and Roosevelt was reelected with 53.5 percent of the nationwide vote. The Democratic coalition retained its hold on government power, and the era of Republican political dominance (1896–1932) slipped further into the past.

Servicemen's Readjustment Act Popularly known as the GI Bill, 1944 legislation authorizing the government to provide World War II veterans with funds for education, housing, and health care, as well as loans to start businesses and buy homes.

> **IN YOUR OWN WORDS** What aspects of the economy and American society were affected by mobilization for war?

Life on the Home Front

The United States escaped the physical devastation that ravaged Europe and East Asia, but the war profoundly changed the country. Americans welcomed wartime prosperity but shuddered when they saw a Western Union boy on his bicycle, fearing that he carried a War Department telegram reporting the death of someone's son, husband, or father. Citizens also grumbled about annoying wartime regulations and rationing but accepted that their lives would be different "for the duration."

"For the Duration"

Spurred by both government propaganda and a desire to serve the war cause, people on the home front took on wartime responsibilities. They worked on civilian defense committees, recycled old newspapers and scrap metal, and served on local rationing and draft boards. About twenty million backyard "victory gardens" produced 40 percent of the nation's vegetables. Various federal agencies encouraged these efforts, especially the Office of War Information (OWI), which disseminated news and promoted patriotism. The OWI urged advertising agencies to link their clients' products to the war effort, arguing that patriotic ads would not only sell goods but also "invigorate, instruct and inspire" citizens (Thinking Like a Historian).

Popular culture, especially the movies, reinforced connections between the home front and the war effort. Hollywood producers, directors, and actors offered their talents to the War Department. Director Frank Capra created a documentary series titled *Why We Fight* to explain war aims to conscripted soldiers. Movie stars such as John Wayne and Spencer Tracy portrayed heroic American fighting men in numerous films, such as *Guadalcanal Diary* (1943) and *Thirty Seconds over Tokyo* (1944). In this pretelevision era, newsreels accompanying the feature films kept the public up-to-date on the war, as did on-the-spot radio broadcasts by Edward R. Murrow and Mary Marvin Breckenridge, the first female radio correspondent for CBS.

For many Americans, the major inconvenience during the war years was the shortage of consumer goods. Beginning in 1942, federal agencies subjected almost everything Americans ate, wore, or used to rationing or regulation. The first major scarcity was rubber. The Japanese conquest of Malaysia and Dutch Indonesia cut off 97 percent of America's imports of that essential raw material. To conserve rubber for the war effort, the government rationed tires, so many of the nation's 30 million car owners put their cars in storage. As more people walked, they wore out their shoes. In 1944, shoes were rationed to two pairs per person a year. By 1943, the government was rationing meat, butter, sugar, and other foods. Most citizens cooperated with the complicated rationing system, but at least one-quarter of the population bought items on the black market, especially meat, gasoline, cigarettes, and nylon stockings.

Migration and the Wartime City

The war determined where people lived. When men entered the armed services, their families often followed them to military bases or points of debarkation. Civilians moved to take high-paying defense jobs. About 15 million Americans changed residences during the war years, half of them moving to another state. One of them was Peggy Terry, who grew up in Paducah, Kentucky; worked in a shell-loading plant in nearby Viola; and then moved to a defense plant in Michigan. There, she recalled, "I met all those wonderful Polacks [Polish Americans]. They were the first people I'd ever known that were any different from me. A whole new world just opened up."

As the center of defense production for the Pacific war, California experienced the largest share of wartime migration. The state welcomed 2.5 million new residents and grew by 35 percent during the war. "The Second Gold Rush Hits the West," announced the *San Francisco Chronicle* in 1943. One-tenth of all federal dollars spent on the war flowed into California, and the state's factories turned out one-sixth of all war materials. People went where the defense jobs were: to Los Angeles, San Diego, and cities around San Francisco Bay. Some towns grew practically overnight; within two years of the opening of the Kaiser Corporation shipyard in Richmond, California, the town's population quadrupled. Other industrial states — notably New York, Illinois, Michigan, and Ohio — also attracted both federal dollars and migrants on a large scale.

The growth of war industries accelerated patterns of rural-urban migration. Cities grew dramatically, as factories, shipyards, and other defense plants drew millions of citizens from small towns and rural areas. This new mobility, coupled with people's distance from their hometowns, loosened the authority of traditional institutions and made wartime cities vibrant and lively. Around-the-clock work shifts kept people on the streets night and day, and bars, jazz clubs, dance halls, and movie theaters proliferated, fed by the ready cash of war workers.

Racial Conflict Migration and more fluid social boundaries meant that people of different races and ethnicities mixed in the booming cities. Over one million African Americans left the rural South for California, Illinois, Michigan, Ohio, and Pennsylvania — a continuation of the Great Migration earlier in the century (Chapters 20 and 21). In a repeat of the events of World War I, as blacks and whites competed for jobs and housing, racial conflicts broke out in more than a hundred cities in 1943. Detroit saw the worst violence. In June 1943, a riot incited by southern-born whites and Polish Americans against African Americans left thirty-four people dead and hundreds injured.

Racial conflict struck the West as well. In Los Angeles, male Mexican American teenagers formed *pachuco* (youth) gangs. Many dressed in "**zoot suits**" — broad-brimmed felt hats, thigh-length jackets with wide lapels and padded shoulders, pegged trousers, and clunky shoes. Pachucas (young women) favored long coats, huarache sandals, and pompadour hairdos. Other working-class teenagers in Los Angeles and elsewhere took up the zoot-suit style to emphasize their rejection of middle-class values. To many adults, the zoot suit symbolized juvenile delinquency. Rumors circulating in Los Angeles in June 1943 that a pachuco gang had beaten an Anglo (white) sailor set off a four-day riot in which hundreds of Anglo servicemen roamed through Mexican American neighborhoods and attacked zoot-suiters, taking special pleasure in slashing their pegged pants. In a stinging display of bias, Los Angeles police officers arrested only Mexican American youth, and the City Council passed an ordinance outlawing the wearing of the zoot suit.

zoot suits
Oversized suits of clothing in fashion in the 1940s, particularly among young male African Americans and Mexican Americans. In June 1943, a group of white sailors and soldiers in Los Angeles, seeking revenge for an earlier skirmish with Mexican American youths, attacked anyone they found wearing a zoot suit in what became known as the zoot-suit riots.

Gay and Lesbian Communities Wartime migration to urban centers created new opportunities for gay men and women to establish communities. Religious and social conventions against gays and lesbians kept the majority of them silent about their sexuality. During the war, however, cities such as New York, San Francisco, Los Angeles, Chicago, and even Kansas City, Buffalo, and Dallas developed vibrant gay neighborhoods, sustained by a sudden influx of migrants and the relatively open wartime atmosphere. These communities became centers of the gay rights movement of the 1960s and 1970s (Chapter 28).

The military tried to screen out homosexuals but had limited success. Once in the service, homosexuals found opportunities to participate in a gay culture often more extensive than that in civilian life. In the last twenty years, historians have documented thriving communities of gay and lesbian soldiers in the World War II military. Some "came out under fire," as one historian put it, but most kept their sexuality hidden from authorities because army officers, doctors, and psychiatrists treated homosexuality as a psychological disorder that was grounds for dishonorable discharge.

Mobilizing the Home Front

The U.S. Office of War Information (OWI) promoted everything from food rationing to carpooling during World War II, and the U.S. Treasury encouraged millions of Americans to buy war bonds. More than 20 million victory gardens were planted by ordinary Americans. By 1944 they were producing more than 40 percent of all vegetables grown in the United States. Through these and other measures, those on the home front were encouraged to see themselves as part of the war effort.

1. **U.S. government advertisement from the *Minneapolis Star Journal*, 1943.**

Source: AdAccess Digital Collection, David M. Rubenstein Rare Book and Manuscript Library Duke University.

2. **Copy from War Advertising Council/U.S. Treasury Department advertisement, 1943.**

Farmer: "Well, there's something we *really* want now — *more than anything else* . . . and I guess everybody does. It's VICTORY IN THIS WAR! We had started saving for a new milking machine and a deep-well pump that we will be needing in a few years. . . . We're still going to have that milking machine and that pump — and a lot of other new improvements after the war. When our son comes home from the fighting front, he'll help us pick them out. And we'll have the cash to pay for them. With the money we are saving now in War Bonds. And we are going to hang on to as many War Bonds as possible to take care of us after our boy takes over on the farm. For after ten years, we get four dollars back for every three we have invested."

3. **Poster from the U.S. Office of Price Administration, 1943.**

Source: United States Office of Price Administration/Northwestern University Library; https://images.northwestern.edu/multiresimages /inu:dil-e099b32d-f48e-42b7-9219-e95ee3884114.

4. Girl Scouts planting a victory garden near San Francisco during the war, 1943.

5. Oral histories about life during the war.

Tessie Hickam Wilson, a young woman from Oklahoma.

It was a hard time, but we felt like we were doing our part, and all the people we knew were doing their part. We had rationing. Sugar, coffee, gasoline and meat were some of the items that were hard to come by. We had ration books every so often, and we had to use them sparingly. We bought savings bonds to help in the war effort.

We also had radios and record players, and when we could afford it, we went to the movies. And even though there were hard times, we did what we could in the war effort, and I will always be glad I was part of it.

Virginia J. Bondra, a student and clothing worker from Ohio.

The only newsreel footage we saw was in the theaters when we went to a movie. And we used to bring scrap metal or cans, and we'd get in the movies free. They needed scrap metal and they — the USA needed scrap fat. My mother used to scrap fat, you know, in a can. She'd save it, and we'd bring it to a certain place. Sugar was rationed. Each member of the family would get one pound of sugar a week. And I always had time to bake because we had sugar. . . .

Different things were rationed. We couldn't buy nylons because it was needed . . . for parachutes. So we'd — we'd — my older sisters would paint their legs with a certain makeup that came out in place of nylons. . . . It was makeup for legs.

They painted a eyebrow pencil line down the back of their leg so it would look like real nylons. And we would write V-mail. I had brother — brothers-in-law in the service. We — we'd write V-mail to them. It was called V-mail. Victory mail. . . . We couldn't put their address on because they were moved around a lot and we didn't want the enemy to know. There were a lot of secrets. They would say "zip your lip was the" — was the word of the days then. "Zip your lip" because we didn't want the enemy to get information.

Sources: (2) Digital Collections, Duke University Libraries; (4) National Park Service, *Rosie the Riveter: Women Working During World War II*, and the Library of Congress Veterans History Project.

ANALYZING THE EVIDENCE

1. Examine sources 1, 2, and 3. Who created these sources, and what does this suggest about the context and purpose of these documents? Can you tell from their content who the intended audience was?

2. Study the photograph (source 4). Who is depicted? What does this suggest about the victory garden program as well as war efforts on the home front more broadly?

3. How do the oral histories in source 5 add to your understanding of home front involvement in the war effort? Does their testimony force you to question the other documents in any way, and if so, how?

PUTTING IT ALL TOGETHER

Analyze some of the ways the U.S. government encouraged ordinary citizens to participate in the war effort, and evaluate the objectives and results of these efforts.

Japanese Removal

Unlike World War I, which evoked widespread harassment of German Americans, World War II produced relatively little condemnation of European Americans. Despite the presence of small but vocal groups of Nazi sympathizers and Mussolini supporters, German American and Italian American communities were largely left in peace during the war; federal officials held only about five thousand potentially dangerous German and Italian aliens. The relocation and temporary imprisonment of Japanese immigrants and Japanese American citizens was a glaring exception to this otherwise tolerant policy. Immediately after the attack on Pearl Harbor, the West Coast remained calm. Then, as residents began to fear spies, sabotage, and further attacks, California's long history of racial animosity toward Asian immigrants surfaced. Local politicians and newspapers whipped up hysteria against Japanese Americans, who numbered only about 112,000, had no political power, and lived primarily in small enclaves in the Pacific coast states.

Early in 1942, President Roosevelt responded to anti-Japanese fears by issuing **Executive Order 9066**, which authorized the War Department to force Japanese Americans from their West Coast homes and hold them in relocation camps for the duration of the war. Although there was no disloyal or seditious activity among the evacuees, few public leaders opposed the plan. "A Jap's a Jap," snapped General John DeWitt, the officer charged with defense of the West Coast. "It makes no difference whether he is an American citizen or not."

The relocation plan shocked Japanese Americans, more than two-thirds of whom were Nisei; that is, their parents were immigrants (Isei), but they were native-born American citizens. Army officials gave families only a few days to dispose of their property. Businesses that had taken a lifetime to build were liquidated overnight. The War Relocation Authority moved the prisoners to hastily built camps in desolate areas in California, Arizona, Utah, Colorado, Wyoming, Idaho, and Arkansas (Map 23.1). Ironically, the Japanese Americans who made up one-third of the population of Hawaii, and presumably posed a greater threat because of their proximity to Japan, were not imprisoned. They provided much of the unskilled labor in the island territory, and the Hawaiian economy could not have functioned without them.

Cracks soon appeared in the relocation policy. An agricultural labor shortage led the government to furlough seasonal farmworkers from the camps as early as 1942. About 4,300 students

Executive Order 9066
An order signed by President Roosevelt in 1942 that authorized the War Department to force Japanese Americans from their West Coast homes and hold them in relocation camps for the rest of the war.

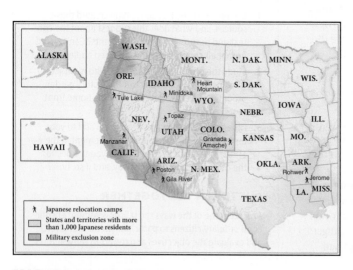

MAP 23.1 Japanese Relocation Camps
In 1942, the government ordered 112,000 Japanese Americans living on the West Coast into internment camps in the nation's interior because of their supposed threat to public safety. Some of the camps were as far away as Arkansas. The federal government rescinded the mass evacuation order in December 1944, but 44,000 people still remained in the camps when the war ended in August 1945.

were allowed to attend colleges outside the West Coast military zone. Other internees were permitted to join the armed services. The 442nd Regimental Combat Team, a unit composed almost entirely of Nisei volunteers, served with distinction in Europe.

Gordon Hirabayashi was among the Nisei who actively resisted incarceration. A student at the University of Washington, Hirabayashi was a religious pacifist who had registered with his draft board as a conscientious objector. He refused to report for evacuation and turned himself in to the FBI. "I wanted to uphold the principles of the Constitution," Hirabayashi later stated, "and the curfew and evacuation orders which singled out a group on the basis of ethnicity violated them." Tried and convicted in 1942, he appealed his case to the Supreme Court in *Hirabayashi v. United States* (1943). In that case and in *Korematsu v. United States* (1944), the Court allowed the removal of Japanese Americans from the West Coast on the basis of "military necessity" but avoided ruling on the constitutionality of the incarceration program. The Court's decision underscored the fragility of civil liberties in wartime. Congress issued a public apology in 1988 and awarded $20,000 to each of the eighty-two thousand surviving Japanese Americans who had once been internees.

> **IN YOUR OWN WORDS** Describe both the short-term and the lasting domestic social changes the war produced.

Fighting and Winning the War

World War II was a war for control of the world. Had the Axis powers triumphed, Germany would have dominated, either directly or indirectly, all of Europe and much of Africa and the Middle East; Japan would have controlled most of East and Southeast Asia. To prevent this outcome, which would have crippled democracy in Europe and restricted American power to the Western Hemisphere, the Roosevelt administration took the United States to war. The combination of American intervention, the perseverance of Britain, and the profound civilian and military sacrifices of the Soviet Union decided the outcome of the conflict and shaped the character of the postwar world.

Wartime Aims and Tensions

Great Britain, the United States, and the Soviet Union were the key actors in the Allied coalition. China, France, and other nations played crucial but smaller roles. The leaders who became known as the Big Three — Prime Minister Winston Churchill of Great Britain, President Franklin Roosevelt, and Premier Joseph Stalin of the Soviet Union — set military strategy. However, Stalin was not a party to the Atlantic Charter, which Churchill and Roosevelt had signed in August 1941, and disagreed fundamentally with some of its precepts, such as a capitalist international trading system. The Allies also disagreed about military strategy and timing. The Big Three made defeating Germany (rather than Japan) the top military priority, but they differed over how best to do it. In 1941, a massive German force had invaded the Soviet Union and reached the outskirts of Leningrad, Moscow, and Stalingrad before being halted in early 1942 by hard-pressed Russian troops. To relieve pressure on the Soviet army, Stalin wanted the British and Americans to open a second front with a major invasion of Germany through France.

Roosevelt informally assured Stalin that the Allies would comply in 1942, but Churchill opposed an early invasion, and American war production was not yet sufficient to support it. For eighteen months, Stalin's pleas went unanswered, and the Soviet Union bore the brunt of the fighting; in the 1943 Battle of Kursk alone, the Soviet army suffered 860,000 casualties, several times what the Allies would suffer for the first two months of the European campaign after D-Day. Then, at a conference of the Big Three in Tehran, Iran, in November 1943, Churchill and Roosevelt agreed to open a second front in France within six months in return for Stalin's promise to join the fight against Japan. Both sides adhered to this agreement, but the long delay angered Stalin, who became increasingly suspicious of American and British intentions.

The War in Europe

Throughout 1942, the Allies suffered one defeat after another. German armies pushed deep into Soviet territory, advancing through the wheat farms of the Ukraine and the rich oil region of the Caucasus. Simultaneously, German forces began an offensive in North Africa aimed at seizing the Suez Canal. In the Atlantic, U-boats devastated American convoys carrying oil and other vital supplies to Britain and the Soviet Union.

Over the winter of 1942–1943, however, the tide began to turn in favor of the Allies. In the epic Battle of Stalingrad, Soviet forces halted the German advance, and by early 1944 Stalin's troops had driven the German army out of the Soviet Union (Map 23.2). Meanwhile, as Churchill's temporary substitute for a second front in France, the Allies launched a counteroffensive in North Africa. Between November 1942 and May 1943, Allied troops under the leadership of General Dwight D. Eisenhower and General George S. Patton defeated the German Afrika Korps, led by General Erwin Rommel.

From Africa, the Allied command followed Churchill's strategy of attacking the Axis through its "soft underbelly": the Italian peninsula. Faced with an Allied invasion, the Italian king ousted Mussolini's fascist regime in July 1943. But German troops, who far outmatched the Allies in skill and organization, took control of Italy and strenuously resisted the Allied invasion. American and British divisions took Rome only in June 1944 and were still fighting German forces in northern Italy when the European war ended in May 1945 (Map 23.3). Churchill's southern strategy proved a time-consuming and costly mistake.

D-Day
June 6, 1944, the date of the Allied invasion of northern France. D-Day was the largest amphibious assault in world history. The invasion opened a second front against the Germans and moved the Allies closer to victory in Europe.

D-Day The long-promised invasion of France came on **D-Day**, June 6, 1944. That morning, the largest armada ever assembled moved across the English Channel under the command of General Eisenhower. When American, British, and Canadian soldiers hit the beaches of Normandy, they suffered terrible casualties but secured a beachhead. Over the next few weeks, more than 1.5 million soldiers and thousands of tons of military supplies and equipment flowed into France. Much to the Allies' advantage, they never faced more than one-third of Hitler's Wehrmacht (armed forces), because the Soviet Union continued to hold down the Germans on the Eastern Front. In August, Allied troops liberated Paris; by September, they had driven the Germans

MAP 23.2 World War II in Europe and North Africa, 1941–1943

Hitler's Germany reached its greatest extent in 1942, by which time Nazi forces had occupied Norway, France, North Africa, central Europe, and much of western Russia. The tide of battle turned in late 1942 when the German advance stalled at Leningrad and Stalingrad. By early 1943, the Soviet army had launched a massive counterattack at Stalingrad, and Allied forces had driven the Germans from North Africa and launched an invasion of Sicily and the Italian mainland.

out of most of France and Belgium. Meanwhile, long-range Allied bombers attacked German cities such as Hamburg and Dresden as well as military and industrial targets. The air campaign killed some 305,000 civilians and soldiers and injured another 780,000 — a grisly reminder of the war's brutality.

The Germans were not yet ready to give up, however. In December 1944, they mounted a final offensive in Belgium, the so-called Battle of the Bulge, before being pushed back across the Rhine River into Germany. American and British troops drove toward Berlin from the west, while Soviet troops advanced east through Poland. On April 30, 1945, as Russian troops massed outside Berlin, Hitler committed suicide; on May 7, Germany formally surrendered.

MAP 23.3 World War II in Europe, 1944–1945
By the end of 1943, the Russian army had nearly pushed the Germans out of the Soviet Union, and by June 1944, when the British and Americans finally invaded France, the Russians had liberated eastern Poland and most of southeastern Europe. By the end of 1944, British and American forces were ready to invade Germany from the west, and the Russians were poised to do the same from the east. Germany surrendered on May 7, 1945.

The Holocaust When Allied troops advanced into Poland and Germany in the spring of 1945, they came face-to-face with Hitler's "final solution" for the Jewish population of Germany and the German-occupied countries: the extermination camps in which 6 million Jews had been put to death, along with another 6 million Poles, Slavs, Gypsies, homosexuals, and other "undesirables." Photographs of the Nazi death camps at Buchenwald, Dachau, and Auschwitz showed bodies stacked like cordwood and survivors so emaciated that they were barely alive. Published in *Life* and other mass-circulation magazines, the photographs of the **Holocaust** horrified the American public and the world.

The Nazi persecution of German Jews in the 1930s was widely known in the United States. But when Jews had begun to flee Europe, the United States refused to relax its strict immigration laws to take them in. In 1939, when the SS *St. Louis*, a German ocean

Holocaust
Germany's campaign during World War II to exterminate all Jews living in German-controlled lands, along with other groups the Nazis deemed "undesirable." In all, some 11 million people were killed in the Holocaust, most of them Jews.

liner carrying nearly a thousand Jewish refugees, sought permission from President Roosevelt to dock at an American port, FDR had refused. Its passengers' futures uncertain, the *St. Louis* was forced to return to Europe, where many would later be deported to Auschwitz and other extermination camps. American officials, along with those of most other nations, continued this exclusionist policy during World War II as the Nazi regime extended its control over millions of Eastern European Jews.

Various factors inhibited American action, but the most important was widespread anti-Semitism: in the State Department, Christian churches, and the public at large. The legacy of the immigration restriction legislation of the 1920s and the isolationist attitudes of the 1930s also discouraged policymakers from assuming responsibility for the fate of the refugees. Taking a narrow view of the national interest, the State Department allowed only 21,000 Jewish refugees to enter the United States during the war. But the War Refugee Board, which President Roosevelt established in 1944 at the behest of Secretary of the Treasury Henry Morgenthau, helped move 200,000 European Jews to safe havens in other countries.

The War in the Pacific

Waging the war against Japan was every bit as arduous as the campaign against Germany. After crippling the American battle fleet at Pearl Harbor, the Japanese quickly expanded into the South Pacific, with seaborne invasions of Hong Kong, Wake Island, and Guam. Japanese forces then advanced into Southeast Asia, conquering the Solomon Islands, Burma, and Malaya and threatening Australia and India. By May 1942, they had forced the surrender of U.S. forces in the Philippine Islands.

At that dire moment, American naval forces scored two crucial victories. These were possible because the attack on Pearl Harbor had destroyed several American battleships but left all aircraft carriers unscathed. In the Battle of the Coral Sea, off southern New Guinea in May 1942, they halted the Japanese offensive against Australia. Then, in June, at the Battle of Midway Island, the American navy severely damaged the Japanese fleet. In both battles, planes launched from American aircraft carriers provided the margin of victory. The U.S. military command, led by General Douglas MacArthur and Admiral Chester W. Nimitz, now took the offensive in the Pacific. For the next eighteen months, American forces advanced slowly toward Japan, taking one island after another in the face of determined Japanese resistance. In October 1944, MacArthur and Nimitz began the reconquest of the Philippines by winning the Battle of Leyte Gulf, a massive naval encounter in which the Japanese lost practically their entire fleet (Map 23.4).

By early 1945, victory over Japan was in sight. Japanese military forces had suffered devastating losses, and American bombing of the Japanese homeland had killed somewhere between 300,000 and 900,000 civilians and crippled the nation's economy. The bloodletting on both sides was horrendous. On the small islands of Iwo Jima and Okinawa, tens of thousands of Japanese soldiers fought to the death, killing 13,000 U.S. Marines and wounding 46,000 more. Desperate to halt the American advance and short on ammunition, Japanese pilots flew suicidal kamikaze missions, crashing their bomb-laden planes into American ships.

Among the grim realities of war in the Pacific was the conflict's racial overtones. The attack on Pearl Harbor reawakened the long tradition of anti-Asian sentiment in the United States. In the eyes of many Americans, the Japanese were "yellow monkeys,"

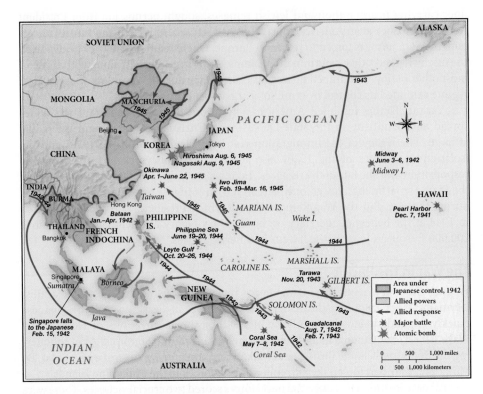

MAP 23.4 World War II in the Pacific

After the attacks on Pearl Harbor in December 1941, the Japanese rapidly extended their domination in the Pacific. The Japanese flag soon flew as far east as the Marshall and Gilbert islands and as far south as the Solomon Islands and parts of New Guinea. Japan also controlled the Philippines, much of Southeast Asia, and parts of China, including Hong Kong. By mid-1942, American naval victories at the Coral Sea and Midway stopped further Japanese expansion. Allied forces retook the islands of the central Pacific in 1943 and 1944 and ousted the Japanese from the Philippines early in 1945. Carrier-launched planes had started bombing Japan itself in 1942, but the capture of these islands gave U.S. bombers more bases from which to strike Japanese targets. As the Soviet army invaded Japanese-occupied Manchuria in August 1945, U.S. planes took off from one of the newly captured Mariana Islands to drop the atomic bombs on Hiroshima and Nagasaki. The Japanese offered to surrender on August 10.

an inferior race whose humanity deserved minimal respect. Racism was evident among the Japanese as well. Their brutal attacks on China (including the rape of Nanjing), their forcing of Korean "comfort women" to have sex with Japanese soldiers, and their treatment of American prisoners in the Philippines flowed from their own sense of racial superiority. Anti-Japanese attitudes in the United States would subside in the 1950s as the island nation became a trusted ally. But racism would again play a major role in the U.S. war in Vietnam in the 1960s.

As the American navy advanced on Japan in the winter of 1945, President Roosevelt returned to the United States from the Yalta Conference, a major meeting of the Big Three at Yalta, a resort town on the Black Sea (Chapter 24). The sixty-three-year-old president was a sick man, visibly exhausted by his 14,000-mile trip and suffering from heart failure and high blood pressure. On April 12, 1945, during a short visit to his vacation home in Warm Springs, Georgia, Roosevelt suffered a cerebral hemorrhage and died.

The Atomic Bomb and the End of the War

When Harry Truman assumed the presidency, he learned for the first time about the top-secret **Manhattan Project**, which was on the verge of testing a new weapon: the atomic bomb. Working at the University of Chicago in December 1942, Enrico Fermi and Leo Szilard, refugees from fascist Italy and Nazi Germany, produced the first controlled atomic chain reaction using highly processed uranium. With the aid of German-born refugee Albert Einstein, the greatest theorist of modern physics and a scholar at Princeton, they persuaded Franklin Roosevelt to develop an atomic weapon, warning that German scientists were also working on such nuclear reactions.

The Manhattan Project cost $2 billion, employed 120,000 people, and involved the construction of thirty-seven installations in nineteen states — with all of its activity hidden from Congress, the American people, and even Vice President Truman. Directed by Lieutenant General Leslie R. Groves Jr. and scientist J. Robert Oppenheimer, the nation's top physicists assembled the first bomb in Los Alamos, New Mexico, and successfully tested it on July 16, 1945. Overwhelmed by its frightening power, as he witnessed the first mushroom cloud, Oppenheimer recalled the words from the Bhagavad Gita, one of the great texts of Hindu scripture: "I am become Death, the Destroyer of Worlds."

Three weeks later, President Truman ordered the dropping of atomic bombs on two Japanese cities: Hiroshima on August 6 and Nagasaki on August 9. Truman's rationale for this order — and the implications of his decision — have long been the subject of scholarly and popular debate (Interpretations). The principal justification was straightforward: Truman and his American advisors, including Secretary of War Henry Stimson and Army Chief of Staff General George Marshall, believed that Japan's military leaders would never surrender unless their country faced national ruin. Moreover, at the Potsdam Conference on the outskirts of Berlin in July 1945, the Allies had agreed that only the "unconditional surrender" of Japan was acceptable — the same terms under which Germany and Italy had been defeated. To win such a surrender, an invasion of Japan itself seemed necessary. Stimson and Marshall told Truman that such an invasion would produce between half a million and a million Allied casualties.

Before giving the order to drop the atomic bomb, Truman considered other options. His military advisors rejected the most obvious alternative: a nonlethal demonstration of the bomb's awesome power, perhaps on a remote Pacific island. If the demonstration failed — not out of

Manhattan Project

Top-secret project authorized by Franklin Roosevelt in 1942 to develop an atomic bomb ahead of the Germans. The Americans who worked on the project at Los Alamos, New Mexico (among other highly secretive sites around the country), succeeded in producing a successful atomic bomb by July 1945.

Hiroshima, March 1946 Though the atomic bomb had been dropped on the port city of Hiroshima six months previous to this photo being taken, the devastation is still apparent. The U.S. Army report on the bombing described the immediate effects of the blast: "At 8:15 A.M., the bomb exploded with a blinding flash in the sky, and a great rush of air and a loud rumble of noise extended for many miles around the city; the first blast was soon followed by the sounds of falling buildings and of growing fires, and a great cloud of dust and smoke began to cast a pall of darkness over the city." The only buildings not leveled were those with concrete reinforcement, meant to withstand earthquakes. The human toll of this weapon was unprecedented: of the estimated population of 350,000, 100,000 were likely killed by the explosion, and many tens of thousands more died slowly of the effects of radiation poisoning. National Archives photo no. 342-FH-4A-49430-KE-6011.

Why Did the United States Drop the Atomic Bomb on Japan?

No president has made a more fateful decision than Harry Truman to drop the atomic bomb on Japan. The cost in human lives was staggering: nearly a third of Hiroshima's 350,000 residents died instantly. Another 60,000 died at Nagasaki three days later. This overpowering demonstration of America's war-making capacity led to Japanese surrender and the end of World War II. At the time and in the decades since, many saw Truman's decision as an unfortunate but necessary one: in the wartime calculus, saving the lives of American soldiers, who may have been called upon to undertake an invasion of Japan had the war dragged on, counted for more than the loss of Japanese lives in these two blast zones.

But was Truman's decision as straightforward as that? For several decades, scholars have been debating Truman's decision. Some scholars have agreed that Truman had few options given Japan's willingness to keep fighting. Others have suggested that Truman's use of atomic weapons was motivated by other geopolitical (some have suggested racist) motivations. Two scholars, Robert P. Newman and Tsuyoshi Hasegawa, wade into this debate with conflicting interpretations of Truman's decision.

ROBERT P. NEWMAN

SOURCE: Robert P. Newman, *Rhetoric & Public Affairs: Truman and the Hiroshima Cult* (East Lansing: Michigan State University Press, 1995), 12–13.

Truman read the [Japanese] intercepts. They were very clear. They did not show a Japan ready to surrender. They show an *elite* ready to negotiate an armistice . . . but . . . [t]he truth is that peace would have been available only had the peace party . . . been in control. They were not. . . . [Those in control in Japan] *never* favored surrender, not after Saipan was lost, not after Iwo Jima was lost, not after the Philippines were lost, not after Okinawa, not even after two atom bombs and a Soviet Declaration of War. They all supported fighting the decisive battle in the homeland during which the American invaders would take such heavy casualties that the Allies would negotiate an armistice.

TSUYOSHI HASEGAWA

SOURCE: Tsuyoshi Hasegawa, *Racing the Enemy: Stalin, Truman, and the Surrender of Japan* (Cambridge: Harvard University Press, 2009), 183.

Soviet entry played an important part in the American decision to speed up the dropping of the atomic bombs. Truman was in a hurry. He was aware that the race was on between the atomic bomb and Soviet entry into the war. That was why he concocted the story of Japan's "prompt rejection" of the Potsdam Proclamation as the justification for the atomic bomb, and that was also the reason he was ecstatic to receive the news of the Hiroshima bomb. The atomic bomb represented to Truman a solution to all the dilemmas he faced: unconditional surrender, the cost of Japan's homeland invasion, and Soviet entry into the war. He was jubilant at news of the atomic bomb on Hiroshima, not because of a perverted joy in killing the Japanese, but because of the satisfaction that everything had gone as he had planned.

QUESTIONS FOR ANALYSIS

1. How do Newman and Hasegawa differ in their interpretation of Truman's decision to use atomic weapons in Japan?
2. How does each scholar weigh moral and strategic concerns in accounting for Truman's decision to bomb Hiroshima and Nagasaki?
3. Based on Chapter 23's discussion of World War II, which of these two interpretations is most compelling as a decisive factor in shaping Truman's decision to use the atomic bomb to end the war with Japan?

the question, as the bomb had been tested only once—it would embolden Japan further. A detailed advance warning designed to scare Japan into surrender was also rejected. Given Japan's tenacious fighting in the Pacific, the Americans believed that only massive devastation or a successful invasion would lead Japan's military leadership to surrender. After all, the deaths of more than 100,000 Japanese civilians in the U.S. firebombing of Tokyo and other cities in the spring of 1945 had brought Japan no closer to surrender.

In any event, the atomic bombs achieved the immediate goal. The deaths of 100,000 people at Hiroshima and 60,000 at Nagasaki prompted the Japanese government to surrender unconditionally on August 15 and to sign a formal agreement on September 2, 1945. Fascism had been defeated, thanks to a fragile alliance between the capitalist nations of the West and the communist government of the Soviet Union. The coming of peace would strain and then destroy the victorious coalition. Even as the global war came to an end, the early signs of the coming Cold War were apparent, as were the stirrings of independence in the European colonies.

The Toll of the War

After the battle of Iwo Jima, one of the fiercest and bloodiest of the Pacific war, a rabbi chaplain in the Marine Corps delivered the eulogy for the fallen. "This shall not be in vain," he said, surveying a battlefield that witnessed the deaths of nearly 30,000 American and Japanese soldiers. Speaking of American losses, he said, "from the suffering and sorrow of those who mourn this, will come — we promise — the birth of a new freedom for the sons of man everywhere." The toll of "suffering and sorrow" from World War II was enormous. Worldwide, more than 50 million soldiers and civilians were killed, nearly 2.5 percent of the globe's population. The Holocaust took the lives of 6 million European Jews, 2.6 million from Poland alone. Nearly 100 million additional soldiers and civilians were wounded, and 30 million people across the globe were rendered homeless. It was one of the most wrenching, disruptive, and terrible wars in human history.

Alongside the human toll stood profound economic and political transformations. Hundreds of cities in Europe and Asia had been bombed. Some of them, like Dresden, Warsaw, Hamburg, and Hiroshima, had been simply obliterated. Much of the industrial infrastructure of Germany and Japan, two of the world's most important industrial economies before the war, lay in ruins. Moreover, despite emerging as one of the victors, Britain was no longer a global power. The independence movement in India was only the most obvious sign of its waning influence. Indeed, throughout the colonized world in Asia and Africa, people had taken the Atlantic Charter, and FDR's insistence that this was a war for *democracy*, seriously. For them, resumption of European imperialism was unacceptable, and the war represented a step toward national self-determination.

In the United States, too, the toll of war was great. More than 400,000 lives were lost, and nearly 300,000 American soldiers were wounded. Yet millions returned home, and in the coming decades veterans would play a central role in national life. Incredibly, in 1950 World War II veterans made up one-third of all American men over the age of nineteen. Only the Civil War involved a comparable commitment of military service from a generation. Americans paid dearly for that commitment—though not, it must be noted, as dearly as other peoples in Europe and Asia — and the legacies of the war shaped families, politics, and foreign policy for the remainder of the century.

> **IN YOUR OWN WORDS** How did Allied strategy against the Axis powers evolve between 1941 and 1945?

Summary

The rise of fascism in Germany, Italy, and Japan led to the outbreak of World War II. Initially, the American public opposed U.S. intervention. But by 1940, President Roosevelt was mobilizing support for the military and preparing the country for war. The Japanese attack on Pearl Harbor in December 1941 brought the nation fully into the conflict. War mobilization dramatically expanded the federal government and led to substantial economic growth. It also boosted geographical and social mobility as women, rural whites, and southern blacks found employment in new defense plants across the country. Government rules assisted both the labor movement and the African American campaign for civil rights. However, religious and racial animosity caused the exclusion of Jewish refugees and the internment of 112,000 Japanese Americans.

By 1942, Germany and Japan seemed to be winning the war. But in 1943, the Allies took the offensive — with advances by the Soviet army in Europe and the American navy in the Pacific — and by the end of 1944, Allied victory was all but certain. Germany finally surrendered in May 1945, and Japan surrendered in August, after the atomic bombing of the Japanese cities Hiroshima and Nagasaki. The United States emerged from the war with an undamaged homeland, sole possession of the atomic bomb, and a set of unresolved diplomatic disputes with the Soviet Union that would soon lead to the four-decade-long Cold War. Federal laws and practices established during the war — the universal income tax, a huge military establishment, and multibillion-dollar budgets, to name but a few — became part of American life. So, too, did the active participation of the United States in international politics and alliances, an engagement intensified by the unresolved issues of the wartime alliance with the Soviet Union and the postwar fate of colonized nations.

CHAPTER 23 REVIEW

TERMS TO KNOW   *Identify and explain the significance of each term below.*

Key Concepts and Events

fascism (p. 748)	Neutrality Act of 1935 (p. 750)	Munich Conference (p. 751)	America First Committee (p. 751)
National Socialist (Nazi) Party (p. 749)	Popular Front (p. 750)	Committee to Defend America by Aiding the Allies (p. 751)	Four Freedoms (p. 752)
Rome-Berlin Axis (p. 750)			Lend-Lease Act (p. 752)

Atlantic Charter (p. 752)

Pearl Harbor (p. 753)

War Powers Act (p. 754)

Revenue Act (p. 756)

code talkers (p. 757)

Executive Order 8802
(p. 759)

Bracero Program (p. 760)

Servicemen's Readjustment
Act (p. 761)

zoot suits (p. 763)

Executive Order 9066
(p. 766)

D-Day (p. 768)

Holocaust (p. 770)

Manhattan Project
(p. 773)

Key People

Benito Mussolini (p. 748)

Adolf Hitler (p. 748)

Hideki Tojo (p. 748)

Charles A. Lindbergh
(p. 750)

Winston Churchill (p. 752)

Harry S. Truman (p. 761)

Gordon Hirabayashi
(p. 767)

Dwight D. Eisenhower
(p. 768)

REVIEW QUESTIONS   *Answer these questions to demonstrate your understanding of the chapter's main ideas.*

1. Explain the steps by which the United States became involved in World War II.

2. What aspects of the economy and American society were affected by mobilization for war?

3. Describe both the short-term and the lasting domestic social changes the war produced.

4. How did Allied strategy against the Axis powers evolve between 1941 and 1945?

5. Review the events listed under "America in the World" on the thematic timeline on page 649. How did World War II change the relationship between the United States and the rest of the world in the first half of the twentieth century?

MAKING CONNECTIONS   *Recognize the larger developments and continuities within and across chapters.*

1. For the United States, the period between World War I (1914–1918) and World War II (1937–1945) was a prolonged series of conflicts and crises, both domestically and internationally. What connections can be drawn between World War I, the Great Depression, and World War II? Did this "long" conflict draw the United States and Europe closer together or drive them further apart? How did American attitudes toward involvement in European affairs change over this period?

2. How did the following developments of World War II change the relationship of the United States to other nations in the world: the Atlantic Charter; fighting a two-front war in Europe and the Pacific; the Manhattan Project and the bombing of Hiroshima and Nagasaki?

3. World War II has popularly been called the "good war." Do you agree with this assessment? Why do you think it earned that nickname?

4. Overall, what effects — positive or negative — did World War II have on social change in the United States, particularly among women and historically marginalized groups?

KEY TURNING POINTS   *Refer to the chapter chronology on page 748 for help in answering the question below.*

Identify the key turning points for the Allies in the European and Pacific campaigns.

8 PART

The Modern State and the Age of Liberalism

1945–1980

Between 1945 and 1980, the United States became the world's leading economic and military power. The dates we've chosen to bookend the period reflect two turning points. In 1945, the United States and its allies emerged victorious from World War II. In 1980, American voters turned away from the robust liberalism of the postwar years and elected a president, Ronald Reagan, backed by a conservative political movement. Each turning point, one international and the other domestic, marked the rise of new developments in American history — and thus our periodization endeavors to capture in these decades a narrative of global power and expanding political liberalism.

Internationally, after 1945 a prolonged period of tension and conflict known as the Cold War drew the United States into an engagement in world affairs unprecedented in the nation's history. Domestically, three decades of sustained economic growth, whose benefits were widely, though imperfectly, distributed, expanded the middle class and brought into being a mass consumer society. These international and domestic developments were intertwined with the predominance of liberalism in American politics and public policy. One might think of an "age of liberalism" in this era, encompassing the social-welfare liberalism that was a legacy of the New Deal and the rights liberalism of the 1960s.

Global leadership abroad and economic prosperity at home were conditioned on further expansions in government power. How that power was used proved controversial. Following World War II, a national security state emerged to investigate so-called subversives in the United States and to destabilize foreign governments abroad. Meanwhile, American troops went to war in Korea and Vietnam. At home, African Americans, women, the poor, and other social groups called for greater equality and sought new government initiatives to make that equality a reality. Here, in brief, are the three key dimensions of this convulsive, turbulent era. ▶

Global Leadership and the Cold War

AP Photo.

When the United States officially joined the combatants of World War II, it entered into an alliance with England and the Soviet Union. That alliance proved impossible to sustain after 1945, as the U.S. and the Soviet Union became competitors to shape postwar Europe, East Asia, and the developing world. The resulting Cold War lasted four decades, during which the U.S. extended its political and military reach onto every continent. Under Harry S. Truman, American officials developed the policy of containment — a combination of economic, diplomatic, and military actions to limit the expansion of communism — that subsequent presidents embraced and expanded.

Intervention abroad was a hallmark of the Cold War. Most American interventions took place in developing countries and in recently independent, decolonized nations. In the name of preventing the spread of communism, the U.S. intervened directly or indirectly in China, Iran, Guatemala, Cuba, Indonesia, and the Dominican Republic, among many other nations, and fought major wars in Korea and Vietnam. This new global role for the U.S. inspired support but also spurred detractors.

The Age of Liberalism

AP Photo/Jack Harris.

In response to the Great Depression, the New Deal expanded federal responsibility for the social welfare of ordinary citizens. Legislators from both parties embraced liberal ideas about the role of government and undertook such measures as the GI Bill, subsidies for home ownership, and investment in infrastructure and education. Poverty, however, affected one-third of Americans in the 1960s, and discrimination denied millions of nonwhites full citizenship. Lack of opportunity became a driving force in the civil rights movement and in the Great Society under Lyndon Johnson.

Inspired by African American civil rights, other social movements sought equality based on gender, sexuality, and ethnicity. If "New Deal liberalism" had focused on social welfare, this "rights liberalism" focused on protecting people from discrimination and ensuring equal citizenship. These struggles resulted in new laws, such as the Civil Rights Act of 1964 and the Voting Rights Act of 1965. Conservative opponents, however, mobilized in the 1960s against what they saw as the excesses of liberal activism. The resulting conflict began to reshape politics in the 1970s and laid the groundwork for a new conservative movement.

Mass Consumption and the Middle Class

Justin Locke/National Geographic/Getty Images.

The postwar American economy was driven by mass consumption and suburbanization. Rising wages and increased access to higher education raised living standards and allowed more Americans than ever to afford consumer goods. Suburbs and the Sunbelt led the nation in population growth. But the new prosperity had mixed results. Cities declined and new racial and ethnic ghettos formed. Mass consumption raised concerns that the nation's rivers, streams, air, and open land were being damaged, and an environmental movement arose in response. And prosperity itself proved short-lived. By the 1970s, deindustrialization had eroded much of the nation's once prosperous industrial base.

A defining characteristic of the postwar decades was the growth of the American middle class predicated on numerous demographic changes. Women worked more outside the home and spurred a new feminism. Children enjoyed more purchasing power, and a "teen culture" arose on television, in popular music, and in film. The family became politicized, too, and by the late 1970s, liberals and conservatives were divided over how best to address the nation's family life.

The Modern State and the Age of Liberalism 1945–1980

AP Photo.

Thematic Understanding

This timeline arranges some of the important events of this period into seven themes. Consider the entries under "America in the World" and "Politics and Power" across all four decades. What connections were there between international developments and domestic politics in this era of the Cold War? Under "American and National Identity" and "Culture and Society," consider how the civil rights movement shaped these decades.

	AMERICAN AND NATIONAL IDENTITY	POLITICS AND POWER	WORK, EXCHANGE, AND TECHNOLOGY
1940	• "To Secure These Rights" (1947) • Desegregation of armed services (1948) • *Shelley v. Kraemer* (1948)	• GI Bill (1944) • Loyalty-Security Program (1947) • Taft-Hartley Act (1947) • Truman reelected (1948) • Truman's Fair Deal (1949)	• Bretton Woods system established: World Bank, International Monetary Fund (1944) • Baby boom establishes new consumer generation
1950	• *Brown v. Board of Education* (1954) • Montgomery Bus Boycott (1955) • Little Rock Central High School desegregation battle (1957) • Southern Christian Leadership Conference founded (1957)	• Cold War liberalism • McCarthyism and Red Scare • Eisenhower's presidency (1953–1961)	• Labor-Management Accord struck in major industries (1950s) • Military-industrial complex begins to rise • National Defense Education Act (1958) spurs development of technology
1960	• Greensboro sit-ins (1960) • *The Feminine Mystique* (1963) • Civil Rights and Voting Rights Acts (1964–1965) • National Organization for Women founded (1966) • Alcatraz occupation (1969) • Black Power (1966) • Student and antiwar activism	• John F. Kennedy's New Frontier • John F. Kennedy assassinated (1963) • Lyndon B. Johnson's landslide victory (1964) • War on Poverty; Great Society • Riots at Democratic National Convention (1968)	• Economic boom • Government spending on Vietnam and Great Society • Medicare and Medicaid created (1965)
1970	• Equal Rights Amendment (1972) • *Roe v. Wade* (1973) • Siege at Wounded Knee (1973) • *Bakke v. University of California* (1978) • Harvey Milk assassinated (1978)	• Richard Nixon's landslide victory (1972) • Watergate scandal; Nixon resigns (1974) • Jimmy Carter elected president (1976) • Moral Majority founded (1979)	• Energy crisis (1973) • Inflation surges, while economy stagnates (stagflation) • Deindustrialization • Tax revolt in California (1978)

CULTURE AND SOCIETY	MIGRATION AND SETTLEMENT	GEOGRAPHY AND THE ENVIRONMENT	AMERICA IN THE WORLD
1940 • World War II migrations produce vibrant, diverse cities • Bebop jazz • Red Scare and anticommunism suppress dissent (1947–1950s) • Advent of television changes entertainment (1940s–1950s)	• War production and expansion of military reshape the Sunbelt • Wartime southern migration (black and white) to northern and western cities • First Levittown opens (1947)	• Continued South-North migration of African Americans • First Levittown opens (1947) • FHA and VA subsidize suburbanization	• Truman Doctrine • Israel created (1947) • Marshall Plan (1948) • Containment strategy emerges • NATO created; West Germany created (1949)
1950 • Emergence of rock 'n' roll and youth culture • Disneyland opens (1955) • McDonald's restaurants lead emergence of fast food • Beat culture flourishes in New York and San Francisco	• Bracero program revived (1951) • Surging middle-class migration to suburbs • Patterns of racial segregation in cities and suburbs reinforced • Migration to Sunbelt (1950s–1970s) • McCarran-Walter Act (1952) • Puerto Rican "great migration" to New York	• Disneyland opens (1955) • National Interstate and Defense Highways Act (1956) • Growth of suburbia and Sunbelt • Atomic bomb testing in Nevada and Pacific Ocean	• Permanent mobilization as a result of NSC-68 • Korean War (1950–1953) • Geneva Accords regarding Vietnam (1954)
1960 • Civil rights movement merges protest and gospel music • Major antiwar protests (1965–1969) • Counterculture • Black Arts movement • Stonewall Inn riot (1969)	• Immigration and Nationality Act of 1965 • Reflecting the new law, immigration from Asia, Latin America, and Africa increases (1960s–1990s) • Rustbelt begins to lose population	• Great Society environmental initiatives • Urban riots (1964–1968) • Kerner Commission Report (1968)	• Cuban missile crisis (1962) • Gulf of Tonkin Resolution (1964) • Johnson sends ground troops to Vietnam; war escalates (1965) • Tet offensive (1968); peace talks begin
1970 • Women's and gay rights movements flourish • Cultural and political conflict over the nuclear family • Evangelical Christian resurgence	• After 1975, Vietnamese refugees fleeing communist regime arrive in U.S. • Rustbelt population decline and Sunbelt population growth produce regional realignment in congressional power (1970s–1990s)	• First Earth Day (1970) • Environmental Protection Agency established (1970) • Endangered Species Act (1973) • Three Mile Island accident (1979)	• Nixon invades Cambodia (1970) • Paris Accords end Vietnam War (1973) • Camp David Accords between Egypt and Israel (1978) • Iranian Revolution (1979) and hostage crisis (1979–1981)

Cold War America
1945–1963

I n the autumn of 1950, a little-known California congressman running for the Senate named Richard M. Nixon stood before reporters in Los Angeles. His opponent, Helen Gahagan Douglas, was a Hollywood actress and a New Deal Democrat. Nixon told the gathered reporters that Douglas had cast "Communist-leaning" votes and that she was "pink right down to her underwear." Gahagan's voting record was not much different from Nixon's. But tarring her with communism made her seem un-American, and Nixon defeated the "pink lady" (meaning nearly *red*, or communist) with nearly 60 percent of the vote.

A few months earlier, U.S. tanks and planes had arrived in French Indochina. A French colony since the nineteenth century, Indochina (present-day Vietnam, Laos, and Cambodia) was home to an independence movement led by Ho Chi Minh and supported by the Soviet Union and China. In the summer of 1950, President Harry S. Truman authorized $15 million worth of military supplies to aid France, which was fighting Ho's army to keep possession of its Indochinese empire. "Neither national independence nor democratic evolution exists in any area dominated by Soviet imperialism," Secretary of State Dean Acheson warned ominously as he announced U.S. support for French imperialism.

Connecting these coincidental historical moments, one domestic and the other international, was a decades-old force in American life that gained renewed strength after World War II: anticommunism. The events in Los Angeles and Vietnam, however different on the surface, were part of the Cold War: the global geopolitical struggle between the capitalist, democratic United States and the communist, authoritarian Soviet Union. Beginning in Europe as World War II ended and extending to Asia, Latin America, the Middle East, and Africa by the mid-1950s, the Cold War reshaped international relations and dominated global politics for more than forty years (Interpretations).

In the United States, the Cold War fostered suspicion of "subversives" in government, education, and the media. The arms race that developed between the two superpowers prompted Congress to boost military expenditures. The resulting military-industrial complex enhanced the power of the corporations that built planes, munitions, and electronic devices. In politics, the Cold War stifled liberal initiatives as the New Deal coalition tried to advance its domestic agenda in the shadow of anticommunism. In these ways, the line between the international and the domestic blurred — and that blurred line was another enduring legacy of the Cold War.

IDENTIFY THE BIG IDEA

In the first two decades of the Cold War, how did competition on the international stage and a climate of fear at home affect politics, society, and culture in the United States?

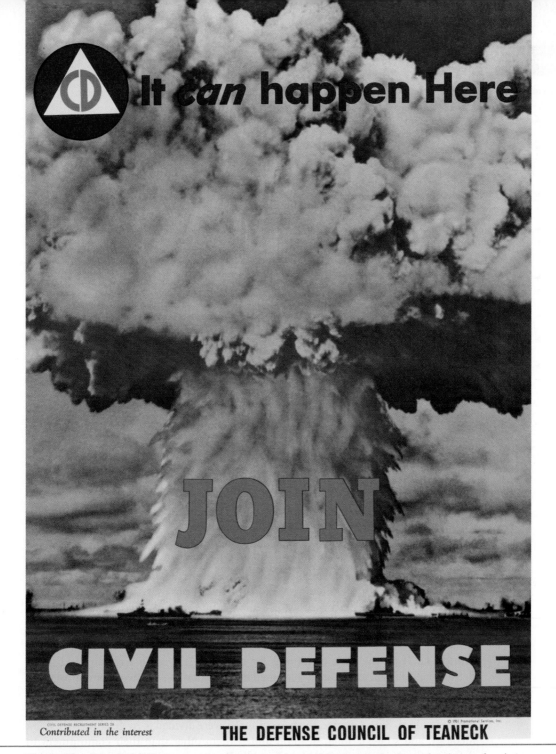

CIVIL DEFENSE RECRUITMENT SERIES 26
Contributed in the interest

© 1951 Promotional Services, Inc.

THE DEFENSE COUNCIL OF TEANECK

The Perils of the Cold War   Americans, like much of the world, lived under the threat of nuclear warfare during the tense years of the Cold War between the United States and the Soviet Union. This 1951 civil defense poster, with the message "It *can* happen Here," suggests that Americans should be prepared for such a dire outcome.   swin ink 2/Corbis via Getty Images.

CHAPTER CHRONOLOGY

As you read, ask yourself why this chapter begins and ends with these dates and identify the links among related events.

1945 ▸ End of World War II; Yalta and Potsdam conferences ▸ Senate approves U.S. participation in United Nations	**1950–** **1953** ▸ Korean War
1946 ▸ George F. Kennan outlines containment policy ▸ U.S. sides with French in war between French and Vietminh over control of Vietnam	**1950** ▸ NSC-68 leads to nuclear buildup ▸ Joseph McCarthy announces "list" of Communists in government
1947 ▸ Truman Doctrine ▸ House Un-American Activities Committee (HUAC) investigates film industry	**1952** ▸ Dwight D. Eisenhower elected president
	1954 ▸ Army-McCarthy hearings on army subversion ▸ Geneva Accords partition Vietnam
1948 ▸ Communist coup in Czechoslovakia ▸ Marshall Plan aids economic recovery in Europe State of Israel created ▸ Stalin blockades West Berlin; Berlin Airlift begins	**1956** ▸ Nikita Khrushchev emerges as Stalin's successor ▸ Suez Canal crisis
	1960 ▸ John F. Kennedy elected president
1949 ▸ North Atlantic Treaty Organization (NATO) founded ▸ Soviet Union detonates atomic bomb ▸ Mao Zedong establishes People's Republic of China	**1961** ▸ Kennedy orders the first contingent of Special Forces ("Green Berets") to Vietnam
	1963 ▸ Ngo Dinh Diem assassinated in South Vietnam

Containment in a Divided Global Order

The Cold War began on the heels of World War II and ended in 1991 with the dissolution of the Soviet Union. While it lasted, this conflict placed two far-reaching questions at the center of global history: Would capitalism or communism shape the nations of Europe and Asia? And how would the European colonies in Asia, the Middle East, and Africa gain their independence and take their places on the world stage? Cold War rivalry framed the possible answers to both questions as it drew the United States into a prolonged engagement with world affairs unprecedented in the nation's history.

Origins of the Cold War

World War II set the basic conditions for the Cold War. With Germany and Japan defeated and Britain and France weakened by years of war, only two geopolitical powers remained standing in 1945. Even had nothing divided them, the United States and the Soviet Union would have jostled each other as they moved to fill the postwar power vacuum. But, of course, the two countries were divided — by geography, history, ideology, and strategic interest. Little united them other than their commitment to defeating the Axis powers. President Franklin Roosevelt understood that maintaining the U.S.-Soviet alliance was essential for postwar global stability. But he also believed

INTERPRETATIONS

Why Was There a Cold War?

During World War II, the United States and the Soviet Union forged a "Grand Alliance" with Great Britain to defeat Hitler's Nazi Germany. In the wake of victory, however, this marriage of necessity quickly dissolved, leaving the Americans and Soviets to face each other in a Cold War that lasted until the dissolution of the Soviet Union (USSR) in 1991. For decades, these superpowers viewed each other's intentions with suspicion and, while avoiding direct and open conflict, waged proxy wars around the globe to advance the security interests they believed the other threatened. But what caused the Cold War, and why was there such hostility between the two nations?

Historians continue to debate these questions. Stephen Ambrose's account of postwar America's rise to global dominance offers a traditional explanation of the Cold War. His argument differs from that of Odd Westad, who shifts the geographical focus of the Cold War rivalry from Europe to the Global South.

STEPHEN AMBROSE

SOURCE: Stephen E. Ambrose, *Rise to Globalism: American Foreign Policy Since 1938* (Baltimore: Penguin Books, 1971), 102–103.

Whatever date is chosen to mark the declaration of [the Cold War], it is certain that the issue that sparked it, gave it life and shaped its early course, was East Europe. For centuries East and West have struggled . . . for control of the huge area running from the Baltic to the Balkans, an area rich in human and industrial resources and one that is strategically vital to both sides. . . . Neither the West nor the East has been willing to allow East Europe to be strong, independent, or neutral. Russia and the West each have wanted the area to be aligned with them and open for their own economic exploitation. . . . [During World War II], the West made no significant contribution to the liberation of East Europe and when the end came the Red Army was in sole possession of the area. . . . This crucial result of World War II destroyed the Grand Alliance and gave birth to the Cold War.

ODD WESTAD

SOURCE: Odd Arne Westad, *The Global Cold War: Third World Interventions and the Making of Our Times* (Cambridge: Cambridge University Press, 2005), 3–5.

[T]he argument that the Cold War conceptually and analytically does not belong in the south [i.e., Africa, South Asia, and Latin America] is wrong. . . . US and Soviet interventionisms . . . shaped both the international and the domestic framework within which political, social, and cultural changes in Third World countries took place. . . . The United States and the Soviet Union were driven to intervene in the Third World by the ideologies inherent in their politics. . . . Washington and Moscow needed to change the world in order to prove the universal applicability of their ideologies, and the elites of the newly independent [Third World] states proved fertile ground for their competition. . . . [B]oth powers saw themselves as assisting natural trends in world history and as defending their own security at the same time. Both saw a specific mission in and for the Third World that only their own state could carry out and which without their involvement would flounder in local hands.

QUESTIONS FOR ANALYSIS

1. Identify the major difference in these two scholars' understanding of the Cold War's geographical focus.
2. To what extent do these scholars agree on the factors driving the Cold War rivalry between the United States and the Soviet Union?
3. Which interpretation of the origins of the Cold War does the narrative in Chapter 24 seem to support?

that permanent peace and long-term U.S. interests depended on the Wilsonian principles of collective security, self-determination, and free trade (Chapter 20).

Yalta Conference
A meeting in Yalta of President Roosevelt, Prime Minister Churchill, and Joseph Stalin in February 1945, in which the leaders discussed the treatment of Germany, the status of Poland, the creation of the United Nations, and Russian entry into the war against Japan.

Yalta   At the **Yalta Conference** of February 1945, Wilsonian principles yielded to U.S.-Soviet power realities. As Allied forces neared victory in Europe and advanced toward Japan in the Pacific, Roosevelt, Churchill, and Stalin met in Yalta, a resort on the Black Sea in southern Ukraine. Roosevelt focused on maintaining Allied unity and securing Joseph Stalin's commitment to enter the war against Japan. But the fate of Eastern Europe divided the Big Three. Stalin insisted that Russian national security required pro-Soviet governments in Eastern European nations. Roosevelt pressed for an agreement, the "Declaration on Liberated Europe," that guaranteed self-determination and democratic elections in Poland and neighboring countries, such as Romania and Hungary. However, given the presence of Soviet troops in those nations, FDR had to

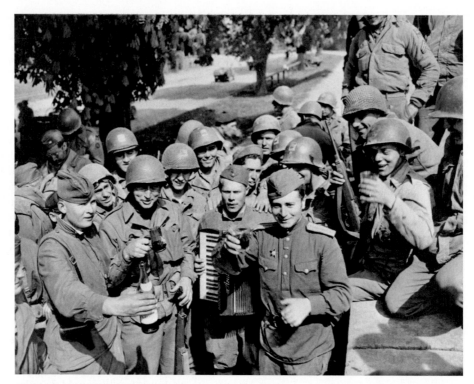

East Meets West   Soviet soldiers celebrate with U.S. soldiers from the First Army near the Elbe River in Torgau, Germany, on April 25, 1945. Soviet and American forces had converged on Hitler's Germany from opposite directions, finally meeting in Torgau. The meeting symbolized the Grand Alliance, in which U.S.-Soviet cooperation was essential, that secured victory over the Axis Powers in World War II. However, as these ordinary infantrymen optimistically toast one another and look forward to the end of fighting, Germany was already being divided in two: between a western sector held by the Allies and an eastern sector held by the Soviet Union. Within a few years, the division of Germany between "East" and "West" would stand at the center of a split in the entire European continent at the dawn of the Cold War. AFP/Getty Images.

accept a lesser pledge from Stalin: to hold "free and unfettered elections" at a future time. The three leaders also formalized their commitment to divide Germany into four zones, each controlled by one of the four Allied powers (including France), and to similarly partition the capital city, Berlin, which was located in the Soviet zone.

At Yalta, the Big Three also agreed to establish an international body to replace the discredited League of Nations. Based on plans drawn up at the 1944 Dumbarton Oaks conference in Washington, D.C., the new organization, to be known as the **United Nations**, would have both a General Assembly, in which all nations would be represented, and a Security Council composed of the five major Allied powers — the United States, Britain, France, China, and the Soviet Union — and seven other nations elected on a rotating basis. The Big Three determined that the five permanent members of the Security Council should have veto power over decisions of the General Assembly. They announced that the United Nations would convene for the first time in San Francisco on April 25, 1945.

Potsdam Following the Yalta Conference, developments over the ensuing year further hardened relations between the Soviets on one side and the Americans and British on the other. At the **Potsdam Conference** outside Berlin in July 1945, Harry Truman replaced the deceased Roosevelt. Inexperienced in world affairs and thrown into enormously complicated negotiations, Truman's instinct was to stand up to Stalin. "Unless Russia is faced with an iron fist and strong language," he said, "another war is in the making." But Truman was in no position to shape events in Eastern Europe, where Soviet-imposed governments in Poland, Hungary, and Romania were backed by the Red Army and could not be eliminated by Truman's bluster. In Poland and Romania, in particular, Stalin was determined to establish communist governments, punish wartime Nazi collaborators, and win boundary concessions that augmented Soviet territory.

Yalta and Potsdam thus set the stage for communist rule to descend over Eastern Europe. The elections called for at Yalta eventually took place in Finland, Hungary, Bulgaria, and Czechoslovakia, with varying degrees of democratic openness. Nevertheless, Stalin got the client regimes he desired in those countries and would soon exert near-complete control over their governments. Stalin's unwillingness to honor self-determination for nations in Eastern Europe was, from the American point of view, the precipitating event of the Cold War.

Germany represented the biggest challenge of all. American officials at Potsdam believed that a revived German economy was essential to ensuring the prosperity of democratic regimes throughout Western Europe — and to keeping ordinary Germans from turning again to Nazism. In contrast, Stalin hoped merely to extract reparations from Germany in the form of industrial machines and goods. In exchange for American recognition of a new German-Polish border, Truman and Secretary of State James Byrnes convinced the Soviet leader to accept German reparations only from the Soviet zone, which was largely rural and promised little wealth or German industry to plunder. The Yalta and Potsdam agreements paved the way for the division of Germany into East and West (Map 24.1).

Yalta and Potsdam demonstrated that in private negotiations the United States and the Soviet Union had starkly different objectives. Public utterances only intensified

United Nations
An international body agreed upon at the Yalta Conference and founded at a conference in San Francisco in 1945, consisting of a General Assembly, in which all nations are represented, and a Security Council of the five major Allied powers — the United States, Britain, France, China, and the Soviet Union — and seven other nations elected on a rotating basis.

Potsdam Conference
The July 1945 conference in which American officials convinced the Soviet Union leader Joseph Stalin to accept German reparations only from the Soviet zone, or far eastern part of Germany. The agreement paved the way for the division of Germany into East and West.

MAP 24.1 Cold War in Europe, 1955
This map vividly shows the Cold War division of Europe. The NATO countries (colored green) are allies of the United States; the Warsaw Pact countries (in purple) are allied to the USSR. In 1955, West Germany had just been admitted to NATO, completing Europe's stabilization into two rival camps. But Berlin remained divided, and one can see from its location deep in East Germany why the former capital was always a flash point in Cold War controversies.

those differences. In February 1946, Stalin delivered a speech in which he insisted that, according to Marxist-Leninist principles, "the unevenness of development of the capitalist countries" was likely to produce "violent disturbance" and even another war. He seemed to blame any future war on the capitalist West. Churchill responded in kind a month later. While visiting Truman in Missouri to be honored for his wartime leadership, Churchill accused Stalin of raising an "iron curtain" around Eastern Europe and allowing "police government" to rule its people. He went further, claiming that "a fraternal association of English-speaking peoples," and not Russians, ought to set the terms of the postwar world.

The cities and fields of Europe had thus barely ceased to run with the blood of World War II before they were menaced again by the tense standoff between the Soviet

Union and the United States. With Stalin intent on establishing client states in Eastern Europe and the United States equally intent on reviving Germany and ensuring collective security throughout Europe, the points of agreement were few and far between. Among the Allies, anxiety about a Nazi victory in World War II had been quickly replaced by fear of a potentially more cataclysmic war with the Soviet Union.

The Containment Strategy

In the late 1940s, American officials developed a clear strategy toward the Soviet Union that would become known as **containment**. Convinced that the USSR was methodically expanding its reach, the United States would counter by limiting Soviet influence to Eastern Europe while reconstituting democratic governments in Western Europe. In 1946–1947, three specific issues worried Truman and his advisors. First, the Soviet Union was pressing Iran for access to oil and Turkey for access to the Mediterranean. Second, a civil war was roiling in Greece, between monarchists backed by England and insurgents supported by the Greek and Yugoslavian Communist parties. Third, as European nations suffered through terrible privation in 1946 and 1947, Communist parties gained strength, particularly in France and Italy. All three developments, as seen from the United States, threatened to expand the influence of the Soviet Union beyond Eastern Europe.

containment
The basic U.S. policy of the Cold War, which sought to contain communism within its existing geographic boundaries. Initially, containment focused on the Soviet Union and Eastern Europe, but in the 1950s it came to include China, North Korea, and other parts of the developing world.

Toward an Uneasy Peace In this anxious context, the strategy of containment emerged in a series of incremental steps between 1946 and 1949. In February 1946, American diplomat George F. Kennan first proposed the idea in an 8,000-word cable — a confidential message within the U.S. State Department — from his post at the U.S. embassy in Moscow. Kennan argued that the Soviet Union was an "Oriental despotism" and that communism was merely the "fig leaf" justifying Soviet aggression. A year after writing this cable (dubbed the Long Telegram), he published an influential *Foreign Affairs* article, arguing that the West's only recourse was to meet the Soviets "with unalterable counter-force at every point where they show signs of encroaching upon the interests of a peaceful and stable world." Kennan called for "long-term, patient but firm and vigilant containment of Russian expansive tendencies." *Containment*, the key word, came to define America's evolving strategic stance toward the Soviet Union.

 To see an excerpt from the Long Telegram, along with other primary sources from this period, see *Sources for America's History*.

Kennan contended that the Soviet system was unstable and would eventually collapse. Containment would work, he reasoned, as long as the United States and its allies opposed Soviet expansion anywhere in the world. Kennan's attentive readers included Stalin himself, who quickly obtained a copy of the classified Long Telegram. The Soviet leader saw the United States as an imperialist aggressor determined to replace Great Britain as the world's dominant capitalist power. Just as Kennan thought that the Soviet system was despotic and unsustainable, Stalin believed that the West suffered from its own fatal weaknesses. Neither side completely understood or trusted the other, and each projected its worst fears onto the other.

In fact, Britain's influence in the world was declining. Exhausted by the war, facing budget deficits and a collapsing economy at home, and confronted with growing independence movements throughout its empire, particularly in India led by Mohandas Gandhi, Britain was waning as a global power. "The reins of world

The Global Cold War

Until 1950, the U.S. policy of containment was confined to economic measures, such as financial assistance to Greece and Turkey and the Marshall Plan, and focused on Europe. That changed between 1950 and 1954. In those years, containment became militarized, and its scope was expanded to include Asia and Latin America. What had begun as a limited policy to contain Soviet influence in war-torn Europe had by the mid-1950s become a global campaign against communism and social revolution.

1. **President Harry S. Truman, address before joint session of Congress, March 12, 1947.** *Known as the Truman Doctrine, this speech outlined Truman's plan to give large-scale assistance to Greece and Turkey as part of a broader anticommunist policy.*

To ensure the peaceful development of nations, free from coercion, the United States has taken a leading part in establishing the United Nations. The United Nations is designed to make possible lasting freedom and independence for all its members. We shall not realize our objectives, however, unless we are willing to help free peoples to maintain their free institutions and their national integrity against aggressive movements that seek to impose upon them totalitarian regimes....

At the present moment in world history nearly every nation must choose between alternative ways of life. The choice is too often not a free one.

One way of life is based upon the will of the majority, and is distinguished by free institutions, representative government, free elections, guarantees of individual liberty, freedom of speech and religion, and freedom from political oppression.

The second way of life is based upon the will of a minority forcibly imposed upon the majority. It relies upon terror and oppression, a controlled press and radio; fixed elections, and the suppression of personal freedoms.

I believe that it must be the policy of the United States to support free peoples who are resisting attempted subjugation by armed minorities or by outside pressures.

I believe that we must assist free peoples to work out their own destinies in their own way.

I believe that our help should be primarily through economic and financial aid which is essential to economic stability and orderly political processes.

2. **Syngman Rhee, president of South Korea, criticizing U.S. policy in 1950.** *The Korean War, 1950–1953, represented the militarization of the Truman Doctrine.*

A few days ago one American friend said that if the U.S. gave weapons to South Korea, she feared that South Korea would invade North Korea. This is a useless worry of some Americans, who do not know South Korea. Our present war is not a Cold War, but a real shooting war. Our troops will take all possible counter-measures. . . . In South Korea the U.S. has one foot in South Korea and one foot outside so that in case of an unfavorable situation it could pull out of the country. I daresay that if the U.S. wants to aid our country, it should not be only lip-service.

3. **Secretary of State Dean Acheson's testimony before the Senate Armed Forces and Foreign Relations Committee, 1951.**

The attack on Korea was . . . a challenge to the whole system of collective security, not only in the Far East, but everywhere in the world. It was a threat to all nations newly arrived at independence....

This was a test which would decide whether our collective security system would survive or would crumble. It would determine whether other nations would be intimidated by this show of force....

As a people we condemn aggression of any kind. We reject appeasement of any kind. If we stood with our arms folded while Korea was swallowed up, it would have meant abandoning our principles, and it would have meant the defeat of the collective security system on which our own safety ultimately depends.

4. **Shigeru Yoshida, prime minister of Japan, speech before the Japanese Diet (parliament), July 14, 1950.**

It is heartening . . . that America and so many members of the United Nations have gone to the rescue of an invaded country regardless of the heavy sacrifices involved. In case a war breaks out on an extensive scale how would Japan's security be preserved [since we are disarmed]? . . . This has been hotly discussed. However, the measures taken by the United Nations have done much to stabilize our people's minds.

5. **John Foster Dulles, secretary of state (1953–1959), June 30, 1954, radio and television address to the American people.** *In 1951, Jacobo Arbenz Guzmán was elected president of Guatemala. Arbenz Guzmán pursued reform policies that threatened large landholders, including the United Fruit Company. In 1954, the United States CIA engineered a coup that overthrew Arbenz Guzmán and replaced him with Carlos Castillo Armas, a colonel in the Guatemalan military.*

Tonight I should like to speak with you about Guatemala. It is the scene of dramatic events. They expose the evil purpose of the Kremlin to destroy the inter-American system, and they test the ability of the American States to maintain the peaceful integrity of the hemisphere.

For several years international communism has been probing here and there for nesting places in the Americas. It finally chose Guatemala as a spot which it could turn into an official base from which to breed subversion which would extend to other American Republics.

This intrusion of Soviet despotism was, of course, a direct challenge to our Monroe Doctrine, the first and most fundamental of our foreign policies.

6. **Guillermo Toriello, Guatemalan foreign minister, speech to delegates at the Tenth Inter-American Conference of the Organization of American States in Caracas, Venezuela, March 5, 1954.**

What is the real and effective reason for describing our government as communist? From what sources comes the accusation that we threaten continental solidarity and security? Why do they [United States] wish to intervene in Guatemala?

The answers are simple and evident. The plan of national liberation being carried out with firmness by my government has necessarily affected the privileges of the foreign enterprises that are impeding the progress and the economic development of the country. . . . With construction of publically owned ports and docks, we are putting an end to the monopoly of the United Fruit Company....

They wanted to find a ready expedient to maintain the economic dependence of the American Republics and suppress the legitimate desires of their peoples, cataloguing as "communism" every manifestation of nationalism or economic independence, any desire for social progress, any intellectual curiosity, and any interest in progressive and liberal reforms.

7. Herblock cartoon from the *Washington Post*, February 11, 1962. *Many Latin American countries were beset by a wide gap between a small wealthy elite and the mass of ordinary, much poorer citizens. American officials worried that this made social revolution an attractive alternative for those at the bottom.*

" —— And His Father Lives Up There"

EXTREME WEALTH

EXTREME POVERTY

REVOLUTION

SOURCE: A 1962 Herblock Cartoon, © The Herb Block Foundation.

SOURCES: (1) The Avalon Project at avalon.law.yale.edu; (2) Reinhard Drifte, "Japan's Involvement in the Korean War," in *The Korean War in History*, ed. James Cotton and Ian Neary (Atlantic Highlands, NJ: Humanities Press International, 1989), 43; (3) Glenn D. Paige, *The Korean Decision* (New York: The Free Press, 1968), 175–176; (4) Drifte, 122; (5) Jonathan L. Fried et al., eds., *Guatemala in Rebellion: Unfinished History* (New York: Grove Press, 1983), 78; (6) Stephen C. Schlesinger and Stephen Kinzer, *Bitter Fruit: The Untold Story of the American Coup in Guatemala* (Garden City, NY: Doubleday, 1982), 143–144.

leadership are fast slipping from Britain's competent but now very weak hands," read a U.S. State Department report. "These reins will be picked up either by the United States or by Russia." The United States was wedded to the notion — dating to the Wilson administration — that communism and capitalism were incompatible on the world stage. With Britain faltering, American officials saw little choice but to fill its shoes.

It did not take long for the reality of Britain's decline to resonate across the Atlantic. In February 1947, London informed Washington that it could no longer afford to support the anticommunists in the Greek civil war. Truman worried that a communist victory in Greece would lead to Soviet domination of the eastern Mediterranean and embolden Communist parties in France and Italy. In response, the president announced what became known as the **Truman Doctrine**. In a speech on March 12, he asserted an American responsibility "to support free peoples who are resisting attempted subjugation by armed minorities or by outside pressures." To that

Truman Doctrine
President Harry S. Truman's commitment to "support free peoples who are resisting attempted subjugation by armed minorities or by outside pressures." First applied to Greece and Turkey in 1947, it became the justification for U.S. intervention into several countries during the Cold War.

end, Truman proposed large-scale assistance for Greece and Turkey (then involved in a dispute with the Soviet Union over the Dardanelles, a strait connecting the Aegean Sea and the Sea of Marmara). "If we falter in our leadership, we may endanger the peace of the world," Truman declared (Thinking Like a Historian). Congress quickly approved Truman's request for $300 million in aid to Greece and $100 million for Turkey.

Soviet expansionism was but one part of a larger story. Europe was sliding into economic chaos. Already devastated by the war, in 1947 the continent suffered the worst winter in memory. People were starving, wages were stagnant, and the consumer market had collapsed. For both humanitarian and practical reasons, Truman's advisors believed something had to be done. A global depression might ensue if the European economy, the largest foreign market for American goods, did not recover. Worse, unemployed and dispirited Western Europeans might fill the ranks of the Communist Party, threatening political stability. Secretary of State George C. Marshall came up with a remarkable proposal: a massive infusion of American capital to rebuild the European economy. In a June 1947 speech, Marshall urged the nations of Europe to work out a comprehensive recovery program based on U.S. aid.

This pledge of financial assistance required approval by Congress, where the plan ran into opposition. Republicans castigated the **Marshall Plan** as a huge "international WPA." But in the midst of the congressional stalemate, on February 25, 1948, Stalin supported a communist-led coup in Czechoslovakia. Congress rallied and voted overwhelmingly to approve the Marshall Plan. Over the next four years, the United States contributed nearly $13 billion to a highly successful recovery effort that benefitted both Western Europe and the United States. European industrial production increased by 64 percent, and the appeal of Communist parties waned in the West. Markets for American goods grew stronger and fostered economic interdependence between Europe and the United States. Notably, however, the Marshall Plan intensified Cold War tensions. U.S. officials invited the Soviets to participate but insisted on restrictions that virtually guaranteed Stalin's refusal. An embittered Stalin rejected participation and ordered Soviet client states to do so as well.

Marshall Plan
Aid program begun in 1948 to help European economies recover from World War II.

East and West in the New Europe The flash point for a hot war remained Germany, the most important industrial economy and the key strategic nation in Europe. When no agreement could be reached with the Soviet Union to unify the four zones of occupation into a single state, the Western allies consolidated their three zones in 1947. They then prepared to establish an independent federal German republic. Marshall Plan funds would jump-start economic recovery. Some of those funds were slated for West Berlin, in hopes of making the city a capitalist showplace 100 miles inside the Soviet zone.

Stung by the West's intention to create a German republic, in June 1948 Stalin blockaded all traffic to West Berlin. Instead of yielding, as Stalin had expected, Truman and the British were resolute. "We are going to stay, period," Truman said plainly. Over the next year, American and British pilots improvised the Berlin Airlift, which flew 2.5 million tons of food and fuel into the Western zones of the city — nearly a ton for

The Berlin Airlift For 321 days U.S. planes like this one flew missions to bring food and other supplies to Berlin after the Soviet Union had blocked all surface routes into the former German capital. The blockade was finally lifted on May 12, 1949, after the Soviets conceded that it had been a failure. AP Photo.

each resident. General Lucius D. Clay, the American commander in Berlin, was nervous and on edge, "drawn as tight as a steel spring," according to U.S. officials. But after a prolonged stalemate, Stalin backed down: on May 12, 1949, he lifted the blockade. Until the Cuban missile crisis in 1962, the Berlin crisis was the closest the two sides came to actual war, and West Berlin became a symbol of resistance to communism.

The crisis in Berlin persuaded Western European nations to forge a collective security pact with the United States. In April 1949, for the first time since the end of the American Revolution, the United States entered into a peacetime military alliance, the **North Atlantic Treaty Organization (NATO)**. Under the NATO pact, twelve nations — Belgium, Canada, Denmark, France, Great Britain, Iceland, Italy, Luxembourg, the Netherlands, Norway, Portugal, and the United States — agreed that "an armed attack against one or more of them in Europe or North America shall be considered an attack against them all." In May 1949, those nations also agreed to the creation of the Federal Republic of Germany (West Germany), which eventually joined NATO in 1955. In response, the Soviet Union established the German Democratic Republic (East Germany); the Council for Mutual Economic Assistance (COMECON); and, in 1955, the **Warsaw Pact**, a military alliance for Eastern Europe that included Albania, Bulgaria, Czechoslovakia, East Germany, Hungary, Poland, Romania, and the Soviet Union. In these parallel steps, the two superpowers formalized the Cold War through a massive division of the continent.

North Atlantic Treaty Organization (NATO)
Military alliance formed in 1949 among the United States, Canada, and Western European nations to counter any possible Soviet threat.

Warsaw Pact
A military alliance established in Eastern Europe in 1955 to counter the NATO alliance; it included Albania, Bulgaria, Czechoslovakia, East Germany, Hungary, Poland, Romania, and the Soviet Union.

By the early 1950s, West and East were the stark markers of the new Europe. As Churchill had observed in 1946, the line dividing the two stretched "from Stettin in the Baltic to Trieste in the Adriatic," cutting off tens of millions of Eastern Europeans from the rest of the continent. Stalin's tactics had often been ruthless, but they were not without reason. The Soviet Union acted out of the sort of self-interest that had long defined powerful nations — ensuring a defensive perimeter of allies, seeking access to raw materials, and pressing the advantage that victory in war allowed.

NSC-68 Atomic developments, too, played a critical role in the emergence of the Cold War. As the sole nuclear power at the end of World War II, the United States entertained the possibility of international control of nuclear technology but did not wish to lose its advantage over the Soviet Union. When the American Bernard Baruch proposed United Nations oversight of atomic energy in 1946, for instance, the plan assured the United States of near-total control of the technology, which further increased Cold War tensions. America's brief tenure as sole nuclear power ended in September 1949, however, when the Soviet Union detonated an atomic bomb. Truman then turned to the U.S. National Security Council (NSC), established by the National Security Act of 1947, for a strategic reassessment.

In April 1950, the NSC delivered its report, known as **NSC-68**. Bristling with alarmist rhetoric, the document marked a decisive turning point in the U.S. approach to the Cold War. The report's authors described the Soviet Union not as a typical great power but as one with a "fanatic faith" that seeks to "impose its absolute authority." Going beyond even the stern language used by George Kennan, NSC-68 cast Soviet ambitions as nothing short of "the domination of the Eurasian landmass."

NSC-68
Top-secret government report of April 1950 warning that national survival in the face of Soviet communism required a massive military buildup.

To prevent that outcome, the report proposed "a bold and massive program of rebuilding the West's defensive potential to surpass that of the Soviet world" (America in Global Context). This included the development of a hydrogen bomb, a thermonuclear device that would be a thousand times more destructive than the atomic bombs dropped on Japan, as well as dramatic increases in conventional military forces. Critically, NSC-68 called for Americans to pay higher taxes to support the new military program and to accept whatever sacrifices were necessary to achieve national unity of purpose against the Soviet enemy. Many historians see the report as having "militarized" the American approach to the Cold War, which had to that point relied largely on economic measures such as aid to Greece and the Marshall Plan. Truman was reluctant to commit to a major defense buildup, fearing that it would overburden the national budget. But shortly after NSC-68 was completed, events in Asia led him to reverse course.

Containment in Asia

As with Germany, American officials believed at the conclusion of World War II that restoring Japan's economy, while limiting its military influence, would ensure prosperity and contain communism in East Asia. After dismantling Japan's military, American occupation forces under General Douglas MacArthur drafted a democratic constitution and paved the way for the restoration of Japanese sovereignty in 1951. Considering the scorched-earth war that had just ended, this was a remarkable achievement, thanks partly to the imperious MacArthur but mainly to the Japanese,

Arming for the Cold War

To fight the Cold War, the United States and the Soviet Union increased overall military spending and assembled massive arsenals of nuclear weapons.

TABLE 24.1

Worldwide Nuclear Stockpiles, 1945–1975

Country	1945	1955	1965	1975
United States	2	3,057	32,135	27,235
USSR	0	200	6,129	19,443
United Kingdom	0	10	310	350
France	0	0	32	188
China	0	0	5	185
Israel	0	0	0	20*

*Estimated

SOURCES: Adapted from *Bulletin of the Atomic Scientists*, National Resources Defense Council, and *Nuclear Weapons and Nonproliferation* (2007).

QUESTIONS FOR ANALYSIS

1. Do you see evidence of the effects of NSC-68 in this table? What kinds of changes did NSC-68 bring about?
2. In what ways does the data in this table suggest the emergence of two "superpowers" after World War II?

who embraced peace and accepted U.S. military protection. However, events on the mainland of Asia proved much more difficult for the United States to shape to its advantage.

Civil War in China A civil war had been raging in China since the 1930s as Communist forces led by Mao Zedong (Mao Tse-tung) fought Nationalist forces under Jiang Jieshi (Chiang Kai-shek). Fearing a Communist victory, between 1945 and 1949 the United States provided $2 billion to Jiang's army. Pressing Truman to "save" China, conservative Republican Ohio senator Robert A. Taft predicted that "the Far East is ultimately even more important to our future peace than is Europe." By 1949, Mao's forces held the advantage. Truman reasoned that to save Jiang, the United States would have to intervene militarily. Unwilling to do so, he cut off aid and left the Nationalists to their fate. The People's Republic of China was formally established under Mao on October 1, 1949, and the remnants of Jiang's forces fled to Taiwan.

Truman expected Mao to take an independent line, as the Communist leader Tito had just done in Yugoslavia. The new Chinese leader, however, aligned himself with the Soviet Union, partly out of fear that the United States would re-arm the

Communist China Chinese Communists carry placards with pictures of Joseph Stalin, premier of the Soviet Union and self-proclaimed leader of global communism. Under the leadership of General Mao Zedong, the Communist Party of China defeated its rivals in a civil war and founded the People's Republic of China in 1949. Mao's victory meant that from East Germany to the Pacific Ocean, much of the Eurasian landmass (including Eastern Europe, the Soviet Union, and China) was ruled by Communist governments. Library of Congress/Corbis/VCG via Getty Images.

Nationalists and invade the mainland. As attitudes hardened, many Americans viewed Mao's success as a defeat for the United States. The pro-Nationalist "China lobby" held Truman's State Department responsible for the "loss" of China. Sensitive to these charges, the Truman administration refused to recognize "Red China" and blocked China's admission to the United Nations. But the United States pointedly declined to guarantee Taiwan's independence, and in fact accepted the outcome on the mainland. (Since 1982, however, the United States has recognized Taiwanese sovereignty.)

The Korean War The United States took a stronger stance in Korea. Truman and Stalin had agreed at the close of World War II to occupy the Korean peninsula jointly, temporarily dividing the former Japanese colony at the 38th parallel. As tensions rose in Europe, the 38th parallel hardened into a permanent demarcation line. The Soviets supported a Communist government, led by Kim Il Sung, in North Korea; the United States backed a right-wing Nationalist, Syngman Rhee, in South Korea. The two sides had waged low-level war since 1945, and both leaders were spoiling for a more

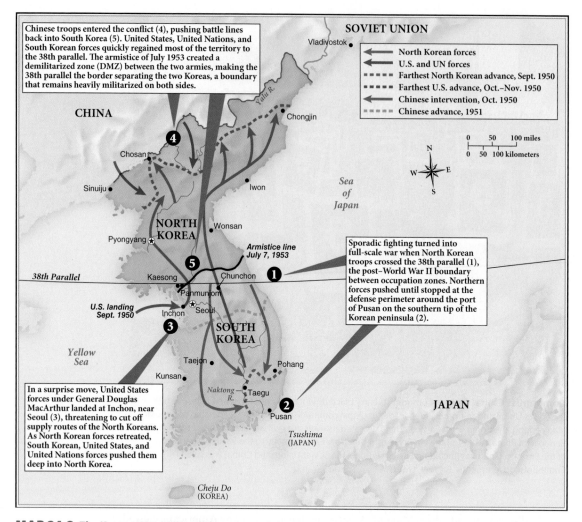

Chinese troops entered the conflict (4), pushing battle lines back into South Korea (5). United States, United Nations, and South Korean forces quickly regained most of the territory to the 38th parallel. The armistice of July 1953 created a demilitarized zone (DMZ) between the two armies, making the 38th parallel the border separating the two Koreas, a boundary that remains heavily militarized on both sides.

Sporadic fighting turned into full-scale war when North Korean troops crossed the 38th parallel (1), the post–World War II boundary between occupation zones. Northern forces pushed until stopped at the defense perimeter around the port of Pusan on the southern tip of the Korean peninsula (2).

In a surprise move, United States forces under General Douglas MacArthur landed at Inchon, near Seoul (3), threatening to cut off supply routes of the North Koreans. As North Korean forces retreated, South Korean, United States, and United Nations forces pushed them deep into North Korea.

MAP 24.2 The Korean War, 1950–1953

The Korean War, which the United Nations officially deemed a "police action," lasted three years and cost the lives of more than 36,000 U.S. troops. South and North Korean deaths were estimated at more than 900,000. Although hostilities ceased in 1953, the South Korean Military (with U.S. military assistance) and the North Korean Army continue to face each other across the demilitarized zone, more than sixty years later.

definitive fight. However, neither Kim nor Rhee could launch an all-out offensive without the backing of his sponsor. Washington repeatedly said no, and so did Moscow. But Kim continued to press Stalin to permit him to reunify the nation. Convinced by the North Koreans that victory would be swift, the Soviet leader finally relented in the late spring of 1950.

On June 25, 1950, the North Koreans launched a surprise attack across the 38th parallel (Map 24.2). Truman immediately asked the UN Security Council to authorize a "police action" against the invaders. The Soviet Union was boycotting the Security Council to protest China's exclusion from the United Nations and therefore could not veto the request. With the Security Council's approval of a "peacekeeping force," Truman ordered U.S. troops to Korea. The rapidly assembled UN army in Korea was overwhelmingly American, with General Douglas MacArthur in command. At first, the North Koreans held a distinct advantage, but MacArthur's surprise amphibious attack at Inchon gave the UN forces control of Seoul, the South Korean capital, and almost all the territory up to the 38th parallel.

The impetuous MacArthur then ordered his troops across the 38th parallel and led them all the way to the Chinese border at the Yalu River. It was a major blunder, certain to draw China into the war. Sure enough, a massive Chinese counterattack forced UN forces into headlong retreat back down the Korean peninsula. Then stalemate set in. With weak public support for the war in the United States, Truman and his advisors decided to work for a negotiated peace. MacArthur disagreed and denounced the Korean stalemate, declaring, "There is no substitute for victory." On April 11, 1951, Truman relieved MacArthur of his command. Truman's decision was highly unpopular, especially among conservative Republicans, but he had likely saved the nation from years of costly warfare with China.

Notwithstanding MacArthur's dismissal, the war dragged on for more than two years. An armistice in July 1953, pushed by the newly elected president, Dwight D. Eisenhower, left Korea divided at the original demarcation line. North Korea remained firmly allied with the Soviet Union; South Korea signed a mutual defense treaty with the United States. It had been the first major proxy war between the Soviet Union and United States, in which they took sides in a civil conflict without directly confronting one another militarily. It would not be the last.

The Korean War had far-reaching consequences. Truman's decision to commit troops without congressional approval set a precedent for future undeclared wars. His refusal to unleash atomic bombs, even when American forces were reeling under a massive Chinese attack, set ground rules for Cold War conflict. The war also expanded American involvement in Asia, transforming containment into a truly global policy. Finally, the Korean War ended Truman's resistance to a major military buildup (Map 24.3). Defense expenditures grew from $13 billion in 1950, roughly one-third of the federal budget, to $50 billion in 1953, nearly two-thirds of the budget. American foreign policy had become more global, more militarized, and more expensive. Even in times of peace, the United States now functioned in a state of permanent military mobilization.

The Munich Analogy Behind much of U.S. foreign policy in the first two decades of the Cold War lay the memory of appeasement (Chapter 23). The generation of politicians and officials who designed the containment strategy had come of age in the era of Munich, the conference in 1938 at which the Western democracies had appeased Hitler by offering him part of Czechoslovakia, paving the road to World War II. Applying the lessons of Munich, American presidents believed that "appeasing" Stalin (and subsequent Soviet rulers Nikita Khrushchev and Leonid Brezhnev) would have the same result: wider war. Thus in Germany, Greece, and Korea, and later in Iran, Guatemala, and Vietnam, the United States staunchly resisted the Soviets — or what it perceived as Soviet influence. The Munich analogy strengthened the U.S. position in a number of strategic conflicts, particularly over the fate of

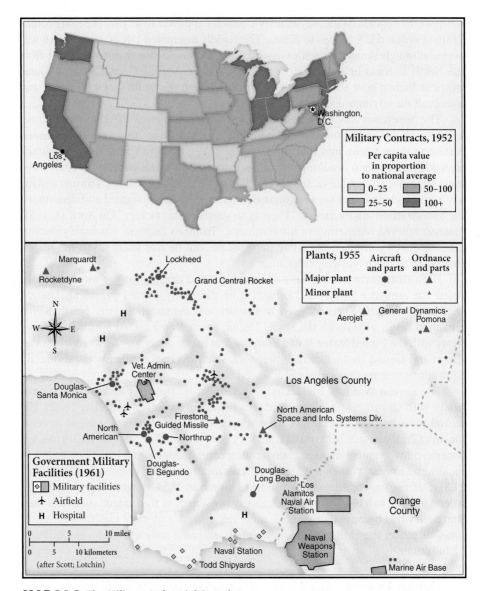

MAP 24.3 The Military-Industrial Complex

Defense spending gave a big boost to the Cold War economy, but, as the upper map suggests, the benefits were by no means equally distributed. The big winners were the Middle Atlantic states, the industrialized Upper Midwest, Washington State (with its aircraft and nuclear plants), and California. The epicenter of California's military-industrial complex was Los Angeles, which, as is evident in the lower map, was studded with military facilities and major defense contractors like Douglas Aircraft, Lockheed, and General Dynamics. There was work aplenty for engineers and rocket scientists.

Germany. But it also drew Americans into armed conflicts — and convinced them to support repressive, right-wing regimes — that compromised, as much as supported, stated American principles.

IN YOUR OWN WORDS What primary factors caused the Cold War?

Cold War Liberalism

As president, Harry Truman cast himself in the mold of his predecessor, Franklin Roosevelt, and hoped to seize the possibilities afforded by victory in World War II to expand the New Deal at home. But the crises in postwar Europe and Asia, combined with the swift rise of anticommunism in the United States, forced him to take a different path. In the end, Truman went down in history as a Cold Warrior rather than a New Dealer. The Cold War consensus that he ultimately embraced — the notion that resisting communism at home and abroad represented America's most important postwar objective — shaped the nation's life and politics for decades to come.

Truman and the End of Reform

Truman and the Democratic Party of the late 1940s and early 1950s forged what historians call **Cold War liberalism**. They preserved the core programs of the New Deal welfare state, developed the containment policy to oppose Soviet influence throughout the world, and fought so-called subversives at home. But there would be no second act for the New Deal. The Democrats adopted this combination of moderate liberal policies and anticommunism — Cold War liberalism — partly by choice and partly out of necessity. A few high-level espionage scandals and the Communist victories in Eastern Europe and China reenergized the Republican Party, which forced Truman and the Democrats to retreat to what historian Arthur Schlesinger called the "vital center" of American politics. However, Americans on both the progressive left and the conservative right accepted this development only reluctantly. Cold War liberalism was a practical centrist program for a turbulent era. But it would not last.

Organized labor remained a key force in the Democratic Party and played a central role in championing Cold War liberalism. Stronger than ever, union membership swelled to more than 14 million by 1945. Determined to make up for their wartime sacrifices, unionized workers made aggressive demands and mounted major strikes in the automobile, steel, and coal industries after the war, as they had after World War I. Republicans responded. They gained control of the House in a sweeping repudiation of Democrats in 1946 and promptly passed — over Truman's veto — the **Taft-Hartley Act** (1947), an overhaul of the 1935 National Labor Relations Act.

Taft-Hartley brought changes in procedures and language that, over time, weakened the right of workers to organize and engage in collective bargaining. Unions especially disliked Section 14b, which allowed states to pass "right-to-work" laws prohibiting the union shop. Additionally, the law forced unions to purge communists, who had been among the most successful labor organizers in the 1930s, from their ranks. Trade unions would continue to support the Democratic Party, but the labor movement would not crack the largely non-union South and would not penetrate the many American industries that remained unorganized. In that sense, Taft-Hartley effectively "contained" the labor movement.

The 1948 Election Democrats would have dumped Truman in 1948 had they found a better candidate. But the party fell into disarray. The left wing split off and formed the Progressive Party, nominating Henry A. Wallace, an avid New Dealer whom Truman had fired as secretary of commerce in 1946 because Wallace opposed America's actions in the

Cold War liberalism
A combination of moderate liberal policies that preserved the programs of the New Deal welfare state and forthright anticommunism that vilified the Soviet Union abroad and radicalism at home. Adopted by President Truman and the Democratic Party during the late 1940s and early 1950s.

Taft-Hartley Act
Law passed by the Republican-controlled Congress in 1947 that overhauled the 1935 National Labor Relations Act, placing restrictions on organized labor that made it more difficult for unions to organize workers.

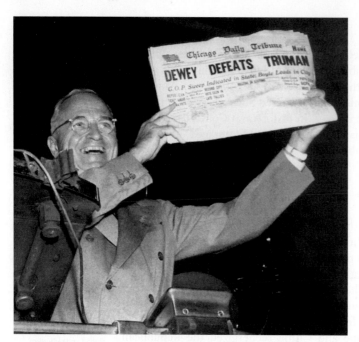

Truman Triumphant   In one of the most famous photographs in U.S. political history, Harry S. Truman gloats over an erroneous headline in the November 3 *Chicago Daily Tribune*. Pollsters had predicted an easy victory for Thomas E. Dewey. Their polling techniques, however, missed the dramatic surge in support for Truman during the last days of the campaign.   Bettmann/ Getty Images.

Cold War. A right-wing challenge came from the South. When northern liberals such as Mayor Hubert H. Humphrey of Minneapolis pushed through a strong civil rights platform at the Democratic convention, the southern delegations bolted and, calling themselves Dixiecrats, nominated for president South Carolina governor Strom Thurmond, an ardent supporter of racial segregation. The Republicans meanwhile renominated Thomas E. Dewey, the politically moderate governor of New York who had run a strong campaign against FDR in 1944.

Truman surprised everyone. He launched a strenuous cross-country speaking tour and hammered away at the Republicans for opposing progressive legislation and, in general, for running a "do-nothing" Congress. By combining these issues with attacks on the Soviet menace abroad, Truman began to salvage his troubled campaign. At his rallies, enthusiastic listeners shouted, "Give 'em hell, Harry!" Truman won, receiving 49.6 percent of the vote to Dewey's 45.1 percent (Map 24.4).

This remarkable election foreshadowed coming political turmoil. Truman occupied the center of FDR's sprawling New Deal coalition. On his left were progressives, civil rights advocates, and peace activists critical of the Cold War. On his right were segregationist southerners, who opposed civil rights and were allied with Republicans on many economic and foreign policy issues. In 1948, Truman performed a delicate balancing act, largely retaining the support of Jewish and Catholic voters in the big cities, black voters in the North, and union voters across the country. But Thurmond's strong showing — he carried four states in the Deep South — demonstrated the fragility of the Democratic coalition and prefigured the revolt of the party's southern wing in the 1960s. As he tried to manage contending forces in his own party, Truman faced mounting pressure from Republicans to denounce radicals at home and to take a tough stand against the Soviet Union.

Fair Deal
The domestic policy agenda announced by President Harry S. Truman in 1949. Including civil rights, health care, and education reform, Truman's initiative was only partially successful in Congress.

The Fair Deal   Despite having to perform a balancing act, Truman and progressive Democrats forged ahead. In 1949, reaching ambitiously to extend the New Deal, Truman proposed the **Fair Deal**: national health insurance, civil rights legislation, aid to education, a housing program, expansion of Social Security, a higher minimum wage, and a new agricultural program. In its attention to civil rights, the Fair Deal reflected the growing influence of African Americans in the Democratic Party.

Congress, however, remained a huge stumbling block, and the Fair Deal fared poorly. The same conservative coalition that had blocked Roosevelt's initiatives in his second term stymied Truman's as well. Cold War pressure shaped political arguments about domestic social programs, while the nation's growing paranoia over internal subversion weakened support for bold extensions of the welfare state. Truman's proposal for national health insurance, for instance, was a popular idea, with strong backing from organized labor. But it was denounced as "socialized medicine" by the American Medical Association and the insurance industry. In the end, the Fair Deal's only significant breakthrough, other than improvements to the minimum wage and Social Security, was the National Housing Act of 1949, which authorized the construction of 810,000 low-income units.

Red Scare: The Hunt for Communists

Cold War liberalism was premised on the grave domestic threat posed, many believed, by Communists and Communist sympathizers. Was there significant Soviet penetration of the American government? Records opened after the 1991 disintegration of the Soviet Union, including the Venona Papers made available in 1995 by the National Security Agency, indicate that there was. Among American suppliers of information to Moscow were FDR's assistant secretary of the treasury, Harry Dexter White; FDR's administrative aide Laughlin Currie; a strategically placed midlevel group in the State Department; key scientists and technicians working on the Manhattan Project; and several hundred more, some identified only by code name, working in a range of government departments and agencies.

How are we to explain this? Many of these enlistees in the Soviet cause had been bright young New Dealers in the mid-1930s, when the Soviet-backed Popular Front suggested that the lines separating liberalism, progressivism, and communism were permeable (Chapter 23). At that time, the United States was not at war and never expected to be. And when war did come, the Soviet Union was an American ally. For critics of the informants, however, there remained the time between the Nazi-Soviet Pact and the German invasion of the Soviet Union, a nearly two-year period during which cooperation with the Soviet Union could be seen in a less positive light. Moreover, passing secrets to another country, even a wartime ally, was simply indefensible to many Americans — particularly when it came to atomic secrets. The lines between U.S. and Soviet interests blurred for some; for others, they remained clear and definite.

Candidate	Electoral Vote	Popular Vote	Percent of Popular Vote
Harry S. Truman (Democrat)	303	24,105,182	49.6
Thomas E. Dewey (Republican)	189	21,970,065	45.1
J. Strom Thurmond (States' Rights)	39	1,169,063	2.5
Henry A. Wallace (Progressive)	—	1,157,326	2.5

MAP 24.4 The Presidential Election of 1948
Truman's electoral strategy in 1948 was to concentrate his campaign in areas where the Democrats had their greatest strength. In an election with a low turnout, Truman held on to enough support from Roosevelt's New Deal coalition of blacks, union members, and farmers to defeat Dewey by more than 2 million votes.

After World War II, however, most suppliers of information to the Soviets apparently ceased spying. For one thing, the professional apparatus of Soviet spying in the United States was disrupted by American counterintelligence work. For another, most of the well-connected amateur spies moved on to other careers. Historians have thus developed a healthy skepticism that there was much Soviet espionage in the United States after 1947, but this was not how many Americans saw it at the time. Legitimate suspicions and real fears, along with political opportunism, combined to fuel the national Red Scare, which was longer and more far-reaching than the one that followed World War I (Chapter 21).

Loyalty-Security Program   To insulate his administration against charges of Communist infiltration, Truman issued Executive Order 9835 on March 21, 1947, which created the **Loyalty-Security Program**. The order permitted officials to investigate any employee of the federal government (some 2.5 million people) for "subversive" activities. Representing a profound centralization of power, the order sent shock waves through every federal agency. Truman intended the order to apply principally to actions designed to harm the United States (sabotage, treason, etc.), but it was broad enough to allow anyone to be accused of subversion for the slightest reason — for marching in a Communist-led demonstration in the 1930s, for instance, or signing a petition endorsing public housing. Along with suspected political subversives, more than a thousand gay men and lesbians were dismissed from federal employment in the 1950s, victims of an obsessive search for anyone deemed "unfit" for government work.

Following Truman's lead, many state and local governments, universities, political organizations, churches, and businesses undertook their own antisubversion campaigns, which often included loyalty oaths. In the labor movement, charges of Communist domination led to the expulsion of a number of unions by the Congress of Industrial Organizations (CIO) in 1949. Civil rights organizations such as the National Association for the Advancement of Colored People (NAACP) and the National Urban League also expelled Communists and "fellow travelers," or Communist sympathizers. Thus the Red Scare spread from the federal government to the farthest reaches of American organizational, economic, and cultural life.

HUAC   The Truman administration had legitimized the vague and malleable concept of "disloyalty." Others proved willing to stretch the concept even further, beginning with the **House Un-American Activities Committee (HUAC)**, which Congressman Martin Dies of Texas and other conservatives had launched in 1938. In 1947, HUAC helped spark the Red Scare by holding widely publicized hearings on alleged Communist infiltration in the movie industry. A group of writers and directors dubbed the Hollywood Ten went to jail for contempt of Congress after they refused to testify about their past associations. Hundreds of other actors, directors, and writers whose names had been mentioned in the HUAC investigation were unable to get work, victims of an unacknowledged but very real blacklist honored by industry executives.

Other HUAC investigations had greater legitimacy. One that intensified the anticommunist crusade in 1948 involved Alger Hiss, a former New Dealer and State Department official who had accompanied Franklin Roosevelt to Yalta. A former

Loyalty-Security Program
A program created in 1947 by President Truman that permitted officials to investigate any employee of the federal government for "subversive" activities.

House Un-American Activities Committee (HUAC)
Congressional committee especially prominent during the early years of the Cold War that investigated Americans who might be disloyal to the government or might have associated with communists or other radicals.

Communist, Whitaker Chambers, claimed that Hiss was a member of a secret Communist cell operating in the government and had passed him classified documents in the 1930s. Hiss denied the allegations, but California Republican congressman Richard Nixon doggedly pursued the case against him. In early 1950, Hiss was found guilty not of spying but of lying to Congress about his Communist affiliations and was sentenced to five years in federal prison. Many Americans doubted at the time that Hiss was a spy. But the Venona transcripts in the 1990s corroborated a great deal of Chambers's testimony, and though no definitive proof has emerged, many historians now recognize the strong circumstantial evidence against Hiss.

McCarthyism The meteoric career of Senator Joseph McCarthy of Wisconsin marked first the apex and then the finale of the Red Scare. In February 1950, McCarthy delivered a bombshell during a speech in Wheeling, West Virginia: "I have here in my hand a list of 205 . . . a list of names that were made known to the Secretary of State as being members of the Communist Party and who nevertheless are still working and shaping policy in the State Department." McCarthy later reduced his numbers, gave different figures in different speeches, and never released any names or proof. But he had gained the attention he sought.

For the next four years, from his position as chair of the Senate Permanent Subcommittee on Investigations, McCarthy waged a virulent smear campaign. Critics who disagreed with him exposed themselves to charges of being "soft" on communism. Truman called McCarthy's charges "slander, lies, [and] character assassination" but could do nothing to curb him. Republicans, for their part, refrained from publicly challenging their most outspoken senator and, on the whole, were content to reap the political benefits. McCarthy's charges almost always targeted Democrats.

Despite McCarthy's failure to identify a single Communist in government, several national developments gave his charges credibility with the public. The dramatic 1951 espionage trial of Julius and Ethel Rosenberg, followed around the world, fueled McCarthy's allegations. Convicted of passing atomic secrets to the Soviet Union, the Rosenbergs were executed in 1953. As in the Hiss case, documents released decades later provided some evidence of Julius Rosenberg's guilt, though not Ethel's. Their execution nevertheless remains controversial — in part because some felt that anti-Semitism played a role in their sentencing. Also fueling McCarthy's charges were a series of trials of American Communists between 1949 and 1955 for violation of the 1940 Smith Act, which prohibited Americans from advocating the violent overthrow of the government. Though civil libertarians and two Supreme Court justices vigorously objected, dozens of Communist Party members were convicted. McCarthy was not involved in either the Rosenberg trial or the Smith Act convictions, but these sensational events gave his wild charges some credence.

In early 1954, McCarthy overreached by launching an investigation into subversive activities in the U.S. Army. When lengthy hearings — the first of their kind broadcast on the new medium of television — brought McCarthy's tactics into the nation's living rooms, support for him plummeted. In December 1954, the Senate voted 67 to 22 to censure McCarthy for unbecoming conduct. He died from an alcohol-related illness three years later at the age of forty-eight, his name forever attached to a period of political repression of which he was only the most flagrant manifestation.

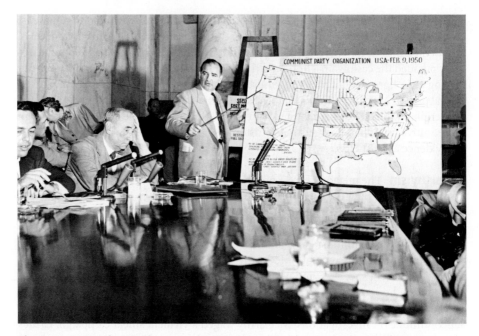

The Army-McCarthy Hearings These 1954 hearings contributed to the downfall of Senator Joseph McCarthy by exposing his reckless accusations and bullying tactics to the huge television audience that tuned in each day. Some of the most heated exchanges took place between McCarthy (center) and Joseph Welch (seated, left), the lawyer representing the army. When the gentlemanly Welch finally asked, "Have you no sense of decency sir, at long last? Have you left no sense of decency?" he fatally punctured McCarthy's armor. The audience broke into applause because someone had finally had the courage to stand up to the senator from Wisconsin. Bettmann/Getty Images.

The Politics of Cold War Liberalism

As election day 1952 approached, the nation was embroiled in the tense Cold War with the Soviet Union and fighting a "hot" war in Korea. Though Americans gave the Republicans victory, radical change was not in the offing. The new president, Dwight D. Eisenhower, embraced what his supporters called modern Republicanism, an updated GOP approach that aimed at moderating, not dismantling, the New Deal. Eisenhower Republicans were as much successors of FDR as of Herbert Hoover. Foreign policy revealed a similar continuity. Like their predecessors, Republicans saw the world in Cold War polarities.

Despite Eisenhower's popularity as the former commander of Allied forces in Europe, divisions in the party persisted. Conservative party activists preferred Robert A. Taft of Ohio, the Republican leader in the Senate who was an outspoken opponent of the New Deal. As a close friend of business, he opposed labor unions. Though an ardent anticommunist, the isolationist-minded Taft criticized Truman's aggressive containment policy and opposed U.S. participation in NATO. Taft ran for president three times, and though he was never the Republican nominee, he won the loyalty of conservative Americans who saw the welfare state as wasteful spending and international affairs as dangerous foreign entanglements.

In contrast, moderate Republicans looked to Eisenhower and even to more liberal-minded party leaders like Nelson Rockefeller, who supported international initiatives such as the Marshall Plan and NATO and were willing to tolerate labor unions and the welfare state. Eisenhower was a man without a political past. Believing that democracy required the military to stand aside, he had never voted. Rockefeller, the scion of one of the richest families in America, was a Cold War internationalist. He served in a variety of capacities under Eisenhower, including as an advisor on foreign affairs. Having made his political name, Rockefeller was elected the governor of New York in 1959 and became the de facto leader of the liberal wing of the Republican Party.

For eight years, between 1952 and 1960, Eisenhower steered a precarious course from the middle of the party, with conservative Taft Republicans on one side and liberal Rockefeller Republicans on the other. His popularity temporarily kept the two sides at bay, though more ardent conservatives considered him a closet New Dealer. "Ike," as he was widely known, proved willing to work with the mostly Democratic-controlled Congresses of those years. Eisenhower signed bills increasing federal outlays for veterans' benefits, housing, highway construction (Chapter 25), and Social Security, and he increased the minimum wage from 75 cents an hour to $1. Like Truman, Eisenhower accepted some government responsibility for the economic security of individuals, part of a broad consensus in American politics in these years.

America Under Eisenhower   The global power realities that had called forth containment guided Eisenhower's foreign policy. New developments, however, altered the tone of the Cold War. Stalin's death in March 1953 precipitated an intraparty struggle in the Soviet Union that lasted until 1956, when Nikita Khrushchev emerged as Stalin's successor. Khrushchev soon startled communists around the world by denouncing Stalin and detailing his crimes and blunders. He also surprised many Americans by calling for "peaceful coexistence" with the West. But the new Soviet leader had his limits, and when Hungarians rose up in 1956 to demand independence from Moscow, Khrushchev crushed the incipient revolution.

With no end to the Cold War in sight, Eisenhower focused on limiting the cost of containment. The president hoped to economize by relying on a nuclear arsenal and deemphasizing expensive conventional forces. Under this **"New Look"** defense policy, the Eisenhower administration stepped up production of the hydrogen bomb and developed long-range bombing capabilities. The Soviets, however, matched the United States weapon for weapon. By 1958, both nations had intercontinental ballistic missiles. When an American nuclear submarine launched an atomic-tipped Polaris missile in 1960, Soviet engineers raced to produce an equivalent weapon. This arms race was another critical feature of the Cold War. American officials believed the best deterrent to Soviet aggression was the threat of an all-out nuclear response by the United States, which was dubbed "massive retaliation" by Secretary of State Dulles.

"New Look"
The defense policy of the Eisenhower administration that stepped up production of the hydrogen bomb and developed long-range bombing capabilities.

Although confident in the international arena, Eisenhower started out as a novice in domestic affairs. Doing his best to set a less confrontational tone after the rancorous Truman years, he was reluctant to speak out against Joe McCarthy, and he was not a leader on civil rights. Democrats meanwhile maintained a strong presence in Congress but proved weak in presidential elections in the 1950s. In the two presidential contests of the decade, 1952 and 1956, Eisenhower defeated the admired but politically inef-fectual liberal Adlai Stevenson. In the 1952 election, Stevenson was hampered by the unpopularity of the Truman administration. The deadlocked Korean War and a series of scandals that Republicans dubbed "the mess in Washington" combined to give the war-hero general an easy victory. In 1956, Ike won an even more impressive victory over Stevenson, an eloquent and sophisticated spokesman for liberalism but no match for Eisenhower's popularity with the public.

During Eisenhower's presidency, new political forces on both the right and the left had begun to stir. But they had not yet fully transformed the party system itself. Particularly at the national level, Democrats and Republicans seemed in broad agree-ment about the realities of the Cold War and the demands of a modern, industrial economy and welfare state. Indeed, respected commentators in the 1950s declared "the end of ideology" and wondered if the great political clashes that had wracked the 1930s were gone forever. Below the apparent calm of national party politics, however, lay profound differences among Americans over the direction of the nation. Those differences would starkly divide the country in the 1960s and bring an end to the brief and fragile Cold War consensus (Chapters 26 and 27).

> **IN YOUR OWN WORDS** What were the components of Cold War liberalism, and why did the Democratic Party embrace them?

Containment in the Postcolonial World

As the Cold War took shape, the world scene was changing at a furious pace. New nations were emerging across Asia, Africa, and the Middle East, created in the wake of successful anticolonial movements whose origins dated to before World War II. Between 1947 and 1962, the British, French, Dutch, and Belgian empires all but disintegrated in a momentous collapse of European global power. FDR had favored the idea of national self-determination, often to the fury of his British and French allies. He expected emerging democracies to be new partners in an American-led, free-market world system. But colonial revolts produced many independent- or socialist-minded regimes in the so-called Third World, as well. *Third World* was a term that came into usage after World War II to describe developing or ex-colonial nations in Asia, Africa, Latin America, and the Middle East that were not aligned with the Western capitalist countries led by the United States or the socialist states of Eastern Europe led by the Soviet Union.

The Cold War and Colonial Independence

Insisting that all nations had to choose sides in the Cold War, the United States drew as many countries as possible into collective security agreements, with the NATO alli-ance in Europe as a model. Secretary of State John Foster Dulles orchestrated the cre-ation of the Southeast Asia Treaty Organization (SEATO), which in 1954 linked the United States and its major European allies with Australia, New Zealand, Pakistan, the Philippines, and Thailand. An extensive system of defense alliances eventually tied the United States to more than forty other countries (Map 24.5). The United States also

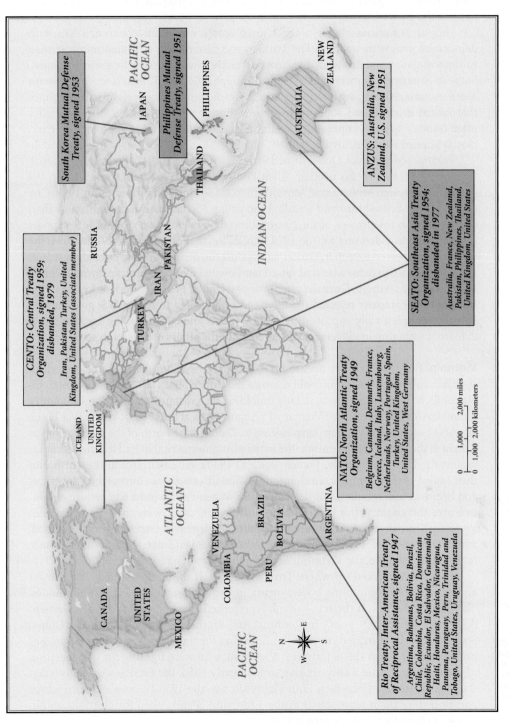

MAP 24.5 American Global Defense Treaties in the Cold War Era

The advent of the Cold War led to a major shift in American foreign policy — the signing of mutual defense treaties. Dating back to George Washington's call "to steer clear of permanent alliances with any portion of the foreign world," the United States had avoided treaty obligations that entailed the defense of other nations. As late as 1919, the U.S. Senate had rejected the principle of "collective security," the centerpiece of the League of Nations established by the Treaty of Versailles that ended World War I. But after World War II, in response to fears of Soviet global expansion, the United States entered defense alliances with much of the non-Communist world.

The following labels appear on the map:

South Korea Mutual Defense Treaty, signed 1953

Philippines Mutual Defense Treaty, signed 1951

ANZUS: Australia, New Zealand, U.S. signed 1951

CENTO: Central Treaty Organization, signed 1959; disbanded, 1979
Iran, Pakistan, Turkey, United Kingdom, United States (associate member)

SEATO: Southeast Asia Treaty Organization, signed 1954; disbanded in 1977
Australia, France, New Zealand, Pakistan, Philippines, Thailand, United Kingdom, United States

NATO: North Atlantic Treaty Organization, signed 1949
Belgium, Canada, Denmark, France, Greece, Iceland, Italy, Luxembourg, Netherlands, Norway, Portugal, Spain, Turkey, United Kingdom, United States, West Germany

Rio Treaty: Inter-American Treaty of Reciprocal Assistance, signed 1947
Argentina, Bahamas, Bolivia, Brazil, Chile, Colombia, Costa Rica, Dominican Republic, Ecuador, El Salvador, Guatemala, Haiti, Honduras, Mexico, Nicaragua, Panama, Paraguay, Peru, Trinidad and Tobago, United States, Uruguay, Venezuela

sponsored a strategically instrumental alliance between Iraq and Iran, on the southern flank of the Soviet Union.

Despite American rhetoric, the United States was often concerned less with democracy than with stability. The Truman and Eisenhower administrations tended to support governments, no matter how repressive, that were overtly anticommunist. Some of America's staunchest allies — the Philippines, South Korea, Iran, Cuba, South Vietnam, and Nicaragua — were governed by dictatorships or right-wing regimes that lacked broad-based support. Moreover, Eisenhower's secretary of state Dulles often resorted to covert operations against governments that, in his opinion, were too closely aligned with the Soviets.

For these covert tasks, Dulles turned to the newly created (1947) Central Intelligence Agency (CIA), run by his brother, Allen Dulles. When Iran's democratically elected nationalist premier, Mohammad Mossadegh, seized British oil properties in 1953, CIA agents helped depose him and installed the young Mohammad Reza Pahlavi as shah of Iran. Iranian resentment of the coup, followed by twenty-five years of U.S. support for the shah, provided fuel for the 1979 Iranian Revolution (Chapter 29). In 1954, the CIA also engineered a coup in Guatemala against the democratically elected president, Jacobo Arbenz Guzmán, who had seized land owned by the American-owned United Fruit Company. Arbenz Guzmán offered to pay United Fruit the declared value of the land, but the company rejected the offer and sought help from the U.S. government. Eisenhower specifically approved those CIA efforts and expanded the agency's mandate from gathering intelligence to intervening in the affairs of sovereign states.

Vietnam But when covert operations failed or proved impractical, the American approach to emerging nations could entangle the United States in deeper, more intractable conflicts. One example was already unfolding on a distant stage, in a small country unknown to most Americans: Vietnam. In August 1945, at the close of World War II, the Japanese occupiers of Vietnam surrendered to China in the north of the country and to Britain in the south. The Vietminh, the nationalist movement that had led the resistance against the Japanese (and the French, prior to 1940), seized control in the north. But their leader, Ho Chi Minh, was a Communist, and this single fact outweighed American and British commitment to self-determination. When France moved to restore its control over the country, the United States and Britain sided with their European ally. President Truman rejected Ho's plea to support the Vietnamese struggle for nationhood, and France rejected Ho's offer of a negotiated independence. Shortly after France returned, in late 1946, the Vietminh resumed their war of national liberation.

Eisenhower picked up where Truman left off. If the French failed, Eisenhower argued, all non-Communist governments in the region would fall like dominoes. This so-called **domino theory** — which represented an extension of the containment doctrine — guided U.S. policy in Southeast Asia for the next twenty years. The United States eventually provided most of the financing for the French war, but money was not enough to defeat the determined Vietminh, who were fighting for the liberation of their country. After a fifty-six-day siege in early 1954, the French were defeated at the huge fortress of Dien Bien Phu. The result was the 1954 Geneva Accords, which partitioned Vietnam temporarily at the 17th parallel and called for elections within two years to unify the strife-torn nation.

domino theory
President Eisenhower's theory of containment, which warned that the fall of a non-Communist government to communism in Southeast Asia would trigger the spread of communism to neighboring countries.

The United States rejected the Geneva Accords and set about undermining them. With the help of the CIA, a pro-American government took power in South Vietnam in June 1954. Ngo Dinh Diem, an anticommunist Catholic living in exile in the United States, returned to Vietnam as premier. The next year, in a rigged election, Diem became president of an independent South Vietnam. Facing certain defeat by the popular Ho Chi Minh, Diem called off the scheduled reunification elections. The Eisenhower administration propped up Diem with an average of $200 million a year in aid and a contingent of 675 American military advisors. This support was just the beginning.

The Middle East If Vietnam was still of minor concern, the same could not be said of the Middle East, an area rich in oil and political complexity. The most volatile area was Palestine, populated by Arabs but also historically the ancient land of Israel and coveted by the Zionist movement as a Jewish national homeland. After World War II, many survivors of the Nazi extermination camps resettled in Palestine, which was still controlled by Britain under a World War I mandate. On November 29, 1947, the UN General Assembly voted to partition Palestine between Jewish and Arab sectors. When the British mandate ended in 1948, Palestinian leaders rejected the partition as a violation of their right to self-determination. When Zionist leaders proclaimed the state of Israel, a coalition of Arab nations known as the Arab League invaded, but Israel survived. Many Palestinians fled or were driven from their homes during the fighting. The Arab defeat left these people permanently stranded in refugee camps. President Truman recognized the new state immediately, which won him crucial support from Jewish voters in the 1948 election but alienated the Arab world.

Southeast of Palestine, Egypt began to assert its presence in the region. Having gained independence from Britain several decades earlier, Egypt remained a monarchy until 1952, when Gamal Abdel Nasser led a military coup that established a constitutional republic. Caught between the Soviet Union and the United States, Nasser sought an independent route: a pan-Arab socialism designed to end the Middle East's colonial relationship with the West. When negotiations with the United States over Nasser's plan to build a massive hydroelectric dam on the Nile broke down in 1956, he nationalized the Suez Canal, which was the lifeline for Western Europe's oil. Britain and France, in alliance with Israel, attacked Egypt and seized the canal. Concerned that the invasion would encourage Egypt to turn to the Soviets for help, Eisenhower urged France and Britain to pull back and applied additional pressure through the UN General Assembly. When the Western nations backed down, however, Egypt reclaimed the Suez Canal and built the Aswan Dam on the Nile with Soviet support. Eisenhower had likely avoided a larger war, but the West lost a potential ally in Nasser.

In early 1957, concerned about Soviet influence in the Middle East, the president announced the **Eisenhower Doctrine**, which stated that American forces would assist any nation in the region that required aid "against overt armed aggression from any nation controlled by International Communism." Invoking the doctrine later that year, Eisenhower helped King Hussein of Jordan put down a Nasser-backed revolt and propped up a pro-American government in Lebanon. The Eisenhower Doctrine was further evidence that the United States had extended the global reach of containment, in this instance accentuated by the strategic objective of protecting the West's access to steady supplies of oil.

Eisenhower Doctrine
President Eisenhower's 1957 declaration that the United States would actively combat communism in the Middle East.

John F. Kennedy and the Cold War

Charisma, style, and personality — these, more than platforms and issues, defined a new brand of politics in the early 1960s. This was John F. Kennedy's natural environment. Kennedy, a Harvard alumnus, World War II hero, and senator from Massachusetts, had inherited his love of politics from his grandfathers — colorful, and often ruthless, Irish Catholic politicians in Boston. Ambitious and deeply aware of style, the forty-three-year-old Kennedy made use of his many advantages to become, as novelist Norman Mailer put it, "our leading man." His one disadvantage — that he was Catholic in a country that had never elected a Catholic president — he masterfully neutralized. And thanks to both media advisors and his youthful attractiveness, Kennedy projected a superb television image.

At heart, Kennedy was a Cold Warrior who had come of age politically in the era of Munich, Yalta, and McCarthyism. He projected an air of idealism, but his years in the Senate (1953–1960) had proved him to be a conventional Cold War politician. Once elected president, Kennedy would shape the nation's foreign policy by drawing both on his ingenuity and on old-style Cold War power politics.

The Election of 1960 and the New Frontier Kennedy's Republican opponent in the 1960 presidential election, Eisenhower's vice president, Richard Nixon, was a seasoned politician and Cold Warrior himself. The great innovation of the 1960 campaign was a series of four nationally televised debates. Nixon, less photogenic than Kennedy, looked sallow and unshaven under the intense studio lights. Voters who heard the first debate on the radio concluded that Nixon had won, but those who viewed it on television favored Kennedy. Despite the edge Kennedy enjoyed in the debates, he won only the narrowest of electoral victories, receiving 49.7 percent of the popular vote to Nixon's 49.5 percent. Kennedy attracted Catholics, African Americans, and the labor vote; his vice-presidential running mate, Texas senator Lyndon Baines Johnson, helped bring in southern Democrats. Yet only 120,000 votes separated the two candidates, and a shift of a few thousand votes in key states would have reversed the outcome.

Kennedy brought to Washington a cadre of young, ambitious newcomers, including Robert McNamara, a renowned systems analyst and former head of Ford Motor Company, as secretary of defense. A host of trusted advisors and academics flocked to Washington to join the New Frontier — Kennedy's term for the challenges the country

The Kennedy Magnetism John F. Kennedy, the 1960 Democratic candidate for president, used his youth and personality (and those of his equally personable and stylish wife) to attract voters. Here the Massachusetts senator draws an enthusiastic crowd on a campaign stop in Elgin, Illinois. AP Photo.

faced. Included on the team as attorney general was Kennedy's younger brother Robert, who had made a name as a hard-hitting investigator of organized crime. Relying on an old American trope, Kennedy's New Frontier suggested masculine toughness and adventurism and encouraged Americans to again think of themselves as exploring uncharted terrain. That terrain proved treacherous, however, as the new administration immediately faced a crisis.

Crises in Cuba and Berlin In January 1961, the Soviet Union announced that it intended to support "wars of national liberation" wherever in the world they occurred. Kennedy took Soviet premier Khrushchev at his word, especially regarding Cuba, where in 1959 Fidel Castro had overthrown the right-wing dictator Fulgencio Batista and declared a revolution. Determined to keep Cuba out of the Soviet orbit, Kennedy followed through on Eisenhower administration plans to dispatch Cuban exiles to launch an anti-Castro uprising. The invaders, trained by the CIA, were ill-prepared for their task. On landing at Cuba's **Bay of Pigs** on April 17, 1961, the force of 1,400 was crushed by Castro's troops. Kennedy prudently rejected CIA pleas for a U.S. air strike. Accepting defeat, Kennedy went before the American people and took full responsibility for the fiasco (Map 24.6).

> **Bay of Pigs**
> A failed U.S.-sponsored invasion of Cuba in 1961 by anti-Castro forces who planned to overthrow Fidel Castro's government.

Already strained by the Bay of Pigs incident, U.S.-Soviet relations deteriorated further in June 1961 when Khrushchev stopped movement between Communist-controlled East Berlin and the city's Western sector. Kennedy responded by dispatching 40,000 more troops to Europe. In mid-August, to stop the exodus of East Germans fleeing to the West, the Communist regime began constructing the Berlin Wall, policed by border guards under shoot-to-kill orders. Kennedy again responded, though this time rhetorically, by delivering a speech in Berlin criticizing the wall in June 1963. Until the 12-foot-high concrete barrier came down in 1989, it served as the supreme symbol of the Cold War.

Perhaps the most perilous Cold War confrontation came in October 1962. In a somber televised address on October 22, Kennedy revealed that U.S. reconnaissance planes had spotted Soviet-built bases for intermediate-range ballistic missiles in Cuba. Some of those weapons had already been installed, and more were on the way. Kennedy announced that the United States would impose a "quarantine on all offensive military equipment" bound for Cuba. As the world held its breath waiting to see if the conflict would escalate into war, on October 25 ships carrying Soviet missiles turned back. After a week of tense negotiations, both sides made concessions: Kennedy pledged not to invade Cuba, and Khrushchev promised to dismantle the missile bases. Kennedy also secretly ordered U.S. missiles to be removed from Turkey, at Khrushchev's insistence. The risk of nuclear war, greater during the **Cuban missile crisis** than at any other time in the Cold War, prompted a slight thaw in U.S.-Soviet relations. As National Security Advisor McGeorge Bundy put it, both sides were chastened by "having come so close to the edge."

> **Cuban missile crisis**
> The 1962 nuclear standoff between the Soviet Union and the United States when the Soviets attempted to deploy nuclear missiles in Cuba.

Kennedy and the World Kennedy also launched a series of bold nonmilitary initiatives. One was the **Peace Corps**, which embodied a call to public service put forth in his inaugural address ("Ask not what your country can do for you, but what you can do for your country"). Thousands of men and women agreed to devote two or more years

> **Peace Corps**
> Program launched by President Kennedy in 1961 through which young American volunteers helped with education, health, and other projects in developing countries around the world.

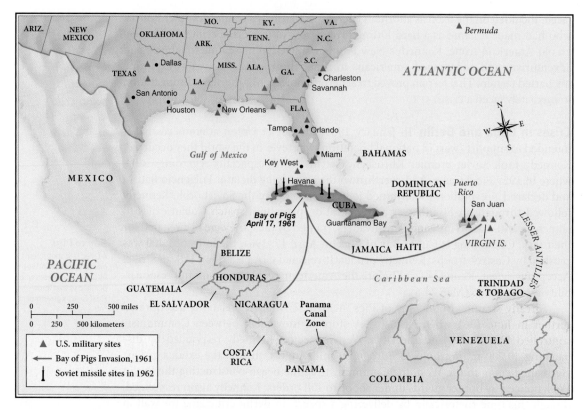

MAP 24.6 The United States and Cuba, 1961–1962

Fidel Castro's 1959 Communist takeover of Cuba brought Cold War tensions to the Caribbean. In 1961, the United States tried unsuccessfully to overthrow Castro's regime by sponsoring the Bay of Pigs invasion of Cuban exiles launched from Nicaragua and other points in the Caribbean. In 1962, the United States confronted the Soviet Union over Soviet construction of nuclear missile sites in Cuba. After President Kennedy ordered a naval blockade of the island, the Soviets backed down from the tense standoff and removed the missiles. Despite the 1991 dissolution of the Soviet Union and the official end of the Cold War, the United States continued to view Cuba, governed by Raúl Castro, Fidel's brother, since 2008, as an enemy nation until 2016, when President Barack Obama began the process of normalizing relations between the two countries.

as volunteers for projects such as teaching English to Filipino schoolchildren or helping African villagers obtain clean water. Exhibiting the idealism of the early 1960s, the Peace Corps was also a low-cost Cold War weapon — and an extension of American "soft power" (Chapter 21) — intended to show the developing world that there was an alternative to communism. Kennedy championed space exploration, as well. In a 1962 speech, he proposed that the nation commit itself to landing a man on the moon within the decade. The Soviets had already beaten the United States into space with the 1957 *Sputnik* satellite and the 1961 flight of cosmonaut Yuri Gagarin. Capitalizing on America's fascination with space, Kennedy persuaded Congress to increase funding for the government's space agency, the National Aeronautics and Space Administration (NASA), enabling the United States to pull ahead of the Soviet Union. Kennedy's ambition was realized when U.S. astronauts arrived on the moon in 1969.

Making a Commitment in Vietnam

When Kennedy became president, he inherited Eisenhower's commitment in Vietnam, which he saw in Cold War terms. But rather than practicing brinksmanship — threatening nuclear war to stop communism — Kennedy sought what at the time seemed a more intelligent and realistic, if nevertheless interventionist, approach. In 1961, he increased military aid to the South Vietnamese and expanded the role of U.S. Special Forces ("Green Berets"), who would train the South Vietnamese army in unconventional, small-group warfare tactics.

South Vietnam's corrupt and repressive Diem regime, propped up by Eisenhower since 1954, was losing ground in spite of American aid. By 1961, Diem's opponents, with backing from North Vietnam, had formed a revolutionary movement known as the National Liberation Front (NLF). NLF guerrilla forces — the Vietcong — found allies among peasants alienated by Diem's "strategic hamlet" program, which had uprooted entire villages and moved villagers into barbed-wire compounds. Furthermore, Buddhists charged Diem, a Catholic, with religious persecution. Starting in May 1963, militant Buddhists staged dramatic demonstrations, including self-immolations (burning to death) recorded by reporters covering the activities of the 16,000 U.S. military personnel then in Vietnam.

The self-immolations, broadcast on television to a shocked global audience, powerfully illustrated the dilemmas of American policy in Vietnam. To ensure a stable southern government and prevent victory for Ho Chi Minh and the North, the United States had to support Diem's authoritarian regime. But the regime's repression of its political opponents made Diem more unpopular. He was assassinated on November 3, 1963. Whether one supported U.S. involvement in Vietnam or not, the elemental paradox remained unchanged: in its efforts to achieve victory over the North, the United States brought defeat ever closer.

> **IN YOUR OWN WORDS** What objectives guided U.S. foreign policy in the so-called Third World during the Cold War?

Summary

The Cold War began as a conflict between the United States and the Soviet Union over Eastern Europe and the fate of post–World War II Germany. Early in the conflict, the United States adopted a strategy of containment, which quickly expanded to Asia after China became a communist state under Mao Zedong. The first effect of that expansion was the Korean War, after which, under Dwight D. Eisenhower, containment of communism became America's guiding principle across the developing world — often called the Third World. Cold War tensions relaxed in the late 1950s but erupted again under John F. Kennedy with the Cuban missile crisis, the building of the Berlin Wall, and major increases in American military assistance to South Vietnam. Cold War imperatives between 1945 and the early 1960s meant a major military buildup, a massive nuclear arms race, and unprecedented entanglements across the globe.

On the domestic front, Harry S. Truman started out with high hopes for an expanded New Deal, only to be confounded by resistance from Congress and the competing demands of the Cold War. The greatest Cold War–inspired development was a climate of fear over internal subversion by Communists that gave rise to McCarthyism. Truman's successor, Eisenhower, brought the Republicans back into power. Although personally conservative, Eisenhower actually proved a New Dealer in disguise. When Eisenhower left office and Kennedy became president, it seemed that a "liberal consensus" prevailed, with old-fashioned, *laissez faire* conservatism mostly marginalized in American political life.

CHAPTER 24 REVIEW

TERMS TO KNOW   *Identify and explain the significance of each term below.*

Key Concepts and Events

Yalta Conference (p. 786)	North Atlantic Treaty Organization (NATO) (p. 794)	Fair Deal (p. 802)	Eisenhower Doctrine (p. 811)
United Nations (p. 787)		Loyalty-Security Program (p. 804)	Bay of Pigs (p. 813)
Potsdam Conference (p. 787)	Warsaw Pact (p. 794)	House Un-American Activities Committee (HUAC) (p. 804)	Cuban missile crisis (p. 813)
containment (p. 789)	NSC-68 (p. 795)		Peace Corps (p. 813)
Truman Doctrine (p. 792)	Cold War liberalism (p. 801)	"New Look" (p. 807)	
Marshall Plan (p. 793)	Taft-Hartley Act (p. 801)	domino theory (p. 810)	

Key People

Joseph Stalin (p. 786)	Joseph McCarthy (p. 805)	Ho Chi Minh (p. 810)	Fidel Castro (p. 813)
George F. Kennan (p. 789)	Nikita Khrushchev (p. 807)	John F. Kennedy (p. 812)	

REVIEW QUESTIONS   *Answer these questions to demonstrate your understanding of the chapter's main ideas.*

1. What primary factors caused the Cold War?

2. What were the components of Cold War liberalism, and why did the Democratic Party embrace them?

3. What objectives guided U.S. foreign policy in the so-called Third World during the Cold War?

4. Review the events listed under "Politics and Power" and "American and National Identity" on the thematic timelines on pages 648 and 780. Radicalism played a significant role in American history between 1890 and 1945. What radical politics took root in the United States during this time, and how did the government, the business community, and different social groups respond to that radicalism?

MAKING CONNECTIONS *Recognize the larger developments and continuities within and across chapters.*

1. How was America's Cold War foreign policy an extension of principles and policies from earlier eras, and in what ways was it a break with those traditions? Was the Cold War inevitable? Why or why not?

2. Look at the map of the military-industrial complex (Map 24.3) on page 800 and the map of population changes (Chapter 25, Map 25.2) on page 844. Where were the majority of military weapons manufactured? What were the connections between weapons and geography? How did those connections affect population distribution in the United States and within individual metropolitan areas?

KEY TURNING POINTS *Refer to the chapter chronology on page 784 for help in answering the question below.*

What turning points and crises defined American containment policy between 1946 and 1953? Explain your answer with evidence from the timeline and chapter.

25

CHAPTER

Triumph of the Middle Class
1945–1963

A t the height of the Cold War, in 1959, U.S. vice president Richard Nixon debated Soviet premier Nikita Khrushchev on the merits of Pepsi-Cola, TV dinners, and electric ovens. Face-to-face at the opening of an American exhibition in Moscow, Nixon and Khrushchev strolled through a model American home, assembled to demonstrate the consumer products available to the typical citizen of the United States. Nixon explained to Khrushchev that although the Soviet Union may have superior rockets, the United States was ahead in other areas, such as color television.

This was Cold War politics by other means — a symbolic contest over which country's standard of living was higher. What was so striking about the so-called **kitchen debate** was Nixon's insistence, to a disbelieving Khrushchev, that a modern home filled with shiny new toasters, televisions, and other consumer products was accessible to the average American worker. "Any steelworker could buy this house," Nixon told the Soviet leader. The kitchen debate settled little in the geopolitical rivalry between the United States and the Soviet Union. But it speaks to us across the decades because it reveals how Americans had come to see themselves by the late 1950s: as home owners and consumers, as a people for whom the middle-class American Dream was a commercial aspiration.

The real story of the postwar period was the growing number of Americans who embraced that aspiration. In the two decades following the end of World War II, a new middle class was born in the United States. *Fortune* magazine estimated that in the 1950s, the middle class — which *Fortune* defined as families with more than $5,000 in annual earnings after taxes (about $45,000 today) — was increasing at the rate of 1.1 million people per year. Riding a wave of rising incomes, American dominance in the global economy, and Cold War federal spending, the postwar middle class enjoyed the highest standard of living in the world.

However, the success of the middle class could not hide deeper troubles. This was an era of neither universal conformity nor diminishing social strife. Jim Crow laws, contradictions in women's lives, a rebellious youth culture, and changing sexual mores were only the most obvious sources of social tension. Suburban growth came at the expense of cities, hastening urban decay and exacerbating racial segregation. Nor was prosperity ever as widespread as the Moscow exhibit implied. The suburban lifestyle was beyond the reach of the working poor, the elderly, immigrants, Mexican Americans, and most African Americans — indeed, the majority of the country. Such contradictions were felt acutely by many Americans but largely ignored by the majority of the country. Not until the 1960s did uneven prosperity become the subject of national debate.

> ## IDENTIFY THE BIG IDEA
>
> **Why did consumer culture become such a fixture of American life in the postwar decades, and how did it affect politics and society?**

kitchen debate
A 1959 debate over the merits of their rival systems between U.S. vice president Richard Nixon and Soviet premier Nikita Khrushchev at the opening of an American exhibition in Moscow.

The Middle-Class Family Ideal   A family eats breakfast at a campground in Zion National Park, Utah.
Americans embraced a middle-class, nuclear family ideal in the postwar decades.   Justin Locke/National Geographic/Getty Images.

CHAPTER CHRONOLOGY

As you read, ask yourself why this chapter begins and ends with these dates and identify the links among related events.

1944 ▶ Bretton Woods economic conference ▶ World Bank and International Monetary Fund (IMF) founded ▶ GI Bill (Servicemen's Readjustment Act)	**1952** ▶ McCarran-Walter Act
	1953 ▶ Kinsey's *Sexual Behavior in the Human Female* published
1946 ▶ First edition of Dr. Spock's *Common Sense Book of Baby and Child Care*	**1954** ▶ Ray Kroc buys the first McDonald's franchise
	1955 ▶ Daughters of Bilitis founded
1947 ▶ First Levittown built	**1956** ▶ National Interstate and Defense Highways Act ▶ Elvis Presley's breakthrough records ▶ Allen Ginsberg's poem "Howl" published
1948 ▶ Beginning of network television ▶ *Shelley v. Kraemer* ▶ Alfred Kinsey's *Sexual Behavior in the Human Male* published	
	1957 ▶ Peak of postwar baby boom
	1961 ▶ Eisenhower warns nation against military-industrial complex
1949 ▶ Billy Graham revival in Los Angeles	
1951 ▶ Bracero Program revived ▶ Mattachine Society founded	**1965** ▶ *Griswold v. Connecticut*

Postwar Prosperity and the Affluent Society

The United States enjoyed enormous economic advantages at the close of World War II. While the Europeans and Japanese were still clearing the war's rubble, America stood poised to enter a postwar boom. As the only major industrial nation not devastated by war, the United States enjoyed an unprecedented global position. The American economy also benefitted from an expanding internal market and heavy investment in research and development. Two additional factors stood out: First, for the first time in the nation's history, employers generally accepted collective bargaining, which for workers translated into rising wages, expanding benefits, and an increasing rate of home ownership. Second, the federal government's outlays for military and domestic programs gave a huge boost to the economy.

Economy: From Recovery to Dominance

Life magazine publisher Henry Luce was so confident in the nation's growing power that during World War II he had predicted the dawning of the "American century." In economic terms, Luce envisioned U.S. corporations, banks, and manufacturers dominating global markets. That vision came to pass after the war. The preponderance of American economic muscle in the postwar decades, however, was not simply an artifact of the world war — it was not an inevitable development. Several key elements came together, internationally and at home, to propel three decades of unprecedented economic growth.

Bretton Woods
An international conference in New Hampshire in July 1944 that established the World Bank and the International Monetary Fund (IMF).

World Bank
An international bank created to provide loans for the reconstruction of war-torn Europe as well as for the development of former colonized nations in the developing world.

The Bretton Woods System American global supremacy rested partly on the economic institutions created at an international conference in **Bretton Woods**, New Hampshire, in July 1944. The first of those institutions was the **World Bank**,

The Kitchen Debate At the American National Exhibition in Moscow in 1959, the United States put on display the technological wonders of American home life. When Vice President Richard Nixon visited, he and Soviet premier Nikita Khrushchev got into a heated debate over the relative merits of their rival systems, with the up-to-date American kitchen as a case in point. This photograph shows the debate in progress. Khrushchev is the bald man pointing his finger. To Nixon's left stands Leonid Brezhnev, who would be Khrushchev's successor. Howard Sochurek/Getty Images.

founded to provide loans for the reconstruction of war-torn Europe as well as for the development of former colonized nations — the so-called Third World or developing world. A second institution, the **International Monetary Fund (IMF)**, was set up to stabilize currencies and provide a predictable monetary environment for trade, with the U.S. dollar serving as the benchmark. The World Bank and the IMF formed the cornerstones of the Bretton Woods system, which guided the global economy after the war. The chief idea of the Bretton Woods system was to make American capital available, on cheap terms, to nations that adopted free-trade capitalist economies.

The Bretton Woods system was joined in 1947 by the first General Agreement on Tariffs and Trade (GATT), which established an international framework for overseeing trade rules and practices. Together, the Bretton Woods system and GATT served America's conception of an open-market global economy and complemented the nation's ambitious diplomatic aims in the Cold War. Critics charged, rightly, that Bretton Woods and GATT favored the United States at the expense of recently independent countries, because the United States could dictate lending and trading terms and stood to benefit as nations purchased more American goods. But the system provided needed economic stability.

International Monetary Fund (IMF)
A fund established to stabilize currencies and provide a predictable monetary environment for trade, with the U.S. dollar serving as the benchmark.

The Military-Industrial Complex A second engine of postwar prosperity was defense spending. In his final address to the nation in 1961, President Dwight D. Eisenhower spoke about the power of what he called the **military-industrial complex**, which by then employed 3.5 million Americans. Even though his administration had fostered this defense establishment, Eisenhower feared its implications: "We must guard against the acquisition of unwarranted influence, whether sought or unsought, by the military-industrial complex," he warned. This complex had its roots in the business-government partnerships of World War II (Chapter 23). After 1945, though the country was nominally at peace, the economy and the government operated in a state of perpetual readiness for war.

Based at the sprawling Pentagon in Arlington, Virginia, the Defense Department evolved into a massive bureaucracy. In the name of national security, defense-related industries entered into long-term relationships with the Pentagon. Some companies did so much business with the government that they in effect became private divisions of the Defense Department. Over 60 percent of the income of Boeing, General Dynamics, and Raytheon, for instance, came from military contracts, and the percentages were even higher for Lockheed and Republic Aviation. In previous peacetime years, military spending had constituted only 1 percent of gross domestic product (GDP); now it represented 10 percent. Economic growth was increasingly dependent on a robust defense sector.

As permanent mobilization took hold, science, industry, and government became intertwined. Cold War competition for military supremacy spawned both an arms race and a space race as the United States and the Soviet Union each sought to develop more explosive bombs and more powerful rockets. Federal spending underwrote 90 percent of the cost of research for aviation and space, 65 percent for electricity and electronics, 42 percent for scientific instruments, and even 24 percent for automobiles. With the government footing the bill, corporations lost little time in transforming new technology into useful products. Backed by the Pentagon, for instance, IBM and Sperry Rand pressed ahead with research on integrated circuits, which later spawned the computer revolution.

When the Soviet Union launched the world's first satellite, *Sputnik*, in 1957, the startled United States went into high gear to catch up in the Cold War space competition. Alarmed that the United States was falling behind in science and technology, Eisenhower persuaded Congress to appropriate additional money for college scholarships and university research. The **National Defense Education Act** of 1958 funneled millions of dollars into American universities, helping institutions such as the University of California at Berkeley, Stanford University, the Massachusetts Institute of Technology, and the University of Michigan become the leading research centers in the world.

Corporate Power Despite its massive size, the defense industry was only one part of the nation's economy. For over half a century, the consolidation of economic power into large corporate firms had characterized American capitalism. In the postwar decades, that tendency accelerated. By 1970, the top four U.S. automakers produced 91 percent of all motor vehicles sold in the country; the top four firms in tires produced 72 percent; those in cigarettes, 84 percent; and those in detergents, 70 percent. Eric Johnston, former president of the American Chamber of Commerce, declared

---

military-industrial complex
A term President Eisenhower used to refer to the military establishment and defense contractors who, he warned, exercised undue influence over the national government.

Sputnik
The world's first satellite, launched by the Soviet Union in 1957. After its launch, the United States funded research and education to catch up in the Cold War space competition.

National Defense Education Act
A 1958 act, passed in response to the Soviet launching of the *Sputnik* satellite, that funneled millions of dollars into American universities, helping institutions such as the University of California at Berkeley and the Massachusetts Institute of Technology, among others, become the leading research centers in the world.

that "we have entered a period of accelerating bigness in all aspects of American life." Expansion into foreign markets also spurred corporate growth. During the 1950s, U.S. exports nearly doubled, giving the nation a trade surplus of close to $5 billion in 1960. By the 1970s, such firms as Coca-Cola, Gillette, IBM, and Mobil made more than half their profits abroad.

To staff their bureaucracies, the postwar corporate giants required a huge white-collar army. A new generation of corporate chieftains emerged, operating in a complex environment that demanded long-range forecasting. Postwar corporate culture inspired numerous critics, who argued that the obedience demanded of white-collar workers was stifling creativity and blighting lives. The sociologist William Whyte painted a somber picture of "organization men" who left the home "spiritually as well as physically to take the vows of organization life." Andrew Hacker, in *The Corporation Take-Over* (1964), warned that a small handful of such organization men "can draw up an investment program calling for the expenditure of several billions of dollars" and thereby "determine the quality of life for substantial segments of society."

Many of these "investment programs" relied on mechanization, or automation — another important factor in the postwar boom. From 1947 to 1975, worker productivity more than doubled across the whole of the economy. American factories replaced manpower with machines, substituting cheap fossil energy for human muscle. As industries mechanized, they could turn out products more efficiently and at lower cost. Mechanization did not come without social costs, however. Over the course of the postwar decades, millions of high-wage manufacturing jobs were lost as machines replaced workers, affecting entire cities and regions. Corporate leaders approved, but workers and their union representatives were less enthusiastic. "How are you going to sell cars to all of these machines?" wondered Walter Reuther, president of the United Auto Workers (UAW).

The Economic Record The American economy produced an extraordinary postwar record. Annual GDP jumped from $213 billion in 1945 to more than $500 billion in 1960; by 1970, it exceeded $1 trillion (Figure 25.1). This sustained economic growth helped produce a 25 percent rise in real income for ordinary Americans between 1946 and 1959. Even better, the new prosperity featured low inflation. After a burst of high prices in the immediate postwar period, inflation slowed to 2 to 3 percent annually, and it stayed low until the escalation of the Vietnam War in the mid-1960s. Feeling secure about the future, Americans were eager to spend and rightly felt that they were better off than ever before. In 1940, 43 percent of American families owned their homes; by 1960, 62 percent did. In that period, moreover, income inequality dropped sharply. The share of total income going to the top tenth — the richest Americans — declined by nearly one-third from the 45 percent it had been in 1940. American society had become not only more prosperous but also more egalitarian.

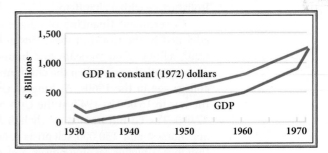

FIGURE 25.1 Gross Domestic Product, 1930–1972

After a sharp dip during the Great Depression, the GDP rose steadily in both real and constant dollars in the postwar period.

However, the picture was not as rosy at the bottom, where tenacious poverty accompanied the economic boom. In ***The Affluent Society*** (1958), which analyzed the nation's successful, "affluent" middle class, economist John Kenneth Galbraith argued that the poor were only an "afterthought" in the minds of economists and politicians, who largely celebrated the new growth. As Galbraith noted, one in thirteen families at the time earned less than $1,000 a year (about $8,300 in today's dollars). Four years later, in ***The Other America*** (1962), the left-wing social critic Michael Harrington chronicled "the economic underworld of American life," and a U.S. government study, echoing a well-known sentence from Franklin Roosevelt's second inaugural address ("I see one-third of a nation ill-housed, ill-clad, ill-nourished"), declared "one-third of the nation" to be poorly paid, poorly educated, and poorly housed. It appeared that in economic terms, as the top and the middle converged, the bottom remained far behind.

A Nation of Consumers

The most breathtaking development in the postwar American economy was the dramatic expansion of the domestic consumer market. The sheer quantity of consumer goods available to the average person was without precedent. In some respects, the postwar decades seemed like the 1920s all over again, with an abundance of new gadgets and appliances, a craze for automobiles, and new types of mass media. Yet there was a significant difference: in the 1950s, consumption became associated with citizenship. Buying things, once a sign of personal indulgence, now meant participating fully in American society and, moreover, fulfilling a social responsibility. What the suburban family consumed, asserted *Life* magazine in a photo essay, would help to ensure "full employment and improved living standards for the rest of the nation."

The GI Bill   The new ethic of consumption appealed to the postwar middle class, the driving force behind the expanding domestic market. Middle-class status was more accessible than ever before because of the Servicemen's Readjustment Act of 1944, popularly known as the GI Bill. In the immediate postwar years, more than half of all U.S. college students were veterans attending class on the government's dime. By the middle of the 1950s, 2.2 million veterans had attended college and another 5.6 million had attended trade school with government financing. Before the GI Bill, commented one veteran, "I looked upon college education as likely as my owning a Rolls-Royce with a chauffeur."

Government financing of education helped make the U.S. workforce the best educated in the world in the 1950s and 1960s. American colleges, universities, and trade schools grew by leaps and bounds to accommodate the flood of students — and expanded again when the children of those students, the baby boomers, reached college age in the 1960s. At Rutgers University, enrollment went from 7,000 before the war to 16,000 in 1947; at the University of Minnesota, from 15,000 to more than 27,000. The GI Bill trained nearly half a million engineers; 200,000 doctors, dentists, and nurses; and 150,000 scientists (among many other professions). Better education meant higher earning power, and higher earning power translated into the consumer spending that drove the postwar economy. One observer of the GI Bill was so impressed with its achievements that he declared it responsible for "the most important educational and social transformation in American history."

The GI Bill stimulated the economy and expanded the middle class in another way: by increasing home ownership. Between the end of World War II and 1966, one of every five single-family homes built in the United States was financed through a GI Bill mortgage—2.5 million new homes in all. In cities and suburbs across the country, the **Veterans Administration** (VA), which helped former soldiers purchase new homes with no down payment, sparked a building boom that created jobs in the construction industry and fueled consumer spending in home appliances and automobiles. Education and home ownership were more than personal triumphs for the families of World War II veterans (and Korean and Vietnam War veterans, after a new GI Bill was passed in 1952). They were financial *assets* that helped lift more Americans than ever before into a mass-consumption-oriented middle class.

Trade Unions Organized labor also expanded the ranks of the middle class. For the first time ever, trade unions and **collective bargaining** became major factors in the nation's economic life. In the past, organized labor had been confined to a narrow band of craft trades and a few industries, primarily coal mining, railroading, and the building and metal trades. The power balance shifted during the Great Depression, and by the time the dust settled after World War II, labor unions overwhelmingly represented America's industrial workforce (Figure 25.2). By the beginning of the 1950s, the nation's major industries, including auto, steel, clothing, chemicals, and virtually all consumer product manufacturing, were operating with union contracts.

That outcome did not arrive without a battle. Unions staged major strikes in nearly all American industries in 1945 and 1946, much as they had done after World War I. Head of the UAW Walter Reuther and CIO president Philip Murray declared that employers could afford a 30 percent wage increase, which would fuel postwar consumption. When employers, led by the giant General Motors, balked at that demand, the two sides seemed set for a long struggle. Between 1947 and 1950, however, a broad "labor-management accord" gradually emerged across most industries. This was not industrial peace—the country still experienced many strikes—but a general acceptance of collective bargaining as the method for setting the terms of employment. The result was rising real income. The average worker with three dependents gained 18 percent in spendable real income in the 1950s.

Veterans Administration
A federal agency that assists former soldiers. Following World War II, the VA helped veterans purchase new homes with no down payment, sparking a building boom that created jobs in the construction industry and fueling consumer spending in home appliances and automobiles.

collective bargaining
A process of negotiation between labor unions and employers, which after World War II translated into rising wages, expanding benefits, and an increasing rate of home ownership.

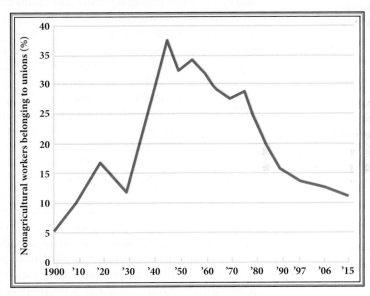

FIGURE 25.2 Labor Union Strength, 1900–2015

Labor unions reached their peak strength immediately after World War II, when they represented close to 40 percent of the nonfarm workforce. Although there was some decline after the mid-1950s, unions still represented nearly 30 percent in 1973. Thereafter, between the 1970s and the 2010s, their decline was precipitous. AFL-CIO Information Bureau, Washington, D.C.

In addition, unions delivered greater leisure (more paid holidays and longer vacations) and, in a startling departure, a social safety net. In postwar Europe, America's allies were constructing welfare states. But having lost the bruising battle in Washington for national health care during Truman's presidency, American unions turned to the bargaining table. By the end of the 1950s, union contracts commonly provided pension plans and company-paid health insurance. Collective bargaining, the process of trade unions and employers negotiating workplace contracts, had become, in effect, the American alternative to the European welfare state and, as Reuther boasted, the passport into the middle class.

This impressive labor-management accord, however, was never as durable or universal as it seemed. Vulnerabilities lurked. For one thing, the sheltered domestic markets — the essential condition for generous contracts, because without competition firms were not pressured to lower wages — were quite fragile. In certain industries, the lead firms were already losing market share. Second, generally overlooked were the many unorganized workers with no middle-class passport — those consigned to unorganized industries, casual labor, or low-wage jobs in the service sector. A final vulnerability was the most basic: the abiding antiunionism of American employers. At heart, business regarded the labor-management accord as a negotiated truce, not a permanent peace. The postwar labor-management accord turned out to be a transitory event, not a permanent condition of American economic life.

Houses, Cars, and Children   Increased educational levels, growing home ownership, and higher wages all enabled more Americans than ever before to become members of what one historian has called a "consumer republic." But what did they buy? The postwar emphasis on nuclear families and suburbs provides the answer. In the emerging suburban nation, three elements came together to create patterns of consumption that would endure for decades: houses, cars, and children.

A feature in a 1949 issue of *McCall's*, a magazine targeting middle-class women, illustrates the connections. "I now have three working centers," a typical housewife explains. "The baby center, a baking center and a cleaning center." Accompanying illustrations reveal the interior of the brand-new house, stocked with the latest consumer products: accessories for the baby's room; a new stove, oven, and refrigerator; and a washer and dryer, along with cleaning products and other household goods. The article does not mention automobiles, but the photo of the house's exterior makes the point clear: father drives home from work in a new car.

Consumption for the home, including automobiles, drove the postwar American economy as much as, or more than, the military-industrial complex did. If we think like advertisers and manufacturers, we can see why. Between 1945 and 1970, more than 25 million new houses were built in the United States. Each required its own supply of new appliances, from refrigerators to lawn mowers. In 1955 alone, Americans purchased 4 million new refrigerators, and between 1940 and 1951 the sale of power mowers increased from 35,000 per year to more than 1 million. Moreover, as American industry discovered planned obsolescence — the encouragement of consumers to replace appliances and cars every few years — the home became a site of perpetual consumer desire.

Children also encouraged consumption. The baby boomers born between World War II and the late 1950s have consistently, throughout every phase of their lives, been the darlings of American advertising and consumption. When they were infants, companies focused on developing new baby products, from disposable diapers to instant formula. When they were toddlers and young children, new television programs, board games, fast food, TV dinners, and thousands of different kinds of toys came to market to supply the rambunctious youth. When they were teenagers, rock music, Hollywood films, and a constantly marketed "teen culture" — with its appropriate clothing, music, hairstyles, and other accessories — bombarded them. Remarkably, in 1956, middle-class American teenagers on average had a weekly income of more than $10, close to the weekly disposable income of an entire family a generation earlier.

Television   The emergence of commercial television in the United States was swift and overwhelming. In the realm of technology, only the automobile and the personal computer were its equal in transforming everyday life in the twentieth century. In 1947, there were 7,000 TV sets in American homes. A year later, the CBS and NBC radio networks began offering regular programming, and by 1950 Americans owned 7.3 million sets. Ten years later, 87 percent of American homes had at least one television set. Having conquered the home, television would soon become the principal mediator between the consumer and the marketplace.

Television advertisers mastered the art of manufacturing consumer desire. TV stations, like radio stations before them, depended entirely on advertising for profits. The first television executives understood that as long as they sold viewers to advertisers they would stay on the air. Early corporate-sponsored shows (such as *General Electric Theater* and *U.S. Steel Hour*) and simple product jingles (such as "No matter what the time or place, let's keep up with that happy pace. 7-Up your thirst away!") gave way by the early 1960s to slick advertising campaigns that used popular music, movie stars, sports figures, and stimulating graphics to captivate viewers.

By creating powerful visual narratives of comfort and plenty, television revolutionized advertising and changed forever how products were sold to American, and global, consumers. On *Queen for a Day*, a show popular in the mid-1950s, women competed to see who could tell the most heartrending story of tragedy and loss. The winner was lavished with household products: refrigerators, toasters, ovens, and the like. In a groundbreaking advertisement for Anacin aspirin, a tiny hammer pounded inside the skull of a headache sufferer. Almost overnight, sales of Anacin increased by 50 percent.

By the late 1950s, what Americans saw on television, both in the omnipresent commercials and in the programming, was an overwhelmingly white, Anglo-Saxon, Protestant world of nuclear families, suburban homes, and middle-class life. A typical show was *Father Knows Best*, starring Robert Young and Jane Wyatt. Father left home each morning wearing a suit and carrying a briefcase. Mother was a stereotypical full-time housewife, prone to bad driving and tears. *Leave It to Beaver*, another immensely popular series about suburban family life, embodied similar late-fifties themes. Earlier in the decade, however, television featured grittier realities. *The Honeymooners*, starring Jackie Gleason as a Brooklyn bus driver, and *The Life of Riley*, a situation comedy featuring a California aircraft worker, treated working-class lives. Two other early-fifties television series, *Beulah*, starring Ethel Waters and then Louise Beavers as an African American maid, and the comedic *Amos 'n' Andy*, were the only shows featuring black actors in major roles. Television was never a showcase for the breadth of American society, but in the second half of the 1950s broadcasting lost much of its ethnic, racial, and class diversity and became a vehicle for the transmission of a narrow range of middle-class tastes and values.

Youth Culture

teenager
A term for a young adult. American youth culture, focused on the spending power of the "teenager," emerged as a cultural phenomenon in the postwar decades.

One of the most striking developments in American life in the postwar decades was the emergence of the **teenager** as a cultural phenomenon. In 1956, only partly in jest, the CBS radio commentator Eric Sevareid questioned "whether the teenagers will take over the United States lock, stock, living room, and garage." Sevareid was grumbling about American youth culture, a phenomenon first noticed in the 1920s and with its roots in the lengthening years of education, the role of peer groups, and the consumer tastes of young people. Market research revealed a distinct teen market to be exploited. *Newsweek* noted with awe in 1951 that the aggregate of the weekly spending money of teenagers was enough to buy 190 million candy bars, 130 million soft drinks, and 230 million sticks of gum. Increasingly, advertisers targeted the young, both to capture their spending money and to exploit their influence on family purchases.

Hollywood movies played a large role in fostering a teenage culture. Young people made up the largest audience for motion pictures, and Hollywood studios learned over the course of the 1950s to cater to them. The success of films such as *The Wild One* (1953), starring Marlon Brando; *Blackboard Jungle* (1955), with Sidney Poitier; and *Rebel Without a Cause* (1955), starring James Dean, convinced movie executives that films directed at teenagers were worthy investments. "What are you rebelling against?" Brando is asked in *The Wild One*. "Whattaya got?" he replies. By the early 1960s, Hollywood had retooled its business model, shifting emphasis away from adults and families, the industry's primary audience since its rise in the 1920s, to teenagers. The "teenpic" soon included multiple genres: horror, rock 'n' roll, dangerous youth, and beach party, among others.

Rock 'n' Roll   What really defined the youth culture, however, was its music. Rejecting the romantic ballads of the 1940s, teenagers discovered rock 'n' roll, which originated in African American rhythm and blues. The Cleveland disc jockey Alan Freed took the lead in introducing white America to the black-created sound by playing what were called "race" records. "If I could find a white man who had the Negro sound and the Negro feel, I could make a billion dollars," a record company owner is quoted as saying. The performer who fit that bill was Elvis Presley, who rocketed into instant celebrity in 1956 with his hit records "Hound Dog" and "Heartbreak Hotel," covers of songs originally recorded by black artists such as Big Mama Thornton. Between 1953 and 1959, record sales increased from $213 million to $603 million, with rock 'n' roll as the driving force.

Many unhappy adults saw in rock 'n' roll music an invitation to interracial dating, rebellion, and a more flagrant sexuality. The media featured hundreds of stories on problem teens, and denunciations of the new music poured forth from many corners. Such condemnation only deflected off the new youth culture or, if anything, increased its popularity. Both Hollywood and the music industry had learned that youth rebellion sold tickets (Interpretations).

Motown   Mary Wilson, Diana Ross, and Florence Ballard (from left to right) were the founding members of the Motown singing group the Supremes (shown here in concert in 1964), which produced twelve number-one singles. Motown, a record label owned by African American entrepreneur Berry Gordy, specialized in so-called cross-over acts: black singers who sold records to white audiences. In the era of Jim Crow, Motown represented a small but noteworthy step toward a less racially segregated American culture.   RB/Getty Images.

Cultural Dissenters   Youth rebellion was only one aspect of a broader discontent with the sometimes saccharine consumer culture of the postwar years. Many artists, writers, and jazz musicians embarked on powerful new experimental projects in a remarkable flowering of intensely personal, introspective art forms. During and just after World War II, black musicians developed a hard-driving improvisational style known as bebop. Whether the "hot" bebop of saxophonist Charlie Parker or the more subdued "cool" sound of the influential trumpeter Miles Davis, postwar jazz was cerebral, intimate, and individualistic. As such, it stood in stark contrast to the commercialized, dance-oriented "swing" bands of the 1930s and 1940s.

Was Rock 'n' Roll an Agent of Social Change?

Many parents of midcentury teens objected to the subversive qualities of rock 'n' roll music: its rebellious lyrics, its overt sexuality, and its origins in an African American rhythm and blues tradition — the latter a concern largely of white parents. Many believed that rock 'n' roll undermined authority and even stoked civil rights agitation. But did this new form of music have the social and political impact parents feared?

In the excerpts included here, two historians address the contradictory impact of rock 'n' roll, particularly as a factor in shaping civil rights. In the first excerpt, historian Suzanne E. Smith discusses the history of Motown, a Detroit-based African American record label that produced a series of hits by black artists, many of whom reached a national white listening audience. In the second excerpt, historian Matthew Delmont assesses the popularity of *American Bandstand*, a nationally broadcast television show originating in Philadelphia that featured mostly white teens dancing to popular rock songs. From the perspective of these historians, did rock 'n' roll have the socially destabilizing impact parents feared?

SUZANNE E. SMITH

Source: Suzanne E. Smith, *Dancing in the Street: Motown and the Cultural Politics of Detroit* (Cambridge: Harvard University Press, 1999), 17–18.

Motown's commercial success put the record company in a unique position to promote a wide range of black cultural expression ... [but its] ... role as a producer of black culture and its ambitions in the business world did not coexist without conflict and contradiction.... [Its] commercial concerns about the marketability of a recording often stalled and sometimes canceled projects that management deemed too politically controversial.... [T]he company wavered between willingness and caution when asked to

Beats

A small group of literary figures based in New York City and San Francisco in the 1950s who rejected mainstream culture and instead celebrated personal freedom, which often included drug consumption and casual sex.

Black jazz musicians found eager fans not only in the African American community but also among young white **Beats**, a group of writers and poets centered in New York and San Francisco who disdained middle-class materialism. In his poem "Howl" (1956), which became a manifesto of the Beat generation, Allen Ginsberg lamented: "I saw the best minds of my generation destroyed by madness, starving hysterical naked, dragging themselves through the negro streets at dawn looking for an angry fix." In works such as Jack Kerouac's novel *On the Road* (1957), the Beats glorified spontaneity, sexual adventurism, drug use, and spirituality. The Beats were apolitical, but their cultural rebellion would, in the 1960s, inspire a new generation of young rebels disenchanted with both the political and cultural status quo.

Religion and the Middle Class

In an age of anxiety about nuclear annihilation and the spread of "godless communism," Americans yearned for a reaffirmation of faith. Church membership jumped from 49 percent of the population in 1940 to 70 percent in 1960. People flocked to produce recordings…that involved overt political or racial messages….[However] popular music audiences, local activists, and national civil rights leaders…had their own ideas and disagreements about the meanings of Motown's music and commercial success….Motown could not avoid becoming a contested symbol of racial progress. Motown's music symbolized the possibility of amicable racial integration through popular culture.

MATTHEW F. DELMONT

Source: Matthew F. Delmont, *The Nicest Kids in Town: American Bandstand, Rock 'n' Roll, and the Struggle for Civil Rights in 1950s Philadelphia* (Berkeley: University of California Press, 2012), 5–6.

American Bandstand encouraged the show's viewers, advertisers, and television affiliates to see it as the thread that stitched together different teenagers in different parts of the country into a coherent and recognizable national youth culture….*American Bandstand* invited viewers to consume the sponsors' snacks and soft drinks along with the latest music and dances….The central problem facing *American Bandstand*'s producers was that their show's marketability depended on both the creative energies of black performers and the erasure of black teenagers….[T]he image of youth culture *American Bandstand* presented to its national audience bore little resemblance to the interracial makeup of Philadelphia's rock and roll scene. As the television program that did the most to define the image of youth in the late 1950s and early 1960s, the exclusionary racial practices of *American Bandstand* marginalized black teens from this imagined national youth culture.

QUESTIONS FOR ANALYSIS

1. To what extent do these historians agree on the impact of rock 'n' roll on America's race relations? What specific passages provide evidence for your answer?

2. According to each historian, how important a factor was the commercial side of rock 'n' roll in promoting or limiting its impact as an agent of social change?

3. Identify two examples from Chapter 25's discussion of midcentury middle-class youth culture that support or challenge the argument for rock 'n' roll as a factor in the American civil rights movement.

---

the evangelical Protestant denominations, beneficiaries of a remarkable new crop of preachers. Most eloquent was the young Reverend Billy Graham, who made brilliant use of television, radio, and advertising. Hundreds of thousands of Americans attended his massive 1949 revival in Los Angeles and his 1957 crusade at Madison Square Garden in New York, establishing Graham as the nation's leading evangelical.

Rather than clashing with the new middle-class ethic of consumption, the religious reawakening was designed to mesh with it. Preachers such as Graham told Americans that so long as they lived moral lives, they deserved the material blessings of modern life. No one was more influential in this regard than the minister and author Norman Vincent Peale, whose best-selling book *The Power of Positive Thinking* (1952) embodied the therapeutic use of religion as an antidote to life's trials and tribulations. Peale taught that with faith in God and "positive thinking," anyone could overcome obstacles and become a success. Graham, Peale, and other 1950s evangelicals laid the foundation for the rise of the televangelists, who created popular television ministries in the 1970s.

The postwar purveyors of religious faith cast Americans as a righteous people opposed to communist atheism. When Julius and Ethel Rosenberg were sentenced to death in 1953, the judge criticized them for "devoting themselves to the Russian ideology of denial of God." Cold War imperatives drew Catholics, Protestants, and Jews into an influential ecumenical movement that downplayed doctrinal differences. The phrase "under God" was inserted into the Pledge of Allegiance in 1954, and U.S. coins carried the words "In God We Trust" after 1956. These religious initiatives struck a distinctly moderate tone, however, in comparison with the politicized evangelism that emerged in the 1960s and 1970s (Chapter 28).

> **IN YOUR OWN WORDS**   What explains the growth of the American economy after World War II?

The American Family in the Era of Containment

Marriage, family structure, and gender roles had been undergoing significant changes since the turn of the twentieth century (Chapter 17). Beginning in the nineteenth century, middle-class Americans increasingly saw marriage as "companionate," that is, based on romantic love and a lifetime of shared friendship. *Companionate* did not mean *equal*. In the mid-twentieth century, family life remained governed by notions of gender inequality, in which men provided economic support and controlled the family's financial resources, while women cared for children and occupied a secondary position in public life.

The resurgent postwar American middle class was preoccupied with the virtues of this paternalist, or patriarchal, vision of family life. Everyone from professional psychologists to television advertisers and every organization from schools to the popular press celebrated nuclear families. Children were prized, and women's caregiving roles were valorized. This view of family life, and especially its emphasis on female "domesticity," was bolstered by Cold War politics. Americans who deviated from prevailing gender and familial norms were not only viewed with scorn but were also sometimes thought to be subversive and politically dangerous.

Yet the model of domesticity so highly esteemed in the postwar middle class hid deeper, longer-term changes in the way marriage, gender roles, women's work, and even sex were understood. To comprehend the postwar decades, we have to keep in mind that while domesticity remained the ideal, in people's daily lives a sometimes different reality held true.

The Baby Boom

A popular 1945 song was called "Gotta Make Up for Lost Time," and Americans did just that. Two things were noteworthy about the families they formed after World War II: First, marriages were remarkably stable. Not until the mid-1960s did the divorce rate begin to rise sharply. Second, married couples were intent on having babies. Everyone expected to have several children — it was part of adulthood, almost a citizen's responsibility. After a century and a half of decline, the birthrate shot up. More babies were born in the six years between 1948 and 1953 than in the previous thirty years (Figure 25.3). Far from "normal," all these developments were anomalies, temporary reversals of long-standing demographic trends. From the perspective of the whole of the twentieth century, the 1950s and early 1960s stand out as exceptions to declining birthrates, rising divorce rates, and the steadily rising marriage age.

One of the reasons for the **baby boom** was a drop in the average marriage age — down to twenty-two for men and twenty for women. Younger parents meant a bumper crop of children. Women who came of age in the 1930s averaged 2.4 children; their counterparts in the 1950s averaged 3.2 children. Such a dramatic turnaround reflected couples' decisions during the Great Depression to limit childbearing and couples' contrasting decisions in the postwar years to have more children. The baby boom peaked in 1957 and remained at a high level until the early 1960s. The passage

FIGURE 25.3 The American Birthrate, 1860–1980
When birthrates are viewed over more than a century, the postwar baby boom is clearly only a temporary reversal of the long-term downward trend in the American birthrate.

of time revealed the ever-widening impact of the baby boom. When baby boomers competed for jobs during the 1970s, the labor market became tight. When career-oriented baby boomers belatedly began having children in the 1980s, the birthrate jumped. And in our own time, as baby boomers begin retiring, huge funding problems threaten to engulf Social Security and Medicare. The intimate decisions of so many couples after World War II continued to shape American life well into the twenty-first century.

Baby boom children benefitted from a host of important advances in public health and medical practice in the postwar years. Formerly serious illnesses became merely routine after the introduction of such "miracle drugs" as penicillin (introduced in 1943), streptomycin (1945), and cortisone (1946). When Dr. Jonas Salk perfected a polio vaccine in 1954, he became a national hero. The free distribution of Salk's vaccine in the nation's schools, followed in 1961 by Dr. Albert Sabin's oral polio vaccine, demonstrated the potential of government-sponsored public health programs.

baby boom
The surge in the American birthrate between 1945 and 1965, which peaked in 1957 with 4.3 million births.

Dr. Benjamin Spock To keep baby boom children healthy and happy, middle-class parents increasingly relied on the advice of experts. Dr. Benjamin Spock's *Common Sense Book of Baby and Child Care* sold 1 million copies every year after its publication in 1946. Spock urged mothers to abandon the rigid feeding and baby-care schedules of an earlier generation. New mothers found Spock's commonsense approach liberating. "Your little paperback is still in my cupboard, with loose pages, rather worn from use because I brought up two babies using it as my 'Bible,'" a California housewife wrote to Spock.

Despite his commonsense approach to child rearing, Spock was part of a generation of psychological experts whose advice often failed to reassure women. If mothers were too protective, Spock and others argued, they might hamper their children's preparation for adult life. On the other hand, mothers who wanted to work outside the home felt guilty because Spock recommended that they be constantly available for their children. As American mothers aimed for the perfection demanded of them seemingly at every turn, many began to question these mixed messages. Some of them would be inspired by the resurgence of feminism in the 1960s.

Women, Work, and Family

Two powerful forces shaped women's relationships to work and family life in the post-war decades. One was the middle-class domestic ideal, in which women were expected to raise children, attend to other duties in the home, and devote themselves to their husbands' happiness. So powerful was this ideal that in 1957 the *Ladies' Home Journal* entitled an article, "Is College Education Wasted on Women?" The second force was the job market. Most working-class women had to earn a paycheck to help their family. And despite their education, middle-class women found that jobs in the professions and business were dominated by men and often closed to them. For both groups, the market offered mostly "women's jobs" — in teaching, nursing, and other areas of the growing service sector — and little room for advancement.

The idea that a woman's place was in the home was, of course, not new. The post-war obsession with femininity and motherhood bore a remarkable similarity to the nineteenth century's notion of domesticity. The updated version drew on new elements of twentieth-century science and culture. Psychologists equated motherhood with "normal" female identity and suggested that career-minded mothers needed therapy. "A mother who runs out on her children to work — except in cases of absolute necessity — betrays a deep dissatisfaction with motherhood or with her marriage," wrote one leading psychiatrist. Television shows and movies depicted career women as social misfits. The postwar consumer culture also emphasized women's domestic role as purchasing agents for home and family. "Can a woman ever feel right cooking on a dirty range?" asked one advertisement.

Despite the postwar domestic ideal, financial necessity increasingly took women outside their homes and into the workforce. In 1954, married women made up half of all women workers. Six years later, the 1960 census reported a stunning fact: the number of mothers who worked had increased four times, and over one-third of these women had children between the ages of six and seventeen. In that same year, 30 percent of wives worked, and by 1970, it was 40 percent. For working-class women, in particular, the economic needs of their families demanded that they work outside the home. Contrary to stereotypes, women's paid work often helped lift many families into the middle class.

Despite rising employment rates, occupational segmentation still haunted women. Until 1964, the classified sections of newspapers separated employment ads into "Help Wanted Male" and "Help Wanted Female." More than 80 percent of all employed women did stereotypical women's work as sales clerks, health-care technicians, waitresses, stewardesses, domestic servants, receptionists, telephone operators, and secretaries. In 1960, only 3 percent of lawyers and 6 percent of physicians were women; on the flip side, 97 percent of nurses and 85 percent of librarians were women. Along with women's jobs went women's pay, which averaged 60 percent of men's pay in 1963.

American society steadfastly upheld the domestic ideal even as so many women entered the workforce. When mothers took jobs outside the home, they still bore full responsibility for child care and household management, contributing to the "double day" of paid work and family work. As one overburdened woman noted, she now had "two full-time jobs instead of just one — underpaid clerical worker and unpaid housekeeper." Meanwhile, the pressures of the Cold War made strong nuclear families with breadwinning fathers and domesticated mothers symbols of a healthy nation. Americans wanted to believe they upheld the domestic ideal even if it did not perfectly describe the reality of their lives.

Challenging Middle-Class Morality

In many ways, the two decades between 1945 and 1965 were a period of cultural conservatism that reflected the values of domesticity. At the dawn of the 1960s, going steady as a prelude to marriage was the fad in high school. College women had curfews and needed permission to see a male visitor. Americans married young; more than half of those who married in 1963 were under the age of twenty-one. After the birth control pill came on the market in 1960, few doctors prescribed it to unmarried women, and even married women did not enjoy unfettered access to contraception until the Supreme Court ruled it a "privacy" right in the 1965 decision *Griswold v. Connecticut.*

Alfred Kinsey Beneath the surface of middle-class morality, Americans were less repressed than confused. They struggled to reconcile new freedoms with older moral traditions. This was especially true with regard to sex. Two controversial studies by an unassuming Indiana University zoologist named Alfred Kinsey forced questions about sexuality into the open. Kinsey and his research team published *Sexual Behavior in the Human Male* in 1948 and followed it up in 1953 with *Sexual Behavior in the Human Female* — an 842-page book that sold 270,000 copies in the first month after its publication. Taking a scientific, rather than moralistic, approach, Kinsey, who became known as "the sex doctor," documented the full range of sexual experiences of thousands of Americans. He broke numerous taboos, discussing such topics as homosexuality and marital infidelity in the detached language of science.

Both studies confirmed that a sexual revolution, although a largely hidden one, had already begun to transform American society by the early 1950s. Kinsey estimated that 85 percent of men had had sex prior to marriage and that more than 25 percent of married

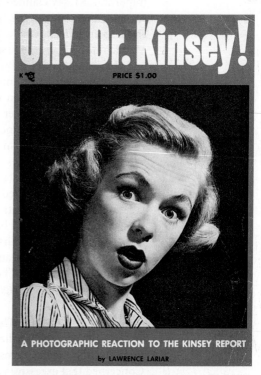

The Kinsey Reports Like the woman on the cover of this lighthearted 1953 book of photographs, many Americans reacted with surprise when Alfred Kinsey revealed the country's sexual habits. In his 1948 book about men and his 1953 book about women, Kinsey wrote about American sexual practices in the detached language of science. But it still made for salacious reading. Evangelical minister Billy Graham (p. 831) warned: "It is impossible to estimate the damage this book will do to the already deteriorated morals of America." Picture Research Consultants & Archives.

women had had sex outside of marriage by the age of forty. These were shocking public admissions in the late 1940s and early 1950s, and "hotter than the Kinsey report" became a national figure of speech. Kinsey was criticized by statisticians — because his samples were not randomly selected — and condemned even more fervently by religious leaders, who charged him with encouraging promiscuity and adultery. But his research opened a national conversation that helped Americans learn to talk more openly about sex.

The Homophile Movement   Among the most controversial of Kinsey's claims was that homosexuality was far more prevalent than most Americans believed. Although the American Psychiatric Association officially defined homosexuality as a mental illness, Kinsey's research found that 37 percent of men had engaged in some form of homosexual activity by early adulthood, as had 13 percent of women. Even more important, Kinsey claimed that 10 percent of American men were *exclusively* homosexual. These claims came as little surprise, but great encouragement, to a group of gay and lesbian activists who called themselves "homophiles." Organized primarily in the Mattachine Society (the first gay rights organization in the country, founded in 1951) and the Daughters of Bilitis (a lesbian organization founded in 1955), homophiles were a small but determined collection of activists who sought equal rights for gays and lesbians. "The lesbian is a woman endowed with all the attributes of any other woman," wrote the pioneer lesbian activist Del Martin in 1956. "The salvation of the lesbian lies in her acceptance of herself without guilt or anxiety."

Building on the urban gay and lesbian communities that had coalesced during World War II, homophiles sought to change American attitudes about same-sex love. They faced daunting obstacles, since same-sex sexual relations were illegal in every state and scorned, or feared, by most Americans. To combat prejudice and change the laws, homophile organizations cultivated a respectable, middle-class image. Members were encouraged to avoid bars and nightclubs, to dress in conservative shirts and ties (for men) and modest skirts and blouses (for women), and to seek out professional psychologists who would attest to their "normalcy." Only in the 1960s did homophiles begin to talk about the "homophile vote" and their "rights as citizens," laying the groundwork for the gay rights movement of the 1970s.

Media and Morality   The homophile movement remained unknown to most Americans. But other challenges to traditional morality received national media attention, and the media themselves became a controversial source of these challenges. Concerned that excessive crime, violence, and sex in comic books were encouraging juvenile delinquency, the U.S. Senate held nationally televised hearings in 1954. The Senate's final report, written largely by the Tennessee Democrat Estes Kefauver, complained of the "scantily clad women" and "penchant for violent death" common in comic books aimed at teenagers. Kefauver's report forced the comics industry to tame its wildest practices but did little to slow the growing frankness about both sex and violence in the nation's print media and films.

A magazine entrepreneur from Chicago named Hugh Hefner played a leading role in that growing frankness. Hefner founded *Playboy* magazine in 1953, in which he created a countermorality to domesticity: a fictional world populated by "hip"

To see an excerpt from the Senate's report on comic books and juvenile delinquency, along with other primary sources from this period, see *Sources for America's History*.

bachelor men and sexually available women. Hefner's imagined bachelors condemned marriage and lived in sophisticated apartments filled with the latest stereo equipment and other consumer products. While domesticated fathers bought lawn mowers and patio furniture, Hefner's magazine encouraged men to spend money on clothing and jazz albums for themselves, and for the "scantily clad women" that filled its pages. Hefner and his numerous imitators became powerful purveyors of sex in the media. But Hefner was the exception that proved the rule: marriage, not swinging bachelorhood, remained the destination for the vast majority of men. Millions of men read *Playboy*, but few adopted its fantasy lifestyle.

IN YOUR OWN WORDS What was the domestic ideal, and how did Americans embrace it in the postwar decades?

A Suburban Nation

Prosperity — how much an economy produces, how much people earn — is more easily measured than is quality of life. During the 1950s, however, the American definition of the good life emerged with exceptional distinctness: a high value on consumption, a devotion to family and domesticity, and a preference for suburban living. In this section, we consider the third dimension of that definition: suburbanization. What drove the nation to abandon its cities for the suburbs, and what social and political consequences did this shift have?

The Postwar Housing Boom

Migration to the suburbs had been going on for a hundred years, but never before on the scale that the country experienced after World War II. Within a decade, farmland on the outskirts of cities filled up with tract housing and shopping malls. Entire counties that had once been rural — such as San Mateo, south of San Francisco, or Passaic and Bergen in New Jersey, west of Manhattan — went suburban. By 1960, one-third of Americans lived in suburbs. Home construction, having ground to a halt during the Great Depression, surged after the war. One-fourth of the country's entire housing stock in 1960 had not even existed a decade earlier.

William J. Levitt and the FHA Two unique postwar developments remade the national housing market and gave it a distinctly suburban shape. First, an innovative Long Island building contractor, William J. Levitt, revolutionized suburban housing by applying mass-production techniques and turning out new homes at a dizzying speed. Levitt's basic four-room house, complete with kitchen appliances, was priced at $7,990 when homes in the first Levittown went on sale in 1947 (about $86,000 today). Levitt did not need to advertise; word of mouth brought buyers flocking to his developments (all called Levittown) in New York, Pennsylvania, and New Jersey. Dozens of other developers were soon snapping up cheap farmland and building subdivisions around the country.

Even at $7,990, Levitt's homes would have been beyond the means of most young families had the traditional home-financing standard — a down payment of half the

The Suburban Landscape of Cold War America

Between the end of World War II and the 1980s, Americans built and moved into suburban homes in an unprecedented wave of construction and migration that changed the nation forever. New home loan rules, and government backing under the Federal Housing Administration and Veterans Administration, made new suburban houses cheaper and brought home ownership within reach of a larger number of Americans than ever before. Commentators cheered these developments as a boon to ordinary citizens, but by the 1960s a generation of urban critics, led by journalist Jane Jacobs, had begun to find fault with the nation's suburban obsession. The following documents provide the historian with evidence of how these new suburban communities arose and how they began to transform American culture.

1. **_Life_ magazine, "A _Life_ Round Table on Housing," January 31, 1949.**

The most aggressive member of _Life_'s Round Table, whether as builder or debater, was William J. Levitt, president of Levitt and Sons, Inc. of Manhasset, NY. He feels that he has started a revolution, the essence of which is size. Builders in his estimation are a poor and puny lot, too small to put pressure on materials manufacturers or the local czars of the building codes or the bankers or labor. A builder ought to be a manufacturer, he said, and to this end must be big. He himself is a nonunion operator.

The Levitt prescription for cheaper houses may be summarized as follows: 1) take infinite pains with infinite details; 2) be aggressive; 3) be big enough to throw your weight around; 4) buy at wholesale; and 5) build houses in concentrated developments where mass-production methods can be used on the site.

2. **Site plan sketch for Park Forest, Illinois, 1946.**

SOURCE: The Park Forest Historical Society.

3. **William H. Whyte Jr., _The Organization Man,_ 1956.** _Whyte, a prominent journalist, wrote about the decline of individualism and the rise of a national class of interchangeable white-collar workers._

And is this not the whole drift of our society? We are not interchangeable in the sense of being people without differences, but in the externals of existence we are united by a culture increasingly national. And this is part of the momentum of mobility. The more people move about, the more similar American environments become, and the more similar they become, the easier it is to move about.

More and more, the young couples who move do so only physically. With each transfer the décor, the architecture, the faces, and the names may change; the people, the conversation, and the values do not — and sometimes the décor and architecture don't either....

Suburban residents like to maintain that their suburbia not only looks classless but is classless. That is, they are apt to add on second thought, there are no extremes, and if the place isn't exactly without class, it is at least a one-class society — identified as the middle or upper middle, according to the inclination of the residents. "We are all," they say, "in the same boat."

4. **Jane Jacobs, _The Death and Life of Great American Cities,_ 1961.** _A classic celebration of vibrant urban neighborhoods by a New York writer and architectural critic._

Although it is hard to believe, while looking at dull gray areas, or at housing projects or at civic centers, the fact is that big cities are natural generators of diversity and prolific incubators of new enterprises and ideas of all kinds....

This is because city populations are large enough to support wide ranges of variety and choice in these things. And again we find that bigness has all the advantages in smaller settlements. Towns and suburbs, for instance, are natural homes for huge supermarkets and for little else in the way of groceries, for standard movie houses or drive-ins and for little else in the way of theater. There are simply not enough people to support further variety, although there may be people (too few of them) who would draw upon it were it there. Cities, however, are the natural homes of supermarkets and standard movie houses plus delicatessens, Viennese bakeries, foreign groceries, art movies, and so on....

The diversity, of whatever kind, that is generated by cities rests on the fact that in cities so many people are so close together, and among them contain so many different tastes, skills, needs, supplies, and bees in their bonnets.

5. Crowded supermarket, early 1960s.

Source: John Dominis/Time Life Pictures/Getty Images.

6. Herbert J. Gans, *The Levittowners*, 1967. *One of the first sociological studies of the new postwar suburbs and their residents.*

The strengths and weakness of Levittown are those of many American communities, and the Levittowners closely resemble other young middle class Americans. They are not America, for they are not a numerical majority of the population, but they represent the major constituency of the latest and more powerful economic and political institutions in American society — the favored customers and voters whom these seek to attract and satisfy....

Although they are citizens of a national polity and their lives are shaped by national economic, social, and political forces, Levittowners deceive themselves into thinking that the community, or rather the home, is the single most important unit of their lives....

In viewing their homes as the center of life, Levittowners are still using a societal model that fit the rural America of self-sufficient farmers and the feudal Europe of self-isolating extended families.

Sources: (2) *Life*, January 31, 1949, 74; (4) William H. Whyte Jr., *The Organization Man* (New York: Simon and Schuster, 1956), 276, 299; (5) Jane Jacobs, *The Death and Life of Great American Cities* (Westminster, MD: Vintage, 1992), 145–147; (6) Herbert J. Gans, *The Levittowners* (New York: Columbia University Press, 1982), 417–418.

ANALYZING THE EVIDENCE

1. Compare sources 3, 4, and 5. How do they reinforce or contradict one another?

2. In source 3, what does Whyte mean by "classless"? Why would suburbanites wish to think of their communities as not beset by class inequality? Were they right in this point of view?

3. Do you see evidence in source 1 of the ways the postwar housing market was transformed? How does Levitt's vision of the home-building industry relate to other kinds of American industries?

4. In source 4, what advantages does Jacobs see in large cities over suburbs? Can you interpret sources 2 and 5 from the perspective that Jacobs outlines?

PUTTING IT ALL TOGETHER

Write an essay in which you use the knowledge you've gained from this chapter and the documents provided above to explore postwar suburbanization. What did it mean to the American economy? To ordinary Americans? What flaws did its critics see?

Hanoch Bartov: Everyone Has a Car

One of Israel's foremost writers and journalists, Hanoch Bartov spent two years in the United States working as a correspondent for the newspaper *Lamerchav*. As a newcomer to Los Angeles in the early 1960s, he was both fascinated and appalled by Americans' love affair with the automobile.

Our immediate decision to buy a car sprang from healthy instincts. Only later did I learn from bitter experience that in California, death was preferable to living without one. Neither the views from the plane nor the weird excursion that first evening hinted at what I would go through that first week.

Very simple — the nearest supermarket was about half a kilometer south of our apartment, the regional primary school two kilometers east, and my son's kindergarten even farther away. A trip to the post office — an undertaking, to the bank — an ordeal, to work — an impossibility....

There are no tramways. No one thought of a subway. Railroads — not now and not in the future. Why? Because everyone has a car. A man invited me to his house, saying, "We are neighbors, within ten minutes of each other." After walking for an hour and a half I realized what he meant — "ten minute drive within the speed limit." Simply put, he never thought I might interpret his remark to refer to the walking distance. The moment a baby sees the light of day in Los Angeles, a car is registered in his name in Detroit....

At first perhaps people relished the freedom and independence a car provided. You get in, sit down, and grab the steering wheel, your mobility exceeding that of any other generation. No wonder people refuse to live downtown, where they can hear their neighbors, smell their cooking, and suffer frayed nerves as trains pass by bedroom windows. Instead, they get a piece of the desert, far from town, at half price, drag a water hose, grow grass, flowers, and trees, and build their dream house.

The result? A widely scattered city, its houses far apart, its streets stretched in all directions. Olympic Boulevard from west to east, forty kilometers. Sepulveda Boulevard, from Long Beach in the south to the edge of the desert, forty kilometers. Altogether covering 1,200 square kilometers. As of now.

SOURCE: "Measures of Affluence" by Hanoch Bartov (1963) in Chapter 16 from *The Outer World,* edited by Oscar Handlin and Lilian Handlin (Cambridge, MA: Harvard University Press, 1997). © 1997. Reprinted by permission of Oscar and Lillian Handlin.

QUESTIONS FOR ANALYSIS

1. From Bartov's observations, what are the pluses and minuses of America's car culture? In what ways was the automobile changing American society?
2. Why did Bartov find that owning a car was necessary, especially in southern California?
3. How would suburbanization have contributed to the construction of new highways in the United States? How would highway construction have facilitated suburbanization?

full price and ten years to pay off the balance — still prevailed. That is where the second postwar development came in. The Federal Housing Administration (FHA) and the Veterans Administration (VA) — that is, the federal government — brought the home mortgage market within the reach of a broader range of Americans than ever before. After the war, the FHA insured thirty-year mortgages with as little as 5 percent down and interest at 2 or 3 percent. The VA was even more generous, requiring only a token $1 down for qualified ex-GIs. FHA and VA mortgages best explain why, after hovering around 45 percent for the previous half century, home ownership jumped to 60 percent by 1960.

What purchasers of suburban houses got, in addition to a good deal, were homogeneous communities. Levitt's houses came with restrictive covenants prohibiting occupancy "by members of other than the Caucasian Race." (Restrictive covenants often applied to Jews and, in California, Asian Americans as well.) Levittowns were hardly alone. Suburban developments from coast to coast exhibited the same age, class, and racial homogeneity (Thinking Like a Historian). In ***Shelley v. Kraemer*** (1948), the Supreme Court outlawed restrictive covenants, but racial discrimination in housing changed little. The practice persisted long after *Shelley*, because the FHA and VA continued the policy of redlining: refusing mortgages to African Americans and members of other minority groups seeking to buy in white neighborhoods. Indeed, no federal law — or even Court decisions like *Shelley* — actually prohibited racial discrimination in housing until Congress passed the Fair Housing Act in 1968.

Interstate Highways Without automobiles, suburban growth on such a massive scale would have been impossible. Planners laid out subdivisions on the assumption that everybody would drive. And they did — to get to work, to take the children to Little League, to shop. With gas plentiful and cheap (15 cents a gallon), no one cared about the fuel efficiency of their V-8 engines or seemed to mind the elaborate tail fins and chrome that weighed down their cars. In 1945, Americans owned twenty-five million cars; by 1965, just two decades later, the number had tripled to seventy-five million (America in Global Context). American oil consumption followed course, tripling as well between 1949 and 1972.

More cars required more highways, and the federal government obliged. In 1956, in a move that drastically altered America's landscape and driving habits, the **National Interstate and Defense Highways Act** authorized $26 billion over a ten-year period for the construction of a nationally integrated highway system — 42,500 miles (Map 25.1). Cast as a Cold War necessity because broad highways made evacuating crowded cities easier in the event of a nuclear attack, the law changed American cities forever. An enormous public works program surpassing anything undertaken during the New Deal, and enthusiastically endorsed by the Republican president, Dwight Eisenhower, federal highways made possible the massive suburbanization of the nation in the 1960s. Interstate highways rerouted traffic away from small towns, bypassed well-traveled main roads such as the cross-country Route 66, and cut wide swaths through old neighborhoods in the cities.

Fast Food and Shopping Malls Americans did not simply fill their new suburban homes with the latest appliances and gadgets; they also pioneered entirely new forms

Shelley v. Kraemer
A 1948 Supreme Court decision that outlawed restrictive covenants on the occupancy of housing developments by African Americans, Asian Americans, and other minorities. Because the Court decision did not actually prohibit racial discrimination in housing, unfair practices against minority groups continued until passage of the Fair Housing Act in 1968.

National Interstate and Defense Highways Act
A 1956 law authorizing the construction of a national highway system.

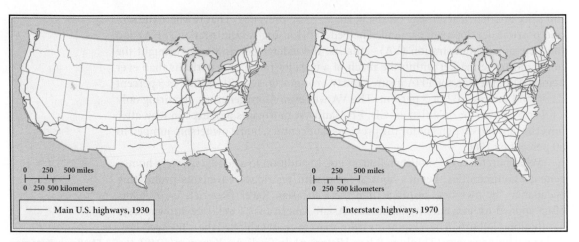

MAP 25.1 Connecting the Nation: The Interstate Highway System, 1930 and 1970
The 1956 National Interstate and Defense Highways Act paved the way for an extensive network of federal highways throughout the nation. The act not only pleased American drivers and enhanced their love affair with the automobile but also benefitted the petroleum, construction, trucking, real estate, and tourist industries. The new highway system promoted the nation's economic integration, facilitated the growth of suburbs, and contributed to the erosion of America's distinct regional identities.

of consumption. Through World War II, downtowns had remained the center of retail sales and restaurant dining with their grand department stores, elegant eateries, and low-cost diners. As suburbanites abandoned big-city centers in the 1950s, ambitious entrepreneurs invented two new commercial forms that would profoundly shape the rest of the century: the shopping mall and the fast-food restaurant.

By the late 1950s, the suburban shopping center had become as much a part of the American landscape as the Levittowns and their imitators. A major developer of shopping malls in the Northeast called them "today's village green," and noted that "the fountain in the mall has replaced the downtown department clock as the gathering place for young and old alike." By centralizing the otherwise dispersed world of suburban consumption, shopping malls brought "the market to the people instead of people to the market," commented the *New York Times*. In 1939, the suburban share of total metropolitan retail trade in the United States was a paltry 4 percent. By 1961, it was an astonishing 60 percent in the nation's ten largest metropolitan regions.

No one was more influential in creating suburban patterns of consumption than a Chicago-born son of Czech immigrants named Ray Kroc. A former jazz musician and traveling salesman, Kroc found his calling in 1954 when he acquired a single franchise of the little-known McDonald's Restaurant, based in San Bernardino, California. In 1956, Kroc invested in twelve more franchises and by 1958 owned seventy-nine. Three years later, Kroc bought the company from the McDonald brothers and proceeded to turn it into the largest chain of restaurants in the world. Based on inexpensive, quickly served hamburgers that hungry families could eat in the restaurant, in their cars, or at home, Kroc's vision transformed the way Americans consumed food. "Drive-in" or "fast" food became a staple of the American diet in the subsequent decades. By the year 2000, fast food was a $100 billion industry, and more children recognized Ronald McDonald, the clown in McDonald's television commercials, than Santa Claus.

Rise of the Sunbelt

Suburban living, although a nationwide phenomenon, was most at home in the **Sunbelt** (the southern and southwestern states), where taxes were low, the climate was mild, and open space allowed for sprawling subdivisions (Map 25.2). Florida added 3.5 million people, many of them retired, between 1940 and 1970. Texas profited from expanding petrochemical and defense industries. Most dramatic was California's growth, spurred especially by the state's booming defense-related aircraft and electronics industries. By 1970, California contained one-tenth of the nation's population and surpassed New York as the most populous state. By the end of the century, if California had been a nation its economy would have ranked among the top ten largest in the world.

A distinctive feature of Sunbelt suburbanization was its close relationship to the military-industrial complex. Building on World War II expansion, military bases proliferated in the South and Southwest in the postwar decades, especially in Florida, Texas, and California. In some instances, entire metropolitan regions — such as San Diego County, California, and the Houston area in Texas — expanded in tandem with nearby military outposts. Moreover, the aerospace, defense, and electronics industries were based largely in Sunbelt metropolitan regions. With government contracts fueling the economy and military bases providing thousands of jobs, Sunbelt politicians had every incentive to support vigorous defense spending by the federal government.

Sunbelt suburbanization was best exemplified by Orange County, California. Southwest of Los Angeles, Orange County was until the 1940s mostly just that — a land of oranges, groves of them. But during World War II, boosters attracted new bases and training facilities for the marines, navy, and air force (at the time the army air corps). Cold War militarization and the Korean War kept those bases humming, and Hughes Aircraft, Ford Aeronautics, and other defense-related manufacturers built new plants in the sunny, sprawling groves. So did subdivision developers, who built so many new homes that the population of the county jumped from 130,760 in 1940 to 703,925 in 1960. Casting his eye on all this development in the early 1950s, an entrepreneurial filmmaker and cartoonist named Walt Disney chose Anaheim in Orange County as the place for a massive new amusement park. Disneyland was to the new generation of suburbanites what Coney Island had been to an earlier generation of urbanites.

Two Societies: Urban and Suburban

While middle-class whites flocked to the suburbs, an opposite stream of working-class migrants, many of them southern African Americans, moved into the cities. In the 1950s, the nation's twelve largest cities lost 3.6 million whites while gaining 4.5 million nonwhites. These urban newcomers inherited a declining economy and a decaying infrastructure. To those enjoying prosperity, the "other America," as the social critic Michael Harrington called it, remained largely invisible. In 1968, however, a report by the National Advisory Commission on Civil Disorders (informally known as the **Kerner Commission** and formed by the president to investigate the causes of the 1967 urban riots), delivered to President Lyndon Johnson, warned that "our nation is moving toward two societies, one black, one white, separate and unequal."

Sunbelt
Name applied to the Southwest and South, which grew rapidly after World War II as a center of defense industries and non-unionized labor.

Kerner Commission
Informal name for the National Advisory Commission on Civil Disorders, formed by the president to investigate the causes of the 1967 urban riots. Its 1968 report warned that "our nation is moving toward two societies, one black, one white, separate and unequal."

MAP 25.2 Shifting Population Patterns, 1950–1980

This map shows the two major, somewhat overlapping, patterns of population movement between 1950 and 1980. Most striking is the rapid growth of the Sunbelt states. All the states experiencing increases of over 100 percent in that period are in the Southwest, plus Florida. The second pattern involves the growth of metropolitan areas, defined as a central city or urban area and its suburbs. The central cities were themselves mostly not growing, however. The metropolitan growth shown in this map was accounted for by the expanding suburbs. And because Sunbelt growth was primarily suburban growth, that's where we see the most rapid metropolitan growth, with Los Angeles the clear leader.

American cities had long been the home of poverty, slum housing, and the hardships and cultural dislocations brought on by immigration from overseas or migration from rural areas. But postwar American cities, especially those in the industrial Northeast and Midwest, experienced these problems with new intensity. By the 1950s, the manufacturing sector was contracting, and mechanization was eliminating thousands upon thousands of unskilled and semiskilled jobs, the kind traditionally taken up by new urban residents. The disappearing jobs were the ones "in which [African Americans] are disproportionately concentrated," noted the civil rights activist Bayard Rustin.

The Urban Crisis The intensification of poverty, the deterioration of older housing stock, and the persistence of racial segregation produced what many at the time called the urban crisis. Unwelcome in the shiny new suburbs built by men such as William J. Levitt, African Americans found low-paying jobs in the city and lived in aging, slumlike apartment buildings. Despite a thriving black middle class — indeed,

Urban Crisis In this photo of a Chicago neighborhood from 1963, a middle-class, high-rise apartment building looms over an older, low-income district. The contrast is emblematic of what many commentators in the 1960s came to call the "urban crisis," the shift of investment, commerce, good jobs, and the middle class away from central cities to either neighboring suburbs or high-rent apartment districts. Racial segregation and continued racial discrimination played a significant role in limiting the economic options available to the black working class. That reality became a major spark to the black freedom struggle in many American cities. Charles E. Knoblock/AP Images.

larger than ever before — for those without resources, upward mobility remained elusive. Racism in institutional forms frustrated African Americans at every turn: housing restrictions, increasingly segregated schools, and an urban infrastructure that stood underfunded and decaying as whites left for the suburbs.

Housing and job discrimination were compounded by the frenzy of urban renewal that hit black neighborhoods in the 1950s and early 1960s. Seeking to revitalize declining city centers, politicians and real estate developers proposed razing blighted neighborhoods to make way for modern construction projects that would appeal to the fleeing middle class. In Boston, almost one-third of the old city — including the historic West End, a long-established Italian neighborhood — was demolished to make way for a new highway, high-rise housing, and government and commercial buildings. In San Francisco, some 4,000 residents of the Western Addition, a predominantly black neighborhood, lost out to an urban renewal program that built luxury housing, a shopping center, and an express boulevard. Between 1949 and 1967, urban renewal nationwide demolished almost 400,000 buildings and displaced 1.4 million people.

The urban experts believed they knew what to do with the dislocated: relocate them to federally funded housing projects, an outgrowth of New Deal housing policy, now much expanded. However well intended, these grim projects too often took the form of cheap high-rises that isolated their inhabitants from surrounding neighborhoods. The impact was felt especially strongly among African Americans, who often found that public housing increased racial segregation and concentrated the poor. The Robert Taylor Homes in Chicago, with twenty-eight buildings of sixteen stories each, housed 20,000 residents, almost all of them black. Despite the planners' wish to build decent affordable apartments, the huge complex became a notorious breeding ground for crime and hopelessness.

Urban Immigrants   Despite the evident urban crisis, cities continued to attract immigrants from abroad. Since the passage of the National Origins Act of 1924 (Chapter 21), U.S. immigration policy had aimed mainly at keeping foreigners out. But World War II and the Cold War began slowly to change American policy. The Displaced Persons Act of 1948 permitted the entry of approximately 415,000 Europeans, many of them Jewish refugees. In a gesture to an important war ally, the Chinese Exclusion Act was repealed in 1943. More far-reaching was the 1952 McCarran-Walter Act, which ended the exclusion of Japanese, Koreans, and Southeast Asians.

After the national-origins quota system went into effect in 1924, Mexico replaced Eastern and Southern Europe as the nation's labor reservoir. During World War II, the federal government introduced the Bracero Program to ease wartime labor shortages (Chapter 23) and then revived it in 1951, during the Korean War. The federal government's ability to force workers to return to Mexico, however, was strictly limited. The Mexican immigrant population continued to grow, and by the time the Bracero Program ended in 1964, many of that group — an estimated 350,000 — had settled permanently in the United States. Braceros were joined by other Mexicans from small towns and villages, who immigrated to the United States to escape poverty or to earn money to return home and purchase land for farming.

As generations of immigrants had before them, Mexicans gravitated to major cities. Mostly, they settled in Los Angeles, Long Beach, San Jose, El Paso, and other southwestern cities. But many also went north, augmenting well-established Mexican American communities in Chicago, Detroit, Kansas City, and Denver. Although still important to American agriculture, Mexican Americans were employed in substantial numbers as industrial and service workers by 1960.

Another major group of Spanish-speaking migrants came from Puerto Rico. American citizens since 1917, Puerto Ricans enjoyed an unrestricted right to move to the mainland United States. Migration increased dramatically after World War II, when mechanization of the island's sugarcane agriculture left many Puerto Ricans jobless. Airlines began to offer cheap direct flights between San Juan and New York City. With the fare at about $50 (two weeks' wages), Puerto Ricans became America's first immigrants to arrive en masse by air. Most Puerto Ricans went to New York, where they settled first in East ("Spanish") Harlem and then scattered in neighborhoods across the city's five boroughs. This massive migration, which increased the Puerto Rican population to 613,000 by 1960, transformed the ethnic composition of the city. More Puerto Ricans now lived in New York City than in San Juan.

Cuban refugees constituted the third largest group of Spanish-speaking immigrants. In the six years after Fidel Castro's seizure of power in 1959 (Chapter 24), an estimated 180,000 people fled Cuba for the United States. The Cuban refugee community grew so quickly that it turned Miami into a cosmopolitan, bilingual city almost overnight. Unlike other urban migrants, Miami's Cubans quickly prospered, in large part because they had arrived with money and middle-class skills.

Spanish-speaking immigrants—whether Mexican, Puerto Rican, or Cuban—created huge barrios in major American cities, where bilingualism flourished, the Catholic Church shaped religious life, and families sought to join the economic mainstream. Though distinct from one another, these Spanish-speaking communities remained largely segregated from white, or Anglo, neighborhoods and suburbs as well as from African American districts.

IN YOUR OWN WORDS What were the major forces that contributed to postwar suburbanization?

Summary

We have explored how, at the same time it became mired in the Cold War, the United States entered an unparalleled era of prosperity in which a new middle class came into being. Indeed, the Cold War was one of the engines of prosperity. The postwar economy was marked by the dominance of big corporations and defense spending.

After years of depression and war-induced insecurity, Americans turned inward toward religion, home, and family. Postwar couples married young, had several children, and—if they were white and middle class—raised their children in a climate of suburban comfort and consumerism. The profamily orientation of the 1950s celebrated traditional gender roles, even though millions of women entered the workforce in those years. Not everyone, however, shared in the postwar prosperity. Postwar cities increasingly became places of last resort for the nation's poor. Black migrants, unlike earlier immigrants, encountered an urban economy that had little use for them. Without opportunity, and faced with pervasive racism, many of them were on their way to becoming an American underclass, even as sparkling new suburbs emerged outside cities to house the new middle class. Many of the smoldering contradictions of the postwar period — Cold War anxiety in the midst of suburban domesticity, tensions in women's lives, economic and racial inequality — helped spur the protest movements of the 1960s.

CHAPTER 25 REVIEW

TERMS TO KNOW   *Identify and explain the significance of each term below.*

Key Concepts and Events

kitchen debate (p. 818)

Bretton Woods (p. 820)

World Bank (p. 820)

International Monetary Fund (IMF) (p. 821)

military-industrial complex (p. 822)

Sputnik (p. 822)

National Defense Education Act (p. 822)

The Affluent Society (p. 824)

The Other America (p. 824)

Veterans Administration (p. 825)

collective bargaining (p. 825)

teenager (p. 828)

Beats (p. 830)

baby boom (p. 833)

Shelley v. Kraemer (p. 841)

National Interstate and Defense Highways Act (p. 841)

Sunbelt (p. 843)

Kerner Commission (p. 843)

Key People

Dwight D. Eisenhower (p. 822)

Miles Davis (p. 829)

Allen Ginsberg (p. 830)

Billy Graham (p. 831)

Dr. Benjamin Spock (p. 833)

William J. Levitt (p. 837)

REVIEW QUESTIONS   *Answer these questions to demonstrate your understanding of the chapter's main ideas.*

1. What explains the growth of the American economy after World War II?

2. What was the domestic ideal, and how did Americans embrace it in the postwar decades?

3. What were the major forces that contributed to postwar suburbanization?

4. Review the events listed under "America in the World" and "Work, Exchange, and Technology" for the periods

1930–1945 and 1945–1960 on the thematic timelines on pages 648–649 and 780–781, respectively. Explain how the United States began the 1930s in deep depression with unemployment near 25 percent and ended the 1950s with an expanded middle class and a consumption-driven economy.

1. Think back to earlier chapters that discussed gender roles, marriage, and American family life in the late nineteenth and early twentieth centuries (Chapters 17, 18, 21, 23). How had the American family changed by the 1950s? What aspects of family life remained similar across many decades? For example, how did the working-class immigrant family of the 1890s differ from the middle-class family of the 1950s?

2. Examine the photograph of urban apartment buildings featured on page 845. What does the image suggest about the American middle class in the 1950s and 1960s — especially its mobility? How would you introduce the theme of race to discuss this image?

KEY TURNING POINTS   *Refer to the chapter chronology on page 820 for help in answering the question below.*

What were the major turning points in the creation of postwar suburbia?

26

CHAPTER

Walking into Freedom Land: The Civil Rights Movement
1941–1973

I n June 1945, as World War II was coming to an end, Democratic senator James O. Eastland of Mississippi stood on the floor of the U.S. Senate and brashly proclaimed that "the Negro race is an inferior race." Raising his arms, his tie askew from vigorous gesturing, Eastland ridiculed black troops. "The Negro soldier was an utter and dismal failure in combat," he said.

Eastland's assertions were untrue. Black soldiers had served honorably; many won medals for bravery in combat. All-black units, such as the 761st "Black Panther" Tank Battalion and the famous Tuskegee Airmen, were widely praised by military commanders. But segregationists like Eastland were a nearly unassailable force in Congress, able to block civil rights legislation and shape national opinion.

In the 1940s, two generations after W. E. B. Du Bois famously wrote that "the problem of the twentieth century is the problem of the color line," few white Americans believed wholeheartedly in racial equality. Racial segregation remained entrenched across the country. Much of the Deep South, like Eastland's Mississippi, was a "closed society": black people had no political rights and lived on the margins of white society, impoverished and exploited. Northern cities proved more hospitable to African Americans, but schools, neighborhoods, public amenities like swimming pools, and many businesses remained segregated and unequal in the North as well.

Across the nation, however, winds of change were gathering. Between World War II and the 1970s, slowly at first, and then with greater urgency in the 1960s, the civil rights movement swept aside systematic racial segregation. It could not sweep away racial inequality in its entirety, but the movement constituted a "second Reconstruction" in which black activism reshaped the nation's laws and practices. Civil rights was the paradigmatic social movement of the twentieth century. Its model of nonviolent protest and its calls for self-determination inspired the New Left, feminism, the Chicano movement, the gay rights movement, the American Indian movement, and many others.

The black-led civil rights movement, joined at key moments by Latinos, Asian Americans, and Native Americans, redefined American *liberalism*. In the 1930s, New Deal liberalism had established a welfare state to protect citizens from economic hardship. The civil rights movement forged a new **rights liberalism**: the idea that individuals deserve state protection from discrimination. This version of liberalism focused on identities — such as race or gender, and eventually sexuality — rather than general social welfare. Rights liberalism proved to be both a necessary expansion of the nation's ideals and a wellspring of political backlash. Indeed, the quest for racial justice would contribute to a crisis of liberalism itself.

IDENTIFY THE BIG IDEA

How did the civil rights movement evolve over time, and how did competing ideas and political alliances affect its growth and that of other social movements?

rights liberalism
The conviction that individuals require government protection from discrimination. This version of liberalism was promoted by the civil rights and women's movements and focused on identities — such as race or gender — rather than the general social welfare of New Deal liberalism.

The March from Selma to Montgomery, 1965 Leading a throng of 25,000 people, Martin Luther King Jr. and his wife, Coretta Scott King, marched from Selma, Alabama, to Montgomery, the state capitol, in March of 1965.
AP Photo.

As you read, ask yourself why this chapter begins and ends with these dates and identify the links among related events.

1941
- A. Philip Randolph proposes march on Washington
- Roosevelt issues Executive Order 8802

1942
- Double V Campaign launched
- Congress of Racial Equality (CORE) founded

1947
- "To Secure These Rights" published
- Jackie Robinson integrates major league baseball
- *Mendez v. Westminster School District*

1948
- States' Rights Democratic Party (Dixiecrats) founded

1954
- *Brown v. Board of Education of Topeka*

1955
- Emmett Till murdered (August)
- Montgomery Bus Boycott begins (December)

1956
- Southern Manifesto issued against *Brown* ruling

1957
- Desegregation of Little Rock Central High School
- Southern Christian Leadership Conference (SCLC) founded

1960
- Greensboro, North Carolina, sit-ins (February)
- Student Nonviolent Coordinating Committee (SNCC) founded (April)

1961
- Freedom Rides (May)

1963
- Demonstrations in Birmingham, Alabama
- March on Washington for Jobs and Freedom (August)

1964
- Civil Rights Act passed by Congress
- Freedom Summer

1965
- Voting Rights Act passed by Congress
- Malcolm X assassinated (February 21)
- Riot in Watts neighborhood of Los Angeles (August)

1966
- Black Panther Party founded

1967
- Riots in Detroit and Newark

1968
- Martin Luther King Jr. assassinated (April 4)

1969
- Young Lords founded
- American Indian Occupation of Alcatraz

1972
- National Black Political Convention
- "Trail of Broken Treaties" protest

The Emerging Civil Rights Struggle, 1941–1957

As it took shape during World War II and the early Cold War, the campaign against racial injustice proceeded along two tracks: at the grass roots and in government institutions (federal courts, state legislatures, and ultimately the U.S. Congress). Labor unions, churches, and organizations such as the Congress of Racial Equality (CORE) inspired hundreds of thousands of ordinary citizens to join the movement. But grassroots protest was not African Americans' only weapon. They also had the Bill of Rights and the Reconstruction amendments to the Constitution. Civil rights lived in those documents — especially in the Fourteenth Amendment, which guaranteed equal protection under the law to all U.S. citizens, and in the Fifteenth, which guaranteed the right to vote regardless of "race, color, or previous condition of servitude" — but had been ignored or violated for nearly a century. The task was to restore the Constitution's legal force. Neither track, grassroots or legal, was entirely independent of the other. Together, they were the foundation of the fight for racial equality in the postwar decades.

Life Under Jim Crow

Racial segregation and economic exploitation defined the lives of the majority of African Americans in the postwar decades. Numbering 15 million in 1950, African Americans were approximately 10 percent of the U.S. population. In the South, however, they constituted between 30 and 50 percent of the population of several states, such as South Carolina and Mississippi. Segregation, commonly known as Jim Crow (Chapter 17), prevailed in every aspect of life in the southern states, where two-thirds of all African Americans lived in 1950. African Americans could not eat in restaurants patronized by whites or use the same waiting rooms at bus stations. All forms of public transportation were rigidly segregated by custom or by law. Public parks and libraries were segregated. Even drinking fountains were labeled "White" and "Colored."

This system of segregation underlay economic and political structures that further marginalized and disempowered black citizens. Virtually no African Americans were allowed to work for city or state government, and the best jobs in the private sector were reserved for whites. Black workers labored "in the back," cleaning, cooking, stocking shelves, and loading trucks for the lowest wages. Rural African Americans labored in a sharecropping system that kept them stuck in poverty, often prevented them from obtaining an education, and offered no avenue of escape. Politically, less than 20 percent of eligible black voters were allowed to vote, the result of poll taxes, literacy tests, intimidation, fraud, and the "white primary" (elections in which only whites could vote). This near-total disfranchisement gave whites power disproportionate to their numbers — black people were one-third of the residents of Mississippi, South Carolina, and Georgia but had basically no political voice in those states.

In the North, racial segregation in everyday life was less acute but just as tangible. Northern segregation took the form of a spatial system in which whites increasingly lived in suburbs or on the outskirts of cities, while African Americans were concentrated in declining downtown neighborhoods. The result was what many called ghettos: all-black districts characterized by high rents, low wages, and inadequate city services. Employment discrimination and their exclusion from job training left many African Americans without any means of support. Few jobs other than the most menial were open to African Americans; journalists, accountants, engineers, and other highly educated men from all-black colleges and universities often labored as railroad porters or cooks because jobs commensurate with their skills remained for whites only. These conditions produced a self-perpetuating cycle that kept far too many black citizens trapped on the social margins.

To be certain, African Americans found a measure of freedom in the

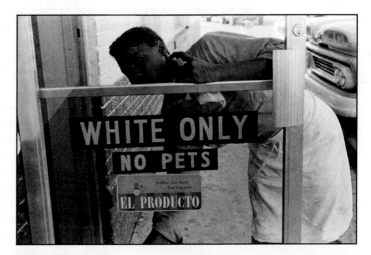

Segregation in Virginia, 1962 As the law of the land in most southern states, racial segregation (known as Jim Crow) required the complete separation of blacks and whites in most public spaces. The "white only" sign on a restaurant door shown in this 1962 photograph in Hampton, Virginia, was typical. Everything from restaurants, drinking fountains, public waiting areas to libraries, public parks, schools, restrooms, and even cola vending machines was subject to strict racial segregation. © Bruce Davidson/Magnum Photos.

North and West compared to the South. They could vote, participate in politics, and, at least after the early 1960s, enjoy equal access to public accommodations. But we err in thinking that racial segregation was only a southern condition or that poverty and racial discrimination were not also deeply entrenched in the North and West. In northern cities such as Detroit, Chicago, and Philadelphia, for instance, white home owners in the 1950s used various tactics — from police harassment to thrown bricks, burning crosses, bombs, and mob violence — to keep African Americans from living near them. Moreover, as we saw in Chapter 25, Federal Housing Administration (FHA) and bank redlining excluded African American home buyers from the all-white suburbs emerging around major cities. Racial segregation was a national, not regional, problem.

Origins of the Civil Rights Movement

Since racial injustice had been part of American life for hundreds of years, why did the civil rights movement arise when it did? After all, the National Association for the Advancement of Colored People (NAACP), founded in 1909, had begun challenging racial segregation in a series of court cases in the 1930s. And other organizations, such as Marcus Garvey's Universal Negro Improvement Association in the 1920s, had attracted significant popular support (Chapter 21). These precedents were important, but several factors came together in the middle of the twentieth century to make a broad movement possible.

An important influence was World War II. "The Jewish people and the Negro people both know the meaning of Nordic supremacy," wrote the African American poet Langston Hughes in 1945. In the war against fascism, the Allies sought to discredit racist Nazi ideology. Committed to fighting racism abroad, Americans increasingly condemned racism at home. The Cold War placed added pressure on U.S. officials. "More and more we are learning how closely our democracy is under observation," President Harry S. Truman commented in 1947. To inspire other nations in the global standoff with the Soviet Union, Truman explained, "we must correct the remaining imperfections in our practice of democracy."

Among the most consequential factors was the growth of the black middle class. Historically small, the black middle class experienced robust growth after World War II. Its ranks produced most of the civil rights leaders: ministers, teachers, trade unionists, attorneys, and other professionals. Churches, for centuries a sanctuary for black Americans, were especially important. Moreover, in the 1960s African American college students — part of the largest expansion of college enrollment in U.S. history — joined the movement, adding new energy and fresh ideas (Table 26.1). With access to education and media, this new middle class had more resources than ever before. Less dependent on white patronage, and therefore less vulnerable to white retaliation, middle-class African Americans were in a position to lead a movement for change.

TABLE 26.1

African American College Enrollment

Year	Number of African Americans Enrolled (rounded to nearest thousand)
1940	60,000
1950	110,000
1960	185,000
1970	430,000
1980	1.4 million
1990	3.6 million

Still other influences assisted the movement. White labor leaders were generally more equality-minded than the rank and file, but the United Auto Workers, the United Steelworkers, and the Communications Workers of America, among many other progressive trade unions, were reliable allies at the national level. The new medium of television, too, played a crucial role. When television networks covered early desegregation struggles — at Little Rock High School in 1957, for instance — Americans across the country saw the violence of white supremacy firsthand. None of these factors alone was decisive. None ensured an easy path. The civil rights movement faced enormous resistance and required dauntless courage and sacrifice from thousands upon thousands of activists for more than three decades. Ultimately, however, the movement changed the nation for the better and improved the lives of millions of Americans.

World War II: The Beginnings

During the war fought "to make the world safe for democracy," the United States was far from ready to extend full equality to its own black citizens. Black workers faced discrimination in wartime employment, and the more than 1 million black troops who served in World War II were placed in segregated units commanded solely by whites. Both at home and abroad, World War II "immeasurably magnified the Negro's awareness of the disparity between the American profession and practice of democracy," NAACP president Walter White observed.

Executive Order 8802 On the home front, activists pushed two strategies. First, A. Philip Randolph, whose **Brotherhood of Sleeping Car Porters** was the most prominent black trade union, called for a march on Washington in early 1941. Randolph planned to bring 100,000 protesters to the nation's capital to call for equal opportunity for black workers in war jobs — then just beginning to expand with President Franklin Roosevelt's pledge to supply the Allies with materiel. To avoid a divisive protest, FDR issued Executive Order 8802 in June of that year, prohibiting racial discrimination in defense industries, and Randolph agreed to cancel the march. The resulting Fair Employment Practice Committee (FEPC) had few enforcement powers, but it set an important precedent: federal action. Randolph's efforts showed that white leaders and institutions could be swayed by concerted African American pressure. It would be a critical lesson for the movement.

> **Brotherhood of Sleeping Car Porters**
> A prominent black trade union of railroad car porters working for the Pullman Company.

The Double V Campaign A second strategy jumped from the pages of the *Pittsburgh Courier*, one of the foremost African American newspapers of the era. It was the brainchild of an ordinary cafeteria worker from Kansas. In a 1942 letter to the editor, James G. Thompson urged that "colored Americans adopt the double VV for a double victory" — victory over fascism abroad and victory over racism at home. Edgar Rouzeau, editor of the paper's New York office, agreed: "Black America must fight two wars and win in both." Instantly dubbed the Double V Campaign, Thompson's notion, with Rouzeau's backing, spread like wildfire through black communities across the country. African Americans would demonstrate their loyalty and citizenship by fighting the Axis powers. But they would also demand, peacefully but emphatically, the defeat of racism at home. "The suffering and privation may be great," Rouzeau told his readers, "but the rewards loom even greater."

The Double V met considerable resistance. In war industries, factories periodically shut down in Chicago, Baltimore, Philadelphia, and other cities because of "hate strikes": the refusal of white workers to labor alongside black workers. Detroit was especially tense. Referring to the potential for racial strife, *Life* magazine reported in 1942 that "Detroit is Dynamite. . . . It can either blow up Hitler or blow up America." In 1943, it nearly did the latter. On a hot summer day, whites from the city's ethnic European neighborhoods taunted and beat African Americans in a local park. Three days of rioting ensued in which thirty-four people were killed, twenty-five of them black. Federal troops were called in to restore order.

Despite such incidents, and to some degree because of them, a generation was spurred into action during the war years. In New York City, employment discrimination on the city's transit lines prompted one of the first bus boycotts in the nation's history, led in 1941 by Harlem minister Adam Clayton Powell Jr. In Chicago, James Farmer and three other members of the Fellowship of Reconciliation (FOR), a nonviolent peace organization, founded the **Congress of Racial Equality (CORE)** in 1942. FOR and CORE embraced the philosophy of nonviolent direct action espoused by Mahatma Gandhi of India. Another FOR member in New York and proponent of direct action, Bayard Rustin, led one of the earliest challenges to southern segregation, the 1947 Journey of Reconciliation. Meanwhile, after the war, hundreds of thousands of African American veterans used the GI Bill to go to college, trade school, or graduate school, placing themselves in a position to push against segregation. At the war's end, Powell affirmed that "the black man . . . is ready to throw himself into the struggle to make the dream of America become flesh and blood, bread and butter."

Cold War Civil Rights

Demands for justice persisted in the early years of the Cold War. African American efforts were propelled by symbolic victories — as when Jackie Robinson broke through the color line in major league baseball by joining the Brooklyn Dodgers in 1947 — but the growing black vote in northern cities proved more consequential. During World War II, more than a million African Americans migrated to northern and western cities, where they joined the Democratic Party of Franklin Roosevelt and the New Deal (Map 26.1). This newfound political leverage awakened northern liberals, many of whom became allies of civil rights advocates. Ultimately, however, the Cold War produced mixed results, as the nation's growing anticommunism opened some avenues for civil rights while closing others.

Civil Rights and the New Deal Coalition   African American leaders were uncertain what to expect from President Truman, inheritor of the New Deal coalition but not opposed to using racist language himself. Though he did not immediately support social equality for African Americans, Truman supported civil rights because he believed in equality before the law. Moreover, he understood the growing importance of the small but often decisive black vote in key northern states such as New York, Illinois, Pennsylvania, and Michigan. Civil rights activists Randolph and Powell — along with vocal white liberals such as Hubert Humphrey, the mayor of Minneapolis, and members of Americans for Democratic Action (ADA), a liberal organization — pressed Truman to act.

Congress of Racial Equality (CORE)
Civil rights organization founded in 1942 in Chicago by James Farmer and other members of the Fellowship of Reconciliation (FOR) that espoused nonviolent direct action. In 1961 CORE organized a series of what were called Freedom Rides on interstate bus lines throughout the South to call attention to blatant violations of recent Supreme Court rulings against segregation in interstate commerce.

"To Secure These Rights"
The 1947 report by the Presidential Committee on Civil Rights that called for robust federal action to ensure equality for African Americans. President Truman asked Congress to make all of the report's recommendations — including the abolition of poll taxes and the restoration of the Fair Employment Practice Committee — into law, leading to discord in the Democratic Party.

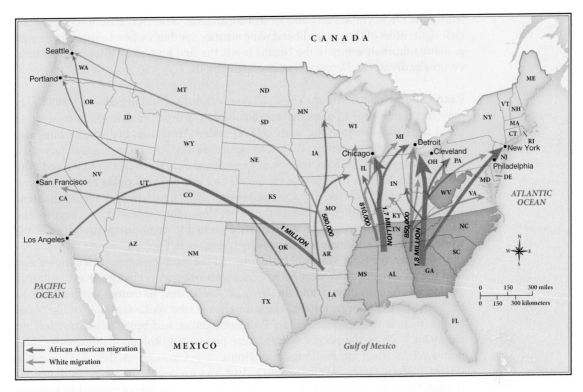

MAP 26.1 Internal Migrations

The migration of African Americans from the South to other regions of the country produced one of the most remarkable demographic shifts of the mid-twentieth century. Between World War I—which marked the start of the Great Migration—and the 1970s, more than 6 million African Americans left the South. Where they settled in the North and West, they helped change the politics of entire cities and even states. Seeking black votes, which had become a key to victory in major cities, liberal Democrats and Republicans alike in New York, Illinois, California, and Pennsylvania, for instance, increasingly made civil rights part of their platform. In this way, migration advanced the political cause of black equality.

With no support for civil rights in Congress, Truman turned to executive action. In 1946, he appointed the Presidential Committee on Civil Rights, whose 1947 report, **"To Secure These Rights,"** called for robust federal action to ensure black equality. With the report's recommendations in mind, in 1948 Truman issued an executive order desegregating employment in federal agencies and, under pressure from Randolph's Committee Against Jim Crow in Military Service, desegregated the armed forces. Truman then sent a message to Congress asking that every one of the report's recommendations—including the abolition of poll taxes and the restoration of the Fair Employment Practice Committee—be made into law. It was the most aggressive and politically bold call for racial equality by the leader of a major political party since Reconstruction.

Truman's boldness was too much for southern Democrats. Under the leadership of Strom Thurmond, governor of South Carolina, white Democrats from the South formed the **States' Rights Democratic Party**, known popularly as the Dixiecrats, for the 1948 election (Chapter 24). This brought into focus an internal struggle developing

States' Rights Democratic Party
Known popularly as the Dixiecrats, a breakaway party of white Democrats from the South that formed for the 1948 election. Its formation shed light on an internal struggle between the civil rights aims of the party's liberal wing and southern white Democrats.

within the Democratic Party and its still-formidable New Deal coalition. Would the civil rights aims of the party's liberal wing alienate southern white Democrats, as well as many suburban whites in the North? It was the first hint of the discord that would eventually divide the Democratic Party in the 1960s.

Race and Anticommunism   The Cold War both helped and impeded the civil rights movement. In a time of growing fear of communist expansionism, Truman worried about America's image in the world. He reminded Americans that when whites and blacks "fail to live together in peace," that failure harmed "the cause of democracy itself in the whole world." Indeed, the Soviet Union used American racism to discredit the United States abroad. "We cannot escape the fact that our civil rights record has been an issue in world politics," the Committee on Civil Rights wrote. International tensions between the United States and the Soviet Union thus appeared to strengthen the hand of civil rights leaders, because America needed to demonstrate to the rest of the world that its racial climate was improving (America in Global Context).

However, the Cold War, McCarthyism, and the hunt for subversives at home also held the civil rights movement back. Civil rights opponents charged that racial integration was "communistic," and the NAACP was banned in many southern states as an "anti-American" organization. Black Americans who spoke favorably of the Soviet Union, such as the actor and singer Paul Robeson, or had been "fellow travelers" in the 1930s, such as the pacifist Rustin, were persecuted. Robeson, whose career was destroyed by such accusations, told House Un-American Activities Committee (HUAC) interrogators, "My father was a slave, and my people died to build this country, and I am going to . . . have a part of it just like you." The fate of people like Robeson showed that the Cold War could work *against* the civil rights cause just as easily as for it.

Mexican Americans and Japanese Americans

African Americans were the most prominent, but not the only, group in American society to organize against racial injustice in the 1940s. In the Southwest, from Texas to California, Mexican immigrants and Mexican Americans endured a "caste" system not unlike the Jim Crow system in the South. In Texas, for instance, poll taxes kept most Mexican American citizens from voting. Decades of discrimination by employers in agriculture and manufacturing — made possible by the constant supply of cheap labor from across the border — suppressed wages and kept the majority of Mexican Americans barely above poverty. Many lived in *colonias* or barrios, neighborhoods separated from Anglos and often lacking sidewalks, reliable electricity and water, and public transportation.

Developments within the Mexican American community set the stage for fresh challenges to these conditions in the 1940s. Labor activism, especially in Congress of Industrial Organizations (CIO) unions with large numbers of Mexican Americans, improved wages and working conditions in some industries and produced a new generation of leaders. More than 400,000 Mexican Americans also served in World War II. Having fought for their country, many returned to the United States determined to challenge their second-class citizenship. Additionally, a new Mexican American middle class began to take shape in major cities such as Los Angeles, San Antonio, El Paso, and Chicago, which, like the African American middle class, gave leaders and resources to the cause.

Freedom in the United States and Africa

HAILOU WOLDE-GIORGHIS

Hailou Wolde-Giorghis was an Ethiopian student who visited the United States at the invitation of the State Department in the early 1960s.

SOURCE: Hailou Wolde-Giorghis, "My Encounters with Racism in the United States," in *Views of America*, ed. Alan F. Westin et al. (New York: Harcourt, Brace, and World, 1966), 228–231.

"Negroes are dirty," say the whites, but in nearly all restaurants I saw Negro waiters and cooks. "They're lazy": I noticed that it is the Negro who does the hardest manual work. They are said to be uncultivated and are therefore denied access to culture. As George Bernard Shaw said, "The haughty American nation makes the Negro shine its shoes, and then demonstrates his physical and mental inferiority by the fact that he is a shoe-cleaner." . . .

What is known as integration in the South is the ability of a Negro to enter a shop and buy a record, or the fact that, of ten thousand students enrolled in a university, two of them are Negroes. "A miracle!" they cry. Real integration, however, does not exist, not even in the North, and by real integration I mean interracial communication, complete equality in the strict sense of the word. Still another example drawn from the South: the manager of a television studio told me in frigid terms that he would not hire Negroes; there would be a scandal and all his sponsors would protest.

MARTIN LUTHER KING JR.

Here, the American civil rights leader celebrates the independence of the African nation of Ghana in 1957.

SOURCE: Martin Luther King Jr., "The Birth of a New Nation," *Liberation* 28 (April 1957).

And it's a beautiful thing, isn't it that . . . [Ghana] is now free and is free without rising up with arms and ammunition. It is free through nonviolent means. Because of that the British Empire will not have the bitterness for Ghana that she has for China, so to speak. Because of that when the British Empire leaves Ghana she leaves with a different attitude than she would have left with if she had been driven out by armies. We've got to revolt in such a way that after revolt is over we can live with people as their brothers and sisters.

KWAME NKRUMAH

Kwame Nkrumah was the first president of the independent nation of Ghana. In the 1930s and 1940s, Nkrumah studied in the United States, earning degrees at Lincoln University and the University of Pennsylvania.

SOURCE: Kwame Nkrumah, *I Speak of Freedom: A Statement of African Ideology* (New York: Praeger, 1961), ix.

The "wind of change" has become a raging hurricane, sweeping away the old colonialist Africa. The year 1960 was Africa's year. In that year alone, seventeen African States emerged as proud and independent sovereign nations. Now the ultimate freedom of the whole of Africa can no more be in doubt.

For centuries, Europeans dominated the African continent. The white man arrogated to himself the right to rule and to be obeyed by the non-white. . . .

All this makes a sad story, but now we must be prepared to bury the past with its unpleasant memories and look to the future. All we ask of the former colonial powers is their goodwill and cooperation to remedy past mistakes and injustices and to grant independence to the colonies in Africa.

QUESTIONS FOR ANALYSIS

1. Wolde-Giorghis is especially critical of southern "integration." As an African, what kind of perspective would he bring to this question?

2. What values and goals do King and Nkrumah seem to share? How were their circumstances and goals different?

3. Compare the circumstances of African Americans in the United States and Africans in nations colonized by Europeans. What were the similarities and differences?

American GI Forum

A group founded by World War II veterans in Corpus Christi, Texas, in 1948 to protest the poor treatment of Mexican American soldiers and veterans.

Community Services Organization (CSO)

A Latino civil rights group founded in Los Angeles in 1947 that trained many Latino politicians and community activists, including Cesar Chavez and Dolores Huerta.

In Texas and California, Mexican Americans created new civil rights organizations in the postwar years. In Corpus Christi, Texas, World War II veterans founded the **American GI Forum** in 1948 to protest the poor treatment of Mexican American soldiers and veterans. Activists in Los Angeles created the **Community Services Organization (CSO)** the same year. Both groups arose to address specific local injustices (such as the segregation of military cemeteries), but they quickly broadened their scope to encompass political and economic justice for the larger community. Among the first young activists to work for the CSO were Cesar Chavez and Dolores Huerta, who would later found the United Farm Workers (UFW) and inspire the Chicano movement of the 1960s.

Activists also pushed for legal change. In 1947, five Mexican American fathers in California sued a local school district for placing their children in separate "Mexican" schools. The case, *Mendez v. Westminster School District*, never made it to the U.S. Supreme Court. But the Ninth Circuit Court ruled such segregation unconstitutional, laying the legal groundwork for broader challenges to racial inequality. Among those filing briefs in the case was the NAACP's Thurgood Marshall, who was then developing the legal strategy to strike at racial segregation in the South. In another significant legal victory, the Supreme Court ruled in 1954 — just two weeks before the landmark *Brown v. Board of Education* decision — that Mexican Americans constituted a "distinct class" that could claim constitutional protection from discrimination.

Also on the West Coast, Japanese Americans accelerated their legal challenge to discrimination. Undeterred by rulings in the *Hirabayashi* (1943) and *Korematsu* (1944) cases upholding wartime imprisonment (Chapter 23), the Japanese American Citizens League (JACL) filed lawsuits in the late 1940s to regain property lost during the war. The JACL also challenged the constitutionality of California's Alien Land Law, which prohibited Japanese immigrants from owning land, and successfully lobbied Congress to enable those same immigrants to become citizens — a right they were denied for fifty years. These efforts by Mexican and Japanese Americans enlarged the sphere of civil rights and laid the foundation for a broader notion of racial equality in the postwar years.

Fighting for Equality Before the Law

With civil rights legislation blocked in Congress by southern Democrats throughout the 1950s, activists looked in two different directions for a breakthrough: to northern state legislatures and to the federal courts. School segregation remained a stubborn problem in northern states, but the biggest obstacle to black progress there was persistent job and housing discrimination. The states with the largest African American populations, and hence the largest share of black Democratic Party voters, became testing grounds for state legislation to end such discriminatory practices.

Winning antidiscrimination legislation depended on coalition politics. African American activists forged alliances with trade unions and liberal organizations such as the American Friends Service Committee (a Quaker group), among many others. Progress was slow and often occurred only after long periods of unglamorous struggle to win votes in state capitals such as Albany, New York; Springfield, Illinois; and Lansing, Michigan. The first fair employment laws had come in New York and New Jersey in 1945. A decade passed, however, before other states with significant black populations passed similar legislation. Antidiscrimination laws in housing were even more difficult to pass, with most progress not coming until the 1960s. These legislative campaigns in northern states received little national attention, but they were instrumental in laying the groundwork for legal equality outside the South.

Thurgood Marshall Because the vast majority of southern African Americans were prohibited from voting, state legislatures there were closed to the kind of organized political pressure possible in the North. Thus activists looked to federal courts for leverage. In the late 1930s, NAACP lawyers Thurgood Marshall, Charles Hamilton Houston, and William Hastie had begun preparing the legal ground in a series of cases challenging racial discrimination. The key was prodding the U.S. Supreme Court to use the Fourteenth Amendment's "equal protection" clause to overturn its 1896 ruling in *Plessy v. Ferguson*, which upheld racial segregation under the "separate but equal" doctrine.

Thurgood Marshall and Daisy Bates Thurgood Marshall was one of the most influential legal thinkers of the twentieth century. As director of the NAACP Legal Defense Fund during the 1940s and 1950s, he helped dismantle the legal underpinnings of racial discrimination and segregation — he argued the *Brown* case, among dozens of others, for the NAACP. In 1967, he was appointed by President Johnson to the U.S. Supreme Court. Daisy Bates was a journalist and black freedom activist whose reporting in the black press in the 1950s was widely read and influential. She headed the Arkansas NAACP and played a prominent role on the national NAACP board. Here, Marshall and Bates sit on the steps of the Supreme Court in 1958 with some of the "Little Rock Nine," the young men and women who risked their lives to desegregate public schools in Arkansas. Bettmann/Getty Images.

Marshall was the great-grandson of slaves. Of modest origins, his parents instilled in him a faith in law and the Constitution. After his 1930 graduation from Lincoln University, a prestigious African American institution near Philadelphia, Marshall applied to the University of Maryland Law School. Denied admission because the school did not accept black applicants, he enrolled at all-black Howard University. There Marshall met Houston, a law school dean, and the two forged a friendship and intellectual partnership that would change the face of American legal history. Marshall, with Houston's and Hastie's critical strategic input, would argue most of the NAACP's landmark cases. (In 1967, President Johnson appointed Marshall to the Supreme Court — the first African American to have that honor.)

Marshall, Houston, Hastie, and six other attorneys filed suit after suit, deliberately selecting each case from dozens of possibilities. The strategy was slow and time-consuming, but progress came. In 1936, Marshall and Houston won a state case that forced the University of Maryland Law School to admit qualified African Americans — a ruling of obvious significance to Marshall. Eight years later, in *Smith v. Allwright* (1944), Marshall convinced the U.S. Supreme Court that all-white primaries were unconstitutional. In 1950, with Marshall once again arguing the case, the Supreme Court ruled in *McLaurin v. Oklahoma* that universities could not segregate black students from others on campus. None of these cases produced swift changes in the daily lives of most African Americans, but they confirmed that civil rights attorneys were on the right track.

Brown v. Board of Education The NAACP's legal strategy achieved its ultimate validation in a case involving Linda Brown, a black pupil in Topeka, Kansas, who had been forced to attend a distant segregated school rather than the nearby white elementary school. In his argument before the court in **Brown v. Board of Education of Topeka** (1954), Marshall contended that such segregation was unconstitutional because it denied Linda Brown the "equal protection of the laws" guaranteed by the Fourteenth Amendment (Map 26.2). In a unanimous decision on May 17, 1954, the Supreme Court agreed, overturning the "separate but equal" doctrine at last. Writing for the Court, the new chief justice, Earl Warren, wrote: "We conclude that in the field of public education the doctrine of 'separate but equal' has no place. Separate educational facilities are inherently unequal." In an implementing 1955 decision known as *Brown II*, the Court declared that desegregation should proceed "with all deliberate speed."

In the South, however, Virginia senator Harry F. Byrd issued a call for "massive resistance." Calling May 17 "Black Monday," the Mississippi segregationist Tom P. Brady invoked the language of the Cold War to discredit the decision, assailing the "totalitarian government" that had rendered the decision in the name of "socialism and communism." That year, half a million southerners joined White Citizens' Councils dedicated to blocking school integration. Some whites revived the old tactics of violence and intimidation, swelling the ranks of the Ku Klux Klan to levels not seen since the 1920s. The "Southern Manifesto," signed in 1956 by 101 members of Congress, denounced the *Brown* decision as "a clear abuse of judicial power" and encouraged local officials to defy it. The white South had declared all-out war on *Brown*.

Enforcement of the Supreme Court's decision was complicated further by Dwight Eisenhower's presence in the White House — the president was no champion of civil

Brown v. Board of Education of Topeka
Supreme Court ruling of 1954 that overturned the "separate but equal" precedent established in *Plessy v. Ferguson* in 1896. The Court declared that separate educational facilities were inherently unequal and thus violated the Fourteenth Amendment.

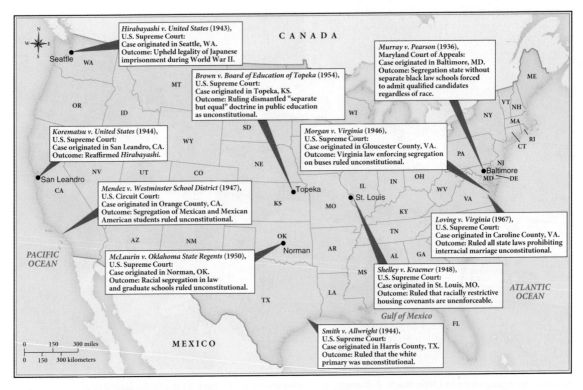

MAP 26.2 Desegregation Court Cases

Desegregation court battles were not limited to the South. Note the important California cases regarding Mexican Americans and Japanese Americans. Two seminal decisions, the 1948 housing decision in *Shelley v. Kraemer* and the 1954 school decision in *Brown v. Board of Education*, originated in Missouri and Kansas, respectively. This map helps show that racial segregation and discrimination were a national, not simply a southern, problem.

rights. Eisenhower accepted the *Brown* decision as the law of the land, but he thought it a mistake. Ike was especially unhappy about the prospect of committing federal power to enforce the decision. A crisis in Little Rock, Arkansas, forced his hand. In September 1957, when nine black students attempted to enroll at the all-white Central High School, Governor Orval Faubus called out the National Guard to bar them. Angry white mobs appeared daily to taunt the students, chanting "Go back to the jungle." As the vicious scenes played out on television night after night, Eisenhower finally acted. He sent 1,000 federal troops to Little Rock and nationalized the Arkansas National Guard, ordering them to protect the black students. Eisenhower thus became the first president since Reconstruction to use federal troops to enforce the rights of African Americans. But Little Rock also showed that southern officials had more loyalty to local custom than to the law—a repeated problem in the post-*Brown* era.

> **IN YOUR OWN WORDS** What factors best explain why and how the civil rights movement developed between 1941 and 1954?

School Desegregation in Little Rock, Arkansas Less well known than the crisis at Little Rock's Central High School the same year, the circumstances at North Little Rock were nonetheless strikingly similar: white resistance to the enrollment of a handful of black students. In this photograph, white students block the doors of North Little Rock High School, preventing six African American students from entering on September 9, 1957. This photograph is noteworthy because it shows a striking new feature of southern racial politics: the presence of film and television cameras that broadcast these images to the nation and the world. AP Photo/William P. Straeter.

Forging a Protest Movement, 1955–1965

By declaring racial segregation integral to the South's "habits, traditions, and way of life," the Southern Manifesto signaled that many whites would not readily accept black equality. As the battle over desegregating Little Rock High School had shown, the unwillingness of local officials to enforce *Brown* could render the decision invalid in practice. If legal victories would not be enough, citizens themselves, black and white, would have to take to the streets and demand justice. Following the *Brown* decision, they did just that, forging a protest movement unique in the history of the United States.

Nonviolent Direct Action

Brown had been the law of the land for barely a year when a single act of violence struck at the heart of black America. A fourteen-year-old African American from the South Side of Chicago, Emmett Till, was visiting relatives in Mississippi in the summer of 1955. Seen talking to a white woman in a grocery store, Till was tortured and murdered under cover of night. His mutilated body was found at the bottom of a river, tied with barbed wire to a heavy steel cotton gin fan. Photos of Till's body in *Jet* magazine brought national attention to the heinous crime.

Two white men were arrested for Till's murder. During the trial, followed closely in black communities across the country, the lone witness to Till's kidnapping — his uncle, Mose Wright — identified both killers. Feeling "the blood boil in hundreds of white people as they sat glaring in the courtroom," Wright said, "it was the first time in my life I had the courage to accuse a white man of a crime." Despite Wright's eyewitness testimony, the all-white jury found the defendants innocent. This miscarriage of justice — later, the killers even admitted their guilt in a *Look* magazine article — galvanized an entire generation of African Americans; no one who lived through the Till incident ever forgot it.

Montgomery Bus Boycott In the wake of the Till murder, civil rights advocates needed some good news. They received it three months later, as southern black leaders embraced an old tactic put to new ends: nonviolent direct action. On December 1, 1955, Rosa Parks, a civil rights activist in Montgomery, Alabama, refused to give up her seat on a bus to a white man. She was arrested and charged with violating a local segregation ordinance. Parks's act was not the spur-of-the-moment decision that it seemed: a longtime NAACP member, she and other female civil rights activists in Montgomery had been contemplating such an act for some time. Parks's arrest became the focal point for the black community's challenge against segregated buses, which were a powerful symbol of the city's racial hierarchy.

Soon after Parks's arrest, the black community turned for leadership to the Reverend Martin Luther King Jr., the recently appointed pastor of Montgomery's Dexter Street Baptist Church. The son of a prominent Atlanta minister, King embraced the teachings of Mahatma Gandhi. Working closely, but behind the scenes, with Bayard Rustin, King deepened his investment in nonviolent philosophy and the practice of direct action, which Rustin and others in the Fellowship of Reconciliation had first used in the 1940s. King and other black ministers endorsed a plan proposed by a local black women's organization to boycott Montgomery's bus system. The **Montgomery Bus Boycott** was inspired by similar boycotts that had taken place in Harlem in 1941 and Baton Rouge, Louisiana, in 1953.

For the next 381 days, Montgomery's African Americans formed car pools or walked to work. "Darling, it's empty!" Coretta Scott King exclaimed to her husband as a bus normally filled with black riders rolled by their living room window on the first day of the boycott. The transit company neared bankruptcy, and downtown stores complained about the loss of business. But only after the Supreme Court ruled in November 1956 that bus segregation was unconstitutional did the city of Montgomery finally comply. "My feets is tired, but my soul is rested," said one woman boycotter.

The Montgomery Bus Boycott catapulted King to national prominence. In 1957, along with the Reverend Ralph Abernathy and dozens of black ministers from across the South, he founded the **Southern Christian Leadership Conference (SCLC)** in Atlanta. The black church, long the center of African American social and cultural life, now lent its moral and organizational strength to the civil rights movement. Black churchwomen were a tower of strength, transferring the skills they had honed during years of church work to the fight for civil rights. The SCLC quickly joined the NAACP at the leading edge of the movement for racial justice.

Montgomery Bus Boycott
Yearlong boycott of Montgomery's segregated bus system in 1955–1956 by the city's African American population. The boycott brought Martin Luther King Jr. to national prominence and ended in victory when the Supreme Court declared segregated seating on public transportation unconstitutional.

Southern Christian Leadership Conference (SCLC)
After the Montgomery Bus Boycott, Martin Luther King Jr. and other civil rights leaders formed the SCLC in 1957 to coordinate civil rights activity in the South.

Student Nonviolent Coordinating Committee (SNCC)
A student civil rights group founded in 1960 under the mentorship of activist Ella Baker. SNCC initially embraced an interracial and nonhierarchical structure that encouraged leadership at the grassroots level and practiced the civil disobedience principles of Martin Luther King Jr. As violence toward civil rights activists escalated nationwide in the 1960s, SNCC expelled nonblack members and promoted "black power" and the teachings of Malcolm X.

Greensboro Sit-Ins The battle for civil rights entered a new phase in Greensboro, North Carolina, on February 1, 1960, when four black college students took seats at the whites-only lunch counter at the local Woolworth's drugstore, which had a diner-style lunch counter, as most southern drugstores in that era did. This simple act was entirely the brainchild of the four students, who had discussed it in their dorm rooms over several preceding nights. A New York–based spokesman for Woolworth's said the chain would "abide by local custom," which meant refusing to serve African Americans at the lunch counter. The students were determined to "sit in" until they were served. For three weeks, hundreds of students inspired by the original foursome took turns sitting at the counters, quietly eating, doing homework, or reading. Taunted and beaten by groups of whites, pelted with food and other debris, the black students — often occupying more than sixty of the sixty-six seats — held strong. Although many were arrested, the tactic worked: the Woolworth's lunch counter was desegregated, and sit-ins quickly spread to other southern cities.

Ella Baker Born in Virginia and educated at Shaw University in Raleigh, North Carolina, Ella Baker was one of the foremost theorists of grassroots, participatory democracy in the United States. Active all her life in the black freedom movement, in 1960 Baker cofounded the Student Nonviolent Coordinating Committee (SNCC). Her advocacy of leadership by ordinary, nonelite people often led her to disagree with the top-down movement strategy of Martin Luther King Jr. and other ministers of the Southern Christian Leadership Conference (SCLC). AP Photo/Jack Harris.

Ella Baker and SNCC Inspired by the developments in Greensboro and elsewhere, Ella Baker, an administrator with the SCLC, helped organize the **Student Nonviolent Coordinating Committee** (**SNCC**, pronounced "Snick") in 1960 to facilitate student sit-ins. Rolling like a great wave across the Upper South, from North Carolina into Virginia, Maryland, and Tennessee, sit-ins had been launched by students in 126 cities by the end of the year. More than 50,000 people participated, and 3,600 went to jail. The sit-ins drew black college students into the movement in significant numbers for the first time. Northern students formed solidarity committees and raised money for bail. SNCC quickly emerged as the most important student protest organization in the country and inspired a generation of students on college campuses across the nation.

Baker took a special interest in these students because she found them receptive to her notion of participatory democracy (Interpretations). The granddaughter of slaves, Baker had moved to Harlem in the 1930s, where she worked for New Deal agencies and then the NAACP. She believed in nurturing leaders from the grass roots, encouraging ordinary people to stand up for their rights rather than depend on charismatic figureheads. "My theory is, strong people don't need strong leaders," she once said. Nonetheless, Baker nurtured a generation of young activists in SNCC, including Stokely Carmichael, Anne Moody, John Lewis, and Diane

INTERPRETATIONS

Was Martin Luther King Jr. a Radical or a Reformer?

In 1983, when Congress established the national holiday that celebrates Martin Luther King Jr.'s birthday each January, members of Congress acknowledged King's pioneering work to advance the cause of black civil rights. But what did King's work involve? For the past few decades, scholars of the civil rights movement have debated how best to understand the movement and King's particular role in it. Some scholars have characterized King as a reformer who "dreamed" of an integrated America where, as he said on the steps of the Lincoln Memorial, "little black boys and black girls will be able to join hands with little white boys and white girls as sisters and brothers." Others have argued that King's vision was far more radical than racial integration alone. So who was King—a radical or a reformer?

In the excerpts below, Thomas F. Jackson and Barbara Ransby present differing portraits of King. In his book, Jackson discusses King's work in the context of a campaign for human rights. Ransby, who wrote a biography of King's civil rights contemporary Ella Baker, draws a distinction between their approaches to the movement.

THOMAS F. JACKSON

SOURCE: Thomas F. Jackson, *From Civil Rights to Human Rights: Martin Luther King, Jr., and the Struggle for Economic Justice* (Philadelphia: University of Pennsylvania Press, 2013), 2.

By 1965, King's radical voice rang more clearly when he confessed that his dream had turned into a "nightmare." The dream shattered when whites murdered voting rights workers in Alabama, when police battled blacks in Los Angeles, when he met jobless and "hopeless" blacks on desperate Chicago streets, and when he saw hunger and poverty in rural Mississippi and Appalachia. But King picked up the shards of his shattered dreams and reassembled them into more radical visions of emancipation for all poor people. . . . Dreams of decent jobs, affordable integrated housing, and adequate family incomes remained central to King's public ministry until his death.

BARBARA RANSBY

SOURCE: Barbara Ransby, *Ella Baker and the Black Freedom Movement* (Chapel Hill: University of North Carolina Press, 2003), 189–191.

The conflict between [King and Baker] reveals more fundamental conflicts between black politics and African American culture over the meanings of American democracy and the pathways toward social change. . . . Baker described [King] as a pampered member of Atlanta's black elite . . . a member of a coddled "silver spoon brigade." . . . In Baker's eyes, King did not identify closely enough with the people he sought to lead. He did not situate himself among them but remained above them. . . . Baker and King . . . translated religious faith into their political identities in profoundly different ways. Above all, they defined the confluence of their roles as individuals and their roles as participants in a mass movement for social change quite distinctly. Baker was a militant egalitarian, and King was a sophisticated southern Baptist preacher.

QUESTIONS FOR ANALYSIS

1. Name one key difference in the way these two historians describe King and his work in the civil rights movement.
2. What qualities does each of these historians use in defining a "radical" and a "reformer"?
3. Based on your reading of the excerpts and Chapter 26's discussion of the civil rights movement, why do you think Congress singled out King from among the many civil rights leaders and activists?

Nash, who went on to become some of the most important civil rights leaders in the United States.

Freedom Rides   Emboldened by SNCC's sit-in tactics, in 1961 the Congress of Racial Equality (CORE) organized a series of what were called Freedom Rides on interstate bus lines throughout the South. The aim was to call attention to blatant violations of recent Supreme Court rulings that had declared segregation in interstate commerce unconstitutional. The activists who signed on — mostly young, both black and white — knew that they were taking their lives in their hands. They found courage in song, as civil rights activists had begun to do across the country, with lyrics such as "I'm taking a ride on the Greyhound bus line. . . . Hallelujah, I'm traveling down freedom's main line!"

Courage they needed. Club-wielding Klansmen attacked the buses when they stopped in small towns. Outside Anniston, Alabama, one bus was firebombed; the Freedom Riders escaped only moments before it exploded. Some riders were then brutally beaten. Freedom Riders and news reporters were also viciously attacked by Klansmen in Birmingham and Montgomery. Despite the violence, state authorities refused to intervene. "I cannot guarantee protection for this bunch of rabble rousers," declared Governor John Patterson of Alabama.

Once again, local officials' refusal to enforce the law left the fate of the Freedom Riders in Washington's hands. The new president, John F. Kennedy, was cautious about civil rights. Despite a campaign commitment, he failed to deliver on a civil rights bill. Elected by a thin margin, Kennedy believed that he could ill afford to lose the support of powerful southern senators. But civil rights was unlike other domestic issues. Its fate was going to be decided not in the halls of Congress, but on the streets of southern cities. Although President Kennedy discouraged the Freedom Rides, beatings shown on the nightly news forced Attorney General Robert Kennedy to dispatch federal marshals. Civil rights activists thus learned the tactical value of nonviolent protest that provoked violent white resistance.

The victories so far had been limited, but the groundwork had been laid for a civil rights offensive that would transform the nation. The NAACP's legal strategy had been followed by the emergence of a major protest movement. And now civil rights leaders focused their attention on Congress.

Legislating Civil Rights, 1963–1965

The first civil rights law in the nation's history came in 1866 just after the Civil War. Its provisions were long ignored (Chapter 14). A second law was passed during Reconstruction in 1875, but it was declared unconstitutional by the Supreme Court. For nearly ninety years, new civil rights legislation was blocked or filibustered by southern Democrats in Congress. Only a weak, largely symbolic act was passed in 1957 during the Eisenhower administration. But by the early 1960s, with legal precedents in their favor and nonviolent protest awakening the nation, civil rights leaders believed the time had come for a serious civil rights bill. The challenge was getting one through a still-reluctant Congress.

The Battle for Birmingham   The road to such a bill began when Martin Luther King Jr. called for demonstrations in "the most segregated city in the United States": Birmingham, Alabama. King and the SCLC needed a concrete victory in Birmingham to validate their strategy of nonviolent direct action. In May 1963, thousands of black marchers protested employment discrimination in Birmingham's department stores. Eugene "Bull" Connor, the city's public safety commissioner, ordered the city's police troops to meet the marchers with violent force: snarling dogs, electric cattle prods, and high-pressure fire hoses. Television cameras captured the scene for the evening news.

While serving a jail sentence for leading the march, King, scribbling in pencil on any paper he could find, composed one of the classic documents of nonviolent direct action: "Letter from Birmingham Jail." "Why direct action?" King asked. "There is a type of constructive, nonviolent tension that is necessary for growth," he began his answer. The civil rights movement sought, King continued, "to create such a crisis and establish such a creative tension." Grounding his appeal in equal parts Christian brotherhood and democratic liberalism, King argued that Americans confronted a moral choice: they could "preserve the evil system of segregation" or take the side of "those great wells of democracy . . . the Constitution and the Declaration of Independence."

Outraged by the brutality in Birmingham and embarrassed by King's imprisonment for leading a nonviolent march, President Kennedy decided that it was time to act. On June 11, 1963, after newly elected Alabama governor George Wallace barred two black students from the state university, Kennedy went on television to denounce racism and promise a new civil rights bill. Many black leaders felt Kennedy's action was long overdue, but they nonetheless hailed this "Second Emancipation Proclamation." That night, Medgar Evers, president of the Mississippi chapter of the NAACP, was shot in the back in his driveway in Jackson by a white supremacist. Evers's martyrdom became a spur to further action (Map 26.3).

The March on Washington To marshal support for Kennedy's bill, civil rights leaders took advantage of a long-planned event set for that August. It was the massive demonstration in Washington that had first been proposed by A. Philip Randolph in 1941. Working with Bayard Rustin, Randolph revived the idea and in early 1963 called for a march to mark the centennial of the Emancipation Proclamation. Under the leadership of Randolph and Rustin, thousands of volunteers across the country coordinated car pools, "freedom buses," and "freedom trains," and on August 28, 1963, delivered a quarter of a million people to the Lincoln Memorial for the **March on Washington**, officially named the March on Washington for Jobs and Freedom.

Although Randolph and Rustin planned the event, Martin Luther King Jr. was the public face of the march. It was King's dramatic "I Have a Dream" speech, beginning with his admonition that too many black people lived "on a lonely island of poverty" and ending with the exclamation from a traditional black spiritual — "Free at last! Free at last! Thank God almighty, we are free at last!" — that captured the nation's imagination. The sight of 250,000 blacks and whites marching solemnly together marked the high point of the civil rights movement and confirmed King's position as the leading spokesperson for the cause.

To have any chance of getting the civil rights bill through Congress, King, Randolph, and Rustin knew they had to sustain this broad coalition of blacks and whites. They could afford to alienate no one. Reflecting a younger, more militant set of activists, however, SNCC member John Lewis had prepared a provocative speech

March on Washington
Officially named the March on Washington for Jobs and Freedom, on August 28, 1963, a quarter of a million people marched to the Lincoln Memorial to demand that Congress end Jim Crow racial discrimination and launch a major jobs program to bring needed employment to black communities.

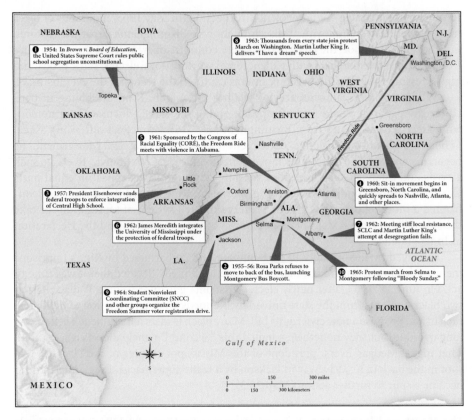

MAP 26.3 The Civil Rights Struggle, 1954–1965

In the postwar battle for black civil rights, the first major victory was the NAACP litigation of *Brown v. Board of Education*, which declared public school segregation unconstitutional. As indicated on this map, the struggle then quickly spread, raising other issues and seeding new organizations. Other organizations quickly joined the battle and shifted the focus away from the courts to mass action and organization. The year 1965 marked the high point, when violence against the Selma, Alabama, marchers spurred the passage of the Voting Rights Act.

for that afternoon. In his original draft of the speech, Lewis wrote, "The time will come when we will not confine our marching to Washington. We will march through the South, through the Heart of Dixie, the way Sherman did." Signaling a growing restlessness among black youth, Lewis warned: "We shall fragment the South into a thousand pieces and put them back together again in the image of democracy." Fearing the speech would alienate white supporters, Rustin and others implored Lewis to tone down his rhetoric. With only minutes to spare before he stepped up to the podium, Lewis agreed. He delivered a more conciliatory speech, but his conflict with march organizers signaled an emerging rift in the movement (Thinking Like a Historian).

Although the March on Washington galvanized public opinion, it changed few congressional votes. Southern senators continued to block Kennedy's legislation. Georgia senator Richard Russell, a leader of the opposition, refused to support any bill that would in his words "bring about social equality and intermingling and amalgamation of the races." Then, tragedies began to pile up, one on another. In September, white supremacists bombed a Baptist church in Birmingham, killing four black girls in Sunday school. Less than two months later, Kennedy himself lay dead, the victim of assassination.

On assuming the presidency, Lyndon Johnson made passing the civil rights bill a priority. A southerner and former Senate majority leader, Johnson was renowned for his fierce persuasive style and tough political bargaining. By appealing to the white South's conscience, invoking the memory of the slain JFK, and practicing his own brand of hardball politics, Johnson overcame the filibuster. In June 1964, Congress approved the most far-reaching civil rights law since Reconstruction. The keystone of the **Civil Rights Act of 1964**, Title VII, outlawed discrimination in employment on the basis of race, religion, national origin, and sex. Another section guaranteed equal access to public accommodations and schools. The law granted new enforcement powers to the U.S. attorney general and established the Equal Employment Opportunity Commission to implement the prohibition against job discrimination.

Civil Rights Act of 1964
Law that responded to demands of the civil rights movement by making discrimination in employment, education, and public accommodations illegal. It was the strongest such measure since Reconstruction and included a ban on sex discrimination in employment.

Freedom Summer   The Civil Rights Act was a law with real teeth, but it left untouched the obstacles to black voting. So protesters went back into the streets. In 1964, in what came to be known as Freedom Summer, black organizations mounted a major campaign in Mississippi. The effort drew several thousand volunteers from across the country, including nearly one thousand white college students from the North. Led by the charismatic SNCC activist Robert "Bob" Moses, the four major civil rights organizations (SNCC, CORE, NAACP, and SCLC) spread out across the state. They established freedom schools for black children and conducted a major voter registration drive. Yet so determined was the opposition that only about twelve hundred black voters were registered that summer, at a cost of four murdered civil rights workers and thirty-seven black churches bombed or burned.

The murders strengthened the resolve of the **Mississippi Freedom Democratic Party** (MFDP), which had been founded during Freedom Summer. Banned from the "whites only" Mississippi Democratic Party, MFDP leaders were determined to attend the 1964 Democratic National Convention in Atlantic City, New Jersey, as the legitimate representatives of their state. Inspired by Fannie Lou Hamer, a former sharecropper turned civil rights activist, the MFDP challenged the most powerful figures in the Democratic Party, including President Johnson himself. "Is this America?" Hamer asked party officials when she demanded that the MFDP, and not the all-white Mississippi delegation, be recognized by the convention. Democratic leaders, however, seated the white Mississippi delegation and refused to recognize the MFDP. Demoralized and convinced that the Democratic Party would not change, Bob Moses told television reporters: "I will have nothing to do with the political system any longer." Freedom Summer began with optimism but ended with bitter disappointment.

Mississippi Freedom Democratic Party
Party founded in Mississippi during the Freedom Summer of 1964. Its members attempted to attend the 1964 Democratic National Convention in Atlantic City, New Jersey, as the legitimate representatives of their state, but Democratic leaders refused to recognize the party.

Selma and the Voting Rights Act   Martin Luther King Jr. and the SCLC did not share Moses's skepticism. They believed that another confrontation with southern injustice could provoke further congressional action. In March 1965, James Bevel of the SCLC called for a march from Selma, Alabama, to the state capital, Montgomery, to protest the murder of a voting-rights activist. As soon as the six hundred marchers left Selma, crossing over the Edmund Pettus Bridge, mounted state troopers attacked them with tear gas and clubs. The scene was shown on national television that night,

Civil Rights and Black Power: Strategy and Ideology

The documents collected below reveal the range of perspectives and ideas at work within the broad civil rights, or "black freedom," struggle in the 1960s.

1. **Martin Luther King Jr., "If the Negro Wins, Labor Wins" speech, 1962.** *King, speaking to a meeting of the nation's trade union leaders, explained the economic objectives of the black freedom struggle.*

If we do not advance, the crushing burden of centuries of neglect and economic deprivation will destroy our will, our spirits and our hopes. In this way labor's historic tradition of moving forward to create vital people as consumers and citizens has become our own tradition, and for the same reasons.

This unity of purpose is not an historical coincidence. Negroes are almost entirely a working people. There are pitifully few Negro millionaires and few Negro employers. Our needs are identical with labor's needs: decent wages, fair working conditions, livable housing, old age security, health and welfare measures, conditions in which families can grow, have education for their children and respect in the community. That is why Negroes support labor's demands and fight laws which curb labor. . . .

The two most dynamic and cohesive liberal forces in the country are the labor movement and the Negro freedom movement. Together we can be architects of democracy in a South now rapidly industrializing.

2. **Police in Birmingham, Alabama, use trained German shepherds against peaceful African American protesters, 1963.**

Source: AP Photo/Bill Hudson.

3. **Bayard Rustin, "From Protest to Politics,"** *Commentary,* **February 1965.**

. . . it would be hard to quarrel with the assertion that the elaborate legal structure of segregation and discrimination, particularly in relation to public accommodations, has virtually collapsed. On the other hand, without making light of the human sacrifices involved in the direct-action tactics (sit-ins, freedom rides, and the rest) that were so instrumental to this achievement, we must recognize that in desegregating public accommodations, we affected institutions which are relatively peripheral both to the American socio-economic order and to the fundamental conditions of life of the Negro people. In a highly-industrialized, 20th-century civilization, we hit Jim Crow precisely where it was most anachronistic, dispensable, and vulnerable — in hotels, lunch counters, terminals, libraries, swimming pools, and the like. . . . At issue, after all, is not civil rights, strictly speaking, but social and economic conditions.

4. James Farmer, *Freedom, When?*, 1965.

"But when will the demonstrations end?" The perpetual question. And a serious question. Actually, it is several questions, for the meaning of the question differs, depending upon who asks it.

Coming from those whose dominant consideration is peace—public peace and peace of mind—the question means: "When are you going to stop tempting violence and rioting?" Some put it more strongly: "When are you going to stop sponsoring violence?" Assumed is the necessary connection between demonstration and violence. . . .

"Isn't the patience of the white majority wearing thin? Why nourish the displeasure of 90 percent of the population with provocative demonstrations? Remember, you need allies." And the assumptions of these Cassandras of the backlash is that freedom and equality are, in the last analysis, wholly gifts in the white man's power to bestow. . . .

What the public must realize is that in a demonstration more things are happening, at more levels of human activity, than meets the eye. Demonstrations in the last few years have provided literally millions of Negroes with their first taste of self-determination and political self-expression.

5. Stokely Carmichael and Charles Hamilton, *Black Power: The Politics of Liberation in America*, 1967.

Black people must redefine themselves, and only they can do that. Throughout this country, vast segments of the black communities are beginning to recognize the need to assert their own definitions, to reclaim their history, their culture; to create their own sense of community and togetherness. There is a growing resentment of the word "Negro," for example, because this term is the invention of our oppressor; it is his image of us that he describes. . . .

The concept of Black Power rests on a fundamental premise: Before a group can enter the open society, it must first close ranks. By this we mean that group solidarity is necessary before a group can operate effectively from a bargaining position of strength in a pluralistic society.

6. Black Power salute at the 1968 Olympics in Mexico City. *Tommie Smith and John Carolos (right) won gold and bronze medals in the 200 meters. The silver medalist, Australian Peter Norman (left), is wearing an Olympic Project for Human Rights badge to show his support.*

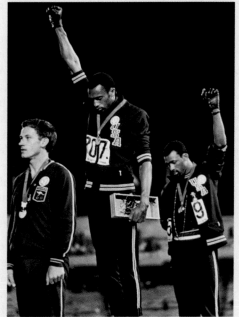

Source: AP Photo.

SOURCES: (1) "If the Negro Wins, Labor Wins," by Martin Luther King Jr. delivered February 12, 1962. Reprinted by arrangement with the Heirs to the Estate of Martin Luther King Jr., c/o Writers House as agent for the proprietor, New York, NY. Copyright © 1962 Martin Luther King Jr. Copyright renewed 1991 Coretta Scott King; (3) *Commentary*, February 1965; (4) James Farmer, *Freedom, When?* (New York: Random House, 1965), 25–27, 42–47; (5) Stokely Carmichael and Charles V. Hamilton, *Black Power: The Politics of Liberation in America* (New York: Vintage, 1992, orig. 1967), 37, 44.

ANALYZING THE EVIDENCE

1. Compare sources 1 and 3. What does Rustin mean when he says that ending segregation in public accommodations has not affected the "fundamental conditions" of African American life? How does King's point in source 1 address such issues?

2. Examine the two photographs. What do they reveal about different kinds of protest? About different perspectives among African Americans?

3. What does "self-determination" mean for Farmer and Carmichael and Hamilton?

PUTTING IT ALL TOGETHER

Compose an essay in which you use the documents above, in addition to your reading of the chapter, to explore and explain different approaches to African American rights in the 1960s. In particular, think about how all of the documents come from a single movement, yet each expresses a distinct viewpoint and a distinct way of conceiving what "the struggle" is about. How do these approaches compare to the tactics of earlier struggles for civil rights?

and the day became known as Bloody Sunday. Calling the episode "an American tragedy," President Johnson went back to Congress.

Voting Rights Act of 1965
Law passed during Lyndon Johnson's administration that empowered the federal government to intervene to ensure minorities' access to the voting booth.

The **Voting Rights Act of 1965**, which was signed by President Johnson on August 6, outlawed the literacy tests and other devices that prevented African Americans from registering to vote, and authorized the attorney general to send federal examiners to register voters in any county where registration was less than 50 percent. Together with the Twenty-Fourth Amendment (ratified in 1964), which outlawed the poll tax in federal elections, the Voting Rights Act enabled millions of African Americans to vote for the first time since Reconstruction.

In the South, the results were stunning. In 1960, only 20 percent of black citizens had been registered to vote; by 1971, registration reached 62 percent (see Map 26.4). Moreover, across the nation the number of black elected officials began to climb, almost quadrupling from 1,400 to 4,900 between 1970 and 1980 and doubling again by the early 1990s. Most of those elected held local offices — from sheriff to county commissioner — but nonetheless embodied a shift in political representation nearly unimaginable a generation earlier. As Hartman Turnbow, a Mississippi farmer who risked his life to register in 1964, later declared, "It won't never go back where it was."

Something else would never go back either: the liberal New Deal coalition. By the second half of the 1960s, the liberal wing of the Democratic Party had won its battle with the conservative, segregationist wing. Democrats had embraced the civil rights movement and made black equality a cornerstone of a new "rights" liberalism. But

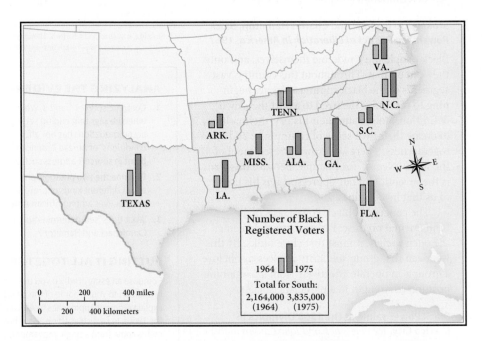

MAP 26.4 Black Voter Registration in the South, 1964 and 1975
After passage of the Voting Rights Act of 1965, black registration in the South increased dramatically. The bars on the map show the number of African Americans registered in 1964, before the act was passed, and in 1975, after it had been in effect for ten years. States in the Deep South, such as Mississippi, Alabama, and Georgia, had the biggest increases.

over the next generation, between the 1960s and the 1980s, southern whites and many conservative northern whites would respond by switching to the Republican Party. Strom Thurmond, the segregationist senator from South Carolina, symbolically led the revolt by renouncing the Democratic Party and becoming a Republican in 1964. The New Deal coalition — which had joined working-class whites, northern African Americans, urban professionals, and white southern segregationists together in a fragile political alliance since the 1930s — was beginning to crumble.

> **IN YOUR OWN WORDS** How did the civil rights movement achieve its major legal and legislative victories between 1954 and 1965?

Beyond Civil Rights, 1966–1973

Supreme Court decisions and new laws do not automatically produce changes in society. But in the mid-1960s, civil rights advocates confronted a more profound issue: perhaps even protests were not enough. In 1965, Bayard Rustin wrote of the need to move "from protest to politics" in order to build institutional black power. Some black leaders, such as the young SNCC activists Stokely Carmichael, Frances Beal, and John Lewis, grew frustrated with the slow pace of reform and the stubborn resistance of whites. Still others believed that addressing black poverty and economic disadvantage remained the most important objective. Neither new laws nor long marches appeared capable of meeting these varied and complex challenges.

The conviction that civil rights alone were incapable of guaranteeing equality took hold in many communities of color in this period. African Americans were joined by Mexican Americans, Puerto Ricans, and American Indians. They came at the problem of inequality from different perspectives, but each group asked a similar question: As crucial as legal equality was, how much did it matter if most people of color remained in or close to poverty, if white society still regarded nonwhites as inferior, and if the major social and political institutions in the country were run by whites? Black leaders and representatives of other nonwhite communities increasingly asked themselves this question as they searched for ways to build on the achievements of the civil rights decade of 1954–1965.

Black Nationalism

Seeking answers to these questions led many African Americans to embrace **black nationalism**. The philosophy of black nationalism signified many things in the 1960s. It could mean everything from pride in one's community to total separatism, from building African American–owned businesses to wearing dashikis in honor of African traditions. Historically, nationalism had emphasized black pride, "self-help" (African Americans creating their own community institutions), and black people's right to shape their own destiny. In the late nineteenth century, Frederick Douglass stood as a primary inspiration, and nationalists founded the Back to Africa movement. In the 1920s the nationalist Marcus Garvey inspired African Americans to take pride in their racial heritage (Chapter 21).

In the early 1960s, the leading exponent of black nationalism was the **Nation of Islam**, which fused a rejection of Christianity with a strong philosophy of self-improvement. Black Muslims, as they were known, adhered to a strict code of personal

black nationalism
A major strain of African American thought that emphasized black racial pride and autonomy. Present in black communities for centuries, it periodically came to the fore, as in Marcus Garvey's pan-Africanist movement in the early twentieth century and in various organizations in the 1960s and 1970s, such as the Nation of Islam and the Black Panther Party.

Nation of Islam
A religion founded in the United States that became a leading source of black nationalist thought in the 1960s. Black Muslims preached an apocalyptic brand of Islam, anticipating the day when Allah would banish the white "devils" and give the black nation justice.

behavior; men were recognizable by their dark suits, white shirts, and ties, women by their long dresses and head coverings. Black Muslims preached an apocalyptic brand of Islam, anticipating the day when Allah would banish the white "devils" and give the black nation justice. Although its full converts numbered only about ten thousand, the Nation of Islam had a wide popular following among African Americans in northern cities.

Malcolm X The most charismatic Black Muslim was Malcolm X (the X stood for his African family name, lost under slavery). A spellbinding speaker, Malcolm X preached a philosophy of militant separatism, although he advocated violence only for self-defense. Hostile to mainstream civil rights organizations, he caustically referred to the 1963 March on Washington as the "Farce on Washington." Malcolm X said plainly, "I believe in the brotherhood of man, all men, but I don't believe in brotherhood with anybody who doesn't want brotherhood with me." Malcolm X had little interest in changing the minds of hostile whites. Strengthening the black community, he believed, represented a surer path to freedom and equality.

In 1964, after a power struggle with founder Elijah Muhammad, Malcolm X broke with the Nation of Islam. While he remained a black nationalist, he moderated his antiwhite views and began to talk of a class struggle uniting poor whites and blacks. Following an inspiring trip to the Middle East, where he saw Muslims of all races worshipping together, Malcolm X formed the Organization of Afro-American Unity to promote black pride and to work with traditional civil rights groups. But he got no further. On February 21, 1965, Malcolm X was assassinated while delivering a speech in Harlem. Three Black Muslims were later convicted of his murder.

Black Power A more secular brand of black nationalism emerged in 1966 when SNCC and CORE activists, following the lead of Stokely Carmichael, began to call for black self-reliance under the banner of Black Power. Advocates of Black Power asked fundamental questions: If alliances with whites were necessary to achieve racial justice, as King believed they were, did that make African Americans dependent on the good intentions of whites? If so, could black people trust those good intentions in the long run? Increasingly, those inclined toward Black Power believed that African Americans should build economic and political power in their own communities. Such power would translate into a less dependent relationship with white America. "For once," Carmichael wrote, "black people are going to use the words they want to use — not the words whites want to hear."

Spurred by the Black Power slogan, African American activists turned their attention to the poverty and social injustice faced by so many black people. President Johnson had declared the War on Poverty, and black organizers joined, setting up day care centers, running community job training programs, and working to improve housing and health care in urban neighborhoods. In major cities such as Philadelphia, New York, Chicago, and Pittsburgh, activists sought to open jobs in police and fire departments and in construction and transportation to black workers, who had been excluded from these occupations for decades. Others worked to end police harassment — a major problem in urban black communities — and to help black entrepreneurs receive small-business loans. CORE leader Floyd McKissick explained, "Black Power is not Black Supremacy; it is a united Black Voice reflecting racial pride."

The attention to racial pride led some African Americans to reject white society and to pursue more authentic cultural forms. In addition to focusing on economic disadvantage, Black Power emphasized black pride and self-determination. Those subscribing to these beliefs wore African clothing, chose natural hairstyles, and celebrated black history, art, and literature. The Black Arts movement thrived, and musical tastes shifted from the crossover sounds of Motown to the soul music of Philadelphia, Memphis, and Chicago.

Black Panther Party One of the most radical nationalist groups was the **Black Panther Party**, founded in Oakland, California, in 1966 by two college students, Huey Newton and Bobby Seale. A militant organization dedicated to protecting African Americans from police violence, the Panthers took their cue from the slain Malcolm X. They vehemently opposed the Vietnam War and declared their affinity for Third World revolutionary movements and armed struggle (Map 26.5). In their manifesto, "What We Want, What We Believe," the Panthers outlined their Ten Point Program for black liberation.

The Panthers' organization spread to other cities in the late 1960s, where members undertook a wide range of community-organizing projects. Their free breakfast program for children and their testing program for sickle-cell anemia, an inherited disease with a high incidence among African Americans, were especially popular. However, the Panthers' radicalism and belief in armed self-defense resulted in violent clashes with police. Newton was charged with murdering a police officer, several Panthers were killed

Black Panther Party
A militant organization dedicated to protecting African Americans from police violence, founded in Oakland, California, in 1966 by Huey Newton and Bobby Seale. In the late 1960s the organization spread to other cities, where members undertook a wide range of community-organizing projects, but the Panthers' radicalism and belief in armed self-defense resulted in violent clashes with police.

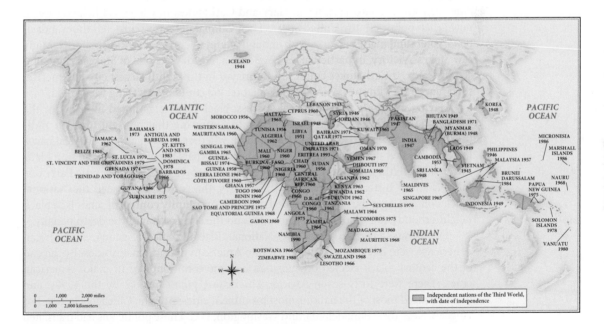

MAP 26.5 Decolonization and the Third World, 1943–1990
In the decades after World War II, African nations threw off the yoke of European colonialism. Some new nations, such as Ghana, the former British colony of Gold Coast, achieved independence rather peacefully. Others, such as Algeria and Mozambique, did so only after bloody anticolonial wars. American civil rights activists watched African decolonization with great enthusiasm, seeing the two struggles as linked. "Sure we identified with the blacks in Africa," civil rights leader John Lewis said. "Here were black people, talking of freedom and liberation and independence thousands of miles away." In 1960 alone, the year that student sit-ins swept across the American South, more than a dozen African nations gained independence.

by police, and dozens went to prison. Moreover, under its domestic counterintelligence program, the Federal Bureau of Investigation (FBI) had begun disrupting party activities.

Young Lords   Among those inspired by the Black Panthers were Puerto Ricans in New York. Their vehicle was the **Young Lords Organization** (YLO), later renamed the Young Lords Party. Like the Black Panthers, YLO activists sought self-determination for Puerto Ricans, both those in the United States and those on the island in the Caribbean. In practical terms, the YLO focused on improving neighborhood conditions: city garbage collection was notoriously poor in East Harlem, where most Puerto Ricans lived, and slumlords had allowed the housing to become squalid. Women in the YLO were especially active, protesting sterilization campaigns against Puerto Rican women and fighting to improve access to health care. As was true of so many nationalist groups, immediate victories for the YLO were few, but their dedicated community organizing produced a generation of leaders (many of whom later went into politics) and awakened community consciousness.

Young Lords Organization
An organization that sought self-determination for Puerto Ricans in the United States and in the Caribbean. Though immediate victories for the YLO were few, their dedicated community organizing produced a generation of leaders and awakened community consciousness.

The New Urban Politics   Black Power also inspired African Americans to work within the political system. By the mid-1960s, black residents neared 50 percent of the population in several major American cities — such as Atlanta, Cleveland, Detroit, and Washington, D.C. Black Power in these cities was not abstract; it counted in real votes. Residents of Gary, Indiana, and Cleveland, Ohio, elected the first black mayors of large cities in 1967. Richard Hatcher in Gary and Carl Stokes in Cleveland helped forge a new urban politics in the United States. Their campaign teams registered thousands of black voters and made alliances with enough whites to create a working majority. Many saw Stokes's victory, in particular, as heralding a new day. As one of Stokes's campaign staffers said: "If Carl Stokes could run for mayor in the eighth largest city in America, then maybe who knows. We could be senators. We could be anything we wanted."

Having met with some political success, black leaders gathered in Gary for the 1972 National Black Political Convention. In a meeting that brought together radicals, liberals, and centrists, debate centered on whether to form a third political party. Hatcher recalled that many in attendance believed that "there was going to be a black third party." In the end, however, delegates decided to "give the Democratic Party one more chance." Instead of creating a third party, the convention issued the National Black Political Agenda, which included calls for community control of schools in black neighborhoods, national health insurance, and the elimination of the death penalty.

Democrats failed to enact the National Black Political Agenda, but African Americans were increasingly integrated into American political institutions. By the end of the century, black elected officials had become commonplace in major American cities. There were forty-seven African American big-city mayors by the 1990s, and blacks had led most of the nation's most prominent cities: Atlanta, Chicago, Detroit, Los Angeles, New York, Philadelphia, and Washington, D.C. These politicians had translated black power not into a wholesale rejection of white society but into a revitalized liberalism that would remain an indelible feature of urban politics for the rest of the century.

Urban Disorder

Black Power was not, fundamentally, a violent political ideology. But violence did play a decisive role in the politics of black liberation in the mid-1960s. Too many

Americans, white and black, had little knowledge or understanding of the rage that existed just below the surface in many poor northern black neighborhoods. That rage boiled over in a wave of riots that struck the nation's cities in mid-decade. The first "long hot summer" began in July 1964 in New York City when police shot a black criminal suspect in Harlem. Angry youths looted and rioted there for a week. Over the next four years, the volatile issue of police brutality set off riots in dozens of cities.

In August 1965, the arrest of a young black motorist in the Watts section of Los Angeles sparked six days of rioting that left thirty-four people dead. "There is a different type of Negro emerging," one riot participant told investigators. "They are not going to wait for the evolutionary process for their rights to be a man." The riots of 1967, however, were the most serious, engulfing twenty-two cities in July and August. Forty-three people were killed in Detroit alone, nearly all of them black, and $50 million worth of property was destroyed. President Johnson called in the National Guard and U.S. Army troops, many of them having just returned from Vietnam, to restore order.

Johnson, who believed that the Civil Rights Act and the Voting Rights Act had immeasurably helped African Americans, was stunned by the rioting. Despondent at the news from Watts, "he refused to look at the cables from Los Angeles," recalled one aide. Virtually all black leaders condemned the rioting, though they understood its origins in poverty and deprivation. At a meeting in Watts, Martin Luther King Jr. admitted that he had "failed to take the civil rights movement to the masses of the people." His appearance appeased few. "We don't need your dreams; we need jobs!" one heckler shouted at King.

Following the gut-wrenching riots in Detroit and Newark in 1967, Johnson appointed a presidential commission, headed by Illinois governor Otto Kerner, to investigate the causes of the violence. Released in 1968, the Kerner Commission Report was a searing look at race in America, the most honest and forthright government document about race since the Presidential Committee on Civil Rights' 1947 report "To Secure These Rights." "Our nation is moving toward two societies," the Kerner Commission Report concluded, "one black, one white — separate and unequal." The report did not excuse the brick-throwing, firebombing, and looting of the previous summers, but it placed the riots in sociological context. Shut out of white-dominated society, impoverished African Americans felt they had no stake in the social order.

Stirred by turmoil in the cities, and seeing the limitations of his civil rights achievements, Martin Luther King Jr. began to expand his vision beyond civil rights to confront the deep-seated problems of poverty and racism in America as a whole. He criticized President Johnson and Congress for prioritizing the war in Vietnam over the fight against poverty at home, and he planned a massive movement called the Poor People's Campaign to fight economic injustice. To advance that cause, he went to Memphis, Tennessee, to support a strike by predominantly black sanitation workers. There, on April 4, 1968, he was assassinated by escaped white convict James Earl Ray. King's death set off a further round of urban rioting, with major violence breaking out in more than a hundred cities.

Tragically, King was murdered before achieving the transformations he sought: an end to racial injustice and a solution to poverty. The civil rights movement had helped set in motion permanent, indeed revolutionary, changes in American race relations. Jim Crow segregation ended, federal legislation ensured black Americans' most basic civil rights, and the white monopoly on political power in the South was broken. However, by 1968, the fight over civil rights had also divided the nation. The Democratic Party was splitting, and a new conservatism was gaining strength. Many whites felt that the issue of civil rights was receiving too much attention, to the detriment of other national concerns. The riots of 1965, 1967, and 1968 further alienated many whites, who blamed the violence on the inability of Democratic officials to maintain law and order.

United Farm Workers (UFW)
A union of farmworkers founded in 1962 by Cesar Chavez and Dolores Huerta that sought to empower the mostly Mexican American migrant farmworkers who faced discrimination and exploitative conditions, especially in the Southwest.

Rise of the Chicano Movement

Mexican Americans had something of a counterpart to Martin Luther King Jr.: Cesar Chavez. In Chavez's case, however, economic struggle in community organizations and the labor movement had shaped his approach to mobilizing society's disadvantaged. He and Dolores Huerta had worked for the Community Service Organization (CSO), a California group founded in the 1950s to promote Mexican political participation and civil rights. Leaving that organization in 1962, Chavez concentrated on the agricultural region around Delano, California. With Huerta, he organized the **United Farm Workers (UFW)**, a union for migrant workers.

Huerta was a brilliant organizer, but the deeply spiritual and ascetic Chavez embodied the moral force behind what was popularly called La Causa. A 1965 grape pickers' strike led the UFW to call a nationwide boycott of table grapes, bringing Chavez huge publicity and backing from the AFL-CIO. In a bid for attention to the struggle, Chavez staged a hunger strike in 1968, which ended dramatically after twenty-eight days with Senator Robert F. Kennedy at his side to break the fast. Victory came in 1970 when California grape growers signed contracts recognizing the UFW.

Mexican Americans shared many economic circumstances with African Americans — especially access to jobs — but they also had unique concerns: the status of the Spanish language in schools, for instance, and immigration policy. Mexican Americans had been politically active since the 1940s, aiming to surmount factors that obstructed their political involvement: poverty, language barriers, and discrimination. Their efforts began to pay off in the 1960s, when the Mexican American Political Association (MAPA) mobilized support for John F. Kennedy and worked successfully with other organizations to elect Mexican American candidates such as Edward Roybal of California and Henry González of Texas to Congress. Two other organizations, the **Mexican American Legal Defense and Education Fund (MALDEF)** and the Southwest Voter Registration and Education Project, carried the fight against discrimination to Washington, D.C., and mobilized Mexican Americans into an increasingly powerful voting bloc.

Younger Mexican Americans grew impatient with civil rights groups such as MAPA and MALDEF,

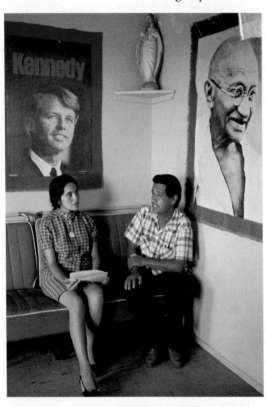

Dolores Huerta and Cesar Chavez Dolores Huerta and Cesar Chavez were two of the leading Mexican American civil rights and social justice advocates of the 1960s. Huerta, influenced by community-organizing traditions, founded two social justice and workers' rights organization before she joined with Chavez in 1962 to cofound the United Farm Workers (UFW), a union of primarily Mexican American agricultural laborers in California. Chavez, influenced equally by the Catholic Church and Mahatma Gandhi, and Huerta led the UFW's massive national grape boycott, an attempt by the UFW to force the nation's grape growers — and, by extension, the larger agriculture industry — to improve wages and working conditions and to bargain in good faith with the union. Arthur Schatz/Getty Images.

however. The barrios of Los Angeles and other western cities produced the militant Brown Berets, modeled on the Black Panthers (who wore black berets). Rejecting their elders' assimilationist approach (that is, a belief in adapting to Anglo society), fifteen hundred Mexican American students met in Denver in 1969 to hammer out a new political and cultural agenda. They proclaimed a new term, *Chicano* (and its feminine form, *Chicana*), to replace *Mexican American*, and later organized a political party, **La Raza Unida** (People United), to promote Chicano interests. Young Chicana feminists formed a number of organizations, including Las Hijas (The Daughters), that organized women both on college campuses and in the barrios. In California and many southwestern states, students staged demonstrations to press for bilingual education, the hiring of more Chicano teachers, and the creation of Chicano studies programs. By the 1970s, dozens of such programs were offered at universities throughout the region.

The American Indian Movement

American Indians, inspired by the Black Power and Chicano movements, organized to address their unique circumstances. Numbering nearly 800,000 in the 1960s, native people were exceedingly diverse—divided by language, tribal history, region, and degree of integration into American life. As a group, they shared a staggering unemployment rate—ten times the national average—and were the worst off in housing, disease rates, and access to education. Native people also had an often troubling relationship with the federal government. In the 1960s, the prevailing spirit of protest swept through Native communities. Young militants challenged their elders in the National Congress of American Indians. Beginning in 1960, the National Indian Youth Council (NIYC), under the slogan "For a Greater Indian America," promoted the ideal of Native Americans as a single ethnic group. The effort to both unite Indians and celebrate individual tribal culture proved a difficult balancing act.

The NIYC had substantial influence within tribal communities, but two other organizations, the militant Indians of All Tribes (IAT) and the **American Indian Movement (AIM)**, attracted more attention in the larger society. These groups embraced the concept of Red Power, and beginning in 1968 they staged escalating protests to draw attention to Indian concerns, especially the concerns of urban Indians, many of whom had been encouraged, or forced, to leave reservations by the federal government in earlier decades. In 1969, members of the IAT occupied the deserted federal penitentiary on Alcatraz Island in San Francisco Bay and proclaimed: "We will purchase said Alcatraz Island for twenty-four dollars in glass beads and red cloth, a precedent set by the white man's purchase of a similar island [Manhattan] about 300 years ago." In 1972, AIM members joined the Trail of Broken Treaties, a march sponsored by a number of Indian groups. When AIM activists seized the headquarters of the hated Bureau of Indian Affairs in Washington, D.C., and ransacked the building, older tribal leaders denounced them.

However, AIM managed to focus national media attention on Native American issues with a siege at Wounded Knee, South Dakota, in February 1973. The site of the infamous 1890 massacre of the Sioux by the U.S. military, Wounded Knee was situated on the Pine Ridge Reservation, where young AIM activists had cultivated ties to sympathetic elders. For more than two months, AIM members occupied a small collection of buildings, surrounded by a cordon of FBI agents and U.S. marshals. Several gun battles left two dead, and the siege was finally brought to a negotiated end. Although upsetting

Mexican American Legal Defense and Education Fund (MALDEF)
A Mexican American civil rights organization founded in 1967 and based on the model of the NAACP Legal Defense and Education Fund. MALDEF focused on legal issues and endeavored to win protections against discrimination through court decisions.

La Raza Unida
An organization founded in Texas in 1970 by Mexican Americans as an alternative to the two major political parties; La Raza Unida (People United) ran candidates for state governor and other local government positions in the 1970s. It was an expression of the Chicano/a movement's attempts to create political unity among American citizens of Mexican descent.

American Indian Movement (AIM)
Organization established in 1968 to address the problems Indians faced in American cities, including poverty and police harassment. AIM organized Indians to end relocation and termination policies and to win greater control over their cultures and communities.

To read the Indians of All Tribes proclamation, along with other primary sources from this period, see *Sources for America's History*.

to many white onlookers and Indian elders alike, AIM protests attracted widespread mainstream media coverage and spurred government action on tribal issues.

> **IN YOUR OWN WORDS**   What social conditions prompted many Americans to seek remedies beyond formal legal equality on the basis of race? How successful were those remedies?

Summary

African Americans and others who fought for civil rights from World War II through the early 1970s sought equal rights and economic opportunity. That quest was also inspired by various forms of nationalism that called for self-determination for minority groups. For most of the first half of the twentieth century, African Americans faced a harsh Jim Crow system in the South and a segregated, though more open, society in the North. Segregation was maintained by a widespread belief in black inferiority and by a southern political system that denied African Americans the vote. In the Southwest and West, Mexican Americans, Native Americans, and Americans of Asian descent faced discriminatory laws and social practices that marginalized them.

The civil rights movement attacked racial inequality in three ways. First, the movement sought equality under the law for all Americans, regardless of race. This required patient work through the judicial system and the more arduous task of winning congressional legislation, such as the Civil Rights Act of 1964 and the Voting Rights Act of 1965. Second, grassroots activists, using nonviolent protest, pushed all levels of government (from city to federal) to abide by Supreme Court decisions (such as *Brown v. Board of Education*) and civil rights laws. Third, the movement worked to open economic opportunity for minority populations. This was embodied in the 1963 March on Washington for Jobs and Freedom. Ultimately, the civil rights movement successfully established the principle of legal equality, but it faced more difficult problems in fighting poverty and creating widespread economic opportunity.

The limitations of the civil rights model led black activists—along with Mexican Americans, Native Americans, and others—to adopt a more nationalist stance after 1966. Nationalism stressed the creation of political and economic power in communities of color, the celebration of racial heritage, and the rejection of white cultural standards.

CHAPTER 26 REVIEW

TERMS TO KNOW   *Identify and explain the significance of each term below.*

Key Concepts and Events

rights liberalism (p. 850)	Brotherhood of Sleeping Car Porters (p. 855)	Congress of Racial Equality (CORE) (p. 856)	"To Secure These Rights" (p. 857)

States' Rights Democratic Party (p. 857)

American GI Forum (p. 860)

Community Services Organization (CSO) (p. 860)

Brown v. Board of Education of Topeka (p. 862)

Montgomery Bus Boycott (p. 865)

Southern Christian Leadership Conference (SCLC) (p. 865)

Student Nonviolent Coordinating Committee (SNCC) (p. 866)

March on Washington (p. 869)

Civil Rights Act of 1964 (p. 871)

Mississippi Freedom Democratic Party (p. 871)

Voting Rights Act of 1965 (p. 874)

black nationalism (p. 875)

Nation of Islam (p. 875)

Black Panther Party (p. 877)

Young Lords Organization (p. 878)

United Farm Workers (UFW) (p. 880)

Mexican American Legal Defense and Education Fund (MALDEF) (p. 880)

La Raza Unida (p. 881)

American Indian Movement (AIM) (p. 881)

Key People

A. Philip Randolph (p. 855)

James Farmer (p. 856)

Cesar Chavez (p. 860)

Dolores Huerta (p. 860)

Thurgood Marshall (p. 860)

Rosa Parks (p. 865)

Martin Luther King Jr. (p. 865)

Stokely Carmichael (p. 866)

Malcolm X (p. 876)

REVIEW QUESTIONS   *Answer these questions to demonstrate your understanding of the chapter's main ideas.*

1. What factors best explain why and how the civil rights movement developed between 1941 and 1954?

2. How did the civil rights movement achieve its major legal and legislative victories between 1954 and 1965?

3. What social conditions prompted many Americans to seek remedies beyond formal legal equality on the basis of race? How successful were those remedies?

4. One of the most significant themes of the period from 1945 to the 1980s is the growth of the power of the federal government. (See "Politics and Power" and "American and National Identity" on the thematic timeline on p. 780.) In what ways is the civil rights movement also part of that story?

MAKING CONNECTIONS   *Recognize the larger developments and continuities within and across chapters.*

1. Why is the decade of the 1960s often referred to as the "second Reconstruction"? Think broadly about the century between the end of the Civil War in 1865 and the passage of the Voting Rights Act of 1965. What are the key turning points in African American history in that long period?

2. Examine the photograph of a confrontation at North Little Rock High School on page 864. How does this photograph reveal the role that the media played in the civil rights struggle? Can you find similar evidence in other photographs from this chapter?

KEY TURNING POINTS   *Refer to the chapter chronology on page 852 for help in answering the question below.*

The history of the civil rights movement is more than a list of significant events. Pick two or three events from this timeline and explain how their timing and the broader historical context contributed to the precise role each played in the movement as a whole.

27

CHAPTER

Uncivil Wars: Liberal Crisis and Conservative Rebirth
1961–1972

The civil rights movement stirred American liberals and pushed them to launch bold new government initiatives to advance racial equality. That progressive spirit inspired an expansive reform agenda that came to include women's rights, new social programs for the poor and the aged, job training, environmental laws, and other educational and social benefits for the middle class. All told, Congress passed more liberal legislation between 1964 and 1972 than in any period since the 1930s. The great bulk of it came during the 1965–1966 legislative session, one of the most active in American history. Liberalism was at high tide.

IDENTIFY THE BIG IDEA

What were liberalism's social and political achievements in the 1960s, and how did debates over liberal values contribute to conflict at home and reflect war abroad?

It did not stay there long. Liberalism quickly came under assault from two directions. First, young, left-leaning activists became frustrated with slow progress on civil rights and rebelled against the Vietnam War. Some of them had been among the young idealists inspired by President John F. Kennedy's inaugural address and the civil rights movement. Now they rejected everything that Cold War liberalism stood for. Their rebellion was symbolized by protests at the 1968 Democratic National Convention in Chicago, where police teargassed and clubbed antiwar demonstrators, who chanted (as the TV cameras rolled), "The whole world is watching!" Inside the convention hall, the proceedings were chaotic, the atmosphere poisonous, the delegates bitterly divided over Vietnam.

A second assault on liberalism came from conservatives, who found their footing after being marginalized during the 1950s. Conservatives opposed the dramatic expansion of the federal government under President Lyndon B. Johnson and disdained the "permissive society" they believed liberalism had encouraged. Advocating law and order, belittling welfare, and resisting key civil rights reforms, conservatives leaped back to political life in the sixties. Their champion was Barry Goldwater, a Republican senator from Arizona, who warned that "a government big enough to give you everything you want is also big enough to take away everything you have."

The clashing of left, right, and center made the years between the inauguration of President Kennedy in 1961 and the landslide reelection of Richard Nixon in 1972 one of the most contentious, complicated, and explosive eras in American history. There were thousands of marches and demonstrations; massive new federal programs aimed at achieving civil rights, ending poverty, and extending the welfare state; and new voices among women, African Americans, Latinos, and gay men and lesbians demanding to be heard. With heated, vitriolic rhetoric on all sides, these developments overlapped with political assassinations and violence both overseas and at home. In this chapter, we undertake to explain how the rekindling of liberal reform under the twin auspices of the civil rights movement and the leadership of President Johnson gave way to a profound liberal crisis and the resurgence of conservatism.

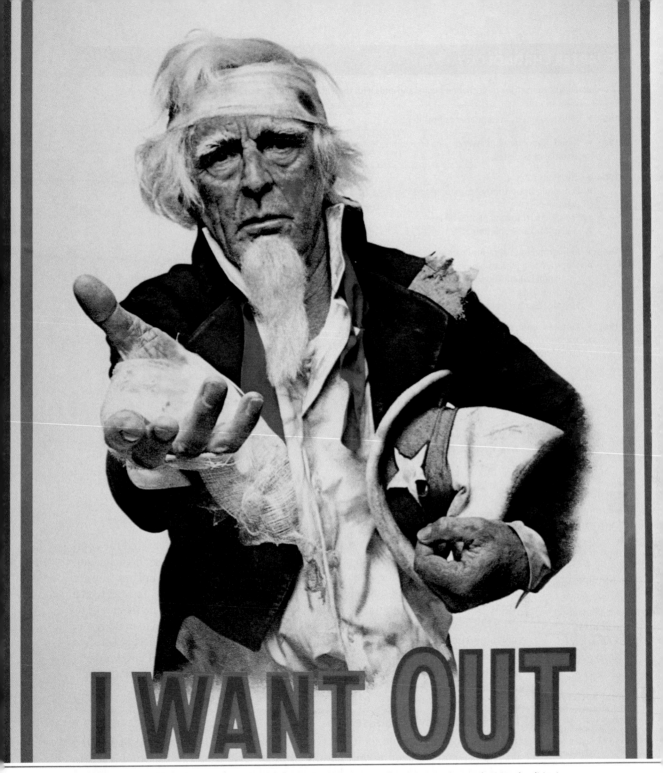

"I Want Out" Protest movements of all kinds shook the foundations of American society and national politics in the 1960s. No issue was more controversial and divisive than the war in Vietnam. *Private Collection/Peter Newark American Pictures/Bridgeman Images.*

As you read, ask yourself why this chapter begins and ends with these dates and identify the links among related events.

1961 ▶ John F. Kennedy inaugurated as president

1963 ▶ John F. Kennedy assassinated; Lyndon B. Johnson assumes presidency

1964 ▶ Civil Rights Act
▶ Economic Opportunity Act inaugurates War on Poverty
▶ Free Speech Movement at Berkeley
▶ Gulf of Tonkin Resolution

1965 ▶ Immigration Act abolishes national quota system
▶ Medicare and Medicaid programs established
▶ Operation Rolling Thunder escalates bombing campaign (March)
▶ First U.S. combat troops arrive in Vietnam

1967 ▶ Counterculture's "Summer of Love"
▶ 100,000 march in antiwar protest in Washington, D.C. (October)

1968 ▶ Tet offensive begins (January)
▶ Martin Luther King Jr. and Robert F. Kennedy assassinated
▶ Women's liberation protest at Miss America pageant
▶ Riot at Democratic National Convention in Chicago (August)
▶ Richard Nixon elected president

1969 ▶ Stonewall riots (June)

1970 ▶ National Women's Strike for Equality

1971 ▶ *Swan v. Charlotte-Mecklenburg* approves countywide busing

1972 ▶ Nixon visits China (February)
▶ Nixon wins a second term (November 7)

1973 ▶ Paris Peace Accords end Vietnam War

1974 ▶ *Milliken v. Bradley* limits busing to school district boundaries

1975 ▶ Vietnam reunified under Communist rule

To see a longer excerpt from President Johnson's "Great Society" speech, along with other primary sources from this period, see **Sources for America's History**.

Great Society
President Lyndon B. Johnson's domestic program, which included civil rights legislation, antipoverty programs, government subsidy of medical care, federal aid to education, consumer protection, and aid to the arts and humanities.

Liberalism at High Tide

In May 1964, Lyndon B. Johnson, president for barely six months, delivered the commencement address at the University of Michigan, where he offered a grand and inspirational vision of a new liberal age. "We have the opportunity to move not only toward the rich society and the powerful society," Johnson continued, "but upward to the **Great Society**." As the graduates listened, Johnson spelled out what he meant: "The Great Society rests on abundance and liberty for all. It demands an end to poverty and racial injustice." Even this, Johnson declared, was just the beginning. He would push to renew American education, rebuild the cities, and restore the natural environment. Ambitious, even audacious, Johnson's vision was a New Deal for a new era. A tragic irony, however, was that he held the presidency at all.

John F. Kennedy's Promise

In 1961, three years before Johnson's Great Society speech, John F. Kennedy declared at his presidential inauguration: "Let the word go forth from this time and place, to friend and foe alike, that the torch has been passed to a new generation of Americans." He challenged his fellow citizens to "ask what you can do for your country," a call to service that inspired many Americans. The British journalist Henry Fairley called

Kennedy's activism "the politics of expectation." Over time, the expectations Kennedy embodied, combined with his ability to inspire a younger generation, encouraged the emerging spirit of liberal reform.

Kennedy's legislative record did not live up to his promising image. This was not entirely his fault; congressional partisanship and resistance stymied many presidents in the twentieth century. Kennedy's domestic advisors devised bold plans for health insurance for the aged, a new antipoverty program, and a tax cut. After enormous pressure from Martin Luther King Jr. and other civil rights leaders — and pushed by the demonstrations in Birmingham, Alabama, in 1963 — they added a civil rights bill. None of these initiatives went anywhere in the Senate, where powerful conservative interests practiced an old legislative art: delay, delay, delay. All Kennedy's bills were at a virtual standstill when tragedy struck.

On November 22, 1963, Kennedy was in Dallas, Texas, on a political trip. As he and his wife, Jacqueline, rode in an open car past the Texas School Book Depository, he was shot through the head and neck by a sniper. He died within the hour. (The accused killer, twenty-four-year-old Lee Harvey Oswald, was himself killed while in custody a few days later by an assassin, a Dallas nightclub owner named Jack Ruby.) Before Air Force One left Dallas to take the president's body back to Washington, a grim-faced Lyndon Johnson was sworn in as Kennedy's successor.

Kennedy's youthful image, the trauma of his assassination, and the nation's sense of loss contributed to a powerful Kennedy mystique. His canonization after death capped what had been an extraordinarily stage-managed presidency. An admiring country saw in Jack and Jackie Kennedy an ideal American marriage (though JFK was, in fact, an obsessive womanizer); in Kennedy the epitome of robust good health (though he was actually afflicted by Addison's disease); and in the Kennedy White House a glamorous world of high fashion and celebrity. No other presidency ever matched the Kennedy aura, but every president after him embraced the idea that image mattered as much as reality in conducting a politically effective presidency.

Lyndon B. Johnson and the Great Society

In many ways, Lyndon Johnson was the opposite of Kennedy. A seasoned Texas politician and longtime Senate leader, Johnson was most at home in the back rooms of power. He was a rough-edged character who had scrambled his way up, with few scruples, to wealth and political eminence. But he never forgot his modest, hill-country origins or lost his sympathy for the downtrodden. Johnson lacked Kennedy's style, but he rose to the political challenge after Kennedy's assassination, applying his astonishing energy and negotiating skills to revive several of Kennedy's stalled programs, and many more of his own, in the ambitious Great Society.

On assuming the presidency, Johnson promptly pushed for civil rights legislation as a memorial to his slain predecessor. His motives were complex. As a southerner who had previously opposed civil rights for African Americans, Johnson wished to prove that he was more than a regional figure — he would be the president of all the people. He also wanted to make a mark on history, telling Martin Luther King Jr. and other black leaders to lace up their sneakers because he would move so fast on civil rights they would be running to catch up. Politically, the choice was risky. Johnson would please the Democratic Party's liberal wing, but because most northern

The Great Society President Lyndon Johnson toured poverty-stricken regions of the country in 1964. Here he visits with Tom Fletcher, a father of eight children in Martin County, Kentucky. Johnson envisioned a dramatic expansion of liberal social programs, both to assist the needy and to strengthen the middle class, that he called the Great Society. Bettmann/Getty Images.

African Americans already voted Democratic, the party would gain few additional votes. Moreover, southern white Democrats would likely revolt, dividing the party at a time when Johnson's legislative agenda most required unanimity. But Johnson pushed ahead, and the 1964 Civil Rights Act stands, in part, as a testament to the president's political risk-taking.

More than civil rights, what drove Johnson hardest was his determination to "end poverty in our time." The president called it a national disgrace that in the midst of plenty, one-fifth of all Americans — hidden from most people's sight in Appalachia, urban ghettos, migrant labor camps, and Indian reservations — lived in poverty. But, Johnson declared, "for the first time in our history, it is possible to conquer poverty."

Economic Opportunity Act
A 1964 act that created a series of programs, including Head Start to prepare disadvantaged preschoolers for kindergarten and the Job Corps and Upward Bound to provide young people with training and employment, aimed at alleviating poverty and spurring economic growth in impoverished areas.

The **Economic Opportunity Act** of 1964, which created a series of programs to reach these Americans, was the president's answer — what he called the War on Poverty. This legislation included several different initiatives. Head Start provided free nursery schools to prepare disadvantaged preschoolers for kindergarten. The Job Corps and Upward Bound provided young people with training and employment. Volunteers in Service to America (VISTA), modeled on the Peace Corps, offered technical assistance to the urban and rural poor. An array of regional development programs focused on spurring economic growth in impoverished areas. On balance, the 1964 legislation provided services to the poor rather than jobs, leading some critics to charge the War on Poverty with doing too little.

The 1964 Election With the Civil Rights Act passed and his War on Poverty initiatives off the ground, Johnson turned his attention to the upcoming presidential election. Not content to govern in Kennedy's shadow, he wanted a national mandate of his own. Privately, Johnson saw himself less as akin Kennedy than as the heir of Franklin Roosevelt, whose political skills he had long admired, and the expansive liberalism of the 1930s. He reminded his advisors never to forget "the meek and the humble and the lowly," because "President Roosevelt never did."

In the 1964 election, Johnson faced Republican Barry Goldwater of Arizona. An archconservative, Goldwater ran on an anticommunist, antigovernment platform, offering "a choice, not an echo" — meaning he represented a genuinely conservative alternative to liberalism rather than the echo of liberalism offered by the moderate wing of the Republican Party (Chapter 24). Goldwater campaigned against the Civil Rights Act of 1964 and promised a more vigorous Cold War foreign policy. Among those supporting him was former actor Ronald Reagan, whose speech on behalf of Goldwater at the Republican convention, called "A Time for Choosing," made him a rising star in the party.

But Goldwater's strident foreign policy alienated voters. "Extremism in the defense of liberty is no vice," he told Republicans at the convention. Moreover, there remained strong national sentiment for Kennedy. Telling Americans that he was running to fulfill Kennedy's legacy, Johnson and his running mate, Hubert H. Humphrey of Minnesota, won in a landslide (Map 27.1). In the long run, Goldwater's candidacy marked the beginning of a grassroots conservative revolt that would eventually transform the Republican Party. In the short run, however, Johnson's sweeping victory gave him a popular mandate and, equally important, congressional majorities that rivaled FDR's in 1935 — just what he and liberal Democrats needed to push the Great Society forward (Table 27.1).

Great Society Initiatives One of Johnson's first successes was breaking a congressional deadlock on education and health care. Passed in April 1965, the Elementary and Secondary Education Act authorized $1 billion in federal funds for teacher training and other educational programs. Standing in his old Texas schoolhouse, Johnson, a former teacher, said: "I believe no law I have signed or will ever sign means more to the future of America." Six months later, Johnson signed the Higher Education Act, providing federal scholarships for college students. Johnson also had the votes he needed to achieve some form of national health insurance. That year, he won passage of two new programs:

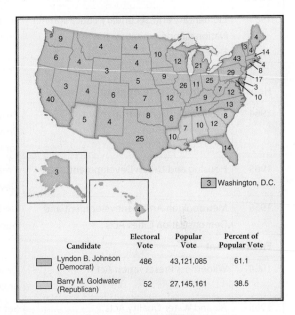

Candidate	Electoral Vote	Popular Vote	Percent of Popular Vote
Lyndon B. Johnson (Democrat)	486	43,121,085	61.1
Barry M. Goldwater (Republican)	52	27,145,161	38.5

MAP 27.1 The Presidential Election of 1964

This map reveals how one-sided was the victory of Lyndon Johnson over Barry Goldwater in 1964. Except for Arizona, his home state, Goldwater won only five states in the Deep South — not of much immediate consolation to him, but a sure indicator that the South was cutting its historic ties to the Democratic Party. Moreover, although soundly rejected in 1964, Goldwater's far-right critique of "big government" laid the foundation for a Republican resurgence in the 1980s.

TABLE 27.1

Major Great Society Legislation

Civil Rights

1964	Twenty-fourth Amendment Civil Rights Act	Outlawed poll tax in federal elections Banned discrimination in employment and public accommodations on the basis of race, religion, sex, or national origin
1965	Voting Rights Act	Outlawed literacy tests for voting; provided federal supervision of registration in historically low-registration areas

Social Welfare

1964	Economic Opportunity Act	Created Office of Economic Opportunity (OEO) to administer War on Poverty programs such as Head Start, Job Corps, and Volunteers in Service to America (VISTA)
1965	Medical Care Act	Provided medical care for the poor (Medicaid) and the elderly (Medicare)
1966	Minimum Wage Act	Raised hourly minimum wage from $1.25 to $1.40 and expanded coverage to new groups

Education

1965	Elementary and Secondary Education Act National Endowment for the Arts and Humanities Higher Education Act	Granted federal aid for education of poor children Provided federal funding and support for artists and scholars Provided federal scholarships for postsecondary education

Housing and Urban Development

1964	Urban Mass Transportation Act Omnibus Housing Act	Provided federal aid to urban mass transit Provided federal funds for public housing and rent subsidies for low-income families
1965	Housing and Urban Development Act	Created Department of Housing and Urban Development (HUD)
1966	Metropolitan Area Redevelopment and Demonstration Cities Acts	Designated 150 "model cities" for combined programs of public housing, social services, and job training

Environment

1964	Wilderness Preservation Act	Designated 9.1 million acres of federal lands as "wilderness areas," barring future roads, buildings, or commercial use
1965	Air and Water Quality Acts	Set tougher air quality standards; required states to enforce water quality standards for interstate waters

Miscellaneous

1964	Tax Reduction Act	Reduced personal and corporate income tax rates
1965	Immigration Act Appalachian Regional and Development Act	Abandoned national quotas of 1924 law, allowing more non-European immigration Provided federal funding for roads, health clinics, and other public works projects in economically depressed regions

Medicare, a health plan for the elderly funded by a surcharge on Social Security pay-roll taxes, and **Medicaid**, a health plan for the poor paid for by general tax revenues and administered by the states.

The Great Society's agenda included environmental reform as well: an expanded national park system, improvement of the nation's air and water, protection for endan-gered species, stronger land-use planning, and highway beautification. Hardly pausing for breath, Johnson oversaw the creation of the Department of Housing and Urban Development (HUD); won funding for hundreds of thousands of units of public hous-ing; made investments in urban rapid transit such as the new Washington, D.C., Metro and the Bay Area Rapid Transit (BART) system in San Francisco; ushered child safety and consumer protection laws through Congress; and helped create the National Endowment for the Arts and the National Endowment for the Humanities to support the work of artists, writers, and scholars.

It even became possible, at this moment of reform zeal, to tackle the nation's dis-criminatory immigration policy. The Immigration Act of 1965 abandoned the quota system that favored northern Europeans, replacing it with numerical limits that did not discriminate among nations. To promote family reunification, the law also stip-ulated that close relatives of legal residents in the United States could be admitted outside the numerical limits, an exception that especially benefitted Asian and Latin American immigrants. Since 1965, as a result, immigrants from those regions have become increasingly prominent in American society (Chapter 30).

Assessing the Great Society   The Great Society enjoyed mixed results. The pro-portion of Americans living below the poverty line dropped from 20 percent to 13 percent between 1963 and 1968. Medicare and Medicaid, the most enduring of the Great Society programs, helped millions of elderly and poor citizens afford necessary health care. Further, as millions of African Americans moved into the middle class, the black poverty rate fell by half. Liberals believed they were on the right track.

Conservatives, however, gave more credit for these changes to the decade's booming economy than to government programs. Indeed, conservative critics accused Johnson and other liberals of believing that every social problem could be solved with a government program. In the final analysis, the Great Society dramat-ically improved the financial situation of the elderly, reached millions of children, and increased the racial diversity of American society and workplaces. However, entrenched poverty remained, racial segregation in the largest cities worsened, and the national distribution of wealth remained highly skewed. In relative terms, the bottom 20 percent remained as far behind as ever. In these arenas, the Great Society made little progress.

Rebirth of the Women's Movement

In the new era of liberal reform the women's movement reawakened. Inspired by the civil rights movement and legislative advances under the Great Society, but frustrated by the lack of attention both gave to women, feminists entered the polit-ical fray and demanded not simply inclusion, but a rethinking of national priorities (Interpretations).

What Are the Origins of 1960s Feminism?

The women's rights movement has a long history, but scholars and activists talk about a "second wave" of feminist activism emerging in the 1960s. Unlike early-twentieth-century feminism, which focused on gaining the right to vote for women, this later phase attacked discrimination and gender inequalities in the workplace, in schools, and within the home and marriage. Many scholars argue that the second wave emerged in response to the 1950s "return to domesticity" following World War II, when women were expected to embrace their roles as wives and mothers. Betty Friedan's 1963 book *The Feminine Mystique* critiqued popular depictions of women's domestic roles and argued that gender discrimination limited women's potential.

Friedan's book was a catalyst for many activists who achieved such milestones as the Equal Pay Act, Title IX, and legalized abortion, but are scholars right to locate the movement's origins there? Were all feminist activists in the 1960s shaped by the constraints of domesticity? Sara Evans and Paula Giddings offer contrasting perspectives on 1960s feminism when they highlight the life experiences, work, and class characteristics of different groups of feminists.

SARA EVANS

SOURCE: Sara Evans, *Personal Politics: The Roots of Women's Liberation in the Civil Rights Movement and the New Left* (New York: Alfred A. Knopf, 1979), 22–23.

Within the context of cultural unrest and the attack on tradition made by women like Friedan, the catalyst for a profounder criticism and a mass mobilization of American women proved to be the young female participants in the social movements of the 1960s. These daughters of the middle class had received mixed, paradoxical messages about what it meant to grow up to be women in America. On the one hand, the cultural ideal . . . informed them that their only true happiness lay in the twin roles of wife and mother. At the same time they could observe the reality that housewifery was distinctly unsatisfactory for millions of suburban women. . . . Such contradictions left young, educated women in the 1960s dry tinder for the spark of revolt. . . . [Their] experiences in the southern civil rights movement and parts of the student new left catalyzed a new feminist consciousness.

PAULA GIDDINGS

SOURCE: Paula Giddings, *When and Where I Enter: The Impact of Black Women on Race and Sex in America* (New York: William Morrow, 1984), 6–7.

In the course of my research, several themes emerged. One of them, clearly exposed through the experience of Black women, is the relationship between sexism and racism. . . . Of course, Black women could understand the relationship between racism and sexism because they had to strive against both. In doing so, they became the linchpin between the two most important social reform movements in American history: the struggles for Black rights and women's rights. In the course of defying the imposed limitations on race and sex, they loosened the chains around both.

QUESTIONS FOR ANALYSIS

1. How do Evans and Giddings differ in their explanation of the chronology and pioneers of 1960s feminism?
2. To what extent do these scholars see the domestic ideal for women as a factor in shaping second-wave feminism?
3. How does the discussion in Chapters 26 and 27 of the civil rights movement and women's activism shed light on the arguments about the origins of feminism that these two scholars make?

Labor Feminists The women's movement had not languished entirely in the postwar years. Feminist concerns were kept alive in the 1950s and early 1960s by working women, who campaigned for such policies as maternity leave and equal pay for equal work. One historian has called these women "labor feminists," because they belonged to trade unions and fought for equality and dignity in the workplace. "It became apparent to me why so many employers could legally discriminate against women — because it was written right into the law," said one female labor activist. Trade-union women were especially critical in pushing for, and winning, congressional passage of the 1963 **Equal Pay Act**, which established the principle of equal pay for equal work.

Labor feminists were responding to the times. More women — including married women (40 percent by 1970) and mothers with young children (30 percent by 1970) — were working outside the home than ever before. But they faced a labor market that undervalued their contributions. Moreover, most working women faced the "double day": they were expected to earn a paycheck and then return home to domestic labor. One woman put the problem succinctly: "The working mother has no 'wife' to care for her children."

Betty Friedan and the National Organization for Women

When Betty Friedan's indictment of suburban domesticity, *The Feminine Mystique*, appeared in 1963, it targeted a different audience: college-educated, middle-class women who found themselves not working for wages but rather stifled by their domestic routine. Tens of thousands of women read Friedan's book and thought, "She's talking about me." *The Feminine Mystique* became a runaway best-seller. Friedan persuaded middle-class women that they needed more than the convenience foods, improved diapers, and better laundry detergents that magazines and television urged them to buy. To live rich and fulfilling lives, they needed education and work outside the home.

Paradoxically, the domesticity described in *The Feminine Mystique* was already crumbling. After the postwar baby boom, women were again having fewer children, aided now by the birth control pill, first marketed in 1960. And as states liberalized divorce laws, more women were divorcing. Educational levels were also rising: by 1970, women made up 42 percent of the college population. All of these changes undermined traditional gender roles and enabled many women to embrace *The Feminine Mystique*'s liberating prescriptions.

Government action also made a difference. In 1961, Kennedy had appointed the **Presidential Commission on the Status of Women**, which issued a 1963 report documenting job and educational discrimination. A bigger breakthrough came when Congress added the word *sex* to the categories protected against discrimination in the Civil Rights Act of 1964. Women suddenly had a powerful legal tool for fighting gender discrimination.

To force compliance with the new act, Friedan and others, including many labor feminists from around the country, founded the **National Organization for Women (NOW)** in 1966. Modeled on the NAACP, NOW intended to be a civil rights organization for women, with the aim of bringing "women into full participation in . . . American society now, exercising all the privileges and responsibilities thereof in truly equal partnership with men." Under Friedan's leadership, membership grew to fifteen thousand by 1971, and NOW became a powerful voice for equal rights.

Equal Pay Act
Law passed in 1963 that established the principle of equal pay for equal work. Trade-union women were especially critical in pushing for, and winning, congressional passage of the law.

The Feminine Mystique
The title of an influential book written in 1963 by Betty Friedan critiquing the ideal whereby women were encouraged to confine themselves to roles within the domestic sphere.

Presidential Commission on the Status of Women
Commission appointed by President Kennedy in 1961, which issued a 1963 report documenting job and educational discrimination.

National Organization for Women (NOW)
Women's civil rights organization formed in 1966. Initially, NOW focused on eliminating gender discrimination in public institutions and the workplace, but by the 1970s it also embraced many of the issues raised by more radical feminists.

One of the ironies of the 1960s was the enormous strain that all of this liberal activism placed on the New Deal coalition. Faced with often competing demands from the civil rights movement, feminists, the poor, labor unions, conservative southern Democrats, the suburban middle class, and urban political machines, the old Rooseveltian coalition had begun to fray. Johnson hoped that the New Deal coalition was strong enough to negotiate competing demands among its own constituents while simultaneously resisting conservative attacks. In 1965, that still seemed possible. It would not remain so for long.

> **IN YOUR OWN WORDS** What explains the surge in liberal politics and social policy in the early 1960s?

The Vietnam War Begins

As the accelerating rights revolution placed strain on the Democratic coalition, the war in Vietnam divided the country. In a CBS interview before his death, Kennedy remarked that it was up to the South Vietnamese whether "their war" would be won or lost. But the young president had already placed the United States on a course that would make retreat difficult. Like other U.S. presidents, Kennedy believed that giving up in Vietnam would weaken America's "credibility." Withdrawal "would be a great mistake," he said.

It is impossible to know how JFK would have managed Vietnam had he lived. What is known is that in the fall of 1963, Kennedy had lost patience with Ngo Dinh Diem, the dictatorial head of South Vietnam whom the United States had supported since 1955 (Chapter 24). The president let it be known in Saigon that the United States would support a military coup. Kennedy's hope was that if Diem, reviled throughout the South because of his brutal repression of political opponents, could be replaced by a popular general or other military figure, a stable government would emerge — one strong enough to repel the South Vietnam National Liberation Front (NLF), or Vietcong.

That calculation proved overly optimistic. Emboldened by Kennedy's approval of their plan, a handful of South Vietnamese generals overthrew Diem on November 1, and then brutally killed him and his brother. Rather than stability, the coup brought chaos. South Vietnam fell into a period of turmoil marked by the increasing ungovernability of both the cities and countryside. Kennedy himself was assassinated in late November and would not live to see the grim results of Diem's murder: American engagement in a long and costly civil conflict in the name of fighting communism.

Escalation Under Johnson

Just as Kennedy had inherited Vietnam from Eisenhower, so Lyndon Johnson inherited Vietnam from Kennedy. Johnson's inheritance was more burdensome, however, for by now only massive American intervention could prevent the collapse of South Vietnam (Map 27.2). Johnson, like Kennedy, was a subscriber to the Cold War tenets of global containment. "I am not going to lose Vietnam," he vowed on taking office. "I am not going to be the President who saw Southeast Asia go the way China went" (Chapter 24).

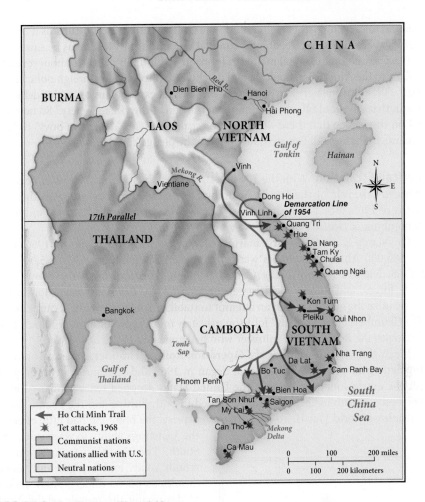

MAP 27.2 The Vietnam War, 1968

The Vietnam War was a guerrilla war, fought in skirmishes rather than set-piece battles. Despite repeated airstrikes, the United States was never able to halt the flow of North Vietnamese troops and supplies down the Ho Chi Minh Trail, which wound through Laos and Cambodia. In January 1968, Vietcong forces launched the Tet offensive, a surprise attack on cities and provincial centers across South Vietnam. Although the attackers were pushed back with heavy losses, the Tet offensive revealed the futility of American efforts to suppress the Vietcong guerrillas and marked a turning point in the war.

Gulf of Tonkin It did not take long for Johnson to place his stamp on the war. During the summer of 1964, the president got reports that North Vietnamese torpedo boats had fired on the U.S. destroyer *Maddox* in the Gulf of Tonkin. In the first attack, on August 2, the damage inflicted was limited to a single bullet hole; a second attack, on August 4, later proved to be only misread radar sightings. To Johnson, it didn't matter if the attack was real or imagined; the president believed a wider war was inevitable and issued a call to arms, sending his national approval rating from 42 to 72 percent. In the entire Congress, only two senators voted against his request for authorization to "take all necessary measures to repel any armed attack against the forces of the United

Gulf of Tonkin Resolution
Resolution passed by Congress in 1964 in the wake of a naval confrontation in the Gulf of Tonkin between the United States and North Vietnam. It gave the president virtually unlimited authority in conducting the Vietnam War. The Senate terminated the resolution in 1970 following outrage over the U.S. invasion of Cambodia.

States and to prevent further aggression." The **Gulf of Tonkin Resolution**, as it became known, gave Johnson the freedom to conduct operations in Vietnam as he saw fit.

Despite his congressional mandate, Johnson was initially cautious about revealing his plans to the American people. "I had no choice but to keep my foreign policy in the wings . . . ," Johnson later said. "I knew that the day it exploded into a major debate on the war, that day would be the beginning of the end of the Great Society." So he ran in 1964 on the pledge that there would be no escalation — no "American boys" fighting Vietnam's fight, he said. Privately, he doubted the pledge could be kept.

American Escalation With the 1964 election safely behind him, Johnson began an American takeover of the war in Vietnam. The escalation, beginning in the early months of 1965, took two forms: deployment of American ground troops and intensive bombing of North Vietnam.

On March 8, 1965, the first marines waded ashore at Da Nang. By 1966, more than 380,000 American soldiers were stationed in Vietnam; by 1967, 485,000; and by 1968, 536,000 (Figure 27.1). General William Westmoreland, the commander of U.S. forces, and Robert McNamara, the secretary of defense, pushed Johnson to Americanize the ground war in an attempt to stabilize South Vietnam. "I can't run and pull a Chamberlain at Munich," Johnson privately told a reporter in early March 1965, referring to the British prime minister who had appeased Hitler in 1938.

Operation Rolling Thunder
Massive bombing campaign against North Vietnam authorized by President Johnson in 1965; against expectations, it ended up hardening the will of the North Vietnamese to continue fighting.

Meanwhile, Johnson authorized **Operation Rolling Thunder**, a massive bombing campaign against North Vietnam that began in 1965 and continued for three years. Over the entire course of the war, the United States dropped twice as many tons of bombs on Vietnam as the Allies had dropped in both Europe and the Pacific during the whole of World War II. To McNamara's surprise, the bombing had little effect on the Vietcong's ability to wage war in the South. The North Vietnamese quickly rebuilt roads and bridges and moved munitions plants underground. Instead of destroying the morale of the North Vietnamese, Operation Rolling Thunder hardened their will to fight. The massive commitment of ground troops and air power devastated Vietnam's countryside, however. After one harsh but not unusual engagement, a commanding officer reported that "it became necessary to destroy the town in order to save it" — a statement that came to symbolize the terrible logic of the war.

The Johnson administration gambled that American superiority in personnel and weaponry would ultimately triumph. This strategy was inextricably tied to political considerations. For domestic reasons, policymakers

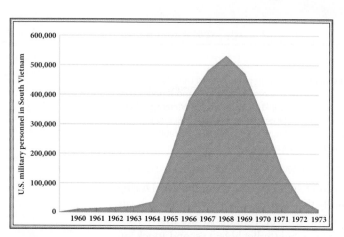

FIGURE 27.1 U.S. Troops in Vietnam, 1960–1973
This figure graphically tracks America's involvement in Vietnam. After Lyndon Johnson decided on escalation in 1964, troop levels jumped from 23,300 to a peak of 543,000 personnel in 1968. Under Richard Nixon's Vietnamization program, beginning in the summer of 1969, levels drastically declined; the last U.S. military forces left South Vietnam on March 29, 1973.

searched for an elusive middle ground between all-out invasion of North Vietnam, which included the possibility of war with China, and disengagement. "In effect, we are fighting a war of attrition," said General Westmoreland. "The only alternative is a war of annihilation."

Public Opinion and the War

Johnson gradually grew more confident that his Vietnam policy had the support of the American people. Both Democrats and Republicans approved Johnson's escalation in Vietnam, and so did public opinion polls in 1965 and 1966. But then opinion began to shift (Thinking Like a Historian).

Every night, Americans saw the carnage of war on their television screens, including images of dead and wounded Americans. One such incident occurred in the first months of fighting in 1965. Television reporter Morley Safer witnessed a marine unit burning the village of Cam Ne to the ground. "Today's operation is the frustration of Vietnam in miniature," Safer explained. America can "win a military victory here, but to a Vietnamese peasant whose home is [destroyed] it will take more than presidential promises to convince him that we are on his side."

With such firsthand knowledge of the war, journalists began to write about a "credibility gap." The Johnson administration, they charged, was concealing bad news about the war's progress. In February 1966, television coverage of hearings by the Senate Foreign Relations Committee (chaired by J. William Fulbright, an outspoken critic of the war) raised further questions about the administration's policy. Johnson complained to his staff in 1966 that "our people can't stand firm in the face of heavy losses, and they can bring down the government." Economic problems put Johnson even more on the defensive. The Vietnam War cost taxpayers $27 billion in 1967, pushing the federal deficit from $9.8 billion to $23 billion. By then, military spending had set in motion the inflationary spiral that would plague the U.S. economy throughout the 1970s.

Out of these troubling developments, an antiwar movement began to crystallize. Little opposition had materialized in 1964, even after Johnson won passage of the Tonkin Resolution. But following the escalation in 1965, groups of students, clergy, civil rights advocates, antinuclear proponents, and even Dr. Benjamin Spock, whose book on child care had helped raise many of the younger activists, began to protest. Their launchpad was an April march of 15,000 people in Washington, D.C., that included a picket line around the White House and speeches denouncing what antiwar activist Paul Potter called "this mad war." Despite their diversity, these opponents of the war shared a skepticism about U.S. policy in Vietnam. They charged variously that intervention was antithetical to American ideals; that an independent, anticommunist South Vietnam was unattainable; and that no American objective justified the suffering that was being inflicted on the Vietnamese people.

The Student Movement

College students, many of them inspired by the civil rights movement, had already begun to organize and agitate for social change prior to the first antiwar march in 1965. In Ann Arbor, Michigan, they founded **Students for a Democratic Society (SDS)** in 1960. Two years later, they held the first national SDS convention in Port Huron,

Students for a Democratic Society (SDS)
An organization for social change founded by college students in 1960.

Debating the War in Vietnam

The war in Vietnam divided Americans and ultimately divided world opinion. A product of the Cold War policy of containment, the war led many to question the application of that policy to Southeast Asia. Yet every American president from Truman to Nixon believed that opposing the unification of Vietnam under communist rule was essential. Historians continue to research, and debate, what led to the war and what effects the war had on both Vietnam and the United States. The following documents help us to consider different views of the war.

1. **President Dwight Eisenhower's "Domino Theory" speech, April 7, 1954.**

Finally, you have broader considerations that might follow what you would call the "falling domino" principle. You have a row of dominoes set up, you knock over the first one, and what will happen to the last one is the certainty that it will go over very quickly. So you could have a beginning of a disintegration that would have the most profound influences. . . .

But when we come to the possible sequence of events, the loss of Indochina, of Burma, of Thailand, of the Peninsula, and Indonesia following, now you begin to talk about areas that not only multiply the disadvantages that you would suffer through loss of materials, sources of materials, but now you're talking about millions and millions and millions of people.

2. **Manifesto of the South Vietnam National Front for Liberation (NLF), 1968.**

Over the past hundred years the Vietnamese people repeatedly rose up to fight against foreign aggression for the independence and freedom of their fatherland. In 1945, the people throughout the country surged up in an armed uprising, overthrew the Japanese and French domination, and seized power. . . .

However, the American imperialists, who had in the past helped the French colonialists to massacre our people, have now replaced the French in enslaving the southern part of our country through a disguised colonial regime. They have been using their stooge — the Ngo Dinh Diem administration — in their downright repression and exploitation of our compatriots,

in their maneuvers to permanently divide our country and to turn its southern part into a base in preparation for war in Southeast Asia.

3. **President Lyndon Johnson, Johns Hopkins University speech, April 7, 1965.**

Over this war — and all Asia — is another reality: the deepening shadow of Communist China. The rulers in Hanoi are urged on by Peiping [Peiking]. This is a regime which has destroyed freedom in Tibet, which has attacked India, and has been condemned by the United Nations for aggression in Korea. It is helping the forces of violence in almost every continent. The contest in Viet-Nam is part of a wider pattern of aggressive purposes.

4. **James Fallows, "What Did You Do in the Class War, Daddy?" Washington Monthly, October 1975.** *The journalist Fallows highlighted the economic unfairness of the Vietnam-era draft.*

The children of the bright, good parents were spared the more immediate sort of suffering that our inferiors were undergoing. And because of that, when our parents were opposed to the war, they were opposed in a bloodless, theoretical fashion, as they might be opposed to political corruption or racism in South Africa. As long as the little gold stars [sent to parents whose son was killed in war] kept going to homes in Chelsea [a working-class part of Boston] and the backwoods of West Virginia, the mothers of Beverly Hills and Chevy Chase and Great Neck and Belmont [all affluent suburbs] were not on the telephone to their congressman screaming, "*You killed my boy.*" . . . It is clear by now that if the men of Harvard had wanted to do the very most they could to help shorten the war, they should have been drafted or imprisoned en masse.

5. Students for a Democratic Society, Call for a March on Washington to End the War, 1965.

The current war in Vietnam is being waged on behalf of a succession of unpopular South Vietnamese dictatorships, not in behalf of freedom. No American-supported South Vietnamese regime in the past few years has gained the support of its people, for the simple reason that the people overwhelmingly want peace, self-determination, and the opportunity for development. American prosecution of the war has deprived them of all three.

The war is fundamentally a *civil* war. . . .
It is a *losing* war. . . .
It is a *self-defeating* war. . . .
It is a *dangerous* war. . . .
It is a war never declared by Congress. . . .
It is a hideously *immoral* war.

6. Richard Nixon, address to the nation on the Vietnam War, November 3, 1969.

. . . President Eisenhower sent economic aid and military equipment to assist the people of South Vietnam in their efforts to prevent a Communist takeover. Seven years ago, President Kennedy sent 16,000 military personnel to Vietnam as combat advisors. Four years ago, President Johnson sent American combat forces to South Vietnam. . . .

For these reasons, I reject the recommendation that I should end the war by immediately withdrawing all our forces. I choose instead to change American policy on both the negotiating front and the battlefront. . . .

7. Evacuation of Vietnamese civilians in a burning village, c. 1965.

Source: Dominique BERRETTY/Gamma-Rapho via Getty Images.

Sources: (1) George Katsiaficas, ed., *Vietnam Documents: American and Vietnamese Views of the War* (Armonk, NY: M. E. Sharpe, Inc., 1992), pp. 120–121. Used by permission of the author; (2) Katsiaficas, 43–44; (3) John Clark Pratt, *Vietnam Voices: Perspectives on the War Years, 1941–1982* (New York: Penguin Books, 1984), 201; (4) *The Washington Monthly*, October 1975, 5–19; (5) Katsiaficas, 120–121; (6) Katsiaficas, 147.

ANALYZING THE EVIDENCE

1. Three of the sources (1, 3, and 6) feature remarks by U.S. presidents. What common feature do they share? Are there differences among the comments? Source 2 is also an attempt by a political figure to persuade. How should historians evaluate such documents?

2. In source 4, which Americans does the author believe have sacrificed the most in fighting the war in Vietnam?

3. Compare sources 2 and 5. What is the intended audience of each? What common features do they share?

4. Journalists and electronic media (photography and television) played an important role in the war. How would images, such as that in source 7, shape opinion about the war both in the United States and globally?

PUTTING IT ALL TOGETHER

Using the knowledge you have gained from this chapter, analyze the documents above to construct an essay in which you explore the Vietnam War's causes and effects, both domestic and international. Choose at least one domestic and one international theme and use the documents to provide evidence for your conclusions.

**Port Huron
Statement**
A 1962 manifesto by
Students for a Democratic
Society from its first
national convention in
Port Huron, Michigan,
expressing students'
disillusionment with the
nation's consumer culture
and the gulf between
rich and poor, as well as
a rejection of Cold War
foreign policy, including
the war in Vietnam.

New Left
A term applied to radical
students of the 1960s and
1970s, distinguishing their
activism from the Old
Left — the communists
and socialists of the 1930s
and 1940s, who tended
to focus on economic and
labor questions rather
than cultural issues.

Michigan. Tom Hayden penned a manifesto, the **Port Huron Statement**, expressing students' disillusionment with the nation's consumer culture and the gulf between rich and poor. "We are people of this generation," Hayden wrote, "bred in at least modest comfort, housed now in universities, looking uncomfortably to the world we inherit." Hayden and SDS sought to shake up what they saw as a complacent nation.

The New Left   The founders of SDS referred to their movement as the **New Left** to distinguish themselves from the Old Left — communists and socialists of the 1930s and 1940s. As New Left influence spread, it hit major university towns first — places such as Madison, Wisconsin, and Berkeley, California. One of the first notable demonstrations erupted in the fall of 1964 at the University of California at Berkeley after administrators banned student political activity on university grounds. In protest, student organizations formed the Free Speech Movement and organized a sit-in at the administration building. Some students had just returned from Freedom Summer in Mississippi, radicalized by their experience. One such student, Mario Savio, spoke for many when he compared the conflict in Berkeley to the civil rights struggle in the South: "The same rights are at stake in both places — the right to participate as citizens in a democratic society and to struggle against the same enemy."

Emboldened by the Berkeley movement, students across the nation were soon protesting their universities' academic policies and then, beginning in 1965, the Vietnam War. Students were on the front lines as the campaign against the war escalated. The 1967 Mobilization to End the War brought 100,000 protesters into the streets of San Francisco, while more than 250,000 followed Martin Luther King Jr. from Central Park to the United Nations in New York. Another 100,000 marched on the Pentagon. President Johnson absorbed the blows and counterpunched — "The enemy's hope for victory . . . is in our division, our weariness, our uncertainty," he proclaimed — but it had become clear that Johnson's war, as many began calling it, was no longer uniting the country.

One spur to student protest was the military's Selective Service System, which in 1967 abolished automatic student deferments. To avoid the draft, some young men enlisted in the National Guard or applied for conscientious objector status; others left the country, most often for Canada or Sweden. In public demonstrations, opponents of the war burned their draft cards, picketed induction centers, and on a few occasions broke into Selective Service offices and destroyed records. Antiwar demonstrators numbered in the tens or, at most, hundreds of thousands — a small fraction of American youth — but they were vocal, visible, and determined.

**Young Americans
for Freedom (YAF)**
The largest student
political organization
in the country, whose
conservative members
defended free enterprise
and supported the war in
Vietnam.

Sharon Statement
Drafted by founding
members of the Young
Americans for Freedom
(YAF), this manifesto
outlined the group's principles and inspired young
conservatives who would
play important roles in the
Reagan administration in
the 1980s.

Young Americans for Freedom   The New Left was not the only political force on college campuses. Conservative students were less noisy but equally numerous. For them, the 1960s was not about protesting Vietnam, staging student strikes, and idolizing Black Power. Inspired by the group **Young Americans for Freedom (YAF)**, conservative students asserted their faith in "God-given free will" and their concern that the federal government "accumulates power which tends to diminish order and liberty." The YAF, the largest student political organization in the country, defended free enterprise and supported the war in Vietnam. Its founding principles were outlined in "The **Sharon Statement**," drafted (in Sharon, Connecticut) two years before the Port

Huron Statement. Young conservatives, many of whom would play important roles in the Reagan administration in the 1980s, rallied to the YAF's call.

The Counterculture While the New Left organized against the political and economic system and the YAF defended it, many other young Americans embarked on a general revolt against authority and middle-class respectability. The "hippie" — identified by ragged blue jeans or army fatigues, flowing skirts, shirts, and blouses, beads, and long unkempt hair — symbolized the new **counterculture**. With roots in the 1950s Beat culture of New York's Greenwich Village and San Francisco's North Beach, the 1960s counterculture was composed largely of white youth alienated from the staid predictability and formality of an older generation. Seeking an ethic of personal freedom and authenticity, they initially turned to folk music for inspiration. Pete Seeger set the tone for the era's idealism with songs such as the 1961 antiwar ballad "Where Have All the Flowers Gone?" In 1963, the year of the civil rights demonstrations in Birmingham and President Kennedy's assassination, Bob Dylan's "Blowin' in the Wind" reflected the impatience of people whose faith in America was wearing thin. Judy Collins and Joan Baez emerged alongside Dylan and pioneered a folk sound that inspired a generation of female musicians.

counterculture
A culture embracing values or lifestyles opposing those of the mainstream culture. Became synonymous with hippies, people who opposed and rejected conventional standards of society and advocated extreme liberalism in their sociopolitical attitudes and lifestyles.

The Counterculture The three-day outdoor Woodstock concert in August 1969 was a defining moment in the rise of the counterculture. The event attracted 400,000 young people, like those pictured here, to Bethel, New York, for a weekend of music, drugs, and sex. The counterculture was distinct from the New Left and was less a political movement than a shifting set of cultural styles, attitudes, and practices. It rejected conformity of all kinds and placed rebellion and contrariness among its highest values. Another concept held dear by the counterculture was, simply, "love." In an era of military violence abroad and police violence at home, many in the counterculture hoped that "peace and love" would prevail instead. Bill Eppridge/The LIFE Picture Collection/Getty Images.

By the mid-1960s, other winds of change in popular music came from the Beatles, four working-class Brits whose awe-inspiring music, by turns lyrical and driving, spawned a commercial and cultural phenomenon known as Beatlemania. American youths' embrace of the Beatles, as well as even more rebellious bands such as the Rolling Stones, the Who, and the Doors, deepened the generational divide between young people and their elders. So did the recreational use of drugs — especially marijuana and the hallucinogen popularly known as LSD or acid — which was celebrated in popular music in the second half of the 1960s.

For a brief time, adherents of the counterculture believed that a new age was dawning. In 1967, the "world's first Human Be-In" drew 20,000 people to Golden Gate Park in San Francisco. That summer — known as the Summer of Love — San Francisco's Haight-Ashbury, New York's East Village, Chicago's Uptown neighborhoods, and the Sunset Strip in Los Angeles swelled with young dropouts, drifters, and teenage runaways whom the media dubbed "flower children." Although most young people had little interest in all-out revolt, media coverage made it seem as though all of American youth was rejecting the nation's social and cultural norms.

> **IN YOUR OWN WORDS**   What led President Johnson to escalate the war in Vietnam, and how did Americans respond?

Days of Rage, 1968–1972

By 1968, a sense of crisis gripped the country. Riots in the cities, campus unrest, and a nose-thumbing counterculture escalated into a general youth rebellion that seemed on the verge of tearing America apart. Calling 1968 "the watershed year for a generation," SDS founder Tom Hayden wrote that it "started with legendary events, then raised hopes, only to end by immersing innocence in tragedy." It was perhaps the most shocking year in all the postwar decades. Violent clashes both in Vietnam and back home in the United States combined with political assassinations to produce a palpable sense of despair and hopelessness (America in Global Context).

War Abroad, Tragedy at Home

President Johnson had gambled in 1965 on a quick victory in Vietnam, before the political cost of escalation came due. But there was no quick victory. North Vietnamese and Vietcong forces fought on, the South Vietnamese government repeatedly collapsed, and American casualties mounted. By early 1968, the death rate of U.S. troops had reached several hundred a week. Johnson and his generals kept insisting that there was "light at the end of the tunnel." Facts on the ground showed otherwise.

The Tet Offensive   On January 30, 1968, the Vietcong unleashed a massive, well-coordinated assault in South Vietnam. Timed to coincide with Tet, the Vietnamese new year, the offensive struck thirty-six provincial capitals and five of the six major cities, including Saigon, where the Vietcong nearly overran the U.S. embassy. In strictly military terms, the Tet offensive was a failure, with very heavy Vietcong losses.

The Global Protests of 1968

Nineteen sixty-eight was a year of youthful protest, political unrest, and violence across the globe. The year of massive antiwar protests at the Democratic National Convention in Chicago as well as the assassinations of Martin Luther King Jr. and Robert Kennedy saw equal or greater turmoil around the world. Half of Italy's universities were occupied; a massive student strike in France turned into a violent confrontation with police; prodemocracy students in Mexico City led huge protests that drew police gunfire; and protests and street battles with police took place in Prague, Berlin, Tokyo, Rome, and London.

RENÉ BOURRIGAUD, FRENCH STUDENT

Source: Ronald Fraser, *1968: A Student Generation in Revolt* (New York: Pantheon Books, 1988), 9.

My most vivid memory of May '68? The new-found ability for everyone to speak — to speak of anything with anyone. In that month of talking during May you learnt more than in the whole of your five years of studying.

THE "TWO THOUSAND WORDS" MANIFESTO, JUNE 27, 1968, PRAGUE, CZECHOSLOVAKIA

Source: Jaromír Navrátil, *The Prague Spring 1968: A National Security Archive Documents Reader* (Budapest: Central European University Press, 1998), 181.

Throughout the spring and summer of 1968, the government of Czechoslovakia, under new communist leadership, pursued reforms pushed by students and other protesters. In August, the Soviet Union invaded and put an end to the new openness.

This spring a great opportunity was given to us once again, as it was at the end of the war [World War II]. Again we have the chance to take into our own hands our common cause, which for working purposes we will call socialism, and give it a form more appropriate to our once-good reputation and to the fairly good opinion we used to have of ourselves.

INTERVIEW WITH PARTICIPANTS IN 1968 PROTESTS IN MEXICO CITY

Source: Produced by Radio Diaries (radiodiaries.org) and originally broadcast on NPR's *All Things Considered*. To hear the entire documentary, visit radiodiaries.org. Used by permission of Radio Diaries.

During the summer of 1968, hundreds of thousands of students protested against Mexico's authoritarian national government and brutal police repression.

Sergio Aguayo: It was, in a symbolic way, the clash of a new Mexico and an old Mexico.

Antonio Azuela: You have a middle class with eyes closed and a group of students saying, this was not a democracy. And this is not working.

Marcela Fernandez de Violante: And so we were together hundreds and hundreds and hundreds. We had these big, big meetings at the campus crowded, crowded. And people singing, Que Vivan los Estudiantes . . . ta-ri-ra-ra-ra-ra.

Marcela Fernandez de Violante: We were very young, very naive. But for the first time, you had this notion that this country was going to be changed by the power of our convictions.

Miguel Breseda: You would get in a bus and give a speech and inform the people. Because newspaper wouldn't publish anything. And people would give you money, they would congratulate you and they would say, "We are with you young people. . . ."

QUESTIONS FOR ANALYSIS

1. Why did free speech figure so prominently in the protests of the 1960s?
2. What do all of these activists seem to be struggling for, or against? How do their struggles seem similar to — or different from — those occurring simultaneously in the United States?

But psychologically, the effect was devastating. Television brought into American homes shocking live images: the American embassy under siege and the Saigon police chief placing a pistol to the head of a Vietcong suspect and executing him.

Tet offensive

Major campaign of attacks launched throughout South Vietnam in January 1968 by the North Vietnamese and Vietcong. A major turning point in the war, it exposed the credibility gap between official statements and the war's reality, and it shook Americans' confidence in the government.

The **Tet offensive** made a mockery of official pronouncements that the United States was winning the war. How could an enemy on the run manage such a large-scale, complex, and coordinated attack? Just before Tet, a Gallup poll found that 56 percent of Americans considered themselves "hawks" (supporters of the war), while only 28 percent identified with the "doves" (war opponents). Three months later, doves outnumbered hawks 42 to 41 percent. Without embracing the peace movement, many Americans simply concluded that the war was unwinnable.

The Tet offensive undermined Johnson and discredited his war policies. When the 1968 presidential primary season got under way in March, antiwar senators Eugene McCarthy of Minnesota and Robert Kennedy of New York, JFK's brother, challenged Johnson for the Democratic nomination. Discouraged, perhaps even physically exhausted, on March 31 Johnson stunned the nation by announcing that he would not seek reelection.

Political Assassinations Americans had barely adjusted to the news that a sitting president would not stand for reelection when, on April 4, James Earl Ray shot and killed Martin Luther King Jr. in Memphis. Riots erupted in more than a hundred cities. The worst of them, in Baltimore, Chicago, and Washington, D.C., left dozens dead and hundreds of millions of dollars in property damaged or destroyed. The violence on the streets of Saigon had found an eerie parallel on the streets of the United States.

One city that did not erupt was Indianapolis. There, Robert Kennedy, in town campaigning in the Indiana primary, gave a quiet, somber speech to the black community on the night of King's assassination. Americans could continue to move toward "greater polarization," Kennedy said, "black people amongst blacks, white amongst whites," or "we can replace that violence . . . with an effort to understand, compassion and love." Kennedy sympathized with African Americans' outrage at whites, but he begged them not to strike back in retribution. Impromptu and heartfelt, Kennedy's speech was a plea to follow King's nonviolent example, even as the nation descended into greater violence.

But two months later, having emerged as the front-runner for the Democratic presidential nomination, Kennedy, too, would be gone. On June 5, as he was celebrating his victory in the California primary over Eugene McCarthy, Kennedy was shot dead by a young Palestinian named Sirhan Sirhan. Amid the national mourning for yet another political murder, one newspaper columnist declared that "the country does not work anymore." *Newsweek* asked, "Has violence become a way of life?" Kennedy's assassination was a calamity for the Democratic Party because only he had seemed able to surmount the party's fissures over Vietnam. In the space of eight weeks, American liberals had lost their two most important national figures, King and Kennedy. The third, Johnson, was unpopular and politically damaged. Without these unifying leaders, the crisis of liberalism had become unmanageable.

The Antiwar Movement and the 1968 Election

Before their deaths, Martin Luther King Jr. and Robert Kennedy had spoken eloquently against the Vietnam War. To antiwar activists, however, bold speeches and marches had not produced the desired effect. "We are no longer interested in merely protesting the war," declared one. "We are out to stop it." They sought nothing short of an immediate American withdrawal. Their anger at Johnson and the Democratic Party — fueled by news of the Tet offensive, the murders of King and Kennedy, and the general youth rebellion — had radicalized the movement.

Democratic Convention In August, at the **1968 Democratic National Convention** in Chicago, the political divisions generated by the war consumed the party. Thousands of protesters descended on the city. The most visible group, led by Jerry Rubin and Abbie Hoffman, a remarkable pair of troublemakers, claimed to represent the Youth International Party (whose members were known as "Yippies"). To mock those inside the convention hall, they nominated a live pig, Pigasus, for president. The Yippies' stunts were geared toward maximum media exposure. But a far larger and more serious group of activists had come to Chicago to demonstrate against the war as well — and they staged what many came to call the Siege of Chicago.

Democratic mayor Richard J. Daley ordered the police to break up the demonstrations. Several nights of skirmishes between protesters and police culminated on the evening of the nominations. In what an official report later described as a "police riot," police officers attacked protesters with tear gas and clubs. As the nominating speeches proceeded, television networks broadcast scenes of the riot, cementing a popular impression of the Democrats as the party of disorder. "They are going to be spending the next four years picking up the pieces," one Republican said gleefully. Inside the hall, the party dispiritedly nominated Hubert H. Humphrey, Johnson's vice president. The delegates approved a middle-of-the-road platform that endorsed continued fighting in Vietnam while urging a diplomatic solution to the conflict.

Richard Nixon On the Republican side, Richard M. Nixon had engineered a remarkable political comeback. After losing the presidential campaign in 1960 and the California gubernatorial race in 1962, he won the Republican presidential nomination in 1968. Sensing weakness in the Democratic Party, Nixon and his advisors believed there were two groups of voters whose long political loyalty to Democrats was wavering: working-class white voters in the North and southern whites of all social classes.

Offended by the antiwar movement and the counterculture, and disturbed by urban riots, northern blue-collar voters, especially Catholics, had drifted away from the Democratic Party. Growing up in the Great Depression, these families were admirers of FDR and perhaps even had his picture on their living-room wall. But times had changed over three decades. To show how much they had changed, the social scientists Ben J. Wattenberg and Richard Scammon profiled blue-collar workers in their study *The Real Majority* (1970). Wattenberg and Scammon asked their readers to consider people such as a forty-seven-year-old working-class woman from Dayton, Ohio: "[She] is afraid to walk the streets alone at night. . . . She has a mixed view about blacks and civil rights." Moreover, they wrote, "she is deeply distressed that her son is going to a community junior college where LSD was found on campus." Such northern blue-collar families were once reliable Democratic voters, but their political loyalties were increasingly up for grabs — a fact Republicans knew well.

George Wallace Working-class anxieties over student protests and urban riots were first exploited by the controversial governor of Alabama, George C. Wallace. Running in 1968 as a third-party presidential candidate, Wallace traded on his fame

1968 Democratic National Convention
A convention held in Chicago during which numerous antiwar demonstrators outside the convention hall were teargassed and clubbed by police. Inside the convention hall, the delegates were bitterly divided over Vietnam.

as a segregationist governor. He had tried to stop the federal government from desegregating the University of Alabama in 1963, and he was equally obstructive during the Selma crisis of 1965. Appealing to whites in both the North and the South, Wallace called for "law and order" and attacked welfare programs; he claimed that mothers on public assistance were, thanks to Johnson's Great Society, "breeding children as a cash crop."

Wallace's hope was that by carrying the South, he could deny a major candidate an electoral majority and force the election into the House of Representatives. He fell short of that objective, finishing with just 13.5 percent of the popular vote. But he had defined hot-button issues — liberal elitism, welfare policies, and law and order — that became hallmarks for the next generation of mainstream conservatives.

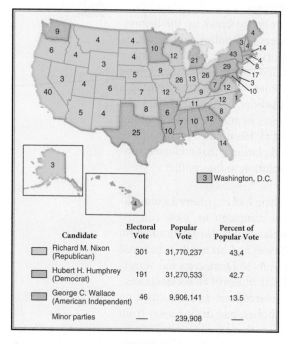

Candidate	Electoral Vote	Popular Vote	Percent of Popular Vote
Richard M. Nixon (Republican)	301	31,770,237	43.4
Hubert H. Humphrey (Democrat)	191	31,270,533	42.7
George C. Wallace (American Independent)	46	9,906,141	13.5
Minor parties	—	239,908	—

MAP 27.3 The Presidential Election of 1968

With Lyndon B. Johnson's surprise withdrawal and the assassination of the party's most charismatic contender, Robert Kennedy, the Democrats faced the election of 1968 in disarray. Governor George Wallace of Alabama, who left the Democrats to run as a third-party candidate, campaigned on the backlash against the civil rights movement. As late as mid-September Wallace held the support of 21 percent of the voters. But in November he received only 13.5 percent of the vote, winning five southern states. Republican Richard M. Nixon, who like Wallace emphasized "law and order" in his campaign, defeated Hubert H. Humphrey with only 43.4 percent of the popular vote, but it was now clear, given that Wallace's southern support would otherwise have gone to Nixon, that the South had shifted decisively to the Republican side.

Nixon's Strategy Nixon offered a subtler version of Wallace's populism in a two-pronged approach to the campaign. He adopted what his advisors called the "southern strategy," which aimed at attracting southern white voters still smarting over the civil rights gains by African Americans. Nixon won over the key southerner, Democrat-turned-Republican senator Strom Thurmond of South Carolina, the 1948 Dixiecrat presidential nominee. Nixon informed Thurmond that while formally he had to support civil rights, his administration would go easy on enforcement. He also campaigned against the antiwar movement, urban riots, and protests, calling for a strict adherence to "law and order." He pledged to represent the "quiet voice" of the "great majority of Americans, the forgotten Americans, the nonshouters, the nondemonstrators." Here Nixon was speaking not just to the South, but to the many millions of anxious suburban voters across the country concerned that social disorder had gripped the nation.

These political strategies — southern and suburban — worked. Nixon received 43.4 percent of the vote to Humphrey's 42.7 percent, defeating him by a scant 500,000 votes out of the 73 million that were cast (Map 27.3). But the numerical closeness of the race could not disguise the devastating blow to the Democrats. Humphrey received almost 12 million fewer votes than Johnson had in 1964. The white South largely abandoned the Democratic Party, an exodus that would accelerate in the 1970s. In the North, meanwhile, Nixon and Wallace made significant inroads among traditionally Democratic voters. The result was that New Deal Democrats lost the unity of purpose that had served them for thirty years. A nation exhausted by months of turmoil and violence had chosen a new direction. Nixon's victory in 1968 foreshadowed — and helped propel — a national electoral realignment in the coming decade.

The Nationalist Turn

Vietnam and the increasingly radical youth rebellion intersected with the turn toward racial and ethnic nationalism by young African American and Chicano activists. As we saw in Chapter 26, the Black Power and Chicano movements broke with the liberal "rights" politics of an older generation of leaders. These new activists expressed fury at the poverty and white racism that were beyond the reach of civil rights laws; they also saw Vietnam as an unjust war against other people of color.

In this spirit, the **Chicano Moratorium Committee** organized demonstrations against the war. Chanting "Viva la Raza, Afuera Vietnam" ("Long live the Chicano people, Get out of Vietnam"), 20,000 Mexican Americans marched in Los Angeles in August 1970. At another rally, Cesar Chavez said: "For the poor it is a terrible irony that they should rise out of their misery to do battle against other poor people." He and other Mexican American activists charged that the draft was biased against those who had little — like most wars in history, Vietnam was, in the words of one retired army colonel, "a poor boy's fight."

Chicano Moratorium Committee
Group founded by activist Latinos to protest the Vietnam War.

Among African Americans, the Black Panther Party and the National Black Antiwar Antidraft League spoke out against the war. "Black Americans are considered to be the world's biggest fools," Eldridge Cleaver of the Black Panther Party wrote in his typically acerbic style, "to go to another country to fight for something they don't have for themselves." Muhammad Ali, the most famous boxer in the world, refused his army induction. Sentenced to prison, Ali was eventually acquitted on appeal. But his action cost him his heavyweight title, and for years he was not allowed to box professionally in the United States.

Women's Liberation and Black and Chicana Feminism

Among women, 1968 also marked a break with the past. The late 1960s spawned new expressions of feminism: **women's liberation** and black and Chicana feminisms. Activists for the former were primarily younger, college-educated women fresh from the New Left, antiwar, and civil rights movements. Those movements' male leaders, they discovered, considered women little more than pretty helpers who typed memos and fetched coffee. Women who tried to raise feminist issues at civil rights and antiwar events were shouted off the platform with jeers such as "Move on, little girl, we have more important issues to talk about here than women's liberation."

women's liberation
A new brand of feminism in the 1960s that attracted primarily younger, college-educated women fresh from the New Left, antiwar, and civil rights movements who sought an end to the denigration and exploitation of women.

Fed up with second-class status, and well versed in the tactics of organization and protest, women radicals broke away and organized on their own. Unlike the National Organization for Women (NOW), the women's liberation movement was loosely structured, comprising an alliance of collectives in New York, San Francisco, Boston, and other big cities and college towns. "Women's lib," as it was dubbed by a skeptical media, went public in 1968 at the Miss America pageant. Demonstrators carried posters of women's bodies labeled as slabs of beef — implying that society treated them as meat. Mirroring the identity politics of Black Power activists and the self-dramatization of the counterculture, women's liberation sought an end to the denigration and exploitation of women. "Sisterhood is powerful!" read one women's liberationist manifesto. The national Women's Strike for Equality in August 1970 brought hundreds of thousands of women into the streets of the nation's cities for marches and demonstrations.

By that year, new terms such as *sexism* and *male chauvinism* had become part of the national vocabulary. As converts flooded in, two branches of the women's movement began to converge. Radical women realized that key feminist goals — child care, equal pay, and reproduction rights — could best be achieved in the political arena. At the same time, more traditional activists, often known as "liberal feminists" and exemplified by Betty Friedan, developed a broader view of women's oppression. They came to understand that women required more than equal opportunity: the culture that regarded women as nothing more than sexual objects and helpmates to men had to change as well. Although still largely white and middle class, feminists began to think of themselves as part of a broad social crusade.

"Sisterhood" did not unite all women, however. Black and Latina women continued to work within the larger framework of the civil rights movement, their feminism linked to the crusade for racial justice. New groups such as the Combahee River Collective and the National Black Feminist Organization arose to speak for the concerns of black women. They criticized sexism but were reluctant to break completely with black men and the struggle for racial equality. Mexican American feminists, or Chicana feminists as they called themselves, came from Catholic backgrounds in which motherhood and family were held in high regard. "We want to walk hand in hand with the Chicano brothers, with our children, our *viejitos* [elders], our Familia de la Raza," one Chicana feminist wrote. Black and Chicana feminists embraced the larger movement for women's rights but carried on their own struggles to address specific needs in their communities.

One of the most important contributions of all the new feminisms was to raise awareness about what feminist Kate Millett called sexual politics. Liberationists, along with black and Chicana feminists, argued that unless women had control over their own bodies, they could not freely shape their destinies. They campaigned for reproductive rights, especially access to abortion, and railed against a culture that blamed women for their own sexual assault and turned a blind eye to sexual harassment in the workplace.

Meanwhile, women's opportunities expanded dramatically in higher education. Dozens of formerly all-male bastions such as Yale, Princeton, and the U.S. military academies admitted women undergraduates for the first time. Colleges started women's studies programs, which eventually numbered in the hundreds, and the proportion of women attending graduate and professional schools rose markedly. With the adoption of **Title IX** in 1972, Congress broadened the 1964 Civil Rights Act to include educational institutions, prohibiting colleges and universities that received federal funds from discriminating on the basis of sex. By requiring comparable funding for sports programs, Title IX made women's athletics a real presence on college campuses.

Women also became increasingly visible in public life. Congresswomen Bella Abzug and Shirley Chisholm joined Betty Friedan and Gloria Steinem, the founder of *Ms.* magazine, to create the National Women's Political Caucus in 1971. Abzug and Chisholm, both from New York, joined Congresswomen Patsy Mink from Hawaii and Martha Griffiths from Michigan to sponsor equal rights legislation. Congress authorized child-care tax deductions for working parents in 1972 and in 1974 passed the

Title IX
A law passed by Congress in 1972 that broadened the 1964 Civil Rights Act to include educational institutions, prohibiting colleges and universities that received federal funds from discriminating on the basis of sex. By requiring comparable funding for sports programs, Title IX made women's athletics a real presence on college campuses.

Equal Credit Opportunity Act, which enabled married women to get credit, including credit cards and mortgages, in their own names.

Stonewall and Gay Liberation

The liberationist impulse transformed the gay rights movement as well. Homophile activists in the 1960s (Chapter 25) had pursued rights by protesting, but they adopted the respectable dress and behavior they knew straight society demanded. Meanwhile, the vast majority of gay men, lesbians, and transgender persons remained "in the closet." So many were closeted because homosexuality was considered immoral and was even illegal in the vast majority of states — sodomy statutes outlawed same-sex relations, and police used other morals laws to harass and arrest gay men and lesbians. In the late 1960s, however, inspired by the Black Power and women's movements, gay activists increasingly demanded immediate and unconditional recognition of their rights. A gay newspaper in New York bore the title *Come Out!*

The new gay liberation found multiple expressions in major cities across the country, but a defining event occurred in New York's Greenwich Village. Police had raided gay bars for decades, making arrests, publicizing the names of patrons, and harassing customers simply for being gay. When a local gay bar called the **Stonewall Inn** was raided by police in the summer of 1969, however, its patrons rioted for two days, setting the establishment on fire and battling with police in the narrow streets of the Village. Decades of police repression had taken their toll. Few commentators excused the violence, and the Stonewall riots were not repeated, but activists celebrated them as a symbolic demand for full citizenship. The gay liberation movement grew quickly after Stonewall. Local gay, lesbian, and transgender organizations proliferated, and activists began pushing for nondiscrimination ordinances and consensual sex laws at the state level. By 1975, the National Gay Task Force and other national organizations were lobbying Congress, serving as media watchdogs, and advancing suits in the courts. Despite all the activity, progress was slow; in most arenas of American life, gay men, lesbians, and transgender people did not enjoy the same legal protections and rights as other Americans.

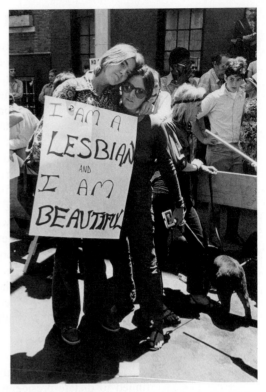

A Lesbian and Gay Rights Protest in Greenwich Village, New York City, 1970 Building on the momentum of the Black Power and women's liberation movements of the late 1960s, a gay liberation movement had emerged by the early 1970s. Its history was longer than most Americans recognized, dating to the homophile movement of the 1950s, but the struggle for gay and lesbian rights and freedoms gained new adherents after the Stonewall riots of 1969. Under the banner of "coming out," lesbian and gay Americans refused to accept second-class citizenship. Rue des Archives/ Getty Images.

Stonewall Inn
A gay bar in New York's Greenwich Village that was raided by police in 1969; the ensuing two-day riot contributed to the rapid rise of a gay liberation movement.

IN YOUR OWN WORDS What factors best explain the rising militancy of social change and protest movements in 1968 and afterward?

Rise of the Silent Majority

Vietnam abroad and the antiwar movement at home tore at the fabric of the Democratic coalition. Lyndon Johnson could not stitch the party back together. Richard Nixon, in contrast, showed himself adept at taking advantage of the nation's unrest through carefully timed speeches and displays of moral outrage. A centrist by nature and temperament, Nixon was not part of the conservative Goldwater wing of the Republican Party. Though he was an ardent anticommunist like Goldwater, Nixon also shared some of Eisenhower's traits, including a basic acceptance of government's role in economic matters. Nixon is thus most profitably viewed as a transitional figure, a national politician who formed a bridge between the liberal postwar era and the much more conservative decades that followed the 1970s.

In late 1969, following a massive antiwar rally in Washington, President Nixon gave a televised speech in which he referred to his supporters as the **silent majority**. It was classic Nixonian rhetoric. In a single phrase, he summed up a generational and cultural struggle, placing himself on the side of ordinary Americans against the rabble-rousers and troublemakers. It was an oversimplification, but the label *silent majority* stuck, and Nixon had defined a political phenomenon. For the remainder of his presidency, Nixon projected himself to the public as the defender of a reasonable middle ground under assault from the radical left.

silent majority
Term derived from the title of a book by Ben J. Wattenberg and Richard Scammon (called *The Real Majority*) and used by Nixon in a 1969 speech to describe those who supported his positions but did not publicly assert their voices, in contrast to those involved in the antiwar, civil rights, and women's movements.

Nixon in Vietnam

In Vietnam, Nixon picked up where Johnson had left off. Cold War assumptions continued to dictate presidential policy. Abandoning Vietnam, Nixon insisted, would damage America's "credibility" and make the country seem "a pitiful, helpless giant." Nixon wanted peace, but only "peace with honor." The North Vietnamese were not about to oblige him. The only reasonable outcome, from their standpoint, was a unified Vietnam under their control.

Vietnamization and Cambodia   To neutralize criticism at home, Nixon began delegating the ground fighting to the South Vietnamese. Under this new policy of **Vietnamization**, American troop levels dropped from 543,000 in 1968 to 334,000 in 1971 to barely 24,000 by early 1973. American casualties dropped correspondingly. But the killing in Vietnam continued. As Ellsworth Bunker, the U.S. ambassador to Vietnam, noted cynically, it was just a matter of changing "the color of the bodies."

Vietnamization
A new U.S. policy, devised under President Nixon in the early 1970s, of delegating the ground fighting to the South Vietnamese in the Vietnam War. American troop levels dropped and American casualties dropped correspondingly, but the killing in Vietnam continued.

Far from abating, however, the antiwar movement intensified. First, in November 1969, half a million demonstrators staged a huge protest in Washington called the Vietnam Moratorium, one of the largest protests ever held in the capital. Then, on April 30, 1970, as part of a secret bombing campaign against Vietcong supply lines, American troops destroyed enemy bases in neutral Cambodia. When news of the invasion of Cambodia came out, American campuses exploded in outrage — and, for the first time, students died. On May 4, 1970, at Kent State University in Ohio, panicky National Guardsmen fired into an antiwar rally, wounding eleven students and killing four. (At least 61 shots were fired in about 13 seconds; of the 13 people hit, the nearest was 60 feet from the Guardsmen.) Less than two weeks later, at Jackson State College in Mississippi,

Guardsmen stormed a dormitory, killing two black students. More than 450 colleges closed in protest. Across the country, the spring semester was essentially canceled.

My Lai Massacre Meanwhile, one of the worst atrocities of the war had become public. In 1968, U.S. Army troops had executed nearly five hundred people in the South Vietnamese village of **My Lai**, including a large number of women and children. The massacre was known only within the military until 1969, when journalist Seymour Hersh broke the story and photos of the massacre appeared in *Life* magazine, discrediting the United States around the world. Americans, *Time* observed, "must stand in the larger dock of guilt and human conscience." Although high-ranking officers participated in the My Lai massacre and its cover-up, only one soldier, a low-ranking second lieutenant named William Calley, was convicted.

Believing that Calley had been made a fall guy for official U.S. policies that inevitably brought death to innocent civilians, a group called Vietnam Veterans Against the War publicized other atrocities committed by U.S. troops. In a controversial protest in 1971, they returned their combat medals at demonstrations outside the U.S. Capitol, literally hurling them onto the Capitol steps. "Here's my merit badge for murder," one vet said. Supporters of the war called these veterans cowardly and un-American, but their heartfelt antiwar protest exposed the deep personal torment that Vietnam had caused many soldiers.

> **My Lai**
> Vietnamese village where U.S. Army troops executed nearly five hundred people in 1968, including a large number of women and children.

Détente As protests continued at home, Nixon pursued two strategies to achieve his declared "peace with honor," one diplomatic and the other military. First, he sought **détente** (a lessening of tensions) with the Soviet Union and a new openness with China. In a series of meetings between 1970 and 1972, Nixon and Soviet premier Leonid Brezhnev resolved tensions over Cuba and Berlin and signed the first Strategic Arms Limitation Treaty (SALT I), the latter a symbolic step toward ending the Cold War arms race. Heavily influenced by his national security advisor, the Harvard professor Henry Kissinger, Nixon believed that he could break the Cold War impasse that had kept the United States from productive dialogue with the Soviet Union.

> **détente**
> The easing of conflict between the United States and the Soviet Union during the Nixon administration, which was achieved by focusing on issues of common concern, such as arms control and trade.

Then, in 1972, Nixon visited China, becoming the first sitting U.S. president to do so. In a televised weeklong trip, the president pledged better relations with China and declared that the two nations — one capitalist, the other communist — could peacefully coexist. This was the man who had risen to prominence in the 1950s by railing against the Democrats for "losing" China and by hounding Communists and fellow travelers. Indeed, the president's impeccable anticommunist credentials gave him the political cover to travel to Beijing. Praised for his efforts to lessen Cold War tensions, Nixon also had tactical objectives in mind. He hoped that by befriending both the Soviet Union and China, he could play one against the other and strike a better deal over Vietnam at the ongoing peace talks in Paris. His second strategy, however, would prove less praiseworthy and cost more lives.

Exit America In April 1972, in an attempt to strengthen his negotiating position, Nixon ordered large-scale bombing raids against North Vietnam. A month later, he approved the mining of North Vietnamese ports, something Johnson had never dared to do. The North Vietnamese were not isolated, however: supplies from China and the Soviet Union continued, and the Vietcong fought on.

With the 1972 presidential election approaching, Nixon sent Kissinger back to the Paris peace talks, which had been initiated under Johnson. In a key concession, Kissinger accepted the presence of North Vietnamese troops in South Vietnam. North Vietnam then agreed to an interim arrangement whereby the South Vietnamese government in Saigon would stay in power while a special commission arranged a final settlement. With Kissinger's announcement that "peace is at hand," Nixon got the election lift he wanted, but the agreement was then sabotaged by General Nguyen Van Thieu, the South Vietnamese president. So Nixon, in one final spasm of bloodletting, unleashed the two-week "Christmas bombing," the most intense of the entire war. On January 27, 1973, the two sides signed the Paris Peace Accords.

Nixon hoped that with massive U.S. aid the Thieu regime might survive. But Congress was in revolt. It refused appropriations for bombing Cambodia after August 15, 1973, and gradually cut back aid to South Vietnam. In March 1975, North Vietnamese forces launched a final offensive, and on April 30, Vietnam was reunited. Saigon, the South Vietnamese capital, was renamed Ho Chi Minh City, after the founding father of the communist regime.

The collapse of South Vietnam in 1975 produced a powerful, and tragic, historical irony: an outcome little different from what would likely have resulted from the unification vote in 1954 (Chapter 24). In other words, America's most disastrous military adventure of the twentieth century barely altered the geopolitical realities in Southeast Asia. The Hanoi regime called itself communist but never intended to be a satellite of any country, least of all China, Vietnam's ancient enemy.

The price paid for the Vietnam War was steep. America's Vietnamese friends lost jobs and property, spent years in "reeducation" camps, or had to flee the country. Millions of Vietnamese died in more than a decade of war, which included some of the most intensive aerial bombing of the twentieth century. In bordering Cambodia, the maniacal Khmer Rouge, followers of Cambodia's ruling Communist Party, took power and murdered 1.7 million people in bloody purges. And in the United States, more than 58,000 Americans had given their lives, and 300,000 had been wounded. On top of the war's $150 billion price tag, slow-to-heal internal wounds divided the country, and Americans increasingly lost confidence in their political leaders.

The Silent Majority Speaks Out

Nixon placed himself on the side of what he called "the nonshouters, the nondemonstrators." But moderate and conservative Americans were not in the mood to simply remain silent. They increasingly spoke out. During Nixon's first presidential term, those opposed to the direction liberalism had taken since the early 1960s focused their discontent on what they believed to be the excesses of the "rights revolution" — the enormous changes in American law and society initiated by the civil rights movement and advanced by feminists and others thereafter.

Law and Order and the Supreme Court The rights revolution had found an ally in an unexpected place: the U.S. Supreme Court. The decision that stood as a landmark in the civil rights movement, *Brown v. Board of Education* (1954), triggered a larger judicial revolution. Following *Brown*, the Court increasingly agreed to hear human rights and civil liberties cases — as opposed to its previous focus on property-related suits. Surprisingly, this shift was led by the man whom President Dwight Eisenhower had appointed chief justice in 1953: Earl Warren. A popular Republican governor of California, Warren surprised many, including Eisenhower himself, with his robust advocacy of civil rights and civil liberties. The **Warren Court** lasted from 1954 until 1969 and established some of the most far-reaching liberal jurisprudence in U.S. history.

Right-wing activists fiercely opposed the Warren Court, which they accused of "legislating from the bench" and contributing to social breakdown. They pointed, for instance, to the Court's rulings that people who are arrested have a constitutional right to counsel (1963, 1964) and, in *Miranda v. Arizona* (1966), that arrestees have to be informed by police of their right to remain silent. Compounding conservatives' frustration was a series of decisions that liberalized restrictions on pornography. Trying to walk the fine line between censorship and obscenity, the Court ruled in *Roth v. United States* (1957) that obscene material had to be "utterly without redeeming social importance" to be banned. The "social importance" test, however, proved nearly impossible to define and left wide latitude for pornography to flourish.

That constitutional test was finally abandoned in 1972, when the Court ruled in *Miller v. California* that "contemporary community standards" were the rightful measure of obscenity. But *Miller*, too, little slowed the proliferation of pornographic magazines, films, and live shows in the 1970s. Conservatives found these decisions especially distasteful, since the Court had also ruled that religious ritual of any kind in public schools — including prayers and Bible reading — violated the constitutional separation of church and state. To many religious Americans, the Court had taken the side of immorality over Christian values.

Supreme Court critics blamed rising crime rates and social breakdown on the Warren Court's liberal judicial record. Every category of crime was up in the 1970s, but especially disconcerting was the doubling of the murder rate since the 1950s and the 76 percent increase in burglary and theft between 1967 and 1976. Sensational crimes had always grabbed headlines, but now "crime" itself preoccupied politicians, the media, and the public. However, no one could establish a direct causal link between increases in crime and Supreme Court decisions, given a myriad of other social factors, including drugs, income inequality, enhanced statistical record-keeping, and the proliferation of guns. But when many Americans looked at their cities in the 1970s, they saw pornographic theaters, X-rated bookstores, and rising crime rates. Where, they wondered, was law and order?

Busing Another major civil rights objective — desegregating schools — produced even more controversy and fireworks. For fifteen years, southern states, by a variety of stratagems, had fended off court directives that they desegregate "with all deliberate speed." In 1968, only about one-third of all black children in the South attended schools with whites. At that point, the federal courts got serious and, in a series of stiff decisions, ordered an end to "dual school systems."

Where schools remained highly segregated, the courts increasingly endorsed the strategy of busing students to achieve integration. Plans differed across the country. In some states, black children rode buses from their neighborhoods to attend previously all-white schools. In others, white children were bused to black or Latino neighborhoods.

Warren Court
The Supreme Court under Chief Justice Earl Warren (1953–1969), which expanded the Constitution's promise of equality and civil rights. It issued landmark decisions in the areas of civil rights, criminal rights, reproductive freedom, and separation of church and state.

An Antibusing Confrontation in Boston Where busing was implemented, it often faced stiff resistance. Many white communities resented judges dictating which children would attend which neighborhood school. In working-class Irish South Boston, mobs attacked African American students bused in from Roxbury in 1974. A police presence was required to keep South Boston High School open. When lawyer and civil rights activist Ted Landsmark tried to enter Boston's city hall during a 1976 antibusing demonstration, he was assaulted. Stanley Forman's Pulitzer Prize–winning photo for the Boston *Herald-American* — titled *The Soiling of Old Glory* — shows Joseph Rakes lunging at Landsmark with an American flag. Busing also had the perverse effect of speeding up "white flight" to city suburbs. Stanley Forman Photo, Pulitzer Prize, 1976.

In an important 1971 decision, *Swan v. Charlotte-Mecklenburg*, the Supreme Court upheld a countywide busing plan for Charlotte-Mecklenburg, a North Carolina school district. Despite local opposition, desegregation proceeded, and many cities in the South followed suit. By the mid-1970s, 86 percent of southern black children were attending school with whites. (In recent years, this trend toward desegregation has reversed.)

In the North, where segregated schooling was also a fact of life — arising from suburban residential patterns — busing orders proved less effective. Detroit dramatized the problem. To integrate Detroit schools would have required merging city and suburban school districts. A lower court ordered just such a merger in 1971, but in *Milliken v. Bradley* (1974), the Supreme Court reversed the ruling, requiring busing plans to remain within the boundaries of a single school district. Without including the largely white suburbs in busing efforts, however, achieving racial balance in Detroit, and other major northern cities, was all but impossible. Postwar suburbanization had produced in the North what law had mandated in the South: entrenched racial segregation of schools.

As the 1972 election approached, President Nixon took advantage of rising discontent over "law and order" and busing. In so doing, he was the political beneficiary of a growing reaction against liberalism that had begun to take hold between 1968 and the early 1970s.

The 1972 Election

Political realignments have been infrequent in American history. One occurred between 1932 and 1936, when many Republicans, despairing over the Great Depression, had switched sides and voted for FDR. The years between 1968 and 1972 were another such pivotal moment. This time, Democrats were the ones who abandoned their party.

After the 1968 elections, the Democrats fell into disarray. Bent on sweeping away the party's old guard, reformers took over, adopting new rules that granted women, African Americans, and young people delegate seats at the convention "in reasonable relation to their presence in the population." In the past, an alliance of urban machines, labor unions, and white ethnic groups — the heart of the New Deal coalition — dominated the presidential nominating process. But at the 1972 convention, few of the party faithful qualified as delegates under the changed rules. The crowning insult came when the convention rejected the credentials of Chicago mayor Richard Daley and his delegation, seating instead an Illinois delegation led by Jesse Jackson, a firebrand young black minister and former aide to Martin Luther King Jr.

Capturing the party was one thing; beating the Republicans was quite another. These party reforms opened the door for George McGovern, a liberal South Dakota senator and favorite of the antiwar and women's movements, to capture the nomination. But McGovern took a number of missteps, including failing to mollify key party backers such as the AFL-CIO, which, for the first time in memory, refused to endorse the Democratic ticket. A weak campaigner, McGovern was also no match for Nixon, who pulled out all the stops. Using the advantages of incumbency, Nixon gave the economy a well-timed lift and proclaimed (prematurely) a cease-fire in Vietnam. Nixon's appeal to the "silent majority" — people who "care about a strong United States, about patriotism, about moral and spiritual values" — was by now well honed.

Nixon won in a landslide, receiving nearly 61 percent of the popular vote and carrying every state except Massachusetts and the District of Columbia (Map 27.4). The returns revealed how fractured traditional Democratic voting blocs had become. McGovern received only 38 percent of the big-city Catholic vote and lost 42 percent of self-identified Democrats overall. The 1972 election marked a pivotal moment in the country's shift to the right. Yet observers legitimately wondered whether the 1972 election results proved the popularity of conservatism or merely showed that the country had grown weary of liberalism and the changes it had wrought in national life.

Candidate	Electoral Vote	Popular Vote	Percent of Popular Vote
Richard Nixon (Republican)	520	47,169,911	60.7
George McGovern (Democrat)	17	29,170,383	37.5
John Hospers (Libertarian)	1	3,674	0.0

MAP 27.4 The Presidential Election of 1972
In one of the most lopsided presidential elections of the twentieth century, Republican Richard Nixon defeated Democrat George McGovern in a landslide in 1972. It was a reversal of the 1964 election, just eight years before, in which Republican Barry Goldwater had been defeated by a similar margin. Nixon hoped that his victory signaled what Kevin Phillips called "the emerging Republican majority," but the president's missteps and criminal actions in the Watergate scandal would soon bring an end to his tenure in office.

> **IN YOUR OWN WORDS** What social issues divided Americans in the early 1970s, and how did those divisions affect the two major political parties?

Summary

In this chapter, we saw that the combined pressures of the Vietnam War and racial, gender, and cultural conflict fractured and split the New Deal coalition. Following John Kennedy's assassination in 1963, Lyndon Johnson advanced the most ambitious liberal reform program since the New Deal, securing not only civil rights legislation but also many programs in education, medical care, transportation, environmental protection, and, above all, his War on Poverty. But the Great Society fell short of its promise as Johnson escalated American involvement in Vietnam.

The war bitterly divided Americans. Galvanized by the carnage of war and the draft, the antiwar movement spread rapidly among young people, and the spirit of rebellion spilled beyond the war. The New Left took the lead among college students, while the more apolitical counterculture preached liberation through sex, drugs, music, and personal transformation. Women's liberationists broke from the New Left and raised new concerns about society's sexism. Conservative students rallied in support of the war and on behalf of conservative principles, but they were often drowned out by the more vocal and demonstrative liberals and radicals.

In 1968, the nation was rocked by the assassinations of Martin Luther King Jr. and Robert F. Kennedy, as well as by a wave of urban riots, fueling a growing popular desire for law and order. Adding to the national disquiet was the Democratic National Convention that summer, which was divided by the Vietnam War and besieged by street riots outside. The stage was set for a new cycle of conservative politics to take hold of the country and a resurgence of the Republican Party under Richard Nixon between 1968 and 1972. President Nixon ended the war in Vietnam, but only after four more years and many more casualties.

CHAPTER 27 REVIEW

TERMS TO KNOW   *Identify and explain the significance of each term below.*

Key Concepts and Events

Great Society (p. 886)

Economic Opportunity Act (p. 888)

Medicare and Medicaid (p. 891)

Equal Pay Act (p. 893)

The Feminine Mystique (p. 893)

Presidential Commission on the Status of Women (p. 893)

National Organization for Women (NOW) (p. 893)

Gulf of Tonkin Resolution (p. 896)

Operation Rolling Thunder (p. 896)

Students for a Democratic Society (SDS) (p. 897)

Port Huron Statement (p. 900)

New Left (p. 900)

Young Americans for Freedom (YAF) (p. 900)

Sharon Statement (p. 900)

counterculture (p. 901)

Tet offensive (p. 904)

1968 Democratic National Convention (p. 905)

Chicano Moratorium Committee (p. 907)

women's liberation (p. 907)

Title IX (p. 908)

Stonewall Inn (p. 909)

silent majority (p. 910)

Vietnamization (p. 910)

My Lai (p. 911)

détente (p. 911)

Warren Court (p. 913)

Key People

Lyndon B. Johnson (p. 886)

Barry Goldwater (p. 889)

Betty Friedan (p. 893)

Ngo Dinh Diem (p. 894)

Robert Kennedy (p. 904)

Richard M. Nixon (p. 905)

George C. Wallace (p. 905)

Henry Kissinger (p. 911)

REVIEW QUESTIONS   *Answer these questions to demonstrate your understanding of the chapter's main ideas.*

1. What explains the surge in liberal politics and social policy in the early 1960s?

2. What led President Johnson to escalate the war in Vietnam, and how did Americans respond?

3. What factors best explain the rising militancy of social change and protest movements in 1968 and afterward?

4. What social issues divided Americans in the early 1970s, and how did those divisions affect the two major political parties?

5. Look at the events listed under "America in the World" on the thematic timeline on page 781. American global leadership is a major theme of Part 8. How did the global role of the United States shift in the 1960s?

MAKING CONNECTIONS   *Recognize the larger developments and continuities within and across chapters.*

1. In what ways was the Great Society an extension of the New Deal? In what ways was it different? What factors made the period between 1932 and 1972 a "liberal" era in American politics? What events and developments would you use to explain your answer?

2. Examine the photographs of the counterculture on page 901 and the gay rights marchers on page 909.

Why did clothing and appearances become so important to many social movements of the 1960s — the women's movements, the Black Power movement, the antiwar movement, and others? How are these visual images historical evidence?

KEY TURNING POINTS   *Refer to the chapter chronology on page 886 for help in answering the question below.*

Which specific developments from the chronology made the years 1964, 1965, and 1968 turning points in politics, foreign policy, and culture, and why?

28

CHAPTER

The Search for Order in an Era of Limits
1973–1980

Early in 1971, a new fictional character appeared on national television. Archie Bunker was a gruff blue-collar worker who berated his wife and bemoaned his daughter's marriage to a bearded hippie. Prone to bigoted and insensitive remarks, Archie and his wife Edith sang "Those Were the Days" at the opening of each episode of *All in the Family*, a half-hour comedy. The song celebrated a bygone era, when "girls were girls and men were men." Disdainful of the liberal social movements of the 1960s, Archie professed a conservative, hardscrabble view of the world.

IDENTIFY THE BIG IDEA

How did the legacy of social changes in the 1960s — such as civil rights, shifting gender roles, and challenges to the family — continue to reverberate in the 1970s, leading to both new opportunities and political clashes?

Archie Bunker became a folk hero to many conservative Americans in the 1970s; he said what they felt. But his significance went beyond his politics. *All in the Family* gave voice to a national search for order. His feminist daughter, liberal son-in-law, and black neighbors brought a changing world into Archie's modest home in Queens, New York. Not all Americans were as resistant to change as Archie. Most were ordinary, middle-of-the-road people confronting the aftermath of the tumultuous late 1960s and early 1970s. The social movements of those years challenged Americans to think in new ways about race, gender roles, sexual morality, and the family. Vietnam and the Watergate scandal had compounded matters by producing a crisis of political authority. An "old order" had seemingly collapsed. But what would take its place was not yet clear.

Alongside cultural dislocation and political alienation, the country confronted economic setbacks. In 1973, inflation began to climb at a pace unprecedented in the post–World War II decades, and economic growth slowed. An energy crisis, aggravated by U.S. foreign policy in the Middle East, produced fuel shortages. Foreign competition in manufacturing brought less expensive, and often more reliable, goods into the U.S. market from nations such as Japan and West Germany. As a result, more American plants closed. The great economic ride enjoyed by the United States since World War II was coming to an end.

What distinguishes the period between the energy crisis (1973) and the election of Ronald Reagan to the presidency (1980) is the collective national search for order in the midst of rapid social change, political realignment, and economic crisis. Virtually all the verities and touchstones of the postwar decades — Cold War liberalism, rising living standards, and the nuclear family — had come into question, and most Americans agreed on the urgency to act. For some, this search demanded new forms of liberal experimentation. For others, it led instead to the conservatism of the emerging New Right.

Shifting Gender Roles As American society underwent dramatic changes in the 1970s, women seized new opportunities and expanded their role in national life. Donna Wright, shown here on break from her work at the Blue Ribbon Mine, was the only woman working at the mine in 1979. Kit Miniciler/*The Denver Post* via Getty Images.

CHAPTER CHRONOLOGY

As you read, ask yourself why this chapter begins and ends with these dates and identify the links among related events.

1970 ▶ Earth Day first observed ▶ Environmental Protection Agency established	**1974** ▶ Nixon resigns over Watergate ▶ Congress imposes 55 miles-per-hour speed limit
1972 ▶ Equal Rights Amendment passed by Congress ▶ Phyllis Schlafly founds STOP ERA ▶ *Furman v. Georgia* outlaws death penalty ▶ Watergate break-in (June)	**1975** ▶ New York City nears bankruptcy ▶ "Watergate babies" begin congressional reform
	1976 ▶ Jimmy Carter elected president
1973 ▶ *Roe v. Wade* legalizes abortion ▶ Endangered Species Act ▶ OPEC oil embargo; gas shortages ▶ Period of high inflation begins ▶ War Powers Act	**1978** ▶ Proposition 13 reduces California property taxes ▶ *Bakke v. University of California* limits affirmative action ▶ Harvey Milk assassinated in San Francisco
	1979 ▶ Three Mile Island nuclear accident

An Era of Limits

The economic downturn of the early 1970s was the deepest slump since the Great Depression. Every major economic indicator — employment, productivity, growth — turned negative, and by 1973 the economy was in a tailspin. Inflation, brought on in part by military spending on the war in Vietnam, proved especially difficult to control. When a Middle East embargo cut oil supplies in 1973, prices climbed even more. Unemployment remained high and productivity growth low until 1982. Overall, the 1970s represented the worst economic decade of the postwar period — what California governor Jerry Brown called an "era of limits."

In this time of distress, Americans were forced to consider other limits to the growth and expansion that had long been markers of national progress. The environmental movement brought attention to the toxic effects of modern industrial capitalism on the natural world. As the urban crisis grew worse, several major cities verged on bankruptcy. Finally, political limits were reached as well: none of the presidents of the 1970s could reverse the nation's economic slide, though each spent years trying.

Energy Crisis

Modern economies run on oil. If the oil supply is drastically reduced, woe follows. Something like that happened to the United States in the 1970s. Once the world's leading oil producer, the United States had become heavily dependent on inexpensive imported oil, mostly from the Persian Gulf (Figure 28.1). French, British, and American companies extracted the oil, a legacy of European colonialism, but they did so under profit-sharing agreements with the Persian Gulf states. In 1960, these nations and other oil-rich developing countries, such as Venezuela, formed a cartel (a business association formed to control prices), the **Organization of Petroleum Exporting Countries (OPEC)**.

Conflict between Israel and the neighboring Arab states of Egypt, Syria, and Jordan prompted OPEC to take political sides between 1967 and 1973. Following Israel's victory in the 1967 Six-Day War, Israeli-Arab tensions in the region grew closer to boiling over with each passing year. In the 1973 Yom Kippur War, Egypt

Organization of Petroleum Exporting Countries (OPEC)
A cartel formed in 1960 by the Persian Gulf states and other oil-rich developing countries that allowed its members to exert greater control over the price of oil.

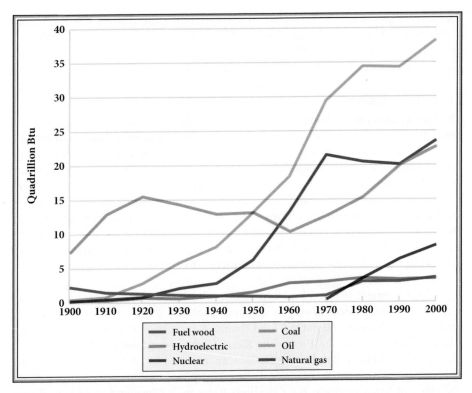

FIGURE 28.1 U.S. Energy Consumption, 1900–2000
Coal was the nation's primary source of energy until the 1950s, when it was surpassed by oil and natural gas. The revival of coal consumption after 1960 stemmed from new open-pit mining in the West that provided cheaper fuel for power plants. The decline in oil consumption in 1980 reflects the nation's response to the oil crisis of the 1970s, including, most notably, fuel-efficient automobiles. Nuclear energy became an important new fuel source, but after 1990 its contribution leveled off as a result of the safety concerns triggered by the Three Mile Island incident.

and Syria invaded Israel to regain territory lost in the 1967 conflict. Israel prevailed, but only after being resupplied by an emergency American airlift. In response to U.S. support for Israel, the Arab states in OPEC declared an oil embargo in October 1973. Gas prices in the United States quickly jumped by 40 percent and heating oil prices by 30 percent. Demand outpaced supply, and Americans found themselves parked for hours in mile-long lines at gasoline stations for much of the winter of 1973–1974. Oil had become a political weapon, and the West's vulnerability stood revealed.

The United States scrambled to meet its energy needs in the face of the oil shortage. Just two months after the OPEC embargo began, Congress imposed a national speed limit of 55 miles per hour to conserve fuel. Americans began to buy smaller, more fuel-efficient cars such as Volkswagens, Toyotas, and Datsuns (later Nissans) — while sales of Detroit-made cars (now nicknamed "gas guzzlers") slumped. With one of every six jobs in the country generated directly or indirectly by the auto industry, the effects rippled across the economy. Compounding the distress was the raging inflation set off by the oil shortage; prices of basic necessities, such as bread, milk, and canned goods, rose by nearly 20 percent in 1974 alone. "THINGS WILL GET WORSE," one newspaper headline warned, "BEFORE THEY GET WORSE."

Environmentalism

energy crisis
A period of fuel shortages in the United States after the Arab states in the Organization of Petroleum Exporting Countries (OPEC) declared an oil embargo in October 1973.

environmentalism
Activist movement begun in the 1960s that was concerned with protecting the environment through activities such as conservation, pollution control measures, and public awareness campaigns. In response to the new environmental consciousness, the federal government staked out a broad role in environmental regulation in the 1960s and 1970s.

Silent Spring
Book published in 1962 by biologist Rachel Carson. Its analysis of the pesticide DDT's toxic impact on the human and natural food chains galvanized environmental activists.

Earth Day
An annual event honoring the environment that was first celebrated on April 22, 1970, when 20 million citizens gathered in communities across the country to express their support for a cleaner, healthier planet.

Environmental Protection Agency (EPA)
Federal agency created by Congress and President Nixon in 1970 to enforce environmental laws, conduct environmental research, and reduce human health and environmental risks from pollutants.

The **energy crisis** drove home the realization that the earth's resources are not limitless. Such a notion was also at the heart of the era's revival of **environmentalism**. The environmental movement was an offshoot of sixties activism, but it had numerous historical precedents: the preservationist, conservationist, and wilderness movements of the late nineteenth century; the conservationist ethos of the New Deal; and anxiety about nuclear weapons and overpopulation in the 1940s. Three of the nation's leading environmental organizations — the Sierra Club, the Wilderness Society, and the Natural Resources Council — were founded in 1892, 1935, and 1942, respectively. Environmental activists in the 1970s expanded on this long history through renewed efforts to ensure a healthy environment and access to unspoiled nature (Thinking Like a Historian).

The movement had received a hefty boost back in 1962 when biologist Rachel Carson published **Silent Spring**, a stunning analysis of the pesticide DDT's toxic impact on the human and natural food chains. A succession of galvanizing developments followed in the late 1960s. The Sierra Club successfully fought two dams in 1966 that would have flooded the Grand Canyon. And in 1969, three major events spurred the movement: an offshore drilling rig spilled millions of gallons of oil off the coast of Santa Barbara; the Cuyahoga River near Cleveland burst into flames because of the accumulation of flammable chemicals on its surface; and Friends of the Everglades protested the construction of an airport that threatened plants and wildlife in Florida. With these events serving as catalysts, environmentalism became a certifiable mass movement on the first **Earth Day**, April 22, 1970, when 20 million people gathered in communities across the country to express their support for a cleaner, healthier planet.

Environmental Protection Agency Earlier that year, on the heels of the Santa Barbara oil spill, Congress passed the National Environmental Policy Act, which created the **Environmental Protection Agency (EPA)**. A bipartisan bill with broad support, including that of President Nixon, the law required developers to file environmental impact statements assessing the effect of their projects on ecosystems. A spate of new laws followed: the Clean Air Act (1970), the Occupational Health and Safety Act (1970), the Water Pollution Control Act (1972), and the Endangered Species Act (1973).

The Democratic majority in Congress and the Republican president generally found common ground on these issues, and *Time* magazine wondered if the environment was "the gut issue that can unify a polarized nation." Despite the broad popularity of the movement, however, *Time*'s prediction was not borne out. Corporations opposed environmental regulations, as did many of their workers, who believed that tightened standards threatened their jobs. "IF YOU'RE HUNGRY AND OUT OF WORK, EAT AN ENVIRONMENTALIST," read one labor union bumper sticker. By the 1980s, environmentalism starkly divided Americans, with proponents of unfettered economic growth on one side and environmental activists preaching limits on the other.

Nuclear Power An early foreshadowing of those divisions came in the brewing controversy over nuclear power. Electricity from the atom — what could be better? That was how Americans had greeted the arrival of power-generating nuclear technology in the 1950s. By 1974, U.S. utility companies were operating forty-two nuclear power plants, with a hundred more planned. Given the oil crisis, nuclear energy might have seemed a godsend; unlike coal- or oil-driven plants, nuclear operations produced no air pollutants.

Environmentalists, however, publicized the dangers of nuclear power plants: a reactor meltdown would be catastrophic, and so, in slow motion, would the dumping of radioactive waste, which would generate toxic levels of radioactivity for hundreds of years. These fears seemed to be confirmed in March 1979, when the reactor core at the **Three Mile Island** nuclear plant near Harrisburg, Pennsylvania, came close to meltdown. More than 100,000 people fled their homes. A prompt shutdown saved the plant, but the near catastrophe enabled environmentalists to win the battle over nuclear energy. After the incident at Three Mile Island, no new nuclear plants were authorized, though a handful with existing authorization were built in the 1980s. Today, nuclear reactors account for 20 percent of all U.S. power generation — substantially less than several European nations, but still fourth in the world.

Three Mile Island
A nuclear plant near Harrisburg, Pennsylvania, where a reactor core came close to a meltdown in March 1979. After the incident at Three Mile Island, no new nuclear plants were authorized in the United States, though a handful with existing authorization were built in the 1980s.

Economic Transformation

In addition to the energy crisis, the economy was beset by a host of longer-term problems. Government spending on the Vietnam War and the Great Society made for a growing federal deficit and spiraling inflation. In the industrial sector, the country faced more robust competition from West Germany and Japan. America's share of world trade dropped from 32 percent in 1955 to 18 percent in 1970 and was headed downward. As a result, in a blow to national pride, nine Western European countries had surpassed the United States in per capita gross domestic product (GDP) by 1980.

Many of these economic woes highlighted a broader, multigenerational transformation in the United States: from an economy based on industrial manufacturing to one based on provision of services. That transformation, which continues to this day, meant that the United States began to produce fewer automobiles, appliances, and televisions and more financial services, health-care services, and management consulting services — not to mention many millions of low-paying jobs in the restaurant, retail, and tourist industries.

In the 1970s, the U.S. economy was hit simultaneously by unemployment, stagnant consumer demand, and inflation — a combination called **stagflation** — which contradicted a basic principle taught by economists: prices were not supposed to rise in a stagnant economy. For ordinary Americans, stagflation meant a noticeable decline in purchasing power, as discretionary income per worker dropped 18 percent between 1973 and 1982. None of the three presidents of the decade — Richard Nixon, Gerald Ford, and Jimmy Carter — had much luck tackling stagflation. Nixon's New Economic Policy was perhaps the most radical attempt. Nixon imposed temporary

stagflation
An economic term coined in the 1970s to describe the condition in which inflation and unemployment rise at the same time.

The Environmental Movement: Reimagining the Human-Earth Relationship

The 1970s witnessed the emergence of the environmental movement in the United States. Environmentalism took a variety of forms and initially was embraced by politicians across the political spectrum, including Republican president Richard Nixon, who signed the National Environmental Policy Act in 1970. Yet environmentalism also proved to be politically divisive. The following documents provide a range of perspectives on an important social and political movement discussed in this chapter.

---

1. **Rachel Carson, *Silent Spring*, 1962.**

   For the first time in the history of the world, every human being is now subjected to contact with dangerous chemicals, from the moment of conception until death. In the less than two decades of their use, synthetic pesticides have been so thoroughly distributed throughout the animate and inanimate world that they occur virtually everywhere. They have been recovered from most of the major river systems and even from streams of groundwater flowing unseen through the earth.

2. **Ralph Nader, foreword to *Ecotactics: The Sierra Club Handbook for Environmental Activists*, 1970.**
   In the Sierra Club's guide to environmental activism, environmental and consumer rights activist Nader discusses "environmental violence."

   Pollution is violence and environmental pollution is environmental violence. It is a violence that has different impacts, styles and time factors than the more primitive kinds of violence such as crime in the streets. Yet in the size of the population exposed and the seriousness of the harm done, environmental violence far exceeds that of street crime. . . .

   To deal with a system of oppression and suppression, which characterizes the environmental violence in this country, the first priority is to deprive the polluters of their unfounded legitimacy.

3. **President Richard Nixon, State of the Union Address, January 22, 1970.**

   I shall propose to this Congress a $10 billion nationwide clean waters program to put modern municipal waste treatment plants in every place in America where they are needed to make our waters clean again, and do it now. . . .

   As our cities and suburbs relentlessly expand [. . .] priceless open spaces needed for recreation areas accessible to their people are swallowed up — often forever. Unless we preserve these spaces while they are available, we will have none to preserve. Therefore, I shall propose new financing methods for purchasing open space and parklands now, before they are lost to us.

   The automobile is our worst polluter of the air. Adequate control requires further advances in engine design and fuel composition. We shall intensify our research, set increasingly strict standards, and strengthen enforcement procedures — and we shall do it now.

   We can no longer afford to consider air and water common property, free to be abused by anyone without regard to the consequences. Instead, we should begin now to treat them as scarce resources, which we are no more free to contaminate than we are free to throw garbage into our neighbor's yard.

4. **"Earthrise" over the moon's surface, December 24, 1968.** *Photo taken by Apollo 8 crewmember Bill Anders, as the Apollo spacecraft orbited the moon.*

Source: NASA.

5. Paul Ehrlich, *The Population Bomb*, 1969. *A best-selling book that warned of a coming global overpopulation straining the world's resources.*

Nothing could be more misleading to our children than our present affluent society. They will inherit a totally different world, a world in which the standards, politics, and economics of the 1960s are dead. As the most powerful nation in the world today, and its largest consumer, the United States cannot stand isolated. We are today involved in the events leading to famine; tomorrow we may be destroyed by its consequences.

Our position requires that we take immediate action at home and promote effective action world-wide. We must have population control at home, hopefully through a system of incentives and penalties, but by compulsion if voluntary methods fail. We must use our political power to push other countries into programs which combine agricultural development and population control. And while this is being done we must take action to reverse the deterioration of our environment before population pressure permanently ruins our planet.

6. President Ronald Reagan, speech at the Republican National Convention, July 17, 1980.

Make no mistake. We will not permit the safety of our people or our environmental heritage to be jeopardized, but we are going to reaffirm that the economic prosperity of our people is a fundamental part of our environment.

Our problems are both acute and chronic, yet all we hear from those in positions of leadership are the same tired proposals for more government tinkering, more meddling, and more control — all of which led us to this state in the first place.

7. "Waste Produced by a Typical Family in a Year."

SOURCE: Martyn Goddard/Getty Images.

SOURCES: (1) Rachel Carson, *Silent Spring* (New York: Mariner Books, 2002), 15; (2) John G. Mitchell and Constance L. Hastings, eds., *Ecotactics: The Sierra Club Handbook for Environmental Activists* (New York: Trident Press, 1970), 13–15; (3 & 6) Gerhard Peters and John T. Woolley, *The American Presidency Project*, presidency.ucsb.edu; (5) Louis Warren, ed., *American Environmental History* (Malden, MA: Blackwell Publishing, 2003), 296.

ANALYZING THE EVIDENCE

1. Compare sources 1, 2, 3, 5, and 7. What are the different ways the environmental threat was understood and characterized? What kinds of solutions were proposed?

2. Source 4 is one of the first photographs of the earth ever taken from space. How would this visual perspective encourage viewers to think of the earth's resources as finite?

3. How does source 6 help us understand the opposition that developed to environmentalism? Why did some Americans oppose the environmental movement?

PUTTING IT ALL TOGETHER

Using what you have learned about the environmental movement in this chapter and the documents above, construct an essay in which you make a historical argument about the origins of the movement, the issues that it raised, and the opposition that developed. How did the movement shape politics in the 1970s?

Why Did the Postwar Boom Bust in the 1970s?

The seventies might be thought of as a lost decade, or at least as a decade of loss. The long post–World War II boom economy busted in the early 1970s, leaving a trail of social, political, and cultural dislocations in its wake. The combination of high unemployment and inflation and the challenges of a globalizing economy deeply affected workers and consumers. A string of events (including Watergate, the end of the Vietnam War, and the Iranian hostage crisis, which ended the decade) exacerbated the sense of decline many Americans were already experiencing. So how do historians explain the crisis of the 1970s? Historians Jefferson Cowie and Meg Jacobs offer similar interpretations of the 1970s economy, but they single out different factors. Cowie, whose work chronicles the struggling American working class in the 1970s, anchors his interpretation within a broad narrative of late-twentieth-century economic transformation. For Jacobs, an international crisis with domestic consequences triggered what she describes as a "panic at the pump."

JEFFERSON COWIE

SOURCE: Jefferson Cowie, *Stayin' Alive: The 1970s and the Last Days of the Working Class* (New York: The New Press, 2010), 12, 209.

Above all, the mid-1970s marked the end of the postwar boom. . . . Starting in the 1973–74 years, real earnings began to stagnate and then slide. . . . By mid-decade the record-breaking strikes, rank-and-file movements, and vibrant organizing drives that had once promised a new day for workers were reduced to a trickle in the new economic climate. They were then replaced by layoffs, plant closures, and union decertification drives. White male workers' incomes . . . stagnated or fell for the next quarter century . . . driven down by oil shocks and inflation; deindustrialization, plant closings, and anti-unionism; and a global restructuring of work itself. . . . By the end of the decade working people would possess less place and meaningful identity within civic life than any time since the industrial revolution.

MEG JACOBS

SOURCE: Meg Jacobs, *Panic at the Pump: The Energy Crisis and the Transformation of American Politics in the 1970s* (New York: Hill and Wang, 2016), 3–4.

Forty years ago, Americans were suffering from what contemporaries called "the energy crisis," a crisis that in many ways defined the decade of the 1970s. During the twin oil shocks of 1973 and 1979, oil supplies dropped and prices soared, and the average citizen understood the energy crisis to mean a panic at the pump — the fear that we would not have enough oil to fill up our gas tanks, heat our homes, or run our factories. . . . [The Arab oil] embargo stunned Americans, as if they had come under a surprise attack . . . because of the serious implications for the economy and the country's security. . . . Americans were vulnerable to scarcity and shortages as well as to higher fuel prices, which rippled through the entire economy and plagued the pocketbooks of all consumers.

QUESTIONS FOR ANALYSIS

1. What factors does each historian identify as causes of the 1970s economic crisis?
2. How do these historians explain the consequences of the economic crisis for Americans living in the 1970s?
3. To what extent does Chapter 28 corroborate, challenge, or supplement the list of factors Cowie and Jacobs present as affecting Americans' sense of crisis in the 1970s?

price and wage controls in 1971 in an effort to curb inflation. Then he took an even bolder step: removing the United States from the gold standard, which allowed the dollar to float in international currency markets and effectively ended the Bretton Woods monetary system established after World War II. The underlying weaknesses in the U.S. economy remained, however, and neither Ford nor Carter had more luck finding a solution. The fruitless search for a new economic order was a hallmark of 1970s politics (Interpretations).

Deindustrialization America's economic woes struck hardest at the industrial sector, which suddenly — shockingly — began to be dismantled. Worst hit was the steel industry, which for seventy-five years had been the economy's crown jewel. Unscathed by World War II, U.S. steel producers had enjoyed an open, hugely profitable market since the 1940s. But lack of serious competition left them without incentives to replace outdated plants and equipment. When West Germany and Japan rebuilt their steel industries, these facilities incorporated the latest technology. Foreign steel flooded into the United States during the 1970s, and the American industry was simply overwhelmed. Formerly titanic steel companies began a massive dismantling; virtually the entire Pittsburgh region, once a national hub of steel production, lost its heavy industry in a single generation. By the mid-1980s, downsizing, automation, and investment in new technologies made the American steel industry competitive again — but it was a shadow of its former self.

The steel industry was the prime example of what became known as **deindustrialization**. The country was in the throes of an economic transformation that left it largely stripped of its industrial base. Steel was hardly alone. A swath of the Northeast and Midwest, the country's manufacturing heartland, became the nation's **Rust Belt** (Map 28.1), strewn with abandoned plants and distressed communities. The automobile, tire, textile, and other consumer durable industries (appliances, electronics, furniture, and the like) all started shrinking in the 1970s. In 1980, *Business Week* bemoaned "plant closings across the continent" and called for the "*re*industrialization of America."

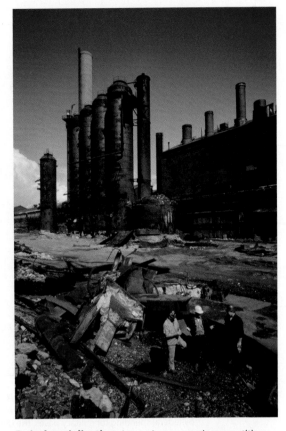

Deindustrialization Increasing economic competition from overseas created hard times for American industry in the 1970s and 1980s. Many of the nation's once-proud core industries, such as steel, declined precipitously in these decades. This photo shows a steel mill in Pittsburgh, Pennsylvania, being demolished in 1982. Once the center of American steel production, Pittsburgh suffered hard times in the 1970s and 1980s. The result of such closures was the creation of the so-called Rust Belt in the Northeast and Midwest (Map 28.1). Lynn Johnson/National Geographic/Getty Images.

deindustrialization

The dismantling of manufacturing — especially in the automobile, steel, and consumer-goods industries — in the decades after World War II, representing a reversal of the process of industrialization that had dominated the American economy from the 1870s through the 1940s.

Organized Labor in Decline Deindustrialization threw many tens of thousands of blue-collar workers out of well-paid union jobs. One study followed 4,100

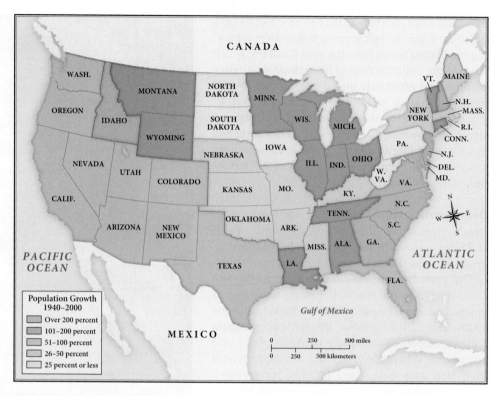

MAP 28.1 **From Rust Belt to Sunbelt, 1940–2000**

One of the most significant developments of the post–World War II era was the growth of the Sunbelt. Sparked by federal spending for military bases, the defense industry, and the space program, states of the South and Southwest experienced an economic boom in the 1950s. This growth was further enhanced in the 1970s, as the heavily industrialized regions of the Northeast and Midwest declined and migrants from what was quickly dubbed the Rust Belt headed to the South and West in search of jobs.

Rust Belt

The once heavily industrialized regions of the Northeast and Midwest that went into decline after deindustrialization. By the 1970s and 1980s, these regions were full of abandoned plants and distressed communities.

steelworkers left jobless by the 1977 shutdown of the Campbell Works of the Youngstown Sheet & Tube Co. Two years later, 35 percent had retired early at half pay; 10 percent had moved; 15 percent were still jobless, with unemployment benefits long gone; and 40 percent had found local work, but mostly in low-paying, service-sector jobs. In another instance, between 1978 and 1981, eight Los Angeles companies — including such giants as Ford, Uniroyal, and U.S. Steel — closed factories employing 18,000 workers. These Ohio and California workers, like hundreds of thousands of their counterparts across the nation, had fallen from their perch in the middle class (America in Global Context).

Deindustrialization dealt an especially harsh blow to the labor movement, which had facilitated the postwar expansion of that middle class. In the early 1970s, as inflation hit, the number of strikes surged; 2.4 million workers participated in work stoppages in 1970 alone. However, industry argued that it could no longer afford union demands, and labor's bargaining power produced fewer and fewer concrete results.

Economic Malaise in the Seventies

Most major economic indicators in the United States turned downward in the 1970s, as the long postwar expansion ground to an unmistakable halt. The figures below offer evidence of how developments in the United States compared with other industrialized countries.

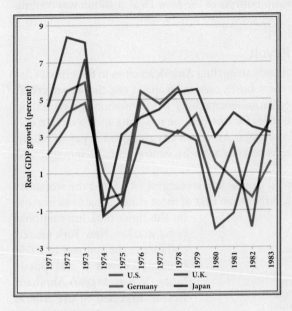

FIGURE 28.2 Falling Gross Domestic Product

FIGURE 28.3 Rising Unemployment

QUESTIONS FOR ANALYSIS

1. In what ways do these figures demonstrate an integrated global economy?
2. What does the GDP graph indicate about how global economic integration affected the U.S. economy? Notice that Japan's GDP growth remained strong in the late 1970s and early 1980s. With what historical development within the U.S. does that correspond?

In these hard years, the much-vaunted labor-management accord of the 1950s, which raised profits and wages by passing costs on to consumers, went bust. Instead of seeking higher wages, unions now mainly fought to save jobs. Union membership went into steep decline, and by the mid-1980s organized labor represented less than 18 percent of American workers, the lowest level since the 1920s. The impact on liberal politics was huge. With labor's decline, a main buttress of the New Deal coalition was coming undone.

Urban Crisis and Suburban Revolt

The economic downturn pushed already struggling American cities to the brink of fiscal collapse. Middle-class flight to the suburbs continued apace, and the "urban crisis" of the 1960s spilled into the "era of limits." Facing huge price inflation and mounting piles of debt — to finance social services for low-income residents and to replace disappearing tax revenue — nearly every major American city struggled to pay its bills in the 1970s. Surrounded by prosperous postwar suburbs, central cities seemingly could not catch a break.

New York, the nation's financial capital and its largest city, fared the worst. Its annual budget was in the billions, larger than that of most states. Unable to borrow on the tightening international bond market, New York neared collapse in the summer of 1975; bankruptcy was a real possibility. When Mayor Abraham Beame appealed to the federal government for assistance, President Ford refused. "Ford to City: Drop Dead" read the headline in the *New York Daily News*. Fresh appeals ultimately produced a solution: the federal government would lend New York money, and banks would declare a three-year moratorium on municipal debt. The arrangement saved the city from defaulting, but the mayor was forced to cut city services, freeze wages, and lay off workers. One pessimistic observer declared that "the banks have been saved, and the city has been condemned."

Cities faced declining fortunes in these years for many reasons, but one key was the

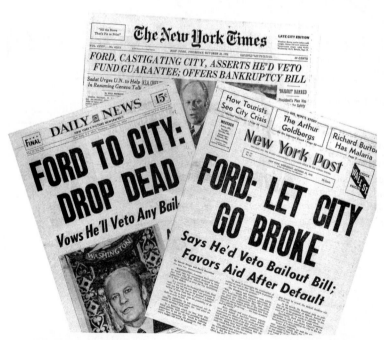

"Ford to City: Drop Dead" In the summer of 1975, New York City nearly went bankrupt. When Mayor Abraham Beame appealed to President Gerald Ford for federal assistance, these newspaper headlines captured the chief executive's response. Though it was ultimately saved from financial ruin, the city's brush with insolvency symbolized the larger problems facing the nation: economic stagnation, high inflation, and unemployment. Hard times had seemingly spared no one. AP Photo.

continued loss of residents and businesses to nearby suburbs. In the 1970s alone, 13 million people (6 percent of the total U.S. population) moved to the suburbs. New suburban shopping centers opened weekly across the country, and other businesses — such as banks, insurance companies, and technology firms — increasingly sought suburban locations. More and more, people lived *and* worked in suburbs. In the San Francisco Bay area, 75 percent of all daily commutes were suburb-to-suburb, and 78 percent of New York's suburban residents worked in nearby suburbs. The 1950s "organization man," commuting downtown from his suburban home, had been replaced by the engineer, teacher, nurse, student, and carpenter who lived in one suburb and worked in another.

Beyond city limits, suburbanization and the economic crisis combined powerfully in what became known as the **tax revolt**, a dramatic reversal of the postwar spirit of generous public investment. The premier example was California. Inflation pushed real estate values upward, and property taxes skyrocketed. Hardest hit were suburban property owners, along with retirees and others on fixed incomes, who suddenly faced unaffordable tax bills. Into this dire situation stepped Howard Jarvis, a conservative anti–New Dealer and a genius at mobilizing grassroots discontent. In 1978, Jarvis proposed **Proposition 13**, an initiative that would roll back property taxes, cap future increases for present owners, and require that all tax measures have a two-thirds majority in the legislature. Despite opposition by virtually the entire state leadership, including politicians from both parties, Californians voted overwhelmingly for Jarvis's measure.

Proposition 13 hobbled public spending in the nation's most populous state. Per capita funding of California public schools, once the envy of the nation, plunged from the top tier to the bottom, where it was second only to Mississippi. Moreover, Proposition 13's complicated formula benefitted middle-class and wealthy home owners at the expense of less-well-off citizens, especially those who depended heavily on public services. Businesses, too, came out ahead, because commercial property got the same protection as residential property. More broadly, Proposition 13 inspired tax revolts across the country and helped conservatives define an enduring issue: low taxes.

In addition to public investment, another cardinal marker of New Deal and Great Society liberalism had been a remarkable decline in income inequality. In the 1970s, that trend reversed, and the wealthiest Americans, those among the top 10 percent, began to pull ahead again. As corporations restructured to boost profits during the 1970s slump, they increasingly laid off high-wage workers, paid the remaining workers less, and relocated overseas. Thus upper-class Americans benefitted, while blue-collar families who had been lifted into the middle class during the postwar boom increasingly lost out. An unmistakable trend was apparent by the end of the 1970s. The U.S. labor market was dividing in two: a vast, low-wage market at the bottom and a much narrower high-wage market at the top, with the middle squeezed smaller and smaller.

tax revolt
A movement to lower or eliminate taxes. California's Proposition 13, which rolled back property taxes, capped future increases for present owners, and required that all tax measures have a two-thirds majority in the legislature, was the result of one such revolt, inspiring similar movements across the country.

Proposition 13
A measure passed overwhelmingly by Californians to roll back property taxes, cap future increases for present owners, and require that all tax measures have a two-thirds majority in the legislature. Proposition 13 inspired "tax revolts" across the country and helped conservatives define an enduring issue: low taxes.

IN YOUR OWN WORDS   What limits did the American economy experience in the 1970s?

Politics in Flux, 1973–1980

A search for order characterized national politics in the 1970s as well. It began with a scandal. Misbehavior is endemic to politics. Yet what became known as the Watergate affair — or simply **Watergate** — implicated President Richard Nixon in illegal behavior severe enough to bring down his presidency. Liberals benefitted from Nixon's fall in the short term, but their long-term retreat continued. Politics remained in flux because while liberals were on the defensive, conservatives had not yet put forth a clear alternative.

Watergate and the Fall of a President

On June 17, 1972, something strange happened at Washington's Watergate office/apartment/hotel complex. Early that morning, five men carrying wiretapping equipment were apprehended there attempting to break into the headquarters of the Democratic National Committee (DNC). Queried by the press, a White House spokesman dismissed the episode as "a third-rate burglary attempt." Pressed further, Nixon himself denied any White House involvement in "this very bizarre incident." In fact, the two masterminds of the break-in, G. Gordon Liddy and E. Howard Hunt, were former FBI and CIA agents currently working for Nixon's Committee to Re-elect the President (CREEP).

The Watergate burglary was no isolated incident. It was part of a broad pattern of abuse of power by a White House obsessed with its political enemies. Liddy and Hunt were on the White House payroll, part of a clandestine squad hired to stop leaks to the press. But they were soon arranging illegal wiretaps at DNC headquarters, part of a campaign of "dirty tricks" against the Democrats. Nixon's siege mentality best explains his fatal misstep. He could have dissociated himself from the break-in by firing his guilty aides or even just by letting justice take its course. But it was election time, and Nixon did not trust his political future to such a strategy. Instead, he arranged hush money for the burglars and instructed the CIA to stop an FBI investigation into the affair. This was obstruction of justice, a criminal offense.

Nixon kept the lid on until after the election, but in early 1973, one of the Watergate burglars began to talk. In the meantime, two reporters at the *Washington Post*, Carl Bernstein and Bob Woodward, uncovered CREEP's links to key White House aides. In May 1973, a Senate investigating committee began holding nationally televised hearings, at which administration officials implicated Nixon in the illegal cover-up. The president kept investigators at bay for a year, but in June 1974, the House Judiciary Committee began to consider articles of impeachment. Certain of being convicted by the Senate, Nixon became, on August 9, 1974, the first U.S. president to resign his office. The next day, Vice President Gerald Ford was sworn in as president. Ford, the Republican minority leader in the House of Representatives, had replaced Vice President Spiro Agnew, who had himself resigned in 1973 for accepting kickbacks while governor of Maryland. A month after he took office, Ford stunned the nation by granting Nixon a "full, free, and absolute" pardon.

Congress pushed back, passing a raft of laws inspired by the abuses of the Nixon administration and designed to limit the power of future presidents: the **War Powers Act** (1973), which reined in the president's ability to deploy U.S. forces without congressional approval; amendments strengthening the **Freedom of Information Act** (1974),

Watergate
Term referring to the 1972 break-in at Democratic Party headquarters in the Watergate complex in Washington, D.C., by men working for President Nixon's reelection campaign, along with Nixon's efforts to cover it up. The Watergate scandal led to President Nixon's resignation.

War Powers Act
A law that limited the president's ability to deploy U.S. forces without congressional approval. Congress passed the War Powers Act in 1973 as a series of laws to fight the abuses of the Nixon administration.

Freedom of Information Act
Passed in the wake of the Watergate scandal, the 1974 act that gave citizens access to federal records.

which gave citizens access to federal records; the **Ethics in Government Act** (1978); and the Foreign Intelligence Surveillance Act (1978), which prohibited domestic wiretapping without a warrant.

Popular disdain for politicians, evident in declining voter turnout, deepened with Nixon's resignation in 1974. "Don't vote," read one bumper sticker in 1976. "It only encourages them." Watergate not only damaged short-term Republican prospects but also shifted the party's balance to the right. Despite mastering the populist appeal to the "silent majority," the moderate Nixon was never beloved by conservatives. His relaxation of tensions with the Soviet Union and his visit to communist China, in particular, won him no friends on the right. His disgraceful exit benefitted the more conservative Republicans, who proceeded to reshape the party in their image.

Watergate Babies As for the Democrats, Watergate granted them a reprieve, a second chance at recapturing their eroding base. Democratic candidates in the 1974 midterm elections made Watergate and Ford's pardon of Nixon their top issues. It worked. Seventy-five new Democratic members of the House came to Washington in 1975, many of them under the age of forty-five, and the press dubbed them Watergate babies.

Young and reform-minded, the Watergate babies solidified huge Democratic majorities in both houses of Congress and quickly set to work. They eliminated the House Un-American Activities Committee (HUAC), which had investigated alleged Communists in the 1940s and 1950s and antiwar activists in the 1960s. In the Senate, Democrats reduced the number of votes needed to end a filibuster from 67 to 60 — a move intended to weaken the power of the minority to block legislation. In both houses, Democrats dismantled the existing committee structure, which had entrenched power in the hands of a few elite committee chairs. Overall, the Watergate babies helped to decentralize power in Washington and bring greater transparency to American government.

In one of the great ironies of American political history, however, the post-Watergate reforms made government *less* efficient and *more* susceptible to special interests — the opposite of what had been intended. Under the new committee structure, smaller subcommittees proliferated, and the size of the congressional staff doubled to more than 20,000. A diffuse power structure actually gave lobbyists more places to exert influence. As the power of committee chairs weakened, influence shifted to party leaders, such as the Speaker of the House and the Senate majority leader. With little incentive to compromise, the parties grew more rigid, and bipartisanship became rare. Finally, filibustering, a seldom-used tactic largely employed by anti–civil rights southerners, increased in frequency. The Congress that we have come to know today — with its partisan rancor, its army of lobbyists, and its slow-moving response to public needs — came into being in the 1970s.

Political Realignment Despite Democratic gains in 1974, the electoral realignment that had begun with Richard Nixon's presidential victories in 1968 and 1972 continued. As liberals proved unable to stop runaway inflation or speed up economic growth, conservatives gained greater traction with the public. The postwar liberal economic formula — sometimes known as the Keynesian consensus — consisted of microadjustments to the money supply coupled with federal spending. When that formula failed to restart the economy in the mid-1970s, conservatives in Congress used this opening to articulate alternatives, especially economic deregulation and tax cuts (Chapter 29).

Ethics in Government Act
Passed in the wake of the Watergate scandal, the 1978 act that forced political candidates to disclose financial contributions and limited the lobbying activities of former elected officials.

On a grander scale, deindustrialization in the Northeast and Midwest and continued population growth in the Sunbelt were changing the political geography of the country. Power was shifting, incrementally but perceptibly, toward the West and South (Table 28.1). As states with strong trade unions at the center of the postwar liberal political coalition — such as New York, Illinois, and Michigan — lost industry, jobs, and people, states with traditions of libertarian conservatism — such as California, Arizona, Florida, and Texas — gained greater political clout. The full impact of this shifting political geography would not be felt until the 1980s and 1990s, but its effects had become apparent by the mid-1970s.

Jimmy Carter: The Outsider as President

"Jimmy who?" was how journalists first responded when James Earl Carter, who had been a naval officer, a peanut farmer, and the governor of Georgia, emerged from the pack to win the Democratic presidential nomination in 1976. When Carter told his mother that he intended to run for president, she had asked, "President of what?"

Jimmy Carter President Jimmy Carter is seen here at his home in Plains, Georgia, in 1975, soon after he'd declared himself a candidate for the Democratic presidential nomination. Carter was content to portray himself as a political outsider, an ordinary American who could restore trust to Washington after the Watergate scandal. A thoughtful man and a born-again Christian, Carter nonetheless proved unable to solve the complex economic problems, especially high inflation, and international challenges of the late 1970s. AP Photo.

Trading on Watergate and his down-home image, Carter pledged to restore morality to the White House. "I will never lie to you," he promised voters. Carter played up his credentials as a Washington outsider, although he selected Senator Walter F. Mondale of Minnesota as his running mate to ensure his ties to traditional Democratic voting blocs. Ford still might have prevailed, but his pardon of Nixon likely cost him enough votes in key states to swing the election to the Democratic candidate. Carter won with 50 percent of the popular vote to Ford's 48 percent.

For a time, Carter got some mileage as an outsider — the common man who walked to the White House after the inauguration and delivered fireside chats in a cardigan sweater. The fact that he was a born-again Christian also played well. But Carter's inexperience began to show. He responded to feminists, an important Democratic constituency, by establishing a new women's commission in his administration. But later he dismissed the commission's concerns and became embroiled in a public fight with prominent women's advocates. Most consequentially, his outsider strategy made for chilly relations with congressional leaders. Disdainful of the Democratic establishment, Carter relied heavily on inexperienced advisors from Georgia. And as a detail-oriented micromanager, he exhausted himself over the fine points of policy better left to his aides.

On the domestic front, Carter's big challenge was managing the economy. The problems that he faced defied easy solution. Most confounding was

TABLE 28.1

Political Realignment: Congressional Seats

State	Apportionment	
	1940	**1990**
Rust Belt		
Massachusetts	14	10
Connecticut	6	6
New York	45	31
New Jersey	14	13
Pennsylvania	33	21
Ohio	23	19
Illinois	26	20
Indiana	11	10
Michigan	17	16
Wisconsin	10	9
Total	**199**	**155**
Sunbelt		
California	23	52
Arizona	2	6
Nevada	1	2
Colorado	4	6
New Mexico	2	3
Texas	21	30
Georgia	10	11
North Carolina	12	12
Virginia	9	11
Florida	6	23
Total	**90**	**156**

In the fifty years between 1940 and 1990, the Rust Belt states lost political clout, while the Sunbelt states gained it — measured here in congressional seats (which are apportioned based on population). Sunbelt states gained 66 seats, with the Rust Belt losing 44. This shifting political geography helped undermine the liberal coalition, which was strongest in industrial states with large labor unions, and paved the way for the rise of the conservative coalition, which was strongest in southern and Appalachian states, as well as California.

SOURCE: Office of the Clerk of the House, clerk.house.gov/art_history/house_history/congApp/bystate.html.

deregulation
The limiting of regulation by federal agencies. Deregulation of prices in the trucking, airline, and railroad industries had begun under President Carter in the late 1970s, and Reagan expanded it to include cutting back on government protections of consumers, workers, and the environment.

📖 To read more of President Carter's television address, along with other primary sources from this period, see *Sources for America's History*.

stagflation. If the government focused on inflation — forcing prices down by raising interest rates — unemployment became worse. If the government tried to stimulate employment, inflation became worse. None of the levers of government economic policy seemed to work. At heart, Carter was an economic conservative. He toyed with the idea of an "industrial policy" to bail out the ailing manufacturing sector, but he moved instead in a free-market direction by lifting the New Deal–era regulation of the airline, trucking, and railroad industries. **Deregulation** stimulated competition and cut prices, but it also drove firms out of business and hurt unionized workers.

The president's efforts failed to reignite economic growth. Then, the Iranian Revolution (see Chapter 29) curtailed oil supplies, and gas prices jumped again. In a major TV address, Carter lectured Americans about the nation's "crisis of the spirit." He called energy conservation "the moral equivalent of war" — or, in the media's shorthand, "MEOW," which aptly captured the nation's assessment of Carter's sermonizing. By then, his approval rating had fallen below 30 percent. And it was no wonder, given an inflation rate over 11 percent, failing industries, and long lines at the pumps. It seemed the worst of all possible economic worlds, and the first-term president could not help but worry about the political costs to him and his party.

> **IN YOUR OWN WORDS**   In what ways was the period between 1973 and 1980 a transitional one in American politics?

Reform and Reaction in the 1970s

Having lived through a decade of profound social and political upheaval — the Vietnam War, protests, riots, Watergate, recession — many Americans were exhausted and cynical by the mid-1970s. But while some retreated to private concerns, others took reform in new directions. Civil rights battles continued, the women's movement achieved some of its most far-reaching aims, and gay rights blossomed. These movements pushed the "rights revolution" of the 1960s deeper into American life. Others, however, pushed back. Social conservatives responded by forming their own organizations and resisting the emergence of what they saw as a permissive society.

affirmative action
Policies established in the 1960s and 1970s by governments, businesses, universities, and other institutions to overcome the effects of past discrimination against specific groups such as racial and ethnic minorities and women. Measures to ensure equal opportunity include setting goals for the admission, hiring, and promotion of minorities; considering minority status when allocating resources; and actively encouraging victims of past discrimination to apply for jobs and other resources.

Civil Rights in a New Era

When Congress banned job discrimination in the 1964 Civil Rights Act, the law required only that employers hire without regard to "race, color, religion, sex, or national origin." But after centuries of slavery and decades of segregation, would nondiscrimination bring African Americans into the economic mainstream? Many liberals thought not. They believed that government, universities, and private employers needed to take positive steps to open their doors to a wider, more diverse range of Americans — including those from other historically underrepresented groups and women.

Among the most significant efforts to address the legacy of exclusion was **affirmative action** — procedures designed to take into account the disadvantaged position of Americans from historically underrepresented groups after centuries of discrimination. First advanced by the Kennedy administration in 1961, affirmative action received a boost under President Lyndon Johnson, whose Labor Department fashioned a series of plans in the late 1960s to encourage government contractors to recruit underrepresented racial groups. Women were added under the last of these plans, when pressure from the women's movement highlighted the problem of sex discrimination. By the early 1970s, affirmative action had been refined by court rulings that identified acceptable procedures: hiring and enrollment goals, special recruitment and training programs, and set-asides (specially reserved slots) for both underrepresented racial groups and women.

Affirmative action, however, did not please many whites, who felt that the deck was being stacked against them. Much of the dissent came from conservative groups that had opposed civil rights all along. They charged affirmative action advocates with "reverse discrimination." Legal challenges abounded, as employees, students, and university applicants went to court to object to these new procedures. Some liberal groups sought a middle position. In a widely publicized 1972 letter, Jewish organizations, seared by the memory of quotas that once kept Jewish students out of elite colleges, came out against all racial quotas but nonetheless endorsed "rectifying the imbalances resulting from past discrimination."

A major shift in affirmative action policy came in 1978. Allan Bakke, a white man, sued the University of California at Davis Medical School for rejecting him in favor of less-qualified minority-group candidates. Headlines across the country sparked anti–affirmative action protest marches on college campuses and vigorous discussion on television and radio and in the White House. Ultimately, the Supreme Court rejected the medical school's quota system, which set aside 16 of 100 places for "disadvantaged" students. The Court ordered Bakke admitted but indicated that a more flexible affirmative action plan, in which race could be considered along with other factors, would still pass constitutional muster. ***Bakke v. University of California*** thus upheld affirmative action but, by rejecting a quota system, also called it into question. Future court rulings and state referenda, in the 1990s and 2000s, would further limit the scope of affirmative action. In particular, California voters passed Proposition 209 in 1996, prohibiting public institutions from using affirmative action to increase diversity in employment and education.

Bakke v. University of California
The 1978 Supreme Court ruling that limited affirmative action by rejecting a quota system.

The Women's Movement and Gay Rights

Unlike the civil rights movement, whose signal achievements came in the 1960s, the women's and gay rights movements flourished in the 1970s. With three influential wings — radical, liberal, and "Third World" — the women's movement inspired both grassroots activism and legislative action across the nation. For their part, gay activists faced a unique set of challenges: they needed to convince Americans that same-sex relationships were natural and that gay men and lesbians deserved the same protection of the law as all other citizens. Neither movement achieved all of its aims in this era, but each laid a strong foundation for the future.

Women's Activism In the first half of the 1970s, the women's liberation movement reached its historic peak. Taking a dizzying array of forms — from lobbying legislatures to marching in the streets and establishing all-female collectives — women's liberation inspired activism on the scale of the earlier black-led civil rights movement.

Women's centers, as well as women-run child-care facilities, began to spring up in cities and towns. A feminist art and poetry movement flourished. Women challenged the admissions policies of all-male colleges and universities — opening such prestigious universities as Yale and Columbia and nearly bringing an end to male-only institutions of higher education. Female scholars began to transform higher education: by studying women's history, by increasing the number of women on college and university faculties, and by founding women's studies programs.

Women's liberationists drew new attention to, and thereby politicized, the female body. Inspired by the Boston collective that first published *Our Bodies, Ourselves* — a groundbreaking book on women's health — the women's health movement founded dozens of medical clinics, encouraged women to become physicians, and educated millions of women about their bodies. To reform antiabortion laws, activists pushed for remedies in more than thirty state legislatures. Women's liberationists established rape crisis centers around the nation and lobbied state legislatures and Congress to reform rape laws. Many of these endeavors and movements began as shoestring operations in living rooms and kitchens: *Our Bodies, Ourselves* was first published as a 35-cent mimeographed booklet, and the antirape movement began in small consciousness-raising groups that met in churches and community centers. By the end of the decade, however, all of these causes had national organizations and touched the lives of millions of American women.

Equal Rights Amendment   Buoyed by this flourishing of activism, the women's movement renewed the fight for an **Equal Rights Amendment (ERA)** to the Constitution. First introduced in 1923, the ERA stated, in its entirety, "Equality of rights under the law shall not be denied or abridged by the United States or any State on the basis of sex." Vocal congressional women from the Democratic Party, such as Patsy Mink (Hawaii), Bella Abzug (New York), and Shirley Chisholm (New York), found enthusiastic male allies — among both Democrats and Republicans — and Congress adopted the amendment in 1972. Within just two years, thirty-four of the necessary thirty-eight states had ratified it, and the ERA appeared headed for adoption. But then, progress abruptly halted (Map 28.2).

Credit for putting the brakes on ERA ratification goes chiefly to a remarkable woman: Phyllis Schlafly, a lawyer long active in conservative causes. Despite her own flourishing career, Schlafly advocated traditional roles for women. The ERA, she proclaimed, would create an unnatural "unisex society," with women drafted into the army and forced to use single-sex restrooms. Abortion, she alleged, could never be prohibited by law. Led by Schlafly's organization, **STOP ERA** (founded in 1972), thousands of women mobilized, showing up at statehouses with home-baked bread and apple pies. As labels on baked goods at one anti-ERA rally expressed it: "My heart and hand went into this dough / For the sake of the family please vote no." It was a message that resonated widely, especially among those troubled by the rapid pace of social change. The ERA never was ratified, despite a congressional extension of the deadline to June 30, 1982.

Roe v. Wade   In addition to the ERA, the women's movement had identified another major goal: winning reproductive rights. Activists pursued two tracks: legislative and

Equal Rights Amendment (ERA)

Constitutional amendment passed by Congress in 1972 that would require equal treatment of men and women under federal and state law. Facing fierce opposition from the New Right and the Republican Party, the ERA was defeated as time ran out for state ratification in 1982.

STOP ERA

An organization founded by Phyllis Schlafly in 1972 to fight the Equal Rights Amendment.

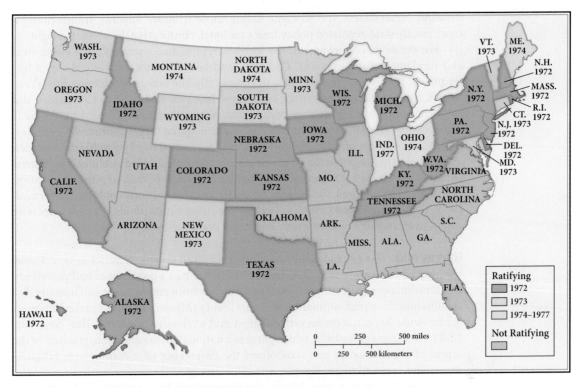

MAP 28.2 States Ratifying the Equal Rights Amendment, 1972–1977
The ratifying process for the Equal Rights Amendment (ERA) went smoothly in 1972 and 1973 but then stalled. The turning point came in 1976, when ERA advocates lobbied extensively, particularly in Florida, North Carolina, and Illinois, but failed to sway the conservative legislatures in those states. After Indiana ratified in 1977, the amendment still lacked three votes toward the three-fourths majority needed for adoption. Efforts to revive the ERA in the 1980s were unsuccessful, and it became a dead issue.

judicial. In the early 1960s, abortion was illegal in virtually every state. A decade later, thanks to intensive lobbying by women's organizations, liberal ministers, and physicians, a handful of states, such as New York, Hawaii, California, and Colorado, adopted laws making legal abortions easier to obtain. But progress after that was slow, and women's advocates turned to the courts. There was reason to be optimistic. The Supreme Court had first addressed reproductive rights in a 1965 case, *Griswold v. Connecticut. Griswold* struck down an 1879 state law prohibiting the possession of contraception as a violation of married couples' constitutional "right of privacy." Following the logic articulated in *Griswold*, the Court gradually expanded the right of privacy in a series of cases in the late 1960s and early 1970s.

Those cases culminated in ***Roe v. Wade*** (1973). In that landmark decision, the justices nullified a Texas law that prohibited abortion under any circumstances, even when the woman's health was at risk, and laid out a new national standard: abortions performed during the first trimester were protected by the right of privacy. At the time and afterward, some legal authorities questioned whether the Constitution recognized any such privacy right and criticized the Court's seemingly arbitrary first-trimester

Roe v. Wade
The 1973 Supreme Court ruling that the Constitution protects the right to abortion, which states cannot prohibit in the early stages of pregnancy. The decision galvanized social conservatives and made abortion a controversial policy issue for decades to come.

timeline. Nevertheless, the Supreme Court chose to move forward, transforming a traditionally state-regulated policy into a national, constitutionally protected right.

For the women's movement, *Roe v. Wade* represented a triumph. For evangelical and fundamentalist Christians, Catholics, and conservatives generally, it was a bitter pill. In their view, abortion was, unequivocally, the taking of a human life. These Americans, represented by groups such as the National Right to Life Committee, did not believe that something they regarded as immoral and sinful could be the basis for women's equality. Women's advocates responded that illegal abortions — common prior to *Roe* — were often unsafe procedures that resulted in physical harm to women and even death. *Roe* polarized what was already a sharply divided public and mobilized conservatives to seek a Supreme Court reversal or, short of that, to pursue legislation that would strictly limit the conditions under which abortions could be performed. In 1976, they convinced Congress to deny Medicaid funds for abortions, an opening round in a campaign against *Roe v. Wade* that continues today.

Harvey Milk The gay rights movement had achieved notable victories as well. These, too, proved controversial. By the mid-1970s, more than a dozen cities had passed gay rights ordinances protecting gay men and lesbians from employment and housing discrimination. One such ordinance in Dade County (Miami), Florida, sparked a protest led by Anita Bryant, a conservative Baptist and a television celebrity. Her "Save Our Children" campaign in 1977, which garnered national media attention, resulted in the repeal of the ordinance and symbolized the emergence of a conservative religious movement opposed to gay rights.

Across the country from Miami, developments in San Francisco looked promising for gay rights advocates, then turned tragic. No one embodied the combination of gay liberation and hard-nosed politics better than a San Francisco camera-shop owner named Harvey Milk. A closeted businessman in New York until he was forty, Milk arrived in San Francisco in 1972 and threw himself into city politics. Fiercely independent, he ran as an openly gay candidate for city supervisor (city council) twice and the state assembly once, both times unsuccessfully.

By mobilizing the "gay vote" into a powerful bloc, Milk finally won a supervisor seat in 1977. He was not the first openly gay elected official in the country — Kathy Kozachenko of Michigan and Elaine Noble of Massachusetts share that distinction — but he became a national symbol of emerging gay political power. Tragically, after he helped to win passage of a gay rights ordinance in San Francisco, he was assassinated in 1978 — along with the city's mayor, George Moscone — by a disgruntled former supervisor named Dan White. When White was convicted of manslaughter rather than murder, five thousand gays and lesbians in San Francisco marched on city hall.

After the Warren Court

In response to what conservatives considered the liberal judicial revolution under the Warren Court, Nixon came into the presidency promising to appoint "strict constructionists" (conservative-minded justices) to the bench. In three short years, between 1969 and 1972, he was able to appoint four new justices to the Supreme Court, including the new chief justice, Warren Burger. Burger and his conservative colleagues did not, suprisingly, immediately seek to overturn Warren Court precedents. Indeed, in

Roe v. Wade the Burger Court extended the "right of privacy" developed under Warren to include women's access to abortion. As we saw above, few Supreme Court decisions in the twentieth century have disappointed conservatives more. Other decisions advanced women's rights further. In 1976, the Court ruled that arbitrary distinctions based on sex in the workplace and other arenas were unconstitutional, and in 1986 that sexual harassment violated the Civil Rights Act. These rulings helped women break employment barriers in the subsequent decades.

In a variety of cases, however, the Burger Court chose a centrist course, particularly in cases regarding criminal law. After first striking down all existing capital punishment laws, in *Furman v. Georgia* (1972), the court shortly restored them, in *Gregg v. Georgia* (1976). Rather than overturning the Warren Court's rulings on the rights of suspected criminals (such as the 1966 decision in *Miranda v. Arizona*), which were deeply unpopular among conservatives, the Burger Court instead limited their reach. Overall, despite its reputation for centrist restraint, the Burger Court helped to ratify the "law and order" politics embraced by many Americans in the years following the 1960s.

In keeping with such centrism, in all of their rulings on privacy rights the Burger Court was reluctant to move ahead of public attitudes toward homosexuality. Gay men and lesbians still had no legal recourse if state laws prohibited same-sex relations. In a controversial 1986 case, *Bowers v. Hardwick*, the Supreme Court upheld a Georgia sodomy statute that criminalized same-sex sexual acts. The majority opinion held that homosexuality was contrary to "ordered liberty" and that extending sexual privacy to gays and lesbians "would be to cast aside millennia of moral teaching." Not until 2003 (*Lawrence v. Texas*) would the Court overturn that decision, recognizing for all Americans the right to sexual privacy.

IN YOUR OWN WORDS How did controversies over new individual rights shape the politics of the 1970s?

The American Family on Trial

In 1973, the Public Broadcasting System (PBS) aired a twelve-part television series that followed the life of a real American family. Producers wanted the show, called simply *An American Family*, to document how a middle-class white family coped with the stresses of a changing society. They did not anticipate that the family would dissolve in front of their cameras. Tensions and arguments raged, and in the final episode, Bill, the husband and father (who had had numerous extramarital affairs), moved out. By the time the show aired, the couple was divorced and Pat, the former wife, had become a single working mother with five children.

An American Family captured a traumatic moment in the twentieth-century history of the family. Between 1965 and 1985, the divorce rate doubled, and children born in the 1970s had a 40 percent chance of spending part of their youth in a single-parent household. As wages stagnated and inflation pushed prices up, more and more families depended on two incomes for survival. Furthermore, the women's movement and the counterculture had called into question traditional sex roles — father as provider and mother as homemaker—and middle-class baby boomers rebelled against what they saw as the puritanical sexual values of their parents' generation. In the midst of such rapid change, where did the family stand?

Working Families in the Age of Deindustrialization

One of the most striking developments of the 1970s and 1980s was the relative stagnation of wages. After World War II, hourly wages had grown steadily ahead of inflation, giving workers more buying power with each passing decade. By 1973, that trend had stopped in its tracks. The decline of organized labor, the loss of manufacturing jobs, and runaway inflation all played a role in the reversal. Hardest hit were blue-collar and pink-collar workers and those without college degrees.

Women Enter the Workforce   Millions of wives and mothers had worked for wages for decades. But many Americans still believed in the "family wage": a breadwinner income, earned by men, sufficient to support a family. After 1973, fewer and fewer Americans had access to that luxury. Between 1973 and the early 1990s, every major income group except the top 10 percent saw their real earnings (accounting for inflation) either remain the same or decline. Over this period, the typical worker saw a 10 percent drop in real wages. To keep their families from falling behind, women streamed into the workforce. Between 1950 and 1994, the proportion of women ages twenty-five to fifty-four working for pay increased from 37 to 75 percent. Much of that increase occurred in the 1970s. Americans were fast becoming dependent on the two-income household.

The numbers tell two different stories of American life in these decades. On one hand, the trends unmistakably show that women, especially in blue-collar and pink-collar families, *had* to work for wages to sustain their family's standard of living: to buy a car, pay for college, afford medical bills, support an aging parent, or simply pay the rent. Moreover, the number of single women raising children nearly doubled between 1965 and 1990. Women's paid labor was making up for the declining earning power or the absence of men in American households. On the other hand, women's real income overall grew during the same period. This increase reflected the opening of professional jobs to educated baby boom women. As older barriers began to fall, women poured into law and medicine, business and government, and, though more slowly, the sciences and engineering. Beneficiaries of feminism, these women pursued careers of which their mothers had only dreamed.

Workers in the National Spotlight   For a brief period in the 1970s, the trials of working men and women made a distinct imprint on national culture. Reporters wrote of the "blue-collar blues" associated with plant closings and the hard-fought strikes of the decade. A 1972 strike at the Lordstown, Ohio, General Motors plant captivated the nation. Holding out not for higher wages but for better working conditions—the plant had the most complex assembly line in the nation—Lordstown strikers spoke out against what they saw as an inhumane industrial system. Across the nation, the number of union-led strikes surged, even as the number of Americans in the labor movement continued to decline. In Lordstown and most other sites of strikes and industrial conflict, workers won a measure of public attention but typically gained little economic ground.

When Americans turned on their televisions in the mid-1970s, the most popular shows reflected the "blue-collar blues" of struggling families. *All in the Family* was joined by *The Waltons*, set during the Great Depression. *Good Times, Welcome Back, Kotter,* and *Sanford and Son* dealt with poverty in the inner city. *The Jeffersons* featured an upwardly mobile black couple struggling to leave their working-class roots behind. *Laverne and Shirley* focused on young working women in the 1950s and *One Day at a Time* on working women in the 1970s making do after divorce. The most-watched television series of the decade, 1977's eight-part *Roots*, explored the history of slavery and the survival of African American culture and family roots despite the oppressive labor system. Not since the 1930s had American culture paid such close attention to working-class life.

The decade also saw the rise of musicians such as Bruce Springsteen, Johnny Paycheck, and John Cougar (Mellencamp), who became stars by turning the hardscrabble lives of people in small towns and working-class communities into rock anthems that filled arenas. Springsteen wrote songs about characters who "sweat it out in the streets of a runaway American dream," and, to the delight of his audience, Paycheck famously sang, "Take this job and shove it!" Meanwhile, on the streets of Harlem and the South Bronx in New York, young working-class African American men experimenting with dance and musical forms invented break dancing and rap music — styles that expressed both the hardship and the creativity of working-class black life in the deindustrialized American city.

Navigating the Sexual Revolution

The economic downturn was not the only force that placed stress on American families in this era. Another such force was what many came to call the "sexual revolution." Hardly revolutionary, sexual attitudes in the 1970s were, in many ways, a logical evolution of developments in the first half of the twentieth century. Beginning in the 1910s, Americans increasingly viewed sex as a component of personal happiness, distinct from reproduction. Attitudes toward sex grew even more lenient in the postwar decades, a fact reflected in the Kinsey studies of the 1940s and 1950s. By the 1960s, sex before marriage had grown more socially acceptable — an especially profound change for women — and frank discussions of sex in the media and popular culture had grown more common.

In that decade, three developments dramatically accelerated this process: the introduction of the birth control pill, the rise of the baby-boomer-led counterculture, and the influence of feminism. First made available in the United States in 1960, the birth control pill gave women an unprecedented degree of control over reproduction. By 1965, more than 6 million American women were taking advantage of this pharmaceutical advance. Rapid shifts in attitude accompanied the technological breakthrough. Middle-class baby boomers embraced a sexual ethic of greater freedom and, in many cases, a more casual approach to sex outside marriage. "I just feel I am expressing myself the way I feel at that moment in the most natural way," a female California college student, explaining her sex life, told a reporter in 1966. The rebellious counterculture encouraged this attitudinal shift by associating a puritanical view of sex with their parents' generation.

Finally, women's rights activists reacted to the new emphasis on sexual freedom in at least two distinct ways. Many feminists felt that the sexual revolution was by and for men: the emphasis on casual sex seemed to perpetuate male privilege — the old double standard; sexual harassment was all too common in the workplace; and the proliferation of pornography continued to commercialize women as sex objects. On the other hand, they remained optimistic that the new sexual ethic could free women from those older moral constraints. They called for a revolution in sexual *values*, not simply behavior, that would end exploitation and grant women the freedom to explore their sexuality on equal terms with men.

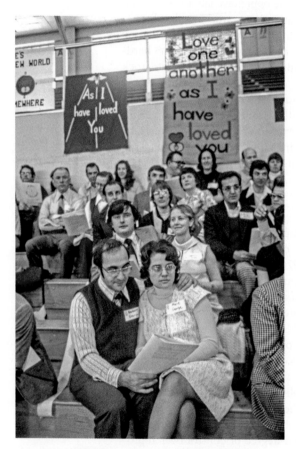

Marriage on the Rocks Couples attending a Marriage Encounter workshop near Boston in 1972. Traditional notions of marriage came under a variety of economic and psychological stresses in the 1970s. Many Americans turned to therapeutic solutions to preserve, or improve, their marriages. Marriage Encounter, founded by priests in the Catholic Church, was one organization that offered couples the opportunity to talk openly about marriage and to learn new skills for navigating the difficulties couples faced. Marriage Encounter was one among dozens of such organizations, both religious and secular, to rise to prominence in the 1970s. Spencer Grant/Getty Images.

Sex and Popular Culture In the 1970s, popular culture was suffused with discussions of the sexual revolution. Mass-market books with titles such as *Everything You Always Wanted to Know About Sex*, *Human Sexual Response*, and *The Sensuous Man* shot up the best-seller list. William Masters and Virginia Johnson became the most famous sex researchers since Alfred Kinsey by studying couples in the act of lovemaking. In 1972, English physician Alex Comfort published *The Joy of Sex*, a guidebook for couples that became one of the most popular books of the decade. Comfort made certain to distinguish his writing from pornographic exploitation. "Sex is the one place where we today can learn to treat people as people," he wrote.

Hollywood took advantage of the new sexual ethic by making films with explicit erotic content that pushed the boundaries of middle-class taste. Films such as *Midnight Cowboy* (1969), *Carnal Knowledge* (1971), and *Shampoo* (1974), the latter starring Hollywood's leading ladies' man, Warren Beatty, led the way. Throughout the decade, and into the 1980s, the Motion Picture Association of America (MPAA) scrambled to keep its guide for parents — the system of rating pictures G, PG, R, and X (and, after 1984, PG-13) — in tune with Hollywood's advancing sexual revolution.

On television, the popularity of social problem shows, such as *All in the Family*, and the fear of losing advertising revenue moderated the portrayal of sex in the early 1970s. However, in the second half of the decade networks both exploited and criticized the new sexual ethic. In frivolous, light-hearted shows such as the popular *Charlie's Angels*, *Three's Company*, and *The Love Boat*, heterosexual couples explored the often confusing, and usually comical, landscape of sexual morality. At the same time, between 1974 and 1981, the major networks produced more than a dozen made-for-TV movies about children in sexual danger — a sensationalized warning to parents of the potential threats to children posed by a less strict sexual morality.

Middle-Class Marriage Many Americans worried that the sexual revolution threatened marriage itself. The notion of marriage as romantic companionship had defined middle-class norms since the nineteenth century. It was also quite common throughout most of the twentieth century for Americans to see sexual satisfaction as a healthy part of the marriage bond. But what defined a healthy marriage in an age of rising divorce rates, changing sexual values, and feminist critiques of the nuclear family? Only a small minority of Americans rejected marriage outright; most continued to create monogamous relationships codified in marriage. But many came to believe that they needed help as marriage came under a variety of economic and psychological stresses.

A therapeutic industry arose in response. Churches and secular groups alike established marriage seminars and counseling services to assist couples in sustaining a healthy marriage. A popular form of 1960s psychotherapy, the "encounter group," was adapted to marriage counseling: couples met in large groups to explore new methods of communicating. One of the most successful of these organizations, Marriage Encounter, was founded by the Catholic Church. It expanded into Protestant and Jewish communities in the 1970s and became one of the nation's largest counseling organizations. Such groups embodied another long-term shift in how middle-class Americans understood marriage. Spurred by both feminism and psychotherapeutic models that stressed self-improvement, Americans increasingly defined marriage not simply by companionship and sexual fidelity but also by the deeply felt emotional connection between two people.

Religion in the 1970s: The New Evangelicalism

For three centuries, American society has been punctuated by intense periods of religious revival — some of which historians have called Great Awakenings (Chapters 4 and 10). These periods have seen a rise in church membership, the appearance of charismatic religious leaders, and the increasing influence of religion, usually of the evangelical variety, on society and politics. One such surge in religiosity and evangelical fervor took shape between the 1960s and 1980s. The "New Evangelicalism" of those decades had many elements, but one of its central features was a growing concern with the family.

In the 1950s and 1960s, many mainstream Protestants had embraced the reform spirit of the age. Some of the most visible Protestant leaders were social activists who condemned racism and opposed the Vietnam War. Organizations such as the National Council of Churches — along with many progressive Catholics and Jews — joined with Martin Luther King Jr. and other African American ministers in the long battle for civil rights. Many mainline Protestant churches, among them the Episcopal, Methodist, and Congregationalist denominations, practiced a version of the "Social Gospel," the reform-minded Christianity of the early twentieth century.

Evangelical Resurgence Meanwhile, **evangelicalism** survived at the grass roots. Evangelical Protestant churches emphasized an intimate, personal salvation (being

evangelicalism
The trend in Protestant Christianity that stresses salvation through conversion, repentance of sin, and adherence to scripture; it also stresses the importance of preaching over ritual.

"born again"); focused on a literal interpretation of the Bible; and regarded the death and resurrection of Jesus as the central message of Christianity. These tenets distinguished evangelicals from mainline Protestants as well as from Catholics and Jews, and they flourished in a handful of evangelical colleges, Bible schools, and seminaries in the postwar decades.

No one did more to keep the evangelical fire burning than Billy Graham. A graduate of the evangelical Wheaton College in Illinois, Graham cofounded Youth for Christ in 1945 and then toured the United States and Europe preaching the gospel. Following a stunning 1949 tent revival in Los Angeles that lasted eight weeks, Graham shot to national fame. His success in Los Angeles led to a popular radio program, but he continued to travel relentlessly, conducting old-fashioned revival meetings he called crusades. A massive sixteen-week 1957 crusade held in New York City's Madison Square Garden made Graham, along with the conservative Catholic priest Fulton Sheen, one of the nation's most visible religious leaders.

Graham and other evangelicals in the 1950s and 1960s laid the groundwork for the New Evangelicalism. But it was a startling combination of events in the late 1960s and early 1970s that dramatically magnified the evangelical revival. First, rising divorce rates, social unrest, and challenges to prevailing values led people to seek the stability of faith. Second, many Americans regarded feminism, the counterculture, sexual freedom, homosexuality, pornography, and legalized abortion not as distinct issues, but as a collective sign of moral decay in society. To seek answers and find order, more and more people turned to evangelical ministries, especially Southern Baptist, Pentecostal, and Assemblies of God churches.

Numbers tell part of the story. As mainline churches lost about 15 percent of their membership between 1970 and 1985, evangelical church membership soared. The Southern Baptist Convention, the largest Protestant denomination, grew by 23 percent, while the Assemblies of God grew by an astounding 300 percent. *Newsweek* magazine declared 1976 "The Year of the Evangelical," and that November the nation made Jimmy Carter the nation's first evangelical president. In a national Gallup poll, a robust one-third of Americans answered yes when asked, "Would you describe yourself as a 'born again' or evangelical Christian?"

Much of this astonishing growth came from the creative use of television. A new generation of preachers brought religious conversion directly into Americans' living rooms through television. These so-called televangelists built huge media empires through small donations from millions of avid viewers — not to mention advertising. Jerry Falwell's *Old Time Gospel Hour*, Pat Robertson's *700 Club*, and Jim and Tammy Bakker's *PTL (Praise the Lord) Club* were the leading pioneers in this televised race for American souls, but another half dozen — including Oral Roberts and Jimmy Swaggart — followed them onto the airwaves. Together, they made the 1970s and 1980s the era of Christian broadcasting.

Religion and the Family   Of primary concern to evangelical Christians was the family. Drawing on selected Bible passages, evangelicals believed that the nuclear family, and not the individual, represented the fundamental unit of society. The family itself was organized along paternalist lines: father was breadwinner and disciplinarian; mother was nurturer and supporter. "Motherhood is the highest form of femininity," the evangelical author Beverly LaHaye wrote in an influential book on Christian women. Another popular Christian author declared, "A church, a family, a nation is only as strong as its men."

Evangelicals spread their message about the Christian family through more than the pulpit and television. They founded publishing houses, wrote books, established foundations, and offered seminars. Helen B. Andelin, for instance, a California house-wife, produced a homemade book called *Fascinating Womanhood* that eventually sold more than 2 million copies. She used the book as the basis for her classes, which by the early 1970s had been attended by 400,000 women and boasted 11,000 trained teachers. *Fascinating Womanhood* led evangelical women in the opposite direction of feminism. Whereas the latter encouraged women to be independent and to seek equality with men, Andelin taught that "submissiveness will bring a strange but righteous power over your man." Andelin was but one of dozens of evangelical authors and educators who encouraged women to defer to men.

Evangelical Christians held that strict gender roles in the family would ward off the influences of an immoral society. Christian activists were especially concerned with sex education in public schools, the proliferation of pornography, legalized abor-tion, and the rising divorce rate. For them, the answer was to strengthen what they called "traditional" family structures. By the early 1980s, Christians could choose from among hundreds of evangelical books, take classes on how to save a marriage or how to be a Christian parent, attend evangelical churches and Bible study courses, watch evangelical ministers on television, and donate to foundations that promoted "Christian values" in state legislatures and the U.S. Congress.

Wherever one looked in the 1970s and early 1980s, American families were under strain. Nearly everyone agreed that the waves of social liberalism and economic trans-formation that swept over the nation in the 1960s and 1970s had destabilized society and, especially, family relationships. But Americans did not agree about how to *resta-bilize* families. Indeed, different approaches to the family would further divide the country in the 1980s and 1990s, as the New Right would increasingly make "family values" a political issue.

IN YOUR OWN WORDS What were the major sources of anxiety about the American family in the decade after the 1960s?

Summary

For much of the 1970s, Americans struggled with economic problems, including infla-tion, energy shortages, income stagnation, and deindustrialization. These challenges highlighted the limits of postwar prosperity and forced Americans to consider lower-ing their economic expectations. A movement for environmental protection, widely supported, led to new laws and an awareness of nature's limits, and the energy crisis highlighted the nation's dependence on resources from abroad, especially oil.

In the midst of this gloomy economic climate, Americans also sought politi-cal and cultural resolutions to the upheavals of the 1960s. In politics, the Watergate scandal led to a brief period of political reform. Meanwhile, the battle for civil rights entered a second stage, expanding to encompass women's rights, gay rights, and the rights of alleged criminals and prisoners and, in the realm of racial justice, focusing on the problem of producing concrete results rather than legislation. Many liberals cheered these developments, but another effect was to strengthen a new, more conservative social mood that began to challenge liberal values in politics and society more generally. Finally, we considered the multiple challenges faced by the American family in the 1970s and how a perception that the family was in trouble helped to spur an evangelical religious revival that would shape American society for decades to come.

CHAPTER 28 REVIEW

TERMS TO KNOW *Identify and explain the significance of each term below.*

Key Concepts and Events

Organization of Petroleum Exporting Countries (OPEC) (p. 920)

energy crisis (p. 922)

environmentalism (p. 922)

Silent Spring (p. 922)

Earth Day (p. 922)

Environmental Protection Agency (EPA) (p. 922)

Three Mile Island (p. 923)

stagflation (p. 923)

deindustrialization (p. 927)

Rust Belt (p. 927)

tax revolt (p. 931)

Proposition 13 (p. 931)

Watergate (p. 932)

War Powers Act (p. 932)

Freedom of Information Act (p. 932)

Ethics in Government Act (p. 933)

deregulation (p. 936)

affirmative action (p. 936)

Bakke v. University of California (p. 937)

Equal Rights Amendment (ERA) (p. 938)

STOP ERA (p. 938)

Roe v. Wade (p. 939)

evangelicalism (p. 945)

Key People

Rachel Carson (p. 922)

Gerald Ford (p. 923)

Howard Jarvis (p. 931)

Jimmy Carter (p. 934)

Phyllis Schlafly (p. 938)

Harvey Milk (p. 940)

Billy Graham (p. 946)

REVIEW QUESTIONS *Answer these questions to demonstrate your understanding of the chapter's main ideas.*

1. What limits did the American economy experience in the 1970s?

2. In what ways was the period between 1973 and 1980 a transitional one in American politics?

3. How did controversies over new individual rights shape the politics of the 1970s?

4. What were the major sources of anxiety about the American family in the decade after the 1960s?

5. Examine the category "Work, Exchange, and Technology" on the thematic timeline on page 780. How did economic developments in the 1970s reverse the course the national economy had been on since World War II? More broadly, can you identify events in each of the timeline categories that made the 1970s a decade of important historical transition?

1. Consider the history of the American economy in the twentieth century. Compare the 1970s with other eras: the Great Depression of the 1930s, the industrial boom of the World War II years, and the growth and rising wages in the 1950s and 1960s. Using these comparisons, construct a historical narrative of the period from the 1920s through the 1970s.

2. Study the photograph on page 927 and the map on page 928. How did the economic downturn of the 1970s affect the lives of ordinary Americans and American culture broadly? What connections can you draw between the photograph and developments in the global economy and the rise of the Sunbelt?

Based on this timeline, what were the three or four major political turning points of the 1970s? Defend your answer by explaining the impact of the changes.

Globalization and the End of the American Century

1980 to the Present

For historians, the recent past can be a challenge to assess. Insufficient time has passed for scholars to weigh the significance of events and to determine which developments will have a lasting effect and which are more fleeting. Nevertheless, scholars generally agree on the era's three most significant developments: the resurgence of political conservatism, the end of the Cold War, and the globalization of communications and the economy. The first of these, as we showed in Part 8, was decades in the making. Conservatism had leaped back to life in the 1960s, but not until the 1980s did American conservatives have the political muscle to reshape national politics in fundamental respects. Conservatism's resurgence occasioned a wide-ranging and divisive internal debate among Americans over what the nation's common values and priorities should be.

The second two developments began to reshape the place of the United States in the world. With the collapse of European communism after 1989, the Cold War came to an end, leaving the U.S. as the world's dominant military power. But military dominance coexisted with shrinking economic influence. What *Time* magazine publisher Henry Luce in 1941 had named the American Century—in his call for the U.S. to assume global leadership after World War II—came to an end in the last quarter of the twentieth century. The U.S. remained the world's largest economy but faced rising competition from a united Europe and a surging China. These decades stand as an era of transition away from the bipolar world of the Cold War.

Contemporary events continue to unfold, and thus Part 9 remains necessarily a work in progress. We've emphasized how through equal parts conflict, struggle, and ingenuity, Americans collectively forged a new era in national history after the 1980s. ▶

Conservative Ascendancy

Ronald Reagan Presidential Library.

In the 1980s, the conservatism of Ronald Reagan and the New Right, consolidated in the Republican Party, challenged the liberalism of the 1960s and 1970s. Conservatives reduced the regulatory power of the federal government, eroded the welfare state of the New Deal and the Great Society, and expanded the military. Evangelical Christians and conservative lawmakers challenged abortion rights, feminism, and gay rights, setting off a "culture war" that sharply divided Americans.

Even as the Reagan coalition brought an end to decades of liberal government activism, much of the legacy of the New Deal was preserved: Medicare, Medicaid, and Social Security grew as a proportion of the federal budget. Conservatives shaped U.S. foreign policy, however, dramatically increasing the defense budget and, under George W. Bush, asserting a new doctrine of "preemptive war." By the election of 2016, national politics seemed as divided as ever. Republican Donald Trump won the presidency, and voters returned a conservative majority to Congress. Polls showed that Americans embraced a moderate liberalism, but the national political system had moved firmly into conservative hands.

End of the Cold War and Rising Conflict in the Middle East

David Turnley/Corbis/VCG via Getty Images.

Under Reagan's direction, the U.S. increased military spending and returned to the sharp Cold War rhetoric of earlier decades. Yet in the second half of the 1980s, as internal reforms swept through the Soviet Union, Reagan engaged in productive dialogue with the Soviet leader Mikhail Gorbachev. Then, in 1991, the Soviet Union stunningly collapsed, and the U.S. emerged in the 1990s as the lone military "superpower" in the world. Absent a clear Cold War enemy, it intervened in civil wars, worked to disrupt terrorist activities, and provided humanitarian aid — but guided more by pragmatism than by principle.

The foremost region that occupied U.S. attention was the Middle East, where strategic interest in oil remained paramount. Between 1991 and 2016, the U.S. fought three wars in the region — two in Iraq and one in Afghanistan — and became even more deeply embedded in its politics. The end of the Cold War thus expanded the U.S. role in the Middle East and renewed debates about the proper American role in the world.

Global Capitalism and Increasing Social Inequality

Hector Mata/AFP/Getty Images.

The post–World War II expansion of the American economy ended in the 1970s, when wages stagnated and inflation skyrocketed. In the 1980s and 1990s, however, productivity grew, military spending boosted production, and new industries — such as computer technology — emerged. These developments led to renewed economic growth. More and more, though, the economy produced *services* rather than *goods* — as Americans increasingly bought the latter from overseas.

The fall of communism had made possible this global expansion of capitalism, as multinational corporations moved production to low-wage countries. Governments across the world facilitated this process by creating new trading zones such as the European Union (EU) and the North American Free Trade Agreement (NAFTA). Conservative tax policies, deindustrialization, the decline of unions, and globalization all contributed to a widening inequality between the wealthiest Americans and the middle class and poor. Globalization thus brought both new economic opportunities and renewed economic insecurity.

Globalization and the End of the American Century
1980 to the Present

Mario Tama/Getty Images

Thematic Understanding

This timeline arranges some of the important events of this period into themes. Consider the entries under "Culture and Society" and "Migration and Settlement." What were the major events of the "culture wars," and how did American attitudes and public policy change over the decades between the 1980s and the 2010s? Next, examine the entries under "American and National Identity" and "America in the World." How did globalization reshape the United States in these decades? How did the U.S. actions affect other regions, particularly the Middle East?

	AMERICAN AND NATIONAL IDENTITY	POLITICS AND POWER	WORK, EXCHANGE, AND TECHNOLOGY
1980	• Ronald Reagan campaigns for presidency (1980), says United States is "greatest country in the world" • Reagan campaigns for reelection (1984) with theme of "It's morning in America"	• New Right helps elect Ronald Reagan president • Iran-Contra scandal (1985–1987) • George H. W. Bush elected president (1988)	• Recession (1981–1982) followed by strong growth (1982–1987) • Reagan tax cut (1981) • Apple IIe personal computer introduced (1983) • National debt triples (1981–1989)
1990	• Americans debate multiculturalism • World Trade Organization (WTO) protests in Seattle against globalization (1999)	• Bill Clinton elected president (1992) • Republican resurgence (1994) • Welfare reform (1996) • Clinton impeached and acquitted (1998–1999)	• Internet gains in popularity • Recession (1990–1991) • NAFTA ratified (1993) • Debt reduction under Bill Clinton
2000	• "War on terror" becomes fixture in American discourse • USA PATRIOT Act authorizes new domestic surveillance to combat terrorism • Abu Ghraib (2004) revelations document U.S. torture practices	• George W. Bush wins presidency in contested election (2000) • USA PATRIOT Act (2001) • Barack Obama elected first African American president (2008)	• Great Recession (2007–2010) • President Bush asks for and receives bank bailout from Congress (2008) • Unemployment hits 10 percent
2010	• Presidential candidates debate whether United States is declining as a nation and the role of international trade and immigration (2016)	• Health-care reform (2010) • Tea Party helps Republicans regain control of House of Representatives • Barack Obama reelected president (2012) • Donald Trump elected president (2016)	• Financial industry accounts for largest share of GDP among all industry sectors

CULTURE AND SOCIETY	MIGRATION AND SETTLEMENT	GEOGRAPHY AND THE ENVIRONMENT	AMERICA IN THE WORLD
1980			
• HIV/AIDS crisis prompts national conversation about homosexuality • Renewed emphasis on material success and the "rich and famous" • *Webster v. Reproductive Health Services* (1989)	• Rise in Latino and Asian immigration • Californians vote to establish English as official language (1986)	• Reagan appoints the antienvironmentalist James Watt as secretary of interior	• Reagan begins arms buildup • United States arms Contras in Nicaragua • Berlin Wall comes down (1989)
1990			
• Pat Buchanan declares "culture war" (1992) • Proposition 209 ends affirmative action in California universities (1996) • Defense of Marriage Act (1998)	• California bans bilingual education in public schools (1998)	• New states emerge in central Asia from dissolution of Soviet Union (1989–1991) • Oil at center of Gulf War • European Union created (1992)	• Persian Gulf War (1990–1991) • USSR breaks apart; end of Cold War • World Trade Center bombed (1993) • NATO begins peacekeeping efforts in Bosnia (1995)
2000			
• *Lawrence v. Texas* (2003) • Massachusetts becomes first state to legalize same-sex marriage (2004); nine states follow by 2012	• California, Texas, Hawaii, and New Mexico become "majority-minority" states (where the majority of the population is composed of different nonwhite groups)	• Kyoto Protocol international treaty on climate change signed by 84 nations (2005) but not by United States	• Al Qaeda attacks World Trade Center and Pentagon (2001) • United States and allies invade Afghanistan (2002) • United States invades Iraq (2003)
2010			
• *Obergefell v. Hodges* (2015) upholds same-sex marriage as legal in all states	• Obama's 2012 electoral coalition heavily African American, Hispanic, Asian American, female, and young • President Donald Trump bans immigrants from six majority-Muslim countries (2017)	• President Obama issues Clean Power Plan through executive action (2015) • President Trump rescinds portions of the Clean Power Plan and orders reconsideration of the remainder (2017)	• Arab Spring (2010–2012) • Osama bin Laden killed (2011) • Last combat troops withdrawn from Iraq (2011) • Syrian civil war and refugee crisis (2011–present)

29

Conservative America in the Ascent
1980–1991

CHAPTER

The decade of the 1970s saw Americans divided by the Vietnam War, wearied by social unrest, and unmoored by economic drift. As a result, many ordinary citizens developed a deep distrust of the muscular Great Society liberalism of the 1960s. Seizing political advantage amid the trauma and divisions, a revived Republican Party, led by a political movement known as the New Right, offered the nation a fresh way forward: economic deregulation, low taxes, Christian morality, and a reenergized Cold War foreign policy. The election of President Ronald Reagan in 1980 symbolized the ascendance of this new political formula, and the president himself helped shape the era.

The New Right revived confidence in "free markets" and called for a smaller government role in economic regulation and social welfare. Reagan famously said, "Government is not the solution to our problem; government *is* the problem." Like the New Right generally, Reagan was profoundly skeptical of the liberal ideology that had informed American public policy since Franklin D. Roosevelt's New Deal. His presidency combined an economically conservative domestic agenda with aggressive anticommunism abroad. Reagan's foreign policy reignited tensions with the Soviet Union, and then, unexpectedly, the president helped orchestrate a thawing of U.S.-Soviet relations, laying the groundwork for the end of the Cold War.

Reagan defined the conservative ascendancy of the 1980s, but he did not create the New Right groundswell that brought him into office. Grassroots conservative activists in the 1960s and 1970s built a formidable right-wing movement that awaited an opportune political moment to contend for national power. That moment came in 1980, when Democratic president Jimmy Carter's popularity plummeted as a result of his mismanagement of two national crises. Raging inflation and the Iranian seizure of U.S. hostages in Tehran undid Carter and provided an opening for the New Right, which would shape the nation's politics for the remainder of the twentieth century and the first decades of the twenty-first.

IDENTIFY THE BIG IDEA

What factors made the rise of the New Right possible, and what ideas about freedom and citizenship did conservatives articulate in the 1980s?

1984 Republican National Convention Ronald Reagan delivers his acceptance speech in this photo from the 1984 Republican National Convention. Reagan's political rise captured the spirit of conservative politics in the late 1970s and 1980s. Ronald Reagan Presidential Library.

CHAPTER CHRONOLOGY

As you read, ask yourself why this chapter begins and ends with these dates and identify the links among related events.

1981	► Ronald Reagan becomes president
	► Republicans gain control of Senate
	► Economic Recovery Tax Act (ERTA) cuts taxes
	► Military expenditures increase sharply
	► Reagan cuts budgets of regulatory agencies
	► Sandra Day O'Connor appointed to the Supreme Court
1981– 1989	► National debt triples
	► Emergence of New Right think tanks: Heritage Foundation, American Enterprise Institute, and the Cato Institute
	► United States assists Iraq in war against Iran (1980–1988)
1985	► Mikhail Gorbachev takes power in Soviet Union

1986	► Iran-Contra scandal weakens Reagan presidency
	► William Rehnquist named chief justice
1987	► United States and USSR agree to limit missiles in Europe
1988	► George H. W. Bush elected president
1989	► Destruction of Berlin Wall
	► "Velvet Revolutions" in Eastern Europe
	► *Webster v. Reproductive Health Services* limits abortion services
1990– 1991	► Persian Gulf War
1991	► Dissolution of Soviet Union ends Cold War

The Rise of the New Right

The Great Depression and World War II discredited the traditional conservative program of limited government at home and diplomatic isolationism abroad. Nevertheless, a right-wing faction survived within the Republican Party. Its adherents continued to oppose the New Deal but reversed their earlier isolationism. In the postwar decades, conservatives pushed for military interventions against communism in Europe, Asia, and the developing world while calling for the broadest possible investigation of subversives at home (Chapter 24).

However, conservatives failed to devise policies that could win the allegiance of American voters in the two decades after World War II. Republicans by and large continued to favor party moderates, such as Dwight Eisenhower, Thomas Dewey, and Nelson Rockefeller. These were politicians, often called liberal Republicans, who supported much of the New Deal, endorsed the containment policy overseas, and steered a middle course through the volatile social and political changes of the postwar era. The conservative faction held out hope, however, that it might one day win the loyalty of a majority of Republicans and remake the party in its image. In the 1960s and 1970s, these conservatives invested their hopes for national resurgence in two dynamic figures: Barry Goldwater and Ronald Reagan. Together, the two carried the conservative banner until the national electorate grew more receptive to right-wing appeals.

Barry Goldwater and Ronald Reagan: Champions of the Right

The personal odyssey of Ronald Reagan embodies the story of New Right Republican conservatism. Before World War II, Reagan was a well-known movie actor as well as a New Deal Democrat and admirer of Roosevelt. However, he turned away from liberalism, partly from self-interest (he disliked paying high taxes) and partly on principle.

As head of the Screen Actors Guild from 1947 to 1952, Reagan had to deal with its Communist members, who formed the extreme left wing of the American labor movement. Dismayed by their hardline tactics and goals, he became a militant anticommunist. After nearly a decade as a spokesperson for the General Electric Corporation, Reagan joined the Republican Party in the early 1960s and began speaking for conservative causes and candidates.

One of those candidates was the forthright conservative Barry Goldwater, a Republican senator from Arizona. Confident in their power, centrist Republicans did not anticipate that grassroots conservatives could challenge the party's old guard and nominate one of their own for president: Goldwater himself. Understanding how they did so in 1964 brings us closer to comprehending the forces that propelled Reagan to the presidency a decade and a half later. Indeed, Reagan the politician came to national attention in 1964 with a televised speech at the Republican convention supporting Goldwater for the presidency. In a dramatic address titled "A Time for Choosing," Reagan warned that if we "trade our freedom for the soup kitchen of the welfare state," the nation would "take the first step into a thousand years of darkness."

The Conscience of a Conservative Like Reagan, Goldwater came from the Sunbelt, home to a libertarian spirit of limited government and great personal freedom. His 1960 book, ***The Conscience of a Conservative***, set forth an uncompromising conservatism. In direct and accessible prose, Goldwater attacked the New Deal state, arguing that "the natural tendency of government [is] to expand in the direction of absolutism." The problem with the Republican Party, as he saw it, was that Eisenhower had been too accommodating to liberalism. When Ike told reporters that he was "liberal when it comes to human problems," Goldwater privately fumed.

The Conscience of a Conservative spurred a Republican grassroots movement in support of Goldwater. By distributing his book widely and mobilizing activists at state party conventions, conservatives hoped to create such a groundswell of support that Goldwater could be "drafted" to run for president in 1964, something he reportedly did not wish to do. Meanwhile, Goldwater further enchanted conservatives with another book, *Why Not Victory?*, in which he criticized the containment policy — the strategy of preventing the spread of communism followed by both Democrats and Republicans since 1947 (Chapter 24). It was, he complained, a policy of "timidly refusing to draw our own lines against aggression . . . unmarked by pride or the prospect of victory." Here was a politician saying exactly what conservatives wanted to hear.

Grassroots Conservatives Because moderates dominated the Republican Party leadership, winning the 1964 nomination for Goldwater required conservative activists to build their campaign from the bottom up. They found thousands upon thousands of Americans willing to hit the streets on behalf of their political hero. Organizations such as the John Birch Society, Young Americans for Freedom, and the Liberty Lobby supplied an army of eager volunteers. They came from such conservative strongholds as Orange County, California, and the fast-growing suburbs of Phoenix, Dallas, Houston, Atlanta, and other Sunbelt metropolises. A critical boost came in the early spring of 1964, when conservatives outmaneuvered moderates at the state convention of the

The Conscience of a Conservative
A 1960 book that set forth an uncompromising conservatism and inspired a Republican grassroots movement in support of its author, Barry Goldwater.

California Republican Party, which then enthusiastically endorsed Goldwater. The fight had been bruising, and one moderate Republican warned that "sinister forces are at work to take over the whole Republican apparatus in California."

Another spur to Goldwater backers was the appearance of a book by Phyllis Schlafly, who was then a relatively unknown conservative activist from the Midwest. Like Goldwater's own book, Schlafly's *A Choice Not an Echo* accused moderate Republicans of being Democrats in disguise (that is, an "echo" of Democrats). Schlafly, who reappeared in the national spotlight in the early 1970s to help halt the ratification of the Equal Rights Amendment, denounced the "Rockefeller Republicans" of the Northeast and encouraged the party to embrace a defiant conservatism. Contrasting Goldwater's "grassroots Republicans" with Rockefeller's "kingmakers," Schlafly hoped to "forestall another defeat like 1940, 1944, 1948, and 1960," Democratic victories all.

The conservative groundswell won the Republican nomination for Goldwater. However, his strident tone and militarist foreign policy were too much for a nation mourning the death of John F. Kennedy and still committed to liberalism. Democrat Lyndon B. Johnson defeated Goldwater in a historic landslide (Chapter 27). Many believed that Goldwater conservatism would wither and die, but instead the nearly four million volunteers who had campaigned for the Arizona senator swung their support to Ronald Reagan and built toward the future. Skilled conservative political operatives such as Richard Viguerie, a Louisiana-born Catholic and antiabortion activist, applied new computer technology to political campaigning. Viguerie took a list of 12,000 Goldwater contributors and used computerized mailing lists, which were new at the time, to solicit campaign funds, rally support for conservative causes, and get out the vote on election day. Conservatism was down but not out.

Backed financially by wealthy southern Californians and supported by Goldwaterites, Reagan won California's governorship in 1966 and again in 1970. His impassioned rhetoric supporting limited government and law and order — referring to campus radicals, he vowed to "clean up the mess in Berkeley" — won broad support among citizens of the nation's most populous state. More significantly, it made him a force in national politics. His supporters believed that he was in line to succeed Nixon as the next Republican president. The Watergate scandal intervened, however, discrediting Nixon and making Gerald Ford the incumbent. After narrowly losing a campaign against Ford for the Republican presidential nomination in 1976, Reagan was forced to bide his time. When Ford lost to Carter in that year's election, as the party's brightest star Reagan was a near lock to be the nominee in 1980.

Free-Market Economics and Religious Conservatism

The last phase of Reagan's rise was the product of several additional developments within the New Right. The burgeoning conservative movement increasingly resembled a three-legged stool. Each leg represented an ideological position and a popular constituency: anticommunism, free-market economics, and religious traditionalism. Uniting all three in a political coalition was no easy feat. Religious traditionalists demanded strong government action to implement their faith-based agenda, while economic conservatives favored limited government and free markets. Both groups, however, were ardent anticommunists — free marketeers loathed the state-directed Soviet economy, and religious conservatives despised the "godless" secularism of the Soviet state. In the end, the success of the New Right would come to depend on balancing the interests of economic and moral conservatives.

Since the 1950s, William F. Buckley, the founder and editor of the conservative magazine *National Review*, and Milton Friedman, the Nobel Prize–winning economist at the University of Chicago, had been the most prominent conservative intellectuals. Convinced that "the growth of government must be fought relentlessly," Buckley used the *National Review* to criticize liberal policy. For his part, Friedman became a national conservative icon with the publication of *Capitalism and Freedom* (1962), in which he argued that "economic freedom is . . . an indispensable means toward the achievement of political freedom." Friedman's free-market ideology, along with that of Friedrich von Hayek, another University of Chicago economist, was taken up by wealthy conservatives, who funded think tanks during the 1980s to disseminate market-based public policy ideas. The Heritage Foundation, the American Enterprise Institute, and the Cato Institute issued policy proposals and attacked liberal legislation and the stranglehold of economic regulation they believed it represented. Followers of Buckley and Friedman envisioned themselves as crusaders working against what one conservative called "the despotic aspects of egalitarianism."

The most striking addition to the conservative coalition was the **Religious Right**. Until the 1970s, politics was an earthly concern of secondary interest to most fundamentalist and evangelical Protestants. But the perception that American society had become immoral, combined with the influence of a new generation of popular ministers, gave politics a new urgent relevance. Conservative Protestants and Catholics joined together in a tentative alliance, as the Religious Right condemned divorce, abortion, premarital sex, and feminism. The route to a moral life and to "peace, pardon, purpose, and power," as one evangelical activist said, was "to plug yourself into the One, the Only One [God]."

Charismatic televangelists such as Pat Robertson and Jerry Falwell emerged as the champions of a morality-based political agenda during the late 1970s. Falwell, founder of Liberty University and host of the *Old Time Gospel Hour* television program, established the Moral Majority in 1979. With 400,000 members and $1.5 million in contributions in its first year, it would be the organizational vehicle for transforming the new evangelicalism into a religious political movement. Falwell made no secret of his views: "If you want to know where I am politically," he told reporters, "I thought Goldwater was too liberal." Falwell was not alone. Phyllis Schlafly's STOP ERA, which became Eagle Forum in 1975, continued to

National Review
A conservative magazine founded by editor William F. Buckley in 1955, who used it to criticize liberal policy.

Religious Right
Politically active religious conservatives, especially Catholics and evangelical Christians, who became particularly vocal in the 1980s against feminism, abortion, and homosexuality and who promoted "family values."

Washington for Jesus During a "Washington for Jesus" rally in 1980, an activist from the Religious Right carries a cross while Pat Robertson, founder of the Christian Broadcasting Network, walks alongside him. AP Photo/Dennis Cook.

advocate for conservative public policy; Focus on the Family was founded in 1977; and a succession of conservative organizations would emerge in the 1980s, including the Family Research Council.

The conservative message preached by Barry Goldwater and Ronald Reagan had appealed to few American voters in 1964. Then came the series of events that undermined support for the liberal agenda of the Democratic Party: the failed war in Vietnam; a judiciary that legalized abortion and pornography, enforced school busing, and curtailed public expression of religion; urban riots; and a stagnating economy. By the late 1970s, the New Right had developed a conservative message that commanded much greater popular support than Goldwater's program had. Religious and free-market conservatives joined with traditional anticommunist hard-liners — alongside whites opposed to black civil rights, affirmative action, and busing — in a broad coalition that attacked welfare-state liberalism, social permissiveness, and an allegedly weak and defensive foreign policy. Ronald Reagan expertly appealed to all of these conservative constituencies and captured the Republican presidential nomination in 1980. It had taken almost two decades, but the New Right appeared on the verge of winning the presidency.

The Carter Presidency

First, the Republican Party had to defeat incumbent president Jimmy Carter. Carter's outsider status and his disdain for professional politicians had made him the ideal post-Watergate president. But his ineffectiveness and missteps as an executive also made him the perfect foil for Ronald Reagan.

Carter had an idealistic vision of American leadership in world affairs. He presented himself as the anti-Nixon, a world leader who rejected Henry Kissinger's "realism" in favor of human rights and peacemaking. "Human rights is the soul of our foreign policy," Carter asserted, "because human rights is the very soul of our sense of nationhood." He established the Office of Human Rights in the State Department and withdrew economic and military aid from repressive regimes in Argentina, Uruguay, and Ethiopia — although, in realist fashion, he still funded equally repressive U.S. allies such as the Philippines, South Africa, and Iran. In Latin America, Carter eliminated a decades-old symbol of Yankee imperialism by signing a treaty on September 7, 1977, turning control of the Panama Canal over to Panama (effective December 31, 1999). Carter's most important efforts came in forging an enduring, although in retrospect limited, peace in the intractable Arab-Israeli conflict. In 1978, he invited Israeli prime minister Menachem Begin and Egyptian president Anwar el-Sadat to Camp David, where they crafted a "framework for peace," under which Egypt recognized Israel and received back the Sinai Peninsula, which Israel had occupied since 1967.

Carter deplored what he called the "inordinate fear of communism," but his efforts at improving relations with the Soviet Union foundered. His criticism of the Kremlin's record on human rights offended Soviet leader Leonid Brezhnev and slowed arms reduction negotiations. When, in 1979, Carter finally signed the second Strategic Arms Limitations Treaty (SALT II), limiting bombers and missiles, Senate hawks objected. Then, when the Soviet Union invaded Afghanistan that December, Carter suddenly endorsed the hawks' position and treated the invasion as the "gravest threat to world peace since World War II." After ordering an embargo on wheat shipments to the Soviet Union and withdrawing SALT II from Senate consideration, Carter called for increased defense spending and declared an American boycott of the 1980 Summer Olympics in Moscow. In a fateful decision, he and Congress began providing covert assistance to anti-Soviet fighters in Afghanistan, some of whom, including Osama bin Laden, would emerge decades later as anti-American Islamic radicals.

Hostage Crisis Carter's ultimate undoing came in Iran, however. The United States had long counted Iran as a faithful ally, a bulwark against Soviet expansion into the Middle East and a steady source of oil. Since the 1940s, Iran had been ruled by Mohammad Reza Shah Pahlavi. Ousted by a democratically elected parliament in the early 1950s, the shah (king) sought and received the assistance of the U.S. Central Intelligence Agency (CIA), which helped him reclaim power in 1953. American intervention soured Iranian views of the United States for decades. Early in 1979, a revolution drove the shah into exile and brought a fundamentalist Shiite cleric, the Ayatollah Ruhollah Khomeini, to power (Shiites represent one branch of Islam, Sunnis the other). When the United States admitted the deposed shah into the country for cancer treatment, Iranian students seized the U.S. embassy in Tehran, taking sixty-six Americans hostage. The captors demanded that the shah be returned to Iran for trial. Carter refused. Instead, he suspended arms sales to Iran and froze Iranian assets in American banks.

For the next fourteen months, the **hostage crisis** paralyzed Carter's presidency. Night after night, humiliating pictures of blindfolded American hostages appeared on television newscasts. An attempt to mount a military rescue in April 1980 had to be aborted because of equipment failures in the desert. Several months later, however, a stunning development changed the calculus on both sides: Iraq, led by Saddam Hussein, invaded Iran, officially because of a dispute over deep-water ports but also to prevent the Shiite-led Iranian Revolution from spreading across the border into Sunni-run Iraq. Desperate to focus his nation's attention on Iraq's invasion, Khomeini began to talk with the United States about releasing the hostages. Difficult negotiations dragged on past the American presidential election in November 1980, and the hostages were finally released the day after Carter left office—a final indignity endured by a well-intentioned but ineffectual president.

hostage crisis
Crisis that began in 1979 after the deposed shah of Iran was allowed into the United States following the Iranian Revolution. Iranians broke into the U.S. embassy in Tehran and took sixty-six Americans hostage. The hostage crisis lasted 444 days and contributed to President Carter's reelection defeat.

The Election of 1980 President Carter's sinking popularity hurt his bid for reelection. When the Democrats barely renominated him over his liberal challenger, Edward (Ted) Kennedy of Massachusetts, Carter's approval rating was historically low: a mere 21 percent of Americans believed that he was an effective president. The reasons were clear. Economically, millions of citizens were feeling the pinch from stagnant wages, high inflation, crippling mortgage rates, and an unemployment rate of nearly 8 percent. In international affairs, the nation blamed Carter for his weak response to Soviet expansion and the Iranians' seizure of American diplomats.

With Carter on the defensive, Reagan remained upbeat and decisive. "This is the greatest country in the world," Reagan reassured the nation in his warm baritone voice.

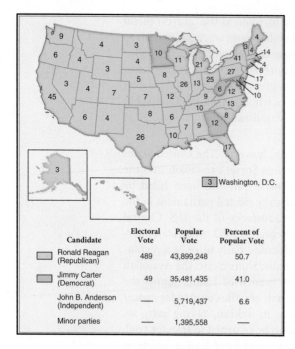

Candidate	Electoral Vote	Popular Vote	Percent of Popular Vote
Ronald Reagan (Republican)	489	43,899,248	50.7
Jimmy Carter (Democrat)	49	35,481,435	41.0
John B. Anderson (Independent)	—	5,719,437	6.6
Minor parties	—	1,395,558	—

MAP 29.1 The Presidential Election of 1980
Ronald Reagan easily defeated Democratic incumbent Jimmy Carter, taking 50.7 percent of the popular vote to Carter's 41.0 percent and winning the electoral vote in all but six states and the District of Columbia. Reagan cut deeply into the traditional Democratic coalition by wooing many southern whites, urban Catholics, and blue-collar workers. More than five million Americans expressed their discontent with Carter's ineffectiveness and Reagan's conservatism by voting for Independent candidate John Anderson, a longtime Republican member of the House of Representatives.

"We have the talent, we have the drive. . . . All we need is the leadership." To emphasize his intention to be a formidable international leader, Reagan hinted that he would take strong action to win the return of the hostages held in Iran. To signal his rejection of liberal policies, he declared his opposition to affirmative action and forced busing and promised to "get the government off our backs." Most important, Reagan effectively appealed to the many Americans who felt financially insecure. In a televised debate with Carter, Reagan emphasized the hardships facing working- and middle-class Americans in an era of stagflation and asked them: "Are you better off today than you were four years ago?"

In November, the voters gave a clear answer. They repudiated Carter, giving him only 41.0 percent of the vote. Independent candidate John Anderson garnered 6.6 percent (with a few minor candidates receiving fractions of a percent), and Reagan won with 50.7 percent of the popular vote (Map 29.1). Moreover, the Republicans elected thirty-three new members of the House of Representatives and twelve new senators, which gave them control of the U.S. Senate for the first time since 1954. The New Right's long road to national power had culminated in an election victory that signaled a new political alignment in the country.

IN YOUR OWN WORDS What were the major characteristics of the political movement that backed Ronald Reagan, known as the New Right?

The Dawning of the Conservative Age

By the time Ronald Reagan took office in 1981, conservatism commanded wider popular support than at any time since the 1920s. As the New Deal Democratic coalition continued to fragment, the Republican Party accelerated the realignment of the American electorate that had begun during the 1960s. Conservatism's ascendancy did more than realign the nation politically. Its emphasis on free markets, low taxes, and individual success shaped the nation's culture and inaugurated an era of conservative individualism. Reagan exhorted Americans, "Let the men and women of the marketplace decide what they want."

The Reagan Coalition

Reagan's decades in public life, especially his years working for General Electric, had equipped him to articulate conservative ideas in easily understandable aphorisms. Speaking against the growing size and influence of government, Reagan said, "Concentrated power has always been the enemy of liberty." In a humorous version of the same sentiment, the president said, "The nine most terrifying words in the English language are: 'I'm from the government, and I'm here to help.'"

Under his leadership, the core of the Republican Party remained the relatively affluent, white, Protestant voters who supported balanced budgets, opposed government activism, feared communism, and believed in a strong national defense. Reagan Republicanism also attracted middle-class suburbanites and migrants to the Sunbelt states who endorsed the conservative agenda of combating crime and limiting social-welfare spending. Suburban growth in particular, a phenomenon that reshaped metropolitan areas across the country in the 1960s and 1970s, benefitted conservatives politically. Suburban traditions of privatization and racial homogeneity, combined with the amenities of middle-class comfort, inclined the residents of suburban cities toward conservative public policies.

This emerging **Reagan coalition** was joined by a large and electorally key group of former Democrats that had been gradually moving toward the Republican Party since 1964: southern whites. Reagan capitalized on the "southern strategy" developed by Richard Nixon's advisors in the late 1960s. Many southern whites had lost confidence in the Democratic Party for a wide range of reasons, but one factor stood out: the party's support for civil rights. When Reagan came to Philadelphia, Mississippi, to deliver his first official speech as the Republican presidential nominee, his ringing endorsement of "states' rights" sent a clear message: he endorsed twenty-five years of southern opposition to federal civil rights legislation. Some of Reagan's advisors had warned him not to go to Philadelphia, the site of the tragic murder of three civil rights workers in 1964, but Reagan believed the opportunity to launch his campaign on a "states' rights" note was too important. After 1980, southern whites would remain a cornerstone of the Republican coalition.

The Religious Right proved crucial to the Republican ascendance as well. Falwell's **Moral Majority** claimed that it had registered two million new voters for the 1980 election, and the Republican Party's platform reflected its influence. That platform called for a constitutional ban on abortion, voluntary prayer in public schools, and a mandatory death penalty for certain crimes. Republicans also demanded an end to court-mandated busing to achieve racial integration in schools, and, for the first time in forty years, opposed the Equal Rights Amendment. Within the Republican Party, conservatism had triumphed.

Reagan's broad coalition attracted the allegiance of another group dissatisfied with the direction of liberalism in the 1970s: blue-collar voters, a high number of Catholics among them, alarmed by antiwar protesters and rising welfare expenditures

President Reagan at His Ranch in Southern California Images of Reagan quickly became vital for the White House to deliver its message of conservative reform to the American people. This photo was taken by a White House photographer. Ronald Reagan Presidential Library.

Reagan coalition
A coalition supporting Ronald Reagan that included the traditional core of Republican Party voters, middle-class suburbanites and migrants to the Sunbelt states, blue-collar Catholics, and a large contingent of southern whites, an electorally key group of former Democrats that had been gradually moving toward the Republican Party since 1964.

Moral Majority
A political organization established by evangelist Jerry Falwell in 1979 to mobilize conservative Christian voters on behalf of Ronald Reagan's campaign for president.

and hostile to feminist demands. Some observers saw these voters, which many called **Reagan Democrats**, as coming from the "silent majority" that Nixon had swung into the Republican fold in 1968 and 1972. They lived in heavily industrialized midwestern states such as Michigan, Ohio, and Illinois and had been a core part of the Democratic coalition for three decades. Reagan's victory in the 1980s thus hinged on both a revival of right-wing conservative activism and broad dissatisfaction with liberal Democrats — a dissatisfaction that had been building since 1968 but had been interrupted by the post-Watergate backlash against the Republican Party.

Reagan Democrats
Blue-collar Catholics from industrialized midwestern states such as Michigan, Ohio, and Illinois who were dissatisfied with the direction of liberalism in the 1970s and left the Democratic Party for the Republicans.

Conservatives in Power

The new president kept his political message clear and uncomplicated. "What I want to see above all," he remarked, "is that this country remains a country where someone can always get rich." Standing in the way, Reagan believed, was government. In his first year in office, Reagan and his chief advisor, James A. Baker III, quickly set new governmental priorities. To roll back the expanded liberal state, they launched a three-pronged assault on federal taxes, social-welfare spending, and the regulatory bureaucracy. To prosecute the Cold War, they advocated a vast increase in defense spending and an end to détente with the Soviet Union. And to match the resurgent economies of Germany and Japan, they set out to restore American leadership of the world's capitalist societies and to inspire renewed faith in "free markets."

Reaganomics   To achieve its economic objectives, the new administration advanced a set of policies, quickly dubbed **Reaganomics**, to increase the production (and thus the supply) of goods. The theory underlying **supply-side economics**, as this approach was called, emphasized investment in productive enterprises. According to supply-side theorists, the best way to bolster investment was to reduce the taxes paid by corporations and wealthy Americans, who could then use these funds to expand production.

supply-side economics (Reaganomics)
Economic theory that tax cuts for individuals and businesses encourage investment and production (supply) and stimulate consumption (demand) because individuals can keep more of their earnings. In reality, supply-side economics created a massive federal budget deficit.

Supply-siders maintained that the resulting economic expansion would increase government revenues and offset the loss of tax dollars stemming from the original tax cuts. Meanwhile, the increasing supply would generate its own demand, as consumers stepped forward to buy ever more goods. Supply-side theory presumed — in fact, gambled — that future tax revenues would make up for present tax cuts. The idea had a growing list of supporters in Congress, led by an ex-professional football player from Buffalo named Jack Kemp. Kemp praised supply-side economics as "an alternative to the slow-growth, recession-oriented policies of the [Carter] administration."

Reagan took advantage of Republican control of the Senate, as well as high-profile allies such as Kemp, to win congressional approval of the 1981 **Economic Recovery Tax Act (ERTA)**, a massive tax cut that embodied supply-side principles. The act reduced income tax rates for most Americans by 23 percent over three years. For the wealthiest Americans — those with millions to invest — the highest marginal tax rate dropped from 70 to 50 percent. The act also slashed estate taxes, levies on inheritances instituted during the Progressive Era to prevent the transmission of huge fortunes from one generation to the next. Finally, the new legislation trimmed the taxes paid by business corporations by $150 billion over a period of five years. As a result of ERTA, by 1986 the annual revenue of the federal government had been cut by $200 billion (nearly half a trillion in 2010 dollars).

Economic Recovery Tax Act (ERTA)
Legislation introduced by President Reagan and passed by Congress in 1981 that authorized the largest reduction in taxes in the nation's history.

David Stockman, Reagan's budget director, hoped to match this reduction in tax revenue with a comparable cutback in federal expenditures. To meet this ambitious goal, he proposed substantial cuts in Social Security and Medicare. But Congress, and even the president himself, rejected his idea; they were not willing to antagonize middle-class and elderly voters who viewed these government entitlements as sacred. As conservative columnist George Will noted ironically, "Americans are conservative. What they want to conserve is the New Deal." After defense spending, Social Security and Medicare were by far the nation's largest budget items; reductions in other programs would not achieve the savings the administration desired. This contradiction between New Right Republican ideology and political reality would continue to frustrate the party into the twenty-first century.

A more immediate embarrassment confronted conservatives, however. In a 1982 *Atlantic* article, Stockman admitted that supply-side theory was based on faith, not economics. To produce optimistic projections of higher tax revenue in future years, Stockman had manipulated the figures. Worse, Stockman told the *Atlantic* reporter candidly that supply-side theory was based on a long-discredited idea: the "trickle-down" notion that helping the rich would eventually benefit the lower and middle classes. Stockman had drawn back the curtain, much to Republicans' consternation, on the flawed reasoning of supply-side theory. But it was too late. The plan had passed Congress, and since Stockman could not cut major programs such as Social Security and Medicare, he had few options to balance the budget.

As the administration's spending cuts fell short, the federal budget deficit increased dramatically. Military spending contributed a large share of the growing **national debt**. But President Reagan remained undaunted. "Defense is not a budget item," he declared. "You spend what you need." Reagan and Defense Secretary Caspar Weinberger pushed through Congress a five-year, $1.2 trillion military spending program in 1981. During Reagan's presidency, military spending accounted for one-fourth of all federal expenditures and contributed to rising annual budget deficits (the amount overspent by the government in a single year) and a skyrocketing national debt (the cumulative total of all budget deficits). By the time Reagan left office, the total federal debt had tripled, rising from $930 billion in 1981 to $2.8 trillion in 1989. The rising annual deficits of the 1980s contradicted Reagan's pledge of fiscal conservatism (Figure 29.1).

national debt
The cumulative total of all budget deficits.

Deregulation Advocates of Reaganomics asserted that excessive regulation by federal agencies impeded economic growth. **Deregulation** of prices in the trucking, airline, and railroad industries had begun under President Carter in the late 1970s, but Reagan expanded the mandate to include cutting back on government protections of consumers, workers, and the environment. Some of the targeted federal bureaucracies, such as the U.S. Department of Labor, had risen to prominence during the New Deal; others, such as the Occupational Safety and Health Administration (OSHA) and the Environmental Protection Agency (EPA), had been created during the Johnson and Nixon administrations. Although these agencies provided many services to business corporations, they also increased their costs — by protecting the rights of workers, mandating safety improvements in factories, and requiring expensive equipment to limit the release of toxic chemicals into the environment. To reduce the reach of

deregulation
The limiting of regulation by federal agencies. Deregulation of prices in the trucking, airline, and railroad industries had begun under President Carter in the late 1970s, and Reagan expanded it to include cutting back on government protections of consumers, workers, and the environment.

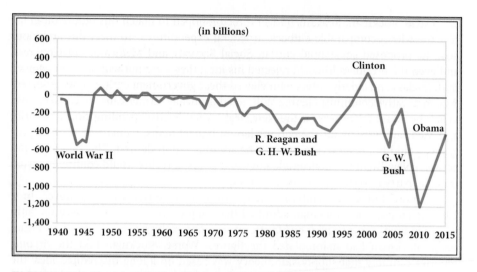

FIGURE 29.1 **The Annual Federal Budget Deficit (or Surplus), 1940–2015**

During World War II, the federal government incurred an enormous budget deficit. But between 1946 and 1965, it ran either an annual budget surplus or incurred a relatively small debt. The annual deficits rose significantly during the Vietnam War and the stagflation of the 1970s, but they really exploded between 1982 and 1994, in the budgets devised by the Ronald Reagan and George H. W. Bush administrations, and again between 2002 and 2005, in those prepared by George W. Bush. The Republican presidents increased military spending while cutting taxes, a budgetary policy that produced deficits.

federal regulatory agencies, the Reagan administration in 1981 cut their budgets, by an average of 12 percent.

Reagan also rendered regulatory agencies less effective by staffing them with leaders who were opposed to the agencies' missions. James Watt, an outspoken conservative who headed the Department of the Interior, attacked environmentalism as "a left-wing cult." Acting on his free-enterprise principles, Watt opened public lands for use by private businesses — oil and coal corporations, large-scale ranchers, and timber companies. Anne Gorsuch Burford, whom Reagan appointed to head the EPA, likewise disparaged environmentalists and refused to cooperate with Congress to clean up toxic waste sites under a program known as the Superfund. The Sierra Club and other environmental groups aroused enough public outrage about these appointees that the administration changed its position. During President Reagan's second term, he significantly increased the EPA's budget and added acreage to the National Wilderness Preservation System and animals and plants to the endangered species lists.

Ultimately, as these adjustments demonstrate, politics in the United States remained "the art of the possible." Savvy politicians know when to advance and when to retreat. Having attained two of his prime goals — a major tax cut and a dramatic increase in defense spending — Reagan did not seriously attempt to scale back big government and the welfare state. When he left office in 1989, federal spending stood at 22.1 percent of the gross domestic product (GDP) and federal taxes at 19 percent of GDP, both virtually the same as in 1981. In the meantime, though, in addition to the tripling of the federal debt, the number of government workers had increased from 2.9 to 3.1 million. This outcome — because it cut against the president's rhetoric about balancing budgets and downsizing government — elicited harsh criticism from some conservative commentators. "There was no Reagan Revolution," one conservative stated flatly. A former Reagan aide offered a more balanced assessment: "Ronald Reagan did far less than he had hoped . . . and a hell of a lot more than people thought he would."

Remaking the Judiciary   Even if he did not achieve everything many of his supporters desired, Reagan left an indelible imprint on politics, public policy, and American culture. One place this imprint was felt in far-reaching ways was the judiciary, where Reagan and his attorney general, Edwin Meese, aimed at reversing the liberal judicial philosophy that had prevailed since the 1950s. During his two terms, Reagan appointed 368 federal court judges — most of them with conservative credentials — and three Supreme Court justices: Sandra Day O'Connor (1981), Antonin Scalia (1986), and Anthony Kennedy (1988). Ironically, O'Connor and Kennedy turned out to be far less devoted to New Right conservatism than Reagan and his supporters imagined. O'Connor, the first woman to serve on the Court, shaped its decision making as a swing vote between liberals and conservatives. Kennedy also emerged as a judicial moderate, leaving Scalia as Reagan's only genuinely conservative appointee.

But Reagan also elevated Justice William Rehnquist, a conservative Nixon appointee, to the position of chief justice. Under Rehnquist's leadership (1986–2005), the Court's conservatives took an activist stance, limiting the reach of federal laws, ending court-ordered busing, and endorsing constitutional protection of property rights. However, on controversial issues such as individual liberties, abortion rights, affirmative action, and the rights of criminal defendants, the presence of O'Connor ensured that the Court adopted a more centrist position. As a result, the justices scaled back, but did not usually overturn, the liberal rulings of the Warren and Burger Courts. In the controversial *Webster v. Reproductive Health Services* (1989), for instance, Scalia pushed for the justices to overturn the abortion-rights decision in *Roe v. Wade* (1973). O'Connor refused, but she nonetheless approved the constitutional validity of state laws that limited the use of public funds and facilities for abortions. A more conservative federal judiciary would remain a significant institutional legacy of the Reagan presidency.

HIV/AIDS   Another conservative legacy was the slow national response to one of the worst disease epidemics of the postwar decades. The human immunodeficiency virus (HIV), a deadly (though slow-acting) pathogen, developed in Africa when a chimpanzee virus jumped to humans; immigrants carried it to Haiti and then to the United States during the 1970s. In 1981, American physicians identified HIV as a new virus — one that caused a disease known as acquired immunodeficiency syndrome (AIDS). Hundreds of gay men, who were prominent among the earliest carriers of the virus, were dying of AIDS. Within two decades, **HIV/AIDS** had spread worldwide, infected more than 50 million people of both sexes, and killed more than 20 million.

Within the United States, AIDS took nearly one hundred thousand lives in the 1980s — more than were lost in the Korean and Vietnam Wars combined. However, because its most prominent early victims were gay men, President Reagan, emboldened

HIV/AIDS
A deadly disease that killed nearly one hundred thousand people in the United States in the 1980s.

HIV/AIDS and the Politics of Public Health The HIV/AIDS epidemic struck the United States in the early 1980s and has remained a major public health issue ever since. The Reagan administration's slow and ineffectual response to the crisis led gay rights activists to found ACT UP (AIDS Coalition to Unleash Power) in 1987, which engaged in militant protests designed to force the federal government to increase support for research and care. In the 1994 New York City Gay Pride parade pictured here, ACT UP supporters hold aloft posters with the ACT UP slogan, "Silence = Death." Allan Tannenbaum/Getty Images.

by New Right conservatives, hesitated in declaring a national health emergency. Some of Reagan's advisors asserted that this "gay disease" might even be God's punishment of homosexuals. Between 1981 and 1986, as the epidemic spread, the Reagan administration took little action — worse, it prevented the surgeon general, C. Everett Koop, from speaking forthrightly to the nation about the disease. Pressed by gay activists and prominent health officials from across the country, in Reagan's last years in office the administration finally began to devote federal resources to treatment for HIV and AIDS patients and research into possible vaccines. But the delay had proved costly, inhumane, and embarrassing.

Morning in America

During his first run for governor of California in 1966, Reagan held a revelatory conversation with a campaign consultant. "Politics is just like the movies," Reagan told him. "You have a hell of an opening, coast for a while, and then have a hell of a close." Reagan indeed had a "hell of an opening." Following a lavish, spectacular inauguration, he quickly won passage of his tax reduction bill and launched his plan to bolster the Pentagon. But then a long "coasting" period descended on his presidency, during which he retreated on tax cuts and navigated a major foreign policy scandal. Finally, toward the end of his two-term presidency, Reagan found his "hell of a close," leaving office as major reforms — which he encouraged from afar — had begun to tear apart the Soviet Union and bring an end to the Cold War. Through all the ups and downs, Reagan remained a master of the politics of symbolism, championing a resurgent American economy and reassuring the country that the pursuit of wealth was noble and that he had the reins of the nation firmly in hand.

Reagan came to symbolize the tax-cutting president, but economic conditions forced him to reverse course on taxes early in his first term. High interest rates set by the Federal Reserve Board had cut the runaway inflation of the Carter years. But these rates — as high as 18 percent — sent the economy into a recession in 1981–1982 that put 10 million Americans out of work and shuttered 17,000 businesses. Unemployment neared 10 percent, the highest rate since the Great Depression. These troubles, combined with the booming deficit, forced Reagan to negotiate a tax increase with Congress in 1982 — to the loud complaints of supply-side diehards. The president's job rating plummeted, and in the 1982 midterm elections Democrats picked up twenty-six seats in the House of Representatives and seven state governorships.

Election of 1984 Fortunately for Reagan, the economy had recovered by 1983, restoring the president's job approval rating just in time for the 1984 presidential election. During the campaign, Reagan emphasized the economic resurgence, touring the country promoting his tax policies and the nation's new prosperity. The Democrats nominated former vice president Walter Mondale of Minnesota. With strong ties to labor unions, a variety of ethnic and racial groups, and party leaders, Mondale epitomized the New Deal coalition. He selected Representative Geraldine Ferraro of New York as his running mate — the first woman to run on the presidential ticket of a major political party. Neither Ferraro's presence nor Mondale's credentials made a difference, however: Reagan won a landslide victory, losing only Minnesota and the District of Columbia. Still, Democrats retained their majority in the House and, in the 1986 midterm elections, regained control of the Senate.

Reagan's 1984 campaign slogan, "It's Morning in America," projected the image of a new day dawning on a confident people. In Reagan mythology, the United States was an optimistic nation of small towns, close-knit families, and kindly neighbors. "The success story of America," he once said, "is neighbor helping neighbor." The mythology may not have reflected the *actual* nation — which was overwhelmingly urban and suburban, and in which the hard knocks of capitalism held down more than opportunity elevated — but that mattered little. Reagan's remarkable ability to produce positive associations and feelings, alongside robust economic growth after the 1981–1982 recession, helped make the 1980s a decade characterized by both backward-looking nostalgia and a future-oriented, aggressive capitalism.

Return to Prosperity Between 1945 and the 1970s, the United States was the world's leading exporter of agricultural products, manufactured goods, and investment capital. Then American manufacturers lost market share, undercut by cheaper and better-designed products from West Germany and Japan. By 1985, for the first time since 1915, the United States registered a negative balance of international payments. It now imported more goods and capital than it exported. The country became a debtor (rather than a creditor) nation. The rapid ascent of the Japanese economy to become the world's second largest was a key factor in this historic reversal (America in Global Context). More than one-third of the American annual trade deficit of $138 billion in the 1980s was from trade with Japan, whose corporations exported huge quantities of electronic goods and made nearly one-quarter of all cars bought in the United States.

Meanwhile, American businesses grappled with a worrisome decline in productivity. Between 1973 and 1992, American productivity (the amount of goods or services per hour of work) grew at the meager rate of 1 percent a year — a far cry from the post–World War II rate of 3 percent. Because managers wanted to cut costs, the wages of most employees stagnated. Further, because of foreign competition, the number of high-paying, union-protected manufacturing jobs shrank. By 1985, more people in the United States worked for McDonald's slinging Big Macs than rolled out rails, girders, and sheet steel in the nation's steel industry.

A brief return to competitiveness in the second half of the 1980s masked the steady long-term transformation of the economy that had begun in the 1970s. The nation's heavy industries — steel, autos, chemicals — continued to lose market share to global competitors. Nevertheless, the U.S. economy grew at the impressive average rate of 2 to 3 percent per year for much of the late 1980s and 1990s (with a short recession in 1990–1991). What had changed was the direction of growth and its beneficiaries. Increasingly, financial services, medical services, and computer technology — **service industries**, broadly speaking — were the leading sectors of growth. This shift in the underlying foundation of the American economy, from manufacturing to service, from making *things* to producing *services*, would have long-term consequences for the global competitiveness of U.S. industries and the value of the dollar.

service industries
Term that includes food, beverage, and tourist industries, financial and medical service industries, and computer technology industries, which were the leading sectors of U.S. growth in the second half of the 1980s. This pattern represented a shift from reliance on the heavy industries of steel, autos, and chemicals.

Culture of Success

The economic growth of the second half of the 1980s popularized the materialistic values championed by the free marketeers. Every era has its capitalist heroes, but Americans in the 1980s celebrated wealth accumulation in ways unseen since the 1920s. When the president christened self-made entrepreneurs "the heroes for the eighties," he probably had people like Lee Iacocca in mind. Born to Italian immigrants and trained as an engineer, Iacocca rose through the ranks to become president of the Ford Motor Corporation. In 1978, he took over the ailing Chrysler Corporation and made it profitable again — by securing a crucial $1.5 billion loan from the U.S. government, pushing the development of new cars, and selling them on TV. His patriotic commercials in the 1980s echoed Reagan's rhetoric: "Let's make American mean something again."

If Iacocca symbolized a resurgent corporate America, high-profile financial wheeler-dealers also captured Americans' imagination. One was Ivan Boesky, a white-collar criminal convicted of insider trading (buying or selling stock based on information from corporate insiders). "I think greed is healthy," Boesky told a business school graduating class. Boesky inspired the fictional character Gordon Gekko, who proclaimed "Greed is good!" in the 1987 film *Wall Street*. A new generation of Wall Street executives, of which Boesky was one example, pioneered the leveraged buyout (LBO).

To see a still from *Wall Street*, along with other primary sources from this period, see **Sources for America's History**.

Yoichi Funabashi: "Japan and America: Global Partners"

Educated at the University of Tokyo and Keio University, Yoichi Funabashi is a prize-winning journalist who specializes in the U.S.-Japan economic relationship. During the 1980s, he lived in the United States as a columnist (and later bureau chief) for the *Asahi Shimbun*, one of Japan's most important daily newspapers.

As Japan struggled to rebuild itself after World War II, the charismatic Shigeru Yoshida, prime minister during the critical years of 1948 to 1952, called on the country to be a good loser. The Japanese have lost the war, he said, but they must not lose heart. Japan must cooperate with the United States, and pull itself out of misery and disgrace. The Japanese did indeed cooperate willingly with the Allied occupation — with the American (and British) "devils" whom they had been taught for years to despise to the very core of their souls. . . .

Postwar Japan went on to prove that it could indeed be a good loser. Under the new constitution promulgated under the guidance of the occupation, it has developed into a democratic country with a relatively moderate disparity between rich and poor and a stable, smoothly functioning political system. . . .

The Japanese-U.S. relationship has thus come to occupy a truly unique position in world history. Never before has a multiethnic, contract-based society and a homogenous, traditional society joined together to form such a powerful team. As global powers, Japan and the United States combined have a decisive impact on world politics; it follows that their future relations will largely determine the blueprints of multilateral cooperation and world stability in the coming century. . . .

Potential sources of bilateral friction are as numerous as ever: the trade imbalance, market liberalization, growing Japanese investment in the United States, heavy U.S. dependence on Japanese technology, and so on. Occasional outbursts of economic nationalism, or "revisionist" thinking are probably inevitable as the debate over these issues unfolds. . . .

Of far greater concern, however, is that Japanese-U.S. relations now face their gravest challenge since 1945. The end of the Cold War has drastically altered the global geopolitical and geoeconomic context that shaped Japanese-U.S. relations. Both countries now face the urgent need to redefine their relationship to suit the new context. . . .

Before they can build a strong bilateral relationship, Americans and Japanese must outgrow their obsession with being Number One. This psychological adjustment is absolutely necessary for both peoples. Projecting the nature of its own hierarchical society, Japan tends to view the rest of the world, it is said, in terms of ranking. This inclination fosters behavior patterns that are oriented more toward what to *be* than what to *do*. Japan is also overly conscious of itself as a late-starter, having entered modern international society only in the mid-nineteenth century, and this history has made catching up with and outpacing other countries a sort of national pastime. . . . It may be even more difficult for the United States, which dominated the free world during the Cold War, to make the psychological adjustments required to enter into a partnership with Japan that is truly equal.

SOURCE: Yoichi Funabashi, "Japan and America: Global Partners," *Foreign Policy* 86 (Spring 1992): 24–39.

QUESTIONS FOR ANALYSIS

1. Among the "sources of bilateral friction" Funabashi lists the trade imbalance and Japanese investment in the United States. Why would these cause friction?

2. How had the U.S.-Japan relationship changed between 1945 and the 1980s?

In a typical LBO, a financier used heavily leveraged (borrowed) capital to buy a company, quickly restructured that company to make it appear spectacularly profitable, and then sold it at a higher price.

Americans had not set aside the traditional work ethic, but the Reagan-era public was fascinated with money and celebrity. (The documentary television show *Lifestyles of the Rich and Famous* began its run in 1984.) One of the most enthralling of the era's money moguls was Donald Trump, a real estate developer who craved publicity. In 1983, the flamboyant Trump built the equally flamboyant Trump Towers in New York City. At the entrance of the $200 million apartment building stood two enormous bronze *T*'s, a display of self-promotion reinforced by the media. Calling him "The Donald," a nickname used by Trump's first wife, TV reporters and magazines commented relentlessly on his marriages, divorces, and glitzy lifestyle. Trading on his celebrity as much as his business acumen, Trump would in later decades forge a career on reality television and, in one of the most unexpected political developments of the early twenty-first century, win the Republican nomination for president in 2016 and ascend to the presidency itself.

The Computer Revolution   While Trump grabbed headlines and made splashy real estate investments, a handful of quieter, less flashy entrepreneurs was busy changing the face of the American economy. Bill Gates, Paul Allen, Steve Jobs, and Steve Wozniak were four entrepreneurs who pioneered the computer revolution in the late 1970s and 1980s (Thinking Like a Historian). They took a technology that had been used exclusively for large-scale enterprises — the military and multinational corporations — and made it accessible to individual consumers. Scientists had devised the first computers for military purposes during World War II. Cold War military research subsequently funded the construction of large mainframe computers. But government and private-sector first-generation computers were bulky, cumbersome machines that had to be placed in large air-conditioned rooms.

Between the 1950s and the 1970s, concluding with the development of the microprocessor in 1971, each generation of computers grew faster and smaller. By the mid-1970s, a few microchips the size of the letter *O* on this page provided as much processing power as a World War II–era computer. The day of the personal computer (PC) had arrived. Working in the San Francisco Bay Area, Jobs and Wozniak founded Apple Computers in 1976 and within a year were producing small, individual computers that could be easily used by a single person. When Apple enjoyed success, other companies scrambled to get into the market. International Business Machines (IBM) offered its first personal computer in 1981, but Apple Corporation's 1984 Macintosh computer (later shortened to "Mac") became the first runaway commercial success for a personal computer.

Meanwhile, two former high school classmates, Gates, age nineteen, and Allen, age twenty-one, had set a goal in the early 1970s of putting "a personal computer on every desk and in every home." They recognized that software was the key. In 1975, they founded the Microsoft Corporation, whose MS-DOS and Windows operating systems soon dominated the software industry. By 2000, the company's products ran nine out of every ten personal computers in the United States and a majority of those around the world. Gates and Allen became billionaires, and Microsoft exploded into a huge company with 57,000 employees and annual revenues of $38 billion. In three decades, the computer had moved from a few military research centers to thousands of corporate offices and then to millions of people's homes. Ironically, in an age that celebrated free-market capitalism, government research and government funding had played an enormous role in the development of the most important technology since television.

> **IN YOUR OWN WORDS** What were the major political successes and failures of the Reagan coalition?

The End of the Cold War

Ronald Reagan entered office determined to confront the Soviet Union diplomatically and militarily. Backed by Republican and Democratic hard-liners alike, Reagan unleashed some of the harshest Cold War rhetoric since the 1950s, labeling the Soviet Union an "evil empire" and vowing that it would end up "on the ash heap of history." In a remarkable turnaround, however, by his second term Reagan had decided that this goal would be best achieved by actively cooperating with Mikhail Gorbachev, the reform-minded Russian Communist leader. The downfall of the Soviet Union in 1991 ended the nearly fifty-year-long Cold War, but a new set of foreign challenges quickly emerged.

U.S.-Soviet Relations in a New Era

When Reagan assumed the presidency in 1981, he broke with his immediate predecessors — Richard Nixon, Gerald Ford, and Jimmy Carter — in Cold War strategy. Nixon regarded himself as a "realist" in foreign affairs. That meant, above all, advancing the national interest without regard to ideology. Nixon's policy of détente with the Soviet Union and China embodied this realist view (Chapter 27). President Carter endorsed détente and continued to push for relaxing Cold War tensions. This worked for a time, but the Soviet invasion of Afghanistan empowered hard-liners in the U.S. Congress and forced Carter to take a tougher line — which he did with the Olympic boycott and grain embargo. This was the relationship Reagan inherited in 1981: a decade of détente that had produced a noticeable relaxation of tensions with the communist world, followed by a year of tense standoffs over Soviet advances into Central Asia, which threatened U.S. interests in the Middle East.

Reagan's Cold War Revival Conservatives did not support détente. Neither did they care much for the containment policy that had guided U.S. Cold War strategy since 1947. Reagan and his advisors wanted to *defeat*, not merely contain, the Soviet Union. His administration pursued a two-pronged strategy toward that end. First, it abandoned détente and set about rearming America. Reagan's military budgets authorized new weapons systems, dramatically expanded military bases, and significantly expanded the nation's nuclear arsenal. This buildup in American military strength, reasoned Secretary of Defense Caspar Weinberger, would force the Soviets into an arms race that would strain their economy and cause domestic unrest. The Reagan

Personal Computing: A Technological Revolution

Considered historically, computers are a strikingly new phenomenon. The ancestors of the first computers were developed in the 1940s using vacuum tubes and transistors. Integrated circuits were introduced in the 1950s and the first microprocessor in the 1970s. Prior to the decade of the 1980s, only the federal government and large corporations and institutions used computers, which were massive in size and expensive to purchase. In the 1980s, inventors and entrepreneurs developed the first "personal" computers, which could fit on desks or tables and were soon within the price range of ordinary families. The computers we know today date from that decade. Another enormous change came in the mid-1990s, when the Internet, whose forerunner was a U.S. Defense Department computer network, became widely available to the public for the first time.

---

1. **Moore's law, 1965.** *In 1965, the electronics engineer Gordon Moore calculated that the number of transistors on an integrated circuit doubled roughly every two years, meaning that the power of computers was increasing at that rate.*

   The complexity for minimum component costs has increased at a rate of roughly a factor of two per year. Certainly over the short term this rate can be expected to continue, if not increase. . . . That means by 1975, the number of components per integrated circuit for minimum cost will be 65,000.

   I believe that such a large circuit can be built on a single wafer.

2. **Scene from** *2001: A Space Odyssey*, **1968.** *In this scene from an acclaimed science fiction film, a space station's computer system, named HAL, defends itself against an astronaut who is determined to shut down the computer.*

   Dave Bowman: Hello, HAL. Do you read me, HAL?

   HAL: Affirmative, Dave. I read you.

   DB: Open the pod bay doors, HAL.

   HAL: I'm sorry, Dave. I'm afraid I can't do that.

   DB: What's the problem?

   HAL: I think you know what the problem is just as well as I do.

   DB: What are you talking about, HAL?

   HAL: This mission is too important for me to allow you to jeopardize it.

   DB: I don't know what you're talking about, HAL.

   HAL: I know that you and Frank were planning to disconnect me, and I'm afraid that's something I cannot allow to happen.

   DB: Where the hell did you get that idea, HAL?

   HAL: Dave, although you took very thorough precautions in the pod against my hearing you, I could see your lips move.

   DB: Alright, HAL. I'll go in through the emergency airlock.

   HAL: Without your space helmet, Dave? You're going to find that rather difficult.

   DB: HAL, I won't argue with you anymore! Open the door!

   HAL: Dave, this conversation can serve no purpose anymore. Goodbye.

3. **Neil Ardley,** *World of Tomorrow: School, Work, and Play*, **1981.** *In this book written for teenagers, Neil Ardley speculated about the future of computers.*

   Imagine you are living in the future, and are doing a project on Halley's comet. It's quite some time since it last appeared in 1986, and you want to find out when it will again be seen from Earth. You also want to know the results of a space mission to the comet, and find out what the comet is made of.

   In the days when the last comet appeared, you would have had to look up Halley's comet in an encyclopedia or a book on astronomy. If you didn't possess these books, you would have gone to the library to get the information. . . .

   People still collect books as valuable antiques or for a hobby, but you get virtually all the information you need from the viewscreen of your home computer. The computer is linked to a library — not a library of books but an electronic library where information on every subject is stored in computer memory banks. . . .

Computers will make the world of tomorrow a much safer place. They will do away with cash, so that you need no longer fear being attacked for your money. In addition, you need not worry that your home will be burgled or your car stolen. The computers in your home and car will guard them, allowing only yourself to enter or someone with your permission.

4. **Scene from *Terminator*, 1984.** *A national defense computer network called Skynet decides to exterminate humanity in the film* Terminator.

Reese: There was a war. A few years from now. Nuclear war. The whole thing. All this — [His gesture includes the car, the city, the world.] — everything is gone. Just gone. There were survivors. Here. There. Nobody knew who started it. (pause) It was the machines.

Sarah: I don't understand. . . .

Reese: Defense network computer. New. Powerful. Hooked into everything. Trusted to run it all. They say it got smart . . . a new order of intelligence. Then it saw all people as a threat, not just the ones on the other side. Decided our fate in a microsecond . . . extermination.

5. **Interview with Steve Jobs, February 1, 1985.** *Apple founder Steve Jobs, one of the pioneers of the personal computer, discusses the future of computers and computer networks.*

Question: Why should a person buy a computer?

Steve Jobs: There are different answers for different people. In business, that question is easy to answer: You can really prepare documents much faster and at a higher quality level, and you can do many things to increase office productivity. A computer frees people from much of the menial work. . . . Remember computers are tools. Tools help us do our work better. In education, computers are the first thing to come along since books that will sit there and interact with you endlessly, without judgment. . . .

Question: What will change?

Steve Jobs: The most compelling reason for most people to buy a computer for the home [in the future] will be to link it into a nationwide communications network. We're just in the beginning stages of what will be a truly remarkable breakthrough for most people — as remarkable as the telephone.

6. **Percentage of Americans Using the Internet.**

SOURCES: (1) G. E. Moore, "Cramming More Components onto Integrated Circuits," *Electronics*, April 19, 1965, 114; (2) *2001: A Space Odyssey*, Screenplay by Stanley Kubrick and Arthur C. Clarke (Hawk Films Ltd. and MGM Studios, 1967); (3) Neil Ardley, *World of Tomorrow: School, Work, and Play* (New York: Franklin Watts, 1981), 20–27; (4) *Terminator*, Screenplay by James Cameron and Gale Anne Hurd, Fifth Draft (Pacific Western Productions, Inc., March 11, 1984), 134; (5) *Playboy*, February 1, 1985, 52.

ANALYZING THE EVIDENCE

1. Compare sources 2 and 4. Anxiety about the extraordinary power of computers has been a regular feature of science fiction, both in writing and in film, since the late 1950s. What do the scenes from these two films tell us about the cultural reactions to computers early in their development?

2. How does source 3 offer a different vision of a future with computers? Why do you think cultural responses to computers tend to swing between extreme anxiety and equally extreme optimism?

3. How does Steve Jobs's assessment of computers in source 5 compare with those in the other documents? Should we trust his judgment more because he is closer to their actual development? Why or why not?

PUTTING IT ALL TOGETHER

Drawing on the history of personal computers discussed in this chapter, as well as on the documents above, write an essay in which you assess the origin of the personal computer. What cultural reactions and predictions surrounded the computer's birth? What economic and social transformations did it have the potential to unleash? You might also consider a comparison of the Industrial Revolution of the second half of the nineteenth century and the "computer revolution" of the late twentieth century. Are there parallels in how each development transformed American society?

administration also proposed the Strategic Arms Reduction Talks (START) with the Soviet Union, in which the United States put forward a plan calculated to increase American advantage in sea- and air-based nuclear systems over the Soviet's ground-based system.

Second, the president supported CIA initiatives to roll back Soviet influence in the developing world by funding anticommunist movements in Angola, Mozambique, Afghanistan, and Central America. To accomplish this objective, Reagan supported repressive, right-wing regimes. Nowhere was this more conspicuous in the 1980s than in the Central American countries of Guatemala, Nicaragua, and El Salvador. Conditions were unique in each country but held to a pattern: the United States sided with military dictatorships and oligarchies if democratically elected governments or left-wing movements sought support from the Soviet Union. In Guatemala, this approach produced a brutal military rule — thousands of opponents of the government were executed or kidnapped. In Nicaragua, Reagan actively encouraged a coup against the left-wing Sandinista government. And in El Salvador, the U.S.-backed government maintained secret "death squads," which murdered members of the opposition. In each case, Reagan blocked Soviet influence, but the damage done to local communities and to the international reputation of the United States, as in Vietnam, was great.

Sandinistas

The democratically elected group in Nicaragua that President Reagan accused of threatening U.S. business interests. Reagan attempted to overthrow them by ordering the CIA to assist an armed opposition group called the Contras.

Contras

An opposition group in Nicaragua that President Reagan ordered the CIA to assist. While Congress banned the CIA and all other government agencies from providing any military support to the Contras, a lieutenant colonel in the U.S. Marines, Oliver North, used the profits from the Iranian arms deal to assist the Contras, resulting in the Iran-Contra affair.

Iran-Contra affair

Reagan administration scandal that involved the sale of arms to Iran in exchange for its efforts to secure the release of hostages held in Lebanon and the redirection — illegal because banned by American law — of the proceeds of those sales to the Nicaraguan Contras.

Iran-Contra Reagan's determination to oppose left-wing movements in Central America engulfed his administration in a major scandal during the president's second term. For years, Reagan had denounced Iran as an "outlaw state" and a supporter of terrorism. But in 1985, he wanted its help. To win its assistance in freeing two dozen American hostages held by Hezbollah, a pro-Iranian Shiite group in Lebanon, the administration sold arms to Iran without public or congressional knowledge. While this secret arms deal was diplomatically and politically controversial, the use of the resulting profits in Nicaragua was explicitly illegal. To overthrow the democratically elected **Sandinistas**, whom the president accused of threatening U.S. business interests, Reagan ordered the CIA to assist an armed opposition group called the **Contras** (Map 29.2). Although Reagan praised the Contras as "freedom fighters," Congress worried that the president and other executive branch agencies were assuming war-making powers that the Constitution reserved to the legislature. In 1984, Congress banned the CIA and all other government agencies from providing any military support to the Contras.

Oliver North, a lieutenant colonel in the U.S. Marines and an aide to the National Security Council, defied that ban. With the tacit or explicit consent of high-ranking administration officials, including the president, North used the profits from the Iranian arms deal to assist the Contras. When asked whether he knew of North's illegal actions, Reagan replied, "I don't remember." The **Iran-Contra affair** came to public light in 1986, resulting in the prosecution of North and several other officials and weakening Reagan domestically — he proposed no bold domestic policy initiatives in his last two years. But the president remained steadfastly engaged in international affairs, where events were unfolding that would bring a dramatic close to the Cold War.

Gorbachev and Soviet Reform The Soviet system of state socialism and central economic planning had transformed Russia from an agricultural to an industrial

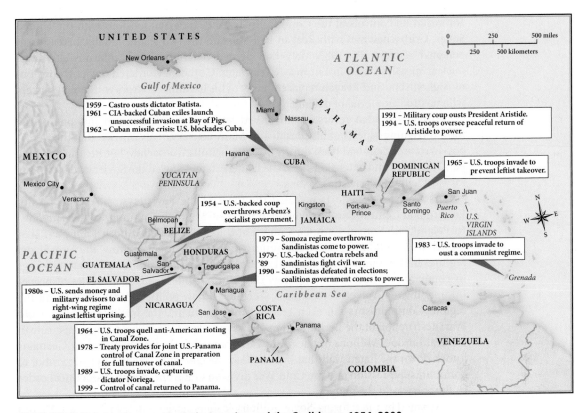

MAP 29.2 U.S. Involvement in Latin America and the Caribbean, 1954–2000

Ever since the Monroe Doctrine (1823), the United States has claimed a special interest in Latin America. During the Cold War, U.S. foreign policy throughout Latin America focused on containing instability and the appeal of communism in a region plagued by poverty and military dictatorships. Providing foreign aid was one approach to addressing social and economic needs, but the United States frequently intervened with military forces (or by supporting military coups) to remove unfriendly or socialist governments. The Reagan administration's support of the Contra rebels in Nicaragua, some of which was contrary to U.S. law, was one of those interventions.

society between 1917 and the 1950s. But it had done so inefficiently. Lacking the incentives of a market economy, most enterprises hoarded raw materials, employed too many workers, and did not develop new products. Except in military weaponry and space technology, the Russian economy fell further and further behind those of capitalist societies, and most people in the Soviet bloc endured a low standard of living. Moreover, the Soviet invasion of Afghanistan in 1979, like the American war in Vietnam, turned out to be a major blunder — an unwinnable war that cost vast amounts of money, destroyed military morale, and undermined popular support of the government.

Mikhail Gorbachev, a relatively young Russian leader who became general secretary of the Communist Party in 1985, recognized the need for internal economic reform and an end to the war in Afghanistan. An iconoclast in Soviet terms, Gorbachev introduced policies of **glasnost** (openness) and **perestroika** (economic restructuring), which encouraged widespread criticism of the rigid institutions and

glasnost
The policy introduced by Soviet president Mikhail Gorbachev during the 1980s that involved greater openness and freedom of expression and that contributed, unintentionally, to the 1991 breakup of the Soviet Union.

perestroika
The economic restructuring policy introduced by Soviet president Mikhail Gorbachev during the 1980s that contributed, unintentionally, to the 1991 breakup of the Soviet Union.

authoritarian controls of the Communist regime. To lessen tensions with the United States, Gorbachev met with Reagan in 1985, and the two leaders established a warm personal rapport. By 1987, they had agreed to eliminate all intermediate-range nuclear missiles based in Europe. A year later, Gorbachev ordered Soviet troops out of Afghanistan, and Reagan replaced many of his hardline advisors with policymakers who favored a renewal of détente.

Reagan's sudden reversal with regard to the Soviet Union remains one of the most intriguing aspects of his presidency. Many conservatives worried that their cowboy-hero president had been duped by a duplicitous Gorbachev, but Reagan's gamble paid off: the easing of tensions with the United States allowed the Soviet leader to press forward with his domestic reforms.

As Gorbachev's efforts revealed the flaws of the Soviet system, the peoples of Eastern and Central Europe demanded the ouster of their Communist governments. In Poland, the Roman Catholic Church and its pope — Polish-born John Paul II — joined with Solidarity, the trade-union movement, to overthrow the pro-Soviet regime. In 1956 and 1964, Russian troops had quashed similar popular uprisings in Hungary and East Germany. Now they did not intervene, and a series of peaceful uprisings — "Velvet Revolutions" — created a new political order throughout the region. Communism's fall even reached into Germany, the birthplace of the Cold War: destruction of the Berlin Wall in 1989 symbolized the end of Communist rule in Central Europe. Millions of television viewers worldwide watched jubilant Germans knock down the hated wall that had divided the city since 1961 — a vivid symbol of communist repression and the Cold War division of Europe. A new geopolitical order in Europe was in the making.

Alarmed by the reforms, Soviet military leaders seized power in August 1991 and arrested Gorbachev. But widespread popular opposition led by Boris Yeltsin, the president of the Russian Republic, thwarted their efforts to oust Gorbachev from office. This failure broke the dominance of the Communist Party. Inspired by the Velvet Revolutions and the weakening of the Communist Party, several Soviet Republics (Estonia, Latvia, Lithuania, Ukraine, and Belarus) broke away as independent nation-states. Finally, on December 25, 1991, the Union of Soviet Socialist Republics formally dissolved to make way for an eleven-member Commonwealth of Independent States (CIS) (Map 29.3). The remarkable and total collapse of the Soviet Union was the result of internal weaknesses of the Communist economy. External pressure from the United States played an important, though secondary, role.

"Nobody — no country, no party, no person — 'won' the cold war," concluded George Kennan, the architect in 1947 of the American policy of containment. The Cold War's cost was enormous, and both sides benefitted greatly from its end. For more than forty years, the United States had fought a bitter economic and ideological battle against its communist foe, a struggle that exerted an enormous impact on American society. Taxpayers had spent some $4 trillion on nuclear weapons and trillions more on conventional arms, placing the United States on a permanent war footing and creating a massive military-industrial complex. The physical and psychological costs were equally high, including anticommunist witch-hunts and a constant fear of nuclear annihilation. Most Americans had no qualms about proclaiming

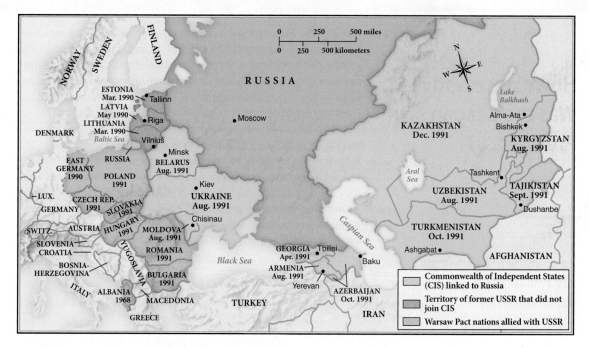

MAP 29.3 The Collapse of the Soviet Union and the Creation of Independent States, 1989–1991
The collapse of Soviet communism dramatically altered the political landscape of Central Europe and Central Asia. The Warsaw Pact, the USSR's answer to NATO, vanished. West and East Germany reunited, and the nations created by the Versailles treaty of 1919 — Estonia, Latvia, Lithuania, Poland, Czechoslovakia, Hungary, and Yugoslavia — reasserted their independence or split into smaller, ethnically defined nations. The Soviet republics bordering Russia, from Belarus in the west to Kyrgyzstan in the east, also became independent states, while remaining loosely bound with Russia in the Commonwealth of Independent States (CIS).

victory, however, and conservative advocates of free-market capitalism celebrated the outcome. The collapse of communism in Eastern Europe and the disintegration of the Soviet Union itself, they argued, demonstrated that they had been right all along.

A New Political Order at Home and Abroad

Ronald Reagan's role in facilitating the end of the Cold War was among his most important achievements. Overall, his presidency left a mixed legacy. Despite his pledge to get the federal government "off our backs," he could not ultimately reduce its size or scope. Social Security and other entitlement programs remained untouched, and increased military spending outweighed cuts in other programs. Determined not to divide the country, Reagan did not actively push controversial policies espoused by the Religious Right. He called for tax credits for private religious schools, restrictions on abortions, and a constitutional amendment to permit prayer in public schools, but he did not expend his political capital to secure these measures (Interpretations).

INTERPRETATIONS

How Conservative Was the Reagan Presidency?

In the 1980s, Ronald Reagan's presidency seemed to define a conservative triumph. The product of a political ground game decades in the making, the conservative victory in the 1980 election fused the mobilization of Christian evangelicals, a libertarian antigovernment individualism, and a probusiness entrepreneurialism into a coalition determined to undermine the expansive legacy of sixties liberalism. Did it work?

Historians are now beginning to offer assessments of Reagan's presidency. Two scholars, Kim Phillips-Fein and Robert O. Self, one of the authors of this textbook, join this debate with perspectives on Reagan's relationship to the Christian evangelical movement. Reacting to what they saw as the permissiveness of the 1960s, the Religious Right pushed a Christian moral agenda into political debate and supported candidates pledged to "return America" to its traditional foundations. To what extent was Reagan their candidate?

KIM PHILLIPS-FEIN

SOURCE: Kim Phillips-Fein, *Invisible Hands: The Making of the Conservative Movement from the New Deal to Reagan* (New York: W. W. Norton, 2009), 256–258.

Reagan worked very hard to show conservative evangelicals that he was their candidate. In August 1980 he appeared at the National Affairs Briefing . . . an event organized by the Religious Roundtable . . . the seeming answer to the prayers of the evangelicals: here was the man who would lead Christians back to the White House. . . . Reagan painted the Christian worldview in broad strokes that made clear its commonalities with the larger antistate agenda of his campaign, denouncing the [Federal Communications Commission] for interfering with religious broadcasting, the IRS for threatening the autonomy of religious schools, and the [National Labor Relations Board] for meddling with church employees. . . . One newspaper described the entire National Affairs Briefing as a "thinly disguised religious pep rally for Ronald Reagan."

ROBERT O. SELF

SOURCE: Robert O. Self, *All in the Family: The Realignment of American Democracy Since the 1960s* (New York: Hill and Wang, 2012), 367, 376–377.

When conservative pragmatists, including Reagan himself, moved slowly or cautiously on many issues, especially abortion, religious and pro-family activists believed they had been betrayed. . . . The president's rhetorical support was unwavering: he gave . . . anti-abortion speeches, appointed right-to-life leaders to his administration, [and] declared support for a Human Life Amendment [an amendment to the Constitution that would have outlawed abortion]. . . . But Reagan watched the polls and chose not to leap too far ahead of public opinion. His support for . . . right-to-life Senate initiatives was calibrated not to disrupt his economic agenda. . . . [H]e seized the opportunity to name the [Supreme] court's first woman, Sandra Day O'Connor, ignoring vocal right-to-life opposition. As an Arizona state senator in 1970, O'Connor had voted to repeal Arizona's abortion law, which had permanently disqualified her from the bench in the minds of right-to-life activists.

QUESTIONS FOR ANALYSIS

1. How do these scholars assess Reagan's commitment to the Religious Right's political agenda?
2. To what extent were evangelical expectations (described by Phillips-Fein) realized during Reagan's presidency (described by Self)?
3. Comparing these excerpts with Chapter 29's discussion of the 1970s and 1980s, identify two examples of the impact the Religious Right had on the era's politics.

While Reagan failed to roll back the social welfare and regulatory state of the New Deal–Great Society era, he changed the dynamic of American politics. The Reagan presidency restored popular belief that the nation — and individual Americans — could enjoy increasing prosperity. And his antigovernment rhetoric won many adherents, as did his bold and fiscally aggressive tax cuts. Social-welfare liberalism, ascendant since 1933, remained intact but was now on the defensive — led by Reagan, conservatives had changed the political conversation.

Election of 1988 George H. W. Bush, Reagan's vice president and successor, was not beloved by conservatives, who did not see him as one of their own. But he possessed an insider's familiarity with government and a long list of powerful allies, accumulated over three decades of public service. Bush's route to the White House reflected the post-Reagan alignments in American politics. In the primaries, he faced a spirited challenge from Pat Robertson, the archconservative televangelist whose influence and profile had grown during Reagan's two terms. After securing the presidential nomination, which he won largely because of his fierce loyalty to Reagan, Bush felt compelled to select as his vice-presidential running mate an unknown and inexperienced Indiana senator, Dan Quayle. Bush hoped that Quayle would help secure the Christian "**family values**" vote upholding the traditional nuclear family and Christian morality. Robertson's challenge and Quayle's selection showed that the Religious Right had become a major force in Republican politics.

family values
Values promoted by the Religious Right, including support for the traditional nuclear family and opposition to same-sex marriage and abortion.

On the Democratic side, Jesse Jackson became the first African American to challenge for a major-party nomination, winning eleven states in primary and caucus voting. However, the much less charismatic Massachusetts governor, Michael Dukakis, emerged as the Democratic nominee. Dukakis, a liberal from the Northeast, proved unable to win back the constituencies Democrats had lost in the 1970s: southern whites, midwestern blue-collar Catholics, and middle-class suburbanites. Indeed, Bush's campaign manager, Lee Atwater, baited Dukakis by calling him a "card-carrying liberal," a not-so-subtle reference to J. Edgar Hoover's 1958 phrase "card-carrying communist." Bush won with 53 percent of the vote, a larger margin of victory than Reagan's in 1980. The election confirmed a new pattern in presidential politics that would last through the turn of the twenty-first century: every four years, Americans would refight the battles of the 1960s, with liberals on one side and conservatives on the other.

Middle East The end of the Cold War left the United States as the world's only military superpower and raised the prospect of what President Bush called a "new world order" dominated by the United States and its European and Asian allies. American officials and diplomats presumed that U.S. interests should prevail in this new environment, but they now confronted an array of regional, religious, and ethnic conflicts that defied easy solutions. None were more pressing or more complex than those in the Middle East — the oil-rich lands stretching from Iran to Algeria. Middle Eastern conflicts would dominate the foreign policy of the United States for the next two decades, replacing the Cold War at the center of American geopolitics.

After Carter's success negotiating the 1979 Egypt-Israel treaty at Camp David, there were few bright spots in U.S. Middle Eastern diplomacy. In 1982, the Reagan administration supported Israel's invasion of Lebanon, a military operation intended to destroy the Palestine Liberation Organization (PLO). But when Lebanese militants, angered at U.S. intervention on behalf of Israel, killed 241 American marines, Reagan abruptly withdrew the forces. Three years later, Palestinians living in the Gaza Strip and along the West Bank of the Jordan River — territories occupied by Israel since 1967 — mounted an intifada, a civilian uprising against Israeli authority. In response, American diplomats stepped up their efforts to persuade the PLO and Arab nations to accept the legitimacy of Israel and to convince the Israelis to allow the creation of a Palestinian state. Neither initiative met with much success. Unable, or unwilling, to solve the region's most intractable problems and burdened by a history of support for undemocratic regimes in Middle Eastern countries, the United States was not seen by residents of the region as an honest broker.

Persian Gulf War

The 1991 war between Iraq and a U.S.-led international coalition that was sparked by the 1990 Iraqi invasion of Kuwait. A forty-day bombing campaign against Iraq followed by coalition troops storming into Kuwait brought a quick coalition victory.

Persian Gulf War American interest in a reliable supply of oil from the region led the United States into a short but consequential war in the Persian Gulf in the early 1990s. Ten years earlier, in September 1980, the revolutionary Shiite Islamic nation of Iran, headed by Ayatollah Khomeini, came under attack from Iraq, a secular state headed by the dictator Saddam Hussein. The fighting was intense and long lasting — a war of attrition that claimed a million casualties. Reagan supported Hussein with military intelligence and other aid — in order to maintain supplies of Iraqi oil, undermine Iran, and preserve a balance of power in the Middle East. Finally, in 1988, an armistice ended the inconclusive war, with both sides still claiming the territory that sparked the conflict.

Two years later, in August 1990, Hussein went to war to expand Iraq's boundaries and oil supply. Believing (erroneously) that he still had the support of the United States, Hussein sent in troops and quickly conquered Kuwait, Iraq's small, oil-rich neighbor, and threatened Saudi Arabia, the site of one-fifth of the world's known oil reserves and an informal ally of the United States. To preserve the balance of power in the region favored by the United States, President George H. W. Bush sponsored a series of resolutions in the United Nations Security Council calling for Iraq to withdraw from Kuwait. When Hussein refused, Bush successfully prodded the UN to authorize the use of force, and the president organized a military coalition of thirty-four nations. Dividing mostly along party lines, the Republican-led House of Representatives authorized American participation by a vote of 252 to 182, and the Democratic-led Senate agreed by the close margin of 52 to 47.

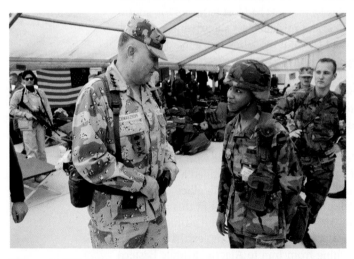

Men — and Women — at War A U.S. soldier with Norman Schwarzkopf, commander of coalition forces in the Persian Gulf War. Women comprised approximately 10 percent of American troops in that conflict. In the last decades of the twentieth century, women increasingly chose military careers and were more frequently assigned to combat zones. David Turnley/Corbis/VCG via Getty Images.

The coalition forces led by the United States quickly won the **Persian Gulf War** for the "liberation of Kuwait." To avoid a protracted struggle and retain French and Russian support for the UN coalition, Bush decided against occupying Iraq and removing Saddam Hussein from power. Instead, he won passage of UN Resolution 687, which imposed economic sanctions against Iraq unless it allowed unfettered inspection of its weapons systems, destroyed all biological and chemical arms, and unconditionally pledged not to develop nuclear weapons. The military victory, the low incidence of American casualties, and the quick withdrawal produced a euphoric reaction at home. "By God, we've kicked the Vietnam syndrome once and for all," Bush announced, and his approval rating shot up precipitously. But Saddam Hussein remained a formidable power in the region, and in March 2003, he would become the pretext for Bush's son, President George W. Bush, to initiate another war in Iraq — one that would be much more protracted, expensive, and bloody for Americans, Iraqis, and the entire Middle East (Chapter 30).

Thus the end of the Cold War brought not peace, but a deeper American involvement in the Middle East. For half a century, the United States and the Soviet Union had tried to divide the world into two rival economic and ideological blocs: communist and capitalist. The next decades promised many new struggles, one of them between a Western-led agenda of economic and cultural globalization and an anti-Western ideology of Muslim and Arab regionalism. Still more post–Cold War shifts were coming into view as well. One was the spectacular emergence of the European Union as a massive united trading bloc, economic engine, and global political force. Another was the equally spectacular economic growth in China, which was just beginning to take off in the early 1990s. The post–Cold War world promised to be a *multi*polar one, with centers of power in Europe, the United States, and East Asia, and seemingly intractable conflict in the Middle East.

> **IN YOUR OWN WORDS**   What were the aims of U.S. foreign policy during the waning years of the Cold War and in its immediate aftermath?

Summary

This chapter examined two central developments of the years 1980–1991: the rise of the New Right in U.S. politics and the end of the Cold War. Each development set the stage for a new era in American life, one that stretches to our own day. Domestically, the New Right, which had been building in strength since the mid-1960s, criticized the liberalism of the Great Society and the permissiveness that conservative activists associated with feminism and the sexual revolution. Shifting their allegiance from Barry Goldwater to Ronald Reagan, right-wing Americans built a conservative movement from the ground up and in 1980 elected Reagan president. Advocating free-market economics, lower taxes, and fewer government regulations, Reagan became a champion of the New Right. His record as president was more mixed than his rhetoric would suggest, however. Reagan's initial tax cuts were followed by tax hikes. Moreover, he frequently dismayed the Christian Right by not pursuing their interests forcefully enough — especially regarding abortion and school prayer.

Reagan played a role in the ending of the Cold War. His massive military buildup in the early 1980s strained an already overstretched Soviet economy, which struggled to keep pace. Reagan then agreed to meet with Soviet leader Mikhail Gorbachev in several summits between 1985 and 1987. More important than Reagan's actions, however, were inefficiencies and contradictions in the Soviet economic structure itself. Combined with the forced military buildup and the disastrous war in Afghanistan, these strains led Gorbachev to institute the first significant reforms in Soviet society in half a century. The reforms stirred popular criticism of the Soviet Union, which formally collapsed in 1991. Beginning the same year with the Gulf War against Iraq, the United States became embroiled in what would become a decades-long series of wars in the Middle East.

CHAPTER 29 REVIEW

TERMS TO KNOW   *Identify and explain the significance of each term below.*

Key Concepts and Events

The Conscience of a Conservative (p. 957)

National Review (p. 959)

Religious Right (p. 959)

hostage crisis (p. 961)

Reagan coalition (p. 963)

Moral Majority (p. 963)

Reagan Democrats (p. 964)

supply-side economics (Reaganomics) (p. 964)

Economic Recovery Tax Act (ERTA) (p. 964)

national debt (p. 965)

deregulation (p. 965)

HIV/AIDS (p. 967)

service industries (p. 970)

Sandinistas (p. 976)

Contras (p. 976)

Iran-Contra affair (p. 976)

glasnost (p. 977)

perestroika (p. 977)

family values (p. 981)

Persian Gulf War (p. 982)

Key People

Barry Goldwater (p. 956)

Ronald Reagan (p. 956)

William F. Buckley (p. 959)

Milton Friedman (p. 959)

David Stockman (p. 965)

Sandra Day O'Connor (p. 967)

Mikhail Gorbachev (p. 973)

George H. W. Bush (p. 981)

REVIEW QUESTIONS   *Answer these questions to demonstrate your understanding of the chapter's main ideas.*

1. What were the major characteristics of the political movement that backed Ronald Reagan, known as the New Right?

2. What were the major political successes and failures of the Reagan coalition?

3. What were the aims of U.S. foreign policy during the waning years of the Cold War and in its immediate aftermath?

4. Review the events listed on the thematic timeline on pages 952–953. In what ways was the New Right "reactive," responding to liberalism, and in what ways was it "proactive," asserting its own agenda?

MAKING CONNECTIONS *Recognize the larger developments and continuities within and across chapters.*

1. Compare the two major periods of liberal legislative accomplishment — the New Deal in the 1930s (Chapter 22) and the Great Society in the 1960s (Chapter 27) — with the Reagan era in the 1980s. Did Reagan undo the legislative gains of those earlier eras? What conservative objectives was he able to accomplish, and what limits or obstacles did he encounter?

2. Examine the images of Reagan in this chapter (pp. 955 and 963). What message do these images convey about Reagan as a person? About his policies? Together, what do they tell us about the image and reality of the Reagan presidency? Do you think that cartoons or photographs are a more accurate source of information for understanding the historical meaning of a particular president and his administration? Why or why not?

KEY TURNING POINTS *Refer to the chapter chronology on page 956 for help in answering the question below.*

Identify some of the key moments in the decline and then end of the Cold War. What part did the United States play in these events, and how did this affect the U.S. role in world affairs more broadly?

30 Confronting Global and National Dilemmas
1989 to the Present

CHAPTER

O n the morning of September 11, 2001, two commercial airliners were deliberately flown into the World Trade Center in lower Manhattan. Millions of Americans, and many more people worldwide, watched live on television and the Internet as the towers burned and collapsed. Simultaneously, a third plane was flown into the Pentagon, and a fourth hijacked plane crashed in rural Pennsylvania. It took Federal Bureau of Investigation officials only a few hours to determine the identity of most of the hijackers, as well as the organization behind the murderous attacks, a radical Islamic group known as **Al Qaeda**.

The attacks were made possible by the new era of globalization. Of the nineteen hijackers, fifteen were from Saudi Arabia, two were from the United Arab Emirates, one was from Egypt, and one was from Lebanon. Many had trained in Afghanistan, in guerrilla warfare camps operated by Osama bin Laden, Al Qaeda's leader. Four had gone to flight school in the United States itself. Several had lived and studied in Germany. They communicated with one another and with planners in Afghanistan through e-mail, Web sites, and cell phones. The most conspicuous crime of the twenty-first century, which left 2,900 people dead and sent waves of shock and anxiety through the American public, would have been impossible without the openness and interconnectivity that are central features of globalization.

The emergence in the Middle East of a radical Islamic movement willing to use terrorism to inflict major damage on the United States and the West testified to the altered realities of global politics. The simple Cold War duality — communism versus capitalism — had for decades obscured regional, ethnic, and religious loyalties and conflicts. Absent the global Cold War rivalry, those loyalties and conflicts moved to center stage. For the United States, the period between the end of the Cold War and the present has been defined by twin dilemmas. The first relates to **globalization**. How would the United States engage in global trade and commerce? How would it engage with the emerging economic strength of Europe and Asia? And how would it conceptualize and address new threats to the nation and to global stability? The second dilemma relates to domestic politics and the economy. In an era of conservative ideological dominance, how would Americans reconcile their political differences, and how would the nation continue to ensure economic opportunity and security for its citizens? As profound geopolitical changes shook the world, these were, as the chapter title suggests, Americans' dilemmas in a global society.

> ## IDENTIFY THE BIG IDEA
>
> How has the post–Cold War era of globalization affected American politics, economics, and society?

Al Qaeda
A network of radical Islamic terrorists organized by Osama bin Laden, who issued a call for holy war against Americans and their allies. Members of Al Qaeda were responsible for the 9/11 terrorist attacks.

globalization
The spread of political, cultural, and economic influences and connections among countries, businesses, and individuals around the world through trade, immigration, communication, and other means.

Energy and the Environment At the dawn of the twenty-first century, few issues were more critical, in the United States and across the globe, than energy and the environment. This wind farm is an example of the search for nonfossil sources of new energy, a search that is among the many challenges facing the globalized world of our century. Raphael GAILLARDE/Gamma-Rapho via Getty Images.

1992
- Democratic moderate Bill Clinton elected president
- *Planned Parenthood of Southeastern Pennsylvania v. Casey*

1993
- North American Free Trade Agreement (NAFTA)
- Clinton budget plan balances federal budget and begins to pay down federal debt

1994
- Clinton health insurance reform effort fails
- Republicans gain control of Congress

1995
- U.S. troops enforce peace in Bosnia

1996
- Personal Responsibility and Work Opportunity Reconciliation Act reforms welfare system

1998
- Bill Clinton impeached by House of Representatives
- Defense of Marriage Act

1999
- Clinton acquitted by Senate
- World Trade Organization (WTO) protests

2000
- George W. Bush wins contested presidential election

2001
- Bush tax cuts
- September 11: Al Qaeda terrorists attack World Trade Center and Pentagon
- Congress passes USA PATRIOT Act

2002
- United States unseats Taliban in Afghanistan
- President Bush declares Iran, North Korea, and Iraq an "axis of evil"

2003
- United States invades Iraq in March

2004
- Torture at Abu Ghraib prison becomes public
- President Bush wins reelection

2007
- Great Recession begins

2008
- Barack Obama elected president

2009
- American Recovery and Reinvestment Act

2010
- Patient Protection and Affordable Care Act

2011
- Osama bin Laden killed by U.S. forces
- Last U.S. combat troops withdrawn from Iraq

2014
- Shooting of Michael Brown and demonstrations in Ferguson, Missouri

2015
- Obama introduces Clean Power Plan

2016
- Donald Trump elected president

America in the Global Economy

In the decade following the collapse of the Soviet Union and the end of the Cold War, Americans rediscovered a long-standing truth: the United States was not an island but was linked in countless ways to a global economy and society. Economic prosperity in the post–World War II decades had obscured for Americans this fundamental reality. Globalization was not itself new—think of the Atlantic economy of the eighteenth century linking Europe, the Americas, and Africa—but a new and distinct era of global integration emerged at the turn of the twenty-first century. This current era has seen the rapid spread of capitalism around the world, huge increases in global trade and commerce, and a diffusion of communications technology, including the Internet, linking the world's people to one another in ways unimaginable a generation earlier (Thinking Like a Historian).

Suddenly, the United States faced a dizzying array of opportunities and challenges, both at home and abroad. "Profound and powerful forces are shaking and remaking our world," said a young President Bill Clinton in his first inaugural address in 1993. "The urgent question of our time is whether we can make change our friend and not our enemy." For many, globalization indeed looked like an enemy. In late 1999, more than 50,000 protesters took to the streets of Seattle, Washington, immobilizing a wide swath of the city's downtown. Police, armed with pepper spray and arrayed in riot gear, worked feverishly to clear the clogged streets, get traffic moving, and usher well-dressed government ministers from around the world into a conference hall. Protesters jeered, chanted, and held hundreds of signs and banners aloft. A radical contingent joined the otherwise peaceful march, and a handful of them began breaking the windows of the chain stores they saw as symbols of global capitalism: Starbucks, Gap, Old Navy.

What aroused such passion in the so-called battle of Seattle was a meeting of the **World Trade Organization (WTO)**, one of the principal institutions pushing unrestrained global trade. Protestors raised a question both fundamental and easily misunderstood: In whose interest was the global economy structured? Many of the Seattle activists took inspiration from the five-point "Declaration for Global Democracy," issued by the human rights organization Global Exchange during the WTO's Seattle meeting. "Global trade and investment," the declaration demanded, "must not be ends in themselves but rather the instruments for achieving equitable and sustainable development, including protections for workers and the environment." This was precisely what the demonstrators charged the WTO with failing to do. The declaration also addressed inequality among nations, calling attention to who benefitted from globalization and who did not.

World Trade Organization (WTO)
International economic body established in 1995 through the General Agreement on Tariffs and Trade to enforce substantial tariff and import quota reductions.

WTO Demonstration, Seattle, 1999 In November 1999, an estimated 50,000 to 100,000 people from many states and foreign nations staged an effective protest at a World Trade Organization (WTO) meeting in Seattle. The goals of the protesters were diffuse; many feared that the trend toward a system of free (capitalist-run) trade would primarily benefit multinational corporations and would hurt both developing nations and the working classes in the industrialized world. Protests have continued at subsequent meetings of the WTO and the World Bank. Hector Mata/AFP/Getty Images.

Globalization: Its Proponents and Its Discontents

Globalization is perhaps one of the most commonly used, yet least understood, concepts in our modern vocabulary. This chapter explores how, while there has long been an international, or global, dimension to trade, migration, and other economic activity, there is nevertheless something distinct about the post–Cold War global order. Economic integration and communications networking have created new opportunities for millions of people. Yet those same processes may not benefit all equally. The following documents offer different perspectives on the broad process called globalization.

1. **Interview with Petra Mata, Mexican immigrant to the United States, 2003.** *An immigrant from a low-wage country who was "insourced," Mata worked as a low-paid garment worker until she lost her job in the United States because it was outsourced — sent abroad to workers paid even less.*

My name is Petra Mata. I was born in Mexico. I have completed no more than the sixth grade in school. In 1969, my husband and I came to the U.S. believing we would find better opportunities for our children and ourselves. We first arrived without documents, then became legal, and finally became citizens. For years I moved from job to job until I was employed in 1976 by the most popular company in the market, Levi Strauss & Company. I earned $9.73 an hour and also had vacation and sick leave. Levi's provided me and my family with a stable situation, and in return I was a loyal employee and worked there for fourteen years.

On January 16, 1990, Levi's closed its plant in San Antonio, Texas, where I had been working, leaving 1,150 workers unemployed, a majority of whom were Mexican-American women. The company moved its factory to Costa Rica. . . .

As a result of being laid off, I personally lost my house, my method of transportation, and the tranquility of my home. My family and I had to face new problems. My husband was forced to look for a second job on top of the one he already had. He worked from seven in the morning to six at night. Our reality was very difficult. At that time, I had not the slightest idea what free trade was or meant. . . .

Our governments make agreements behind closed doors without participation from the working persons who are most affected by these

decisions — decisions that to my knowledge only benefit large corporations and those in positions of power.

2. **iPhone global supply chain, 2011.**

E.U. profits 1.1%
Chinese labor costs 1.8%
Non-Apple U.S. profits 2.4%
Non-Chinese labor costs 3.5%
S. Korea profits 4.7%
Unidentified profits 5.3%
Japan profits .5%
Taiwan profits .5%
Apple profits 58.5%
Cost of materials 21.9%

FIGURE 30.1

3. **Seattle Chapter, National Lawyers Guild, "Bringing in an Undemocratic Institution Brings an Undemocratic Response," 2000.**

Many of the businesses that most promote the WTO [World Trade Organization] and its allied institutions rely on undemocratic practices to promote their business interest. In recent years these policies have included not only monopolistic business practices but also outright interference with local governments. Frequently, to promote the interests of business, a militaristic type of government is either promoted, or even created. The effects these governments and their policies have on the citizenry of these nations are disastrous.

Farms and forests are ruined and denuded. Low cost toxic waste dumps are created near population centers to service skyrocketing debts. . . .

The WTO was nominally chartered as a dispute resolution organization. The problem is it is an organization with no real oversight or accountability, and a process that favors the most powerful corporations.

4. World Trade Organization press release, 2000.

- Extreme poverty is a huge problem. 1.2 billion people survive on less than a dollar a day. A further 1.6 billion, more than a quarter of the world's population, make do with one to two dollars a day.

- To alleviate poverty, developing economies need to grow faster, and the poor need to benefit from this growth. Trade can play an important part in reducing poverty, because it boosts economic growth and the poor tend to benefit from that faster growth.

- The study finds that, in general, living standards in developing countries are not catching up with those in developed countries. But some developing countries are catching up. What distinguishes them is their openness to trade. The countries that are catching up with rich ones are those that are open to trade; and the more open they are, the faster they are converging.

5. Stuart Carlson, political cartoon from the Milwaukee Journal-Sentinel, 2005.

6. Former president Bill Clinton, speech at Guildhall, London, 2006.

I spent a lot of time working on globalization when I was president, coming to terms with the fundamental fact of interdependence that goes far beyond economics: open border, easy travel, easy immigration, free flow of money as well as people, products, and services. I tried to figure out how to maximize the dynamism of global interdependence and still broaden its impact in terms of economics and opportunity. The one thing that I am quite sure of is that interdependence is not a choice, it's not a policy, it is the inevitable condition of our time. So, divorce is not an option. . . .

Therefore, the mission of the moment clearly is to build up the positive and reduce the negative forces of global interdependence in a way that enables us to keep score in the right way. Are people going to be better off, will our children have a better chance, will we be more united than divided?

Sources: (1) From *Shafted: Free Trade and America's Working Poor*, by Christine Ahn (Food First Books, 2003). Reprinted by permission of the Institute for Food and Development Policy, 398 60th Street, Oakland, CA 94618; (2) Kenneth L. Kraemer, Greg Linden, and Jason Dedrick, "Capturing Value in Global Networks: Apple's iPad and iPhone" (Paul Merage School of Business, University of California, Irvine, July 2011). Used by permission of the authors; (3) Seattle Chapter, National Lawyers Guild, "Bringing in an Undemocratic Institution Brings an Undemocratic Response," July 5, 2000, ii, 5; (4) WTO press release, June 13, 2000, quoting a WTO Special Study No. 5, "Trade, Income Disparity, and Poverty," June 2000. Used by permission of the World Trade Organization; (6) collegeofpublicspeaking.co.uk/Clinton-London-2006.html.

ANALYZING THE EVIDENCE

1. Free trade means that goods can move between countries without restriction or taxation (such as tariffs or duties). Compare sources 1, 3, 5, and 6. How do these different sources explain the effects of freer trade across the globe? How would you interpret the WTO's optimism about free trade alongside Petra Mata's personal experience of displacement?

2. How is increased global communication important to the trade relationships described in source 2? According to source 4, what are some other effects associated with the trade relationships shown here?

3. What tension in globalization is the cartoonist in source 5 attempting to capture? What kind of change over time has the cartoonist identified?

PUTTING IT ALL TOGETHER

Based on this chapter's discussion of globalization, and using the above documents, write an essay in which you examine the economic effects of recent global integration. In particular, use your essay to define globalization and to outline some of its potential positive and negative effects.

The Rise of the European Union and China

During the Cold War, the United States and the Soviet Union oversaw what observers called a bipolar world — two powerful poles, one capitalist and the other communist, around which global geopolitics were organized. Since the early 1990s, however, a multipolar world has emerged — with centers of power in Europe, Japan, China, and the United States, along with rising regional powers such as India and Brazil (America in Global Context).

In 1992, the nations of Western Europe created the European Union (EU) and moved toward the creation of a single federal state, somewhat like the United States. By the first decades of the twenty-first century, the European Union included twenty-eight countries and 500 million people — collectively, the third largest population in the world, behind China and India — and accounted for a fifth of all global imports and exports. In 2002, the EU introduced a single currency, the euro, which soon rivaled the dollar and the Japanese yen as a major international currency (Map 30.1). The EU has remained an economic juggernaut and trading rival of the United States, but following the Great Recession of 2007–2008, it pursued a policy of austerity largely unpopular outside of Germany, its dominant economic member. In a stunning referendum in 2016, the voters of the United Kingdom rejected EU membership on the grounds that it compromised national sovereignty and permitted unregulated immigration. Whatever its future, the EU has presented a number of new dilemmas for American officials, especially economic competition and the strength of the EU currency.

China has also presented dilemmas. A vast nation of 1.3 billion people that was the world's fastest-rising economic power in the first decade of the twenty-first century, China *quadrupled* its gross domestic product (GDP) between 2000 and 2008. Economic growth rates during those years were consistently near 10 percent — higher than the United States achieved during its periods of furious economic growth in the 1950s and 1960s. Although still governed by the Communist Party, China embraced capitalism, and its factories produced inexpensive products that Americans eagerly purchased — everything from children's toys and television sets to clothing, household appliances, and video games. To maintain this symbiotic relationship, China deliberately kept its currency weak against the American dollar, ensuring that its exports remained cheap in the United States.

Although this relationship has been beneficial to American consumers in the short run, its implications for the future may be less promising. Two such implications stand out. First, as more and more goods that Americans buy are produced in China, the manufacturing base in the United States continues to shrink, costing jobs and adversely affecting communities. Second, until quite recently China kept its currency low against the dollar primarily by purchasing American debt. China now owns 7 percent of total U.S. debt, making it the largest foreign holder alongside Japan. Many economists believe that it is unwise to allow a single country to wield so much influence over the U.S. currency supply. Should this relationship continue unchanged, Americans may find their manufacturing sector contracting even more severely in the coming decades.

A New Era of Globalization

Americans have long depended on foreign markets to which they export their goods and have long received imported products and immigrants from other countries. But the *intensity* of international exchange has varied over time. The end of the Cold War

Global Trade, 1960–2009

One of the major consequences of economic globalization is an increase in trade among nations. The figures below show imports and exports for four of the world's largest economies.

FIGURE 30.2 Imports, 1960–2009

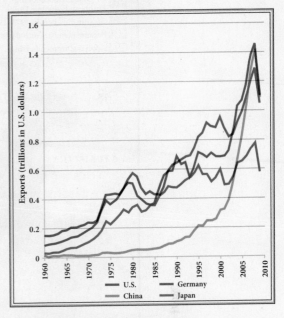

FIGURE 30.3 Exports, 1960–2009

Legislation inspired by nativism slowed the influx of immigrants after 1920, as did the dislocations brought on by economic depression and war in the 1930s and 1940s. Note the high rate of non-European immigration since the 1970s, the result of new eligibility rules in the Immigration and Nationality Act of 1965 (Chapter 27). The dramatic increase since 1980 in the number of migrants from Latin America and Asia reflects American economic prosperity, traditionally a magnet for migrants, and the rapid acceleration of illegal immigration.

QUESTIONS FOR ANALYSIS

1. Notice how U.S. imports rose at roughly the same rate as those of other countries until the 1970s. What accounts for the acceleration of U.S. imports thereafter?
2. China's exports rose spectacularly after the 1990s. Germany increased its exports in this period dramatically as well. What evidence do you see here for increasing competition for the United States in a globalizing economy?

MAP 30.1 Growth of the European Community, 1951–2016
The European Community (EU) began in the 1950s as a loose organization of Western European nations. Over the course of the following decades, it created stronger common institutions, such as the European Parliament in Strasbourg, the EU Commission in Brussels, and the Court of Justice in Luxembourg. With the collapse of communism, the EU expanded to include the nations of Eastern and Central Europe. It now includes twenty-eight nations and over 500 million people. Many states have applied for membership and are awaiting official ascension into the union, while in 2016 the United Kingdom voted to exit the EU.

shattered barriers that had restrained international trade and impeded capitalist development of vast areas of the world. New communications systems — satellites, fiber-optic cables, global positioning networks — were shrinking the world's physical spaces to a degree unimaginable at the beginning of the twentieth century. Perhaps most important, global financial markets became integrated to an unprecedented extent, allowing investment capital to "flow" into and out of nations and around the world in a matter of moments.

International Organizations and Corporations International organizations, many of them created in the wake of World War II, set the rules for capitalism's worldwide expansion: the World Bank, the International Monetary Fund (IMF), and the General Agreement on Tariffs and Trade (GATT). During the final decades of the Cold War, the leading capitalist industrial nations formed the Group of Seven (G7) to manage global economic policy. Russia joined in 1997, creating the **Group of Eight (G8)**. The G8 nations — the United States, Britain, Germany, France, Italy, Japan, Canada, and Russia — largely controlled the major international financial organizations (Russia was suspended from the G8 in 2014). In 1995, GATT evolved into the World Trade Organization (WTO), with nearly 150 participating nations that regulate and formalize trade agreements with member states.

As globalization accelerated, so did the integration of regional economies. To offset the economic clout of the European bloc, in 1993 the United States, Canada, and Mexico signed the **North American Free Trade Agreement (NAFTA)**. This treaty, as ratified by the U.S. Congress, envisioned the eventual creation of a free-trade zone covering all of North America. In East Asia, the capitalist nations of Japan, South Korea, Taiwan, and Singapore consulted on economic policy; as China developed a quasi-capitalist economy and became a major exporter of manufactures, its Communist-led government joined their deliberations.

International organizations set the rules, but globalization was made possible by the proliferation of **multinational corporations** (MNCs). In 1970, there were 7,000 corporations with offices and factories in multiple countries; by 2000, the number had exploded to 63,000. Many of the most powerful MNCs were, and continue to be, based in the United States. Walmart, the biggest American retailer, is also one of the world's largest corporations, with 6,000 stores in other nations and more than $475 billion in sales in 2015. Apple, maker of the iPhone and iPad, grew spectacularly in the 2000s and now has more than $170 billion in annual global sales. The McDonald's restaurant chain had 1,000 outlets outside the United States in 1980; twenty years later, there were nearly 13,000, and "McWorld" had become a popular shorthand term for globalization.

Globalization was driven by more than a quest for new markets. Corporations also sought ever-cheaper sources of labor. Many American MNCs closed their factories in the United States and outsourced manufacturing jobs to plants in Mexico, Eastern Europe, and especially Asia. The athletic sportswear firm Nike was a prime example. By 2005, Nike had established 700 factories worldwide that employed more than 650,000 workers, most of whom received low wages, endured harsh working conditions, and had no health or pension benefits. Highly skilled jobs were outsourced as well.

Financial Deregulation One of the principal differences between this new era of globalization and previous eras has been the opening of national financial and currency markets to investment from around the world. The United States and Britain led the way. Both countries came under the sway of powerful political forces in the 1980s calling for the total deregulation of banks, brokerage houses, investment firms, and financial markets — letting the free market replace government oversight. Together, the United States and Britain led a quiet revolution in which investment markets around the world were gradually set free.

Financial deregulation led to spectacular profits for investors but produced a more fragile, crash-prone global economy. On the profit side, financial-industry profits in the United States rose from less than 10 percent of total business profits in the 1950s to more than 40 percent beginning in the 1990s. But the costs were becoming clear as well: the bankruptcy of the American savings and loan industry in the 1980s; the "lost decade" in Japan in the 1990s; the near bankruptcy of Russia in the late 1990s

Group of Eight (G8)
An international organization of the leading capitalist industrial nations: the United States, Britain, Germany, France, Italy, Japan, Canada, and Russia. The G8 largely control the world's major international financial organizations: the World Bank, the International Monetary Fund (IMF), and the World Trade Organization (WTO). In 2014 Russia was suspended because of its invasion of Crimea.

North American Free Trade Agreement (NAFTA)
A 1993 treaty that eliminated all tariffs and trade barriers among the United States, Canada, and Mexico.

multinational corporations
Corporations with offices and factories in multiple countries, which expanded to find new markets and cheaper sources of labor. Globalization was made possible by the proliferation of these multinational corporations.

and of Argentina in 2001; the 1997 Asian financial crisis, centered in Thailand and Indonesia; and the Great Recession, which affected the entire global economy in 2008. These and other episodes dramatized the extraordinary risks that financial globalization has introduced.

Revolutions in Technology

The technological advances of the 1980s and 1990s changed the character of everyday life for millions of Americans, linking them with a global information and media environment unprecedented in world history. Not since television was introduced to American homes in the years following World War II had technology so profoundly changed the way people lived their lives. Personal computers, cell phones and smartphones, the Internet and the World Wide Web, and other electronic devices and systems altered work, leisure, and access to knowledge in stunning ways. Like unimpeded trade, these advances in communications and personal technologies enhanced globalization.

Advanced Research Projects Agency Network (ARPANET)
A decentralized computer network developed in the late 1960s by the U.S. Department of Defense in conjunction with the Massachusetts Institute of Technology. The Internet grew out of the ARPANET.

World Wide Web
A collection of interlinked computer servers that debuted in 1991, allowing access by millions to documents, pictures, and other materials.

During the 1990s, personal computers, which had emerged in the late 1970s, grew even more significant with the spread of the Internet and the World Wide Web. Like the computer itself, the Internet was the product of military-based research. During the late 1960s, the U.S. Department of Defense, in conjunction with the Massachusetts Institute of Technology, began developing a decentralized computer network, the **Advanced Research Projects Agency Network (ARPANET)**. The Internet, which grew out of the ARPANET, was soon used by government scientists, academic specialists, and military contractors to exchange data, information, and electronic mail (e-mail). By the 1980s, the Internet had spread to universities, businesses, and the general public. The debut in 1991 of the graphics-based **World Wide Web** — a collection of servers that allowed access to millions of documents, pictures, and other materials — enhanced the popular appeal and commercial possibilities of the Internet. By 2011, 78 percent of all Americans and more than two billion people worldwide used the Internet to send messages, view information, and buy and sell products and services.

> **IN YOUR OWN WORDS**   How did globalization redefine the relationship of the United States to the rest of the world after the end of the Cold War?

Politics and Partisanship in a Contentious Era

culture war
A term used by Patrick Buchanan in 1992 to describe a long-standing political struggle, dating to the 1920s, between religious traditionalists and secular liberals. Social issues such as abortion rights and the rights of lesbians and gay men divided these groups.

Standing at the podium at the 1992 Republican National Convention, his supporters cheering by the thousands, Patrick Buchanan did not mince words. Buchanan was a former speechwriter for President Richard Nixon and a White House aide to President Ronald Reagan. Despite having lost the nomination for president, Buchanan still hoped to shape the party's message to voters. This election, he told the audience — including millions watching on television — "is about what we stand for as Americans." Citing Democratic support for abortion rights and the rights of lesbians and gay men, Buchanan claimed there was "a religious war going on in our country for the soul of America." He also called it "a cultural war," and his address became known as the "**culture war**" speech.

Buchanan's war was another name for a long-standing political struggle, dating to the 1920s, between religious traditionalists and secular liberals (Chapter 21). This time, however, Americans struggled over these questions in the long shadow of the 1960s, which had taken on an exaggerated meaning in the nation's politics. Against the backdrop of globalization, American politics in the 1990s and early 2000s careened back and forth between contests over divisive social issues and concern over the nation's economic future.

An Increasingly Plural Society

Exact estimates vary, but demographers predict that at some point between 2040 and 2050 the United States will become a "majority-minority" nation: no single ethnic or racial group will be in the numerical majority. This was already the case in four states by 2010 — California, Texas, Hawaii, and New Mexico — where African Americans, Latinos, and Asians together constituted a majority of the state's residents. As this unmistakable trend became apparent in the 1990s, it fueled renewed debates over ethnic and racial identity and over public policies such as affirmative action.

New Immigrants According to the Census Bureau, the population of the United States grew from 203 million in 1970 to 280 million in 2000. Of that 77-million-person increase, immigrants accounted for 28 million, with documented entrants numbering 21 million and undocumented entrants adding another 7 million (Figure 30.4). As a result, by 2010, 27 percent of California's population was foreign-born, as was 20 percent of New York's and 17 percent each of New Jersey's and Florida's (these percentages

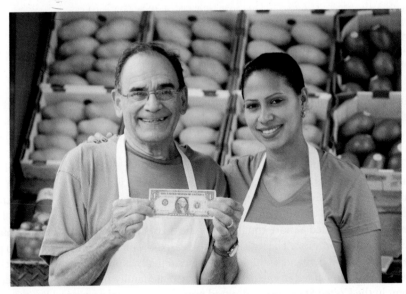

New Immigrants In the early years of the 2000s, more immigrants lived in the United States than at any time since the first decades of the twentieth century. Most came from Asia, Latin America, and Africa. Many, like those pictured here, started small businesses that helped revive the economies of urban and suburban neighborhoods across the country. Blend Images/SuperStock.

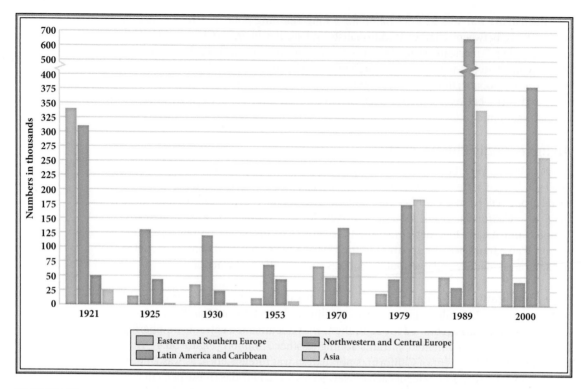

FIGURE 30.4 **American Immigration, 1920–2000**

Legislation inspired by nativism slowed the influx of immigrants after 1920, as did the dislocations brought on by economic depression and war in the 1930s and 1940s. Note the high rate of non-European immigration since the 1970s, the result of new eligibility rules in the Immigration and Nationality Act of 1965 (Chapter 27). The dramatic increase since 1980 in the number of migrants from Latin America and Asia reflects American economic prosperity, traditionally a magnet for migrants, and the rapid acceleration of undocumented immigration.

declined somewhat in the 2010 Census). Relatively few immigrants came from Europe, which had dominated immigration to the United States between 1880 and 1924. The overwhelming majority — some 25 million — now came from Latin America (16 million) and East Asia (9 million) (Map 30.2).

Immigration and Nationality Act
A 1965 law that eliminated the discriminatory 1924 nationality quotas, established a slightly higher total limit on immigration, included provisions to ease the entry of immigrants with skills in high demand, and allowed immediate family members of legal residents in the United States to be admitted outside of the total numerical limit.

This extraordinary inflow of immigrants was the unintended result of the **Immigration and Nationality Act** of 1965, one of the less well-known but most influential pieces of Great Society legislation (Chapter 27). Known as the Hart-Celler Act, the legislation eliminated the 1924 quota system, which had favored Northern Europe. In its place, Congress created a more equal playing field among nations and a slightly higher total limit on immigration. The legislation also eased the entry of immigrants who possessed skills in high demand in the United States. Finally, a provision with far-reaching implications was included in the new law: immediate family members of those legally resident in the United States were admitted outside of the total numerical limit.

American residents from Latin America and the Caribbean were best positioned to take advantage of the family provision. Millions of Mexicans came to the United States to join their families, and U.S. residents from El Salvador and Guatemala — tens

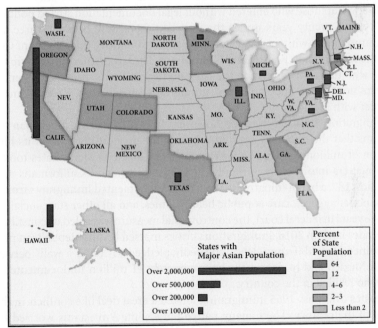

MAP 30.2 Latino and Asian Populations, 2000

In 2000, people of Latin American descent made up more than 11 percent of the American population, and they now outnumber African Americans as the largest minority group. Asian Americans accounted for an additional 4 percent of the population. Demographers predict that by the year 2050 only about half of the U.S. population will be composed of non-Latino whites. Note the high percentage of Latinos and Asians in California and certain other states.

of thousands of whom had arrived seeking sanctuary or asylum during the civil wars of the 1980s — and the Dominican Republic now brought their families to join them. Nationally, there were now more Latinos than African Americans. Many of these immigrants profoundly shaped the emerging global economy by sending substantial portions of their earnings, called remittances, back to family members in their home countries. In 2015, for instance, workers in the United States sent $25 billion to Mexico, a massive remittance flow that constituted Mexico's third largest source of foreign exchange.

Asian immigrants came largely from China, the Philippines, South Korea, India, and Pakistan. In addition, 700,000 refugees came to the United States from Southeast Asia (Vietnam, Laos, and Cambodia) after the Vietnam War. This immigration signaled more than new flows of people into the United States. Throughout much of its history, the United States had oriented itself toward the Atlantic. Indeed, at the end of the nineteenth century, American secretary of state John Hay observed, "The Mediterranean is the ocean of the past; the Atlantic the ocean of the present." He added, presciently, "The Pacific [is] the ocean of the future." By the last decades of the twentieth century, Hay's future had arrived. As immigration from Asia increased, as Japan and China grew more influential economically, and as more and more transnational trade crossed the Pacific, commentators on both sides of the ocean began speaking of the Pacific Rim as an important new region.

Multiculturalism and Its Critics   Most new immigrants arrived under the terms of the 1965 law. But those who entered without legal documentation stirred political controversy. After twenty years under the new law, there were between three and five million immigrants without legal status. In 1986, to remedy this situation, Congress passed the Immigration Reform and Control Act. The law granted citizenship to many of those who had arrived outside the law's numerical limits, provided incentives for employers not to hire undocumented immigrants, and increased surveillance along the border with Mexico.

Immigration critics persisted, however. In 1992, Patrick Buchanan warned Americans that their country was "undergoing the greatest invasion in its history, a migration of millions of illegal aliens a year from Mexico." Many states took immigration matters into their own hands. In 1994, for instance, Californians approved Proposition 187, a ballot initiative that barred undocumented immigrants from public schools, nonemergency care at public health clinics, and all other state social services (after five years in federal court, the controversial measure was ruled unconstitutional). Two decades later, in 2016, immigration's critics massed behind Republican presidential nominee Donald Trump, who repeatedly pledged to "build a wall" between the U.S. and Mexico and to deport the approximately 11 million undocumented immigrants who resided in the country.

To see a portion of Proposition 187, along with other primary sources from this period, see **Sources for America's History**.

Debates over post-1965 immigration looked a great deal like conflicts in the early decades of the century. Then, many native-born white Protestants worried that the largely Jewish and Catholic immigrants from Southern and Eastern Europe, along with African American migrants leaving the South, could not assimilate and threatened the "purity" of the nation. Although the conflicts looked the same, the cultural paradigm had shifted. In the earlier era, the *melting pot* — a term borrowed from the title of a 1908 play — became the metaphor for how American society would accommodate its newfound diversity. Some native-born Americans found solace in the melting-pot concept because it implied that a single "American" culture would predominate. In the 1990s, however, a different concept, **multiculturalism**, emerged to define social diversity. Americans, this concept suggested, were not a single people into whom others melted; rather, they comprised a diverse set of ethnic and racial groups living and working together. A shared set of public values held the multicultural society together, even as different groups maintained unique practices and traditions.

multiculturalism
The promotion of diversity in gender, race, ethnicity, religion, and sexual preference. This political and social policy became increasingly popular in the United States during the 1980s post–civil rights era.

Critics, however, charged that multiculturalism sowed division and conferred preferential treatment on minority groups. Many government policies, as well as a large number of private employers, for instance, continued to support affirmative action programs designed to bring African Americans and Latinos into public- and private-sector jobs and universities in larger numbers. Conservatives argued that such governmental programs were deeply flawed because they promoted "reverse discrimination" against white men and women and resulted in the selection and promotion of less qualified applicants for jobs and educational advancement.

California stood at the center of the debate. In 1995, under pressure from Republican governor Pete Wilson, the regents of the University of California scrapped their entire affirmative action admissions policy. A year later, California voters approved **Proposition 209**, which outlawed affirmative action in state employment and public education. At the height of the 1995 controversy, President Bill Clinton delivered a major speech defending affirmative action. He reminded Americans that Richard Nixon, a Republican president, had endorsed affirmative action, and he concluded by saying the nation should "mend it," not "end it." However, as in the *Bakke* decision of the 1970s (Chapter 28), it was the U.S. Supreme Court that spoke loudest on the subject. In two parallel 2003 cases, the Court invalidated one affirmative action plan at the University of Michigan but allowed racial preference policies that promoted a "diverse" student body. Thus diversity became the law of the land, the constitutionally acceptable basis for affirmative action. The policy had been narrowed but preserved.

Proposition 209
A proposition approved by California voters in 1996 that outlawed affirmative action in state employment and public education.

Additional anxieties about a multicultural nation centered on language. In 1998, Silicon Valley software entrepreneur Ron Unz sponsored a California initiative calling for an end to bilingual education in public schools. Unz argued that bilingual education had failed because it did not adequately prepare Spanish-speaking students to succeed in an English-speaking society. The state's white, Anglo residents largely approved of the measure; most Mexican American, Asian American, and civil rights organizations opposed it. When Unz's measure, Proposition 227, passed with a 61 percent majority, it seemed to confirm the limits of multiculturalism in the nation's most diverse state.

Clashes over "Family Values"

If the promise of a multicultural nation was one contested political issue, another was American families. New Right conservatives charged that the "abrasive experiments of two liberal decades," as a Reagan administration report put it, had eroded respect for marriage and what they had called, since the 1970s, "family values." They pointed to the 40 percent rate of divorce among whites and the nearly 60 percent rate of out-of-wedlock pregnancies among African Americans. To conservatives, there was a wide range of culprits: legislators who enacted liberal divorce laws, funded child care, and allowed welfare payments to unmarried mothers, as well as judges who condoned abortion and banished religious instruction from public schools.

Abortion   Abortion was central to the battles between feminists and religious conservatives and a defining issue between Democrats and Republicans. Feminists who described themselves as prochoice viewed the issue from the perspective of the pregnant woman; they argued that the right to a legal, safe abortion was crucial to her autonomy over her body and life. Conversely, religious conservatives, who pronounced themselves prolife, viewed abortion from the perspective of the unborn fetus and claimed that its rights trumped those of the mother. That is where the debate had stood since the U.S. Supreme Court's 1973 decision in *Roe v. Wade.*

By the 1980s, fundamentalist Protestants had assumed leadership of the antiabortion movement, which became increasingly confrontational and politically powerful. In 1987, the religious activist Randall Terry founded **Operation Rescue**, which mounted protests outside abortion clinics and harassed their staffs and clients. While such vocal protests took shape outside clinics, antiabortion activists also won state laws that limited public funding for abortions, required parental notification before minors could obtain abortions, and mandated waiting periods before any woman could undergo an abortion procedure. Such laws further restricted women's reproductive choices.

Operation Rescue
A movement founded by religious activist Randall Terry in 1987 that mounted protests outside abortion clinics and harassed their staffs and clients.

Gay Rights   The issue of homosexuality stirred equally deep passions. As more gay men and women came out of the closet in the years after Stonewall (Chapter 27), they demanded legal protections from discrimination in housing, education, and employment. Public opinion about these demands varied by region, but by the 1990s, many cities and states had banned discrimination on the basis of sexual orientation. Gay rights groups also sought legal rights for same-sex couples — such as the eligibility for workplace health-care coverage — that were akin to those enjoyed by married heterosexuals. In later years, activists pushed to have transgender persons included in such protections. Many of the most prominent national gay rights organizations, such as the Human Rights Campaign, focused on full marriage equality: a legal recognition of same-sex marriage that was on par with opposite-sex marriages.

The Religious Right had long condemned homosexuality as morally wrong, and public opinion remained sharply divided. In 1992, Colorado voters approved an amendment to the state constitution that prevented local governments from enacting ordinances protecting gays and lesbians — a measure that the Supreme Court subsequently overturned as unconstitutional. That same year, however, Oregon voters defeated a more radical initiative that would have prevented the state from using any funds "to promote, encourage or facilitate" homosexuality. In 1998, Congress entered the fray by enacting the **Defense of Marriage Act**, which allowed states to refuse to recognize gay marriages or civil unions formed in other jurisdictions. Following the lead of Massachusetts, which legalized same-sex marriage in 2004, in the first decades of the twenty-first century, ten states approved gay unions: California, Connecticut, Iowa, Maine, Maryland, New Hampshire, New York, Vermont, Washington, and Rhode Island. Then, in *Obergefell v. Hodges* in 2015, the Supreme Court ruled that states could not prohibit same-sex marriage under the constitution. Remarkably, in a generation, marriage equality had prevailed.

Defense of Marriage Act
A law enacted by Congress in 1998 that allowed states to refuse to recognize gay marriages or civil unions formed in other jurisdictions. The Supreme Court ruled that DOMA was unconstitutional in 2013.

Culture Wars and the Supreme Court Divisive rights issues increasingly came before the U.S. Supreme Court. Abortion led the way, with abortion rights activists challenging the constitutionality of the new state laws limiting access to the procedure. In **Webster v. Reproductive Health Services** (1989), the Supreme Court upheld the authority of state governments to limit the use of public funds and facilities for abortions. Then, in the important case of **Planned Parenthood of Southeastern Pennsylvania v. Casey** (1992), the Court upheld a law requiring a twenty-four-hour waiting period prior to an abortion. Surveying these and other decisions, a reporter suggested that 1989 was "the year the Court turned right," with a conservative majority ready and willing to limit or invalidate liberal legislation and legal precedents.

This observation was only partly correct. The Court was not yet firmly conservative. Although the *Casey* decision upheld certain restrictions on abortions, it affirmed the "essential holding" in *Roe v. Wade* (1973) that women had a constitutional right to control their reproduction. Justice David Souter, appointed to the Court by President George H. W. Bush in 1990, voted with Reagan appointees Sandra Day O'Connor and Anthony Kennedy to uphold *Roe*. Souter, like O'Connor, emerged as an ideologically moderate justice on a range of issues. Moreover, in a landmark decision, **Lawrence v. Texas** (2003), the Supreme Court limited the power of states to prohibit private homosexual activity between consenting adults and, more recently, in *Windsor v. United States* (2013) declared the Defense of Marriage Act unconstitutional. The Court had crept incrementally, rather than lurched, to the right while signaling its continued desire to remain within the broad mainstream of American public opinion, particularly on the issues of reproduction and marriage equality.

Bill Clinton and the New Democrats

The culture wars contributed to a new, divisive partisanship in national politics. Rarely in the twentieth century had the two major parties so adamantly refused to work together. Also rare was the vitriolic rhetoric that politicians used to describe their opponents. The fractious partisanship was filtered through — or, many would argue, created by — the new twenty-four-hour cable news television networks, such as Fox News and CNN. Commentators on these channels, finding that nothing drew viewers like aggressive partisanship, increasingly abandoned their roles as conveyors of information and became entertainers and provocateurs.

That divisiveness was a hallmark of the presidency of William (Bill) Jefferson Clinton. In 1992, Clinton, the governor of Arkansas, styled himself a New Democrat who would bring Reagan Democrats and middle-class voters back to the party. Only forty-six, he was an energetic, ambitious policy wonk — extraordinarily well informed about the details of public policy. To win the Democratic nomination in 1992, Clinton had to survive charges that he embodied the permissive social values conservatives associated with the 1960s: namely, that he dodged the draft to avoid service in Vietnam, smoked marijuana, and cheated repeatedly on his wife. The charges were damaging, but Clinton adroitly talked his way into the presidential nomination: he had charisma and a way with words. When he chose Albert A. Gore, a senator from Tennessee, as his running mate, they became the first baby boom national ticket as well as the nation's first all-southern major-party ticket.

Webster v. Reproductive Health Services
A 1989 Supreme Court ruling that upheld the authority of state governments to limit the use of public funds and facilities for abortions.

Planned Parenthood of Southeastern Pennsylvania v. Casey
A 1992 Supreme Court case that upheld a law requiring a twenty-four-hour waiting period prior to an abortion. Although the decision upheld certain restrictions on abortions, it affirmed the "essential holding" in *Roe v. Wade* (1973) that women had a constitutional right to control their reproduction.

Lawrence v. Texas
A 2003 landmark decision by the Supreme Court that limited the power of states to prohibit private homosexual activity between consenting adults.

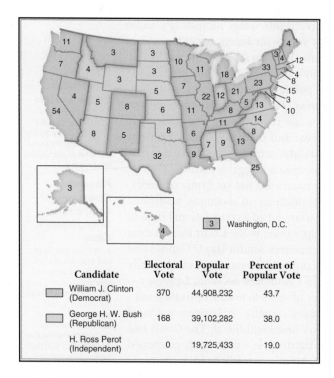

Candidate	Electoral Vote	Popular Vote	Percent of Popular Vote
William J. Clinton (Democrat)	370	44,908,232	43.7
George H. W. Bush (Republican)	168	39,102,282	38.0
H. Ross Perot (Independent)	0	19,725,433	19.0

MAP 30.3 The Presidential Election of 1992
The first national election after the end of the Cold War focused on the economy, which had fallen into a recession in 1991. The first-ever all-southern Democratic ticket of Bill Clinton (Arkansas) and Al Gore (Tennessee) won support across the country but won the election with only 43.7 percent of the popular vote. The Republican candidate, President George H. W. Bush, ran strongly in his home state of Texas and the South, an emerging Republican stronghold. Independent candidate H. Ross Perot, a wealthy technology entrepreneur, polled an impressive 19.0 percent of the popular vote by capitalizing on voter dissatisfaction with the huge federal deficits of the Reagan-Bush administrations.

President George H. W. Bush won renomination over his lone opponent Pat Buchanan. The Democrats mounted an aggressive campaign that focused on Clinton's domestic agenda: he promised a tax cut for the middle class, universal health insurance, and a reduction of the huge Republican budget deficit. It was an audacious combination of traditional social-welfare liberalism and fiscal conservatism. For his part, Bush could not overcome voters' discontent with the weak economy and conservatives' disgust at his tax hikes. He received only 38.0 percent of the popular vote as millions of Republicans cast their ballots for independent businessman Ross Perot, who won more votes (19.0 percent) than any independent candidate since Theodore Roosevelt in 1912. With 43.7 percent of the vote, Clinton won the election (Map 30.3). Among all post–World War II presidents, only Richard Nixon (in 1969) entered the White House with a comparably small share of the national vote.

New Democrats and Public Policy
Clinton tried to steer a middle course through the nation's increasingly divisive partisanship. On his left was the Democratic Party's weakened but still vocal liberal wing. On his right were party moderates influenced by Reagan-era notions of reducing government regulation and the welfare state. Clinton's "third way," as he dubbed it, called for the new president to tailor his proposals to satisfy these two quite different — and often antagonistic — political constituencies. Clinton had notable successes as well as spectacular failures pursuing this course.

The spectacular failure came first. Clinton's most ambitious social-welfare goal was to provide a system of health care that would cover all Americans and reduce the burden of health-care costs on the larger economy. It was an objective that had eluded every Democratic president since Harry Truman. Recognizing the potency of Reagan's attack on "big government," Clinton's health-care task force — led by First Lady Hillary Clinton — proposed a system of "managed competition." Private insurance companies and market forces were to rein in health-care expenditures. The cost of this system would fall heavily on employers, and many smaller businesses campaigned strongly against it. So did the health insurance industry and the American Medical Association, powerful lobbies with considerable influence in Washington.

By mid-1994, Democratic leaders in Congress declared that the Clintons' universal health-care proposal was dead. Forty million Americans, or 15 percent of the population, remained without health insurance coverage.

More successful was Clinton's plan to reduce the budget deficits of the Reagan-Bush presidencies. In 1993, he secured a five-year budget package that would reduce the federal deficit by $500 billion. Republicans unanimously opposed the proposal because it raised taxes on corporations and wealthy individuals, and liberal Democrats complained because it limited social spending. But shared sacrifice led to shared rewards. By 1998, Clinton's fiscal policies had balanced the federal budget and begun to pay down the federal debt — at a rate of $156 billion a year between 1999 and 2001. As fiscal sanity returned to Washington, the economy boomed, thanks in part to the low interest rates stemming from deficit reduction.

The Republican Resurgence The midterm election of 1994 confirmed that the Clinton presidency had not produced an electoral realignment: conservatives still had a working majority. In a well-organized campaign, in which grassroots appeals to the New Right dominated, Republicans gained fifty-two seats in the House of Representatives, giving them a majority for the first time since 1954. They also retook control of the Senate and captured eleven governorships. Leading the Republican charge was Representative Newt Gingrich of Georgia, who revived calls for significant tax cuts, reductions in welfare programs, anticrime initiatives, and cutbacks in federal regulations. These initiatives, which Gingrich promoted under the banner of a "**Contract with America**," had been central components of the conservative-backed Reagan Revolution of the 1980s, but Gingrich believed that under the presidency of George H. W. Bush Republicans had not emphasized them enough.

In response to the massive Democratic losses in 1994, Clinton moved to the right. Claiming in 1996 that "the era of big government is over," he avoided expansive social-welfare proposals for the remainder of his presidency and sought Republican support for a centrist New Democrat program. The signal piece of that program was reforming the welfare system, a measure that saved relatively little money but carried a big ideological message. Many taxpaying Americans believed — with some supporting evidence — that the Aid to Families with Dependent Children (AFDC) program encouraged female recipients to remain on welfare rather than seek employment. In August 1996, the federal government abolished AFDC, achieving a long-standing goal of conservatives when Clinton signed the **Personal Responsibility and Work Opportunity Reconciliation Act**. Liberals were furious with the president.

Clinton's Impeachment Following a relatively easy victory in the 1996 election, Clinton's second term unraveled when a sex scandal led to his impeachment. Clinton denied having had a sexual affair with Monica Lewinsky, a former White House intern, and Republicans concluded that Clinton had committed perjury and obstructed justice and that these actions were grounds for impeachment. Viewed historically, Americans have usually defined "high crimes and misdemeanors" — the constitutional standard for impeachment — as involving a serious abuse of public trust that endangered the republic. In 1998, conservative Republicans favored a much lower standard because of their total opposition to the Clinton presidency. On December 19,

Contract with America
Initiatives by Representative Newt Gingrich of Georgia for significant tax cuts, reductions in welfare programs, anticrime measures, and cutbacks in federal regulations.

Personal Responsibility and Work Opportunity Reconciliation Act
Legislation signed by President Clinton in 1996 that replaced Aid to Families with Dependent Children, the major welfare program dating to the New Deal era, with Temporary Assistance for Needy Families, which provided grants to the states to assist the poor and which limited welfare payments to two years, with a lifetime maximum of five years.

the House of Representatives narrowly approved two articles of impeachment. Only a minority of Americans supported the House's action; according to a CBS News poll, 38 percent favored impeachment while 58 percent opposed it. Chastened by the lack of public support, in early 1999 Republicans in the Senate fell well short of the two-thirds majority they needed to remove the president. But like Andrew Johnson, the only other president to be tried by the Senate, Clinton and the Democratic Party paid a high price for his acquittal. Preoccupied with defending himself, the president was unable to fashion a Democratic alternative to the Republicans' domestic agenda.

Post–Cold War Foreign Policy

Politically weakened after 1994, Clinton believed he could nonetheless make a difference on the international stage. There, post–Cold War developments gave him historic opportunities. The 1990s was a decade of stunning change in Europe and Central Asia. A great arc of newly independent states emerged as the Soviet empire collapsed. The majority of the 142 million people living in the former Soviet states were poor, but the region had a sizable middle class and was rich in natural resources, especially oil and natural gas.

Among the challenges for the United States was the question of whether to support the admission of some of the new states into the North Atlantic Treaty Organization (NATO) (Chapter 24). Many observers believed, with ample justification, that extending the NATO alliance into Eastern Europe, right up to Russia's western border, would damage U.S-Russian relations. However, Czechoslovakia, Poland, and Hungary were also eager to become NATO members — three nations that Stalin had decisively placed in the Soviet sphere of influence at the close of World War II. Clinton encouraged NATO admission for those three countries but stopped short of advocating a broader expansion of the alliance. Nonetheless, by 2010, twelve new nations — most of them in Eastern Europe — had been admitted to the NATO alliance. Nothing symbolized the end of the Cold War more than the fact that ten of those nations were former members of the Warsaw Pact. As some observers had feared, however, NATO's expansion damaged U.S.-Russian relations. Russia's leader since 2000, Vladimir Putin, has made no secret of his disdain for the West's encroachment.

The Breakup of Yugoslavia Two of the new NATO states, Slovenia and Croatia, emerged from an intractable set of conflicts that led to the dissolution of the communist nation of Yugoslavia. In 1992, the heavily Muslim province of Bosnia-Herzegovina declared its independence, but its substantial Serbian population refused to live in a Muslim-run multiethnic state. Slobodan Milosevic, an uncompromising Serbian nationalist, launched a ruthless campaign of "ethnic cleansing" to create a Serbian state. In November 1995, Clinton organized a NATO-led bombing campaign and peacekeeping effort, backed by 20,000 American troops, that ended the Serbs' vicious expansionist drive. Four years later, a new crisis emerged in Kosovo, another province of the Serbian-dominated Federal Republic of Yugoslavia. Again led by the United States, NATO intervened with air strikes and military forces to preserve Kosovo's autonomy. By 2008, seven independent nations had emerged from the wreckage of Yugoslavia.

America and the Middle East No post–Cold War development proved more challenging than the emergence of radical Islamic movements in the Middle East. Muslim nations there had a long list of grievances against the West. Colonialism — both British and French — in the early decades of the twentieth century had been thoroughly exploitive. A U.S.-sponsored overthrow of Iran's government in 1953 — and twenty-five years of American support for the Iranian shah — was also a sore point. America's support for Israel in the 1967 Six-Day War and the 1973 Yom Kippur War and its near-unconditional backing of Israel in the 1980s were particularly galling to Muslims. The region's religious and secular moderates complained about these injustices, but many of them had political and economic ties to the West that constrained their criticism.

This situation left an opening for radical Islamic fundamentalists to build a movement based on fanatical opposition to Western imperialism and consumer culture. These groups interpreted the American presence in Saudi Arabia as signaling new U.S. colonial ambitions in the region. Clinton had inherited from President George H. W. Bush a defeated Iraq and a sizable military force — about 4,000 Air Force personnel — in Saudi Arabia. Clinton also enforced a UN-sanctioned embargo on trade with Iraq, a policy designed to constrain Saddam Hussein's military that ultimately denied crucial goods to the civilian population. Spurred by their opposition to U.S. intervention in the region, Muslim fundamentalists soon began targeting Americans. In 1993, radical Muslim immigrants set off a bomb beneath the World Trade Center in New York City, killing six people and injuring more than a thousand. Terrorists used truck bombs to blow up U.S. embassies in Kenya and Tanzania in 1998, and they bombed the USS *Cole* in the Yemeni port of Aden in 2000.

The Clinton administration knew these attacks were the work of Al Qaeda, a network of radical Islamic terrorists organized by the wealthy Saudi exile Osama bin Laden. In February 1998, bin Laden had issued a call for a global struggle — a "Jihad against Jews and Crusaders," in which it was said to be the duty of every Muslim to kill Americans and their allies. After the embassy attacks, Clinton ordered air strikes on Al Qaeda bases in Afghanistan, where an estimated 15,000 operatives had been trained since 1990. The strikes failed to disrupt this growing terrorist network, and when Clinton left office, the Central Intelligence Agency (CIA), the State Department, and the Pentagon were well aware of the potential threat posed by bin Laden's followers. That was where things stood on September 10, 2001.

IN YOUR OWN WORDS What were the sources of domestic division in the United States after 1988, and how did they reshape the political landscape?

Into a New Century

In the second decade of the new century, Americans can reflect on three significant developments that have profoundly shaped their own day: the long war in the Middle East that began with the terrorist attack on September 11, 2001; the election of the nation's first African American president in 2008, Barack Obama (reelected in 2012); and the election of the brazenly contrarian businessman and television personality,

Donald Trump, as president on November 8, 2016. Too little time has passed for us to assess exactly how these events will help to define the twenty-first century, but all three have indelibly marked our present.

The Ascendance of George W. Bush

The 2000 presidential election briefly offered the promise of a break with the intense partisanship of the final Clinton years. The Republican nominee, George W. Bush, the son of President George H. W. Bush, cast himself as a "uniter, not a divider" against his opponent, Al Gore, Clinton's vice president. The election of 2000 would join those of 1876 and 1960 as the closest and most contested in American history. Gore won the popular vote, amassing 50.9 million votes to Bush's 50.4 million, but fell short in the electoral college, 267 to 271.

Late on election night, the vote tally in Florida gave Bush the narrowest of victories. As was their legal prerogative, the Democrats demanded hand recounts in several counties. A month of tumult followed, until the U.S. Supreme Court, splitting directly along conservative-liberal lines, ordered the recount stopped and let Bush's victory stand. Recounting ballots without a consistent standard to determine "voter intent," the Court reasoned, violated the rights of Floridian voters under the Fourteenth Amendment's equal protection clause. As if acknowledging the frailty of this argument, the Court declared that *Bush v. Gore* was not to be regarded as precedent. But in a dissenting opinion, Justice John Paul Stevens warned that the transparently partisan decision undermined "the Nation's confidence in the judge as an impartial guardian of the rule of law."

Although Bush had positioned himself as a moderate, countertendencies drove his administration. His vice president, the uncompromising conservative Richard (Dick) Cheney, became, with Bush's consent, virtually a copresident. Bush also brought into the administration his campaign advisor, Karl Rove, who argued that a permanent Republican majority could be built on the party's conservative base. On Capitol Hill, Rove's hard line was reinforced by Tom DeLay, the House majority leader, who in 1995 had declared "all-out war" on the Democrats. To win that war, DeLay pushed congressional Republicans to endorse a fierce partisanship. The Senate, although more collegial, went through a similar hardening process. After 2002, with Republicans in control of both Congress and the White House, bipartisan lawmaking came to an end.

Economic Growth and Tax Relief Act
Legislation introduced by President George W. Bush and passed by Congress in 2001 that slashed income tax rates, extended the earned income credit for the poor, and marked the estate tax to be phased out by 2010.

Tax Cuts The domestic issue that most engaged President Bush, as it had Ronald Reagan, was taxes. Bush's **Economic Growth and Tax Relief Act** of 2001 had something for everyone. It slashed income tax rates, extended the earned income credit for the poor, and marked the estate tax to be phased out by 2010. A second round of cuts in 2003 targeted dividend income and capital gains. Bush's signature cuts — those favoring big estates and well-to-do owners of stocks and bonds — skewed the distribution of tax benefits upward (Table 30.1) and pushed far beyond those of any other postwar president, even Reagan.

Critics warned that such massive tax cuts would plunge the federal government into debt. By 2006, federal expenditures had jumped 33 percent, at a faster clip than under any president since Lyndon Johnson. Huge increases in health-care costs were the main culprit. Two of the largest federal programs, Medicare and Medicaid — health

TABLE 30.1						
Impact of the Bush Tax Cuts, 2001–2003						
Income in 2003	**Taxpayers**	**Gross Income**	**Total Tax Cut**	**% Change in Tax Bill**	**Tax Bill**	**Tax Rate**
Less than $50,000	92,093,452	$19,521	$435	−48%	$474	2%
$50,000 to 100,000	26,915,091	70,096	1,656	−21	6,417	9
$100,000 to 200,000	8,878,643	131,797	3,625	−17	18,281	14
$200,000 to 500,000	1,999,061	288,296	7,088	−10	60,464	21
$500,000 to 1,000,000	356,140	677,294	22,479	−12	169,074	25
$1,000,000 to 10,000,000	175,157	2,146,100	84,666	−13	554,286	26
$10,000,000 or more	6,126	25,975,532	1,019,369	−15	5,780,926	22

SOURCE: *New York Times*, April 5, 2006.

care for the elderly and the poor, respectively — could not contain runaway medical costs. Midway through Bush's second term, the national debt stood at over $8 trillion — much of it owned by foreign investors, who also financed the nation's huge trade deficit. On top of that, staggering Social Security and Medicare obligations were beginning to come due for retiring baby boomers, burdens the tax cuts passed on to future generations.

September 11, 2001 As a candidate in 2000, George W. Bush had said little about foreign policy. He had assumed that his administration would rise or fall on his domestic program. But nine months into his presidency, an altogether different political scenario unfolded. On a sunny September morning, nineteen Al Qaeda terrorists hijacked four commercial jets and flew two of them into New York City's World Trade Center, destroying its twin towers and killing nearly 2,900 people. A third plane crashed into the Pentagon, near Washington, D.C. The fourth, presumably headed for the White House or possibly the U.S. Capitol, crashed in Pennsylvania when the passengers fought back and thwarted the hijackers. As an outburst of patriotism swept the United States in the wake of the September 11 attacks, George W. Bush proclaimed a "war on terror" and vowed to carry the battle to Al Qaeda.

Operating out of Afghanistan, where they had been harbored by the fundamentalist Taliban regime, the elusive Al Qaeda briefly offered a clear target. In October 2001, while Afghani allies carried the ground war, American planes attacked the enemy. By early 2002, this lethal combination had ousted the Taliban, destroyed Al Qaeda's training camps, and killed or captured many of its operatives. However, the big prize, Al Qaeda leader Osama bin Laden, had retreated to a mountain hideout. Inexplicably, U.S. forces failed to press the attack, and bin Laden escaped over the border into Pakistan.

The Invasion of Iraq On the domestic side, Bush declared the terrorist threat too big to be contained by ordinary law-enforcement means. He wanted the government's

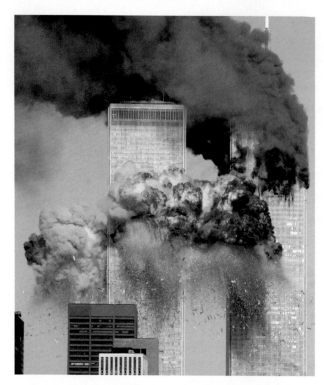

September 11, 2001 Photographers at the scene after a plane crashed into the north tower of New York City's World Trade Center on September 11 found themselves recording a defining moment in the nation's history. When a second airliner approached and then slammed into the building's south tower at 9:03 A.M., the nation knew this was no accident. The United States was under attack. Of the nearly 2,900 people killed on that day, 2,600 died at the World Trade Center. Spencer Platt/Getty Images.

USA PATRIOT Act
A 2001 law that gave the government new powers to monitor suspected terrorists and their associates, including the ability to access personal information.

powers of domestic surveillance placed on a wartime footing. With little debate, in 2001 Congress passed the **USA PATRIOT Act**, granting the administration sweeping authority to monitor citizens and apprehend suspected terrorists. On the international front, Bush used the war on terror as the premise for a new policy of preventive war. Under international law, only an imminent threat justified a nation's right to strike first, but with what became known as the Bush doctrine, the United States lowered the bar. It reserved for itself the right to act in "anticipatory self-defense." In 2002, President Bush singled out Iran, North Korea, and Iraq — "an axis of evil" — as the targeted states.

Of the three, Iraq was the preferred mark. Officials in the Pentagon regarded Iraq as unfinished business, left over from the Gulf War of 1991. More grandly, Bush administration officials saw in Iraq an opportunity to fulfill what they believed to be America's mission to democratize the world. Iraqis, they contended, would abandon the tyrant Saddam Hussein and embrace democracy if given the chance. The democratizing effect would spread across the Middle East, toppling or reforming other unpopular Arab regimes and stabilizing the region. That, in turn, would secure the Middle East's oil supply, whose fragility Hussein's 1990 invasion of Kuwait had made all too clear. It was the oil, in the end, that was of vital interest to the United States (Map 30.4).

None of these considerations, either singly or together, met Bush's declared threshold for preventive war. So the president reluctantly acceded to the demand by anxious European allies that the United States go to the UN Security Council, which demanded that Saddam Hussein allow the return of the UN weapons inspectors expelled in 1998. Hussein surprisingly agreed. Anxious to invade Iraq for its own reasons, the Bush administration insisted that Hussein's regime constituted a "grave and gathering danger" and ignored further UN deliberations. American forces invaded in March 2003 in what newspapers in France, which refused to cooperate with its longtime ally, called simply "Bush's war." America's one major ally in the rush to war was Great Britain. Relations with France and Germany became poisonous. Even neighboring Mexico and Canada condemned the invasion, and Turkey, a key military ally, refused transit permission, ruining the army's plan for a northern thrust into Iraq. As for the Arab world, it exploded in anti-American demonstrations.

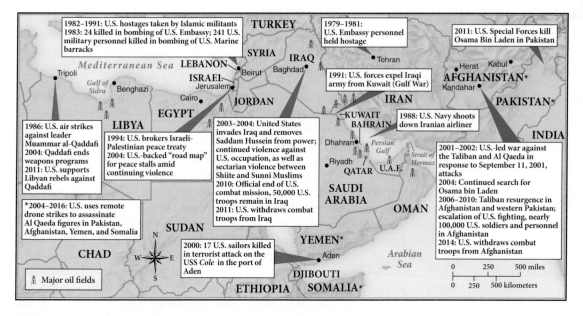

MAP 30.4 U.S. Involvement in the Middle East, 1979–2016
The United States has long played an active role in the Middle East, driven by the strategic importance of that region and, most important, by America's need to ensure a reliable supply of oil from the Persian Gulf states. This map shows the highlights of that troubled involvement, from the Tehran embassy hostage taking in 1979 to the invasion and occupation of both Iraq and Afghanistan. President Obama withdrew most combat troops from Iraq in 2011 and from Afghanistan in 2014, but U.S. involvement in the region, in the form of drone strikes, material assistance to various states and factions, and other forms of diplomatic and military assistance continues.

Within three weeks, American troops had taken the Iraqi capital. The regime collapsed, and its leaders went into hiding (Saddam Hussein was captured nine months later). But despite meticulous military planning, the Pentagon had made no provision for postconflict operations. The war shattered the infrastructure of Iraq's cities, leaving them without reliable supplies of electricity and water. In the midst of this turmoil, an insurgency began, sparked by Sunni Muslims, a minority religious faction who had nonetheless dominated Iraq under Hussein's Baathist regime. Iraq's Shiite majority, long oppressed by Hussein, at first welcomed the Americans, but extremist Shiite elements soon turned hostile, and U.S. forces found themselves under fire from both sides. With the borders unguarded, Al Qaeda supporters flocked in from all over the Middle East, eager to do battle with the infidel Americans.

Blinded by their own nationalism, dominant nations tend to underestimate the strength of religious and national identities in other people. Although it was hard for Bush administration officials to believe, Iraqis of all stripes viewed the U.S. forces as invaders. Moreover, in a war against insurgents, no occupation force comes out with clean hands. In 2004 in Iraq, that painful truth burst forth graphically in photographs showing American guards at Baghdad's **Abu Ghraib prison** abusing and torturing suspected insurgents. The ghastly images shocked the world. For Muslims, they offered final proof of American treachery. At that low point, in 2004, the United States had

Abu Ghraib prison
A prison just outside Baghdad, Iraq, where American guards were photographed during the Iraq War abusing and torturing suspected insurgents.

spent upward of $100 billion. More than 1,000 American soldiers had died, and 10,000 others had been wounded, many maimed for life. But if the United States pulled out, Iraq would descend into chaos. So, as Bush took to saying, the United States had to "stay the course."

The 2004 Election As the 2004 presidential election approached, Karl Rove, Bush's top advisor, theorized that stirring the culture wars and emphasizing patriotism and Bush's war on terror would mobilize conservatives to vote for Bush. Rove encouraged activists to place antigay initiatives on the ballot in key states to draw conservative voters to the polls; in all, eleven states would pass ballot initiatives that wrote bans on gay marriage equality into state constitutions that year. The Democratic nominee, Senator John Kerry of Massachusetts, was a Vietnam hero, twice wounded and decorated for bravery — in contrast to the president, who had spent the Vietnam years in the Texas Air National Guard. But when Kerry returned from service in Vietnam, he had joined the antiwar group Vietnam Veterans Against the War and in 1971 had delivered a blistering critique of the war to the Senate Armed Services Committee. In the logic of the culture wars, this made him vulnerable to charges of being weak and unpatriotic. Nearly 60 percent of eligible voters — the highest percentage since 1968 — went to the polls. Bush beat Kerry, with 286 electoral votes to Kerry's 252. In exit polls, Bush did well among voters for whom moral "values" and national security were top concerns. Voters told interviewers that Bush, a wartime president, made them feel "safer."

Violence Abroad and Economic Collapse at Home

George Bush's second term was defined by crisis management. In 2005, Hurricane Katrina — one of the deadliest hurricanes in the nation's history — devastated New Orleans. Chaos ensued as floodwaters breached earthen barricades surrounding the city. Many residents remained without food, drinking water, or shelter for days following the storm, and deaths mounted — the final death toll stood at more than 2,000. Initial emergency responses to the catastrophe by federal and local authorities were uncoordinated and inadequate. Because the hardest-hit parts of the city were poor and African American, Katrina had revealed the poverty and vulnerability, alongside decaying and vulnerable infrastructure, at the heart of American cities.

The run of crises did not abate after Katrina. Increasing violence and a rising insurgency in Iraq made the war there even more unpopular in the United States. In 2007, changes in U.S. military strategy helped quell some of the worst violence, but the war dragged into its fifth and sixth years under Bush. Then, in 2008, the American economy began to stumble. By the fall, the Dow Jones Industrial Average had lost half its total value, and major banks, insurance companies, and financial institutions were on the verge of collapse. The entire automobile industry was near bankruptcy. Millions of Americans lost their jobs, and the unemployment rate surged to 10 percent. Housing prices dropped by as much as 40 percent in some parts of the country, and millions of Americans defaulted on their mortgages. The United States had entered the worst economic recession since the 1930s, what soon became known as the Great Recession — technically, the recession had begun in 2007, but its major effects were not felt until the fall of 2008.

The 2008 presidential election took shape in that perilous context. In a historically remarkable primary season, the Democratic nomination was contested between the first woman and the first African American to be viable presidential contenders, Hillary R. Clinton and Barack H. Obama. In a close-fought contest, Obama emerged by early summer as the nominee.

Meanwhile, the Bush administration confronted an economy in free fall. In September, less than two months before the election, Secretary of the Treasury Henry Paulson urged Congress to pass the Emergency Economic Stabilization Act, commonly referred to as the bailout of the financial sector. Passed in early October, the act dedicated $700 billion to rescuing many of the nation's largest banks and brokerage houses. Between Congress's actions and the independent efforts of the Treasury Department and the Federal Reserve, the U.S. government invested close to $1 trillion in saving the nation's financial system.

Reform and Stalemate in the Obama Years

During his campaign for the presidency against Republican senator John McCain, Barack Obama, a Democratic senator from Illinois, established himself as a unique figure in American politics. The son of an African immigrant-student and a young white woman from Kansas, Obama was raised in Hawaii and Indonesia, and he easily connected with an increasingly multiracial America (Interpretations). A generation younger than Bill Clinton and George W. Bush, Obama (born in 1961) seemed at once a product of the 1960s, especially civil rights gains, and outside its heated conflicts. He took the oath of office of the presidency on January 21, 2009, amid the deepest economic recession since the Great Depression and with the United States mired in two wars in the Middle East. From the podium, the new president recognized the crises and, striking an optimistic tone, encouraged the country to "begin again the work of remaking America."

"Remaking America" A nation that a mere two generations ago would not allow black Americans to dine with white Americans had elected a black man to the highest office. Obama himself was less taken with this historic accomplishment — which was also part of his deliberate strategy to downplay race — than with developing a plan to deal with the nation's innumerable challenges, at home and abroad. With explicit comparisons to Franklin Roosevelt, Obama used the "first hundred days" of his presidency to lay out an ambitious agenda: an economic stimulus package of federal spending to invigorate the economy; plans to draw down the war in Iraq and refocus American military efforts in Afghanistan; a reform of the nation's health insurance system; and new federal laws to regulate Wall Street.

Remarkably, the president accomplished much of that agenda. The Democratic-controlled Congress elected alongside Obama passed the **American Recovery and Reinvestment Act**, an economic stimulus bill that provided $787 billion to state and local governments — one of the largest single packages of government spending in American history. Congress next passed the Wall Street Reform and Consumer Protection Act, a complex law that added new regulations limiting the financial industry and new consumer protections. The president's signal accomplishment, however, was the first major reform of the nation's health-care system since the introduction of Medicare in 1965: the **Patient Protection and Affordable Care Act**, signed into law by Obama on March 23, 2010. Political opposition and the powerful lobbying of the private health insurance industry ensured that the new law contained enough compromises that few could predict its long-term impact.

American Recovery and Reinvestment Act
An economic stimulus bill passed in 2009, in response to the Great Recession, that provided $787 billion to state and local governments for schools, hospitals, and transportation projects. It was one of the largest single packages of government spending in American history.

Patient Protection and Affordable Care Act
Sweeping 2010 health-care reform bill championed by President Obama that established nearly universal health insurance by providing subsidies and compelling larger businesses to offer coverage to employees.

How Should Historians Write the History of Current Events?

At what point does the present become the past? Today's headlines become the primary sources for the historian of the future, but what about the historian of today? Is it advisable for historians to interpret current events? This final chapter, which brings America's history to the 2017 presidential inauguration, includes events in the living memory and experience of everyone writing and reading these words. What do we say about our own time? What historical interpretation is possible?

In the excerpts below, two scholars, Thomas J. Sugrue and Michael Eric Dyson, attempt historical interpretations of Barack Obama's presidency. Specifically, both scholars offer an assessment of President Obama by placing him and his presidency in the context of America's racial history. How does their historical lens shape their perspective of America's most recent past?

THOMAS J. SUGRUE

SOURCE: Thomas J. Sugrue, *Not Even Past: Barack Obama and the Burden of Race* (Princeton: Princeton University Press, 2010), 54–55.

Situating himself in a current of civil rights history that emphasized its radical currents would be political suicide. But there was something deeper than simple political instrumentality at work. During his journey through the polarized racial world of late twentieth-century America, Obama discovered his calling . . . to overcome the acrimonious history of racial polarization — whether it be black power or the culture wars . . . to act on the understanding that such polarization was anathema to national unity. . . . By the time that Obama was inaugurated president, he had recast himself as an agent of national unification, one who could finally bring to fruition the few lingering, unmet promises of the civil rights movement. . . . From the cacophony of the recent past, from its messiness and tumult, Obama extracts a powerful, reassuring message of progress . . . both true and mythological at the same time. Thus Barack Obama's own quest for identity and the distinctive history of the black freedom struggle, of urban politics, of civil rights and

black power, became the American story. What Obama called "my story" became "our story."

MICHAEL ERIC DYSON

SOURCE: Michael Eric Dyson, *The Black Presidency: Barack Obama and the Politics of Race in America* (Boston: Houghton Mifflin Harcourt, 2016), 156.

It is understandable that Obama prefers being seen as the black *president* rather than the *black* president. But his refusal to address race except when he has no choice — a kind of racial procrastination — leaves him little control of the conversation. When he is boxed into a racial corner, often as a result of black social unrest sparked by claims of police brutality, Obama has been mostly uninspiring: he has warned (black) citizens to obey the law and affirmed the status quo. Yet Obama energetically peppers his words to blacks with talk of responsibility in one public scolding after another. When Obama upbraids black folks while barely mentioning the flaws of white America, he leaves the impression that race is the concern solely of black people, and that blackness is full of pathology.

QUESTIONS FOR ANALYSIS

1. What tone does each of these scholars adopt in assessing Obama's approach to issues of race in America?
2. Name two ways in which Sugrue and Dyson diverge in their assessment of Obama's relationship to race during his presidency.
3. From your reading of Chapter 30's discussion of Obama's two terms in office, which assessment — Sugrue's or Dyson's — is more convincing and why?

Following the legislative accomplishments of his first two years in office, President Obama faced a divided Congress. During the fierce debate over health-care reform, a coalition of far-right groups, known collectively as the Tea Party, emerged to catalyze Republican opposition to the president. Democrats lost their majority in the House of Representatives in 2010 and in the Senate in 2014. With **Tea Party**–backed Republicans leading the way, the GOP refused to consider virtually any Democratic legislation. In the face of the legislative stalemate, Obama turned to executive authority to advance his broader, cautiously liberal, agenda. In 2011, for instance, the president ordered that gay men and lesbians be allowed to serve openly in the armed forces, a reversal of decades of military policy. He made two appointments to the Supreme Court: Sonia Sotomayor in 2009, the first Latina to serve on the high court, and Elena Kagan in 2010. Both are committed liberals. And in 2015, Obama directed the Environmental Protection Agency (EPA) to adopt the Clean Power Plan to combat greenhouse gases (an action blocked by a Supreme Court stay and further limited by President Trump).

Tea Party
A set of far-right opposition groups that emerged during President Obama's first term and gave voice to the extreme individualism and antigovernment sentiment traditionally associated with right-wing movements in the United States.

Climate Change Obama took the executive action on climate change because of congressional inaction on that issue. A scientific consensus has existed for decades that the production of energy through the burning of carbon-based substances (especially petroleum and coal) increases the presence of greenhouse gases in the atmosphere, warming the earth. Increasing temperatures have begun to produce dramatically new weather patterns and promise rising sea levels in this century, developments that threaten agriculture, the global distributions of plant and animal life, and whole cities and regions at or near the current sea level. How to halt, or at least mitigate, climate change has been one of the most pressing public policy issues of the twenty-first century.

Arriving at the scientific consensus on climate change has proven easier than developing government policies to address it. This has been especially true in the United States, where oil company lobbyists, defenders of free-market capitalism, and conservatives who deny global warming altogether have been instrumental in blocking action. For instance, the United States is not a signatory to the major international treaty — the so-called Kyoto Protocol — designed to reduce carbon emissions. Legislative proposals have not fared better. Cap-and-trade legislation, so named because it places a cap on individual polluters' emissions but allows those companies to trade for more emission allowances from low polluters, has stalled in Congress. Another proposal, a tax on carbon emissions, has likewise gained little political support. There is little doubt, however, that global climate change, and the role of the United States in both causing and mitigating it, will remain among the most critical questions of the next decades.

War and Instability in the Middle East Even as he pursued an ambitious domestic agenda, Obama faced two wars in the Middle East that he inherited from his predecessor. Determined to end American occupation of Iraq, in 2010 the president began to draw down troops stationed there, and the last convoy of U.S. soldiers departed in late 2011. The nine-year war in Iraq, begun to find alleged weapons of mass destruction, had followed a long and bloody arc to its end. That same year, in May, U.S. Special Forces found and killed Osama bin Laden in Pakistan, where he had been hiding for many years, an action for which the president won a great deal of praise domestically. More controversial has been the president's use of "drone" strikes to assassinate Al Qaeda leaders and other U.S. enemies in Afghanistan, Pakistan, and elsewhere in the region.

Whatever the nature of the president's efforts, disengaging from Afghanistan proved difficult. Early in his first term, and despite his campaign promise to end the war there, the president ordered an additional 30,000 American troops to prevent further Taliban victories. The surge temporarily stabilized the country, but securing long-term political and military stability eluded Obama in the long run, and he left office in 2017 having been unable to withdraw the remaining 8,000 to 10,000 U.S. troops stationed there.

Meanwhile, a host of events in the Middle East deepened the region's volatility. In late 2010, a series of multicountry demonstrations and protests, dubbed the Arab Spring, toppled autocratic rulers in Egypt, Tunisia, Libya, and Yemen. Obama and the U.S. State Department cautiously supported the uprisings but were unable to significantly shape events thereafter. In Syria, for instance, the Arab Spring insurgency produced a brutal civil war that has resulted in hundreds of thousands of deaths, nearly five million refugees, and the internal displacement of nearly six million Syrian citizens. Syria has also been plagued by the Islamic State, an ultraviolent, fundamentalist Sunni group that emerged in the chaos of war-torn Iraq. It has conquered territory and sown instability and fear among populations across northern Iraq and northern Syria since 2011. Between 2001, when the war against the Taliban began in Afghanistan, and 2016, when the Syrian refugee crisis and the Islamic State dominated headlines, the United States demonstrated that it could make war far more readily and easily than it could control the events that followed.

Domestic Crisis   Much as in the era of the Vietnam War, violence abroad came to have an eerie echo at home. African Americans have long endured, and have long resisted, police brutality, in cycles of pain and protest dating to the nineteenth century. One such cycle began in 2014 with the killing of an unarmed black teenager named Michael Brown in Ferguson, Missouri. Weeks of demonstrations followed, as black activists, joined by many white and Latino supporters, converged on Ferguson from around the country. Many groups and leaders articulated calls for police reform and a renewed struggle against racism.

Amid this increased activism, an organization called Black Lives Matter (BLM) emerged at the fore of a broader movement. Formed two years earlier, in response to the 2012 killing of Trayvon Martin, an unarmed black teenager, by a civilian neighborhood watch captain, BLM put forth a comprehensive agenda of police reform, economic justice, political empowerment, and, echoing Black Power activists from the 1960s, black community control. Between 2014 and 2016, BLM and other activists staged protests in more than one hundred American cities, as the shooting and/or killing of black men by police came to the public's attention through cell phone, surveillance, and police videos. Many activists stressed that the ongoing crisis disproved the notion that electing a black president represented a fundamental transformation in American racial history. Indeed, many activists claimed that the Tea Party's opposition to the president was racially charged. Evidence for such a claim could be found in the appearance of "go back to Kenya" signs directed at Obama at Tea Party rallies or in the so-called "birther" movement, which questioned the president's U.S. citizenship.

The 2016 Election From one political vantage point, President Obama and the Democratic Party looked like the beneficiaries of an electoral shift in a liberal direction. Between 1992 and 2012, Democrats won the popular vote in five of the six presidential elections, and in 2008 Obama won a greater share of the popular vote (53 percent) than any Democratic nominee since Lyndon Johnson in 1964. He won the support of 93 percent of African Americans, 71 percent of Hispanics, 73 percent of Asian Americans, 55 percent of women, and 60 percent of Americans under the age of thirty. His coalition was multiracial, heavily female, and young.

That coalition appears strong enough to win popular majorities for Democratic presidential nominees into the foreseeable future. Yet the nation's peculiar constitutional method of awarding the presidency through the electoral college allows for the possibility, as in 2000 and again in 2016, that a candidate with the lower national vote total can win. Moreover, the Constitution's awarding of two senators to each state regardless of population means that a fiercely conservative state with a small population, like North Dakota, has as much influence in the U.S. Senate as a fiercely liberal state with a massive population, like California. In that context, the Democratic coalition has struggled to sustain Senate majorities. Furthermore, changes in House districts after the 2010 Census have further disadvantaged Democrats (Table 30.2). In 2012, Democratic candidates for the House of Representatives won more votes nationally than Republican candidates did (59.6 million to 58.2 million), but Republicans still won a majority of seats. Thus, heading into the 2016 election, the long-term fate of the liberal Obama coalition remained unclear.

Few historians can predict the future of the Obama coalition, but in the short term the outcome of the 2016 presidential election proved to be a stunning surprise to many Americans. First, the presidential campaign itself looked nothing like recent contests. The Republican nominee was Donald Trump, a political novice who had never held elective office and who defeated a series of more experienced, and traditionally conservative, politicians for the Republican nomination. A Manhattan real estate developer and symbol of the "rich and famous" celebrity culture of the 1980s, Trump was primarily known for building a series of failed casinos in Atlantic City, New Jersey, and for starring in the reality television show *The Apprentice*. As a candidate, Trump secured ample media coverage with disparaging remarks about immigrants and his oft-recited promise to "build a wall" along the U.S.-Mexico border, alongside other nationalist slogans. His speeches, impromptu and off-the-cuff, railed against globalization, President Obama, the media, the political establishment, and the Democratic nominee, Hillary Clinton.

Clinton had secured the Democratic nomination after a spirited primary campaign against the social-democratic Bernie Sanders, a U.S. senator from Vermont. The first woman to lead a major-party ticket for U.S. president, Clinton boasted a resume with decades of high-level political service, including eight years as First Lady, eight years as a U.S. senator, and four years as secretary of state. In the general election campaign against Trump, Clinton emphasized this experience and proposed detailed plans of action on a wide range of issues, including climate change, criminal justice reform, workers' rights, early childhood education, tax reform, the nation's deteriorating infrastructure, and many more. For its part, the Trump campaign issued no specific proposals and instead ran a populist campaign that featured few substantive

TABLE 30.2

Political Realignment: Congressional Seats

As Table 28.1 (p. 935) demonstrated, between 1940 and 1990 the Rust Belt states lost population and political representation in Congress, and the Sunbelt states gained both. That trend continued between 1990 and 2010. Geographic shifts in population, especially continued population growth in California, Texas, and Florida, shaped which parts of the country had the loudest voice in Congress. In 1940, the major industrial states accounted for 45 percent of congressional seats. By 2010, they accounted for only 31 percent. Meanwhile, the Sunbelt moved in the opposite direction: in 1940, those ten states had only 20 percent of congressional seats, but by 2010 they held 40 percent. Political influence had shifted geographically over the course of seven decades.

State	Apportionment	
	1990	2010
Rust Belt		
Massachusetts	10	9
Connecticut	6	5
New York	31	27
New Jersey	13	12
Pennsylvania	21	18
Ohio	19	16
Illinois	20	18
Indiana	10	9
Michigan	16	14
Wisconsin	9	8
Total	**155**	**136**
Sunbelt		
California	52	53
Arizona	6	9
Nevada	2	4
Colorado	6	7
New Mexico	3	3
Texas	30	36
Georgia	11	14
North Carolina	12	13
Virginia	11	11
Florida	23	27
Total	**156**	**177**

SOURCE: Office of the Clerk of the House, clerk.house.gov/art_history/house_history/congApp/bystate.html.

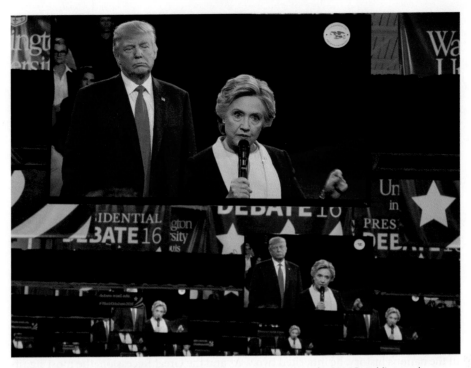

Donald Trump and Hillary Clinton Television monitors capture the 2016 Republican and Democratic presidential nominees in their second debate, at Washington University in St. Louis. Timothy A. Clary/AFP/Getty Images.

issues—the exception being global trade policy—and relied on inaccurate claims about the threat of immigration and urban crime along with promises to restore a romanticized American past. Trump remained a viable presidential candidate despite revelations that many observers believed were disqualifying: that he likely avoided paying federal income taxes for decades, for instance, and his bragging in a 2005 video about sexually assaulting women.

National polls predicted a close election, with many indicating a likely Clinton victory. But in one of the most surprising presidential elections in more than a generation, Trump achieved an electoral college majority and won the presidency. As in 2000, the Democratic nominee, Clinton, won the popular vote (by more than 2.8 million votes) but could not secure a majority in enough key states to emerge victorious. Between Trump's election in November 2016 and his inauguration on January 20, 2017, Americans debated the meaning of that victory, the fate of the Obama coalition, and the capacity of the nation's governing institutions to successfully address the major national and global challenges of the twenty-first century. As we go to press, history is unfolding at a furious pace, as President Trump has begun his administration with a series of unprecedented executive orders, while anti-Trump protests, both massive and small-scale, roil American cities.

IN YOUR OWN WORDS How did wars abroad and political contest at home shape the United States in the first decades of the twenty-first century?

Summary

This chapter has stressed how globalization — the worldwide flow of capital, goods, and people — entered a new phase after the end of the Cold War. The number of multinational corporations, many of them based in the United States, increased dramatically, and people, goods, and investment capital moved easily across political boundaries. Financial markets, in particular, grew increasingly open and interconnected across the globe. Technological innovations strengthened the American economy and transformed daily life. The computer revolution and the spread of the Internet changed the ways in which Americans shopped, worked, learned, and stayed in touch with family and friends. Globalization also facilitated the immigration of millions of Asians and Latin Americans into the United States.

In the decades since 1989, American life has been characterized by the dilemmas presented by the twin issues of globalization and divisive cultural politics. Conservatives spoke out strongly, and with increasing effectiveness, against multiculturalism and what they viewed as serious threats to "family values." Debates over access to abortion, affirmative action, and the legal rights of homosexuals intensified. The terrorist attacks of September 11, 2001, diverted attention from this increasingly bitter partisanship, but that partisanship was revived after President Bush's decision to invade Iraq (a nation not involved in the events of 9/11) in 2003 led to a protracted war. When Barack Obama was elected in 2008, the first African American president in the nation's history, he inherited two wars and the Great Recession, the most significant economic collapse since the 1930s. His, and the nation's, efforts to address these and other pressing issues enjoyed initial success before stalling in a deepening partisan stalemate, especially after his reelection in 2012. Finally, bringing matters nearly to the present, the election of the celebrity businessman Donald Trump to the presidency in 2016 confirmed that globalization and domestic cultural divisions remain at the core of American politics. Trump won the election (over Democrat Hillary Clinton), as George W. Bush had in 2000, while losing the popular vote, giving his presidency a fragile legitimacy and leaving the country as divided politically as it has been since the 1960s.

CHAPTER 30 REVIEW

TERMS TO KNOW   *Identify and explain the significance of each term below.*

Key Concepts and Events

Al Qaeda (p. 986)

globalization (p. 986)

World Trade
   Organization
   (WTO) (p. 989)

Group of Eight (G8)
   (p. 995)

North American Free
   Trade Agreement
   (NAFTA) (p. 995)

multinational corporations
   (p. 995)

Advanced Research Projects
   Agency Network
   (ARPANET) (p. 996)

World Wide Web (p. 996)

culture war (p. 996)

Immigration and
   Nationality Act (p. 998)

multiculturalism (p. 1001)

Proposition 209 (p. 1001)

Operation Rescue (p. 1002)

Defense of Marriage Act (p. 1002)

Webster v. Reproductive Health Services (p. 1003)

Planned Parenthood of Southeastern Pennsylvania v. Casey (p. 1003)

Lawrence v. Texas (p. 1003)

Contract with America (p. 1005)

Personal Responsibility and Work Opportunity Reconciliation Act (p. 1005)

Economic Growth and Tax Relief Act (p. 1008)

USA PATRIOT Act (p. 1010)

Abu Ghraib prison (p. 1011)

American Recovery and Reinvestment Act (p. 1013)

Patient Protection and Affordable Care Act (p. 1013)

Tea Party (p. 1015)

Key People

William (Bill) Jefferson Clinton (p. 1003)

Hillary Clinton (p. 1004)

Newt Gingrich (p. 1005)

Saddam Hussein (p. 1007)

Osama bin Laden (p. 1007)

George W. Bush (p. 1008)

Barack Obama (p. 1013)

REVIEW QUESTIONS *Answer these questions to demonstrate your understanding of the chapter's main ideas.*

1. How did globalization redefine the relationship of the United States to the rest of the world after the end of the Cold War?

2. What were the sources of domestic division in the United States after 1988, and how did they reshape the political landscape?

3. How did wars abroad and political contest at home shape the United States in the first decades of the twenty-first century?

4. Review the events included on the thematic timeline on pages 952–953. In what ways does the period between 1992 (Bill Clinton's election) and 2016 (Donald Trump's election) suggest a postliberal era in American politics? In what ways was the conservative resurgence under Reagan preserved, and in what ways was it not?

MAKING CONNECTIONS *Recognize the larger developments and continuities within and across chapters.*

1. How would you compare the Iraq War with previous wars in U.S. history? Compare in particular the reasons for entering the war, support for the war abroad and at home, and the outcome of the conflict.

2. How would you explain the geography of American politics after World War II? Compare Table 28.1

(p. 935) and Table 30.2 (p. 1018), which show how population gains and losses over several decades shaped which states and regions had greater representation in Congress. How would you explain the significance of those changes?

KEY TURNING POINTS *Refer to the chapter chronology on page 988 for help in answering the question below.*

What were the major domestic and foreign policy challenges between the 1990s and 2016?

Documents

The Declaration of Independence

In Congress, July 4, 1776,
The Unanimous Declaration of the Thirteen
United States of America

When in the Course of human events, it becomes necessary for one people to dissolve the political bands which have connected them with another, and to assume among the Powers of the earth, the separate and equal station to which the Laws of Nature and of Nature's God entitle them, a decent respect to the opinions of mankind requires that they should declare the causes which impel them to the separation.

We hold these truths to be self-evident, that all men are created equal, that they are endowed by their Creator with certain unalienable rights, that among these are Life, Liberty, and the pursuit of Happiness. That to secure these rights, Governments are instituted among Men, deriving their just powers from the consent of the governed. That whenever any Form of Government becomes destructive of these ends, it is the Right of the People to alter or to abolish it, and to institute new Government, laying its foundation on such principles and organizing its powers in such form, as to them shall seem most likely to effect their Safety and Happiness. Prudence, indeed, will dictate that Governments long established should not be changed for light and transient causes; and accordingly all experience hath shown, that mankind are more disposed to suffer, while evils are sufferable, than to right themselves by abolishing the forms to which they are accustomed. But when a long train of abuses and usurpations, pursuing invariably the same Object evinces a design to reduce them under absolute Despotism, it is their right, it is their duty, to throw off such Government, and to provide new Guards for their future security. — Such has been the patient sufferance of these Colonies; and such is now the necessity which constrains them to alter their former Systems of Government. The history of the present King of Great Britain is a history of repeated injuries and usurpations, all having in direct object the establishment of an absolute Tyranny over these States. To prove this, let Facts be submitted to a candid world.

He has refused his Assent to Laws, the most wholesome and necessary for the public good.

He has forbidden his Governors to pass Laws of immediate and pressing importance, unless suspended in their operation till his Assent should be obtained; and, when so suspended, he has utterly neglected to attend to them.

He has refused to pass other Laws for the accommodation of large districts of people, unless those people would relinquish the right of Representation in the Legislature, a right inestimable to them and formidable to tyrants only.

He has called together legislative bodies at places unusual, uncomfortable, and distant from the depository of their public Records, for the sole purpose of fatiguing them into compliance with his measures.

He has dissolved Representative Houses repeatedly, for opposing with manly firmness his invasions on the rights of the people.

He has refused for a long time, after such dissolutions, to cause others to be elected; whereby the Legislative powers, incapable of Annihilation, have returned to the People at large for their exercise; the State remaining in the mean time exposed to all the dangers of invasion from without and convulsions within.

He has endeavoured to prevent the population of these States; for that purpose obstructing the Laws of Naturalization of Foreigners; refusing to pass others to encourage their migrations hither, and raising the conditions of new Appropriations of Lands.

He has obstructed the Administration of Justice, by refusing his Assent to Laws for establishing Judiciary powers.

He has made Judges dependent on his Will alone, for the tenure of their offices, and the amount and payment of their salaries.

He has erected a multitude of New Offices, and sent hither swarms of Officers to harass our People, and eat out their substance.

He has kept among us, in times of peace, Standing Armies without the Consent of our legislature.

He has affected to render the Military independent of and superior to the Civil Power.

He has combined with others to subject us to a jurisdiction foreign to our constitution, and unacknowledged by our laws; giving his Assent to their Acts of pretended Legislation:

For quartering large bodies of armed troops among us:

For protecting them, by a mock Trial, from Punishment for any Murders which they should commit on the Inhabitants of these States:

For cutting off our Trade with all parts of the world:

For imposing taxes on us without our Consent:

For depriving us, in many cases, of the benefits of Trial by jury:

For transporting us beyond Seas to be tried for pretended offences:

For abolishing the free System of English Laws in a neighbouring Province, establishing therein an Arbitrary government, and enlarging its Boundaries so as to render it at once an example and fit instrument for introducing the same absolute rule into these Colonies:

For taking away our Charters, abolishing our most valuable Laws, and altering fundamentally the Forms of our Governments:

For suspending our own Legislatures, and declaring themselves invested with Power to legislate for us in all cases whatsoever.

He has abdicated Government here, by declaring us out of his Protection and waging War against us.

He has plundered our seas, ravaged our Coasts, burnt our towns, and destroyed the lives of our people.

He is at this time transporting large armies of foreign mercenaries to compleat the works of death, desolation, and tyranny, already begun with circumstances of Cruelty & perfidy scarcely paralleled in the most barbarous ages, and totally unworthy the Head of a civilized nation.

He has constrained our fellow Citizens taken Captive on the high Seas to bear Arms against their Country, to become the executioners of their friends and Brethren, or to fall themselves by their Hands.

He has excited domestic insurrections amongst us, and has endeavoured to bring on the inhabitants of our frontiers, the merciless Indian Savages, whose known rule of warfare, is an undistinguished destruction of all ages, sexes, and conditions.

In every stage of these Oppressions We have Petitioned for Redress in the most humble terms: Our repeated Petitions have been answered only by repeated injury. A Prince, whose character is thus marked by every act which may define a Tyrant, is unfit to be the ruler of a free people.

Nor have We been wanting in attention to our British brethren. We have warned them from time to time of attempts by their legislature to extend an unwarrantable jurisdiction over us. We have reminded them of the circumstances of our emigration and settlement here. We have appealed to their native justice and magnanimity, and we have conjured them by the ties of our common kindred to disavow these usurpations, which would inevitably interrupt our connections and correspondence. They too have been deaf to the voice of justice and of consanguinity. We must, therefore, acquiesce in the necessity, which denounces our Separation, and hold them, as we hold the rest of mankind, Enemies in War, in Peace Friends.

We, therefore, the Representatives of the United States of America, in General Congress, Assembled, appealing to the Supreme Judge of the world for the rectitude of our intentions, do, in the Name, and by Authority of the good People of these Colonies, solemnly publish and declare, That these United Colonies are, and of Right ought to be FREE AND INDEPENDENT STATES; that they are Absolved from all Allegiance to the British Crown, and that all political connection between them and the State of Great Britain, is and ought to be totally dissolved; and that as Free and Independent States, they have full Power to levy War, conclude Peace, contract Alliances, establish Commerce, and to do all other Acts and Things which Independent States may of right do. And for the support of this Declaration, with a firm reliance on the Protection of Divine Providence, we mutually pledge to each other our Lives, our Fortunes, and our sacred Honor.

John Hancock

Button Gwinnett	**Thos. Stone**	**Benja. Franklin**
Lyman Hall	**Charles Carroll of**	**John Morton**
Geo. Walton	**Carrollton**	**Geo. Clymer**
Wm. Hooper	**George Wythe**	**Jas. Smith**
Joseph Hewes	**Richard Henry Lee**	**Geo. Taylor**
John Penn	**Th. Jefferson**	**James Wilson**
Edward Rutledge	**Benja. Harrison**	**Geo. Ross**
Thos. Heyward, Junr.	**Thos. Nelson, Jr.**	**Caesar Rodney**
Thomas Lynch, Junr.	**Francis Lightfoot Lee**	**Geo. Read**
Arthur Middleton	**Carter Braxton**	**Thos. M'Kean**
Samuel Chase	**Robt. Morris**	**Wm. Floyd**
Wm. Paca	**Benjamin Rush**	**Phil. Livingston**

Frans. Lewis	Josiah Bartlett	Step. Hopkins
Lewis Morris	Wm. Whipple	William Ellery
Richd. Stockton	Matthew Thornton	Roger Sherman
John Witherspoon	Saml. Adams	Sam'el Huntington
Fras. Hopkinson	John Adams	Wm. Williams
John Hart	Robt. Treat Paine	Oliver Wolcott
Abra. Clark	Elbridge Gerry	

The Constitution of the United States of America

Agreed to by Philadelphia Convention, September 17, 1787
Implemented March 4, 1789

We the People of the United States, in Order to form a more perfect Union, establish Justice, insure domestic Tranquility, provide for the common defence, promote the general Welfare, and secure the Blessings of Liberty to ourselves and our Posterity, do ordain and establish this Constitution for the United States of America.

Article I

Section 1. All legislative Powers herein granted shall be vested in a Congress of the United States, which shall consist of a Senate and a House of Representatives.

Section 2. The House of Representatives shall be composed of Members chosen every second Year by the People of the several States, and the Electors in each State shall have the Qualifications requisite for Electors of the most numerous Branch of the State Legislature.

No Person shall be a Representative who shall not have attained to the Age of twenty-five Years, and been seven Years a Citizen of the United States, and who shall not, when elected, be an Inhabitant of that State in which he shall be chosen.

Representatives and direct Taxes shall be apportioned among the several States which may be included within this Union, according to their respective Numbers, *which shall be determined by adding to the whole Number of free Persons, including those bound to Service for a Term of Years, and excluding Indians not taxed, three fifths of all other Persons.** The actual Enumeration shall be made within three Years after the first Meeting of the Congress of the United States, and within every subsequent Term of ten Years, in such Manner as they shall by Law direct. The Number of Representatives shall not exceed one for every thirty Thousand, but each State shall have at Least one Representative; and *until such enumeration shall be made, the State of New Hampshire shall be entitled to chuse three, Massachusetts eight, Rhode Island and Providence Plantations one, Connecticut five, New York six, New Jersey four, Pennsylvania eight, Delaware one, Maryland six, Virginia ten, North Carolina five, South Carolina five, and Georgia three.*

When vacancies happen in the Representation from any State, the Executive Authority thereof shall issue Writs of Election to fill such Vacancies.

The House of Representatives shall chuse their Speaker and other Officers; and shall have the sole Power of Impeachment.

Section 3. The Senate of the United States shall be composed of two Senators from each State, *chosen by the Legislature thereof,*† for six Years; and each Senator shall have one Vote.

Note: The Constitution became effective March 4, 1789. Provisions in italics are no longer relevant or have been changed by constitutional amendment.

*Changed by Section 2 of the Fourteenth Amendment.

†Changed by Section 1 of the Seventeenth Amendment.

Immediately after they shall be assembled in Consequence of the first Election, they shall be divided as equally as may be into three Classes. The Seats of the Senators of the first Class shall be vacated at the Expiration of the second Year, of the second Class at the Expiration of the fourth Year, and of the third Class at the Expiration of the sixth Year, so that one-third may be chosen every second Year; and if Vacancies happen by Resignation, or otherwise, during the Recess of the Legislature of any State, the Executive thereof may make temporary Appointments until the next Meeting of the Legislature, which shall then fill such Vacancies.‡

No person shall be a Senator who shall not have attained to the Age of thirty Years, and been nine Years a Citizen of the United States, and who shall not, when elected, be an Inhabitant of that State for which he shall be chosen.

The Vice President of the United States shall be President of the Senate, but shall have no Vote, unless they be equally divided.

The Senate shall chuse their other Officers, and also a President pro tempore, in the absence of the Vice President, or when he shall exercise the Office of President of the United States.

The Senate shall have the sole Power to try all Impeachments. When sitting for that Purpose, they shall be on Oath or Affirmation. When the President of the United States is tried, the Chief Justice shall preside: And no Person shall be convicted without the Concurrence of two-thirds of the Members present.

Judgment in Cases of Impeachment shall not extend further than to removal from Office, and disqualification to hold and enjoy any Office of honor, Trust or Profit under the United States: but the Party convicted shall nevertheless be liable and subject to Indictment, Trial, Judgment and Punishment, according to Law.

Section 4. The Times, Places and Manner of holding Elections for Senators and Representatives, shall be prescribed in each State by the Legislature thereof; but the Congress may at any time by Law make or alter such Regulations, except as to the Places of Chusing Senators.

The Congress shall assemble at least once in every Year, and such Meeting *shall be on the first Monday in December, unless they shall by Law appoint a different Day.**

Section 5. Each House shall be the Judge of the Elections, Returns and Qualifications of its own Members, and a Majority of each shall constitute a Quorum to do Business; but a smaller number may adjourn from day to day, and may be authorized to compel the Attendance of absent Members, in such Manner, and under such Penalties, as each House may provide.

Each House may determine the Rules of its Proceedings, punish its Members for disorderly Behavior, and, with the Concurrence of two-thirds, expel a Member.

Each House shall keep a Journal of its Proceedings, and from time to time publish the same, excepting such Parts as may in their Judgment require Secrecy; and the Yeas and Nays of the Members of either House on any question shall, at the Desire of one-fifth of those Present, be entered on the Journal.

---

‡Changed by Clause 2 of the Seventh Amendment.
*Changed by Section 2 of the Twentieth Amendment.

Neither House, during the Session of Congress, shall, without the Consent of the other, adjourn for more than three days, nor to any other Place than that in which the two Houses shall be sitting.

Section 6. The Senators and Representatives shall receive a Compensation for their Services, to be ascertained by Law, and paid out of the Treasury of the United States. They shall in all Cases, except Treason, Felony and Breach of the Peace, be privileged from Arrest during their Attendance at the Session of their respective Houses, and in going to and returning from the same; and for any Speech or Debate in either House, they shall not be questioned in any other Place.

No Senator or Representative shall, during the Time for which he was elected, be appointed to any civil Office under the Authority of the United States, which shall have been created, or the Emoluments whereof shall have been increased, during such time; and no Person holding any Office under the United States, shall be a Member of either House during his Continuance in Office.

Section 7. All Bills for raising Revenue shall originate in the House of Representatives; but the Senate may propose or concur with Amendments as on other Bills.

Every Bill which shall have passed the House of Representatives and the Senate, shall, before it becomes a Law, be presented to the President of the United States; If he approve he shall sign it, but if not he shall return it, with his Objections to that House in which it shall have originated, who shall enter the Objections at large on their Journal, and proceed to reconsider it. If after such Reconsideration two-thirds of that House shall agree to pass the Bill, it shall be sent, together with the Objections, to the other House, by which it shall likewise be reconsidered, and if approved by two-thirds of that House, it shall become a Law. But in all such Cases the Votes of both Houses shall be determined by Yeas and Nays, and the Names of the Persons voting for and against the Bill shall be entered on the Journal of each House respectively. If any Bill shall not be returned by the President within ten Days (Sundays excepted) after it shall have been presented to him, the Same shall be a Law, in like Manner as if he had signed it, unless the Congress by their Adjournment prevent its Return, in which Case it shall not be a Law.

Every Order, Resolution, or Vote to which the Concurrence of the Senate and the House of Representatives may be necessary (except on a question of Adjournment) shall be presented to the President of the United States; and before the Same shall take Effect, shall be approved by him, or being disapproved by him, shall be repassed by two-thirds of the Senate and House of Representatives, according to the Rules and Limitations prescribed in the Case of a Bill.

Section 8. The Congress shall have Power To lay and collect Taxes, Duties, Imposts and Excises, to pay the Debts and provide for the common Defence and general Welfare of the United States; but all Duties, Imposts and Excises shall be uniform throughout the United States;

To borrow Money on the credit of the United States;

To regulate Commerce with foreign Nations, and among the several States, and with the Indian Tribes;

To establish an uniform Rule of Naturalization, and uniform Laws on the subject of Bankruptcies throughout the United States;

To coin Money, regulate the Value thereof, and of foreign Coin, and fix the Standard of Weights and Measures;

To provide for the Punishment of counterfeiting the Securities and current Coin of the United States;

To establish Post Offices and post Roads;

To promote the Progress of Science and useful Arts, by securing for limited Times to Authors and Inventors the exclusive Right to their respective Writings and Discoveries;

To constitute Tribunals inferior to the supreme Court;

To define and punish Piracies and Felonies committed on the high Seas, and Offenses against the Law of Nations;

To declare War, grant Letters of Marque and Reprisal, and make Rules concerning Captures on Land and Water;

To raise and support Armies, but no Appropriation of Money to that Use shall be for a longer Term than two Years;

To provide and maintain a Navy;

To make Rules for the Government and Regulation of the land and naval Forces;

To provide for calling forth the Militia to execute the Laws of the Union, suppress Insurrections and repel Invasions;

To provide for organizing, arming, and disciplining the Militia, and for governing such Part of them as may be employed in the Service of the United States, reserving to the States respectively, the Appointment of the Officers, and the Authority of training the Militia according to the discipline prescribed by Congress;

To exercise exclusive Legislation in all Cases whatsoever, over such District (not exceeding ten Miles square) as may, by Cession of particular States, and the acceptance of Congress, become the Seat of Government of the United States, and to exercise like Authority over all Places purchased by the Consent of the Legislature of the State in which the Same shall be, for the Erection of Forts, Magazines, Arsenals, dock-Yards, and other needful Buildings; — And

To make all Laws which shall be necessary and proper for carrying into Execution the foregoing Powers, and all other Powers vested by this Constitution in the Government of the United States, or in any Department or Officer thereof.

Section 9. The Migration or Importation of such Persons as any of the States now existing shall think proper to admit, shall not be prohibited by the Congress prior to the Year one thousand eight hundred and eight but a tax or duty may be imposed on such Importation, not exceeding ten dollars for each Person.

The privilege of the Writ of Habeas Corpus shall not be suspended, unless when in Cases of Rebellion or Invasion the public Safety may require it.

No Bill of Attainder or ex post facto Law shall be passed.

*No capitation, or other direct, Tax shall be laid, unless in Proportion to the Census or Enumeration herein before directed to be taken.**

No Tax or Duty shall be laid on Articles exported from any State.

No Preference shall be given by any Regulation of Commerce or Revenue to the Ports of one State over those of another: nor shall Vessels bound to, or from, one State, be obliged to enter, clear, or pay Duties in another.

---

*Changed by the Sixteenth Amendment.

No Money shall be drawn from the Treasury, but in Consequence of Appropriations made by law; and a regular Statement and Account of the Receipts and Expenditures of all public Money shall be published from time to time.

No Title of Nobility shall be granted by the United States: And no Person holding any Office of Profit or Trust under them, shall, without the Consent of the Congress, accept of any present, Emolument, Office, or Title, of any kind whatever, from any King, Prince, or foreign State.

Section 10. No State shall enter into any Treaty, Alliance, or Confederation; grant Letters of Marque and Reprisal; coin Money; emit Bills of Credit; make any Thing but gold and silver Coin a Tender in Payment of Debts; pass any Bill of Attainder, ex post facto Law, or Law impairing the Obligation of Contracts, or grant any Title of Nobility.

No State shall, without the Consent of the Congress, lay any Imposts or Duties on Imports or Exports, except what may be absolutely necessary for executing its inspection Laws: and the net Produce of all Duties and Imposts, laid by any State on Imports or Exports, shall be for the Use of the Treasury of the United States; and all such Laws shall be subject to the Revision and Control of the Congress.

No State shall, without the Consent of the Congress, lay any duty of Tonnage, keep Troops, or Ships of War in time of Peace, enter into any Agreement or Compact with another State, or with a foreign Power, or engage in War, unless actually invaded, or in such imminent Danger as will not admit of delay.

Article II

Section 1. The executive Power shall be vested in a President of the United States of America. He shall hold his Office during the Term of four Years, and, together with the Vice President, chosen for the same Term, be elected, as follows:

Each State shall appoint, in such Manner as the Legislature thereof may direct, a Number of Electors, equal to the whole Number of Senators and Representatives to which the State may be entitled in the Congress; but no Senator or Representative, or Person holding an Office of Trust or Profit under the United States, shall be appointed an Elector.

The Electors shall meet in their respective States, and vote by Ballot for two Persons, of whom one at least shall not be an Inhabitant of the same State with themselves. And they shall make a List of all the Persons voted for, and of the Number of Votes for each; which List they shall sign and certify, and transmit sealed to the Seat of the Government of the United States, directed to the President of the Senate. The President of the Senate shall, in the Presence of the Senate and House of Representatives, open all the Certificates, and the Votes shall then be counted. The Person having the greatest Number of Votes shall be the President, if such Number be a Majority of the whole Number of Electors appointed; and if there be more than one who have such Majority, and have an equal Number of Votes, then the House of Representatives shall immediately chuse by Ballot one of them for President; and if no Person have a Majority, then from the five highest on the List the said House shall in like Manner chuse the President. But in chusing the President, the Votes shall be taken by States, the Representation from each State having one Vote; a quorum for this Purpose shall consist of a Member or Members from two thirds of the States, and a Majority of all the States shall be necessary to a Choice. In every Case, after the Choice of the President, the

Person having the greatest Number of Votes of the Electors shall be the Vice President. But if there should remain two or more who have equal Votes, the Senate shall chuse from them by Ballot the Vice President.*

The Congress may determine the Time of chusing the Electors, and the Day on which they shall give their Votes; which Day shall be the same throughout the United States.

No Person except a natural born Citizen, or a Citizen of the United States, at the time of the Adoption of this Constitution, shall be eligible to the Office of President; neither shall any Person be eligible to that Office who shall not have attained to the Age of thirty five Years, and been fourteen Years a Resident within the United States.

In Case of the Removal of the President from Office, or of his Death, Resignation, or Inability to discharge the Powers and Duties of the said Office, the same shall devolve on the Vice President, *and the Congress may by Law provide for the Case of Removal, Death, Resignation, or Inability, both of the President and Vice President, declaring what Officer shall then act as President, and such Officer shall act accordingly, until the Disability be removed, or a President shall be elected.*†

The President shall, at stated Times, receive for his Services a Compensation, which shall neither be increased nor diminished during the Period for which he shall have been elected, and he shall not receive within that Period any other Emolument from the United States, or any of them.

Before he enter on the Execution of his Office, he shall take the following Oath or Affirmation: — "I do solemnly swear (or affirm) that I will faithfully execute the Office of President of the United States, and will to the best of my Ability, preserve, protect and defend the Constitution of the United States."

Section 2. The President shall be Commander in Chief of the Army and Navy of the United States, and of the Militia of the several States, when called into the actual Service of the United States; he may require the Opinion, in writing, of the principal Officer in each of the executive Departments, upon any Subject relating to the Duties of their respective Offices, and he shall have Power to Grant Reprieves and Pardons for Offences against the United States, except in Cases of Impeachment.

He shall have Power, by and with the Advice and Consent of the Senate, to make Treaties, provided two thirds of the Senators present concur; and he shall nominate, and by and with the Advice and Consent of the Senate, shall appoint Ambassadors, other public Ministers and Consuls, Judges of the supreme Court, and all other Officers of the United States, whose Appointments are not herein otherwise provided for, and which shall be established by Law: but the Congress may by Law vest the Appointment of such inferior Officers, as they think proper, in the President alone, in the Courts of Law, or in the Heads of Departments.

The President shall have Power to fill up all Vacancies that may happen during the Recess of the Senate, by granting Commissions which shall expire at the End of their next Session.

---

*Superseded by the Twelfth Amendment.
†Modified by the Twenty-Fifth Amendment.

Section 3. He shall from time to time give to the Congress Information of the State of the Union, and recommend to their Consideration such Measures as he shall judge necessary and expedient; he may, on extraordinary Occasions, convene both Houses, or either of them, and in Case of Disagreement between them, with Respect to the Time of Adjournment, he may adjourn them to such Time as he shall think proper; he shall receive Ambassadors and other public Ministers; he shall take Care that the Laws be faithfully executed, and shall Commission all the Officers of the United States.

Section 4. The President, Vice President and all civil Officers of the United States, shall be removed from Office on Impeachment for, and Conviction of, Treason, Bribery, or other high Crimes and Misdemeanors.

Article III

Section 1. The judicial Power of the United States, shall be vested in one supreme Court, and in such inferior Courts as the Congress may from time to time ordain and establish. The Judges, both of the supreme and inferior Courts, shall hold their Offices during good Behaviour, and shall, at stated Times, receive for their Services a Compensation, which shall not be diminished during their Continuance in Office.

Section 2. The judicial Power shall extend to all Cases, in Law and Equity, arising under this Constitution, the Laws of the United States, and Treaties made, or which shall be made, under their Authority; — to all Cases affecting Ambassadors, other public Ministers and Consuls; — to all Cases of admiralty and maritime Jurisdiction; — to Controversies to which the United States shall be a Party; — to Controversies between two or more States; — *between a State and Citizens of another State*;‡ — between Citizens of different States; — between Citizens of the same State claiming Lands under Grants of different States, and between a State, or the Citizens thereof, and foreign States, Citizens or Subjects.

In all Cases affecting Ambassadors, other public Ministers and Consuls, and those in which a State shall be Party, the supreme Court shall have original Jurisdiction. In all the other Cases before mentioned, the supreme Court shall have appellate Jurisdiction, both as to Law and Fact, with such Exceptions, and under such Regulations as the Congress shall make.

The trial of all Crimes, except in Cases of Impeachment, shall be by Jury; and such Trial shall be held in the State where said Crimes shall have been committed; but when not committed within any State, the Trial shall be at such Place or Places as the Congress may by Law have directed.

Section 3. Treason against the United States, shall consist only in levying War against them, or in adhering to their Enemies, giving them Aid and Comfort. No Person shall be convicted of Treason unless on the Testimony of two Witnesses to the same overt Act, or on Confession in open Court.

The Congress shall have Power to declare the Punishment of Treason, but no Attainder of Treason shall work Corruption of Blood, or Forfeiture except during the Life of the Person attainted.

---

‡Restricted by the Eleventh Amendment.

Article IV

Section 1. Full Faith and Credit shall be given in each State to the public Acts, Records, and judicial Proceedings of every other State. And the Congress may by general Laws prescribe the Manner in which such Acts, Records, and Proceedings shall be proved, and the Effect thereof.

Section 2. The Citizens of each State shall be entitled to all Privileges and Immunities of Citizens in the several States.

A Person charged in any State with Treason, Felony, or other Crime, who shall flee from Justice, and be found in another State, shall on demand of the executive Authority of the State from which he fled, be delivered up, to be removed to the State having Jurisdiction of the Crime.

No Person held to Service or Labour in one State, under the Laws thereof, escaping into another, shall, in Consequence of any Law or Regulation therein, be discharged from such Service or Labour, but shall be delivered up on Claim of the Party to whom such Service or Labour may be due.*

Section 3. New States may be admitted by the Congress into this Union; but no new State shall be formed or erected within the Jurisdiction of any other State; nor any State be formed by the Junction of two or more States, or parts of States, without the Consent of the Legislatures of the States concerned as well as of the Congress.

The Congress shall have Power to dispose of and make all needful Rules and Regulations respecting the Territory or other Property belonging to the United States; and nothing in this Constitution shall be so construed as to Prejudice any Claims of the United States, or of any particular State.

Section 4. The United States shall guarantee to every State in this Union a Republican Form of Government, and shall protect each of them against Invasion; and on Application of the Legislature, or of the Executive (when the Legislature cannot be convened) against domestic Violence.

Article V

The Congress, whenever two-thirds of both Houses shall deem it necessary, shall propose Amendments to this Constitution, or, on the Application of the Legislatures of two-thirds of the several States, shall call a Convention for proposing Amendments, which, in either Case, shall be valid to all Intents and Purposes, as Part of this Constitution, when ratified by the Legislatures of three-fourths of the several States, or by Conventions in three-fourths thereof, as the one or the other Mode of Ratification may be proposed by the Congress; *Provided that no Amendment which may be made prior to the Year One thousand eight hundred and eight shall in any Manner affect the first and fourth Clauses in the Ninth Section of the first Article; and* that no State, without its Consent, shall be deprived of its equal Suffrage in the Senate.

Article VI

All Debts contracted and Engagements entered into, before the Adoption of this Constitution, shall be as valid against the United States under this Constitution, as under the Confederation.

---

*Superseded by the Thirteenth Amendment.

This Constitution, and the Laws of the United States which shall be made in Pursuance thereof; and all Treaties made, or which shall be made, under the Authority of the United States, shall be the supreme Law of the Land; and the Judges in every State shall be bound thereby, any Thing in the Constitution or Laws of any State to the Contrary notwithstanding.

The Senators and Representatives before mentioned, and the Members of the several State Legislatures, and all executive and judicial Officers, both of the United States and of the several States, shall be bound by Oath or Affirmation, to support this Constitution; but no religious Test shall ever be required as a Qualification to any Office or public Trust under the United States.

Article VII

The Ratification of the Conventions of nine States shall be sufficient for the Establishment of this Constitution between the States so ratifying the Same.

Done in Convention by the Unanimous Consent of the States present the Seventeenth Day of September in the Year of our Lord one thousand seven hundred and Eighty seven and of the Independence of the United States of America the Twelfth. In Witness whereof We have hereunto subscribed our Names.

Go. Washington President and deputy from Virginia

New Hampshire
John Langdon
Nicholas Gilman

Massachusetts
Nathaniel Gorham
Rufus King

Connecticut
Wm. Saml. Johnson
Roger Sherman

New York
Alexander Hamilton

New Jersey
Wil. Livingston
David Brearley
Wm. Paterson
Jona. Dayton

Pennsylvania
B. Franklin
Thomas Mifflin
Robt. Morris
Geo. Clymer
Thos. FitzSimons
Jared Ingersoll
James Wilson
Gouv. Morris

Delaware
Geo. Read
Gunning Bedford jun
John Dickinson
Richard Bassett
Jaco. Broom

Maryland
James McHenry
Dan. of St. Thos. Jenifer
Danl. Carroll

Virginia
John Blair
James Madison, Jr.

North Carolina
Wm. Blount
Richd. Dobbs Spaight
Hu Williamson

South Carolina
J. Rutledge
Charles Cotesworth
    Pinckney
Charles Pinckney
Pierce Butler

Georgia
William Few
Abr. Baldwin

Amendments to the Constitution (Including the Six Unratified Amendments)

Amendment I [1791]*

Congress shall make no law respecting an establishment of religion, or prohibiting the free exercise thereof; or abridging the freedom of speech, or of the press; or the right of the people peaceably to assemble, and to petition the Government for a redress of grievances.

Amendment II [1791]

A well regulated Militia, being necessary to the security of a free State, the right of the people to keep and bear Arms shall not be infringed.

Amendment III [1791]

No Soldier shall, in time of peace, be quartered in any house, without the consent of the Owner, nor in time of war, but in a manner to be prescribed by law.

Amendment IV [1791]

The right of the people to be secure in their persons, houses, papers, and effects, against unreasonable searches and seizures, shall not be violated, and no Warrants shall issue, but upon probable cause, supported by Oath or affirmation, and particularly describing the place to be searched, and the persons or things to be seized.

Amendment V [1791]

No person shall be held to answer for a capital or otherwise infamous crime, unless on a presentment or indictment of a Grand Jury, except in cases arising in the land or naval forces, or in the Militia, when in actual service in time of War or public danger; nor shall any person be subject for the same offence to be twice put in jeopardy of life or limb; nor shall be compelled in any criminal case to be a witness against himself, nor be deprived of life, liberty, or property, without due process of law; nor shall private property be taken for public use, without just compensation.

Amendment VI [1791]

In all criminal prosecutions, the accused shall enjoy the right to a speedy and public trial, by an impartial jury of the State and district wherein the crime shall have been committed, which district shall have been previously ascertained by law, and to be informed of the nature and cause of the accusation; to be confronted with the witnesses against him; to have compulsory process for obtaining witnesses in his favor, and to have the Assistance of Counsel for his defence.

---

*The dates in brackets indicate when the amendment was ratified.

Amendment VII [1791]

In suits at common law, where the value in controversy shall exceed twenty dollars, the right of trial by jury shall be preserved, and no fact tried by a jury, shall be otherwise reexamined in any Court of the United States, than according to the Rules of the common law.

Amendment VIII [1791]

Excessive bail shall not be required, nor excessive fines imposed, nor cruel and unusual punishments inflicted.

Amendment IX [1791]

The enumeration in the Constitution, of certain rights, shall not be construed to deny or disparage others retained by the people.

Amendment X [1791]

The powers not delegated to the United States by the Constitution, nor prohibited by it to the States, are reserved to the States respectively, or to the people.

Unratified Amendment

Reapportionment Amendment (proposed by Congress September 25, 1789, along with the Bill of Rights)

After the first enumeration required by the first article of the Constitution, there shall be one Representative for every thirty thousand, until the number shall amount to one hundred, after which the proportion shall be so regulated by Congress, that there shall be not less than one hundred Representatives, nor less than one Representative for every forty thousand persons, until the number of Representatives shall amount to two hundred; after which the proportion shall be so regulated by Congress, that there shall not be less than two hundred Representatives, nor more than one Representative for every fifty thousand persons.

Amendment XI [1795]

The Judicial power of the United States shall not be construed to extend to any suit in law or equity, commenced or prosecuted against one of the United States by Citizens of another State, or by Citizens or subjects of any foreign state.

Amendment XII [1804]

The Electors shall meet in their respective States and vote by ballot for President and Vice-President, one of whom, at least, shall not be an inhabitant of the same State with themselves; they shall name in their ballots the person voted for as President, and in distinct ballots the person voted for as Vice-President, and they shall make distinct lists of all persons voted for as President, and of all persons voted for as Vice-President, and of the number of votes for each, which lists they shall sign and certify, and transmit sealed to the seat of government of the United States, directed to the President of the Senate; — the President of the Senate shall, in the presence of the Senate and House of Representatives, open all the certificates and the votes shall then be counted; — The person having the greatest number of votes for President, shall be the President, if such number be a majority of the whole number of Electors appointed; and if no person have such majority, then from the persons having the highest numbers not exceeding three on the list of those voted for as President, the House of Representatives shall choose immediately, by ballot, the President. But in choosing the President, the votes shall be taken by States, the representation from each State having one vote; a quorum for this purpose shall consist of a member or members from two-thirds of the States, and a majority of all the States shall be necessary to a choice. And if the House of Representatives shall not choose a President whenever the right of choice shall devolve upon them, before *the fourth day of March* next following, then the Vice-President shall act as President, as in the case of the death or other constitutional disability of the President.* — The person having the greatest number of votes as Vice-President, shall be the Vice-President, if such number be a majority of the whole number of Electors appointed; and if no person have a majority, then from the two highest numbers on the list, the Senate shall choose the Vice-President; a quorum for the purpose shall consist of two-thirds of the whole number of Senators, and a majority of the whole number shall be necessary to a choice. But no person constitutionally ineligible to the office of President shall be eligible to that of Vice-President of the United States.

Unratified Amendment

Titles of Nobility Amendment (proposed by Congress May 1, 1810)

If any citizen of the United States shall accept, claim, receive or retain any title of nobility or honor or shall, without the consent of Congress, accept and retain any present, pension, office or emolument of any kind whatever, from any emperor, king, prince or foreign power, such person shall cease to be a citizen of the United States, and shall be incapable of holding any office of trust or profit under them, or either of them.

Unratified Amendment

Corwin Amendment (proposed by Congress March 2, 1861)

No amendment shall be made to the Constitution which will authorize or give to Congress the power to abolish or interfere, within any State, with the domestic institutions thereof, including that of persons held to labor or service by the laws of said State.

Amendment XIII [1865]

Section 1. Neither slavery nor involuntary servitude, except as a punishment for crime whereof the party shall have been duly convicted, shall exist within the United States, or any place subject to their jurisdiction.

Section 2. Congress shall have power to enforce this article by appropriate legislation.

---

*Superseded by Section 3 of the Twentieth Amendment.

Amendment XIV [1868]

Section 1. All persons born or naturalized in the United States, and subject to the jurisdiction thereof, are citizens of the United States and of the State wherein they reside. No State shall make or enforce any law which shall abridge the privileges or immunities of citizens of the United States; nor shall any State deprive any person of life, liberty, or property, without due process of law; nor deny to any person within its jurisdiction the equal protection of the laws.

Section 2. Representatives shall be apportioned among the several States according to their respective numbers, counting the whole number of persons in each State, excluding Indians not taxed. But when the right to vote at any election for the choice of electors for President and Vice-President of the United States, Representatives in Congress, the Executive and Judicial officers of a State, or the members of the Legislature thereof, is denied to any of the *male* inhabitants of such State, being *twenty-one* years of age and citizens of the United States, or in any way abridged, except for participation in rebellion, or other crime, the basis of representation therein shall be reduced in the proportion which the number of such *male* citizens shall bear to the whole number of *male* citizens *twenty-one* years of age in such State.

Section 3. No person shall be a Senator or Representative in Congress, or Elector of President and Vice-President, or hold any office, civil or military, under the United States, or under any State, who, having previously taken an oath, as a member of Congress, or as an officer of the United States, or as a member of any State legislature, or as an executive or judicial officer of any State, to support the Constitution of the United States, shall have engaged in insurrection or rebellion against the same, or given aid or comfort to the enemies thereof. Congress may, by a vote of two-thirds of each house, remove such disability.

Section 4. The validity of the public debt of the United States, authorized by law, including debts incurred for payment of pensions and bounties for services in suppressing insurrection or rebellion, shall not be questioned. But neither the United States nor any State shall assume or pay any debt or obligation incurred in aid of insurrection or rebellion against the United States, or any claim for the loss or emancipation of any slave; but all such debts, obligations, and claims shall be held illegal and void.

Section 5. The Congress shall have power to enforce, by appropriate legislation, the provisions of this article.

Amendment XV [1870]

Section 1. The right of citizens of the United States to vote shall not be denied or abridged by the United States or by any State on account of race, color, or previous condition of servitude —

Section 2. The Congress shall have power to enforce this article by appropriate legislation.

Amendment XVI [1913]

The Congress shall have power to lay and collect taxes on incomes, from whatever source derived, without apportionment among the several States, and without regard to any census or enumeration.

Amendment XVII [1913]

Section 1. The Senate of the United States shall be composed of two Senators from each State, elected by the people thereof, for six years; and each Senator shall have one vote. The electors in each State shall have the qualifications requisite for electors of [voters for] the most numerous branch of the State legislatures.

Section 2. When vacancies happen in the representation of any State in the Senate, the executive authority of such State shall issue writs of election to fill such vacancies: Provided, that the Legislature of any State may empower the executive thereof to make temporary appointments until the people fill the vacancies by election as the Legislature may direct.

Section 3. *This amendment shall not be so construed as to affect the election or term of any Senator chosen before it becomes valid as part of the Constitution.*

Amendment XVIII [1919; repealed 1933 by Amendment XXI]

Section 1. *After one year from the ratification of this article the manufacture, sale, or transportation of intoxicating liquors within, the importation thereof into, or the exportation thereof from the United States and all territory subject to the jurisdiction thereof, for beverage purposes, is hereby prohibited.*

Section 2. *The Congress and the several States shall have concurrent power to enforce this article by appropriate legislation.*

Section 3. *This article shall be inoperative unless it shall have been ratified as an amendment to the Constitution by the legislatures of the several States, as provided by the Constitution, within seven years from the date of the submission thereof to the States by the Congress.*

Amendment XIX [1920]

Section 1. The right of citizens of the United States to vote shall not be denied or abridged by the United States or by any State on account of sex.

Section 2. Congress shall have the power to enforce this article by appropriate legislation.

Unratified Amendment

Child Labor Amendment (proposed by Congress June 2, 1924)

Section 1. *The Congress shall have power to limit, regulate, and prohibit the labor of persons under eighteen years of age.*

Section 2. *The power of the several States is unimpaired by this article except that the operation of State laws shall be suspended to the extent necessary to give effect to legislation enacted by Congress.*

Amendment XX [1933]

Section 1. The terms of the President and Vice-President shall end at noon on the 20th day of January, and the terms of Senators and Representatives at noon on the 3rd day of January, of the years in which such terms would have ended if this article had not been ratified; and the terms of their successors shall then begin.

Section 2. The Congress shall assemble at least once in every year, and such meeting shall begin at noon on the 3rd day of January, unless they shall by law appoint a different day.

Section 3. If, at the time fixed for the beginning of the term of the President, the President-elect shall have died, the Vice-President-elect shall become President. If a President shall not have been chosen before the time fixed for the beginning of his term, or if the President-elect shall have failed to qualify, then the Vice-President-elect shall act as President until a President shall have qualified; and the Congress may by law provide for the case wherein neither a President-elect nor a Vice-President-elect shall have qualified, declaring who shall then act as President, or the manner in which one who is to act shall be selected, and such person shall act accordingly until a President or Vice-President shall have qualified.

Section 4. The Congress may by law provide for the case of the death of any of the persons from whom the House of Representatives may choose a President whenever the right of choice shall have devolved upon them, and for the case of the death of any of the persons from whom the Senate may choose a Vice-President whenever the right of choice shall have devolved upon them.

Section 5. Sections 1 and 2 shall take effect on the 15th day of October following the ratification of this article.

Section 6. This article shall be inoperative unless it shall have been ratified as an amendment to the Constitution by the Legislatures of three-fourths of the several States within seven years from the date of its submission.

Amendment XXI [1933]

Section 1. The eighteenth article of amendment to the Constitution of the United States is hereby repealed.

Section 2. The transportation or importation into any State, Territory, or Possession of the United States for delivery or use therein of intoxicating liquors, in violation of the laws thereof, is hereby prohibited.

Section 3. This article shall be inoperative unless it shall have been ratified as an amendment to the Constitution by conventions in the several States, as provided in the Constitution, within seven years from the date of the submission thereof to the States by the Congress.

Amendment XXII [1951]

Section 1. No person shall be elected to the office of the President more than twice, and no person who has held the office of President, or acted as President, for more than two years of a term to which some other person was elected President shall be elected to the office of President more than once. But this article shall not apply to any person holding the office of President when this Article was proposed by the Congress, and shall not prevent any person who may be holding the office of President, or acting as President, during the term within which this Article becomes operative from holding the office of President or acting as President during the remainder of such term.

Section 2. This article shall be inoperative unless it shall have been ratified as an amendment to the Constitution by the legislatures of three-fourths of the several States within seven years from the date of its submission to the States by the Congress.

Amendment XXIII [1961]

Section 1. The District constituting the seat of Government of the United States shall appoint in such manner as the Congress may direct: A number of electors of President and Vice-President equal to the whole number of Senators and Representatives in Congress to which the District would be entitled if it were a State, but in no event more than the least populous State; they shall be in addition to those appointed by the States, but they shall be considered for the purposes of the election of President and Vice-President, to be electors appointed by a State; and they shall meet in the District and perform such duties as provided by the twelfth article of amendment.

Section 2. The Congress shall have the power to enforce this article by appropriate legislation.

Amendment XXIV [1964]

Section 1. The right of citizens of the United States to vote in any primary or other election for President or Vice-President, for electors for President or Vice-President, or for Senator or Representative in Congress, shall not be denied or abridged by the United States or any State by reason of failure to pay any poll tax or other tax.

Section 2. The Congress shall have the power to enforce this article by appropriate legislation.

Amendment XXV [1967]

Section 1. In case of the removal of the President from office or of his death or resignation, the Vice-President shall become President.

Section 2. Whenever there is a vacancy in the office of the Vice-President, the President shall nominate a Vice-President who shall take office upon confirmation by a majority vote of both Houses of Congress.

Section 3. Whenever the President transmits to the President pro tempore of the Senate and the Speaker of the House of Representatives his written declaration that he is unable to discharge the powers and duties of his office, and until he transmits to them a written declaration to the contrary, such powers and duties shall be discharged by the Vice-President as Acting President.

Section 4. Whenever the Vice-President and a majority of either the principal officers of the executive departments or of such other body as Congress may by law provide, transmit to the President pro tempore of the Senate and the Speaker of the House of Representatives their written declaration that the President is unable to discharge the powers and duties of his office, the Vice-President shall immediately assume the powers and duties of the office as Acting President.

Thereafter, when the President transmits to the President pro tempore of the Senate and the Speaker of the House of Representatives his written declaration that no inability exists, he shall resume the powers and duties of his office unless the Vice-President and a majority of either the principal officers of the executive department[s] or of such other body as Congress may by law provide, transmit within four days to the President pro tempore of the Senate and the Speaker of the House of Representatives their written declaration that the President is unable to discharge the powers and duties of his office.

Thereupon Congress shall decide the issue, assembling within forty-eight hours for that purpose if not in session. If the Congress, within twenty-one days after receipt of the latter written declaration, or, if Congress is not in session, within twenty-one days after Congress is required to assemble, determines by two-thirds vote of both Houses that the President is unable to discharge the powers and duties of his office, the Vice-President shall continue to discharge the same as Acting President; otherwise, the President shall resume the powers and duties of his office.

Amendment XXVI [1971]

Section 1. The right of citizens of the United States, who are eighteen years of age or older, to vote shall not be denied or abridged by the United States or by any State on account of age.

Section 2. The Congress shall have power to enforce this article by appropriate legislation.

Unratified Amendment

Equal Rights Amendment (proposed by Congress March 22, 1972; seven-year deadline for ratification extended to June 30, 1982)

Section 1. Equality of rights under the law shall not be denied or abridged by the United States or by any State on account of sex.

Section 2. The Congress shall have the power to enforce, by appropriate legislation, the provisions of this article.

Section 3. This amendment shall take effect two years after the date of ratification.

Unratified Amendment

District of Columbia Statehood Amendment (proposed by Congress August 22, 1978)

Section 1. For purposes of representation in the Congress, election of the President and Vice President, and article V of this Constitution, the District constituting the seat of government of the United States shall be treated as though it were a State.

Section 2. The exercise of the rights and powers conferred under this article shall be by the people of the District constituting the seat of government, and as shall be provided by Congress.

Section 3. The twenty-third article of amendment to the Constitution of the United States is hereby repealed.

Section 4. This article shall be inoperative, unless it shall have been ratified as an amendment to the Constitution by the legislatures of three-fourths of the several states within seven years from the date of its submission.

Amendment XXVII [1992]

No law varying the compensation for the services of the Senators and Representatives, shall take effect, until an election of Representatives shall have intervened.

Glossary

1968 Democratic National Convention: A convention held in Chicago during which numerous antiwar demonstrators outside the convention hall were tear-gassed and clubbed by police. Inside the convention hall, the delegates were bitterly divided over Vietnam. (p. 905)

Abu Ghraib prison: A prison just outside Baghdad, Iraq, where American guards were photographed during the Iraq War abusing and torturing suspected insurgents. (p. 1011)

Advanced Research Projects Agency Network (ARPANET): A decentralized computer network developed in the late 1960s by the U.S. Department of Defense in conjunction with the Massachusetts Institute of Technology. The Internet grew out of the ARPANET. (p. 996)

affirmative action: Policies established in the 1960s and 1970s by governments, businesses, universities, and other institutions to overcome the effects of past discrimination against specific groups such as racial and ethnic minorities and women. Measures to ensure equal opportunity include setting goals for the admission, hiring, and promotion of minorities; considering minority status when allocating resources; and actively encouraging victims of past discrimination to apply for jobs and other resources. (p. 936)

The Affluent Society: A 1958 book by John Kenneth Galbraith that analyzed the nation's successful middle class and argued that the poor were only an "afterthought" in the minds of economists and politicians. (p. 824)

Agricultural Adjustment Act: New Deal legislation passed in May 1933 that aimed at cutting agricultural production to raise crop prices and thus farmers' income. (p. 720)

Al Qaeda: A network of radical Islamic terrorists organized by Osama bin Laden, who issued a call for holy war against Americans and their allies. Members of Al Qaeda were responsible for the 9/11 terrorist attacks. (p. 986)

America First Committee: A committee organized by isolationists in 1940 to oppose the entrance of the United States into World War II. The membership of the committee included senators, journalists, and publishers and such well-respected figures as the aviator Charles Lindbergh. (p. 751)

American Civil Liberties Union: An organization formed during the Red Scare to protect free speech rights. (p. 698)

American exceptionalism: The idea that the United States has a unique destiny to foster democracy and civilization on the world stage. (p. 653)

American Federation of Labor: Organization created by Samuel Gompers in 1886 that coordinated the activities of craft unions and called for direct negotiation with employers in order to achieve benefits for skilled workers. Like other trade unions, the AFL called for the closed shop—all employees had to be union members—to keep out low-wage competition and strengthen unions' bargaining power with employers. (p. 553)

American GI Forum: A group founded by World War II veterans in Corpus Christi, Texas, in 1948 to protest the poor treatment of Mexican American soldiers and veterans. (p. 860)

American Indian Movement (AIM): Organization established in 1968 to address the problems Indians faced in American cities, including poverty and police harassment. AIM organized Indians to end relocation and termination policies and to win greater control over their cultures and communities. (p. 881)

American Liberty League: A group of Republican business leaders and conservative Democrats who banded together to fight what they called the "reckless spending" and "socialist" reforms of the New Deal. (p. 722)

American Plan: Strategy by American business in the 1920s to keep workplaces free of unions, which included refusing to negotiate with trade unions and requiring workers to sign contracts (known as "yellow dog" contracts) pledging not to join a union. (p. 687)

American Protective Association: A powerful political organization of militant Protestants, which for a brief period in the 1890s counted more than two million members. In its virulent anti-Catholicism and calls for restrictions on immigrants, the APA prefigured the revived Ku Klux Klan of the 1920s. (p. 561)

American Recovery and Reinvestment Act: An economic stimulus bill passed in 2009, in response to the Great Recession, that provided $787 billion to state and local governments for schools, hospitals, and transportation projects. It was one of the largest single packages of government spending in American history. (p. 1013)

American Woman Suffrage Association: A women's suffrage organization led by Lucy Stone, Henry Blackwell, and others who remained loyal to the Republican Party, despite its failure to include women's voting rights in the Reconstruction amendments. Stressing the urgency of voting rights for African American men, AWSA leaders held out hope that once Reconstruction had been settled, it would be women's turn. (p. 471)

anarchism: The advocacy of a stateless society achieved by revolutionary means. Feared for their views, anarchists became scapegoats for the 1886 Haymarket Square bombing. (p. 550)

Antiquities Act: A 1906 act that allowed the U.S. president to use executive powers to set aside, as federal monuments, sites of great environmental or cultural significance. Theodore Roosevelt, the first president to invoke the act's powers, used them to preserve the Grand Canyon. (p. 574)

associated state: A system of voluntary business cooperation with government. The Commerce Department helped create two thousand trade associations representing companies in almost every major industry. (p. 689)

Atlanta Compromise: An 1895 address by Booker T. Washington that urged whites and African Americans to work together for the progress of all. Delivered at the Cotton States Exposition in Atlanta, the speech was widely interpreted as approving racial segregation. (p. 577)

Atlantic Charter: A press release by President Roosevelt and British prime minister Winston Churchill in August 1941 calling for economic cooperation, national self-determination, and guarantees of political stability after the war. (p. 752)

baby boom: The surge in the American birthrate between 1945 and 1965, which peaked in 1957 with 4.3 million births. (p. 833)

Bakke v. University of California: The 1978 Supreme Court ruling that limited affirmative action by rejecting a quota system. (p. 937)

Battle of Little Big Horn: The 1876 battle begun when American cavalry under George Armstrong Custer attacked an encampment of Sioux, Arapaho, and Cheyenne Indians who were resisting removal to a reservation. Custer's force was annihilated, but with whites calling for U.S. soldiers to retaliate, the Native American military victory was short-lived. (p. 518)

Bay of Pigs: A failed U.S.-sponsored invasion of Cuba in 1961 by anti-Castro forces who planned to overthrow Fidel Castro's government. (p. 813)

Beats: A small group of literary figures based in New York City and San Francisco in the 1950s who rejected mainstream culture and instead celebrated personal freedom, which often included drug consumption and casual sex. (p. 830)

Beecher-Tilton scandal: A trial, triggered by revelations made by free love advocate and journalist Victoria Woodhull, that exposed unconventional sexual relationships among a leading New York abolitionist pastor and his congregants, discrediting radical Reconstruction by associating some of its advocates with alleged sexual immorality. (p. 472)

Black Codes: Laws passed by southern states after the Civil War that denied ex-slaves the civil rights enjoyed by whites, punished vague crimes such as "vagrancy" or failing to have a labor contract, and tried to force African Americans back to plantation labor systems that closely mirrored those in slavery times. (p. 465)

black nationalism: A major strain of African American thought that emphasized black racial pride and autonomy. Present in black communities for centuries, it periodically came to the fore, as in Marcus Garvey's pan-Africanist movement in the early twentieth century and in various organizations in the 1960s and 1970s, such as the Nation of Islam and the Black Panther Party. (p. 875)

Black Panther Party: A militant organization dedicated to protecting African Americans from police violence, founded in Oakland, California, in 1966 by Huey Newton and Bobby Seale. In the late 1960s the organization spread to other cities, where members undertook a wide range of community-organizing projects, but the Panthers' radicalism and belief in armed self-defense resulted in violent clashes with police. (p. 877)

blues: A form of American music that originated in the Deep South, especially from the black workers in the cotton fields of the Mississippi Delta. (p. 597)

Bonus Army: A group of fifteen thousand to twenty thousand unemployed World War I veterans who set up camps near the Capitol building in 1932 to demand immediate payment of pension awards due to be paid in 1945. (p. 717)

Bracero Program: Officially the Mexican Farm Labor Agreement (signed with Mexico), a federal program that brought hundreds of thousands of Mexican agricultural workers to the United States during and after World War II. The program continued until 1964 and was a major spur of Mexican immigration to the United States. (p. 760)

Bretton Woods: An international conference in New Hampshire in July 1944 that established the World Bank and the International Monetary Fund (IMF). (p. 820)

Brotherhood of Sleeping Car Porters: A prominent black trade union of railroad car porters working for the Pullman Company. (p. 855)

Brown v. Board of Education of Topeka: Supreme Court ruling of 1954 that overturned the "separate but equal" precedent established in *Plessy v. Ferguson* in 1896. The Court declared that separate educational facilities were inherently unequal and thus violated the Fourteenth Amendment. (p. 862)

Burlingame Treaty: An 1868 treaty that guaranteed the rights of U.S. missionaries in China and set official terms for the emigration of Chinese laborers to work in the United States. (p. 497)

Chicago school: A school of architecture dedicated to the design of buildings whose form expressed, rather than masked, their structure and function. (p. 592)

Chicano Moratorium Committee: Group founded by activist Latinos to protest the Vietnam War. (p. 907)

Chinese Exclusion Act: The 1882 law that barred Chinese laborers from entering the United States. It continued in effect until the 1940s. (p. 546)

"City Beautiful" movement: A turn-of-the-twentieth-century movement that advocated landscape beautification, playgrounds, and more and better urban parks. (p. 606)

Civilian Conservation Corps: Federal relief program that provided jobs to millions of unemployed young men who built thousands of bridges, roads, trails, and other structures in state and national parks, bolstering the national infrastructure. (p. 721)

Civil Rights Act of 1866: Legislation passed by Congress that nullified the Black Codes and affirmed that African Americans should have equal benefit of the law. (p. 467)

Civil Rights Act of 1875: A law that required "full and equal" access to jury service and to transportation and public accommodations, irrespective of race. (p. 482)

Civil Rights Act of 1964: Law that responded to demands of the civil rights movement by making discrimination in employment, education, and public accommodations illegal. It was the strongest such measure since Reconstruction and included a ban on sex discrimination in employment. (p. 871)

Civil Rights Cases: A series of 1883 Supreme Court decisions that struck down the Civil Rights Act of 1875, rolling back key Reconstruction laws and paving the way for later decisions that sanctioned segregation. (p. 487)

classical liberalism or laissez-faire: The political ideology of individual liberty, private property, a competitive market economy, free trade, and limited government. The ideal is a *laissez faire* or "let alone" policy, in which government does the least possible, particularly in reference to economic policies such as tariffs and incentives for industrial development. Attacking corruption and defending private property, late-nineteenth-century liberals generally called for elite governance and questioned the advisability of full democratic participation. (pp. 483, 726)

Clayton Antitrust Act: A 1914 law that strengthened federal definitions of "monopoly" and gave more power to the Justice Department to pursue antitrust cases; it also specified that labor unions could not generally be prosecuted for "restraint of trade," ensuring that antitrust laws would apply to corporations rather than unions. (p. 641)

code talkers: Native American soldiers trained to use native languages to send messages in battle during World War II. Neither the Japanese nor the Germans could decipher the codes used by these Navajo, Comanche, Choctaw, and Cherokee speakers, and the messages they sent gave the Allies great advantage in the battle of Iwo Jima, among many others. (p. 757)

Cold War liberalism: A combination of moderate liberal policies that preserved the programs of the New Deal welfare state and forthright anticommunism that vilified the Soviet Union abroad and radicalism at home. Adopted by President Truman and the Democratic Party during the late 1940s and early 1950s. (p. 801)

collective bargaining: A process of negotiation between labor unions and employers, which after World War II translated into rising wages, expanding benefits, and an increasing rate of home ownership. (p. 825)

Committee to Defend America by Aiding the Allies: A group of interventionists who believed in engaging with, rather than withdrawing from, international developments. Interventionists became increasingly vocal in 1940 as war escalated in Europe. (p. 751)

Community Services Organization (CSO): A Latino civil rights group founded in Los Angeles in 1947 that trained many Latino politicians and community activists, including Cesar Chavez and Dolores Huerta. (p. 860)

Comstock Act: An 1873 law that prohibited circulation of "obscene literature," defined as including most information on sex, reproduction, and birth control. (p. 576)

Comstock Lode: A vein of silver ore discovered in Nevada in 1859, leading to one of the West's most important mining booms. The lode was so rich that a Confederate expedition tried unsuccessfully to capture it during the Civil War; its output significantly altered the ratio of silver in circulation, leading to changes in monetary policy. (p. 503)

Congress of Racial Equality (CORE): Civil rights organization founded in 1942 in Chicago by James Farmer and other members of the Fellowship of Reconciliation (FOR) that espoused nonviolent direct action. In 1961 CORE organized a series of what were called Freedom Rides on interstate bus lines throughout the South to call attention to blatant violations of recent Supreme Court rulings against segregation in interstate commerce. (p. 856)

The Conscience of a Conservative: A 1960 book that set forth an uncompromising conservatism and inspired a Republican grassroots movement in support of its author, Barry Goldwater. (p. 957)

consumer credit: New forms of borrowing, such as auto loans and installment plans, that flourished in the 1920s but helped trigger the Great Depression. (p. 691)

containment: The basic U.S. policy of the Cold War, which sought to contain communism within its existing geographic boundaries. Initially, containment focused on the Soviet Union and Eastern Europe, but in the 1950s it came to include China, North Korea, and other parts of the developing world. (p. 789)

Contract with America: Initiatives by Representative Newt Gingrich of Georgia for significant tax cuts, reductions in welfare programs, anticrime measures, and cutbacks in federal regulations. (p. 1005)

Contras: An opposition group in Nicaragua that President Reagan ordered the CIA to assist. While Congress banned the CIA and all other government agencies from providing any military support to the Contras, a lieutenant colonel in the U.S. Marines, Oliver North, used the profits from the Iranian arms deal to assist the Contras, resulting in the Iran-Contra affair. (p. 976)

convict leasing: Notorious system, begun during Reconstruction, whereby southern state officials allowed private companies to hire out prisoners to labor under brutal conditions in mines and other industries. (p. 480)

counterculture: A culture embracing values or lifestyles opposing those of the mainstream culture. Became synonymous with hippies, people who opposed and rejected conventional standards of society and advocated extreme liberalism in their sociopolitical attitudes and lifestyles. (p. 901)

Crédit Mobilier: A sham corporation set up by shareholders in the Union Pacific Railroad to secure government grants at an enormous profit. Organizers of the scheme protected it from investigation by providing gifts of its stock to powerful members of Congress. (p. 484)

"Crime of 1873": A term used by those critical of an 1873 law directing the U.S. Treasury to cease minting silver dollars, retire Civil War–era greenbacks, and replace them with notes backed by the gold standard from an expanded system of national banks. (p. 501)

Cuban missile crisis: The 1962 nuclear standoff between the Soviet Union and the United States when the

Soviets attempted to deploy nuclear missiles in Cuba. (p. 813)

culture war: A term used by Patrick Buchanan in 1992 to describe a long-standing political struggle, dating to the 1920s, between religious traditionalists and secular liberals. Social issues such as abortion rights and the rights of lesbians and gay men divided these groups. (p. 996)

Dawes Severalty Act: The 1887 law that gave Native Americans severalty (individual ownership of land) by dividing reservations into homesteads. The law was a disaster for Native peoples, resulting over several decades in the loss of 66 percent of lands held by Indians at the time of the law's passage. (p. 517)

D-Day: June 6, 1944, the date of the Allied invasion of northern France. D-Day was the largest amphibious assault in world history. The invasion opened a second front against the Germans and moved the Allies closer to victory in Europe. (p. 768)

Defense of Marriage Act: A law enacted by Congress in 1998 that allowed states to refuse to recognize gay marriages or civil unions formed in other jurisdictions. The Supreme Court ruled that DOMA was unconstitutional in 2013. (p. 1002)

deindustrialization: The dismantling of manufacturing — especially in the automobile, steel, and consumer-goods industries — in the decades after World War II, representing a reversal of the process of industrialization that had dominated the American economy from the 1870s through the 1940s. (p. 927)

deregulation: The limiting of regulation by federal agencies. Deregulation of prices in the trucking, airline, and railroad industries had begun under President Carter in the late 1970s, and Reagan expanded it to include cutting back on government protections of consumers, workers, and the environment. (p. 965)

deskilling: The elimination of skilled labor under a new system of mechanized manufacturing, in which workers completed discrete, small-scale tasks rather than crafting an entire product. With deskilling, employers found they could pay workers less and replace them more easily. (p. 537)

détente: The easing of conflict between the United States and the Soviet Union during the Nixon administration, which was achieved by focusing on issues of common concern, such as arms control and trade. (p. 911)

dollar diplomacy: Policy emphasizing the connection between America's economic and political interests overseas. Business would gain from diplomatic efforts on its behalf, while the strengthened American economic presence overseas would give added leverage to American diplomacy. (p. 688)

domino theory: President Eisenhower's theory of containment, which warned that the fall of a non-Communist government to communism in Southeast Asia would trigger the spread of communism to neighboring countries. (p. 810)

dust bowl: An area including the semiarid states of Oklahoma, Texas, New Mexico, Colorado, Arkansas, and Kansas that experienced a severe drought and large dust storms from 1930 to 1941. (p. 739)

Earth Day: An annual event honoring the environment that was first celebrated on April 22, 1970, when 20 million citizens gathered in communities across the country to express their support for a cleaner, healthier planet. (p. 922)

Economic Growth and Tax Relief Act: Legislation introduced by President George W. Bush and passed by Congress in 2001 that slashed income tax rates, extended the earned income credit for the poor, and marked the estate tax to be phased out by 2010. (p. 1008)

Economic Opportunity Act: A 1964 act that created a series of programs, including Head Start to prepare disadvantaged preschoolers for kindergarten and the Job Corps and Upward Bound to provide young people with training and employment, aimed at alleviating poverty and spurring economic growth in impoverished areas. (p. 888)

Economic Recovery Tax Act (ERTA): Legislation introduced by President Reagan and passed by Congress in 1981 that authorized the largest reduction in taxes in the nation's history. (p. 964)

Eighteenth Amendment: The ban on the manufacture and sale of alcohol that went into effect in January 1920. Also called "prohibition," the amendment was repealed in 1933. (p. 698)

Eisenhower Doctrine: President Eisenhower's 1957 declaration that the United States would actively combat communism in the Middle East. (p. 811)

energy crisis: A period of fuel shortages in the United States after the Arab states in the Organization of Petroleum Exporting Countries (OPEC) declared an oil embargo in October 1973. (p. 922)

Enforcement Laws: Acts passed in Congress in 1870 and signed by President U. S. Grant that were designed to protect freedmen's rights under the Fourteenth and Fifteenth Amendments. Authorizing federal prosecutions, military intervention, and martial law to suppress terrorist activity, the Enforcement Laws largely succeeded in shutting down Klan activities. (p. 486)

environmentalism: Activist movement begun in the 1960s that was concerned with protecting the environment through activities such as conservation, pollution control measures, and public awareness campaigns. In response to the new environmental consciousness, the federal government staked out a broad role in environmental regulation in the 1960s and 1970s. (p. 922)

Environmental Protection Agency (EPA): Federal agency created by Congress and President Nixon in 1970 to enforce environmental laws, conduct environmental research, and reduce human health and environmental risks from pollutants. (p. 922)

Equal Pay Act: Law passed in 1963 that established the principle of equal pay for equal work. Trade-union women were especially critical in pushing for, and winning, congressional passage of the law. (p. 893)

Equal Rights Amendment (ERA): Constitutional amendment passed by Congress in 1972 that would require equal treatment of men and women under federal and state law. Facing fierce opposition from the New Right and the Republican Party, the ERA was defeated as time ran out for state ratification in 1982. (p. 938)

Ethics in Government Act: Passed in the wake of the Watergate scandal, the 1978 act that forced political candidates to disclose financial contributions and limited the lobbying activities of former elected officials. (p. 933)

eugenics: An emerging "science" of human breeding in the late nineteenth century that argued that mentally deficient people should be prevented from reproducing. (p. 560)

evangelicalism: The trend in Protestant Christianity that stresses salvation through conversion, repentance of sin, and adherence to scripture; it also stresses the importance of preaching over ritual. (p. 945)

Executive Order 8802: An order signed by President Roosevelt in 1941 that prohibited "discrimination in the employment of workers in defense industries or government because of race, creed, color, or national origin" and established the Fair Employment Practices Commission (FEPC). (p. 759)

Executive Order 9066: An order signed by President Roosevelt in 1942 that authorized the War Department to force Japanese Americans from their West Coast homes and hold them in relocation camps for the rest of the war. (p. 766)

Exodusters: African Americans who walked or rode out of the Deep South following the Civil War, many settling on farms in Kansas in hopes of finding peace and prosperity. (p. 506)

Fair Deal: The domestic policy agenda announced by President Harry S. Truman in 1949. Including civil rights, health care, and education reform, Truman's initiative was only partially successful in Congress. (p. 802)

Fair Labor Standards Act: One of the final major laws of the New Deal, it outlawed child labor, made the 40-hour workweek standard (and mandated overtime pay), and established a national minimum wage. (p. 728)

family values: Values promoted by the Religious Right, including support for the traditional nuclear family and opposition to same-sex marriage and abortion. (p. 981)

Farmers' Alliance: A rural movement founded in Texas during the depression of the 1870s that spread across the plains states and the South. The Farmers' Alliance advocated cooperative stores and exchanges that would circumvent middlemen, and it called for greater government aid to farmers and stricter regulation of railroads. (p. 551)

fascism: An authoritarian system of government characterized by dictatorial rule, extreme nationalism, disdain for civil society, and a conviction that imperialism and warfare are the principal means by which nations attain greatness. The United States went to war against fascism when it faced Nazi Germany under Adolf Hitler and Italy under Benito Mussolini during World War II. (p. 748)

Federal Housing Administration: An agency established by the Federal Housing Act of 1934 that refinanced home mortgages for mortgage holders facing possible foreclosure. (p. 722)

Federal Reserve Act: The central bank system of the United States, created in 1913. The Federal Reserve helps set the money supply level, thus influencing the rate of growth of the U.S. economy, and seeks to ensure the stability of the U.S. monetary system. (p. 640)

Federal Writers' Project: A program under the Works Progress Administration (WPA) from 1935 to 1939 in which historians, teachers, editors, novelists, poets, and playwrights were employed by the federal government to produce a variety of materials — this included, for example, interviews with hundreds of former slaves; a major survey of American foodways; and state-by-state guidebooks to history, geography, and culture. (p. 742)

The Feminine Mystique: The title of an influential book written in 1963 by Betty Friedan critiquing the ideal whereby women were encouraged to confine themselves to roles within the domestic sphere. (p. 893)

feminism: The ideology that women should enter the public sphere not only to work on behalf of others, but also for their own equal rights and advancement. Feminists moved beyond advocacy of women's voting rights to seek greater autonomy in professional careers, property rights, and personal relationships. (p. 584)

Fetterman massacre: A massacre in December 1866 in which 1,500 Sioux warriors lured Captain William Fetterman and 80 soldiers from a Wyoming fort and attacked them. With the Fetterman massacre the Sioux succeeded in closing the Bozeman Trail, the main route into Montana. (p. 512)

Fifteenth Amendment: Constitutional amendment ratified in 1870 that forbade states to deny citizens the right to vote on grounds of race, color, or "previous condition of servitude." (p. 470)

fireside chats: A series of informal radio addresses Franklin Roosevelt made to the nation in which he explained New Deal initiatives. (p. 719)

flapper: A young woman of the 1920s who defied conventional standards of conduct by wearing short skirts and makeup, freely spending the money she earned on the latest fashions, dancing to jazz, and flaunting her liberated lifestyle. (p. 691)

Four Freedoms: Identified by President Franklin D. Roosevelt as the most basic human rights: freedom of speech, freedom of religion, freedom from want, and freedom from fear. The president used these ideas of freedom to justify support for England during World War II, which in turn pulled the United States into the war. (p. 752)

Four-Minute Men: Name given to thousands of volunteers enlisted by the Committee on Public Information to deliver short prowar speeches at movie theaters to galvanize public support for the war. Their work, as part of the broader objectives of the CPI, helped create a political climate intolerant of dissent. (p. 670)

Fourteen Points: Principles for a new world order proposed in 1919 by President Woodrow Wilson as a basis for peace negotiations at Versailles. Among them were open diplomacy, freedom of the seas, free trade, territorial integrity, arms reduction, national self-determination, and creation of the League of Nations. (p. 674)

Fourteenth Amendment: Constitutional amendment ratified in 1868 that made all native-born or naturalized persons U.S. citizens and prohibited states from abridging the rights of national citizens, thus giving primacy to national rather than state citizenship. (p. 467)

Freedmen's Bureau: Government organization created in March 1865 to aid displaced blacks and other war refugees. Active until the early 1870s, it was the first federal agency in history that provided direct payments to assist those in poverty and to foster social welfare. (p. 467)

Freedom of Information Act: Passed in the wake of the Watergate scandal, the 1974 act that gave citizens access to federal records. (p. 932)

free silver: A policy of loosening the money supply by expanding federal coinage to include silver as well as gold. Advocates of the policy thought it would encourage borrowing and stimulate industry, but the defeat of Democratic presidential candidate William Jennings Bryan ended the "free silver" movement and gave Republicans power to retain the gold standard. (p. 625)

fundamentalism: A term adopted by Protestants, between the 1890s and the 1910s, who rejected modernism and historical interpretations of scripture and asserted the literal truth of the Bible. Fundamentalists have historically seen secularism and religious relativism as markers of sin that will be punished by God. (p. 563)

Ghost Dance movement: Religion of the late 1880s and early 1890s that combined elements of Christianity and traditional Native American religion. It fostered Plains Indians' hope that they could, through sacred dances, resurrect the great bison herds and call up a storm to drive whites back across the Atlantic. (p. 520)

glasnost: The policy introduced by Soviet president Mikhail Gorbachev during the 1980s that involved greater openness and freedom of expression and that contributed, unintentionally, to the 1991 breakup of the Soviet Union. (p. 977)

Glass-Steagall Act: A 1933 law that created the Federal Deposit Insurance Corporation (FDIC), which insured deposits up to $2,500 (and now up to $250,000). The act also prohibited banks from making risky, unsecured investments with customers' deposits. (p. 720)

globalization: The spread of political, cultural, and economic influences and connections among countries, businesses, and individuals around the world through trade, immigration, communication, and other means. (p. 986)

gold standard: The practice of backing a country's currency with its reserves of gold. In 1873 the United States, following Great Britain and other European nations, began converting to the gold standard. (p. 501)

Gospel of Wealth: Andrew Carnegie's argument that corporate leaders' success showed their "fitness" to lead society and that poverty demonstrated, on the contrary, lack of "fitness" to compete in the new economy. Carnegie advocated, however, that wealthy men should use their fortunes for the public good. (p. 530)

Granger laws: Economic regulatory laws passed in some midwestern states in the late 1870s, triggered by pressure from farmers and the Greenback-Labor Party. (p. 549)

Great Migration: The migration of over 400,000 African Americans from the rural South to the industrial cities of the North during and after World War I. (p. 670)

Great Railroad Strike of 1877: A nationwide strike of thousands of railroad workers and labor allies, who protested the growing power of railroad corporations and the steep wage cuts imposed by railroad managers amid a severe economic depression that had begun in 1873. (p. 548)

Great Society: President Lyndon B. Johnson's domestic program, which included civil rights legislation, antipoverty programs, government subsidy of medical care, federal aid to education, consumer protection, and aid to the arts and humanities. (p. 886)

Greenback-Labor Party: A national political movement calling on the government to increase the money supply in order to assist borrowers and foster economic growth; "Greenbackers" also called for greater regulation of corporations and laws enforcing an eight-hour workday. (p. 549)

Group of Eight (G8): An international organization of the leading capitalist industrial nations: the United States, Britain, Germany, France, Italy, Japan, Canada, and Russia. The G8 largely control the world's major international financial organizations: the World Bank, the International Monetary Fund (IMF), and the World Trade Organization (WTO). In 2014 Russia was suspended because of its invasion of Crimea. (p. 995)

Gulf of Tonkin Resolution: Resolution passed by Congress in 1964 in the wake of a naval confrontation in the Gulf of Tonkin between the United States and North Vietnam. It gave the president virtually unlimited authority in conducting the Vietnam War. The Senate terminated the resolution in 1970 following outrage over the U.S. invasion of Cambodia. (p. 896)

Harlem Renaissance: A flourishing of African American artists, writers, intellectuals, and social leaders in the 1920s, centered in the neighborhoods of Harlem, New York City. (p. 704)

Haymarket Square: The May 4, 1886, conflict in Chicago in which both workers and policemen were killed or wounded during a labor demonstration called by local anarchists. The incident created a backlash against all labor organizations, including the Knights of Labor. (p. 550)

Hepburn Act: A 1906 antitrust law that empowered the federal Interstate Commerce Commission to set railroad shipment rates wherever it believed that railroads were unfairly colluding to set prices. (p. 631)

HIV/AIDS: A deadly disease that killed nearly one hundred thousand people in the United States in the 1980s. (p. 967)

Hollywood: The city in southern California that became synonymous with the American movie industry in the 1920s. (p. 691)

Holocaust: Germany's campaign during World War II to exterminate all Jews living in German-controlled lands, along with other groups the Nazis deemed "undesirable." In all, some 11 million people were killed in the Holocaust, most of them Jews. (p. 770)

Homestead Act: The 1862 act that gave 160 acres of free western land to any applicant who occupied and improved the property. This policy led to the rapid development of the American West after the Civil War; facing arid conditions in the West, however, many homesteaders found themselves unable to live on their land. (p. 502)

Homestead lockout: The 1892 lockout of workers at the Homestead, Pennsylvania, steel mill after Andrew Carnegie refused to renew the union contract. Union supporters attacked the guards hired to close them out and protect strikebreakers who had been employed by the mill, but the National Guard soon suppressed this resistance and Homestead, like other steel plants, became a non-union mill. (p. 528)

horizontal integration: A business concept invented in the late nineteenth century to pressure competitors and force rivals to merge their companies into a conglomerate. John D. Rockefeller of Standard Oil pioneered this business model. (p. 532)

hostage crisis: Crisis that began in 1979 after the deposed shah of Iran was allowed into the United States following the Iranian Revolution. Iranians broke into the U.S. embassy in Tehran and took sixty-six Americans hostage. The hostage crisis lasted 444 days and contributed to President Carter's reelection defeat. (p. 961)

House Un-American Activities Committee (HUAC): Congressional committee especially prominent during the early years of the Cold War that investigated Americans who might be disloyal to the government or might have associated with communists or other radicals. (p. 804)

Hull House: One of the first and most famous social settlements, founded in 1889 by Jane Addams and her companion Ellen Gates Starr in an impoverished, largely Italian immigrant neighborhood on Chicago's West Side. (p. 609)

Hundred Days: A legendary session during the first few months of Franklin Roosevelt's administration in which Congress enacted fifteen major bills that focused primarily on four problems: banking failures, agricultural overproduction, the business slump, and soaring unemployment. (p. 719)

Immigration and Nationality Act: A 1965 law that eliminated the discriminatory 1924 nationality quotas, established a slightly higher total limit on immigration, included provisions to ease the entry of immigrants with skills in high demand, and allowed immediate family members of legal residents in the United States to be admitted outside of the total numerical limit. (p. 998)

Indian Reorganization Act: A 1934 law that reversed the Dawes Act of 1887. Through the law, Indians won a greater degree of religious freedom, and tribal governments regained their status as semisovereign dependent nations. (p. 737)

Industrial Workers of the World: An umbrella union and radical political group founded in 1905, dedicated to organizing unskilled workers to oppose capitalism. Nicknamed the Wobblies, it advocated direct action by workers, including sabotage and general strikes. (p. 635)

Insular Cases: A set of Supreme Court rulings in 1901 that declared that the U.S. Constitution did not automatically extend citizenship to people in acquired territories; only Congress could decide whether to grant citizenship. (p. 658)

International Monetary Fund (IMF): A fund established to stabilize currencies and provide a predictable monetary environment for trade, with the U.S. dollar serving as the benchmark. (p. 821)

Interstate Commerce Act: An 1887 act that created the Interstate Commerce Commission (ICC), a federal regulatory agency designed to oversee the railroad industry and prevent collusion and unfair rates. (p. 551)

Iran-Contra affair: Reagan administration scandal that involved the sale of arms to Iran in exchange for its efforts to secure the release of hostages held in Lebanon and the redirection — illegal because banned by American law — of the proceeds of those sales to the Nicaraguan Contras. (p. 976)

jazz: Unique American musical form that arose in New Orleans and other parts of the South before

World War I. Jazz musicians developed an ensemble improvisational style. (p. 705)

Jim Crow: Laws that required separation of the races, especially blacks and whites, in public facilities. This system of racial segregation in the South lasted a century, from after the Civil War until the 1960s. (p. 568)

Kerner Commission: Informal name for the National Advisory Commission on Civil Disorders, formed by the president to investigate the causes of the 1967 urban riots. Its 1968 report warned that "our nation is moving toward two societies, one black, one white, separate and unequal." (p. 843)

Keynesian economics: The theory, developed by British economist John Maynard Keynes in the 1930s, that purposeful government intervention in the economy (through lowering or raising taxes, interest rates, and government spending) can affect the level of overall economic activity and thereby prevent severe depressions and runaway inflation. (p. 728)

kitchen debate: A 1959 debate over the merits of their rival systems between U.S. vice president Richard Nixon and Soviet premier Nikita Khrushchev at the opening of an American exhibition in Moscow. (p. 818)

Knights of Labor: The first mass labor organization created among America's working class. Founded in 1869 and peaking in strength in the mid-1880s, the Knights of Labor attempted to bridge boundaries of ethnicity, gender, ideology, race, and occupation to build a "universal brotherhood" of all workers. (p. 549)

Ku Klux Klan: Secret society that first undertook violence against African Americans in the South after the Civil War but was reborn in 1915 to fight the perceived threats posed by African Americans, immigrants, radicals, feminists, Catholics, and Jews. (pp. 485, 700)

land-grant colleges: Authorized by the Morrill Act of 1862, land-grant colleges were public universities founded to broaden educational opportunities and foster technical and scientific expertise. These universities were funded by the Morrill Act, which authorized the sale of federal lands to raise money for higher education. (p. 502)

La Raza Unida: An organization founded in Texas in 1970 by Mexican Americans as an alternative to the two major political parties; La Raza Unida (The United Race) ran candidates for state governor and other local government positions in the 1970s. It was an expression of the Chicano/a movement's attempts to create political unity among American citizens of Mexican descent. (p. 881)

Lawrence v. Texas: A 2003 landmark decision by the Supreme Court that limited the power of states to prohibit private homosexual activity between consenting adults. (p. 1003)

League of Nations: The international organization bringing together world governments to prevent future hostilities, proposed by President Woodrow Wilson in the aftermath of World War I. Although the League of Nations did form, the United States never became a member state. (p. 675)

Lend-Lease Act: Legislation in 1941 that enabled Britain to obtain arms from the United States without cash but with the promise to reimburse the United States when the war ended. The act reflected Roosevelt's desire to assist the British in any way possible, short of war. (p. 752)

Lochner v. New York: A 1905 Supreme Court ruling that New York State could not limit bakers' workday to ten hours because that violated bakers' rights to make contracts. (p. 630)

Lodge Bill: Also known as the Federal Elections Bill of 1890, a bill proposing that whenever 100 citizens in any district appealed for intervention, a bipartisan federal board could investigate and seat the rightful winner. The defeat of the bill was a blow to those seeking to defend African American voting rights and to ensure full participation in politics. (p. 622)

Lone Wolf v. Hitchcock: A 1903 Supreme Court ruling that Congress could make whatever Indian policies it chose, ignoring all existing treaties. (p. 516)

Loyalty-Security Program: A program created in 1947 by President Truman that permitted officials to investigate any employee of the federal government for "subversive" activities. (p. 804)

management revolution: An internal management structure adopted by many large, complex corporations that distinguished top executives from those responsible for day-to-day operations and departmentalized operations by function. (p. 531)

Manhattan Project: Top-secret project authorized by Franklin Roosevelt in 1942 to develop an atomic bomb ahead of the Germans. The Americans who worked on the project at Los Alamos, New Mexico (among other highly secretive sites around the country), succeeded in producing a successful atomic bomb by July 1945. (p. 773)

March on Washington: Officially named the March on Washington for Jobs and Freedom, on August 28, 1963, a quarter of a million people marched to the Lincoln Memorial to demand that Congress end Jim Crow racial discrimination and launch a major jobs program to bring needed employment to black communities. (p. 869)

Marshall Plan: Aid program begun in 1948 to help European economies recover from World War II. (p. 793)

maternalism: The belief that women should contribute to civic and political life through their special talents as mothers, Christians, and moral guides. Maternalists put this ideology into action by creating dozens of social reform organizations. (p. 578)

Medicaid: A health plan for the poor passed in 1965 and paid for by general tax revenues and administered by the states. (p. 891)

Medicare: A health plan for the elderly passed in 1965 and funded by a surcharge on Social Security payroll taxes. (p. 891)

Mexican American Legal Defense and Education Fund (MALDEF): A Mexican American civil rights organization founded in 1967 and based on the model of the NAACP Legal Defense and Education Fund. MALDEF focused on legal issues and endeavored to win protections against discrimination through court decisions. (p. 880)

military-industrial complex: A term President Eisenhower used to refer to the military establishment and defense contractors who, he warned, exercised undue influence over the national government. (p. 822)

Minor v. Happersett: A Supreme Court decision in 1875 that ruled that suffrage rights were not inherent in citizenship and had not been granted by the Fourteenth Amendment, as some women's rights advocates argued. Women were citizens, the Court ruled, but state legislatures could deny women the vote if they wished. (p. 471)

Mississippi Freedom Democratic Party: Party founded in Mississippi during the Freedom Summer of 1964.

Its members attempted to attend the 1964 Democratic National Convention in Atlantic City, New Jersey, as the legitimate representatives of their state, but Democratic leaders refused to recognize the party. (p. 871)

modernism: A movement that questioned the ideals of progress and order, rejected realism, and emphasized new cultural forms. Modernism became the first great literary and artistic movement of the twentieth century and remains influential today. (p. 564)

Montgomery Bus Boycott: Yearlong boycott of Montgomery's segregated bus system in 1955–1956 by the city's African American population. The boycott brought Martin Luther King Jr. to national prominence and ended in victory when the Supreme Court declared segregated seating on public transportation unconstitutional. (p. 865)

Moral Majority: A political organization established by evangelist Jerry Falwell in 1979 to mobilize conservative Christian voters on behalf of Ronald Reagan's campaign for president. (p. 963)

mothers' pensions: Progressive Era government support provided to mothers whose husbands had died, been disabled, or abandoned the family. Recipients had to meet standards of "respectability" defined by middle-class home visitors, but those who met approval got help in raising their young children. (p. 634)

muckrakers: A critical term, first applied by Theodore Roosevelt, for investigative journalists who published exposés of political scandals and industrial abuses. (p. 599)

Muller v. Oregon: A 1908 Supreme Court case that upheld an Oregon law limiting women's workday to ten hours, based on the need to protect women's health for motherhood. *Muller* complicated the earlier decision in *Lochner v. New York*, laying out grounds on which states could intervene to protect workers. It divided women's rights activists, however, because some saw its provisions as discriminatory. (p. 633)

multiculturalism: The promotion of diversity in gender, race, ethnicity, religion, and sexual preference. This political and social policy became increasingly popular in the United States during the 1980s post–civil rights era. (p. 1001)

multinational corporations: Corporations with offices and factories in multiple countries, which expanded to find new markets and cheaper sources of labor. Globalization was made possible by the proliferation of these multinational corporations. (p. 995)

Munich Conference: A conference in Munich held in September 1938 during which Britain and France agreed to allow Germany to annex the Sudetenland — a German-speaking border area of Czechoslovakia — in return for Hitler's pledge to seek no more territory. (p. 751)

Munn v. Illinois: An 1877 Supreme Court case that affirmed that states could regulate key businesses, such as railroads and grain elevators, if those businesses were "clothed in the public interest." (p. 500)

mutual aid society: An urban aid society that served members of an ethnic immigrant group, usually those from a particular province or town. The societies functioned as fraternal clubs that collected dues from members in order to pay support in case of death or disability. (p. 593)

My Lai: Vietnamese village where U.S. Army troops executed nearly five hundred people in 1968, including a large number of women and children. (p. 911)

National American Woman Suffrage Association: Women's suffrage organization created in 1890 by the union of the National Woman Suffrage Association and the American Woman Suffrage Association. Up to national ratification of suffrage in 1920, the NAWSA played a central role in campaigning for women's right to vote. (p. 584)

National Association for the Advancement of Colored People (NAACP): An organization founded in 1909 by leading African American reformers and white allies as a vehicle for advocating equal rights for African Americans, especially through the courts. (p. 635)

National Association of Colored Women: An organization created in 1896 by African American women to provide community support. Through its local clubs, the NACW arranged for the care of orphans, founded homes for the elderly, advocated temperance, undertook public health campaigns, campaigned for women's suffrage, and raised awareness of racial injustice (such as lynching, segregated facilities, and disfranchisement). (p. 583)

National Association of Manufacturers: An association of industrialists and business leaders opposed to government regulation. In the era of the New Deal, the group promoted free enterprise and capitalism through a publicity campaign of radio programs, motion pictures, billboards, and direct mail. (p. 722)

National Child Labor Committee: A reform organization that worked (unsuccessfully) to win a federal law banning child labor. The NCLC hired photographer Lewis Hine to record brutal conditions in mines and mills where thousands of children worked. (p. 633)

National Consumers' League: Begun in New York, a national progressive organization that encouraged women, through their shopping decisions, to support fair wages and working conditions for industrial laborers. (p. 610)

national debt: The cumulative total of all budget deficits. (p. 965)

National Defense Education Act: A 1958 act, passed in response to the Soviet launching of the *Sputnik* satellite, that funneled millions of dollars into American universities, helping institutions such as the University of California at Berkeley and the Massachusetts Institute of Technology, among others, become the leading research centers in the world. (p. 822)

National Interstate and Defense Highways Act: A 1956 law authorizing the construction of a national highway system. (p. 841)

National Municipal League: A political reform organization that advised cities to elect small councils and hire professional city managers who would direct operations like a corporate executive. (p. 605)

National Organization for Women (NOW): Women's civil rights organization formed in 1966. Initially, NOW focused on eliminating gender discrimination in public institutions and the workplace, but by the 1970s it also embraced many of the issues raised by more radical feminists. (p. 893)

National Origins Act: A 1924 law limiting annual immigration from each country to no more than 2 percent of that nationality's percentage of the U.S. population as it had stood in 1890. The law severely limited immigration, especially from Southern and Eastern Europe. (p. 699)

National Park Service: A federal agency founded in 1916 that provided comprehensive oversight of the growing system of national parks. (p. 573)

National Recovery Administration: Federal agency established in June 1933 to promote industrial recovery during the Great Depression. It encouraged industrialists to voluntarily adopt codes that defined fair working conditions, set prices, and minimized competition. (p. 720)

National Review: A conservative magazine founded by editor William F. Buckley in 1955, who used it to criticize liberal policy. (p. 959)

National Socialist (Nazi) Party: German political party led by Adolf Hitler, who became chancellor of Germany in 1933. The party's ascent was fueled by huge World War I reparation payments, economic depression, fear of communism, labor unrest, and rising unemployment. (p. 749)

National War Labor Board: A federal agency founded in 1918 that established an eight-hour day for war workers (with time-and-a-half pay for overtime), endorsed equal pay for women, and supported workers' right to organize. (p. 667)

National Woman's Party: A political party founded in 1916 that fought for an Equal Rights Amendment to the U.S. Constitution in the early twentieth century. (p. 671)

National Woman Suffrage Association: A suffrage group headed by Elizabeth Cady Stanton and Susan B. Anthony that stressed the need for women to lead organizations on their own behalf. The NWSA focused exclusively on women's rights — sometimes denigrating men of color in the process — and took up the battle for a federal women's suffrage amendment. (p. 471)

Nation of Islam: A religion founded in the United States that became a leading source of black nationalist thought in the 1960s. Black Muslims preached an apocalyptic brand of Islam, anticipating the day when Allah would banish the white "devils" and give the black nation justice. (p. 875)

Negro Leagues: Professional baseball teams formed for and by black players, after the main national leagues began to exclude all African American players in the 1890s. Enduring until the desegregation of baseball after World War II, the leagues enabled black men to showcase athletic ability and race pride, but their working conditions and wages were much less desirable than those of players in the white leagues. (p. 571)

Neutrality Act of 1935: Legislation that sought to avoid entanglement in foreign wars while protecting trade. It imposed an embargo on selling arms to warring countries and declared that Americans traveling on the ships of belligerent nations did so at their own risk. (p. 750)

Newlands Reclamation Act: A 1902 law, supported by President Theodore Roosevelt, that allowed the federal government to sell public lands to raise money for irrigation projects that expanded agriculture on arid lands. (p. 632)

New Left: A term applied to radical students of the 1960s and 1970s, distinguishing their activism from the Old Left — the communists and socialists of the 1930s and 1940s, who tended to focus on economic and labor questions rather than cultural issues. (p. 900)

"New Look": The defense policy of the Eisenhower administration that stepped up production of the hydrogen bomb and developed long-range bombing capabilities. (p. 807)

New Nationalism: In a 1910 speech, Theodore Roosevelt called for a "New Nationalism" that promoted government intervention to enhance public welfare, including a federal child labor law, more recognition of labor rights, a national minimum wage for women, women's suffrage, and curbs on the power of federal courts to stop reform. (p. 636)

New South: A nickname for the former Confederate states, used by boosters to describe the region's economic diversification and growth of industrial jobs in the post–Civil War era. Because of the region's poverty, many of those industries were extractive (such as coal and timber), and some (like textiles) were low-wage and involved considerable child labor. (p. 539)

North American Free Trade Agreement (NAFTA): A 1993 treaty that eliminated all tariffs and trade barriers among the United States, Canada, and Mexico. (p. 995)

North Atlantic Treaty Organization (NATO): Military alliance formed in 1949 among the United States, Canada, and Western European nations to counter any possible Soviet threat. (p. 794)

NSC-68: Top-secret government report of April 1950 warning that national survival in the face of Soviet communism required a massive military buildup. (p. 795)

Omaha Platform: An 1892 statement by the Populists calling for stronger government to protect ordinary Americans. (p. 623)

"open door" policy: A claim put forth by U.S. Secretary of State John Hay that all nations seeking to do business in China should have equal trade access. (p. 658)

Operation Rescue: A movement founded by religious activist Randall Terry in 1987 that mounted protests outside abortion clinics and harassed their staffs and clients. (p. 1002)

Operation Rolling Thunder: Massive bombing campaign against North Vietnam authorized by President Johnson in 1965; against expectations, it ended up hardening the will of the North Vietnamese to continue fighting. (p. 896)

Organization of Petroleum Exporting Countries (OPEC): A cartel formed in 1960 by the Persian Gulf states and other oil-rich developing countries that allowed its members to exert greater control over the price of oil. (p. 920)

The Other America: A 1962 book by left-wing social critic Michael Harrington, chronicling "the economic underworld of American life." His study made it clear that in economic terms the bottom class remained far behind. (p. 824)

Palmer raids: A series of raids led by Attorney General A. Mitchell Palmer on radical organizations that peaked in January 1920, when federal agents arrested six thousand citizens and aliens and denied them access to legal counsel. (p. 685)

pan-Africanism: The idea that people of African descent, in all parts of the world, have a common heritage and destiny and should cooperate in political action. (p. 706)

Panama Canal: A canal across the Isthmus of Panama connecting trade between the Atlantic and Pacific oceans. Built by the U.S. Army Corps of Engineers and opened in 1914, the canal gave U.S. naval vessels quick access to the Pacific and provided the United States with a commanding position in the Western Hemisphere. (p. 661)

Patient Protection and Affordable Care Act: Sweeping 2010 health-care reform bill championed by President Obama that established nearly universal health insurance by providing subsidies and compelling larger businesses to offer coverage to employees. (p. 1013)

Peace Corps: Program launched by President Kennedy in 1961 through which young American volunteers helped with education, health, and other projects in developing countries around the world. (p. 813)

Pearl Harbor: A naval base in Pearl Harbor, Hawaii, that was attacked by Japanese bombers on December 7, 1941; more than 2,400 Americans were killed. The following day, President Roosevelt asked Congress for a declaration of war against Japan. (p. 753)

Pendleton Act: An 1883 law establishing a nonpartisan Civil Service Commission to fill federal jobs by examination. The Pendleton Act dealt a major blow to the "spoils system" and sought to ensure that government positions were filled by trained, professional employees. (p. 620)

perestroika: The economic restructuring policy introduced by Soviet president Mikhail Gorbachev during the 1980s that contributed, unintentionally, to the 1991 breakup of the Soviet Union. (p. 977)

Persian Gulf War: The 1991 war between Iraq and a U.S.-led international coalition that was sparked by the 1990 Iraqi invasion of Kuwait. A forty-day bombing campaign against Iraq followed by coalition troops storming into Kuwait brought a quick coalition victory. (p. 982)

Personal Responsibility and Work Opportunity Reconciliation Act: Legislation signed by President Clinton in 1996 that replaced Aid to Families with Dependent Children, the major welfare program dating to the New Deal era, with Temporary Assistance for Needy Families, which provided grants to the states to assist the poor and which limited welfare payments to two years, with a lifetime maximum of five years. (p. 1005)

Planned Parenthood of Southeastern Pennsylvania v. Casey: A 1992 Supreme Court case that upheld a law requiring a twenty-four-hour waiting period prior to an abortion. Although the decision upheld certain restrictions on abortions, it affirmed the "essential holding" in *Roe v. Wade* (1973) that women had a constitutional right to control their reproduction. (p. 1003)

Platt Amendment: A 1902 amendment to the Cuban constitution that blocked Cuba from making a treaty with any country except the United States and gave the United States the right to intervene in Cuban affairs. The amendment was a condition for U.S. withdrawal from the newly independent island. (p. 658)

Plessy v. Ferguson: An 1896 Supreme Court case that ruled that racially segregated railroad cars and other public facilities, if they claimed to be "separate but equal," were permissible according to the Fourteenth Amendment. (p. 567)

political machines: Complex, hierarchical party organizations such as New York's Tammany Hall, whose candidates remained in office on the strength of their political organization and their personal relationship with voters, especially working-class immigrants who had little alternative access to political power. (p. 602)

Popular Front: A small but vocal group of Americans who pushed for greater U.S. involvement in Europe. American Communist Party members, African American civil rights activists, and trade unionists, among other members of the Popular Front coalition, encouraged Roosevelt to take a stronger stand against European fascism. (p. 750)

Port Huron Statement: A 1962 manifesto by Students for a Democratic Society from its first national convention in Port Huron, Michigan, expressing students' disillusionment with the nation's consumer culture and the gulf between rich and poor, as well as a rejection of Cold War foreign policy, including the war in Vietnam. (p. 900)

Potsdam Conference: The July 1945 conference in which American officials convinced the Soviet Union leader Joseph Stalin to accept German reparations only from the Soviet zone, or far eastern part of Germany. The agreement paved the way for the division of Germany into East and West. (p. 787)

Presidential Commission on the Status of Women: Commission appointed by President Kennedy in 1961, which issued a 1963 report documenting job and educational discrimination. (p. 893)

producerism: The argument that real economic wealth is created by workers who make their living by physical labor, such as farmers and craftsmen, and that merchants, lawyers, bankers, and other middlemen unfairly gain their wealth from such "producers." (p. 549)

progressivism: A loose term for the cause of political reformers — especially those from the elite and middle classes — who worked to improve the political system, fight poverty, conserve environmental resources, and increase government involvement in the economy.

Giving their name to the "Progressive Era," such reformers were often prompted to act by fear that mass, radical protests by workers and farmers would spread, as well as by their desire to enhance social welfare and social justice. (p. 605)

Proposition 13: A measure passed overwhelmingly by Californians to roll back property taxes, cap future increases for present owners, and require that all tax measures have a two-thirds majority in the legislature. Proposition 13 inspired "tax revolts" across the country and helped conservatives define an enduring issue: low taxes. (p. 931)

Proposition 209: A proposition approved by California voters in 1996 that outlawed affirmative action in state employment and public education. (p. 1001)

protective tariff: A tax or duty on foreign producers of goods coming into or imported into the United States; tariffs gave U.S. manufacturers a competitive advantage in America's gigantic domestic market. (p. 496)

Public Works Administration: A New Deal construction program established by Congress in 1933. Designed to put people back to work, the PWA built the Boulder Dam (renamed Hoover Dam) and Grand Coulee Dam, among other large public works projects. (p. 721)

Pure Food and Drug Act: A 1906 law regulating the conditions in the food and drug industries to ensure a safe supply of food and medicine. (p. 610)

race riot: A term for an attack on African Americans by white mobs, triggered by political conflicts, street altercations, or rumors of crime. In some cases, such "riots" were not spontaneous but planned in advance by a group of leaders seeking to enforce white supremacy. (p. 595)

"rain follows the plow": An unfounded theory that settlement and farming of the Great Plains caused an increase in rainfall. (p. 505)

Reagan coalition: A coalition supporting Ronald Reagan that included the traditional core of Republican Party voters, middle-class suburbanites and migrants to the Sunbelt states, blue-collar Catholics, and a large contingent of southern whites, an electorally key group of former Democrats that had been gradually moving toward the Republican Party since 1964. (p. 963)

Reagan Democrats: Blue-collar Catholics from industrialized midwestern states such as Michigan, Ohio, and

Illinois who were dissatisfied with the direction of liberalism in the 1970s and left the Democratic Party for the Republicans. (p. 964)

realism: A movement that called for writers and artists to picture daily life as precisely and truly as possible. (p. 564)

Reconstruction Act of 1867: An act that divided the conquered South into five military districts, each under the command of a U.S. general. To reenter the Union, former Confederate states had to grant the vote to freedmen and deny it to leading ex-Confederates. (p. 467)

Red Scare: A term for anticommunist hysteria that swept the United States, first after World War I, and led to a series of government raids on alleged subversives and a suppression of civil liberties. (p. 685)

Red Summer: The summer and fall of 1919, in which anti-black riots by white Americans in more than two dozen cities led to hundreds of deaths. So named because of the bloody clashes. The worst occurred in Chicago, in which 38 people were killed (23 blacks, 15 whites), 537 injured, and 1,000 black families made homeless. (p. 686)

Religious Right: Politically active religious conservatives, especially Catholics and evangelical Christians, who became particularly vocal in the 1980s against feminism, abortion, and homosexuality and who promoted "family values." (p. 959)

Revenue Act: A 1942 act that expanded the number of people paying income taxes from 3.9 million to 42.6 million. These taxes on personal incomes and business profits paid half the cost of World War II. (p. 756)

rights liberalism: The conviction that individuals require government protection from discrimination. This version of liberalism was promoted by the civil rights and women's movements and focused on identities — such as race or gender — rather than the general social welfare of New Deal liberalism. (p. 850)

Roe v. Wade: The 1973 Supreme Court ruling that the Constitution protects the right to abortion, which states cannot prohibit in the early stages of pregnancy. The decision galvanized social conservatives and made abortion a controversial policy issue for decades to come. (p. 939)

Rome-Berlin Axis: A political and military alliance formed in 1936 between German dictator Adolf Hitler and the Italian dictator Benito Mussolini. (p. 750)

Roosevelt Corollary: The 1904 assertion by President Theodore Roosevelt that the United States would act as a "policeman" in the Caribbean region and intervene in the affairs of nations that were guilty of "wrongdoing or impotence" in order to protect U.S. interests in Latin America. (p. 661)

Roosevelt recession: A recession from 1937 to 1938 that occurred after President Roosevelt cut the federal budget. (p. 728)

Root-Takahira Agreement: A 1908 agreement between the United States and Japan confirming principles of free oceanic commerce and recognizing Japan's authority over Manchuria. (p. 660)

Rural Electrification Administration: An agency established in 1935 to promote nonprofit farm cooperatives that offered loans to farmers to install power lines. (p. 741)

Rust Belt: The once heavily industrialized regions of the Northeast and Midwest that went into decline after deindustrialization. By the 1970s and 1980s, these regions were full of abandoned plants and distressed communities. (p. 927)

Sand Creek massacre: The November 29, 1864, massacre of more than one hundred peaceful Cheyennes, largely women and children, by John M. Chivington's Colorado militia. (p. 512)

Sandinistas: The democratically elected group in Nicaragua that President Reagan accused of threatening U.S. business interests. Reagan attempted to overthrow them by ordering the CIA to assist an armed opposition group called the Contras. (p. 976)

scientific management: A system of organizing work developed by Frederick W. Taylor in the late nineteenth century. It was designed to coax maximum output from the individual worker, increase efficiency, and reduce production costs. (p. 537)

Scopes trial: The 1925 trial of John Scopes, a biology teacher in Dayton, Tennessee, for violating his state's ban on teaching evolution. The trial created a nationwide media frenzy and came to be seen as a showdown between urban and rural values. (p. 698)

Securities and Exchange Commission: A commission established by Congress in 1934 to regulate the stock market. The commission had broad powers to determine how stocks and bonds were sold to the public, to set rules for margin (credit) transactions, and to prevent stock sales by those with inside information about corporate plans. (p. 722)

Sedition Act of 1918: Wartime law that prohibited any words or behavior that might promote resistance to the United States or help in the cause of its enemies. (p. 670)

service industries: Term that includes food, beverage, and tourist industries, financial and medical service industries, and computer technology industries, which were the leading sectors of U.S. growth in the second half of the 1980s. This pattern represented a shift from reliance on the heavy industries of steel, autos, and chemicals. (p. 970)

Servicemen's Readjustment Act: Popularly known as the GI Bill, 1944 legislation authorizing the government to provide World War II veterans with funds for education, housing, and health care, as well as loans to start businesses and buy homes. (p. 761)

sharecropping: The labor system by which landowners and impoverished southern farmworkers, particularly African Americans, divided the proceeds from crops harvested on the landowner's property. With local merchants providing supplies—in exchange for a lien on the crop—sharecropping pushed farmers into cash-crop production and often trapped them in long-term debt. (p. 476)

Sharon Statement: Drafted by founding members of the Young Americans for Freedom (YAF), this manifesto outlined the group's principles and inspired young conservatives who would play important roles in the Reagan administration in the 1980s. (p. 900)

Shelley v. Kraemer: A 1948 Supreme Court decision that outlawed restrictive covenants on the occupancy of housing developments by African Americans, Asian Americans, and other minorities. Because the Court decision did not actually prohibit racial discrimination in housing, unfair practices against minority groups continued until passage of the Fair Housing Act in 1968. (p. 841)

Sheppard-Towner Federal Maternity and Infancy Act: The first federally funded health-care legislation that provided federal funds for medical clinics, prenatal education programs, and visiting nurses. (p. 696)

Sherman Antitrust Act: Landmark 1890 act that forbade anticompetitive business activities, requiring the federal government to investigate trusts and any companies operating in violation of the act. (p. 622)

Sierra Club: An organization founded in 1892 that was dedicated to the enjoyment and preservation of America's great mountains (including the Sierra Nevadas) and wilderness environments. Encouraged by such groups, national and state governments began to set aside more public lands for preservation and recreation. (p. 573)

silent majority: Term derived from the title of a book by Ben J. Wattenberg and Richard Scammon (called *The Real Majority*) and used by Nixon in a 1969 speech to describe those who supported his positions but did not publicly assert their voices, in contrast to those involved in the antiwar, civil rights, and women's movements. (p. 910)

Silent Spring: Book published in 1962 by biologist Rachel Carson. Its analysis of the pesticide DDT's toxic impact on the human and natural food chains galvanized environmental activists. (p. 922)

Slaughter-House Cases: A group of decisions begun in 1873 in which the Court began to undercut the power of the Fourteenth Amendment to protect African American rights. (p. 487)

Smoot-Hawley Tariff: A high tariff enacted in 1930 during the Great Depression. By taxing imported goods, Congress hoped to stimulate American manufacturing, but the tariff triggered retaliatory tariffs in other countries, which further hindered global trade and led to greater economic contraction. (p. 715)

Social Darwinism: An idea, actually formulated not by Charles Darwin but by British philosopher and sociologist Herbert Spencer, that human society advanced through ruthless competition and the "survival of the fittest." (p. 559)

Social Gospel: A movement to renew religious faith through dedication to public welfare and social justice, reforming both society and the self through Christian service. (p. 563)

Social Security Act: A 1935 act with three main provisions: old-age pensions for workers; a joint federal-state system of compensation for unemployed workers; and a program of payments to widowed mothers and the blind, deaf, and disabled. (p. 725)

social settlement: A community welfare center that investigated the plight of the urban poor, raised funds to address urgent needs, and helped neighborhood residents advocate on their own behalf. Social settlements became a nationally recognized reform strategy during the Progressive Era. (p. 609)

soft power: The exercise of popular cultural influence abroad, as American radio and movies became popular around the world in the 1920s, transmitting American cultural ideals overseas. (p. 691)

Southern Christian Leadership Conference (SCLC): After the Montgomery Bus Boycott, Martin Luther King Jr. and other civil rights leaders formed the SCLC in 1957 to coordinate civil rights activity in the South. (p. 865)

Sputnik: The world's first satellite, launched by the Soviet Union in 1957. After its launch, the United States funded research and education to catch up in the Cold War space competition. (p. 822)

stagflation: An economic term coined in the 1970s to describe the condition in which inflation and unemployment rise at the same time. (p. 923)

Standard Oil decision: A 1911 Supreme Court decision that directed the breakup of the Standard Oil Company into smaller companies because its overwhelming market dominance and monopoly power violated antitrust laws. (p. 632)

States' Rights Democratic Party: Known popularly as the Dixiecrats, a breakaway party of white Democrats from the South that formed for the 1948 election. Its formation shed light on an internal struggle between the civil rights aims of the party's liberal wing and southern white Democrats. (p. 857)

Stonewall Inn: A gay bar in New York's Greenwich Village that was raided by police in 1969; the ensuing two-day riot contributed to the rapid rise of a gay liberation movement. (p. 909)

STOP ERA: An organization founded by Phyllis Schlafly in 1972 to fight the Equal Rights Amendment. (p. 938)

Student Nonviolent Coordinating Committee (SNCC): A student civil rights group founded in 1960 under the mentorship of activist Ella Baker. SNCC initially embraced an interracial and nonhierarchical structure that encouraged leadership at the grassroots level and practiced the civil disobedience principles of Martin Luther King Jr. As violence toward civil rights activists escalated nationwide in the 1960s, SNCC expelled

nonblack members and promoted "black power" and the teachings of Malcolm X. (p. 866)

Students for a Democratic Society (SDS): An organization for social change founded by college students in 1960. (p. 897)

Sunbelt: Name applied to the Southwest and South, which grew rapidly after World War II as a center of defense industries and non-unionized labor. (p. 843)

supply-side economics (Reaganomics): Economic theory that tax cuts for individuals and businesses encourage investment and production (supply) and stimulate consumption (demand) because individuals can keep more of their earnings. In reality, supply-side economics created a massive federal budget deficit. (p. 964)

Taft-Hartley Act: Law passed by the Republican-controlled Congress in 1947 that overhauled the 1935 National Labor Relations Act, placing restrictions on organized labor that made it more difficult for unions to organize workers. (p. 801)

talented tenth: A term used by Harvard-educated sociologist W. E. B. Du Bois for the top 10 percent of educated African Americans, whom he called on to develop new strategies to advocate for civil rights. (p. 634)

tax revolt: A movement to lower or eliminate taxes. California's Proposition 13, which rolled back property taxes, capped future increases for present owners, and required that all tax measures have a two-thirds majority in the legislature, was the result of one such revolt, inspiring similar movements across the country. (p. 931)

Tea Party: A set of far-right opposition groups that emerged during President Obama's first term and gave voice to the extreme individualism and antigovernment sentiment traditionally associated with right-wing movements in the United States. (p. 1015)

Teapot Dome: Nickname for scandal in which Interior Secretary Albert Fall accepted $300,000 in bribes for leasing oil reserves on public land in Teapot Dome, Wyoming. It was part of a larger pattern of corruption that marred Warren G. Harding's presidency. (p. 689)

teenager: A term for a young adult. American youth culture, focused on the spending power of the "teenager," emerged as a cultural phenomenon in the postwar decades. (p. 828)

Teller Amendment: An amendment to the 1898 U.S. declaration of war against Spain disclaiming any intention by the United States to occupy Cuba. The amendment assured the public that the United States would uphold democracy abroad as well as at home. (p. 654)

tenement: A high-density, cheap, five- or six-story housing unit designed for working-class urban populations. In the late nineteenth and early twentieth centuries, tenements became a symbol of urban immigrant poverty. (p. 595)

Tennessee Valley Authority: An agency funded by Congress in 1933 that integrated flood control, reforestation, electricity generation, and agricultural and industrial development in the Tennessee Valley area. (p. 740)

Ten Percent Plan: A plan proposed by President Abraham Lincoln during the Civil War, but never implemented, that would have granted amnesty to most ex-Confederates and allowed each rebellious state to return to the Union as soon as 10 percent of its voters had taken a loyalty oath and the state had approved the Thirteenth Amendment. (p. 464)

Tet offensive: Major campaign of attacks launched throughout South Vietnam in January 1968 by the North Vietnamese and Vietcong. A major turning point in the war, it exposed the credibility gap between official statements and the war's reality, and it shook Americans' confidence in the government. (p. 904)

Three Mile Island: A nuclear plant near Harrisburg, Pennsylvania, where a reactor core came close to a meltdown in March 1979. After the incident at Three Mile Island, no new nuclear plants were authorized in the United States, though a handful with existing authorization were built in the 1980s. (p. 923)

Title IX: A law passed by Congress in 1972 that broadened the 1964 Civil Rights Act to include educational institutions, prohibiting colleges and universities that received federal funds from discriminating on the basis of sex. By requiring comparable funding for sports programs, Title IX made women's athletics a real presence on college campuses. (p. 908)

"To Secure These Rights": The 1947 report by the Presidential Committee on Civil Rights that called for robust federal action to ensure equality for African Americans. President Truman asked Congress to make all of the report's recommendations — including the abolition of poll taxes and the restoration of the Fair Employment Practice Committee — into law, leading to discord in the Democratic Party. (p. 857)

Townsend Plan: A plan proposed by Francis Townsend in 1933 that would give $200 a month (about $3,600 today) to citizens over the age of sixty. Townsend Clubs sprang up across the country in support of the plan, mobilizing mass support for old-age pensions. (p. 723)

transcontinental railroad: The railway line completed on May 10, 1869, that connected the Central Pacific and Union Pacific lines, enabling goods to move by railway from the eastern United States all the way to California. (p. 494)

"treat": A form of heterosexual dating in which, given the male partner's higher wage level, he is expected to pay for food and entertainment, and the young woman is expected to provide sexual favors in return. (p. 598)

Treaty of Versailles: The 1919 treaty that ended World War I. The agreement redrew the map of the world, assigned Germany sole responsibility for the war, and saddled it with a debt of $33 billion in war damages. Its long-term impact around the globe — including the creation of British and French imperial "mandates" — was catastrophic. (p. 675)

Triangle Fire: A devastating fire that quickly spread through the Triangle Shirtwaist Company in New York City on March 25, 1911, killing 146 people. In the wake of the tragedy, fifty-six state laws were passed dealing with such issues as fire hazards, unsafe machines, and wages and working hours for women and children. The fire also provided a national impetus for industrial reform. (p. 611)

Truman Doctrine: President Harry S. Truman's commitment to "support free peoples who are resisting attempted subjugation by armed minorities or by outside pressures." First applied to Greece and Turkey in 1947, it became the justification for U.S. intervention into several countries during the Cold War. (p. 792)

trust: A small group of associates that hold stock from a group of combined firms, managing them as a single entity. Trusts quickly evolved into other centralized business forms, but progressive critics continued to refer to giant firms like U.S. Steel and Standard Oil as "trusts." (p. 532)

Tydings-McDuffie Act: A 1934 law that provided for the independence of the Philippines, after a ten-year transition period. Though it granted Philippine independence, its origins were nativist, because the law's proponents wished to classify Filipinos as "alien" and reduce their immigration to the United States. (p. 739)

United Farm Workers (UFW): A union of farmworkers founded in 1962 by Cesar Chavez and Dolores Huerta that sought to empower the mostly Mexican American migrant farmworkers who faced discrimination and exploitative conditions, especially in the Southwest. (p. 880)

United Nations: An international body agreed upon at the Yalta Conference and founded at a conference in San Francisco in 1945, consisting of a General Assembly, in which all nations are represented, and a Security Council of the five major Allied powers — the United States, Britain, France, China, and the Soviet Union — and seven other nations elected on a rotating basis. (p. 787)

Universal Negro Improvement Association: A Harlem-based group, led by charismatic, Jamaican-born Marcus Garvey, that arose in the 1920s to mobilize African American workers and champion black separatism. (p. 705)

USA PATRIOT Act: A 2001 law that gave the government new powers to monitor suspected terrorists and their associates, including the ability to access personal information. (p. 1010)

U.S. Fisheries Commission: A federal bureau established in 1871 that made recommendations to stem the decline in wild fish. Its creation was an important step toward wildlife conservation and management. (p. 509)

vaudeville theater: A type of professional stage show popular in the 1880s and 1890s that included singing, dancing, and comedy routines; it created a form of family entertainment for the urban masses that deeply influenced later forms, such as radio shows and television sitcoms. (p. 596)

vertical integration: A business model in which a corporation controlled all aspects of production from raw materials to packaged products. "Robber barons," or industrial innovators such as Gustavus Swift and Andrew Carnegie, pioneered this business form at the end of the Civil War. (p. 531)

Veterans Administration: A federal agency that assists former soldiers. Following World War II, the VA helped veterans purchase new homes with no down payment, sparking a building boom that created jobs in the construction industry and fueling consumer spending in home appliances and automobiles. (p. 825)

Vietnamization: A new U.S. policy, devised under President Nixon in the early 1970s, of delegating the ground fighting to the South Vietnamese in the Vietnam War. American troop levels dropped and American casualties dropped correspondingly, but the killing in Vietnam continued. (p. 910)

Volstead Act: Officially the National Prohibition Act, passed by Congress in 1920 to enforce the provisions of the Eighteenth Amendment banning the sale of alcohol. (p. 698)

Voting Rights Act of 1965: Law passed during Lyndon Johnson's administration that empowered the federal government to intervene to ensure minorities' access to the voting booth. (p. 874)

Wade-Davis Bill: A bill proposed by Congress in July 1864 that required an oath of allegiance by a majority of each state's adult white men, new governments formed only by those who had never taken up arms against the Union, and permanent disenfranchisement of Confederate leaders. The plan was passed but pocket vetoed by President Abraham Lincoln. (p. 464)

Wagner Act: A 1935 act that upheld the right of industrial workers to join unions and established the National Labor Relations Board (NLRB), a federal agency with the authority to protect workers from employer coercion and to guarantee collective bargaining. (p. 725)

War Industries Board: A federal board established in July 1917 to direct military production, including allocation of resources, conversion of factories to war production, and setting of prices. (p. 667)

War Powers Act (1941): The law that gave President Roosevelt unprecedented control over all aspects of the war effort during World War II. (p. 754)

War Powers Act (1973): A law that limited the president's ability to deploy U.S. forces without congressional approval. Congress passed the War Powers Act in 1973 as a series of laws to fight the abuses of the Nixon administration. (p. 932)

Warren Court: The Supreme Court under Chief Justice Earl Warren (1953–1969), which expanded the Constitution's promise of equality and civil rights. It issued landmark decisions in the areas of civil rights, criminal rights, reproductive freedom, and separation of church and state. (p. 913)

Warsaw Pact: A military alliance established in Eastern Europe in 1955 to counter the NATO alliance; it included Albania, Bulgaria, Czechoslovakia, East Germany, Hungary, Poland, Romania, and the Soviet Union. (p. 794)

Watergate: Term referring to the 1972 break-in at Democratic Party headquarters in the Watergate complex in Washington, D.C., by men working for President Nixon's reelection campaign, along with Nixon's efforts to cover it up. The Watergate scandal led to President Nixon's resignation. (p. 932)

Webster v. Reproductive Health Services: A 1989 Supreme Court ruling that upheld the authority of state governments to limit the use of public funds and facilities for abortions. (p. 1003)

welfare capitalism: A system of labor relations that stressed management's responsibility for employees' well-being. (p. 687)

welfare state: A term applied to industrial democracies that adopt various government-guaranteed social-welfare programs. The creation of Social Security and other measures of the Second New Deal fundamentally changed American society and established a national welfare state for the first time. (p. 725)

Williams v. Mississippi: An 1898 Supreme Court ruling that allowed states to impose poll taxes and literacy tests. By 1908, every southern state had adopted such measures. (p. 627)

Wisconsin Idea: A policy promoted by Republican governor Robert La Follette of Wisconsin for greater government intervention in the economy, with reliance on experts, particularly progressive economists, for policy recommendations. (p. 633)

Woman's Christian Temperance Union: An organization advocating the prohibition of liquor that spread rapidly after 1879, when charismatic Frances Willard became its leader. Advocating suffrage and a host of reform activities, it launched tens of thousands of women into public life and was the first nationwide organization to identify and condemn domestic violence. (p. 579)

women's liberation: A new brand of feminism in the 1960s that attracted primarily younger, college-educated women fresh from the New Left, antiwar, and

civil rights movements who sought to end to the denigration and exploitation of women. (p. 907)

Women's Trade Union League: A labor organization for women founded in New York in 1903 that brought elite, middle-class, and working-class women together as allies. The WTUL supported union organizing efforts among garment workers. (p. 611)

Works Progress Administration: Federal New Deal program established in 1935 that provided government-funded public works jobs to millions of unemployed Americans during the Great Depression in areas ranging from construction to the arts. (p. 726)

World Bank: An international bank created to provide loans for the reconstruction of war-torn Europe as well as for the development of former colonized nations in the developing world. (p. 820)

World Trade Organization (WTO): International economic body established in 1995 through the General Agreement on Tariffs and Trade to enforce substantial tariff and import quota reductions. (p. 989)

World Wide Web: A collection of interlinked computer servers that debuted in 1991, allowing access by millions to documents, pictures, and other materials. (p. 996)

Wounded Knee: The 1890 massacre of Sioux Indians by American cavalry at Wounded Knee Creek, South Dakota. Sent to suppress the Ghost Dance, soldiers caught up with fleeing Lakotas and killed as many as three hundred. (p. 520)

Yalta Conference: A meeting in Yalta of President Roosevelt, Prime Minister Churchill, and Joseph Stalin in February 1945, in which the leaders discussed the treatment of Germany, the status of Poland, the creation of the United Nations, and Russian entry into the war against Japan. (p. 786)

yellow journalism: A derogatory term for newspapers that specialize in sensationalistic reporting. Yellow journalism is associated with the inflammatory reporting by the Hearst and Pulitzer newspapers leading up to the Spanish-American War in 1898. (p. 599)

Yellowstone National Park: Established in 1872 by Congress, Yellowstone was the United States's first national park. (p. 508)

Young Americans for Freedom (YAF): The largest student political organization in the country, whose conservative members defended free enterprise and supported the war in Vietnam. (p. 900)

Young Lords Organization: An organization that sought self-determination for Puerto Ricans in the United States and in the Caribbean. Though immediate victories for the YLO were few, their dedicated community organizing produced a generation of leaders and awakened community consciousness. (p. 878)

Young Men's Christian Association: Introduced in Boston in 1851, the YMCA promoted muscular Christianity, combining evangelism with athletic facilities where men could make themselves "clean and strong." (p. 568)

Zimmermann telegram: A 1917 intercepted dispatch in which German foreign secretary Arthur Zimmermann urged Mexico to join the Central Powers and promised that if the United States entered the war, Germany would help Mexico recover Texas, New Mexico, and Arizona. Published by American newspapers, the telegram outraged the American public and help precipitate the move toward U.S. entry in the war on the Allied side. (p. 664)

zoot suits: Oversized suits of clothing in fashion in the 1940s, particularly among young male African Americans and Mexican Americans. In June 1943, a group of white sailors and soldiers in Los Angeles, seeking revenge for an earlier skirmish with Mexican American youths, attacked anyone they found wearing a zoot suit in what became known as the zoot-suit riots. (p. 763)

Index

CANADA

MINNESOTA

Lake Superior

MINNESOTA

WISCONSIN

St. Paul
Minneapolis

Lake Michigan

Lake Huron

MICHIGAN

Lansing

Milwaukee

Madison

Detroit

Lake Erie

IOWA

Des Moines

CENTRAL
LOWLAND

Chicago

Cleveland

Omaha

Missouri River

MISSOURI

INDIANA

Indianapolis

OHIO

Columbus

Cincinnati

Wheeling

Pittsburgh

Charleston

Frankfort

W.
VA.

Springfield

ILLINOIS

St. Louis

Louisville

APPALACHIAN MTS.

Kansas City

Topeka

Jefferson
City

KENTUCKY

Cumberland
River

Knoxville

Richmond

VIRGINIA

Norfolk

Raleigh

Tulsa

Nashville

Mt. Mitchell
(6,684 ft.; 2,037 m)

NORTH CAROLINA

ARKANSAS

TENNESSEE

Charlotte

Little
Rock

Memphis

Tennessee River

SOUTH CAROLINA

Columbia

Birmingham

Atlanta

Charleston

Dallas

MISSISSIPPI

ALABAMA

GEORGIA

TIDEWATER

LOUISIANA

Jackson

Montgomery

Houston

Baton Rouge

New Orleans

Tallahassee

Jacksonville

Gulf
of
Mexico

FLORIDA

Orlando

Lake
Okeechobee

Miami

VERMONT

Burlington

Montpelier

Mt. Washington
(6,288 ft.; 1,917 m)

Concord

MAINE

Augusta

Portland

NEW
HAMPSHIRE

Manchester

Boston

Albany

NEW
YORK

Buffalo

Lake Ontario

St. Lawrence River

Hudson River

Hartford

MASS.

Providence

R.I.

CONNECTICUT

New York

Trenton

PENNSYLVANIA

Harrisburg

Philadelphia

NEW JERSEY

Baltimore

Dover

DELAWARE

Annapolis

WASHINGTON, D.C.

MARYLAND

Chesapeake
Bay

Potomac
River

ATLANTIC
OCEAN

BAHAMAS

CUBA

THE
UNITED STATES

Elevation

Feet	Meters
Over 13,001	Over 3,001
6,561–13,000	2,001–3,000
3,281–6,560	1,001–2,000
1,641–3,280	501–1,000
661–1,640	201–500
0–660	0–200
Below sea level	Below sea level

0   150   300 miles
0   150   300 kilometers

N
S
E
W

90°W   80°W   70°W

ATLANTIC OCEAN

San Juan

PUERTO
RICO

18°N

67°W   65°W

VIRGIN
ISLANDS

Caribbean Sea

0   50   100 miles
0   50   100 kilometers

ARCTIC OCEAN

80°N

Greenland
(Den.)

Alaska

ICELAND

60°N

CANADA

UNITED
KINGDOM

IRELAND

BEL.
FRANCE
SWITZ.
SPAIN

40°N

UNITED STATES

ATLANTIC
OCEAN

Azores
(Port.)

PORTUGAL

ALGERIA

MOROCCO

Canary Is.
(Sp.)

Western Sahara
(Mor.)

BAHAMAS

DOMINICAN

HAITI REPUBLIC

Hawaii

MEXICO

20°N

CUBA
JAMAICA
BELIZE

Puerto Rico (U.S.)
ST. KITTS AND NEVIS
ANTIGUA AND BARBUDA
DOMINICA

MAURITANIA

CAPE
VERDE

MALI

GUATEMALA
EL SALVADOR

HONDURAS
NICARAGUA

Guadeloupe (Fr.)
Martinique (Fr.)
ST. LUCIA

ST. VINCENT AND THE GRENADINES
BARBADOS
GRENADA

SENEGAL

GAMBIA

GUINEA-BISSAU

COSTA RICA

TRINIDAD AND TOBAGO
GUYANA

GUINEA

SIERRA LEONE

PANAMA

VENEZUELA

SURINAME

LIBERIA

PACIFIC OCEAN

COLOMBIA

French Guiana (Fr.)

CÔTE D'IVOIRE

BURKINA FASO

GHANA

0°

Equator

Galápagos Is.
(Ec.)

ECUADOR

SAMOA

PERU

BRAZIL

TONGA

Easter I.
(Chile)

BOLIVIA

20°S

PARAGUAY

CHILE

ATLANTIC
OCEAN

0   1,500   3,000 miles

0   1,500   3,000 kilometers

URUGUAY

ARGENTINA

40°S

Falkland Is.
(U.K.)

60°S

80°S

160°W   140°W   120°W   100°W   80°W   60°W   40°W   20°W

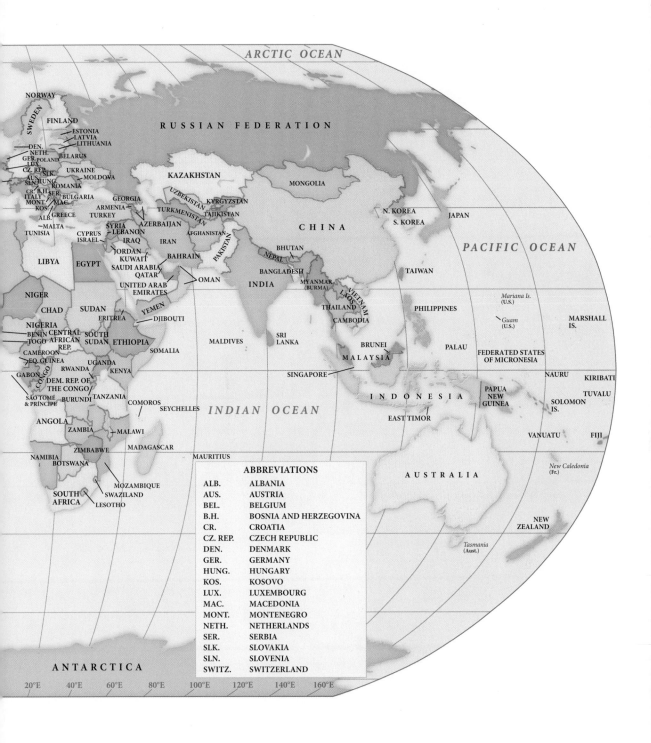

ARCTIC OCEAN

NORWAY
SWEDEN
FINLAND
ESTONIA
LATVIA
LITHUANIA
DEN.
NETH.
GER. POLAND
LUX. BELARUS
CZ. REP.
SLK. UKRAINE
AUS. MOLDOVA
SLN. HUNG. ROMANIA
CR. B.H. SER. BULGARIA
ITALY MONT. MAC.
KOS. GREECE
ALB.
MALTA
TUNISIA

RUSSIAN FEDERATION

KAZAKHSTAN

MONGOLIA

N. KOREA
S. KOREA
JAPAN

PACIFIC OCEAN

UZBEKISTAN KYRGYZSTAN
GEORGIA
ARMENIA TURKMENISTAN TAJIKISTAN
TURKEY AZERBAIJAN
CYPRUS SYRIA AFGHANISTAN
ISRAEL LEBANON
IRAQ IRAN
JORDAN
KUWAIT BAHRAIN
SAUDI ARABIA QATAR
OMAN
UNITED ARAB
EMIRATES
YEMEN

CHINA

TAIWAN

PAKISTAN

NEPAL BHUTAN
BANGLADESH
INDIA MYANMAR
(BURMA)
LAOS
VIETNAM
THAILAND
CAMBODIA

Mariana Is.
(U.S.)
Guam
(U.S.)

MARSHALL
IS.

PHILIPPINES

LIBYA EGYPT

NIGER
CHAD SUDAN
ERITREA
NIGERIA DJIBOUTI
BENIN CENTRAL SOUTH ETHIOPIA
TOGO AFRICAN SUDAN
REP.
CAMEROON
EQ. GUINEA SOMALIA
UGANDA
GABON RWANDA KENYA
DEM. REP. OF
THE CONGO
SÃO TOMÉ BURUNDI TANZANIA
& PRÍNCIPE COMOROS SEYCHELLES

MALDIVES

SRI
LANKA

BRUNEI

MALAYSIA

PALAU

FEDERATED STATES
OF MICRONESIA

NAURU KIRIBATI

TUVALU

SINGAPORE

INDONESIA

SOLOMON
IS.

INDIAN OCEAN

EAST TIMOR

PAPUA
NEW
GUINEA

VANUATU FIJI

ANGOLA
ZAMBIA
MALAWI
ZIMBABWE MADAGASCAR
NAMIBIA
BOTSWANA MAURITIUS

New Caledonia
(Fr.)

AUSTRALIA

MOZAMBIQUE
SOUTH SWAZILAND
AFRICA LESOTHO

NEW
ZEALAND

Tasmania
(Aust.)

ANTARCTICA

ABBREVIATIONS	
ALB.	ALBANIA
AUS.	AUSTRIA
BEL.	BELGIUM
B.H.	BOSNIA AND HERZEGOVINA
CR.	CROATIA
CZ. REP.	CZECH REPUBLIC
DEN.	DENMARK
GER.	GERMANY
HUNG.	HUNGARY
KOS.	KOSOVO
LUX.	LUXEMBOURG
MAC.	MACEDONIA
MONT.	MONTENEGRO
NETH.	NETHERLANDS
SER.	SERBIA
SLK.	SLOVAKIA
SLN.	SLOVENIA
SWITZ.	SWITZERLAND

20°E   40°E   60°E   80°E   100°E   120°E   140°E   160°E

About the Authors

Rebecca Edwards is Eloise Ellery Professor of History at Vassar College, where she teaches courses on nineteenth-century politics, the Civil War, the frontier West, and women, gender, and sexuality. She is the author of, among other publications, *Angels in the Machinery: Gender in American Party Politics from the Civil War to the Progressive Era*; *New Spirits: Americans in the "Gilded Age," 1865–1905*; and the essay "Women's and Gender History" in *The New American History*. She is currently working on a book about the role of childbearing in the expansion of America's nineteenth-century empire.

Eric Hinderaker is Professor of History at the University of Utah. His research explores early modern imperialism, relations between Europeans and Native Americans, military-civilian relations in the Atlantic world, and comparative colonization. His most recent book, *Boston's Massacre*, was published in 2017. His other publications include *Elusive Empires: Constructing Colonialism in the Ohio Valley, 1673–1800*; *The Two Hendricks: Unraveling a Mohawk Mystery*, which won the Herbert H. Lehman Prize for Distinguished Scholarship in New York History from the New York Academy of History; and, with Peter C. Mancall, *At the Edge of Empire: The Backcountry in British North America*.

Robert O. Self is Mary Ann Lippitt Professor of American History at Brown University. His research focuses on urban history, American politics, and the post-1945 United States. He is the author of *American Babylon: Race and the Struggle for Postwar Oakland*, which won four professional prizes, including the James A. Rawley Prize from the Organization of American Historians, and *All in the Family: The Realignment of American Democracy Since the 1960s*. He is currently at work on a book about the centrality of houses, cars, and children to family consumption in the twentieth-century United States.

James A. Henretta is Professor Emeritus of American History at the University of Maryland, College Park. His publications include *The Evolution of American Society, 1600–1815*, *The Origins of American Capitalism*, and an edited volume, *Republicanism and Liberalism in America and the German States, 1750–1850*. His most recent publications include two long articles, "Magistrates, Common Law Lawyers, Legislators: The Three Legal Systems of British America" and "Charles Evans Hughes and the Strange Death of Liberal America," derived from his ongoing research on the liberal state in America, and in particular New York, 1820–1975.

About the cover image

Queensboro Bridge, New York

Blendon Reed Campbell (1872–1969), an American artist who studied in Paris, celebrated American technology in this 1935 image of boats being loaded on the East River under the Queensboro Bridge, which links New York's Manhattan and Long Island. The bridge, which originally carried pedestrians and elevated railway lines as well as carriages, was built in 1909 and modified over time for auto traffic. Completed soon after New York's consolidation of five boroughs into a single municipality, the Queensboro Bridge symbolized the city's emergence as a great world metropolis. It also nearly became a casualty of labor unrest: during construction, protesters dynamited one of the pilings.